OUTSTANDING WOMEN ATHLETES

Who They Are and How They Influenced Sports in America

Second Edition

Janet Woolum

Oryx Press
1998

The rare Arabian Oryx is believed to have inspired the myth of the unicorn. This desert antelope became virtually extinct in the early 1960s. At that time several groups of international conservationists arranged to have 9 animals sent to the Phoenix Zoo to be the nucleus of a captive breeding herd. Today the Oryx population is over 1,000, and over 500 have been returned to the Middle East.

© 1998 by The Oryx Press
4041 North Central at Indian School Road
Phoenix, Arizona 85012-3397

Cover photos © Allsport USA

Published simultaneously in Canada
Printed and Bound in the United States of America

∞ The paper used in this publication meets the minimum requirements of
American National Standard for Information Science—Permanence
of Paper for Printed Library Materials, ANSI Z39.48, 1984.

Library of Congress Cataloging-in-Publication Data

Woolum, Janet, 1955–
    Outstanding women athletes : who they are and how they influenced
sports in America / by Janet Woolum. —2nd ed.
    Includes bibliographical references and index.
    ISBN 1-57356-120-7 (alk. paper)
    1. Women athletes—United States—Biography—Dictionaries
2. Sports for women—United States—History. I. Title.
GV697.A1W69 1998
796'.082'092273—dc21
    [B]   98-17076
                                                                      CIP

To Risa, Alissa, Erin, and Mykah

Contents

Foreword   Nancy Lieberman-Cline   vii

Preface   ix

Part I: History of Women's Sports   1

    Chapter 1—Women in American Sports   3

    Chapter 2—Women in the Olympics   35

Part II: Biographies and Teams   75

    Chapter 3—Outstanding Women Athletes Who Influenced American Sports   77

Michelle Akers (soccer player)   77

Tenley Albright (figure skater)   79

Constance M.K. Applebee (field hockey coach)   81

Evelyn Ashford (track and field sprinter)   82

Tracy Austin (tennis player)   85

Senda Berenson (basketball innovator)   86

Patty Berg (golfer)   88

Bonnie Blair (speed skater)   90

Fanny Blankers-Koen (track and field star)   92

Susan Butcher (sled-dog racer)   94

Connie Carpenter-Phinney (cyclist)   96

Florence Chadwick (long-distance swimmer)   98

Nadia Comaneci (gymnast)   99

Maureen Connolly (tennis player)   102

Donna de Varona (swimmer)   103

Gail Devers (track and field sprinter)   105

Jean Driscoll (wheelchair athlete)   107

Camille Duvall (water-skier)   109

Amelia Earhart (aviator)   110

Gertrude Ederle (long-distance swimmer)   113

Teresa Edwards (basketball player)   115

Janet Evans (swimmer)   117

Chris Evert (tennis player)   119

Lisa Fernandez (softball player)   122

Peggy Fleming (figure skater)   124

Juli Furtado (mountain bike racer)   126

Althea Gibson (tennis player)   127

Lucy Giovinco (bowler)   131

Diana Golden (disabled ski racer)   132

Michelle Gould (racquetball player)   135

Steffi Graf (tennis player)   136

Janet Guthrie (auto racer)   138

Dorothy Hamill (figure skater)   141

Alison Hargreaves (mountain climber)   143

Carol Heiss (figure skater)   144

Sonja Henie (figure skater)   146

Lynn Hill (rock climber)   148

Flo Hyman (volleyball player)   150

Charmayne James (barrel racer)   152

Lynn Jennings (distance runner)   153

Joan Joyce (softball player)   155

Florence Griffith Joyner (track and field sprinter)   156

Jackie Joyner-Kersee (track and field heptathlete)   158

Billie Jean King (tennis player)   161

Micki King (diver)   164

Olga Korbut (gymnast)   166

Julie Krone (jockey)   169

Marion Ladewig (bowler)   171

Andrea Mead Lawrence (Alpine skier)   173

Nancy Lieberman-Cline (basketball player)   175

Nancy Lopez (golfer)   177

Alice Marble (tennis player)   179

Christy Martin (boxer)   181

Helene Mayer (fencer)   183

Patricia McCormick (diver)   184

Floretta Doty McCutcheon (bowler)   186
Ann Meyers (basketball player)   188
Cheryl Miller (basketball player)   190
Shannon Miller (gymnast)   192
Helen Wills Moody (tennis player)   194
Shirley Muldowney (drag racer)   195
Martina Navratilova (tennis player)   198
Cindy Nelson (Alpine skier)   201
Paula Newby-Fraser (triathlete)   203
Mary Lou Retton (gymnast)   204
Manon Rheaume (ice hockey goalie)   207
Cathy Rigby (gymnast)   208
Wilma Rudolph (track and field
    sprinter)   210
Joan Benoit Samuelson (marathon run-
    ner)   213
Cristina Sánchez (bullfighter)   214
Eleonora Sears (all-around athlete)   216
Monica Seles (tennis player)   218
Mary Decker Slaney (middle-distance
    runner)   220

Francie Larrieu Smith (middle-distance
    runner)   222
Vivian Stringer (basketball coach)   223
Patricia Head Summitt (basketball
    coach)   225
Wyomia Tyus (track and field sprinter)   227
Glenna Collett Vare (golfer)   229
Grete Andersen Waitz (marathon run-
    ner)   231
Kathy Whitworth (golfer)   233
Hazel Hotchkiss Wightman (tennis
    player)   235
Lynette Woodard (basketball player)   237
Mickey Wright (golfer)   239
Kristi Yamaguchi (figure skater)   241
Sheila Young (speed skater and cyclist)   243
Mildred "Babe" Didrikson Zaharias (all-
    around athlete)   245

Chapter 4—Outstanding Women's Teams   252

    All American Girls Professional Baseball League   253

    America^3 258

    1994 Colorado Silver Bullets   265

    Raybestos Brakettes   271

    Tennessee State University Tigerbelles   276

    U.S. Olympic Synchronized Swimming Team   280

    U.S. Women's Gymnastics Team   285

    U.S. Women's National Soccer Team   289

    USA Basketball Women's National Team   295

    USA Softball Women's National Team   301

Part III: Basic Resources   309

    Chapter 5—Selected Bibliography   311

    Chapter 6—Directory of Organizations   322

Part IV: Appendixes   331

    Appendix A—Olympic Gold Medalists   333

    Appendix B—Selected National Award Winners and Champions   346

    Appendix C—National Collegiate Athletic Association (NCAA) Champions—
        Division I   368

    Appendix D—Athletes Profiled in *Outstanding Women Athletes,* Arranged by Sport   377

    Appendix E—List of Organization Abbreviations   379

    Appendix F—Selected Reference Sources   381

Index   385

Foreword

by Nancy Lieberman-Cline

As I prepare my expansion team, the Detroit Shock, for its inaugural season in the two-year-old Women's National Basketball Association (WNBA), I am struck by the changes in women's sports in the last 25 years. With professional sport opportunities finally opening to women, it is easy to forget that within my own lifetime, opportunities for women in sport were severely limited—not just on the professional level, but on every level. The few pro sports opportunities that were available to women and girls emphasized individual talents over team competition. Even as women began to be accepted as individual competitors, the idea of a woman making a living in a team sport was seen as ludicrous.

Today, young female athletes take it for granted that they have access to teams, facilities, coaching, and careers in sport, but as this book by Janet Woolum, *Outstanding Women Athletes: Who They Are and How They Influenced Sports,* second edition, outlines, this access is a recent phenomenon. Tireless advocacy by leading women athletes, coaches, and educators in the early 1970s resulted in the passage of Title IX, which outlawed gender discrimination in education activities, including sports. This legis-

lation, and the constant support of high profile athletes and ordinary women and men, has created opportunities for girls and women that athletes of my generation only dreamed about. Many of these beneficiaries, however, have no idea of the struggles that were fought to win their right to play. This book helps fill that knowledge void.

My own story illustrates the changes that have occurred in the years since Title IX was passed in 1972. When I was growing up, girls were not allowed to play in New York's Public School Athletic League. If I wanted to play basketball, I had to break into a pick-up game at the local YMCA or playground, often enduring the hostile attitudes of players who thought that a girl playing in a male-dominated sport was ridiculous. By the time I entered Old Dominion University, the climate had improved somewhat. Sports scholarships were finally offered to women in the 1970s; I was fortunate enough to receive a scholarship to play basketball at ODU and helped lead my team to national titles in 1979 and 1980. Attendance at our games increased each year I was at ODU. By my senior year, we drew nearly 10,000 spectators for a game against the Soviet Union.

Nancy Lieberman-Cline is coach and general manager of the Detroit Shock

Despite my success in college basketball, including winning the Wade Trophy as the player of the year in 1979 and 1980, the riches and professional opportunities that awaited my male counterparts eluded me and my fellow women stars. For us, college was supposed to be the pinnacle of our sports careers. Basketball was my life, though, and I was determined to make a living in the sport I loved. This determination served me well, because the chances for a woman in professional basketball were few and far between. I played in two short-lived professional leagues in the 1980s, the Women's Professional Basketball League and the Women's American Basketball Association, both of which folded after a year. In between, I worked in a number of sports-related ventures, including stints as a television commentator. In 1986, I played in a men's professional summer league, and, in 1988, I toured with the Washington Generals, playing the Harlem Globetrotters in a European tour. While these jobs brought me great experience, it was frustrating to have to work so hard off the court, never sure where the next opportunities would be.

In 1997, my basketball career came full circle. I once again joined a fledgling women's professional basketball league, the WNBA. This time around, however, the league was a success from the beginning. Attendance surpassed everyone's expectations and games were regularly shown on national television. Female basketball stars coming out of college had two professional leagues in this country to choose from, and throughout the sporting world, people were taking notice of strong women's teams in various sports. Many of the myths regarding the perceived lack of interest in women's team sports began to crumble as attendance figures at women's sporting events soared. Now as I prepare for my second year in the league, this time as a coach, I'm excited at the prospect of the coming years.

Unfortunately, my story of struggle in sports is not a unique one. In reading through *Outstanding Women Athletes*, I came across story after story of women who faced similar obstacles to the ones I overcame. These athletes refused to take no for answer and broke through barrier after barrier. Not only is it satisfying to read the stories of these trailblazers, but it is also very rewarding to learn of the exploits of the first generation of women to benefit from the efforts of their foremothers. In this second edition, women are profiled who, thanks to tireless advocacy and struggle on and off the playing fields, had full access to top facilities and coaching, who had opportunities to play both individual and team sports at every level, and who had the chance to make a living doing what they love.

It is important to read the stories and history in this book, and even while we rejoice in the progress so far, plenty of room is left for improvement. Women's sports at all levels still receive less coverage than men's sports in both print and electronic media. The salaries of women athletes are still lower than their male counterparts, and in some sports, leagues have yet to form. Professional leagues need to be supported, and young girls growing up need role models to emulate. *Outstanding Women Athletes* provides the role models; it is up to you to fight for your opportunities, and to support those who want to play—whether in the school, playground, or professional arena.

Preface

As we near the twenty-first century, more women than ever before will have the chance to reach their potential as athletes. The road for full and complete acceptance of women in the sports world, however, has been a long and arduous one. Sports in America emerged in the nineteenth century as a strictly male domain. Women were discouraged from participating in anything more than recreational activities because of myths about women being the weaker sex, unable physically and emotionally to handle the pressures and strains of competition. But beginning in the latter part of the previous century, women began to challenge these myths, proving that they belonged in sports and that they could benefit from full participation. In June 1997, America celebrated the 25th anniversary of the passage of Title IX, legislation that helped provide opportunities for thousands of young female athletes to reach their potential on sports fields around the country.

Early in the twentieth century, sports pioneers like Eleonora Sears, Helen Wills Moody, and Gertrude Ederle challenged the sexist barriers and broke down many of the restrictive notions about women's physi-

cal abilities. These women opened doors for future generations of female athletes—athletes such as Chris Evert, Nancy Lopez, and Jackie Joyner-Kersee—who took advantage of the efforts of the early sportswomen to forge new ground of their own.

Outstanding Women Athletes: Who They Are and How They Influenced Sports in America, second edition, provides, under one cover, a resource combining history, biography, bibliography, and statistics about women's sporting experiences in America. Part 1 consists of two historical chapters. Competitive sports, in which women entered tournaments and contests that pitted their skills against those of other women, are primarily a twentieth-century phenomenon. The female "athlete" emerged in the twentieth century and brought with her dress reform and an interest in fitness as an empowering force. Women who participated in sports early in the twentieth century, such as Hazel Hotchkiss Wightman, Glenna Collett Vare, and Babe Didrikson Zaharias, generally did so outside the strict confines of proper behavior set by society; despite all the restrictions, these women garnered near-hero status because of their exceptional talents and endearing personalities. During these years, college women were introduced to sports as part of their educational programs, but competitive sports were frowned upon and discouraged by the nation's physical educators for nearly a quarter of a century more. Professional opportunities for women in sports didn't come until after World War II; more recently, a revolution in sports, spurred by the women's movement, education legislation (Title IX), and television, opened the doors wider for sportswomen in America.

Chapter 1 offers a narrative history of women's sports in America, focusing on the female experience in competitive sports at the collegiate, amateur, and professional levels. A chronological list of women's sporting milestones is presented at the end of this chapter, which provides a look at the women who took the first steps in breaching the male-dominated sports world.

The Olympics also played an important role in the development of women's sports in America. Chapter 2 describes important events as they relate to the women's Olympic program and acknowledges outstanding performances of female Olympians at each successive Olympiad. (Although the focus is on American women, international athletes who impacted the sports world with their outstanding performances also receive recognition.) The success of Olympians such as Wilma Rudolph, Olga Korbut, and Joan Benoit Samuelson had a tremendous impact on creating an atmosphere of acceptance for women in all sports. Again, the path to participation was not an easy one. From the outset, modern Olympic Games' founders opposed women's participation in the sports festival. In response to this opposition, sportswomen from around the world developed and participated in four innovative and highly successful Women's Olympics (1922,

1926, 1930, 1934), which became a forum for women's track and field athletes to exhibit their talents. The success of the Women's Olympics contributed to greater inclusion of women in the Olympics in the 1920s, and for the next 60 years, the number of women's sports and events increased at a moderate pace.

Every Olympic venue to date is listed in chapter 2. Each section offers a description of the venue, a comparison of the number of female and male competitors, and a list of new events added for women, which shows the progress of women in the Olympic movement. In this second edition, the data on the number of nations, events, and athletes in the respective Olympic Games have been updated to reflect those used by the United States Olympic Committee (USOC) as reported in the *USOC Fact Book*.

The history outlined in the first two chapters sets a foundation for an appreciation of the challenges female athletes faced in establishing themselves in the sports world. Overcoming the sexist barriers and reaching excellence have made women sports stars of the twentieth century role models for young women striving to succeed not only in sports, but in whatever endeavors they choose.

Part 2 includes biographical essays about some of the female athletes who shaped and influenced the course of women's sports in America. The biographies include information on the lives of 86 athletes—representing 30 different sports, spanning the years from the late nineteenth century through 1997—who in some way influenced the development of women's sports in America. Since it was impossible to include all the women who deserve to be in this book, I chose to include women who had won titles in the sport's major events, such as the Olympics, world or national championships, and who had a significant impact on sports in America. Although American athletes are emphasized again, exceptions were made for foreign-born figures who greatly influenced sports in America, such as Sonja Henie, Olga Korbut, Nadia Comaneci, Manon Rheaume, and Monica Seles. Each biography presents basic information about the woman's life including her birth date and place and parents' names (when available); information about how she became involved in her sport(s); her achievements, records set, and championships earned; and honors or awards received. For those athletes still competing, information is current through 1997. Because women may enter the record books under their maiden or married names, athletes have been listed alphabetically by the names by which they are best known. Cross-references to maiden or married names are provided in the indexes to accommodate name changes. Organizations and events also often undergo name changes over time. For example, in tennis, the U.S. Open was known as the U.S. National Championship until 1968, when the event went from an amateur to a professional tournament. This edition includes a list of organization and event abbreviations.

The selection of the athletes to include was at times a difficult task. The 86 athletes who were chosen should in no way diminish the accomplishments of the hundreds of women who have achieved distinction in sports over the last century.

Since the first edition of this book was published, women's sports teams have taken a more visible role in the sporting world. Chapter 4 profiles 10 of America's most outstanding women's teams. Over the last hundred years, women have banded together to wage battles, overcome defeat,

and share victory in the name of equality on and off the sports field. But female athletes faced enormous obstacles in their efforts to get women's team sports accepted into the sports world. Since the turn of the century, individual sports like swimming, badminton, golf, tennis, and bowling were emphasized and considered much more acceptable than team sports like volleyball, basketball, and softball. But powerful women's teams made up of strong individual players emerged throughout the twentieth century, and after a century of struggle, U.S. women's teams made their most dramatic mark at the 1996 Olympic Summer Games.

Chapter 4 includes brief histories of the teams, how and when they were formed, lists of their accomplishments in national and/or international competitions, followed by brief biographies of team members. The biographies profile team members during the height of their respective successes, most particularly the five gold-medal-winning teams at the 1996 Olympics (basketball, gymnastics, softball, soccer, synchronized swimming). The Tennessee State University Tigerbelles (track) and the Raybestos Brakettes (softball) have fielded strong women's teams for more than three decades. Athletes selected from those teams have been successful in national and world competition. The Colorado Silver Bullets (baseball) section provides information about the inaugural team, which in no way should diminish the achievements of other team members.

Part 3 provides basic resources for the reader who is searching for more information on these women and their sports. One of the exciting trends in women in sports is the growing number of publications on women in sports, including histories, biographies, and autobiographies. The selected annotated bibliography, arranged by sport, includes books that focus on the biography of women in sports. It does not include instructional or health and fitness books for women. The list has been updated in this second edition to include books that are currently available. A completely updated directory of sports organizations and foundations that promote women's sports in the United States is also included.

The final section of the book contains a complete list of Olympic gold-medal winners, lists of award winners and women champions in 20 sports, and National Collegiate Athletic Association (NCAA) Division I champions in eight sports—cross-country, fencing, golf, gymnastics, swimming and diving, tennis, track, and field. This section ends with a list, arranged by sport, of the athletes profiled in the book.

This second edition has been completed revised. Chapters 1 and 2 have been updated to include important developments since the last edition was published in 1991, including a reflection on the impact of Title IX 25 years after its passage, as well as descriptions of the 1992, 1994, 1996, and 1998 Olympic Games. As previously mentioned, biographies of still active athletes have been updated through 1997. In addition, 26 new biographies have been added to chapter 3. Chapter 4 is completely new to this edition, as are two new appendixes—a NCAA champions list and a list of selected references. The other bibliographies, directories, and lists have been updated through 1997, with the exception of the listing of gold medal winners, which includes 1998 Nagano gold medalists.

A 1985 Miller Lite/Women's Sports Foundation survey suggested that one of the remaining barriers to women's participation in sports and fitness activities was a lack of prominent role models. Throughout history, in sports and in other areas, talented and accomplished individuals have awakened in others a sense of their own capabilities and a desire to fulfill their own potential. Anyone who aspires to achieve their full potential as an athlete can look to sports pioneers for inspiration and possibly find that the lives behind the statistics may not be so different from their own.

Acknowledgments

Many people have helped in getting this project completed. I would like to thank the media relations departments of numerous organizations, sports associations, clubs and governing bodies that assisted in providing with information and verifying facts, most particularly the American Softball Association and the National Softball Hall of Fame, Colorado Silver Bullets, U.S. Synchronized Swimming, USA Gymnastics, U.S. Swimming, USA Basketball, U.S. Figure Skating, U.S. Skiing, USA Track and Field, Ladies Professional Golf Association, National Collegiate Athletic Association, Corel WTA Tour, USA Bowling, U.S. Fencing, Women's Professional Rodeo Association, the America[3] Foundation, United States Olympic Committee, U.S. Archery, and U.S. Soccer.

From the outset, the editiorial and production staff at The Oryx Press have shown enormous enthusiasm and support for this project. I especially thank my editor Sean Tape, who worked diligently in putting the pieces together and skillfully guiding the manuscript through production, and Lori Kennedy, who had the daunting task of locating photos.

Part I

History of Women's Sports

Chapter 1
Women in American Sports

"Achievement is not about what you've done, but what you've gained from your experience."
Lynn Hill, world class rock climber

Throughout the history of sports in America, women have had to battle society's strict conventions to participate in competitive sports. The Victorian attitudes of the nineteenth century created an atmosphere that discouraged women from participating in the "masculine" world of sports. For more than a century, women had limited or no access to facilities, training, and coaching. The opportunities available to sportswomen in the 1990s and into the twenty-first century were created by female athletes whose competitive spirit and athletic skill forced changes that opened doors for future generations. Those women who achieved success despite the odds shaped women's history and sports' history in America. This chapter is their history.

RECREATION IN EARLY AMERICA

Women have participated in recreational activities in the United States since the founding of the country. Recreation in early America played an important role in the social life of the female colonists. Recreational pursuits during this time often par-alleled the role of women in society, with social class and cultural sex roles dictating women's participation. In the pre-industrial family, all the subsistence living, food production, and social activities centered around the home and the community. Women's daily work routines included clothing, cooking for, and educating the children, as well as economic tasks such as growing and preserving food. This lifestyle left little leisure time for the female settlers working to establish their homes. People often played games directly related to their daily lives: economic-type activities such as barn-raising, corn-husking, or quilting bees; family games of cards and charades that centered around the home; and ceremonial activities such as dancing at holiday celebrations.

Dancing prevailed as the most socially acceptable and popular recreational activity for women of all classes. The gentry attended balls and lavish parties, while frontier women held barn dances and outdoor barbecues where they danced vigorous jigs and reels. Dances provided a public place for young women and men to socialize. Fishing, boating, sleighing, ice skating, and horseback riding accentuated the public life of upper-class women, who had more leisure time to pursue these activities.

Early in the nineteenth century, the country began to industrialize, and men moved into the public work force, taking their traditional work into the factories. Industrialization and the subsequent urbanization resulted in a new middle class with more time and money for leisure activities. But within this middle class also developed the notion of "true womanhood," based on the ideal that emerged during the reign of Queen Victoria of England (1837–1901). The Victorian ideal meant women should be gentle, passive, pure, and moral. Generally, according to the ideal, women stayed inside the home to maintain their purity; rebuffed any strenuous exercise; and maintained the appearance of a petite, delicate, and frail body. Many believed that women could not take the strain of any physical exertion and any overt activity would have negative effects on female sexuality and the ability to give birth, which was held to be the foremost task in women's lives during the Victorian period in America.

By the mid-1850s, however, medical doctors, such as America's first female doctor Elizabeth Blackwell (1821–1910), and educators, such as Catherine Beecher (1800–1878), became concerned with the poor quality of women's health and began to advocate moderate exercise. Women's rights advocates began to encourage dress reform, arguing that the rigid corsets and layers of petticoats women wore contributed to many women's ailments, but the Victorian attitude toward women continued until after the Civil War. Dancing, ice skating, and mild exercises remained the only real physical outlets for women.

Although middle-class women did not compete in sports in the mid-1800s, they did accompany their fathers, husbands, and brothers to sporting events such as horse races and baseball games. As spectators, women gave these events more respectability, and promoters encouraged women to attend in all their finery. And like dances were to earlier generations, these events provided a socially acceptable place for young women to socialize with the community's young men. As a result, women became increasingly interested in actually competing in the sports they viewed rather than being mere spectators.

POST-CIVIL WAR

Between 1861 and 1865, the United States engaged in a devastating Civil War that tore the country apart. Women took on jobs as nurses, cooks, and merchants to support the fighting men. After the war, as the country went through the reconstruction process, women engaged in an ever-increasing range of activities in the public sphere, primarily through the formation of women's clubs and organizations. Women's recreation evolved into women's sport as more competitive opportunities opened up through club tournaments and sponsored events.

Organized Sports for Women

In this period of urbanization and organization after the Civil War, women often formed their own athletic clubs. Thirty women from New York formed the Ladies Club for Outdoor Sports in 1877, and club members enjoyed tennis, archery, and other sports. The women had their own clubhouse that contained a reception room, a locker room, and a bathroom with showers. Women also formed clubs for archery, bicycling, rowing, and fencing, and by the early 1880s, they joined their husbands as members in country clubs that provided golf, tennis, and riding. The recreational activities quickly turned into sports competitions, particularly in tennis, golf, archery, and baseball.

Tennis. Mary Ewing Outerbridge (1856–1924) is credited with introducing lawn tennis to the United States in 1874. In January of that year, Outerbridge traveled to Bermuda for her annual holiday. While on the island, she watched British Army officers hitting a rubber ball across an outstretched net using spoon-shaped paddles strung with catgut. Fascinated by the game, Outerbridge brought a box of the tennis equipment with her when she returned to New York in the spring.

Outerbridge and her family set up a court on the corner of one of the cricket fields at the Staten Island Cricket and Baseball Club. This first court was an hour-glass shape, 24-feet wide at the net and 30-feet wide at the baseline. Outerbridge introduced the game to her friends, and the women played tennis while the men pursued baseball and cricket. The game quickly became popular with the men as well and rapidly spread throughout the Northeast as a favorite pastime.

In 1887, women from the Philadelphia Cricket Club organized a national tennis tournament by inviting women players from outside their own club to participate. Ellen Hansell won the first U.S. national tournament, and Bertha Townsend won the following year. The United States Lawn Tennis Association (USLTA) formed in 1881 and opened its membership to women in 1889. The USLTA took over sponsorship of the national tournament and offered its first women's championship in 1889, won by Bertha Townsend.

Golf. Women played golf in America as early as 1889, when the first mixed-foursome event was played at St. Andrews Golf Club at Yonkers, New York. Miss Carrie Low and her partner John Reid defeated Mrs. Reid and Henry Upham in the match. Shinnecock Hills in New York and the Chicago Golf Club opened their doors to women in 1891 and 1892, respectively, followed by several other courses in the New York/Philadelphia area. In 1894, an article in the *Ladies Home Journal* noted that "There is no reason why the middle-aged woman should fasten herself in a rocking chair. . . . Instead, she can, with her golfing club, follow her ball from link to link, renewing her beauty and youth by exercise in the open air." [1]

In 1894, an enthusiastic group of women in Morristown, New Jersey, got together to plan their own golf course—one for women only. The women formed a new club, the Morris County Golf Club, and granted honorary memberships to 200 men as "associate members." The women commissioned the design and building of an 18-hole course. In the summer of 1894, with nine holes completed, the members held a grand opening, attended by European royalty and members of New York's society crowd. Unfortunately, the women golfers became victims of their own success. The male "associate" members, who saw the potential of turning the club into a successful business, used their voting power to replace the female officers and effectively took over running of the course from the women.

In 1895, Meadowbrook Club in Hempstead, New York, hosted the first United States Golf Association (USGA) Women's Amateur Championship. Thirteen women competed in the event, won by Mrs. Charles S. Brown (first name unknown). The Morris County Golf Club hosted the second USGA Women's Amateur Championship in 1896, won by Beatrix Hoyt.

Archery. The sport of archery also grew in popularity with women after the Civil War. The National Archery Association (NAA) of the United States formed in 1879 and held its first national championships for men and women that same year. Twenty women entered the first National Archery Championships—the first national tournament for American women in any sport. Mrs. Spalding Brown won the first championship, and in 1893, Lydia Scott Howell won the first of her 13 national archery titles.

Baseball. After the Civil War, men's professional baseball became a popular sport in the eastern cities. Although the male players considered the game "too strenuous for womankind," women began playing the game at all-female colleges around the country. In the 1890s, male promoters formed a number of women's baseball teams and charged the public admission to watch them play. Known as "bloomer teams" for the bloomer uniforms the women wore, these barnstorming teams toured the country, challenging local men's teams and playing other bloomer teams. Although not considered "professional," women were paid for their play and were serious about offering the public exciting baseball. Hundreds of bloomer teams played between 1890 and 1920, and the opportunity to earn a living transformed the lives of thousands of athletic women at the turn of the century.

Adventurers. Adventurers also emerged in the world of sport. Anne Smith Peck (1850–1935) gained international attention in 1895 when she wore knickers to climb the Matterhorn in Switzerland. In 1911, at the age of 61, Peck was the first to climb Peru's 21,250-foot Mt. Corropuna, where she placed a pennant proclaiming "Votes for Women."

Dress Reform

Fashion played an important role in determining the extent of women's abilities and opportunities in the sports they played. The croquet craze that hit the Atlantic seaboard in the 1860s was an acceptable sport for women to play because they could do so while wearing their hooped skirts and layers of clothing. Tennis quickly became a favorite pastime, yet the country club set considered it "unfeminine" to "run" after the ball. Often four or five women stood on each side of the net waiting for the ball to come to them. Even if women wanted to run, their restrictive clothing prohibited them from any real vigorous activity. As one turn-of-the-century player described: "No girl would appear unless upholstered with a corset, a starched petticoat, a starched skirt, heavily button-trimmed blouse, a starched shirtwaist with long sleeves and cuff links, a high collar and four-in-hand necktie; a belt with silver buckle; and sneakers with large silk bows." [2]

Women golfers wore similar outfits. One reporter noted that at the first women's amateur championship, women came dressed in long tweed skirts that reached to their ankles, heavy leather belts with buckles, blouses with long sleeves and starched collars, bright-colored jackets over the blouses, broad-brimmed hats held in place by hat pins or veils tucked under the chin, and heavy shoes or boots.

One of the most significant events in speeding up dress reform for women was the invention of the safety bicycle in 1888. The crude vehicle was a toy for hundreds of upper-class citizens initially, but as it grew in popularity, its use as a type of recreation and a mode of transportation became more prevalent among the middle and lower classes. In 1892, Frances Willard (1839–1898), president of the Women's Christian Temperance Union (WCTU), learned how to ride a bicycle, and in 1895, she wrote *A Wheel Within a Wheel* to describe her efforts to learn to ride and to extol its benefits for other women: "I wanted to help women to a wider world, for I hold that the more interests women and men have in common, in thought, word, and deed, the happier will it be for the home."[3]

Women took to the new contraption readily. Riding a bicycle challenged the Victorian mores of the time, creating a feeling of independence and control for the female riders. Riding a bicycle also demanded physical exertion that women of the Victorian era had been warned against and required new, radical attire. Female cyclists adopted the split skirt or knickers because their ankle-length dresses would get caught in the spokes, pedal cranks, sprockets, and other mechanisms. Some riders ventured out in bloomers—baggy trousers worn under a long-sleeved, mid-calf dress—which had become standard gymnasium attire, but initially women were ridiculed for wearing the outfit in public. After the Civil War, however, bloomers became popular among most sportswomen. Gymnastics outfits, developed for more freedom of movement, went from knee-length, long-sleeved dresses with pants underneath to bloomers under a skirt, and gradually to below-the-knee knickers. Dress reform spurred by women's interest in the bicycle and other sporting activities was one of the great social changes for women at the turn of the century.

COLLEGE/PHYSICAL EDUCATION

The presence of many women in sports came from their participation in the physical education classes at the nation's colleges and universities. The newly opened women's seminaries and academies became a major source of physical activity for young American women. When Catherine Beecher opened the Hartford Female Seminary in 1823, she included calisthenics as part of the curriculum. Beecher later wrote *Letters on Health and Happiness* and quickly followed it with the publication of *Physiology and Calisthenics for Schools and Families*. She promoted her books throughout the Midwest, where other educators embraced her ideas with great enthusiasm.

Mount Holyoke College, established in 1837 in Massachusetts, also required physical education as part of the curriculum for its female students. By the end of the nineteenth century, nearly every college had a physical education program. Early proponents of physical education for women, such as Beecher, Lydia Huntley Sigourney, and Horace Mann, wrote that good health was essential to academic success. Physical education began as individual class instruction in hygiene, calisthenics, and gymnastics, but grew into intramurals and interclass competitions, and finally evolved into extramural contests.

The newly invented sport of basketball swept the country in 1891 and emerged as the most popular sport for women after Senda Berenson introduced the game to her female students at Smith College in 1892. One year later, Berenson and her students modified the rules of the men's game, which many deemed too rough for girls to play. According to Berenson's rules, players could not grab the ball from another player's hands and could only dribble the ball three times before having to pass or shoot. Berenson's rules also divided the court into three sections and players had to stay in their designated section, preventing any overexertion from running the length of the court. (The court would later be divided into two sections in 1914; the six-player split-court game remained the norm until well into the 1960s.)

The apparent concern for "appropriate" standards of play for women in basketball and other team sports led to the formation of the first in a series of physical educators' organizations to oversee women's athletics at the college level. In 1899, the Women's Basketball Rules Committee published the first basketball rules based on Berenson's revisions, and in 1905, this group became the National Women's Basketball Committee, functioning within the American Physical Education Association (APEA). In 1917, the APEA formed the Committee on Women's Athletics (CWA) because of the insistent and increasing demands for assistance in solving issues connected with the athletic activities for girls and women; the APEA believed the requests demonstrated the need for a set of standards that would be based on the limitations, abilities, and needs of women. The notion that game rules and standards of play for women should be different from the standards set for men became the dominant philosophy for the next 60 years. Women physical educators wanted control of both physical education classes and extramural competition left in their hands to ensure the programs would be run properly with the best interests of the female student in mind.

Early basketball players and coaches set up interclass and intramural competitions that subsequently led to extramural games between local colleges. However, these extramural competitions were not so quick to receive the approval of the administration. Faculty were against any competition that might cause the young students emotional and physical exhaustion, fearing that young women could not handle the competitive nature of sports. In 1894, Bryn Mawr College challenged Vassar College to a tennis tournament, but the faculty from both schools refused to let the match take place. The first intercollegiate competitions for women on the basketball courts took place two years later when the University of California, Berkeley, played Stanford at Armory Hall in San Francisco. Stanford won the game 2–1.

Field hockey appeared on the scene in 1901 when Constance M.K. Applebee brought the favorite sport of her native England to the United States. She presented the game to women at Vassar and took the exhibition to five other sister schools. Physical educators considered the game quite acceptable for female college students and promoted it in their daily classes. The first interclass contests took place in 1902.

TWENTIETH-CENTURY SPORTS

The enthusiasm of sportswomen continued to grow outside the education system at the dawn of the new century. Within the world of sports, 1870 to 1920 was a period of standardizing rules and intensive organization of sports at different skill levels. Women who participated in early physical education programs often took their interest in sport with them upon graduation. Unfortunately, these women faced considerable opposition in their efforts to develop their athletic skills beyond the recreational level. Female golfers were not allowed to use the public courses during prime playing hours, and tennis players had to relinquish the courts to men during daytime hours.

The development of elite female athletes often came in the private or special clubs formed by and for women. These clubs provided women with their own space to continue competing and to develop their skills. In 1903, wealthy Chicago women organized the Chicago Sports Club, a sports facility that included a gymnasium, swimming pool, and bowling lanes. Club members participated in competitive tournaments in fencing, basketball, bowling, water polo, and swimming. By 1920, a number of national sports organizations were offering national championship tournaments for women.

Forty bowling enthusiasts from 11 Midwestern and Northeastern cities traveled to St. Louis on November 30, 1916, and formed the Women's National Bowling Association (WNBA), now the Women's International Bowling Congress (WIBC). The WNBA was one of the first attempts to organize an association to promote a specific sport for women, and the WNBA was the first national sports organization created for and run by women. A year later, a group of swimmers formed the Women's Swimming Association of New York (WSA) to promote interest in swimming, to provide instruction in all phases of aquatics including lifesaving, and to offer the opportunity for competition. For the most part, swimmers from this New York swim club made up the Olympic teams in the early years of women's swimming competition.

The Amateur Athletic Union (AAU), which formed in 1888 to promote men's amateur athletics outside the educational setting and to preserve the concept of amateurism in American sports, offered the opportunity for sports clubs around the country to send their top athletes to national championships in a variety of sports. The AAU took an interest in women's sports just after World War I. It began sanctioning women's competition in 1914 with women's swimming and diving, and in 1923, authorized women's track and field competitions. By 1926, the AAU sponsored women's competitions in basketball, track and field, swimming and diving, and handball. The AAU also played an important role in securing American women's inclusion into the Olympics in 1916. (See chapter 2.)

African American Women

Although the AAU worked to promote sports for women after World War I, African American women were hard-pressed to find opportunities to play. The doctrine of the 1896 Supreme Court ruling in the *Plessy v. Ferguson* case, which permitted "separate but equal" facilities for Whites and Blacks on railroad cars, soon spread to other public facilities including sports fields. Many facilities, including golf courses, public tennis courts, basketball facilities, and gymnasiums, were off-limits to Blacks. Few African Americans were accepted into the mainstream women's and coed colleges where basketball, field hockey, and other women's sports developed. Black women and girls, therefore, were forced to develop their athletic abilities outside of school, generally at the local "colored" YWCAs.

Despite this discrimination, African Americans also joined in on the wave of sports clubs being formed after the Civil War and at the turn of the century. In 1916, tennis players from the Washington, DC, area came together to form the American Tennis Association (ATA) to develop tennis among Black people—men and women—in the United States. Lucy Diggs Slowe (1885–1936) won the first ATA Nationals, held at Baltimore's Druid Hill Park, in August 1917, becoming the first Black female national champion in any sport.

In 1926, a group of African American golfers formed the United Golf Association (UGA). Marie Thompson of Chicago won the UGA's first event. The first all-women's club for Blacks, Wake Robin Golf Club, formed in Washington, DC, in 1927.

THE GOLDEN AGE OF SPORTS

The expanding role of women in the workforce during World War I (1914–1917) showed that women were capable of doing jobs commonly believed too difficult or next to impossible for them. After the war, women significantly helped in gaining passage of important reform bills at the local and national levels. Their involvement in the political process proved to many women that they also had power to effect social change. This sense of power, combined with a new sense of freedom that grew as women worked for the right to vote, was influential in changing the lives of many women.

The postwar economy boomed and provided more money for leisure activities—activities the nation embraced en masse after the strenuous and lean war years. After the turmoil of World War I, the nation was ready to relax from the tensions of the past decade. From this era emerged what journalists called the "Golden Age of Sport in America," when sports flourished and sports stars made headlines. Male sports figures emerged as heroes in popular culture, and sportswomen like aviator Amelia Earhart, tennis star Helen Wills Moody, golfer Glenna Collett Vare, and swimmer Gertrude Ederle challenged the remnants of the "true woman" stereotype and the rigid divisions of the male-female physical worlds. With the 18th Amendment ratified in January 1919, prohibiting the manufacture, sale, or transportation of intoxicating liquors, more women ventured into ballparks, racetracks, and other sporting venues that once were considered disreputable places because of their association with the "evil" libations.

The 19th Amendment to the Constitution granting women the right to vote also helped the cause of women in sports. Women's suffrage was expected to bring equality to women, which would carry over into all aspects of public life. In reality, it did not bring equality, but it was an important sign that more women were accepted into public life and men's traditional domains, including sports.

Amelia Earhart captured the imagination of the country when she flew solo across the Atlantic in 1932. Her exploits helped to break down many of the stereotypes of women's physical limitations. While Earhart made news in the sky, Gertrude Ederle achieved recognition for her success in the water. In 1926, Ederle became the first woman to swim the 20 miles across the English Channel and did so over an hour faster than any man had. She was an inspirational role model for women and girls pursuing competitive athletics in the early twentieth century, challenging her own abilities as well as those of male swimmers. After Ederle completed her swim, thousands of females took to the water as a swimming craze swept the country.

Golfer Glenna Collett Vare dominated her sport, winning the first of her six national amateur tournaments in 1922. She helped popularize golf among American women and brought it from the private country club onto the public courses. Tennis star Helen Wills Moody won seven U.S. singles titles at Forest Hills, eight Wimbledon singles titles, and a gold medal in the 1924 Paris Olympics. Nicknamed "Little Miss Poker Face" for her cool, calm demeanor on the tennis court, Moody quickly became a favorite of the press. She introduced an aggressive, serve-and-volley style of play, making women's tennis much more competitive and more interesting for spectators to watch. She also successfully challenged tennis's rigid dress code by wearing sleeveless dresses and no stockings on the court. This bold step led to many dress reforms in sports and built upon the re- forms begun by women before the turn of the century.

Ora Washington (1898–1971) estab- lished herself as the best female player on the American Tennis Association circuit. Washington won eight ATA national singles titles between 1929 and 1937, and the doubles title every year from 1928 through 1936. Her exploits were well known in the African American community; she was also an outstanding basketball player. Washing- ton once challenged White tennis cham- pion Helen Wills Moody to a match, but Moody refused.

All of these sportswomen received publicity that proved to be important in acknowledging the endeavors of women in competitive athletics and in bringing other women into sports. Suddenly, America had female role models in the male-oriented world of sports.

ANTI-COMPETITION MOVEMENT

As activities for women became more vig- orous, competitive, and organized, a clear division developed between public sport and sport offered in colleges and universi- ties. As the skill level of the women in- creased, so did their desire for more intense competition. The nation's physical educa- tors, however, disapproved of women par- ticipating in competitive sports that ap- peared to focus on the elite athlete at the expense of the less skilled. College classes emphasized team sports, such as softball, basketball, volleyball, and field hockey, and discouraged individual sports like track and field.

Meanwhile, the preparations for World War I showed that a large number of the inductees were physically unfit to serve, and the subsequent concern over the physi-

cal fitness of the nation's youth created an interest in developing a nationwide pro- gram to promote physical activity and the general well-being of the country's citizens. After World War I, the War Department took an active role in organizing the Na- tional Amateur Athletic Federation (NAAF) in the hope that it could promote desirable sport practices that would lead to a more fit nation. The federation included a women's division, and federation leaders asked Lou Henry Hoover (wife of future president Herbert Hoover) to organize it. Because of the success of the fitness programs in the nation's public and private schools, Hoover called upon the nation's physical educators to help her organize the Women's Divi- sion.

With the expressed purpose of pro- moting physical activity and fitness, mem- bers of the NAAF reiterated the concern that as sports got more competitive and more people came to see women play, the highly skilled women would be exploited and their games would fall to commercial- ization. Additionally, NAAF organizers wanted more women involved, and they believed that the glorification of the highly skilled athlete would discourage less-skilled players.

In the April 1923 organizing meeting of the Women's Division of the NAAF, the group set out their official position in a 16-point directive that stated: "The Women's Division believes in the spirit of play for its own sake and works for the promotion of physical activity for the larg- est possible proportion of persons in any given group, in forms suitable to individual needs and capacities, under leadership and environmental conditions that foster health, physical efficiency, and the development of good citizenship."[4]

The NAAF meeting also gave physical educators the opportunity to voice their concerns publicly about what they perceived to be the AAU's attempted takeover of women's sports, and to again set standards for women's competitive athletics in U.S. colleges and universities. The Women's Division wanted the country to realize the importance of developing the "sport for the girl" and not the girl for the sport, and the necessity of keeping women's competitive athletics in the physical education departments of the nation's colleges and universities.

In addition to controlling women's athletics through the independent NAAF, the same women physical educators continued to have a strong voice on the Committee on Women's Athletics division of the American Physical Education Association. Educators such as Mabel Lee of the University of Nebraska and Blanche Trilling of the University of Wisconsin wrote articles and books and attended meetings to promote their philosophies of athletics for all women. At a time when physical education departments within the universities were becoming more autonomous, these women leaders created a tight-knit, independent group that nearly took complete control of all of women's college sports, both inside and outside the classroom.

Despite the clear objectives of the Women's Division, many perceived its stance as a movement to eliminate any form of competition in college programs. But Agnes Wayman, one of the foremost educators of the time, explained that "it isn't the competition which so many of us decry, but the highly intensive type of do-or-die play, motivated not so much by a desire to 'play the game' as by a desire to 'defeat someone,'" and she added that "the highly skilled girl could compete all she wants after college, but while in school competitive athletics would only interfere with her academics."[5] Any concerns related to physical harm imposed by competition, as espoused in the mid-nineteenth century, seemed secondary in the educators' argument against competition. Again Wayman articulated the consensus regarding this issue: "Since there was no scientific proof that highly intensive competition [did not produce] harmful physiological or psychological effects on the women, it was best to be on the safe side and discourage any intense activity."[6]

Play Days and Sports Days

To meet the needs of their students, physical educators came up with play days, telegraphic meets, and sports days to satisfy the competitive urges of their students. The play day brought together women from a number of schools for a day of sports activities ranging from basketball, volleyball, field hockey, and swimming to hopscotch, dodgeball, relays, and folk dancing. Individual schools would not compete against one another; rather, teams composed of players from a number of schools would play. Scores were not recorded. Officials de-emphasized competition to maximize the social aspects of the get-togethers by encouraging numerous breaks in play for reading and refreshments.

The telegraphic meet soon became a popular form of competition with the educators. In a telegraphic meet, the contestants participated on their own campuses in accordance with agreed-upon conditions. The competitors telegraphed the results of bowling games, archery rounds, and track and field times and distances to a designated official who determined the winner. The meets eliminated the expense and effort of traveling, allowing any number of women to take part in individual sports without competing directly against another student.

Despite their efforts, physical educators could not quell the increasing desire of their students to compete rather than just recreate. The educators developed sports days that permitted teams to represent their own institutions. However, to ensure that the contests did not turn intensely competitive, officials often modified the rules to shorten the games or offered less challenging round-robin formats. Sports days were the most widespread form of competition promoted by the physical educators between 1925 and 1950. Some small, rural colleges of the Midwest and West allowed intercollegiate competition in basketball, softball, and baseball, but on a very limited basis.

THE DEPRESSION, WORLD WAR II, AND CIVIL RIGHTS

The 1930s opened with an economic crisis that would last for more than a decade, not ending until the onslaught of World War II. The prosperity and hope of the 1920s were dealt a big blow with the stock market crash in October 1929. In 1930, the jobless numbered 7 million; by 1931, their ranks had swelled to 12 million; and in 1932, the unemployed totaled 15 million out of a total labor force of 45 million. Women left many of the jobs they had taken in the economic prosperity of the 1920s and returned to the home and private life.

The early 1930s saw a decline in the attendance at public events, travel, and club membership, but as the Depression wore on, more people began looking for diversions from the tensions of daily life. Going to the movies, listening to the radio, playing bridge, and participating in and watching different sports became favorite activities of many citizens who had an abundance of leisure time and little money to spend. New Deal legislation of Franklin D. Roosevelt helped to promote mass-participation sports with government aid through the Works Progress Administration (WPA), which contributed more than $1.17 billion to develop recreation facilities and programs in the United States. This new emphasis on low-cost activities attracted many new sports enthusiasts. Softball, volleyball, tennis, and bowling gained thousands of female participants. Floretta McCutcheon toured the country giving bowling instruction and setting up leagues for women. Former national tennis champion Hazel Hotchkiss Wightman held free tennis clinics for women at the Longwood Cricket Club in New York and ran tournaments for all skill levels in New England. These women contributed to the growing number of women who became involved in sports during the Depression-ridden 1930s.

Basketball. In the 1920s, companies began sponsoring baseball, basketball, and track teams that participated in league competitions and tournaments throughout the country. In Texas, an entire network of more than 40 basketball teams played tournaments around the state. The teams used men's rules whenever they played. In 1926, the AAU sponsored the first national women's basketball championships, which also played with men's rules.

Two female African American teams featured some of the best female athletes in the country. The *Philadelphia Tribune*–sponsored team, which formed in 1931, included Ora Washington, the ATA tennis champion. Her teammates were Gladys Walker, Virginia Woods, Lavinia Moore, Myrtle Wilson, Rose Wilson, Marie Leach, Florence Campbell, and Sarah Latimore. The Tribunes toured the South, giving clinics and playing exhibitions to demonstrate women's ability to play high-quality sports. Their Midwest counterparts, the Chicago Romas, included a line-up that featured

Isadore Channels, a four-time winner of the ATA women's singles title, and included Corrine Robison, Mignon Burns, Lillian Ross, Virginia Wills, and Lula Porters.

Baseball. The bloomer teams of the early twentieth century continued to barnstorm the country. The bloomer outfits, however, gave way to standard baseball uniforms, and the women began to play a more aggressive style. But as major league baseball attendance soared during the 1920s, bloomer teams faced increased competition for the baseball audience. Baseball owners used their money to support men's semipro teams to develop players for their major league teams rather than the bloomer teams. By the mid-1930s, baseball for women gave way to softball, and women's baseball nearly disappeared from the sporting scene.

Track and Field. With AAU support, America's elite track and field female athletes had gained entry into the Olympics by 1928. Despite NAAF and CWA objections, the AAU first sent a track and field team to the 1922 Women's Olympics. The AAU then argued to include a U.S. women's track and field team at the 1928 Olympics, which occurred only after unprecedented male support for women's inclusion by a threatened American men's team boycott. (See chapter 2.)

Most African American sports clubs did not belong to the Amateur Athletic Union so their athletes did not compete in the national championships unless by special invitation, and so Black sports enthusiasts began to organize their own meets. On May 7, 1927, the all-Black Tuskegee Institute began its Relay Carnival. Organizer Cleveland Abbott, Tuskegee's athletic director, opened two events for women, the 100-yard dash and a 440-yard relay. In

1930, he added the 50-yard dash and the discus. Abbott set out to build a powerhouse women's track team at Tuskegee. He hired Amelia C. Roberts to coach the team. In 1937, the team won the AAU nationals and began the Black female domination of some track and field events.

Mildred "Babe" Didrikson

One American woman emerged as an Olympic superstar in 1932 and is perhaps the greatest female athlete America has known. Mildred "Babe" Didrikson (Zaharias) began her sports career at the age of 16 with the Golden Cyclone Athletic Club of Dallas in an industry-sponsored basketball league. In the off-season, Didrikson entered AAU competitions in track and field, where she single handedly won the national title for her sponsor, Employers Casualty of Dallas, by winning five of the eight events she entered. In 1932, Didrikson captured three track and field medals at the Los Angeles Olympics, and she quickly became a headline maker. The attention she received for her Olympic exploits led her into other areas. She excelled at nearly every sport she tried. Between 1932 and 1934, Didrikson traveled across the United States performing exhibitions of her athletic skill in a wide range of sports. She formed the Babe Didrikson All-American Basketball team (she was one of three females) that barnstormed the country playing exhibitions against local teams. She pitched at a baseball game against the St. Louis Cardinals and gave demonstrations of pitching, billiards, and swimming. Her tours were a great success; thousands paid to see her perform her athletic feats.

In 1935, Didrikson took up golf and went on an exhibition tour with the leading men's professional golfer Gene Sarazen for $1,000 a week. She had lost her amateur status when she allowed her name to be used in an automobile advertisement upon her return from the Olympics. With no professional opportunities for women golfers in the late 1930s, Didrikson had to wait three years to regain her amateur status in order to play competitive golf. She won her first golf tournament, the Texas State Amateur Championship, in 1940. Between 1944 and 1947, she won 22 amateur tournaments, 14 of them in a row. Her presence on the golf course gave the game visibility, and Didrikson, along with Patty Berg, was instrumental in the formation of the Ladies Professional Golf Association (LPGA) in 1949. Didrikson showed that women could participate in competitive athletics and reach excellence unharmed.

World War II

The entry of the United States into World War II in 1941 and the ensuing four years of fighting dramatically affected the lives of most Americans. As men were called to fight the war, thousands of women joined the nation's labor force in the government's all-out push to establish an efficient wartime economy. By the wartime peak in July 1944, 19 million women were employed, an increase of 47 percent over prewar levels. Almost 50 percent of all women were employed at some point during 1944.

As in the World War I emergency, women's participation in war production and homefront activities necessitated an increase in the general level of health and fitness, which was vigorously encouraged by the government and supported by the country's physical educators. The Women's Bureau of the Department of Labor recommended that companies set up recreation programs to boost workers' morale, and the physical fitness division of the Office of Civilian Defense encouraged fit-

ness through sports competition. Bowling and softball leagues for women workers flourished during the war, as did sports programs in basketball and volleyball.

One of the first professional team sports leagues for women debuted during the war with the formation of the All-American Girls Professional Baseball League (AAGPBL). Chicago Cubs owner Philip K. Wrigley (of chewing gum fame), concerned that fans would lose interest in the national pastime while the men were at war, organized the league in 1943 to attract fans to the major league ballparks until the men returned. (See chapter 4.)

Wrigley and other team sponsors invited the top women softball players to try out for their teams. Players were taught how to use a regulation nine-inch baseball, pitch overhand, and play on a field with the longer 85-foot base paths. Great pains were taken to ensure that the players retained their femininity. In preseason training, the players learned game fundamentals during the day and went to charm school at night to learn etiquette and makeup techniques. During regular season games, players wore uniform dresses that could be no more than six inches above the knee. Players could not wear slacks, shorts, or jeans in public; they could not cut their hair; and each team had a chaperon for the players as the league strove to give the public the image of complete femininity.

The league was a success for more than a decade. Between 1943 and 1954, more than 600 women played a schedule of 110 to 160 games a year for the 10 teams from Wisconsin, Indiana, Minnesota, Michigan, and Illinois. Nearly one million fans flocked to the games in 1948. Top players included Helen Callaghan, who led the league in batting in 1945 with a .299 average; Sophie Kurys, whose 201 stolen bases in a single season still stands as a professional record (71 more than Rickey Henderson's 1982 record); and Jean Faut, who pitched two perfect games and had a career record of 132 wins and 61 losses. The league folded in 1954 because of financial troubles brought on by the return of men's baseball and the subsequent popularity of television and televised major league games. Nonetheless, for more than 10 years, the nation had a successful professional women's team sport that entertained millions.

The absence of men during the war had expanded women's involvement in more than just the workforce and the baseball field, and despite a resurgence of traditional values of home and family after the war, women's roles continued to grow in educational, civic, and cultural activities. In sports, Babe Didrikson dominated women's golf as the fledgling LPGA struggled to establish itself. Women bowlers formed the Professional Women's Bowling Association (PWBA) in 1959, with more than 100 women bowling in the first PWBA tournament the following year. Teenager Maureen Connolly led an impressive group of female tennis players in the world's top amateur events (professional tennis would not begin until the open era of the early 1970s), while skier Andrea Mead Lawrence and figure skaters Tenley Albright and Carol Heiss brought home the gold in the Winter Olympics.

The publicity given to the exploits of these women helped reinforce the postwar notion pushed by elite athletes and feminists that women were physically capable of doing just about anything. Additionally, the "sport for every girl" philosophy of the 1920s and 1930s produced a whole generation of women wanting and expecting opportunities in sport upon leaving the nation's colleges and universities. How-

ever, after nearly a century of sports participation, women still faced challenges in entering the male-controlled sports establishment. After World War II, working women were encouraged to return to the home, giving their jobs back to men returning from the battlefields. Society encouraged women to go back to life as it was before the war. Women's sports suffered the same sort of blacklash. Although not completely discouraged from sports, women were encouraged to participate in sports that emphasized individual talent or grace and beauty, such as golf, tennis, and figure skating, as opposed to sports that required teamwork and strength and endurance, such as baseball and track and field.

College Athletics

In the nation's physical education departments, female college athletes still did not have access to coaching, facilities, or training opportunities. Those students who chose to pursue competitive athletics had to look to the Amateur Athletic Union, industrial and business sponsorship, and professional organizations to develop their skills.

By the mid-1950s, however, the noncompetition attitudes for women's collegiate sports slowly began to change. Most of the sports-day activities in colleges and universities were curtailed during the war, but intercollegiate contests for women increased in number after the war. Finally, after years of review, the majority of physical educators conceded that varsity-type competition had no adverse effect on intramural and physical education programs.

The physical educators modified their position and considered sanctioning intercollegiate events for college women. In 1941, against the wishes of the NAAF and CWA, Gladys Palmer hosted an intercollegiate golf championship at Ohio State University as a one-time experiment. Under the watchful eye of the women's groups, Ohio State continued to sponsor the annual tournament until 1956. In 1957, the Division for Girls' and Women's Sport (DGWS), formerly named the Women's Division of the NAAF, took over sponsorship of the tournament and for the first time began to address the issue of women's intercollegiate competition in earnest.

Thus, the 1960s proved to be a period of rapid change in women's collegiate sport. The DGWS outlined standards for collegiate competition while reaffirming the philosophy that student athletes should not be treated specially, i.e., they should not receive financial aid or scholarships for their superior skill alone, and that any programs should remain in the women's physical education departments to ensure that the competition would not interfere with the students' academic programs. In 1963, the DGWS and the Women's Board of the Olympic Development Committee sponsored a series of five institutes for improving high-level teaching and coaching in many Olympic sports. This cooperative effort signaled the first time in nearly 40 years that the DGWS directly promoted women's participation in the Olympics and encouraged women's competitive sports *outside* the educational framework.

In 1967, the DGWS formed the Commission on Intercollegiate Athletics for Women (CIAW) to establish a platform for conducting intercollegiate athletics for college women and began offering national championships in golf, tennis, gymnastics, and track and field, among others. So popular were the championships, among competitors and spectators alike, that CIAW officials decided that a separate membership organization to oversee women's intercollegiate contests was needed. In 1971,

the CIAW reorganized and became the Association of Intercollegiate Athletics for Women (AIAW) to govern women's athletics at the college level as an independent group *outside* college physical education departments. The AIAW developed rules, policies, and procedures for holding tournaments, competitions, and national championships. In 1973, the AIAW allowed universities to offer athletic scholarships for female athletes based on athletic skill.

Civil Rights

The growing opportunities for women to participate in sport were mirrored by changes in society in general. The 1954 Supreme Court decision in the *Brown v Board of Education* of Topeka, Kansas, held that segregated public schools were unconstitutional, and in 1955, the Court ordered that the desegregation of public schools should begin "with all deliberate speed." Following the ruling by the Supreme Court, Congress passed the Civil Rights Act of 1960 to ensure voting rights for all citizens.

This legislation was the first of many legislative and civil actions in the fight for equality, but by this time, women had already begun efforts to remove racial barriers in sports. Althea Gibson broke the color barrier in tennis in 1950 when she played in the U.S. National Championships. The same year, the Women's International Bowling Congress (WIBC), the largest sports organization for women in the world, opened its membership to women of color, and in 1956, the United States Golf Association (USGA) allowed African American women to enter the U.S. Women's Amateur Championship. Anne Gregory of Gary, Indiana, considered the best Black female golfer ever—she won the UGA title in 1950, 1953, 1957, 1965, and 1966—entered the 1956 U.S. Women's Amateur Championships held in Indianapolis, breaking down barriers for minority players on golf courses around the country. The success of the Tennessee State University Tigerbelles in track and field, as seen in the success of Olympic athletes Wilma Rudolph, Mae Faggs, and Wyomia Tyus, also helped to open doors for many African American athletes. (See chapter 4.)

A REVOLUTION IN SPORTS

The burgeoning women's movement of the 1960s that sought to address the inequities in society also provided the catalyst for involving more women in education and in sports. The changes that took place in sports for women during the 1960s and 1970s were a direct result of these social changes that created new attitudes about and toward women. The women's movement supported equal opportunity on the playing field, and women demanded the equal opportunity, facilities, and equipment that previously had been denied them.

High school girls challenged existing state laws prohibiting them from competing in sports with boys. In 1971, Julia Barash of Monroe, New York, and Phyllis Graber of Jamaica, New York, wanted to play on the boys' tennis teams because there were no girls' teams. They challenged the state law prohibiting them from playing on a boys' team, awakening state and local officials to the lack of opportunities for girls in sports. The discriminatory regulations of high school athletic associations in California, Connecticut, Illinois, Indiana, Kansas, Michigan, and numerous other states were all challenged in the courts, with most decisions in favor of the girls.

Title IX

All the court cases and women's advocacy expanded opportunities to play, but the most influential piece of legislation to af-

fect women's athletics, the Education Amendments of 1972, was signed into law on June 23, 1972, by President Nixon. Included among these amendments was Title IX, a provision outlawing sex discrimination in education, which stated that:

> No person in the United States shall, on the basis of sex, be excluded from participation in, be denied the benefits of, or be subjected to discrimination under any education program or activity receiving federal financial assistance.

The legislation required schools and universities receiving money from the federal government to offer equal programs, facilities, and opportunities for women. The law covered all aspects of curricular and extra-curricular programs, meaning that in sports, women were to have equal access to the equipment, training, and competitive opportunities that men had been receiving for more than half a century.

Title IX had an immediate and enormous impact on high school sports programs. The National Federation of State High School Associations reported that in 1970 there were fewer than 300,000 female participants in interscholastic athletics, but by 1972, when Title IX passed, there were nearly 800,000 female participants. Participation rates for high school girls jumped approximately 616 percent between 1971 and 1982.

Women's sports on the college and university level were also dramatically changed by the passage of Title IX. In 1970, women received only one percent of the total athletic budgets in American colleges and universities. Women's intercollegiate athletics had never been a major concern of male university administrators and athletic directors. With Title IX, women's share of the athletic budget rose from 1 percent in 1971 to nearly 20 percent by 1982, and participation increased nearly

150 percent in the same period. With a larger presence, both physically and financially, in the college and university athletic departments, women had access to better training facilities and state-of-the-art equipment and could hire more experienced coaches at better salaries.

Governance of Women's Sports

During that 10-year period, the AIAW successfully regulated the growing sporting opportunities for the nation's elite female athletes. At the height of its influence, 1981–82, more than 125,000 female athletes participated in AIAW events. That year, the AIAW offered 39 national championships in 19 sports to more than 6,000 teams at nearly 1,000 member colleges and universities. However, as women's sports grew in popularity and gained more television coverage in the mid-1970s, the National Collegiate Athletic Association (NCAA), which governed men's sports on the collegiate level, began to challenge AIAW's control and threatened to take over women's college athletics.

Back in 1905, a group of college presidents and administrators had formed the NCAA to standardize rules for all college sports and to set policies related to eligibility, recruiting, and scholarships for athletes. Although the NCAA implied in its policy statement that it covered men's *and* women's athletics, women's programs were not included until the 1980s. In 1974, the NCAA lifted its ban against women and in 1975 voted to take over governance of women's intercollegiate sports despite strong protests from the majority of women athletes, coaches, and administrators who believed they would lose their autonomy. The AIAW held its position as the governing body of women's intercollegiate athletics until 1980, when the NCAA membership voted to offer national championships for women athletes in five sports in three divisions. With the vote, the NCAA implemented a four-year plan that allowed member colleges and universities to operate their women's programs under either existing NCAA or AIAW rules until 1985. However, after 1985, member schools that wanted to participate in NCAA-sponsored women's athletics had to belong exclusively to the NCAA and had to be governed by NCAA rules. Pressure on member schools to adhere to this directive led to the demise of the AIAW—the first and only autonomous governing body exclusively for women's college athletics. In 1982, the women's group lost a court battle to prevent NCAA sponsorship of women's championships, and the AIAW was finished for all practical purposes.

Television

Other factors contributed to the changing nature of women's sports. Television coverage of sporting events in the 1950s revolutionized sports in America by bringing sports and sports heroes into American living rooms. Major League Baseball, National Football League, and National Basketball Association games filled valuable airtime on the new medium, but elite female athletes rarely received any television coverage. However, in 1960, live, via satellite, the world saw American Wilma Rudolph sprint to three gold medals in track and field at the Rome Olympics. Suddenly, TV discovered women's sports, and the number of televised women's events began to grow. Live television coverage of the Olympic efforts of Wyomia Tyus, Donna de Varona, Peggy Fleming, Dorothy Hamill, and Nadia Comaneci, among others, all contributed to further acceptance of women's athletics in the United States. During the 1972 Summer Olympics, television introduced the world to Olga Korbut, whose athletic ability sparked a worldwide interest in gymnastics among young girls, initiating a whole generation of tumblers and dancers.

Women's Professional Tennis and the "Battle of the Sexes"

Perhaps the most significant televised sports event for both the women's movement and women's sports in the 1970s occurred on September 20, 1973, when Billie Jean King, the top woman tennis player in the world, faced Bobby Riggs in what the media billed as the "Battle of the Sexes."

King had been working to promote a professional women's tennis tour since the advent of open (professional) tennis in 1968. From the initiation of open tennis, women faced unequal treatment in prize money offered at the most prestigious tournaments. In the 1968 Wimbledon and the 1968 English Hard Court Championships at Bournemouth, the first two professional events, the men's winners received $56,000 and $28,000, respectively, while the women's winner received a paltry $2,100 and $840. In addition to unequal prize money, the male-controlled USLTA, the governing body for tennis in the United States, failed to schedule any women's tournaments in 1970. This move incited King, *World Tennis* magazine publisher Gladys Heldman, and eight other players to take action to set up a separate women's tour that would guarantee a full tournament schedule and equitable prize money. The group of tennis professionals convinced Virginia Slims of Houston to sponsor eight professional tournaments that year. By the end of 1970, the Virginia Slims circuit had nearly 40 members, up from its original nine; an independent women's professional tennis tour was born.

In 1971, women professional tennis players competed in 19 tournaments for a total of more than $300,000 in prize money. The successful appearance of a full-blown Slims circuit in 1971 became a direct economic threat to the USLTA. Attendance at the USLTA events dropped, while the women's tournaments became more popular. Eleven of the 19 tournaments made a profit in the first year as spectators filled the stands to see the top women players.

Just as the new women's professional circuit was getting off the ground, Bobby Riggs, a 55-year-old former tennis star, challenged Billie Jean King to a five-set match. Millions of television viewers worldwide watched as King won the match easily. A victory for women's sports everywhere! After the match, with television cameras blazing, King took the opportunity in the limelight to speak out for equal pay in women's tennis and equal opportunity for all women in sport.

Opportunities for Women in Other Sports

In addition to tennis, other women's professional sports made strides in numbers, organization, sponsorship money, press coverage, and general acceptance. Nancy Lopez moved women's golf into the public's consciousness with her remarkable performances in her first year on the LPGA tour. Her rookie earnings of $153,000 in 1978 were a record not only for women, but also for men. She came to symbolize women's professional sports and was an icon of the revolution in women's sports.

Professional opportunities also opened in other sports. Wyomia Tyus headlined the Professional International Track Association (PITA), a professional track and field tour begun in 1973; Joan Joyce and Billie Jean King created the International Women's Professional Softball Association (IWPSA) in 1975; and Mary Jo Peppler and

Kathy Gregory starred in the International Volleyball Association (IVA), a league of four-men, two-women volleyball teams initiated in 1975.

Throughout the 1970s, women continually challenged the barriers to enter sports that had traditionally belonged to men. Ann Meyers signed a one-year contract with the Indiana Pacers of the National Basketball Association; jockey Diane Crump raced in the Kentucky Derby; and Janet Guthrie sped around the oval track at nearly 200 miles per hour in the 1977 Indianapolis 500.

Running and fitness for women also exploded onto the scene in the 1970s. A decade earlier, in April 1966, Roberta Gibb Bingay, disguised in a hooded sweatshirt, crossed the finish line at the 69th annual Boston Marathon as the first woman to unofficially run in the prestigious event. (Women were not allowed to enter the nation's premier distance running event.) A year later, Kathrine Switzer officially entered the race as K. Switzer, but an official tried to pull her off the track during the course of the race. Switzer and her running partners fought off the official, and she went on to finish the race. When photos of the incident flashed across the newswire, women runners across the country expressed their outrage. After pressure from the growing number of female distance runners, the Boston Marathon established the women's division in 1972; Nina Kuscsik was its first winner.

To encourage young athletes to forge new ground in sports, Billie Jean King, Donna de Varona, Micki King, Wyomia Tyus, and Sheila Young founded the Women's Sports Foundation (WSF) in 1974 as a nonprofit, educational organization dedicated to promoting and enhancing the sports experience for all girls and women.

Among many of its activities, the WSF acts as a resource clearinghouse on women's sports and related topics, maintains a speakers bureau referral service, sponsors the International Women's Sports Hall of Fame, provides sport camp scholarships for deserving and financially needy girls, and publishes and distributes information to assist in sports programming. Members of WSF and other concerned citizens were instrumental in the passage of the Amateur Sports Act of 1978 to promote and provide financial support for developmental sports for girls and women and to provide the elite athlete with training and world-class experience.

Team Sports

Women's basketball underwent a series of rule changes in the 1960s and 1970s. In 1961, roving players were allowed unlimited dribbles (previously they had been allowed only three before passing to a teammate), and in 1971, the AAU adopted the five-player, full-court game, which allowed players to run the length of the court. Women's basketball and field hockey were added to the 1976 Olympics, joining volleyball as the only team sports for women on the Olympic schedule, and the Raybestos Brakettes dominated the Amateur Softball Association major league fast-pitch softball championships by winning 10 out of 12 championships between 1966 and 1978. (See chapter 4.)

The Title IX Generation and Beyond

Title IX mandated equal opportunity in educational programs and in institutions supported by federal funds and contributed to an enormous surge in participation rates in the last two decades. The first generation of Title IX athletes has now begun to make its mark on women's sports. Outstanding female athletes like speed skater Bonnie Blair, swimmer Janet Evans, softball pitcher Lisa Fernandez, figure skater Kristi Yamaguchi, and heptathlete Jackie Joyner-Kersee have excelled in their sports in part because of the opportunities afforded them by Title IX legislation; these women have become role models for the next generation of female athletes.

In conjunction with Title IX, women's sports benefited from increased media coverage, though equal coverage for women's sports is still not a reality. The United States hosted the 1984 Olympics in Los Angeles, which provided hours of television coverage for female athletes. Mary Lou Retton tumbled and danced into the hearts and minds of millions of young girls, just as Olga Korbut had done a dozen years earlier. Four years later, Florence Griffith Joyner flashed to world records in the 100- and 200-meter races with amazing style and grace. Joan Benoit Samuelson's triumphant finish of the 26-mile, 385-yard marathon before a crowd of 70,000 in the Los Angeles Coliseum and a worldwide television audience of millions forever changed the face of women's running in the United States.

Media acceptance of women athletes was also bolstered by the extraordinary 15-year rivalry of tennis superstars Chris Evert and Martina Navratilova. Evert, with her mental tenacity and relentless baseline play, battled Navratilova's superior athleticism and serve-and-volley style in a match-up of two distinct talents and personalities. The rivalry, which began in 1973 and ended in 1989 with Evert's retirement from tennis, vaulted women's tennis into one of the top sports attractions in the world. (See table 1.) The two competitors met in 60 tournament finals, with Navratilova winning 36

and Evert winning 24. The world may never again see an individual rivalry of this magnitude and influence.

In 1987, 17-year-old Steffi Graf burst on the scene and won the Grand Slam of tennis (winning the Australian, French, and U.S. Opens and Wimbledon), the first Grand Slam since Margaret Court achieved the feat in 1970, then added a gold medal in 1988, when tennis regained its status as a full-medal sport in the Olympics. Back in 1971, Virginia Slims sponsored the women's professional tennis tour with a total prize fund of just more than $300,000; in 1997, Corel® pledged sponsorship of $38 million. As Billie Jean King titled her 1988 book: "We *Have* Come a Long Way."

While professional tennis and golf continue to thrive (the annual LPGA Tour prize money reaches over $30.2 million), professional sports opportunities are becoming available for women in basketball, softball, and baseball. Two basketball leagues, the American Basketball League (ABL) and the Women's National Basketball Association (WNBA), have given female players the opportunity to play in the United States, no longer having to travel overseas to play professionally. The WNBA's New York Liberty broke the attendance record for a women's professional basketball game in the United States when 17,780 turned out for their home opener against the Phoenix Mercury. Women's professional softball and baseball leagues began play in 1997.

In addition to greater recognition and rewards in women's sports in the last two decades, sports physiologists began publishing research that squashed many of the prevailing myths about women's physical limitations and offered a clearer understanding of the genetic differences between male and female athletes. This research led to the development of more precise medi-

Table 1.

NAVRATILOVA vs. EVERT HEAD-TO-HEAD

YEAR	TOURNAMENT	SURFACE	ROUND	WINNER	SCORE
1973	Akron, Ohio, USA	Indoor	1r	CE	7-6, 6-3
1973	St. Petersburg, Florida, USA	Clay	SF	CE	7-5, 6-3
1974	San Francisco, California, USA	Indoor	1r	CE	6-7, 6-3, 6-1
1974	Italian Open	Clay	F	CE	6-3, 6-3
1975	San Francisco, California, USA	Indoor	SF	CE	6-4, 6-3
1975	Washington, D.C., USA	Indoor	QF	MN	3-6, 6-4, 7-6
1975	Akron, Ohio, USA	Indoor	QF	CE	6-3, 6-1
1975	Chicago, Illinois, USA	Indoor	SF	MN	6-4, 6-0
1975	Philadelphia, Pennsylvania, USA	Indoor	SF	CE	7-6, 6-4
1975	Los Angeles, California, USA	Indoor	F	CE	6-4, 6-2
1975	Amelia Island, Florida, USA	Clay	F	CE	7-5, 6-4
1975	Italian Open	Clay	F	CE	6-1, 6-0
1975	French Open	Clay	F	CE	2-6, 6-2, 6-1
1975	U.S. Open	Clay	SF	CE	6-4, 6-4
1975	Atlanta, Georgia, USA	Indoor	F	CE	2-6, 6-2, 6-0
1976	Austin, Texas, USA	Cement	SF	CE	6-0, 6-3
1976	Houston, Texas, USA	Indoor	F	MN	6-3, 6-4
1976	Wimbledon	Grass	SF	CE	6-3, 4-6, 6-4
1977	Washington, D.C., USA	Indoor	F	MN	6-2, 6-3
1977	Seattle, Washington, USA	Indoor	F	CE	6-2, 6-4
1977	Los Angeles, California, USA	Indoor	F	CE	6-2, 2-6, 6-1
1977	Philadelphia, Pennsylvania, USA	Indoor	F	CE	6-4, 4-6, 6-3
1977	Tucson, Arizona, USA	Cement	F	CE	6-3, 7-6
1977	Palm Springs, California, USA	Cement	RR	CE	6-4, 6-1
1978	Eastbourne	Grass	F	MN	6-4, 4-6, 9-7
1978	Wimbledon	Grass	F	MN	2-6, 6-4, 7-5
1978	Atlanta, Georgia, USA	Indoor	F	CE	7-6, 0-6, 6-3
1978	Palm Springs, California, USA	Cement	F	CE	6-3, 6-3
1978	Tokyo	Indoor	F	CE	7-5, 6-2
1979	Oakland, California, USA	Indoor	F	MN	7-5, 7-5
1979	Los Angeles, California, USA	Indoor	F	CE	6-3, 6-4
1979	Dallas, Texas, USA	Indoor	F	MN	6-4, 6-4
1979	Eastbourne	Grass	F	CE	7-5, 5-7, 13-11
1979	Wimbledon	Grass	F	MN	6-4, 6-4
1979	Phoenix, Arizona, USA	Cement	F	MN	6-1, 6-3
1979	Brighton	Indoor	F	MN	6-3, 6-3
1980	Chicago, Illinois, USA	Indoor	F	MN	6-4, 6-4
1980	Wimbledon	Grass	SF	CE	4-6, 6-4, 6-2
1980	Brighton	Indoor	F	CE	6-4, 5-7, 6-3
1980	Tokyo Lion's Cup	Indoor	SF	MN	7-6, 6-2
1981	Amelia Island, Florida, USA	Clay	F	CE	6-0, 6-0
1981	U.S. Open	Cement	SF	MN	7-5, 4-6, 6-4
1981	Tokyo Lion's Cup	Indoor	F	MN	6-3, 6-2
1981	Sydney	Grass	F	CE	6-4, 2-6, 6-1
1981	Australian Open	Grass	F	MN	6-7 (4-7), 6-4, 7-5
1982	Wimbledon	Grass	F	MN	6-1, 3-6, 6-2
1982	Brighton	Indoor	F	MN	6-1, 6-4
1982	Australian Open	Grass	F	CE	6-3, 2-6, 6-3
1982	Toyota Championships	Indoor	F	MN	4-6, 6-1, 6-2
1983	Dallas, Texas, USA	Indoor	F	MN	6-4, 6-0
1983	Virginia Slims Championships	Indoor	F	MN	6-2, 6-0
1983	Los Angeles, California, USA	Cement	F	MN	6-1, 6-3
1983	Canadian Open	Cement	F	MN	6-4, 4-6, 6-1
1983	U.S. Open	Cement	F	MN	6-1, 6-3
1983	Tokyo Lion's Cup	Cement	F	MN	6-2, 6-2
1984	U.S. Indoors	Indoor	F	MN	6-2, 7-6 (7-4)
1984	Virginia Slims Championships (Best of 5)	Indoor	F	MN	6-3, 7-5, 6-1
1984	Amelia Island, Florida, USA	Clay	F	MN	6-2, 6-0
1984	French Open	Clay	F	MN	6-3, 6-1
1984	Wimbledon	Grass	F	MN	7-6 (7-5), 6-2
1984	U.S. Open	Cement	F	MN	4-6, 6-4, 6-4
1985	Key Biscayne, Florida, USA	Cement	F	CE	6-2, 6-4
1985	Lipton International Players Championships	Cement	F	MN	6-2, 6-4
1985	Dallas, Texas, USA	Indoor	F	MN	6-3, 6-4
1985	French Open	Clay	F	CE	6-3, 6-7 (4-7), 7-5
1985	Wimbledon	Grass	F	MN	4-6, 6-3, 6-2
1985	Australian Open	Grass	F	MN	6-2, 4-6, 6-2
1986	Dallas, Texas, USA	Indoor	F	MN	6-2, 6-1
1986	French Open	Clay	F	CE	2-6, 6-3, 6-3
1986	Los Angeles, California, USA	Cement	F	MN	7-6 (7-5), 6-3
1987	Houston, Texas, USA	Clay	F	CE	3-6, 6-1, 7-6 (7-4)
1987	French Open	Clay	SF	MN	6-2, 6-2
1987	Wimbledon	Grass	SF	MN	6-2, 5-7, 6-4
1987	Los Angeles, California, USA	Cement	SF	CE	6-2, 6-1
1987	Filderstadt	Indoor	F	MN	7-5, 6-1
1988	Australian Open	Cement	SF	CE	6-2, 7-5
1988	Houston, Texas, USA	Clay	F	CE	6-0, 6-4
1988	Wimbledon	Grass	SF	MN	6-1, 4-6, 7-5
1988	Filderstadt	Indoor	F	MN	6-2, 6-3
1988	Chicago, Illinois, USA	Indoor	F	MN	6-2, 6-2

Total: Navratilova leads 43-37.

From Women's Tennis Association, *1990 Media Guide.*

cal treatment of athletic injuries; better performance-testing techniques; and advanced coaching and training methods for female athletes. Women have benefited from advances in sports medicine such as arthroscopic surgery, and from specialized equipment changes such as new clothing like the sports bra for comfort and protection, specialized athletic shoes, and bicycles and golf clubs sized for women's smaller frames.

The advances in equipment and training have had a positive effect on the promotion of women's participation at all levels of sport in the United States, particularly in women's endurance sports such as the marathon, triathlon, and mountain climbing. In 1988, Paula Newby-Fraser set a world record in the Ironman Triathlon—an event that includes a 2.4-mile swim, 112-mile bike ride, and 26.2-mile run—of 8 hours, 55 minutes, 28 seconds; Alison Hargreaves climbed the 29,028-foot Mount Everest without supplementary oxygen in 1995; and Lynn Hill free climbed the 3,000-foot Nose of El Capitán in a single day in 1994. All these feats of amazing stamina and endurance permanently put to rest any notions of female athletic inferiority.

Women are not just successfully challenging physical barriers; they are breaking down more gender barriers as well. In 1988, Julie Croteau took the field for NCAA Division III St. Mary's College of Maryland as the first woman to play on a men's collegiate baseball team. She later joined the Colorado Silver Bullets, the first and only all-female professional baseball team to be officially recognized by the National Association of Professional Baseball Leagues. The Colorado Silver Bullets began their inaugural season on Mother's Day, May 8, 1994, and averaged 7,000 fans per game in their first season. Croteau is currently an assistant men's baseball coach at the University of Massachusetts.

Other pioneering women in the post–Title IX period include Manon Rheaume, who, on September 23, 1992, played in an exhibition game between the Tampa Bay Lightning and the St. Louis Blues, becoming the first woman to play in the National Hockey League (NHL). The all-woman crew of America[3], sailed *Mighty Mary* to a second place finish in the final round of the 1995 America's Cup Defenders Series. Since its first defense over 100 years ago, only seven women had sailed in the America's Cup competition. The pioneering crew missed the opportunity to sail for the America's Cup by just two boat lengths (about 52 seconds).

Women also are emerging in many leadership positions traditionally held by men. In 1986, Anita DeFrantz became the first U.S. woman elected to the International Olympic Committee (IOC) and in 1997 was elected a vice president of the IOC. The National Collegiate Athletic Association elected Judy Sweet as its first female president in 1991, and Barbara Hedges was named athletic director for the University of Washington—the first female athletic director of a NCAA Division I school that has a football program. In June 1990, Bernadette Locke became the first woman to coach a major college men's sport when she accepted the position of assistant coach on the University of Kentucky men's basketball team. At Kingsboro Community College in Brooklyn, New York, Kerri McTiernan was hired as head coach of the men's basketball team in October 1995. She is the first and only female head coach in the men's college basketball ranks.

On February 6, 1997, America celebrated its Eleventh Annual National

Women in Sports Day, an event first sponsored by Senators Bob Packwood and Bill Bradley and Congresswoman Olympia Snow in 1987 to recognize and celebrate women's participation in and contributions to sport. As the millennium approaches, more women will enjoy sports and turn in more previously unimaginable performances than ever before. The pioneers in women's sport have helped to destroy the myths about women's abilities in sport by their skill and determination, and by their example. Following the examples set by their predecessors in effecting change, women now must work to continue opening doors to better coaching, training, facilities, and professional opportunities that will one day make women truly equal in the sports arena.

The next generation of female runners, swimmers, bowlers, golfers, tennis players, and other sportswomen are already a step closer to reaching their full potential as athletes thanks to the efforts of their predecessors. To see the future of women's sports is to remember the sportswomen of the past.

MILESTONES IN WOMEN'S SPORTS

1804, August 25—The first woman jockey was an English woman named Alicia Meynell. She rode against Captain William Flint in a four-mile race in York, England (result unavailable).

1876—The first woman to cross the Niagara Rapids on a cable was Maria Spelterina.

1876, March 16—Nell Saunders defeated Rose Harland in the first U.S. women's boxing match.

1877, June 13—The new Ladies Club for Outdoor Sports held its first meeting at New Brighton, Staten Island, New York. Club members played archery, lawn tennis, and croquet.

1880—New Orleans women organized the Pearl Archery Club as one of the first sports organizations for women in the southern United States.

1883, June 16—The New York Gothams baseball team held the first "Ladies' Day," allowing women into baseball parks either at a reduced rate or free of charge, signaling the acceptance of women spectators at public sporting events.

1895, November 9—Thirteen women participated in the first U.S. women's amateur golf championship played at the Meadowbrook Club, Hempstead, New York. Mrs. Charles B. Brown won the event, playing the 18 holes in 132 strokes.

1896, January 6–11—Madison Square Garden in New York hosted the first bicycle marathon for women. Frankie Nelson traveled 418 miles over the six days to win the race.

1896, April 4—The first women's intercollegiate basketball game took place at the Armory Hall in San Francisco between Stanford and the University of California at Berkeley. Stanford won the contest 2-1.

1902, August 31—Mrs. Adolph Ladenburg of Saratoga, New York, introduced an innovative horse show riding outfit, wearing a split skirt rather than the traditional ankle-length attire. She rode her horse astride rather than side-saddle, one of the first women to do so in public.

1905—May Sutton Bundy defeated Doris K. Douglas of Great Britain to become the first American woman to win the ladies singles championship at Wimbledon. She won the title again in 1907.

1907—Annette Kellerman appeared on Revere Beach in Boston in a one-piece bathing suit, one of the first women to appear in public in such attire.

1910—Blanche Scott of Dayton, Ohio, became the first woman to pilot an airplane solo.

1912—The Amateur Fencers League of America sponsored the first women's national fencing championship in 1912. A. Baylis of the Fencers Club won the foils competition.

1913, July—Harriet D. Hammond organized the first trapshooting club for women in Wilmington, Delaware.

1914—The Amateur Athletic Union (AAU) permitted the registration of women swimmers. In 1915, the AAU began recording women's swimming records.

1916, April 1—The AAU held its first national championships in women's swimming, both indoors and outdoors, with four events including races at 440 and 880 yards, one mile, and one diving contest.

1916, November 29—Forty women organized the Women's National Bowling Association, now the Women's International Bowling Congress, now the largest sports organization for women in the world, in St. Louis, Missouri. The Progress team of St. Louis won the first team championship, and Mrs. A. J. Koester, also of St. Louis, won the all-events title.

1917—Lucy Slowe became the first Black woman tennis champion in the United States, winning the women's singles title at a Baltimore tournament.

1919—Suzanne Lenglen revolutionized women's tennis dress by appearing for a match in a short-sleeved, one-piece pleated dress, without a petticoat.

1920—Marjorie Voorhies won the first national tournament for women horseshoe pitchers.

1923—The AAU sponsored the first major outdoor track and field meet for women at Newark, New Jersey. Winners in the 1923 meet were 100-yard dash: Frances Rupert (12 seconds); 80-yard hurdles: Hazel Kirk (9.6 seconds); 440-yard relay: the Meadowbrook Club team of Philadelphia (52.4 seconds); high jump: Catherine Wright (4 feet, 7½ inches); long jump: Helen Dinnehey (15 feet, 4 inches); eight-pound shot put: Bertha Christophel (30 feet, 10½ inches); discus throw: Babe Wolbert (71 feet, 9½ inches); javelin: Roberta Ranck (59 feet, 7¾ inches); softball throw: Elinor Churchill (284 feet, 5¾ inches).

1923—Hazel Hotchkiss Wightman established the international women's tennis team competition known as the Wightman Cup. The United States and Great Britain played the first match at Forest Hills, New York; the U.S. team won 7–0.

1924—Sybil Bauer became the first woman to break an existing men's world swimming record when she won the 1924 Olympic 100-meter backstroke competition in 1:23.2.

1925, July 11—The first woman to clear the five-foot barrier in the high jump was Phyllis Green of Great Britain.

1926, August 6—American Gertrude Ederle swam across the English Channel from Cap Gris-Nez, France, to Dover, England, in record time—14 hours, 39 minutes—the first woman to cross the Channel.

1927—Violet Cordery was the first woman to drive around the world, traveling 10,266 miles across five continents at an average speed of just over 24 miles per hour.

1928—Eleanora Sears won the first U.S. women's squash racquets singles championship at the Round Hill Club in Greenwich, Connecticut.

1930, February 12—Jennie Kelleher of Madison, Wisconsin, was the first woman to bowl a perfect 300 game.

1931, April 1—Verne "Jackie" Mitchell, the first woman to play in major league baseball, signed a contract to pitch for the Memphis Lookouts of the Southern Association. In an exhibition game against the New York Yankees, she struck out both Babe Ruth and Lou Gehrig.

1931, June 23—Lili de Alvarez appeared on center court at Wimbledon wearing shorts, the first woman to don such radical attire in the prestigious tennis event.

1932, May 22—Amelia Earhart piloted her own plane from Newfoundland to Ireland, the first woman to fly solo across the Atlantic.

1932—Helene Madison of Seattle, Washington, became the first woman ever to swim 100 yards in less than one minute.

1935—The Jockey Club of the United States licensed Mary Hirch, the first woman trainer of thoroughbred race horses.

1936, May 27—Sally Stearns, the first woman coxswain of a men's college varsity crew, led Rollins College's shell in a race against Marietta College.

1937, September 4—The National Amateur Bicycling Association held its first U.S. women's bicycling championship in Buffalo, New York. Doris Kopsky of Belleville, New Jersey, won the one-mile race in 4 minutes, 22.4 seconds.

1938—Ernestine Bayer founded the first U.S. women's rowing club.

1940, May 2—Belle Martell of Van Nuys, California, the first woman boxing referee, officiated her first card, eight bouts in San Bernardino, California.

1941, July 3—Eleanor Dudley won the first women's national intercollegiate golf championship sponsored by Ohio State University.

1943, April 27—An English woman, Judy Johnson, rode Lone Gallant to a 10th place finish in a field of 11 horses in a steeplechase event at the Pimlico Racetrack at Baltimore, Maryland, the first woman steeplechase jockey to race at a major U.S. racetrack.

1944—Swimmer Ann Curtis was the first woman to receive the prestigious James E. Sullivan Award, honoring the outstanding amateur athlete of the year.

1944—Hope Seignious, Elizabeth (Betty) Hicks, and Ellen Griffin founded and incorporated the Women's Professional Golf Association (WPGA).

1946, September 1—Patty Berg defeated Betty Jameson in the final round to win the first U.S. Women's Open golf tournament.

1947—Babe Didrikson Zaharias was the first American to win the British Women's Golf Championship.

1947, October 23—The United States Women's Curling Association was founded in Milwaukee, Wisconsin.

1949, May 29—Wilson Sporting Goods agreed to sponsor the formation of the Ladies Professional Golf Association. The group became an officially chartered organization in 1950.

1950—Althea Gibson broke the color barrier in tennis playing at the U.S. National Tennis Championship at Forest Hills, New York.

1950—Florence Chadwick was the first woman to swim both ways across the English Channel. She swam from France to England in 1950, setting a new record of 13 hours, 20 minutes; and the next year, she swam from England to France, completing her round trip.

1952—Sponsored by the National Rifle Association, the first match was held for the Randle Women's International Team Trophy, which goes to the winning 10-woman team in a small-bore rifle match. The United States women's team won for the first 13 years before the British triumphed in 1965.

1952, January 15—The St. Andrew Golf Club hosted the first bonspiel for women curlers in the New York area.

1953, February 15—Tenley Albright was the first U.S. woman to win the World Figure Skating Championship.

1953, September 7—Maureen Connolly of the United States won the Australian, French, American, and British tennis titles to become the first woman to win tennis's Grand Slam.

1956—The College Rodeo Nationals featured a women's event for the first time; the barrel race was won by Kathleen Younger of Colorado A&M.

1957, January 20—In Ciudad Juarez, Mexico, Patricia McCormick entered the arena as North America's first woman bullfighter.

1957, July 6—Althea Gibson was the first Black woman player to win a Wimbledon title in the women's tennis singles.

1957, July 21—Althea Gibson won the first national clay court singles championship, the first Black woman to win a major U.S. tennis title.

1958, October 18—The first woman to clear six feet in the high jump was Romanian Iolanda Balas.

1958—An Italian, Maria-Teresa de Filippis, was the first woman to compete in a modern European Grand Prix auto race.

1963—The International Lawn Tennis Federation inaugurated the Federation Cup, an international team competition. The U.S. women's team won the first Federation Cup, beating the Australian team, 2-1, at London, England.

1964—Donna Mae Mins became the first woman to win a Sports Car Club of America championship, beating out 31 men in the Class II production category for imported two-seaters.

1964, April 17—Jerrie Mock was the first woman to fly around the world solo. She began the trip on March 19, made 21 stops, and flew a total of 22,858.8 miles in her single-engine plane.

1965, November 4—Margaret Laneive "Lee" Breedlove set a women's land speed record of 308.65 miles per hour on the Bonneville Salt Flats, Utah.

1966, April 19—Roberta Gibb Bingay was the first woman to run in a Boston Marathon, finishing ahead of more than half the 415 men in the race. She wore a hood sweatshirt to disguise her appearance because women were not allowed to run in the race.

1967—Kathrine Switzer entered the Boston Marathon and finished despite objections of race officials. Pictures of an official trying to remove her number created an uproar.

1968—Enriqueta Basilio became the first woman to light the Olympic flame in the stadium.

1968—Fencer Janice Lee York Romary of San Mateo, California, was the first woman to carry the U.S. flag in the opening ceremonies of the Olympic Games.

1968—The first licensed woman jockey in the United States was Kathy Kusner.

1969—American Sharon Sites sailed her 25-foot sloop 5,000 miles from Yokohama, Japan, to San Diego, California, in 74 days, becoming the first woman to sail solo across the Pacific Ocean.

1969—Cyclist Audrey McElmury won the Women's World Road Racing Championship in Bruno, Czechoslovakia. With her victory, McElmury became the first American, man or woman, to win a world road racing title.

1969, February 7—Diane Crump became the first U.S. woman jockey to ride at a pari-mutuel track; she rode her first mount to a 10th-place finish at a Hialeah, Florida, race track.

1969, February 22—Barbara Jo Rubin rode Cohesion to victory at the Charles Town, West Virginia, track to become the first woman jockey to win a race at a U.S. thoroughbred track.

1970, May—Jockey Diane Crump was the first woman to ride in the Kentucky Derby.

1970, June 13—Chi Cheng of Taiwan was the first woman to run 100 yards in 10 seconds flat.

1970, August 15—Pat Palinkas signed with the Orlando Panthers in the Atlantic Coast Professional Football League, holding the ball for the point-after-touchdown kicks. She was the first woman to play in a professional football game.

1970, September 23—Billie Jean King; Gladys Heldman, publisher of *World Tennis* magazine; and eight other players organized the Virginia Slims Tennis Tournament in Houston, Texas, the first tournament for women professional tennis players held separate from male players.

1971—Tennis star Billie Jean King was the first female athlete in any sport to earn more than $100,000 in a single season.

1971, May 27—A New York State Education Department Law went into effect, permitting girls to compete as members of boys' teams in noncontact sports.

1971, June 30—Mary Bacon was the first woman jockey to ride 100 winners, posting her 100th victory at the Thistledown Race Track in Cleveland, Ohio, aboard California Lassie.

1972, March 2—The New York State Athletic Commission decided to allow women journalists into dressing rooms at boxing and wrestling matches.

1972, March 19—The Association for Intercollegiate Athletics for Women (AIAW) held its first women's collegiate basketball championship. Immaculata College defeated West Chester State, 52-48.

1972, April 17—In the 76th annual Boston Marathon, Nina Kuscsik of Long Island, New York, won the first women's competition with a time of 3 hours, 8 minutes, 58 seconds.

1972, June—Bernice Gera became the first woman to umpire a professional baseball game. She took the field in a game between minor league teams, the Auburn Phillies and the Geneva Rangers.

1972, June 23—President Richard Nixon signed into law Title IX of the Higher Education Act banning sex bias in athletics and other activities at all educational institutions receiving federal assistance.

1973—Marcia Frederick became the first U.S. woman to win a world gymnastics title, taking the gold in the uneven parallel bars.

1973—Lynne Cox swam the English Channel in 9 hours, 36 minutes, setting a new world record for women and men.

1973—Terry Williams was the first woman to receive a full-tuition athletic scholarship to the University of Miami, Coral Gables, Florida.

1973, February—The first Women's World Invitational Swim Meet was held at East Los Angeles College.

1973, March 1—Robyn Smith became the first woman jockey to win a stakes race when she rode North Sea to victory in the $27,450 Paumanauk Handicap at Aqueduct Raceway, Queens, New York.

1973, July 19—The United States Tennis Association announced that the U.S. Open tennis championships would award equal prize money to women and men.

1973, August 26—Mary Boitano won the 6.8-mile Dipsea Race in Marin County, California, the first time a female runner had won the race in its 68-year history.

1974, June 12—Little League baseball announced that its teams would be open to girls.

1975—Shirley Muldowney was the first woman licensed in the United States to drive top fuel dragsters.

1975—Diana Nyad swam around Manhattan Island in 7 hours, 57 minutes, breaking a record set by Bryon Somers almost 50 years before.

1976—Judy Rankin was the first professional female golfer to win more than $100,000 in a single season.

1976—Runner Madeline Manning Mims became the first American woman to break two minutes in the 800 meters.

1976, March 28—Krystyna Choynowski-Liskiewicz of Poland was the first woman to sail around the world solo.

1977—Jan Todd bench-pressed 176¼ pounds, dead lifted 441 pounds, and lifted 424¼ pounds from a squat to become the first woman ever to lift more than 1,000 pounds in three power lifts.

1977, March 5—At age 50, Betty Cook became the first woman to win a major offshore motorboat race when she won the Bushmills Grand Prix off Newport Beach, California.

1977, May 29—At the 61st Indianapolis 500, Janet Guthrie became the first woman to compete in auto racing's premier event.

1977, September 29—Eva Shain was the first woman to officiate a heavyweight championship fight; the match was between Muhammad Ali and Ernie Shavers.

1978, September 25—In a suit brought by *Sports Illustrated* reporter Melissa Ludtke, U.S. District Court Judge Constance Baker Motley ruled that Major League Baseball could not legally bar a woman sportswriter from the locker room after a game.

1978, October 26—Beverly Johnson of Wyoming became the first woman to scale El Capitán in Yosemite National Park.

1978, December 9—The first game of the Women's Professional Basketball League took place between the Chicago Hustle and the Milwaukee Does.

1979, August 30—Ann Meyers became the first woman to sign a contract to play in the National Basketball Association, signing a one-year contract with the Indiana Pacers.

1980, June—For the first time, the Professional Golf Association (PGA) allowed female caddies in the U.S. Open at the Baltusrol Golf Club in Springfield, New Jersey. Pamela Shuttleworth of Santa Monica, California, caddied for PGA player Jim Dent.

1981, April 4—Sue Brown from Oxford, England, became the first woman to cox against Cambridge in the 152-year history of the Oxford-Cambridge race. Brown coxed the Oxford crew to an eight-length victory over Cambridge.

1981, April 27—The first professional female soccer game official, Betty Ellis, was hired by the North American Soccer League.

1981, August—Thirteen-year-old Tonia Schlegel of Hamilton, Ohio, was the first girl to win the All-American Soap Box Derby.

1982, March 28—Louisiana Tech defeated Cheyney State 76–62 to win the first NCAA-sponsored women's basketball championship.

1985, March 20—In Alaska, Libby Riddles became the first woman to win the 1,827-kilometer, Anchorage-to-Nome Iditarod Trail Sled Dog Race.

1985, October 7—Former University of Kansas basketball star Lynette Woodard signed as the first female player on the Harlem Globetrotters.

1986—The International Olympic Committee (IOC) appointed former Olympic rower Anita DeFrantz to lifetime membership in the IOC. DeFrantz became the only U.S. woman, and one of only five women, on the 91-member committee.

1986, May 1—Ann Bancroft became the first woman to the top of the world when she and her five male companions reached the North Pole by dogsled.

1987, February 4—The first National Girls and Women in Sports Day was celebrated in Washington, DC.

1987—Gayle Sierens was the first woman broadcaster to do play-by-play for an NFL game, Kansas City vs. Seattle.

1988—Julie Croteau took the field for NCAA Division III St. Mary's College of Maryland as the first woman to play on a men's collegiate baseball team.

1988, August 1—Phyllis Holmes began her term as president of the National Association of Intercollegiate Athletics (NAIA), the first woman to serve as president of any national coed sports organization.

1988, October 2—In a "Battle of the Sexes" match race at Canterbury Downs in Shakopee, Minnesota, Julie Krone rode Don't Fool With Me to a narrow victory over Willie Shoemaker on Dakota Stew for a $30,000 purse.

1988—The Women's International Bowling Congress Championship tournament in Reno/Carson City, Nevada, broke all participation records with 77,735 bowlers competing.

1989—Lori Norwood became the first American woman to win the individual title at the World Modern Pentathlon Championships.

1990, June—Bernadette Locke became the first woman to coach a major college men's sport when she accepted the position of assistant coach on the University of Kentucky men's basketball team.

1990, December—Juli Inkster of Los Altos, California, became the first woman to win the only professional golf tournament in the world in which women and men compete head-to-head. Juli parred the 18th hole of the Spalding Invitational Pro-Am at Pebble Beach for a one-stroke victory over PGA tour member Mark Brooks.

1991, January—The National Collegiate Athletic Association elected Judy Sweet as its first female president.

1991, February—Tonya Harding became the first American female to land a triple axel in figure skating competition.

1991, May—Barbara Hedges was named athletic director for the University of Washington—the first female athletic director of an NCAA Division I school that has a football program.

1991, June 8—Julie Krone became the first female jockey to ride in the 123-year-old Belmont Stakes, the third leg of horse racing's Triple Crown.

1991, July 15—Sandra Ortiz-Del Valle officiated the United States Basketball League (USBL) game between the New Haven Skyhawks and the Philadelphia Spirit, making her the first woman to officiate a men's professional basketball game.

1991—Jo Ann Fairbanks served as a lineswoman in the women's qualifying rounds for the North & Central American and Caribbean regional soccer tournament in Haiti, becoming the first U.S. female referee at an international soccer event.

1991, September 13—Fifteen-year-old gymnast Kim Zmeskal captured the gold medal in the individual all-around to become the first American woman to win an individual all-around gold medal in the world championships.

1991, December—The U.S. women's soccer team defeated Norway to claim the first women's world soccer championship.

1992—Tricia Saunders of Phoenix, Arizona, became the first U.S. wrestler to earn a gold medal at the women's world championships, claiming the 50 kilograms title at the 1992 world championships in Willeurbanne, France.

1992, September 23—Manon Rheaume played in an exhibition game between the Tampa Bay Lightning and the St. Louis Blues, becoming the first woman to play in the National Hockey League (NHL).

1993, November 1—Dallas Malloy won the first amateur boxing fight ever sanctioned for women in the United States.

1994, May 29—The Colorado Silver Bullets defeated the Richfield Rockets 7–2 to post the first victory by a professional women's baseball team over an all-male professional squad.

1995—Fourteen-year-old Iris Zimmerman of Rush, New York, won the 1995 World Under-17 Championship in women's foil, becoming the first U.S. fencer in history to win a world championship.

1995, June 24—WFAN radio sportscaster Suzyn Waldman became the first woman to broadcast a network baseball game with coverage of the Texas Rangers/New York Yankees game.

1995, October 21—Heather McDaniel was the first female referee to officiate in a professional ice hockey game when she worked the Central Hockey League exhibition between the Tulsa Oilers and Oklahoma City Blazers.

1996—LPGA rookie Karrie Webb became the first player in LPGA history to surpass $1 million in earnings in one season.

1996, May 15—Tammy Holes was the first woman to homer in an organized professional baseball game against men, hitting an inside-the-park grand slam in the Colorado Silver Bullets' 14–11 win against the Atlanta Mustangs.

1996, November 16—Heidi Pascoe won the first-ever women's diving competition at the famed cliffs of Acapulco, Mexico. She performed two cleanly executed dives from 68 feet to outscore five other female divers.

1997, March 9—Stacy Dragila of the United States won the first-ever world championship pole vault competition at the International Amateur Athletic Federation (IAAF) World Indoor Championships. Dragila cleared 4.40 meters (approx. 14 1/2 feet) on her second attempt to win the title.

1997, March 24—Tara Lipinski of the United States won the world figure skating championships in Lausanne, Switzerland. At age 14, she was the youngest women's champion in history.

1997, May 31—Ila Borders became the first woman to pitch in a regular-season Major League Baseball game when she came in during the sixth inning of the St. Paul Saints' Northern League game against the host Sioux Falls Canaries.

1997, June 29—The Women's National Basketball Association's New York Liberty broke the attendance record for a women's professional basketball game when 17,780 turned out for their home opener against the Phoenix Mercury.

1997, July 3— Teresa Gordon-Dick of Redwood Valley, California, won the Greco-Roman gold medal in the 100-pound division of the USA Wrestling Kids National Tournament becoming USA Wrestling's first female national champion in a coed bracket.

1997, October 17—Liz Heaston, a junior at Willamette University in Salem, Oregon, became the first woman ever to play in a college football game. Heaston kicked two extra points as Willamette beat Linfield College, 27–0.

1997, December 19—University of Texas women's basketball coach Jody Conradt got her 700th coaching victory in a 89–86 win over Northwestern. Conradt was the first women's college coach and only the eighth—men's or women's—to reach the 700-victory milestone.

NOTES TO CHAPTER 1

1. Rhonda Glenn, *The Illustrated History of Women's Golf* (Dallas, TX: Taylor Publishing, 1991), p. 16.

2. Marie Wagner, "Women Play Indoors," *Fifty Years of Lawn Tennis in the United States* (New York: United States Lawn Tennis Association, 1931), p. 108.

3. Quoted in Sue Heinemann, *Timelines of American Women's History* (New York: The Berkley Publishing Group, 1996), p. 276.

4. L. Schoedler, "Report of Progress, Women's Division, National Amateur Athletic Federation of America," *American Physical Education Review*, June 1924, pp. 308–09.

5. Quoted in Reet Howell, ed. *Her Story in Sport: A Historical Anthology of Women in Sports* (West Point, NY: Leisure Press, 1982), p. 452.

6. Howell, pp. 452–53.

Chapter 2
Women in the Olympics

"If a young female sees my dreams and goals come true, they will realize their dreams and goals might also come true."
—Jackie Joyner-Kersee, three time Olympic Gold Medalist

The Olympics are the premier forum for athletes from hundreds of sports to display their athletic skills, and Olympic success has become the standard of perfection. For nearly a century, the Olympics have been the primary way for women athletes to receive recognition for their achievements as well as to take part in international competition. But women's inclusion into the modern Olympic Games did not come without a struggle.

The founder of the modern Olympic Games, Pierre de Coubertin of France, believed the Olympics should be for men only, and outwardly opposed women's participation in the Games, as did the all-male International Olympic Committee (IOC), the governing body of the event. Not until 1908 did women actually have officially recognized sports competitions in the festival, and throughout the twentieth century, women athletes have fought to convince officials to include a full register of events. In spite of the slow and uphill struggle to gain acceptance in the international games, women have had a rich history of participation in the Olympics. The Olympics have produced female role models who signifi-

cantly influenced their sports and women's sport in the United States.

With increased coaching and training in the 1990s, women continue to better Olympic records, providing spectators with a new appreciation for the talents of the world's elite female athletes. The publicity that female athletes receive from their participation in the Olympics has contributed to society's acceptance of high-level competition for women and has been an important factor in increasing participation for women at all levels of sport. As the modern Olympics move into their second century, women's roles in the Games will continue to grow.

This chapter explores both women's exclusion from and women's participation in the Olympics. The struggle to include women's events forms an important part of this chapter. It also highlights the influential events and athletes that helped shape the Olympic Games for nearly a century and describes some of the outstanding accomplishments of Olympic pioneers worldwide with a focus on the efforts of U.S. female athletes. (See appendix A for a complete list of women Olympic gold medalists.)

Olympic Summer Games

PERIOD OF ORGANIZATION
1896-1912

When Baron Pierre de Coubertin proposed a revival of the Olympic Games, he wanted to promote the development of the physical and moral qualities of amateur sport and to bring together the athletes of the world in a festival of sports, creating international respect and goodwill and thus helping to construct a better and more peaceful world.

High ideals indeed, but Coubertin and the IOC opposed women's participation, stating that the Olympic Games should be reserved for the "solemn and periodic exaltation of male athleticism with internationalism as a base, loyalty as a means, arts for its setting, and *female applause* as reward."

By the end of the nineteenth century, however, the impact of industrialization, urbanization, and women's reform movements contributed to the increased role of women in sport. The worldwide bicycling craze helped spur dress reform that loosened women's restrictive clothing. This new clothing meant more freedom of movement, and in sports the freer movement meant better, more active performances. Local and national organizations formed that encouraged competition in a variety of sports, such as golf, tennis, and sailing. Although women lacked the international support to request full inclusion in the Olympics, their participation in leisure-time activities contributed to an initial appearance in the Games, helping women get a small foothold into the world of international athletics.

I. Athens, Greece—1896

Competitors: women, 0; men, 311

The first Games of the modern Olympics opened on April 6, 1896, in Athens, Greece, with 311 competitors representing 13 nations. Coubertin's belief that the Olympics should be strictly a masculine event meant that no women participated in the inaugural Games. However, as legend has it, one female runner, a Greek woman named Melpomene, wanted to run in the special event, the Olympic marathon, but the organizers refused her request to enter. She had trained for three weeks prior to the event, so she ran anyway, starting behind the 25 male contestants and completing the race in four and a half hours. As an unofficial entrant and excluded from the ceremonial finish afforded marathon runners inside the stadium, she ran her final lap alone around the outside of the stadium.

II. Paris, France—1900

Competitors: women, 11; men, 1,319
New women's events (unofficial):
Golf
Tennis: singles and mixed doubles
Yachting

Second Olympiad. The Second Olympiad moved to Coubertin's home country in 1900. The French Athletic Association held the athletic events in connection with the Paris World's Fair. Casually organized, the events of the Paris Games occurred over a six-month period, May to October, often in adverse conditions and using poor facilities. Sporting events held in and around Paris during the year were arbitrarily recognized as Olympic events, and many of the champions were never notified that they had actually won Olympic medals.

Tennis and Golf. In the original Olympic charter, the local organizing committee had the right to determine the events to be included in the Olympic program so the French Organizing Committee selected two women's events, lawn tennis and golf, as Olympic competitions. A yachting event was registered as a mixed event, which allowed women to sail, but no women entered.

Eleven women from Britain, France, and the United States competed in the Paris Games. In winning the International Tournament held at the Société de Sport de Compiegne, golfer Margaret Abbott of the United States became the first American woman to win an Olympic gold medal.

The lawn tennis matches were strictly a British and French affair. Three-time Wimbledon champion Charlotte Cooper of Great Britain defeated Helen Prevost of France to claim the singles championship, and Cooper paired with Reginald Doherty to win the mixed doubles competition.

III. St. Louis, USA—1904

Competitors: women, 6; men, 681
New women's event (unofficial):
Archery: double round

The Games of the Third Olympiad centered around the St. Louis World's Fair, in the same manner as the previous Olympics in Paris. Again, the Olympic events were poorly organized with the events spread out over four and a half months. Most European nations skipped the Games; only 13 countries sent representatives to St. Louis. The only event for women contested at the fair was archery. Rival archery clubs from Cincinnati and Washington, DC, held a tournament that included a Double Columbia Round (48 arrows at 50, 40, and 30 yards) and a Double National Round (48 arrows at 60 and 50 yards). Lida Howell won both events and also received a gold medal as part of the Cincinnati Archery Club team, becoming the first U.S. female to win three gold medals in one Olympic sport.

Interim Games. Athens, Greece—1906

Competitors: women, 7; men, 877
New women's events: none

The first three Olympiads, unorganized and informal, were not as Coubertin had envisioned in his plan to present a grand sports festival. To get better organized, Coubertin and the IOC planned the Interim Games in 1906. Athens, Greece, hosted the Games, and although the events were not recognized in the official Olympic record books, the Interim Games are important because they helped reestablish the goals of the International Olympic Committee.

Tennis. The only women's events contested at the Interim Games were singles and mixed doubles tennis. Seven women, representing Greece and France, entered in the tennis matches.

IV. London, Great Britain—1908

Competitors: women, 36; men, 1,999
New women's events:
Figure skating: singles and pairs

Athletes from 22 countries traveled to London for the 1908 Games. The Amateur Athletic Association of London held the Games at Shepherd's Bush Stadium, a unique sporting facility built specially for the Games, which included a cycle track; running track; soccer field; swimming pool; and a platform for wrestling, fencing, and gymnastics.

Official Recognition. At the 1908 London Games, the Olympic Committee officially recognized women's events as part of the sports festival for the first time. Women's events took place in tennis, archery, and figure skating. Winter sports for women appeared on the Olympic schedule for the first time, as women from Great Britain, Germany, and Sweden took to the ice in the figure skating singles and pairs events. Thousands of spectators watched noncompetitive exhibitions in gymnastics, fencing, swimming, and diving.

U.S. Women. U.S. women did not participate in the London Games. The all-male American Olympic Committee (AOC) opposed American women's participation in events in which women did not wear long skirts, and so no women were sent to London to represent the United States.

Yachting. Yachtswoman Frances Clytie Rivett-Carnac of Great Britain teamed with her husband Charles Rivett-Carnac, Norman Bingley, and Richard Dixon to win the gold medal in the 7-meter class, making her the first woman to win an event not restricted to women or mixed pairs.

V. Stockholm, Sweden—1912

Competitors: women, 57; men, 2,490
New women's events:
Equestrian
Swimming: 100-meter freestyle, 4x100-meter freestyle relay, platform diving

Swimming. The popularity of the swimming exhibitions at the London Games carried over to the Stockholm Games in 1912, when three swimming contests for women—two swimming and one diving—became official events. In 1910, the International Swimming Federation (ISF) accepted events for women in their competitions, the first international sports group to do so, setting a precedent for other federations. International federation sponsorship was critical in getting women's events included in the Olympics.

Forty-two women from nine countries swam in the first official swimming events. Obtaining recognition for swimming events was a major breakthrough for women in the Olympic movement. It was the first acknowledgment of women's increasing involvement in competitive sport by a major international sports organization.

U.S. Swimmers. U.S. women swimmers did not compete in the swimming events in Stockholm. Although the ISF recognized women's swimming on a worldwide basis, U.S. women still did not have a national sports organization to represent them. The Amateur Athletic Union (AAU) did not begin sanctioning women's swimming in the United States until 1914.

Gymnastics. The gymnastics demonstrations continued to be a crowd favorite, but there was no indication that they would soon become official events.

Equestrian. Count Clarence von Rosen, the Master of the Horse to the King of Sweden, requested that equestrian events be added to the program of the Stockholm Games. The three-day event, consisting of dressage, endurance, and show jumping, allowed women to compete directly with the male athletes, yet it was not until 1952 that a woman actually qualified for the event.

VI. Berlin, Germany—1916

Cancelled due to World War I

STRUGGLE FOR INCLUSION
1920-1936

In the organizing years of the modern Olympic Games, women participated in golf, tennis, and figure skating, and in 1912, swimming and equestrian were added to the schedule. The popularity of the demonstration events in gymnastics and fencing indicated that more women's sports were gaining worldwide acceptance by both participants and spectators. The popularity of women's sports, however, did not lead to immediate inclusion in the Olympic Games.

When the Games resumed after World War I in 1920 in Antwerp, Belgium, women began to demand that track and field events be included in the Olympic schedule. Track and field, the cornerstone of every Olympic Games, and other sports had gained popularity among European and American women after the war. However, Coubertin and the IOC remained staunch in their opposition to women competing in the Games.

The Women's Olympics

The difficulty in gaining acceptance for women's international competition was compounded by the lack of international federations willing to recognize women's sports. In an effort to get women's track and field events into the Olympics, Alice Milliat of France organized the Fédération Sportive Féminine Internationale (FSFI) in 1921 to regulate women's sports and to stage a separate Women's Olympic Games. For 12 years (1922-34), the FSFI conducted four successful Women's Games. (See table 1.) The success of the Women's Games presented a challenge to the traditional Olympics and ultimately forced IOC officials to accept women's track and field events into the Games.

The First Women's Olympic Games took place in Paris in 1922, in front of nearly 20,000 spectators. Women representing seven countries, including the United States, took part in 11 track and field events, including the 1,000-meter run. Organized

and administered entirely by women, the First Women's Olympic Games proved to be enormously successful and plans for the 1926 Games began in earnest.

Renamed the Second International Ladies Games, the women's event held in Gothenburg, Sweden, in 1926 was as successful as the first. The number of track and field events increased to 15, with women from eight member countries competing.

Meanwhile, the IOC and International Amateur Athletic Federation (IAAF) could not ignore the fact that women's track and field had gained a strong following. The IAAF recommended a full program of events for women in track and field in the 1928 Olympics, but when the proposal came to a vote, the IAAF committee only agreed to five events for women—100 meters, 800 meters, high jump, discus, and 80-meter hurdles. Still opposed to women's track and field in the Olympics, the IOC made it clear that the women would be included only as an "experiment."

After all of the hard work in getting the events included, the "experiment" nearly failed. Upon completion of the women's 800-meter event, journalists from the London *Daily Mail*, the *New York Times*, and other newspapers reported that several female competitors collapsed in exhaustion after the race and had to be carried off the field. In fact, all the women completed the race. But the reports caused a furor in Olympic circles, and the officials who had been opposed to women in the Olympics

Table 1.

The Women's Olympics or The Women's World Games			
First Women's Olympic Games	1922,	Paris,	7 countries
Second International Ladies Games	1926,	Gothenburg,	8 countries
Third Women's World Games	1930,	Prague,	17 countries
Fourth Women's World Games	1934,	London,	19 countries

used the exaggerated reports as evidence against continuing the women's program.

At its annual meeting in 1929, the IOC voted to withdraw the women's program in track and field, but a threatened boycott from the U.S. team in 1932 forced Olympic officials to reverse their earlier vote. Women's track and field stayed on the schedule, but the 800 meters was eliminated from the program and did not return until 1960.

The women's federation continued to sponsor the separate Women's Games until women got a full program of events in the Olympics. Held in Letna Stadium in Prague, Czechoslovakia, in 1930, the Third Women's World Games hosted more than 200 athletes from 17 countries. The three-day festival drew more than 15,000 spectators. In 1934, the FSFI invited women from 19 countries to compete in the Fourth Women's World Games in London. By 1936, the FSFI reported a membership of 30 nations.

In 1936, the IAAF agreed to recognize world records reported by the FSFI and to sponsor an international championship in track and field. The FSFI disbanded after 16 years of championing the cause of women's track and field in international competition, but their efforts did result in women's Olympic participation.

U.S. Women and Olympic Participation

The burgeoning women's sports movement in the United States benefited from the worldwide fight to include women's events in the Games. The Amateur Athletic Union (AAU), the governing body for amateur sports in the United States, supported and encouraged women's participation in the Olympics.

Initially, however, the AAU did not recognize women's sports and even voted against allowing women's swimming and diving in the 1912 Olympics, due in part to the personal objection of then– AAU President James Sullivan. However, following Sullivan's death in 1914, the AAU reversed its position and agreed to recognize women's swimming competitions; thus in 1920 the United States sent its first official team of women athletes, 15 swimmers and 2 figure skaters, to the Olympics. In 1916, the AAU took control of track and field events and by 1920 had immersed itself in the dispute over allowing track and field events in the Olympics.

When the AAU declared its intention to send a team of female athletes to compete in the 1922 Women's Olympic Games, many people opposed the move. The Committee on Women's Athletics (CWA) of the American Physical Education Association (APEA) opposed the participation of U.S. women in the Games. The group believed that the nation's physical educators should direct the policies of women's athletics in the United States, not the AAU with their nonschool programs, and that women's track and field promoted the training and participation of a few highly skilled women rather than promoting the participation of many unskilled women. In April 1923, the Women's Division of the National Amateur Athletic Federation (NAAF) formed to promote a national policy for governing girls' and women's sports. (See chapter 1.)

Part of that national policy was to oppose women's participation in the Olympic Games. The Women's Division petitioned the IOC to eliminate women's athletics in the 1932 Los Angeles Games. The petition was denied, but the physical educators continued to oppose any focus on the highly skilled athlete. Prospective Olympic athletes had to fund their own training and organize their own competitions. This situation made participation more difficult and limited the potential pool of female Olympic talent for nearly 30 years.

The actions of the Women's Division did not deter America's female athletes, for they had the support of the AAU. The governing body promoted national and international programs in swimming, track and field, basketball, and gymnastics. The AAU's interest in women's athletics provided the sponsorship that U.S. athletes needed to gain entry into the Olympics.

VII. Antwerp, Belgium—1920

Competitors: women, 64; men, 2,543
New women's events:
Figure skating (reinstated, not held in 1912)
Swimming: 300-meter freestyle, springboard diving
Tennis: doubles
Yachting: mixed, finn class

After World War I, the Olympics resumed with a full schedule of events. The IOC awarded the Games to Antwerp, Belgium, in recognition of the sacrifices the country made during the war. For their part in the war, Austria, Bulgaria, Germany, Hungary, and Turkey were not allowed to send athletes. Doves, signifying peace, and the official Olympic flag became a part of the opening ceremonies for the first time.

For the first time in 16 years, the United States sent a contingent of women athletes to participate in the Olympics. The 1920 Games marked a new competitive spirit among U.S. team members. Ethelda Bleibtrey won the 100-meter freestyle to become the first U.S. woman to win a gold medal in swimming; and at age 14, Aileen Riggin, the youngest member of the U.S. team, won the first Olympic springboard diving competition, establishing America's dominance in the event.

VIII. Paris, France—1924

Competitors: women, 136; men, 2,956
New women's events:
Fencing: foil, individual
Swimming: 200-meter breaststroke, 400-meter freestyle replaced the 300-meter freestyle

By 1924, the Olympics had become a major force in international sports. The postwar euphoria translated into a revolution in amateur sports competition worldwide, with the Olympics as the focal point. The eighth Olympiad in Paris was well attended, with athletes from 44 nations taking part.

Swimming. U.S. women continued to dominate the swimming events despite the restrictions placed on the team by the

American Olympic Committee. U.S. officials, concerned about protecting their young swimmers from the temptations of the city, housed the women outside of Paris, nearly three hours away from the Olympic pool. Despite having to travel five to six hours a day to compete, the U.S. swimmers swept through the five swimming events, winning four gold, three silver, and three bronze medals. Gertrude Ederle won three medals for the United States: bronze in the 100- and 400-meter freestyles and a gold as a member of the winning freestyle relay team. Just two years later, Ederle made history as the first woman to swim across the 20-mile English Channel. (See her biography, p. 113.)

In Paris, U.S. divers swept all three springboard diving medals and won gold and silver medals in platform diving. American Aileen Riggin, who had won an Olympic gold in 1920, became the first person in Olympic history to win medals for both swimming and diving. She placed third in the 100-meter backstroke and second in the springboard diving competition.

Tennis. In tennis, U.S. national champion Helen Wills (Moody) won the ladies singles gold then teamed with former U.S. national champion Hazel Hotchkiss Wightman to win the doubles title. Wightman then paired with R. Norris Williams to capture the mixed doubles gold. After a dispute with the International Lawn Tennis Association over player treatment and scheduling, the IOC dropped tennis from the Olympic schedule after the 1924 Games. It returned to the Olympics as a full medal sport in 1988.

IX. Amsterdam, Holland—1928

Competitors: women, 290; men, 2,724
New women's events:
Track and field: 100 meters, 800 meters, 4x100-meter relay,
high jump, discus throw
Gymnastics: team combined competition
Discontinued women's events:
Tennis

The "Golden Age of Sport" was in full bloom when the 1928 Olympics commenced in Amsterdam. The exploits of Amelia Earhart and swimmer Gertrude Ederle in the years prior to the Amsterdam Games brought more attention to women's sport and the excitement surrounding the first track and field events for women gave another boost to women's participation.

Track and Field. The track and field events appeared to proceed without any problems, as 121 women entered the competition. In the sprints, Elizabeth "Betty" Robinson, a 16-year-old high school student from Riverdale, Illinois, won the 100 meters, the first women's track and field event to be contested in the Olympics. The Canadian team of Fanny Rosenfield, Ethel Smith, Florence Bell, and Myrtle Cook won the 4x100-meter relay in world record time.

The 800 meters, however, touched off a major controversy in the athletic world. Lina Radke of Germany won the race in 2 minutes, 16.8 seconds, setting a world record that lasted for more than 16 years. Although all the contestants finished the race, journalists reported that several of the competitors collapsed after the race. These reports caused a worldwide furor and brought forth claims from doctors and sports officials that women were not capable of running such a long distance. In response, the IOC banned all races for women longer than 200 meters, a rule that lasted nearly 32 years.

Gymnastics. On a happier note, the 12-woman Dutch team won the team combined exercises in the first Olympic gymnastics competition. In addition to Holland, other countries represented in the women's gymnastics competition included Italy, Great Britain, Hungary, and France.

X. Los Angeles, USA—1932

Competitors: women, 127; men, 1,281
New women's events:
Track and field: 80-meter hurdles, javelin throw
Yachting: mixed, star class

The Olympic Games came to the United States in 1932 for the first time in more than 20 years. The worldwide economic depression and the geographic isolation of southern California caused the lowest participation in the Olympics since 1906. But the hosts went all out to stage a dramatic Olympic Games. More than 105,000 spectators crowded the Los Angeles Coliseum to watch the two-hour opening ceremonies. The Los Angeles Organizing Committee built the first-ever Olympic Village near the Coliseum, which housed only the men. Female competitors and their chaperons stayed at the Chapman Park Hotel in Los Angeles.

The U.S. women physical educators who objected to women's participation staged a last-ditch effort to get the women's events cancelled in Los Angeles. The Women's Division of the National Amateur Athletic Federation (NAAF) petitioned the IOC to exclude women from the 1932 Games, and then proposed that Los Angeles host a festival that would include singing, dancing, music, *mass* sports and games, banquets, and exhibitions.

The lack of support from U.S. physical educators nearly halted women's track and field in the United States, as evidenced by the fact that all the members of the U.S. women's team came from independent athletic clubs rather than educational institutions. Women's track and field events remained on precarious ground in 1932, but the women who did compete excelled at every turn with a new world record set in nearly every women's event.

Babe Didrikson. The 1932 Games belonged to American Mildred "Babe" Didrikson. Olympic rules limited Didrikson to only three individual events, even though she had qualified for five at the AAU trials. She chose to compete in her three best events—the 80-meter hurdles, the javelin throw, and the high jump. She won two gold medals and one silver in the hurdles, javelin, and high jump, respectively, setting world records in each event. In the high jump, Jean Shiley and Didrikson had a jump-off to determine the winner and both cleared the world-record height of 5 feet, 5¾ inches. But officials disqualified

Didrikson for her western-roll style jump that caused her head to clear the bar before her body. The judges awarded the gold medal to Shiley, but declared that both women would share the world record. The epitome of the Olympic motto, *Citius, Altius, Fortius* (Faster, Higher, Stronger), Didrikson is the only athlete in Olympic history to win individual medals in throwing, running, and jumping events. (See her biography, p. 245.)

Swimming. American swimmers won six of the seven swimming and diving events held in Los Angeles. Georgia Coleman of the United States successfully executed a 2½ forward somersault in springboard diving, the first woman to accomplish the feat in Olympic competition. Soon after the competition, the International Swimming Federation banned dives it thought were too daring for the women's competition, like the 2½ somersault.

XI. Berlin, Germany—1936

Competitors: women, 328; men, 3,738
New women's events: none

The 1936 Olympics, known as the Nazi Olympics, went to Berlin just three years after Hitler took power in Germany. Hitler and the German people staged an elaborate sports festival, the first to be shown on television with broadcasts throughout Berlin. The Berlin Organizing Committee initiated the ritual of the Olympic torch relay, a lighted torch carried from Olympia to the current Games to ignite the Olympic flame.

More than 300 women, many of them from Germany and other European countries, competed in the five-sport program, and for the first time in nearly 30 years, no new events were added for women.

Helene Mayer. Just as the anti-Nazi movement used male-sprinter Jesse Owens's victories to discredit Hitler's "superior white race" theories, so too did a woman athlete find herself in the middle of a political chess game. As a condition for hosting the 1936 Olympics, the German Organizing Committee assured IOC members that they would comply with the IOC policy of not discriminating on the basis of race or religion. The German government also agreed that German Jews would not be excluded from the German teams. Under pressure from the IOC, the German government invited 1928 Olympic fencing champion Helene Mayer to compete as a member of the German team. (See her biography, page 183.) Dropped from her German fencing club in 1933 because she was Jewish, Mayer had moved to California to escape the violent anti-Semitic atmosphere that pervaded Germany. IOC officials urged her to return to the German team; they were eager to dispel charges that holding the Olympics in Berlin was acceding to the racism sweeping the country. Despite the anti-Semitic stance of the German government, Mayer quickly accepted the opportunity to recapture the gold medal and to see the family she had left behind. In an electrifying duel, Mayer finished second to Hungarian Ilona Schacherer-Elek (who was also Jewish) in the foil competition. After the Olympics, Mayer returned to California, where she continued to compete in U.S. national championships. She never returned to Germany.

U.S. Track and Field. The AAU fielded a small women's team for the 1936 Games. The American squad of Harriet Bland, Annette Rogers, Elizabeth Robinson, and Helen Stephens staged an upset victory in the 4x100-meter relay event after the world-record-holding German team dropped their baton on the final pass. American Helen Stephens beat defending champion Stella Walsh for the 100-meter gold medal.

Eleanor Holm. For American women, the 1936 Berlin Olympics will be remembered for the treatment afforded champion swimmer Eleanor Holm, who was removed from the team by AAU and American Olympic Committee (AOC) president Avery Brundage. On the nine-day voyage to Germany aboard the *S.S. Manhattan*, Holm, married and accustomed to first-class accommodations and a lively social life, took offense to the strict regulations and curfews instituted by the AOC. On the second night of the trip, Holm attended an on-board party hosted by the owner of the passenger ship, where she stayed drinking until 6:00 A.M. Warned by Olympic officials to tone down her behavior, Holm continued to drink in public. The following day, U.S. officials voted to remove her from the team for her training violations and discipline problems. Although she was the defending champion and the favorite to win backstroke events in the swimming competition, Holm spent her days in Berlin as a spectator. She returned to the United States after the Olympics to begin a successful acting career.

XII. Tokyo, Japan; Helsinki, Finland—1940

Cancelled due to World War II

XIII. London, Great Britain—1944

Cancelled due to World War II

POSTWAR OLYMPICS
1948–1964

The advent of World War II caused the cancellation of two Olympic Games. When the Games resumed in 1948, the image of the female athlete had changed. New levels of athletic performance attained by women reflected the physical stamina, endurance, and ability that their sisters exhibited as part of the workforce during the war. Female athletes developed a new awareness of their abilities and were eager to demonstrate them on the international playing field.

Between 1948 and 1964, the only new sport for women that was added to the Olympic schedule was volleyball, but several new events in swimming, track and field, and gymnastics found their way into the Olympic program. The most important event was the return of the 800-meter run in 1960.

Cold War Politics. During this period, Cold War politics dictated that sport become an arena for nationalism. Competitions between Communist and non-Communist countries became the focal point as more and more money and attention went to developing Olympic athletes.

Cold War politics directly contributed to the development of female Olympic talent in the United States. The United States Olympic Committee (USOC) became increasingly concerned about the poor showing of U.S. female athletes compared to the dominating posture of the athletes from the Soviet Bloc countries in the 1952 and 1956 Games. With no support in the nation's education system, the USOC could only enter 10 athletes in the women's track and field events in those years.

Believing that women's Olympic success was tied to the nation's educational system, the United States Olympic Development Committee created a Women's Advisory Board with representatives from the AAU and the Women's Division of the NAAF in 1958 to discuss competitive sports in the high schools and colleges. Philanthropist Doris Duke Cromwell donated $500,000 to help develop women's Olympic sports, and the Women's Division designed a series of sports institutes to train physical educators on coaching and officiating expertise in the various sports. By 1963, the Women's Division had completely reversed its decision on competitive sports and began a cooperative effort to coach and train highly skilled female athletes for international competition.

The success of the Tennessee State University (TSU) Tigerbelles proved that supervised and university-sponsored coaching would result in Olympic gold. Under the coaching of Ed Temple, the TSU program produced Olympic track and field sprinting champions Madeline Manning, Wilma Rudolph, Edith McGuire, and Wyomia Tyus. (See chapter 4.)

Television also became a significant influence in promoting advances in women's sport in the postwar period. The outstanding performance of Wilma Rudolph, broadcast worldwide in 1960, contributed to an awakening of the American public to the skills of the nation's female athletes.

XIV. London, Great Britain—1948

Competitors: women, 385; men, 3,714
New women's events:
Track and field: 200 meters, long jump, shot put
Canoeing: kayak singles, 500 meters

Soon after the end of World War II, the IOC selected London as the site for the first Olympic Games to be held in 12 years. With Britain still recovering from the war, London hosted more than 4,000 competitors from 59 countries in the 14th Olympiad. For their part in the war, Germany and Japan were not invited to attend.

More than 80,000 spectators witnessed the athletic events on the temporary track at Wembley Stadium. With the new events added, the women had a total of nine track and field events. Thirty-year-old Fanny Blankers-Koen of Holland emerged as the star of the track and field events and of the entire London Games.

Fanny Blankers-Koen. Blankers-Koen first participated in the 1936 Olympics where she competed in the high jump and 4x100-meter relay. She continued to train during the Nazi occupation of Holland, during which time she got married and had two children. In 1948, Blankers-Koen entered four of the nine women's events, foregoing her other specialties, the long jump and the high jump. She won gold in the 100 meters, the 80-meter hurdles, the 200 meters, and as the anchor of the Dutch 4x100-meter relay team. The "Flying Dutch Housewife" returned to Holland a national hero after her stunning Olympic performance. (See her biography, p. 92.)

Blankers-Koen's success in the four running events left little for American women. Alice Coachman of the United States outjumped Great Britain's Dorothy Odam Tyler to win the high jump competition, setting a new Olympic record at 5 feet, 6¼ inches.

Swimming. In the swimming events, Ann Curtis won the women's 100-meter freestyle and swam the anchor leg of the 4x100-meter relay to give the U.S. team the gold. U.S. women continued their domination of the diving competition. Victoria Draves came from behind on her last two dives to win the springboard competition, and with her win in platform diving, she became the first woman in Olympic history to win both diving gold medals in the same Games.

Gymnastics. The gymnastics finals, originally planned for Wembley Stadium, were forced inside by torrential rains. The eight-woman U.S. team finished third for a bronze medal in the team combined exercises, the first Olympic gymnastics medal for the United States in women's gymnastics. It would be 36 years before the U.S. women would win another gymnastics medal.

XV. Helsinki, Finland—1952

Competitors: women, 518; men, 4,407
New women's events:
Gymnastics: individual all-around, side horse vault, uneven bars, balance beam, floor exercise

Before the start of World War II, the IOC offered the 1940 Olympics to Helsinki after banning Tokyo from holding the Games because of Japan's involvement in the Sino-Japanese War. The cancellation of the 1940 Games delayed Helsinki's chance to play Olympic host, but when the Games finally made their way to Scandinavia in 1952, the Finns conducted the sports festival in the manner expressed in the original Olympic ideals.

Soviet Athletes. Soviet athletes entered the Olympics for the first time in 40 years. The Soviet Union's presence at the Helsinki Games had an immediate impact on the women's events. The gymnastics competition for women had been expanded to include four individual events, and the Soviet women immediately established their dominance in the sport. The Soviet team won the team combined title, their first of eight consecutive gold medals in that event. Three of the five individual apparatus golds also went to Soviet women.

Track and Field. The Soviet women also competed well in the track and field events with a strong showing in the three throwing events. With only 10 women on the U.S. track team in Helsinki, the Americans managed only one medal: a gold in the 4x100-meter relay. The team of Mae Faggs, Barbara Jones, Janet Moreau, and Catherine Hardy set a new world record in the relay in defeating the favored Australian team. As a member of the triumphant team, 15-year-old Barbara Jones was the youngest person ever to win a gold medal in track and field.

Equestrian Events. For the first time in Olympic history, women competed directly with men in the equestrian event. Four women entered in individual dres-

sage, which requires the rider to put the horse through a series of movements that display communication and cooperation between horse and rider. Paralyzed from the knees down after a bout with polio, Lis Hartel of Denmark had to be helped on and off her horse, but she had enormous command of her animal, Jubilee. She rode Jubilee to a silver medal in dressage.

XVI. Melbourne, Australia—1956

Competitors: women, 384; men, 2,958
New women's event:
Swimming: 100-meter butterfly

For the first time in the modern era, the Olympics were held in the Southern Hemisphere. Melbourne hosted the Games amid worldwide political controversy that resulted in three boycotts. Holland, Spain, and Switzerland boycotted the 1956 Games to protest the Soviet invasion of Hungary. Egypt, Iraq, and Lebanon withdrew to protest the Israeli-led takeover of the Suez Canal, and the People's Republic of China withdrew from the Games because Taiwan was allowed to compete. The Chinese would not send a team to the Olympics until 1984.

Quarantine. Australia had strict animal quarantine laws, and so the equestrian events had to be held in Stockholm, Sweden. Competing directly against the men, the all-woman dressage team from Germany won the silver medal, and Lis Hartel of Denmark and Liselott Linsenhoff of Germany won the silver and bronze individual medals, respectively. Women participated in the show jumping competition for the first time. Patricia Smythe, a member of the British team, won a bronze medal in the Nation's Cup (Prix des Nations) event.

Track and Field. The United States continued to field a small team of women tracksters. The only track and field medals for the United States came from Mildred McDaniel, who won the gold in the high jump, and the 4x100-meter relay team, which took home the bronze.

Swimming and Diving. Swimming and diving, however, remained strong events for U.S. women. They swept the 100-meter butterfly, and the U.S. team took silver in the 4x100-meter freestyle, finishing two seconds behind the record-setting Australian team. American Carin Cone won the silver in the 100-meter backstroke and her teammate Sylvia Ruuska finished third in the 400-meter freestyle. Patricia McCormick of Long Beach, California, defended her 1952 Olympic titles by winning the platform and springboard diving contests, becoming the only woman in Olympic history to win both diving events in consecutive Olympics. (See her biography, p. 184.)

XVII. Rome, Italy—1960

Competitors: women, 610; men, 4,738
New women's events:
Track and field: 800 meters (reinstated)
Canoeing: kayak pairs, 500 meters
Fencing: foil, team
Swimming: 4x100-meter medley relay
Yachting, mixed: flying dutchman class

The Olympic Games returned to the European continent in 1960, to the site that hosted the final ancient Games some two thousand years earlier. The Rome Organizing Committee spent more than $50 million on new facilities for the sporting events, while using facilities of the ancient Games like the Basilica of Maxentius for wrestling and the Terme di Caracalla for gymnastics. Romans supported the athletes with enormous crowds at each venue; even Pope John XXIII became a spectator, watching the canoeing events from a window of his summer residence.

Television. Millions of viewers tuned their televisions for coverage of the Olympics as the summer event was broadcast worldwide for the first time. Television brought recognition to the athletes; for the first time, fans in their home countries could see the outstanding performances of their female athletes. The women's program continued to expand slowly with four new events and the reinstatement of the 800-meter run.

Black Track Stars. The first generation of Black American female track stars emerged in these Games. Wilma Rudolph, representing the United States, won three gold medals—in the 100 meters, the 200 meters, and as anchor of the 4x100-meter relay team. As a child, Rudolph had contracted polio, and doctors predicted she would never walk normally again. She learned to walk at age 7 and began running at age 12. Her clear domination in the sprint events by age 19 ranked her as the world's fastest female; her exciting performance, watched by millions of TV viewers, stimulated an interest in women's track and field worldwide. (See her biography, p. 210.)

With her trio of victories, Rudolph became the first U.S. woman to win three track and field events in the same Olympic Games. Also in 1960, Earlene Brown of the United States won the bronze in the shot put, and through 1996 was still the only U.S. woman to win a medal in that event.

Teenage Swimmers. An American squad of teenagers dominated the swimming events, winning five of the six contests. Sixteen-year-old Chris Von Saltza won three golds and a silver medal as the outstanding performer on the U.S. team. For the first time in the modern Games, the Americans lost the diving contests; Ingrid Kramer of the strong East German team won both the springboard and platform diving events.

XVIII. Tokyo, Japan—1964

Competitors: women, 683; men, 4,457
New women's events:
Track and field: 400 meters, pentathlon
Swimming: 400-meter individual medley
Volleyball

In 1964, the Olympics went to the Land of the Rising Sun, as Japan became the first country in the Far East to host the Games. The Tokyo Games were an enormous success for both spectators and competitors. Ninety-four nations participated, and the Games were telecast live to 39 countries.

Volleyball. The first team sport for women, volleyball, was added to the Olympic schedule in 1964. Excited fans from the host country watched as the Japanese women's team stormed through the first Olympic volleyball tournament relatively unchallenged on its way to the gold.

Track and Field. All-around athletic ability marked the new events for women in Tokyo. Women's track and field added the pentathlon, which measured all-around athletic ability with competition in five events— the 80-meter hurdles, shot put, high jump, long jump, and 200 meters—over a two-day period. Irina Press of the Soviet Union won the first pentathlon.

Swimming. All-around ability in swimming was needed for success in the most grueling of events, the 400-meter individual medley, which requires 100 meters each of the butterfly, backstroke, breaststroke, and freestyle. World-record-holder Donna de Varona of the United States breezed to a six-second victory over teammate Sharon Finneran. In other swimming events, Australian Dawn Fraser won her third consecutive 100-meter freestyle gold medal, becoming the first Olympic swimmer of either sex to win the same event three times.

Equestrian Events. In the equestrian contests, the Olympic three-day event—a combination class for individuals and teams of jumping, dressage, and speed and endurance tests in cross-country and steeplechase—was open to women to compete directly with men for Olympic medals. Helen Dupont of the United States was the only woman to compete in the three-day event in the 1964 Olympics; she finished in 33rd place in the mixed competition.

THE OLYMPIC REVOLUTION IN WOMEN'S SPORTS
1968–2000

Throughout the 1960s and 1970s, female athletes and women's sports advocates lobbied hard to get more sports and more events for women in the Olympics. This effort, combined with the increasing interest and participation in women's sports, resulted in an expanded Olympic program for women. Although volleyball was the only new sport added between 1948 and 1964, the number of events during that period increased to 14. Since 1968, 11 new sports have been introduced: rowing, basketball, and team handball in 1976; field hockey in 1980; cycling in 1984; table tennis in 1988; badminton and judo in 1992; and softball, soccer, and beach volleyball in 1996. Tennis was also reintroduced as a full medal sport in 1988. Women may also try out and compete with men in equestrian, shooting, and yachting events. The number of women participating and the percentage of women also increased in this period.

Sex Testing. With more and better training opportunities, women's performances improved noticeably over those of the men during this period. (See table 2.)

Women trained hard and became more muscular and, although muscular women had always taken part in the Olympics, by the 1960s the gender of these women came into question. To address the concern, in 1968 the IOC initiated a sex-testing program "to protect women against unfair competition." The IOC based their reasons for sex testing on the idea of male superiority in Olympic events: females would not have an advantage over men in the men's competition, but men competing in women's events would have a definite advantage; therefore, women should be protected against men entering their events. Thus, any athlete entering women's events must undergo a chromosome test to determine the sex of the athlete. A controversy continues today over the necessity of such tests.

Table 2.
Performance Changes in Olympics, 1936–96.

	1936	1956	1976	1996
100 meters	11.5 sec.	11.5 sec.	11.08 sec.	10.94 sec.
High jump	5' 3"	5' 9¼"	6' 4 "	6'8¾"
Discus throw	156' 3"	176' 1"	226' 4"	228' 6"

XIX. Mexico City, Mexico—1968

Competitors: women, 781; men, 4,750
New women's events:
Shooting, mixed: skeet shooting
Swimming: 200-meter freestyle, 800-meter freestyle, 200-meter backstroke, 100-meter breaststroke, 200-meter butterfly, 200-meter individual medley

Olympic Flame. The Mexico City Olympics presented both new opportunities and new scrutiny for female athletes. Enriqueta Basilio became the first woman to light the Olympic flame in the stadium, and Janice Lee York Romary of San Mateo, California, a 40-year-old fencer competing in her sixth Olympic Games, was the first woman to carry the U.S. flag in the opening ceremonies.

Mixed Events. Women competed in men's shooting events for the first time. Eulalia Rolinska of Poland and Gladys de Seminario of Peru were the first women to compete in Olympic shooting; they finished 22nd and 31st, respectively, in the small-bore rifle, prone position. And women continued their success in the equestrian events. In capturing second place, Marion Coakes of Great Britain became the first woman to win an individual medal for show jumping.

Track and Field. Wyomia Tyus led the American women's track and field effort. She successfully defended her 100-meter title, the first woman to do so in a sprint event. She also anchored the victori-ous U.S. 4x100-meter relay team. Madeline Manning won the gold medal in the 800 meters, establishing a world record and becoming the first American to win the event.

Swimming. With five new events, the women's swimming program expanded to 14 contests. U.S. swimmers won 11 of the 14 races. Debbie Meyer of Sacramento, California, won three individual golds as did Claudia Kolb of Hayward, California.

XX. Munich, West Germany—1972

Competitors: women, 1,171; men, 6,659

New women's events:

Track and field: 1,500 meters, 100-meter hurdles (replaced the 80-meter hurdles), 4x400-meter relay

Archery: individual single-round

Canoeing: kayak slalom singles

Yachting, mixed: soling class

The Games returned to Germany for the first time since the Nazi Olympics in 1936. The hosts in Munich built lavish sporting and housing facilities for their guests to stage the most elaborate Olympics to date. But the two-week affair was permanently scarred when eight Palestinian terrorists broke into the Olympic Village, killing two Israeli athletes and taking nine others hostage. A shoot-out at the Munich airport left all nine hostages and five terrorists dead. The IOC postponed the Olympics for 24 hours and held a memorial service at the main stadium attended by 80,000; the Games continued that afternoon.

Nearly 1,200 women participated in the Munich Games. Archery returned to the Olympic schedule for the first time since 1920, and more events were added in track and field, including the 1,500 meters, the longest distance race for women to date. The East Germans emerged as the dominant track and field team, winning six gold medals.

Swimming. Just as the East Germans controlled track and field, the Americans continued their domination in the water. The U.S. swimming squad won eight gold medals, including three from super swimmer Melisse Belote. Swimmers broke every existing Olympic record in Munich.

Shooting. Margaret Murdock, a 33-year-old nurse from Topeka, Kansas, won a silver medal in the small-bore rifle, three positions event in the shooting contest, the first woman to win a shooting medal competing directly against the men. Murdock finished in a tie with U.S. teammate Lanny Bassham at 1,162 points. Bassham was awarded the gold medal because he had scored three 100s to Murdock's two. At the medal ceremony, he pulled Murdock up to the first-place platform where they stood together for the playing of the national anthem.

Equestrian. Twenty-one of the 33 riders in individual dressage were women, including Liselott Linsenhoff of West Germany, the first female individual gold medalist in an equestrian event.

Olga Korbut. In every Summer Games, one personality emerges that captures the attention of the media and the spectators. In 1972, that person was Soviet gymnast Olga Korbut. As an alternate replacing an injured teammate, Korbut wowed the crowds at the gymnastic venue with her daring moves on the individual apparatus. Her perky personality endeared her to the arena crowd and to the television audience worldwide. In these Olympics, Korbut won three gold medals and sparked a growing interest in women's gymnastics worldwide. (See her biography, p. 166.)

XXI. Montreal, Canada—1976

Competitors: women, 1,274; men, 4,915
New women's events:
Basketball
Team handball
Rowing: single sculls, double sculls, quadruple sculls, pairs without coxswain, fours with coxswain, eights
Yachting, mixed: tornado class

The Games of the 21st Olympiad held in Montreal, Canada, were conducted under tight security to prevent a recurrence of the tragic events of Munich. The more than 6,000 athletes from 100 countries who came to participate were treated to elaborate housing facilities and sporting venues. The Games suffered yet another boycott when the African nations withdrew in protest of New Zealand's participation in the Games. The New Zealand rugby team had made a tour of South Africa prior to the Olympics, which many felt violated the ban on Olympic athletes competing in apartheid-torn South Africa.

Team Sports. Two more women's team events became full medal sports at the Montreal Games: basketball and team handball. The Soviet basketball team had not lost a game in five years and was undefeated in international tournament competition since 1958, and so as expected they breezed to a gold medal in the inaugural basketball tournament. The 12-woman U.S. team, which included Ann Meyers, Nancy Lieberman (-Cline), and Patricia Head (Summitt), defeated Bulgaria 95-79 to win the silver medal.

Rowing. Women also got six new rowing events added to the schedule, and the East Germans initiated the sport by winning all but two of the events.

The Summer Games of Montreal were dominated by the Eastern Europeans. In addition to success in the rowing events, East German women won 11 swimming and nine track and field gold medals out of a possible 14 in each of the sports.

Nadia Comaneci. Fourteen-year-old gymnast Nadia Comaneci of Romania replaced Olga Korbut as the star of the Olympics. She received seven perfect scores for her daring and innovative routines on the individual gymnastic apparatus, taking Olympic gymnastics to a new level of performance and expectation.

XXII. Moscow, USSR—1980

Competitors: women, 1,192; men, 4,320
New women's event:
Field hockey

The 1980 Summer Games went to the Soviet Union for the first time since the USSR began competing in 1952. The Games suffered a major loss when 35 nations, led by the United States and including Canada, Japan, and West Germany, withdrew to protest the Soviet invasion of Afghanistan. Despite the absence of the top Western athletes, many remarkable performances were recorded.

East German Women's Team. The East German women continued their streak of victories in swimming, while the Soviet team delighted its hometown crowd with outstanding performances in track and field. With several world-record holders missing from the competition, the East Germans sped through the swimming contests, winning an average of two out of three medals per event. In the 100-meter freestyle, Barbara Krause of East Germany won the gold medal and became the first woman to break the 55-second barrier. She repeated her gold-medal performance in the 200-meter freestyle, and finished first as part of the winning 4x100-meter freestyle relay team,

making hers one of the outstanding performances of the 1980 Summer Games.

Field Hockey. When five of the six nations scheduled to compete in the inaugural women's field hockey tournament withdrew from the Olympics, the Moscow Organizing Committee and the IOC contacted Zimbabwe to fill the field just five weeks before the start of the Games. The members of the team were not selected until the weekend before the Olympics opened. Amazingly, the Zimbabwe women's field hockey team went undefeated in the tournament to win the Olympic gold medal.

Gymnastics. The 1980 gymnastics competition became a battle between members of the Soviet Union and the Romanian teams. Nadia Comaneci returned to defend her all-around and individual titles. Although she lost the all-around to Soviet gymnast Yelena Davydova in a controversial judges' decision, Comaneci went on to capture gold in the balance beam and floor exercise.

XXIII. Los Angeles, USA—1984

Competitors: women, 1,620; men, 5,458

New women's events:

Track and field: 3,000 meters, marathon, 400-meter hurdles, heptathlon (7 events)
replaced the pentathlon (5 events)
Canoeing: kayak fours, 500 meters
Cycling: road race
Gymnastics: rhythmic all-around
Shooting: sport pistol; small-bore rifle, three positions; air rifle
(now separate women's events)
Swimming: synchronized swimming, solo; synchronized swimming, duet
Yachting, mixed: windglider

Boycott. For the third time in 12 years, the modern Olympic Games suffered a major boycott. In retaliation for the U.S.-led boycott in 1980, the Soviet Union and Communist Bloc countries (except Romania) withdrew from the Summer Games. Nonetheless, Los Angeles hosted more than 7,000 athletes from 140 countries, more than ever before, including the Chinese who made their first appearance since 1956. The Los Angeles Olympic Organizing Committee conducted elaborate opening and closing ceremonies, relying on corporate sponsors rather than government subsidies to finance the undertaking.

New Women's Events. The hard work and lobbying efforts of the athletes and advocates to get more events included in the program paid off as 13 new events were added to the women's program in Los Angeles, making a total of 75 events exclusively for women. In track and field, the pentathlon gave way to the heptathlon, which added the javelin and restored the 200-meter dash (which had been replaced by the 800 meters in 1980) to the already grueling event, and two more women's distance races filled out the women's track and field schedule. These two events, the 3,000 meters and the marathon, garnered

the attention of the world in the 1984 Olympics for two very different reasons.

Mary Decker, Zola Budd, and the 3,000-Meter Race. The 3,000-meter run had a less than triumphant beginning. The race featured Mary Decker (Slaney), America's premier middle-distance runner, and South African teenager Zola Budd. The media indulged in enormous pre-race hype over Budd's citizenship and the "Decker Olympic jinx." Because South African athletes were banned from Olympic competition over their government's racial policies, Budd could not compete as a citizen of South Africa. In order to compete, she established British citizenship via her paternal grandfather who was British. This move did not sit well with the media and anti-apartheid groups around the world. For "Little Mary Decker," as she was affectionately called by the U.S. press, this Olympics was her chance to go for the gold that had eluded her for more than a decade. Although already a top runner as a teenager, Decker could not compete in the 1972 Olympics because she was too young; in 1976, she sat out because of injuries; and in 1980, she was forced to stay home due to the U.S. boycott.

During the final of the 3,000 meters, Decker took the early lead and set a fast pace, followed closely by Budd. With less than two laps to go the two bumped each other on the inside lane, causing Decker to lose her balance and fall into the infield. The race continued but Budd fell off the pace and finished seventh; Maricica Puica of Romania won the race. Controversy raged across the Atlantic as to who was at fault. Track officials immediately disqualified Budd for obstruction, but after reviewing the videotapes, determined that no one was at fault. Decker was not so forgiving. The collision put a damper on the new distance event for women, but the women's marathon restored the excitement to women's track and field.

Women's Marathon. One of the most watched events at the 1984 Games was the women's marathon. The long struggle to achieve recognition for women's long-distance running reached fruition with the first women's Olympic marathon featuring the best female distance runners in the world, including world-record-holder Joan Benoit (Samuelson) of the United States and former world-record-holder Grete Waitz of Norway. However, what was expected to be a classic battle between the two never materialized. In the heat of the Los Angeles summer, Benoit moved ahead of the pack after only 14 minutes and never looked back. Many of the runners, including Waitz, were leery of the heat and ran more conservative races. Benoit entered the tunnel leading to the Coliseum track more than a minute ahead of the pack. The 77,000 fans in the LA Coliseum cheered her around the last lap on her way to the gold medal, finishing the race in 2:24:52.

Other Track and Field Events. In other track and field events, American Valerie Brisco-Hooks won three gold medals—

in the 200 meters, 400 meters, and 4x400-meter relay; and Evelyn Ashford sprinted to a new Olympic record in the 100 meters.

New Stars. The Soviet boycott of the Olympics left the door open for a new gymnastics star to emerge. Mary Lou Retton electrified the world on her way to the all-around title in women's gymnastics, the first individual medal for a U.S. female gymnast. With the East Germans absent from the Games, U.S. swimmers dominated the aquatics events, winning nine gold medals, including golds in the two new synchronized swimming events. U.S. team members Tracy Calkins, Mary T. Meagher, and Nancy Hogshead each won three swimming gold medals in Los Angeles.

Cycling. Cycling, the sport that emancipated women around the world at the turn of the century, came full circle with its inclusion in the Olympic Games. American Connie Carpenter-Phinney won the inaugural road race in a dramatic finish, coming from behind to defeat teammate Rebecca Twigg by less than half a wheel length.

Equestrian and Archery Events. In other events, Karen Stives became the first U.S. woman to win an individual equestrian medal, riding Ben Arthur to a second-place finish in the individual three-day event. Finishing 35th in the women's archery competition was New Zealand's Neroli Fairhall, the first paraplegic athlete to take part in the Olympics.

Overall. Despite the boycott of the strong East German and Soviet teams, the success of U.S. athletes on U.S. soil went a long way to inspire another generation of sportswomen. The new and exciting events added to the increased recognition of women as athletes. As Joan Benoit stated after winning the marathon: "This win is a triumph for women's athletics."

XXIV. Seoul, South Korea—1988

Competitors: women, 2,438; men, 6,983
New women's events:
Track and field: 10,000 meters; 800-meter wheelchair
Archery: team competition
Cycling: 1,000-meter sprint
Shooting: air pistol
Swimming: 50-meter freestyle
Table tennis: singles, doubles
Tennis: singles, doubles
Yachting: 470 class

For the first time in 30 years, the three major sports world powers (the Soviet Union, China, and the United States) would meet in an Olympic competition. With no terrorism and no boycotts, nearly 10,000 athletes from 160 countries came to Seoul, South Korea, to compete in the 24th Olympiad. The Koreans hosted a spectacular and colorful Olympics, marred only by the suspension of several athletes for using performance-enhancing drugs.

Growing Women's Program. The women's program continued to grow as tennis returned to the Games as a full-medal sport and women got their own yachting event. The success of the 1984 women's marathon led the IOC to add the 10,000 meters to the track and field schedule. Spectators at the Olympic velodrome venue watched the first-ever women's cycling sprint event, and the inclusion of table tennis increased the number of women's sports to 18.

Otto and Evans. Two of the outstanding female athletes at the Seoul Games were swimming sensations Kristin Otto of East Germany and Janet Evans of the United States. Otto won six gold medals, four individual and two in the sprint relays. Evans won three golds, setting Olympic records in the 400-meter freestyle and the 800-meter freestyle.

Griffith Joyner and Joyner-Kersee. The traditional strength of the U.S. team continued in track and field. The Seoul Games were a family affair with the success of Florence "FloJo" Griffith Joyner and her sister-in-law Jackie Joyner-Kersee. Griffith Joyner became an instant media star in capturing three track gold medals, setting a world record in the 200-meter dash, setting an Olympic record in the 100 meters, and winning the 4x100-meter relay. (In the finals of the 100 meters, Griffith Joyner ran faster than 12 of the competitors in the men's second round of the 100-meter preliminaries.) Joyner-Kersee, one of the world's finest all-around female athletes, set a world record in the grueling heptathlon, and then went on to establish a new Olympic mark in the women's long jump. (See their biographies, pages 156 and 158.)

Sharon Hedrick of the United States won the first-ever women's 800-meter wheelchair race in 2:11.49.

The Return of Tennis. Tennis returned as a full-medal sport with the world's top players vying for medals. U.S. superstar Chris Evert made her Olympic debut losing to unseeded Raffaella Reggi of Italy in the second round. The number one player in the world, Steffi Graf turned her Grand Slam into a Golden Grand Slam by defeating Gabriela Sabatini of Argentina in the women's singles final. Sabatini's silver medal was her country's first Olympic medal since 1972.

Women's Yachting. Women from more than 30 nations traveled to Seoul to compete in the first women's-only yachting event. The 470 class is a race involving a lightweight, 15½-foot boat ridden by two. Each class in yachting runs seven races over a marked course with points awarded depending on order of finish. U.S. sailors Allison Jolly and Lynne Jewell led after the first six races and had only to finish in the top 14 in the last race to win the gold. But horrendous winds forced the team to stop dead in the water for five minutes to make repairs; when they started moving again, they had dropped to 15th place. Still, they forged ahead, finished ninth in the race, and claimed the gold.

Equestrian. The equestrian events are just one of two sports in which women compete directly against men for individual medals. In the individual dressage, the rider takes her horse through a series of prearranged movements to demonstrate the horse's responsiveness to the rider's commands. In 1988, Nicole Uphoff of Germany won the gold, Margi Ott-Crepin of France won the silver, and Christine Stuckelberger of Switzerland won the bronze. This Olympics was the first time all three dressage medals were won by women.

XXV. Barcelona, Spain—1992

Competitors: women, 3,008; men, 7,555
New women's events:
Cycling: 3,000-meter individual pursuit
Judo
Badminton

The 1992 Olympics came to Barcelona, Spain, the home of IOC President Juan Antonio Samaranch. The newly built sports venues were mixed amongst the captivating architecture and distinctly European flavor of the Catalonian city.

Worldwide Political Changes. A number of worldwide political changes had occurred in the years since the previous Olympics. Apartheid was repealed in South Africa, allowing that nation to return to the Olympics. West and East Germany were united, and with the collapse of Communism in the Soviet Union, the USSR split into 15 separate countries. In 1992, independent teams from Estonia and Latvia made their first appearance since 1936, and Lithuania fielded its first team since 1928.

The remaining republics of the former Soviet Union competed at the Barcelona Games as the Unified Team, although individual winners were honored by the raising of the flag of their own republic. Cuba, North Korea, and Ethiopia ended their Olympic boycotts. All told, 172 nations sent athletes to compete in the Barcelona Olympics.

Gymnastics. The Barcelona Olympics was the last time that the republics of the former Soviet Union would compete as one team. They continued their dominance of the team gymnastics competition by winning their 10th gold medal. Shannon Miller of the United States won a silver medal in the all-around competition, becoming the first female U.S. gymnast to earn a silver medal in a nonboycotted Olympics. Miller medalled in five of the six gymnastics events.

Track and Field. The 100-meter final in Barcelona was the closest in Olympic history. Gail Devers of the United States and Russian Irna Privalova ran even for most of the race, with Gwen Torrence (USA), Juliet Cuthbert (Jamaica), and Merlene Ottey (Jamaica) at their heels. A slow-motion replay of the finish showed that Devers had edged Cuthbert for the gold. Only .06 seconds separated the top five finishers in the race.

In the 1,500 meters, Hassiba Boulmerka of Algeria upset the field to win the gold medal. Boulmerka, a devout Muslim, became a symbol for Arab women who wanted to break away from traditional Islamic restrictions, but she was denounced by Islamic fundamentalists for "running with naked legs in front of thousands of men."

XXVI. Atlanta, USA— 1996

Competitors: women, 3,684; men, 7,060
New women's events:
Beach volleyball
Softball
Soccer
Team synchronized swimming (replaced solo and duet)
Track and field: 5,000 meters
Badminton: mixed doubles
Cycling: points race, road time trial, cross-country race (mountain biking)
Fencing: épée, individual; épée, team
Rhythmic gymnastics: team
Rowing: lightweight: double sculls
Shooting: double trap
Swimming: 4x200-meter freestyle relay; 4x100-meter medley relay

Athletes from 197 countries came to Atlanta, Georgia, to participate in the Centennial Olympic Summer Games. One of the most memorable aspects of these Olympic Games was the extraordinary success of the U.S. women, particularly in the team sports. U.S. women's teams won all three swimming relays, both track relays, and gold in gymnastics, synchronized swimming, softball, soccer, and basketball.

Gymnastics. The 1996 Centennial Olympic Games in Atlanta found their defining moment in the women's gymnastics competition. Kerri Strug's heroic final vault capped the end of the Olympic reign of the Russian women's team, as the U.S. women defeated the world gymnastics power for the United States' first team gold medal in Olympic history. In the individual events, Shannon Miller won a gold medal in the balance beam, Amy Chow took a silver on the uneven bars, and Dominique Dawes won bronze in the floor exercise.

Swimming. Amy Van Dyken became the first U.S. woman to win four gold medals in one Olympics when she won the 50-meter freestyle, the 100-meter butterfly, and two relays. The United States swept the relays for the first time since 1972.

Track and Field. Gail Devers of the United States became the first woman to win back-to-back 100-meter titles since Wyomia Tyus in 1964-68. Two-time heptathlon champion Jackie Joyner-Kersee withdrew after one heptathlon event with a sore leg, but she made a courageous comeback to win the bronze medal in the long jump.

Basketball. The U.S. women's basketball team drew crowds of over 30,000 in all six of its games played at the Georgia Dome, including a women's basketball world record attendance figure of 33,952 in the game versus Australia on July 27. Led by team captain Teresa Edwards, appearing in her fourth Olympic Games, the U.S. team won the gold medal at the Centennial Olympics in dominating fashion. They posted victories over Cuba (101-84), Ukraine (98-65), Zaire (107-47), Australia (96-79), and South Korea (105-64) in preliminary-round play, and they defeated Japan 108-93 to advance to the medal round semifinals. The United States defeated Australia 93-71 in the semifinal game, and dominated current world champion Brazil in the gold-medal game, winning in overwhelming fashion 111-87. Team USA outscored their opponents by an average of 28.6 points a game, and outrebounded their opponents by 15.1 boards per game. (See chapter 4.)

Soccer and Softball. Both soccer and softball were new Olympic events in 1996. The U.S. women's soccer team captured the first-ever women's Olympic soccer gold medal by defeating China 2-1 on August 1, 1996, before a crowd of 76,481 at Sanford Stadium in Athens, Georgia, the largest crowd ever to see a women's Olympic event.

In the softball competition, the U.S. team defeated China 3-1 to capture the first-ever gold medal in women's Olympic softball. A crowd of over 8,500 watched the United States win behind the strong pitching of Michele Granger and Lisa Fernandez. Thirty-four-year-old shortstop and orthopedic surgeon Dot Richardson hit a two-run home run to key the victory over China for the gold medal.

XXVII. Sydney, Australia—2000

New women's events:
Shooting: skeet and trap
Water polo
Triathlon
Tae kwon do
Swimming: synchronized swimming, duet (reinstated)
Weightlifting

Olympic Winter Games

The first winter sports appeared unofficially on the Olympic program in 1908 when the British Olympic Council sponsored figure skating events for women and men at the Prince's Skating Rink in London as part of the Fourth Olympiad. However, modern Olympic Games founder Coubertin opposed a separate Games for winter events because he believed they would bring disunity within the overall Olympic movement. In 1920, when the Summer Games resumed after World War I, figure skating appeared on the schedule as did men's ice hockey, although both were still exhibition sports and not an official part of the Olympic program.

Alpine Skiing. The popularity of competitive winter sports had increased by the 1920s with the invention of downhill and slalom skiing. The Norwegian Skiing Federation put pressure on the International Olympic Committee (IOC) to designate a separate Winter Games to contest their sports. That pressure combined with the well-attended and competitive winter events of 1920 convinced the IOC to establish the Olympic Winter Games.

First Olympic Winter Games. The first Winter Games began in 1924 with a modest program of five sports, but only one sport, figure skating, was open to women. Like their experiences in the Summer Games, women had difficulty getting a full schedule of events on the Olympic program and had only one event in the Winter Games until 1936. Thirteen women entered the first Winter Olympics in 1924; by 1994, more than 500 participated. The shortage of events did not keep female athletes from turning in outstanding performances. Women have skied and skated into Olympic history, turning in stellar performances along the way.

Figure Skating. The ladies' figure skating event became an official event in 1924 and quickly became the focal point of the winter sports festival. The sport of figure skating, a popular recreation worldwide, initially held little attraction as a competitive sport. That changed in 1924 when Sonja Henie of Norway entered her first Olympic competition. By 1928, she had revolutionized the sport, transforming it into an event with athletic jumps, turns, and spins. Henie skated with grace and athleticism, which attracted the attention of skating enthusiasts. Much of the success of the early Winter Games was due to the popularity of Sonja Henie and the ladies' figure skating event. (See her biography, p. 146.)

U.S. Team. U.S. women have had a consistent presence in the Winter Olympics, but because of the limited opportunity to participate in winter sports in most of the country, the success of American women in the Winter Olympics has fallen behind that of the strong Scandinavian, German, and Soviet women's teams, especially in the cross-country skiing and luge events.

I. Chamonix, France—1924

Competitors: women, 13; men, 281
New women's event:
Figure skating: singles and pairs

Chamonix, France, hosted the first official Winter Olympic Games in 1924. Sixteen nations took part in the inaugural Winter Games, initially staged by the French Olympic Committee as the International Winter Sports Week.

Figure Skating. Thirteen women competed in figure skating, which included both singles and mixed pairs. Herma Planck-Szabo of Austria won the singles event, receiving first-place votes from all seven judges and outscoring U.S. champion Beatrix Loughran by nearly 20 points. Most notable, however, was 11-year-old Sonja Henie making her first appearance at the Olympics. Because Henie was so young, the IOC allowed her to wear shorter skirts than the other competitors, causing somewhat of a scandal. Wearing a skirt just above the knees made it easier for her to complete the jumps and spins she had developed.

Despite her last-place finish, young Henie created a stir among figure skating fans with her athletic style and gracious manner on the ice. Her abbreviated skating costume promoted more freedom of movement and the apparent acceptance of a shorter skirt contributed to advancing women's Olympic figure skating.

II. St. Moritz, Switzerland—1928

Competitors: women, 27; men, 366
New women's events: none

The success of each Winter Olympics generally depends on the cooperation of the weather. Throughout their history, the Winter Olympics have been plagued with weather problems that often disrupted events; such was the case at the second Winter Games. The 1928 Winter Olympics opened in St. Moritz, Switzerland, on February 11, 1928, amid below-zero temperatures that warmed to nearly 77 degrees four days later. The evening of the 14th brought a downpour of warm rain, causing every competition on February 15th to be postponed. The next day, a sudden freeze set in, and the Games continued on schedule.

Alpine Skiing. Winter sports came of age during the 1920s with the flourish of

Alpine skiing competitions. The IOC included downhill and slalom events as exhibition matches; they would not become official events until 1936.

Sonja Henie. The 1928 St. Moritz Games marked the debut of 15-year-old Sonja Henie as the world's premier women's figure skater. The defending world champion was awarded first place by six of the seven judges to win her first gold medal. The skirt length of the ladies figure skating entrants continued to cause a mild furor. Three of the contestants wore their skirts above the knee, causing considerable concern among the spectators in St. Moritz.

III. Lake Placid, USA—1932

Competitors: women, 30; men, 277
New women's events: none

The United States hosted the third Winter Games amidst a worldwide economic depression that kept many athletes from attending and kept the number of spectators down as well. Again the weather wreaked havoc on the Games, and at one point snow

had to be trucked in from Canada to help repair the cross-country track. Despite the economic and weather conditions, the state of New York spent more than $1 million to stage the 1932 Winter Games at Lake Placid. These Winter Olympics provided many

Americans with a firsthand view of sports they might have only read about, which helped to stimulate American interest in the winter sports, particularly figure skating and skiing.

New Facilities. The people of New York spent more than $200,000 to build a new skating rink for the 1932 Games, the first time that Olympic figure skating events went indoors. Sonja Henie successfully defended her Olympic figure skating title, this time the unanimous first choice of the seven judges. In the pairs competition, Andrée Joly and her husband Pierre Brunet of France also defended their titles as figure skating pairs gold medalists.

Speed Skating Demonstrations. Women's speed skating made its debut in Lake Placid, with demonstration events in the 500-, 1,000-, and 1,500-meter races. Five U.S. women entered the competition finishing first in the 1,000- and 1,500-meter races, second in the 500 meters, and third in all three.

IV. Garmisch-Partenkirchen, Germany—1936

Competitors: women, 76; men, 680
New women's event:
Alpine skiing: alpine combined (downhill and slalom)

The efforts of Hitler's Nazi regime to stage an extravagant event and the introduction of Alpine skiing combined to make the fourth Winter Games the first with mass appeal. Thousands of spectators invaded the neighboring villages of Garmisch and Partenkirchen in the German Alps to watch the competitions.

Alpine Skiing. Alpine skiing made its official debut in the 1936 Games, with medals awarded for the best combined times (finishes) in the slalom and downhill races. The United States sent a women's team that members of the Amateur Ski Club of New York had formed in 1934. The inexperienced U.S. racers could not contend with the more experienced Europeans. Christl Cranz of Germany turned in two outstanding slalom runs to capture the first women's alpine gold medal, followed closely by her German teammate Kathe Grasegger.

Figure Skating. Twenty-six women battled to dethrone two-time champion Sonja Henie for the ladies' figure skating gold medal. Up to the challenge and skating better than ever, Henie skated to her third consecutive gold medal. To the delight of her rivals, she retired from competitive skating shortly after her victory.

Sapporo, Japan; St. Moritz, Switzerland—1940

Cancelled due to World War II

Cortina d'Ampezzo, Italy—1944

Cancelled due to World War II

The IOC selected Sapporo, Japan, to host the fifth Winter Games for 1940, but because of Japan's involvement in the Sino-Japanese war, the IOC withdrew its invitation and offered the Games first to St. Moritz then to Garmisch-Partenkirchen. The 1944 Games had been awarded to Cortina d'Ampezzo, Italy. The outbreak of World War II postponed the Games for eight years.

V. St. Moritz, Switzerland—1948

Competitors: women, 77; men, 636
New women's events:
Alpine skiing: downhill, slalom

The Games Resume. The Winter Games resumed in 1948, hosted for the second time by St. Moritz, Switzerland. Twenty-eight countries sent athletes to St. Moritz; athletes from Germany and Japan were not invited to compete because of their countries' involvement in the war.

Alpine Skiing. Olympic medals were awarded in individual Alpine skiing events, the slalom and the downhill, for both women and men. Gretchen Fraser of the United States won the inaugural slalom event for women, Hedy Schlunegger of Switzerland won the downhill, and Trude Beiser of Austria had the best combined times in both events to take home the gold medal in the Alpine combined.

New Skating Champion. With the retirement of Sonja Henie, a new ladies' figure skating champion was crowned at the 1948 Olympics. The current world champion Barbara Ann Scott of Canada received seven of the nine first-place votes to win the gold medal.

VI. Oslo, Norway—1952

Competitors: women, 108; men, 624
New women's events:
Alpine skiing: giant slalom
Cross-country skiing: 10 kilometers

Discontinued events:
Alpine skiing: Alpine combined

Athletes from 30 countries traveled to the homeland of skiing, Oslo, Norway, to compete in the sixth Winter Games. More than 500,000 spectators watched the 11-day festival amid excellent weather conditions.

Cross-Country Skiing. Cross-country skiing, which has been the mainstay of the Winter Games for nearly a quarter of a century, opened to women in 1952. Twenty women competed in the inaugural 10-kilo-meter race; the women's team from Finland swept the medals in the event.

New Alpine Events. The Alpine combined event gave way to the giant slalom in women's Alpine ski racing. Andrea Mead Lawrence of the United States won the giant slalom and six days later captured the gold in the slalom after recovering from a fall on her first run. She was the first U.S. skier to win two gold medals in the Winter Olympics. (See her biography, p. 173.)

VII. Cortina d'Ampezzo, Italy—1956

Competitors: women, 132; men, 687
New women's event:
Cross-country skiing: 3x5-kilometer relay

The small Italian village of Cortina d'Ampezzo had been awarded the 1944 Games, but the war postponed their opportunity to host the event until 1956. Cortina set some important milestones in the history of Olympic winter sport. The seventh Winter Olympics was the first televised Winter Games. A whole generation saw the color and pageantry of the Games via satellite. Thirty-two countries sent representatives to Cortina, including the Soviet Union, which entered athletes for the first time.

Olympic Oath. Guiliana Minuzzo of Italy, the 1952 downhill skiing bronze medalist, became the first woman to recite the Olympic oath for all athletes.

Women's Program. The women's program grew with an additional cross-country event, but women still had only eight events in three sports to contest. In their first Winter Olympics, Soviet women won gold and silver in the cross-country 10-kilometer race and gold in the 3x5-kilometer relay race. Swiss and Austrian women dominated the Alpine events, while Tenley Albright of the United States captured the gold in figure skating, with teenager Carol Heiss, also of the United States, finishing second to take home a silver medal. (See their biographies, pp. 79 and 144.)

VIII. Squaw Valley, USA—1960

Competitors: women, 146; men, 502
New women's events:
Speed skating: 500 meters, 1,000 meters, 1,500 meters, 3,000 meters

In the Sierra Nevada Mountains about 200 miles from San Francisco, the tiny ski resort of Squaw Valley, California, built an impressive Olympic Village specially for the 1960 Games. This self-contained village included an all-purpose center for the skating events and a housing complex that kept the competitors in close touch with practice facilities and training rooms.

Speed Skating. Women's speed skating events, which had not been held since they were demonstrated in 1932, reached full-medal status in 1960. These additional events were a real boost to the women's Olympic program. The Soviet women flexed their muscles in the speed skating events, winning three of the four new contests. They continued to dominate the Winter Games with a victory in the cross-country 10-kilometer race and a second-place finish in the 3x5-kilometer relay.

Figure Skating. The figure skating events belonged to the North Americans. World champion Carol Heiss of the United States, who had finished second to Tenley Albright in 1956, won her first gold medal as the unanimous first-place choice of the nine judges. Canadian skaters Barbara Wagner and Robert Paul won the gold in pairs competition.

IX. Innsbruck, Austria—1964

Competitors: women, 175; men, 758
New women's events:
Luge: single
Cross-country skiing: 5 kilometers

Innsbruck, Austria, welcomed nearly 1,200 athletes from 36 countries to the ninth Olympic Winter Games. More than a million spectators crowded the city and the news coverage of the daily events took on a greater importance. The increased popularity of the winter sports brought more media personnel than Olympic competitors to Innsbruck. In addition to newspaper and radio reporters, 34 television networks from around the world sent journalists to cover the events. For the first time the Games became fully computerized, using computers to calculate scores, figure standings, and print results.

Alpine Skiing. Women played a prominent role in these Games. A sibling rivalry emerged in the Alpine events, capturing the attention of the media. The Goitschel sisters, Marielle and Christine, of France waged a duel for first and second in the slalom events. Marielle won the giant slalom with Christine second; Christine won the slalom with Marielle finishing second.

Speed Skating. Lydia Skobilkova of the Soviet Union performed brilliantly in the speed skating events, winning gold in all four of the women's events.

Figure Skating. The U.S. Olympic figure skating team was in a rebuilding period after the team had been virtually wiped out by a tragic plane crash in 1961. Thus the women's figure skating team failed to win a medal for the first time since 1948. Sjoukje Dijkstra of Holland won the gold.

X. Grenoble, France—1968

Competitors: women, 230; men, 1,063
New women's events: none

To conduct the Winter Games on a grand scale, the people of Grenoble spent more than $200 million in a building program that included housing, motorways, and a state-of-the-art Olympic indoor ice stadium seating nearly 12,000 spectators for the figure skating and ice hockey competitions. Controversy erupted over the sponsor advertising on skis and other equipment, and for the first time in history, Olympic organizers ordered female competitors to take a sex test.

Figure Skating. For the first time since 1932, no new events for women were added to the schedule, although a record number of women athletes traveled to Grenoble to compete. One bright spot for the U.S. Olympic team came from Peggy Fleming, who won the women's figure skating gold medal, the only U.S. gold-medal winner of the Grenoble Games.

Luge Competition. Olympic officials disqualified three of East Germany's leading women sledders from the luge competition after discovering that the women had been heating the runners of their sleds to obtain greater speed. Italy's Erica Lechner was awarded first place and the gold medal.

Speed Skating. The United States scored a "triple" of sorts in the women's 500-meter speed skating event when Jennifer Fish, Dianne Holum, and Mary Meyers tied for second place, each skating the distance in 46.3 seconds.

XI. Sapporo, Japan—1972

Competitors: women, 218; men, 927
New women's events: none

Sapporo, Japan, had been awarded the Games in 1940 but because of World War II, delayed hosting the games until 1972. The Japanese city welcomed athletes from 35 countries for the 10-day sports festival. The press outnumbered the competitors by nearly two-to-one, taking advantage of new Japanese technology in the broadcasting center. Located on the northernmost island of Japan, Sapporo offered a beautiful setting to stage the winter events.

U.S. Female Victories. For the second Winter Olympics in a row, all the U.S. gold medals were won by women. Anne Henning and Dianne Holum, both from Northbrook, Illinois, near Chicago, won speed skating gold medals in the 500 meters and 1,500 meters, respectively, and Barbara Cochran added a gold in Alpine skiing slalom. American women entered their first cross-country events, although none finished in medal contention.

XII. Innsbruck, Austria—1976

Competitors: women, 248; men, 1,013
New women's events:
Figure skating: ice dancing for mixed pairs
Cross-country skiing: 4x5-kilometer relay (changed from 3x5-kilometer)

The IOC originally selected Denver to host the 1976 Olympic Winter Games, but the Rocky Mountain city turned down the event after environmentalists protested and state residents failed to pass a state referendum to fund the Games. With only three years to prepare, Innsbruck, Austria, hosted the Games for the second time. The city spent approximately $17 million in modernizing its 12-year-old Olympic facilities. The Austrian army was enlisted to prepare the venues, run the events, and provide extensive security measures.

Women's Program. Women made up about 20 percent of all participants, were included in 26 out of the 36 participating Olympic delegations, and could participate in 14 out of 37 events. For the first time in 12 years, a new event for women was added to the program, ice dancing for mixed pairs.

Skating Events. U.S. women fared well in the skating events. Dorothy Hamill succeeded previous U.S. champions Tenley Albright, Carol Heiss, and Peggy Fleming as the women's figure skating gold medalist. Detroit's Sheila Young skated to a gold, silver, and bronze medal in the speed skating events to add to her world championship in cycling.

Alpine Skiing. Rosi Mittermaier of West Germany stole the show in the Alpine events, winning gold in the downhill and the slalom, and finished a mere .012 second behind Kathy Kreiner of Canada in the giant slalom for a silver medal. No woman has ever won all three Alpine events in one Olympics.

XIII. Lake Placid, USA—1980

Competitors: women, 271; men, 1,012
New women's events: none

When the village of Lake Placid, New York, hosted the third Olympic Winter Games in 1932, the world was in the midst of an economic depression. The cost to stage the Olympics was $1.1 million, and the number of competitors was 307. When the Games returned to Lake Placid in 1980, the budget was nearly $80 million, and the number of competitors had increased to 1,283 from 37 countries. Despite transportation and weather problems throughout the 11-day event, the 1980 Olympics proved memorable for the outstanding performances by the world's premier athletes.

Rugged Whiteface Mountain played host to the women's Alpine ski events, which saw Hanni Wenzel of Liechtenstein score two gold medals in the slalom and giant slalom. With two silver medals from the 1972 Games, Annemarie Moser-Pröll returned to competitive skiing after a short retirement to capture the women's downhill event.

Skating Events. The U.S. women's team was shut out in its efforts to medal in the Alpine events and did not win a single gold medal in 1980. In speed skating, American Leah Mueller won two silver medals and her teammate Beth Heiden captured a bronze. And the ladies' figure skating champion was decided on the strength of East German Anett Poetzsch's compulsory skating. Rival Linda Fratianne of Los Angeles came in a close second to garner the silver. The real story of the figure skating competition came in the mixed pairs, where Soviet skater Irina Rodnina, paired with husband Aleksandr Zaitsev, won her third Olympic gold medal. With three gold medals and 10 world championships, Rodnina tied the record of major championship titles set by Sonja Henie dating back to 1936. Rodnina and Zaitsev expected to be challenged by current world champions Tai Babilonia and Randy Gardner of the United States for the gold. Unfortunately, Gardner suffered an injury prior to the competition that forced the U.S. team to withdraw.

XIV. Sarajevo, Yugoslavia—1984

Competitors: women, 283; men, 1,127
New women's event:
Cross-country skiing: 20 kilometers

For the first time in Olympic history, the IOC selected an Eastern European city to host the Winter Games. Until the 1984 Games, Sarajevo, Yugoslavia, was best known as the city where, in 1914, Archduke Franz Ferdinand was assassinated, setting off World War I. Seventy years later, Sarajevo welcomed more than 1,400 athletes from 49 countries to the 14th Winter Olympic Games.

Figure Skating. In figure skating, the most exciting moments came from the pairs competitions. Ice dancers Jayne Torvill and Christopher Dean of Great Britain lit up the scoreboard with 12 perfect marks for their dramatic performance to Ravel's *Bolero*. In an upset, Americans Kitty and Peter Carruthers skated a near flawless routine to win the silver medal in the pairs competition behind the strong Soviet couple Elena Valova and Oleg Vasiliev. The Carruthers' medal was the first U.S. medal in pairs since their coach Ron Ludington and his wife Nancy won the bronze in 1960.

Alpine Skiing. On the slopes, U.S. women's Alpine team members Debbie Armstrong and Christin Cooper finished 1-2 to win gold and silver in the giant slalom event.

Speed Skating. In speed skating the East Germans continued their domination; Karin Enke led the way with two golds and two silvers.

Cross-Country Skiing. One of the most outstanding performances for women in the 1984 Winter Games came from 28-year-old Marja-Liisa Haemaelaeinen of Finland who won all three individual gold medals and took home a bronze in the 4x5-kilometer relay in cross-country skiing.

XV. Calgary, Canada—1988

Competitors: women, 317; men, 1,270
New women's events:
Speed skating: 5,000 meters
Alpine skiing: Super G., Alpine combined (reinstated)

The tranquil plains of southern Alberta provided the setting for the 15th Olympic Winter Games. Calgary, Canada, staged a magnificent show with athletes from 59 nations participating in the 15-day event. By 1988, women had 17 events in five sports, compared to 26 events in eight sports for men, and women still made up only 22 percent of the total competitors.

Figure Skating. In ladies' figure skating, Katarina Witt of East Germany won her second consecutive Olympic gold, while hometown favorite Elizabeth Manley skated brilliantly to a silver. Nineteen eighty-six world champion Debi Thomas of the United States finished third for the bronze medal.

Speed Skating. In speed skating, Holland's Therese van Gennip won three gold medals putting a halt to East Germany's long domination in the sport. Bonnie Blair sped to a gold and a bronze medal in the 500 meters and the 1,000 meters, respectively, the United States' only double-medal winner in the Calgary Games.

XVI. Albertville, France—1992

Competitors: women, 488; men, 1,313
New women's events:
Short-track speed skating: 500 meters, 3,000-meter relay
Freestyle skiing: moguls
Biathlon

Only 18 of the 57 official events included in the Albertville Olympics were actually held in Albertville. Seven other towns hosted medal competitions, which made for interesting logistics in moving athletes and spectators around.

The U.S. contingent equaled its best Olympic performance ever on foreign soil, led by the U.S. women who collected all 5 gold medals and 9 of the 11 U.S. medals overall, including the inaugural freestyle skiing event. Skiing in a snowstorm to the accompaniment of "Rock 'n' Roll High School" by the Ramones, Donna Weinbrecht took home the gold in moguls.

Speed Skating. Speed skaters Bonnie Blair and Cathy Turner each won two medals at the Albertville Games. Blair became the first U.S. woman to win gold medals in consecutive Winter Olympics by taking the 500-meter title in 1988 and 1992 in addition to her 1,000-meter crown in 1992. Turner dominated the short track competition, winning the gold medal in the 500-meter event and the silver in the 3,000-meter relay.

Figure Skating. The U.S. women's figure skaters recorded the best showing ever in Olympic history by a single country as Kristi Yamaguchi captured the gold medal, Nancy Kerrigan won the bronze, and Tonya Harding finished fourth. Yamaguchi became the first U.S. woman to win a figure skating Olympic gold medal since Dorothy Hamill in 1976.

Luge. The United States improved its best previous Olympic finish ever on the luge course in La Plagne. Cammy Myler recorded the best showing ever for any American in luge by placing fifth in women's singles while teammate Erica Terwillegar also cracked the top 10 with a ninth-place finish.

Cross-Country Skiing. As a member of the gold-medal-winning 4x5-kilometer relay team, Soviet skier Raisa Smetanina became the first winter athlete to earn 10 Olympic medals. She also became the only athlete to win medals in five Winter Olympics.

XVII. Lillehammer, Norway—1994

Competitors: women, 542; men, 1,302
New women's events:
Freestyle skiing: aerials
Short-track speed skating: 1,000 meters

After the 1992 Summer Olympic Games, the International Olympic Committee (IOC) made the decision to alter the dates of the Summer and Winter Games so they would not be held in the same year. This meant there would be only two years separating the 1992 and 1994 events. Many of the athletes from the 1992 Albertville Games returned to compete in the Games in Lillehammer.

Figure Skating. The main events of these Olympics were overshadowed by the scandal surrounding the attack on U.S. figure skater Nancy Kerrigan and the involvement of her U.S. teammate and rival Tonya Harding. Just 60 days before the start of the Lillehammer Olympics, Kerrigan was viciously assaulted prior to the start of the U.S. national championships and was forced to withdraw from the competition. Harding's ex-husband confessed to plotting the attack and implicated Tonya in the plan. Kerrigan recovered in time to compete in the Olympics, and although she skated brilliantly, she was edged out for the gold by Oksana Baiul of the Ukraine. Harding was allowed to skate and finished 12th.

Speed Skating. Bonnie Blair equaled her gold-medal-winning performances in both the 500- and 1,000-meter events. With five gold medals and one bronze medal, Blair became the most decorated female Winter Olympian in U.S. history. (See her biography, p. 90).

Cross-Country Skiing. Manuela Di Centra of Italy was the most decorated athlete at the Lillehammer Games. She won five medals at these Olympics—two golds, two silvers, and one bronze in cross-country skiing events.

XVIII. Nagano, Japan—1998

New women's events:
Curling
Ice hockey
Snowboarding: giant slalom, halfpipe

The Olympics returned to the Asian continent when more than 3,000 athletes descended on Nagano, Japan, for the 18th Winter Olympiad. Building on the momentum of the women's success at the 1996 Summer Games, U.S. women won four of the six golds and eight of the 13 U.S. medals.

Ice Hockey. Women's ice hockey made its debut at the Nagano Games. In the first-ever gold medal game in Olympic women's ice hockey competition, the United States defeated Canada, 3–1. The victory gave the U.S. Olympic Women's Ice Hockey Team the tournament's only unbeaten and untied record at 6-0-0.

Alpine Skiing. Weather posed a problem for many of the Alpine skiing events, causing the races to be postponed for several days due to heavy snow. When the competition finally got underway, Picabo Street of the United States, just weeks after recovering from a severe knee injury, surprised the competition with a gold medal performance in the Super G. Germany's Katja Seizinger won two gold medals, in the downhill and Alpine combined.

Figure Skating. At age 15, Tara Lipinski of the United States became the youngest Winter Olympic gold medalist in an individual sport by winning the women's figure skating title. Michelle Kwan, also of the United States, captured the silver medal as both turned in near flawless performances. This finish marks the first time that the United States has won the gold and silver medals in women's figure skating since the 1956 Olympic Winter Games when Tenley Albright and Carol Heiss accomplished that feat.

XIX. Salt Lake City, USA—2002

Part II

Biographies and Teams

Chapter 3
Outstanding Women Athletes Who Influenced American Sports

"I don't think anyone who is a true pioneer thinks of themselves as one. They're just doing something they have a passion for."
—Susan Butcher, four-time winner of the Iditarod Trail Sled Dog Race

When Susan Butcher won her fourth Iditarod Trail Sled Dog Race, she brought worldwide attention to the challenge of the Iditarod, making it one of the most intriguing sporting events to emerge in the 1980s. She became a symbol of women's stamina and endurance in the toughest of sports. Butcher is just one of the many women who have shaped and influenced the course of women's sports in the United States by participating, and excelling, in their chosen athletic endeavors. From tennis player Martina Navratilova's 1,438 career match victories to Kathy Whitworth's 88 LPGA tournament titles, America's elite female athletes have established incredible performance records and have amassed numerous awards and honors. These elite female athletes followed their own course to success in spite of many restrictions placed on them by society—lack of coaching, facilities, equipment, and finances, and the myth of women being the weaker sex.

Heroines in a wide variety of sports—from basketball, bicycling, and bowling to swimming, track, and rock climbing—the 86 women profiled in this chapter have, through their unique qualities and skills, contributed to the history of women's sports in America. Most importantly, they have become role models for female athletes all over the world. Through their pioneering efforts and brilliant careers, these athletes have brought the next generation of sportswomen a step closer to fulfilling their potential as fine athletes.

Michelle Akers (soccer player)

Born February 1, 1966, Santa Clara, California

A member of the U.S. Women's National Soccer Team since 1985, Michelle Akers is the all-time leading goal scorer for both men's and women's U.S. national teams; she has scored more than 90 goals in over 100 international matches. Many consider her one of the best female soccer players in the history of the sport. She led her team-

Michelle Akers
©Allsport USA/Al Bello

Association (NCAA) All-American (1984, 1986, 1987, 1988). In 1988, she was named the winner of the Hermann Trophy as the best female collegiate soccer player.

Akers joined the U.S. national team in 1985. She traveled with the squad to Italy for its first international competition. In 1991, at the first-ever FIFA Women's World Championship in China, she scored 10 goals in six games, leading the U.S. Women's National Soccer Team to the gold medal. In the finals against Norway, with the score tied 1-1 and less than three minutes to play, Akers drove home the game-winning goal to give the United States its first world soccer championship since 1862. She was named the Gold Boot Winner (highest scorer) in the tournament. Akers was selected U.S. Soccer's Female Athlete of the Year in 1990 and 1991.

After graduating from UCF in 1989 with a degree in liberal studies/health, Akers played professionally overseas for three seasons (1990, 1992, 1994) in Sweden with the Tyreso Football Club. While competing with Tyreso in 1992, she scored 43 goals and was the leading goal scorer—male or female—from any of Sweden's professional divisions.

She returned to the United States to compete for the national team, but in 1993, after collapsing during a match at the Olympic Sports Festival in San Antonio, Akers was diagnosed with the Epstein-Barr virus, also known as chronic fatigue syndrome. The virus attacks the immune system and drains the body of strength. "When it was bad, I couldn't sit up in a chair. All I could do was lie in bed. And the migraine headaches pounded. Boom! Boom! Boom!" she told *Sports Illustrated*.[2]

For nearly two years, Akers continued to be a key offensive weapon for the national team while she battled her illness. She was the MVP of the 1994 CONCACAF Qual-

mates to the first-ever Women's World Cup championship in 1991 and to the first-ever Olympic gold medal in women's soccer at the 1996 Summer Olympic Games in Atlanta, Georgia.

Born in Santa Clara, California, Akers was raised in the Pacific Northwest near Seattle. Her dream as a little girl was to be a wide receiver for the Pittsburgh Steelers. "I practiced Hail Mary catches daily with my father and brother in the backyard and at school during recess with the guys," she said. "Then one day, my first grade teacher pulled me aside and told me 'Girls don't play football.' I was crushed."[1] But girls did play a kind of football: soccer.

Akers played soccer for Shorecrest High School in Seattle. She was a four-time All-American (1980-84) and earned a scholarship to the University of Central Florida (UCF) in Orlando. While at UCF, she was a four-time National Collegiate Athletic ifying Championship in Montreal, where she tied with Mia Hamm as the tournament's second-leading goal scorer. The win helped the United States qualify for the 1995 FIFA Women's World Championship in Sweden. At the 1995 championships, Akers was injured in the opening game and did not play again until the semifinal loss to Norway. The U.S. team finished third.

After the loss to Norway, Akers and the U.S. team set their sights on the first-ever Olympic soccer tournament. "I always craved the opportunity to play in the Olympics," she said. "It will do so much for the future of our sport."[3] As a member of the U.S. Women's National Soccer Team at the 1996 Centennial Olympic Games, Akers started all five matches of the tournament, scoring a crucial goal in the U.S. semifinal victory over Norway. The U.S. team captured the first-ever women's Olympic gold medal by defeating China 2-1 on August 1, 1996, before a crowd of 76,481 at Sanford Stadium in Athens, Georgia, the largest crowd to watch a women's Olympic event.

Michelle Akers led the U.S. team in becoming a world powerhouse in international soccer. She has started as center forward for the U.S. team in more than 100 international competitions and is the most prolific scorer in U.S. soccer history. Akers remains one of the top players in the world. She is still playing on the national team and continues to battle chronic fatigue syndrome.

Tenley Albright (figure skater)

Born July 18, 1935, Newton Center, Massachusetts

In 1944, Hollis and Elin Albright of Newton Center, Massachusetts, bought their nine-year-old daughter Tenley a pair of ice skates, which she used on their flooded rink in the backyard. Within a decade, Albright would go from turning figure eights on her backyard rink to turning the heads of the audience and the judges at the 1953 Women's World Figure Skating Championship. Albright became the first U.S. woman figure skater to win the world championship, and went on to become the first U.S. woman to win an Olympic figure skating gold medal, signaling the emergence of the United States as an international power in women's figure skating.

Born in Newton Center, Massachusetts, Albright joined the Skating Club of Boston shortly after she got her first pair of skates. At age 11, she suffered an attack of poliomyelitis, also known as infantile paralysis. Her doctors encouraged her to continue skating as a therapy for her weakened muscles. Just four months after her recovery from the bout with polio, Albright entered and won her first skating competition, the Eastern U.S. Junior Ladies' Championship. She proceeded through the ranks of U.S. figure skating by winning the U.S. Ladies' Novice Singles Championship in 1949, and the U.S. Ladies' Junior Singles title in 1950.

A serious student from the outset, Albright had to schedule practice time around her studies at Manter Hall School in Cambridge, Massachusetts. She practiced her compulsory figures at the local indoor rink at four o'clock each morning, then would return home in time for breakfast and the start of the school day. Practicing the compulsories was tedious work; she much preferred free-skating: "I like the creative side of skating, the opportunity to practice new jumps or dance steps, to fit them to music my own way, and then to perfect the whole thing."[4] During her summer breaks, Albright traveled to wherever indoor skating rinks were available. Her determination, dedication, and hard work paid off when she stormed into the senior ranks with unprecedented success.

In 1952, Albright represented the United States in the Olympic Winter Games held at Oslo, Norway. In her first international competition, the 16-year-old won the Olympic silver medal, the nation's first silver medal in women's figure skating since Beatrix Loughran won hers in 1924.

Later that year, Albright won her first U.S. Ladies' Seniors title, and in February 1953, she skated a nearly flawless performance to capture America's first Women's World Figure Skating Championship. She followed her world title with the North American crown and a second national title to complete skating's triple crown, the first American to accomplish the feat. Albright continued to dominate U.S. figure skating, winning the national titles again in 1954 and 1955. She lost her world title to Gundi Busch of West Germany in 1954 but regained the crown in 1955.

Two weeks before the 1956 Olympics, Albright fell in training and severely injured her right ankle. Despite the pain, she performed a marvelous free-skate exhibition and won the Olympic gold medal, narrowly defeating her U.S. teammate and closest rival, Carol Heiss. With the Olympic victory, Albright became the first U.S. woman to win a figure skating gold medal. "She did a courageous job," observed her coach, former U.S. champion Maribel Vinson. "She was a true champion to forget her injury under pressure and not to make it an excuse."[5]

Tenley Albright
Courtesy of the World Figure Skating Museum

Following her Olympic success, Albright went to Garmisch-Partenkirchen, Germany, to defend her world title, but with her ankle still not totally healed, she lost the championship to Heiss. The rivals met again in Philadelphia for the 1956 U.S. championships, where Albright won her sixth consecutive title. Soon after the U.S. championships, Albright retired from competitive skating to pursue her medical career.

While Albright worked to achieve skating's highest honors, she continued to pursue her lifelong goal of becoming a doctor. She enrolled in Radcliffe College in 1953 and took summer school and extra courses to keep up with her studies. Often at competitions she could be found studying German or English literature while waiting for her turn to skate. She graduated from Radcliffe in 1957 and at age 21 was accepted at Harvard Medical School, one of six women in a class of 130. She graduated from Harvard in 1960 and established herself as a skilled and successful surgeon. She married

Tudor Gardiner in 1962 and has three children. In 1979, Albright became the first woman officer of the U.S. Olympic Committee, and she was named to the International Women's Sports Hall of Fame in 1983.

Throughout her successful skating career, Tenley Albright understood the importance of dedication and determination.

She took to the ice with confidence earned after hours of practice, and her success on the ice carried over to success in the classroom, and in life. As a sportswoman, she initiated the emergence of the United States as a world figure skating power by becoming the first U.S. woman figure skater to win the world championship and the Olympic gold medal.

Constance M.K. Applebee (field hockey coach)

Born June 4, 1873, Chigivall, Essex, England; died January 26, 1981

Englishwoman Constance M.K. Applebee first came to the United States in the summer of 1901 to attend the Harvard Summer School of Physical Education under the direction of Dr. Dudley A. Sargent. While at the school, she demonstrated field hockey to female students at Vassar College, promoting it as a healthy recreation for college girls. Later that same summer, she taught the game to the physical educators at Wellesley, Radcliffe, Smith, Mt. Holyoke, and Bryn Mawr. With physical educators Senda Berenson and Lucile E. Hill, she founded the American Field Hockey Association, which established the game's official rules.

Constance Applebee (back row on far left) with Bryn Mawr College hockey team, 1905
Courtesy of Bryn Mawr College Archives

For the next 70 years, "the Apple," as she was affectionately nicknamed, taught her favorite sport to players around the world. In 1922, she presided over the inaugural meeting of the U.S. Field Hockey Association (USFHA) and began her Pocono Hockey Camp on the grounds of Camp Tegawitha in Pennsylvania. While in the United States, she coached thousands of junior and senior high school and college students, as well as nearly 50,000 club sport players.

While coaching at Bryn Mawr College, she edited and published America's first women's sports magazine, *The Sportswoman*, which reported on the world of field hockey and contained articles on lacrosse, fenc-ing, archery, swimming, bowling, and skating.

Constance M.K. Applebee, field hockey's most outspoken proponent, lived a life devoted to field hockey and believed her sport gave girls physical and mental strength. She was inducted into the USFHA Hall of Fame, and she received the Distinguished Service Award from the American Association for Health, Physical Education, and Recreation, and the Award of Merit from the Association of Intercollegiate Athletics for Women. Applebee was a 1991 inductee into the International Women's Sports Hall of Fame. She coached field hockey until she was 95 years old and lived to be 107 years old.

Evelyn Ashford (track and field sprinter)

Born April 15, 1957, Shreveport, Louisiana

President Jimmy Carter's decision to boycott the 1980 Moscow Olympics affected hundreds of U.S. athletes who had been training for years to compete at the world's most prestigious athletic event. None was more affected than Evelyn Ashford, America's top female sprinter. Initially, she took the boycott announcement hard, but her disappointment quickly turned to a renewed dedication to earn the title of the world's fastest woman. A member of five U.S. Olympic Track and Field Teams (1976, 1980, 1984, 1988, 1992), Ashford flew by her competition in U.S. and international meets, breaking numerous records on her way. She epitomized speed, power, endurance, and dedication, becoming one of America's best track athletes in the 1980s.

Born in Shreveport, Louisiana, the daughter of U.S. Air Force Sergeant Samuel Ashford and Vietta Ashford, Ashford had a nomadic childhood, living a military life. Her family settled in Roseville, California, near Sacramento when she was a teenager. While at Roseville High School, Ashford's mathematics teacher, who knew of her great running ability, arranged some races against the boys in her school. She beat them all, and the coach promptly invited her to join the boys' track squad. Ashford sprinted against boys in high school meets, winning the majority of her races; during her senior year, she was named co-captain of the team.

Ashford's success in high school caught the attention of the UCLA track coach Pat Connolly. In 1975, the university offered her one of its first women's athletic scholarships. While at UCLA, she trained with Connolly, and by the end of her freshman year, she had qualified for the 1976 U.S. Olympic team. In Montreal, the relatively unknown 19-year-old ran the 100 meters in 11.24 seconds to finish in a respectable fifth place.

Evelyn Ashford
© Allsport/Michael King

the finals she reinjured her hamstring and fell to the ground while Göhr sped by.

Despite the tender hamstring, Ashford continued to train for the 1984 Los Angeles Games. She qualified for the Olympic team, and although she had hoped to win three gold medals at the Olympics, she chose to withdraw from the 200-meter competition to protect her leg from further injury.

The time finally came for Ashford to go for the gold. With Göhr and the East Germans boycotting the 1984 Los Angeles Olympics, Ashford breezed through the preliminary rounds. In the finals, she dominated the field, running to an Olympic gold and setting a new Olympic record of 10.97 seconds, the first woman to run the 100 meters under 11 seconds in the Olympics. She also anchored the U.S. 4x100-meter relay team to victory for her second gold medal.

She had great success at UCLA, earning All-American honors in 1977 and 1978; she won the Association of Intercollegiate Athletics for Women (AIAW) National Championships in 1977 in the 100 meters, the 200 meters, and the 800-meter relay, and defended her 200-meter championship a year later. Ashford left UCLA in 1978 to train on her own full-time.

In 1979, Ashford set a U.S. record in the 200 meters, running the distance in 21.83 seconds. Just months before the start of the 1980 Olympics, Ashford won the World Cup 100 meters and 200 meters, beating East German world-record holders in both events. She was favored to win Olympic gold in the two events before Carter made the boycott announcement. Despite her disappointment, Ashford continued to race. But things would get worse before they got better. Not long after the boycott, she tore her hamstring muscle at a meet in Los Angeles. She took 1980 off to recuperate and reevaluate her career. What she wanted, she decided, was Olympic gold.

Ashford returned to competition in 1981 with a new commitment to track and a new quest for gold in 1984. She repeated her World Cup double in 1981, and in 1983, she recorded 20 of the 23 fastest times for the 100 meters in U.S. track and field history. In June 1983, Marlies Göhr of East Germany, who would become Ashford's greatest rival, defeated her in a Los Angeles meet; but one week later, Ashford set a new world record of 10.79 seconds at the National Sports Festival in Colorado, beating Göhr's previous record of 10.81. Following her record-setting performance, Ashford traveled to Helsinki for the 1983 World Track and Field Championships, ready to face Göhr to see who would claim the title of the fastest woman in the world. Ashford streaked through the quarterfinals and semifinals with overwhelming victories, but in

Although Ashford had focused her eight-year sprinting career on Olympic gold, she was not finished after Los Angeles. She still had not beaten Göhr in the 100 meters. Throughout the summer of 1984, the two traded 100-meter victories in separate meets, with Göhr clocking 10.95, and Ashford following with times of 10.94 and 10.92. Finally, on August 22, the two met head-to-head in Zurich. Göhr jumped out of the blocks quickly, but Ashford surged past her in the final 40 meters of the race, winning with a new world record of 10.76 seconds.

For her record-setting Olympic and world championship performances, Ashford was named Track and Field Athlete of the Year in 1984. She sat out the 1985 season to have her daughter Raina (she was pregnant when she set the world record in Zurich), and after a 17-month layoff, she returned to competition with a third-place finish in the 100 meters at the 1986 U.S. championships. She continued her winning ways with a victory in the 100-meter dash at the Goodwill Games in Moscow, USSR, and participated on the winning 4x100-meter relay team. Following her outstanding return to competition, she was honored with the Vitalis Award for excellence in track and field in January 1987.

In 1987, Ashford suffered recurring problems with her right hamstring and was forced to withdraw from the U.S. Olympic Sports Festival and the World Track and Field Championships in Rome, Italy. But she came back strong in 1988, qualifying for her fourth U.S. Olympic team and was chosen to carry the U.S. flag at the opening ceremonies of the 1988 Seoul Olympics. In Seoul, at age 31, she captured the silver medal in the 100 meters, finishing .29 of a second behind teammate Florence Griffith Joyner. In one of the highlights of the 1988 Summer Games, Ashford overcame a sizable lead by the East German team in the anchor leg of the 4x100-meter relay to win the gold for the United States. In 1991, she finished third in the 100 meters at the U.S. nationals and qualified for participation at the 1991 World Track and Field Championships in Tokyo, Japan.

Ashford made her fifth Olympic track and field team in 1992. Although she failed to qualify for the finals in the 100 meters at the Barcelona Games, she led the U.S. team to a first-place finish and the gold medal in the 4x100-meter relay. This victory brought her career medal total to four golds and one silver.

Evelyn Ashford defined women's sprinting in the 1980s. For more than 10 years, she battled Marlies Göhr to claim the title of fastest woman in the world. Despite the disappointment of the 1980 boycott and a delicate right hamstring muscle, Ashford committed herself to excellence. She won four golds and one silver medal in a career that spanned four Olympic Games. In 1989, the Women's Sports Foundation awarded Ashford the Flo Hyman Trophy for commitment to excellence in supporting women's advancements in sports.

Tracy Austin (tennis player)

Born December 12, 1962, Palos Verdes Peninsula, California

In 1992, Tracy Austin became the youngest member ever elected to the International Tennis Hall of Fame, just one of a number of "youngest" records that she established in her career as one of tennis's all-time great players. She won her first professional title at age 14 and was ranked number one in the world at 17. When she retired in July 1994, she had an overall record of 348-87, with 29 professional titles, including two U.S. Open titles. Austin was the first of the tennis prodigies and ushered in an era of young superstars in women's tennis.

The daughter of George and Jeannie Austin, Tracy was born on December 12, 1962, in Palos Verdes Peninsula, California. The entire family—her parents, three brothers, and a sister—all played tennis, and so Tracy had an early introduction to the sport. "I was born to play tennis," she wrote in her autobiography *Beyond Center Court*. "I was the last of five children in a family totally devoted to the game."[6] When she was two years old, she enrolled in a program for kids ages three to eight at the Jack Kramer Club in Rolling Hills, California. At age seven, she played in the 12-and-under age group in her first tournament, in Long Beach, California, where she soundly lost her first match. At age nine, she played in Long Beach's age-group championships and won the 10-and-under and the 12-and-under titles in the same day. Beginning with these first city titles, Austin experienced a meteoric rise to tennis stardom. She captured a total of 25 junior national titles from the 12-and-under singles title in 1972 to the girls' 18-and-under singles title in 1978. The tennis prodigy won more than 150 tournaments as an amateur player.

On January 10, 1977, the 14-year-old phenom won her first professional tourna-ment at the Avon Futures, a satellite tour-nament of the main women's professional tour, in Portland, Oregon, when she defeated Stacy Margolin in three sets. She retained her amateur status by refusing the prize money. Continuing to play as an amateur, Austin became the youngest player to compete at the All-England Championships at Wimbledon the following July. She won her first- and second-round matches but lost to Chris Evert, 6-1, 6-1, in the third round. Austin also played in the U.S. Open that year, reaching the quarterfinals before losing, 6-2, 6-2, to Betty Stove of the Netherlands.

Austin turned professional on October 23, 1978, less than two months before her 16th birthday. She won her first major

Tracy Austin
Courtesy of the International Tennis Hall of Fame

international title, the Italian Open, in May 1979. The following July, at age 16 years, 9 months, she defeated Chris Evert 6-4, 6-3, to become the youngest player to win the U.S. Open. Using strong baseline strokes, steely determination, and unwavering concentration, she defeated Martina Navratilova to regain the title in 1981. In 1980, she and brother John captured the mixed doubles championships at Wimbledon, the first sister-brother team to do so. Austin also represented the United States in the Wightman Cup, competition between Great Britain and the United States (1978-1979, 1981), and the Federation Cup, the international team championship for women (1978-1980).

By the time she was 17 years old, Austin had earned more than $1 million in prize money and was ranked number one in the world. She was named Women's Tennis Association (WTA) Player of the Year in 1980, Women's Sports Foundation Sportswoman of the Year in 1980, and Associated Press Female Athlete of the Year in 1979 and 1981.

Beginning in 1981, Austin suffered a series of injuries—including a stress fracture in her back, sciatic nerve damage, and a shoulder injury—that halted her remarkable career. In August 1989, as she was preparing for a comeback appearance at the U.S. Open, she was involved in a serious car accident, which resulted in a broken leg and a shattered knee that required surgery and months of physical therapy. The injuries forced her off the professional tour until her return in February 1993, when she played in the Matrix Essentials/Evert Cup in Indian Wells, California. She reappeared in the WTA rankings August 16, 1993, at No. 159; by the time she retired from the professional tour in July 1994, she had moved up to No. 81 in the world. On July 11, 1992, at 29 years, 7 months, Tracy Austin became the youngest member ever elected to the International Tennis Hall of Fame.

"At eight I decided that I wanted to be the best tennis player in the world. From then on, it was always in the back of my mind," wrote Austin in her autobiography.[7] She reached her goal—the number one ranking—while still a teenager. She stormed on to the tennis scene in the late 1970s, and ushered in the era of teenage champions from which many of the legends of women's tennis, including Steffi Graf, Monica Seles, and Martina Hingis, followed. Her talent and perseverance make her one of the most enduring role models in women's tennis.

Further Reading

Austin, Tracy, with Christine Brennan. *Beyond Center Court: My Story*. New York: William Morrow & Company, 1992. 224 pp.

Senda Berenson (basketball innovator)

Born March 19, 1868, Biturmansk, Lithuania; died February 16, 1954

After reading about James Naismith's newly invented game of basketball in the YMCA publication *The Triangle*, physical education instructor Senda Berenson introduced the game to her students at Smith College in 1892. Berenson and her enthusiastic students quickly adopted the game and modified its rules for women's play. The game quickly spread to other physical education classes at normal schools and colleges throughout the country. Berenson's rules remained in use with only slight modifications until the 1960s as women's basketball became one of the most popular team sports for women in the United States.

Born in Lithuania to future Jewish immigrants to the United States, Albert and Julie Valvrojenski, Senda Berenson (the

Senda Berenson
Courtesy of Smith College Archives

family name was changed when her father arrived in the United States in 1875) enrolled in the Boston Normal School of Gymnastics, a female teachers' college, where in 1890 she began studying physical education under Amy Morris Homans and Mary Hemenway. Berenson left the Boston Normal School in 1892 to teach physical training at Smith College. When Berenson arrived at Smith College in 1892, the college had just opened Alumnae Gymnasium, housing administrative offices, dressing rooms, the latest Swedish gymnastic equipment, and a swimming pool.

A year earlier, James Naismith, an instructor at the YMCA Training School at Springfield, Massachusetts, developed basket ball (the original name was two words), a new game played by two teams of men in a gymnasium. In the January 1892 issue of *The Triangle,* Naismith described the game and listed the rules. Berenson read Naismith's article and thought his game might be a good activity for women.

Berenson organized the first basketball match between her freshman and sophomore classes on March 23, 1893. She wrote, "I read in a small magazine that an indoor game was invented called Basket Ball. We no sooner tried it than we liked it."[8]

After the game, with help from her students, she modified Naismith's original 13 rules for her female students. These modifications included a court divided into three sections that kept players from crossing the dividing lines, and rules forbidding stealing the ball from other players, holding the ball for more than three seconds, and dribbling more than three times. In 1899, she established the first official rules for girls, and chaired the American Association for the Advancement of Physical Education (AAAPE) Committee on Basketball for Girls, a position she held for 12 years. In 1901, she wrote *Line Basket Ball for Women,* the first published rules for women's basketball, which included Berenson's prevailing philosophy about the sport and articles on the psychological and physiological effects of basketball on women.

She led the women's physical education department at Smith College for 19 years and was the director of Physical Education at the Mary A. Burnham School in Northampton, Massachusetts, for 10 years after that. As a physical educator, she introduced fencing and folk dancing as part of her physical education program and brought remedial gymnastics to students with special physical needs.

On January 15, 1911, Berenson married Smith College English professor Herbert Vaughn Abbott. After retiring from teaching in 1921, she traveled to Europe to study art and music, then moved to California in 1934, where she lived until her death. In 1984, Senda Berenson was inducted into the Naismith Memorial Basketball Hall of Fame and the International Women's Sports Hall of Fame for her contributions to the game of women's basketball.

Patty Berg (golfer)

Born February 13, 1918, Minneapolis, Minnesota

When Patty Berg was 12, her father gave her younger brother a golf club membership. "Where's mine?" she said. "Just because I'm a girl is no reason not to give me one."[9] Herman Berg gave his daughter a set of golf clubs and a golf membership, and with them sent her on her way to golf history. In a career that spanned nearly four decades, Berg won 29 amateur titles before turning pro in 1940. Her professional career was even more impressive. She earned more than 57 professional titles, including 44 Ladies Professional Golf Association (LPGA) titles in a 14-year period (1948–62). Along with Babe Didrikson Zaharias, Berg helped organize the LPGA and served as the group's first president. Berg's leadership in the early years of the LPGA were crucial to its success; her pioneering efforts gave women's golf a firm place in the world of professional sports. Her contributions to advancing the game for women at the nonprofessional level were equally impressive and led to thousands of women learning and enjoying the game; she introduced and taught golf to more women than any other player.

Growing up in Minneapolis, Minnesota, Berg had always been active in sports. The daughter of Herman and Therese Berg, Patty played numerous sports as a youngster. She quarterbacked the 50th Street Tigers football team to an undefeated season and played sandlot baseball. She participated in the National Junior Speed Skating Championships and ran the 30-yard dash for the track team at the John Burroughs elementary school. In 1930, she read about Bobby Jones winning the U.S. Open at the Interlachen course near her home. The story of the great golf champion winning so close to home inspired Berg to learn more about the game.

In 1932, Berg got her first set of golf clubs, and her family joined the Interlachen Country Club so she could practice. She began taking lessons from Willie Kidd, Sr., and Jim Pringle, who helped her become a strong, all-around golfer. She attributes her early success to playing at Interlachen: "I think that did more for my golf game than anything because it was so great a test of golf. The course required every conceivable kind of golf shot."[10]

Berg qualified for the Minneapolis City Championship in 1933 with a round of 122. Disappointed in her score, she said, "After that, all I could think about was next year's championship. I decided right then and there I was going to dedicate the next 365 days of the year to improving my golf game."[11] Improve she did. In 1935, the 17-

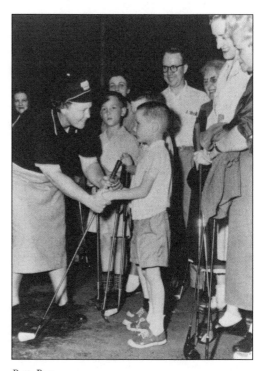

Patty Berg
Courtesy of the Ladies Professional Golf Association

year-old won the Minnesota State Championships, a title she won again in 1936 and 1938. Also in 1935, the women's national tournament was held on her home course. She played brilliantly in the early rounds, amazing the crowds with her 200-yard drives. She fought her way to the finals, where she met legend Glenna Collett Vare. Although she lost to Vare that day, Berg attracted media attention for her exploits. They predicted greatness for the 17-year-old; she did not let them down.

By the time Berg was 20, she was considered the foremost woman golfer in the United States. In 1938, she won the U.S. Amateur title and 10 of the 13 tournaments she entered, including the Women's Western, Trans-Mississippi, and Women's Western Derby events. For her achievements, the Associated Press named her the Outstanding Female Athlete of 1938.

Berg won more than 40 tournaments as an amateur and represented the United States on two Curtis Cup teams before deciding to give up her amateur status at age 22. Although the women had no professional tour in 1940, Berg signed with the Wilson Sporting Goods Company at a salary of approximately $7,500 a year. Berg made appearances at summer camps for girls and offered golf clinics and schools. As she recalled: "When I turned professional, there were three tournaments—the Women's Western Open, the Women's Titleholders (Master's), and the Asheville Invitational—prize money of $500 and about five women professionals."[12] At the 1941 Women's Western Open, Berg won a $100 savings bond. She went on to capture that title in 1943 and 1948. Adding to her early professional titles, she claimed the first U.S. Women's National Open in 1946.

By 1949, Berg and others decided it was time to expand the women's professional tour. Along with "Babe" Didrikson and George Zaharias and their manager Fred Corcoran, Berg met with the president of Wilson Sporting Goods who agreed to sponsor the women golfers. The Ladies Professional Golf Association (LPGA), officially chartered in 1950, quickly increased the number of professional tournaments from three to nine, with a total purse of about $45,000. The women gave golf clinics to bring out the crowds and to attract much-needed publicity. Berg served as the LPGA's president from 1949 to 1952. She won 39 tournaments in the group's first decade, including seven Women's Titleholders.

Despite the LPGA's relatively low amount of prize money in the early lean years, Berg managed to make money on the tour. She was the tour's leading money winner three times—in 1954, 1956, and 1957—and was the first woman golfer to reach $100,000 in career earnings. She also won the Vare Trophy, presented to the player with the lowest annual scoring average, in 1953, 1955, and 1956. In 1952, Berg shot a 64 in the Richmond Open at Richmond, California, to set an LPGA scoring record that stood for 12 years. She averaged 75.5 strokes per round during her peak years.

The honors and awards bestowed upon Berg are numerous. In addition to her induction into the LPGA Hall of Fame (1951), she was voted into the World Golf Hall of Fame (1974) and the International Women's Sports Hall of Fame (1980). She is one of only two women in the Professional Golf Association (PGA) Hall of Fame (inducted in 1978). She won the Associated Press Female Athlete of the Year Award three times (1938, 1943, 1955) and was named "Golfer of the Decade" for the period 1938–47 by GOLF Magazine.

Her contributions to the game garnered her countless accolades. Berg received the 1963 Bob Jones Award "honoring the person whose contribution to the game is most completely described by the term distinguished sportsmanship." She was awarded the Ben Hogan Award in 1975, for overcoming cancer surgery to play again.

The awards Berg has won represent the contributions she made to advance the game of golf for women. Along these lines, she has written three instructional books for women and continues to tour the country for Wilson Sporting Goods, giving golf clinics. She travels approximately 60,000 miles per year to conduct classes and playing exhibitions. In 1978, the LPGA established the Patty Berg Award in her honor, given to a person making outstanding contributions to women's golf.

Early in her amateur career Berg played exhibitions for charity every Saturday and Sunday. Her father told her, "If you're going to play the game, you're going to do some charity work for the people. So get started."[13] Berg's charitable work left its mark on the LPGA. Each tournament sponsors a charity organization, and the LPGA annually raises nearly $4 million for local and national charities.

Patty Berg's sense of fair play was evident at an early age. A natural athlete, Berg loved many sports, but golf became her passion. She picked up the game quickly, and dominated women's amateur golf in the 1930s and then the ladies' professional tour in the 1940s and 1950s. Always a favorite of the crowds, Berg proved to be as great an attraction for golf as her friend and chief rival, Babe Didrikson Zaharias. Together these two defined women's professional golf, and their efforts to legitimize golf as an acceptable professional sport for women laid the foundation for the multi-million-dollar prizes being earned by today's LPGA members.

Further Reading

Berg, Patty, with Marsh Schiewe. *Inside Golf for Women*. Chicago: Contemporary Books, 1977. 104 pp.

Hahn, James, and Lynn Hahn. *Patty! The Sports Career of Patty Berg*. Mankato, MN: Crestwood House, 1981. 47 pp.

Bonnie Blair (speed skater)

Born March 18, 1964, Cornwall, New York

With victories in both the 500- and 1,000-meter races at the 1994 Winter Olympic Games in Lillehammer, Norway, Bonnie Blair became the United States' most decorated female Winter Olympian ever with a total of five gold medals and one bronze in her career. She is also the only U.S. woman to win gold medals in the same event at three consecutive Olympic Winter Games. Considered by many to be the greatest U.S. woman speed skater ever, Blair is the standard-bearer for future female speed skaters and women who strive to win Olympic gold.

The youngest of Charlie and Eleanor Blair's six children, Bonnie was born on March 18, 1964, in Cornwall, New York. She joined a close-knit family of competitive speed skaters and took up the sport when she was just two years old. Blair entered her first competition at the age of four and won her first race at age seven.

As a teenager, Blair began to take the sport more seriously. She started working with coach Cathy Priestner Faminow to develop stronger technique and a regular training schedule. At just 15 years old, Blair qualified for the U.S. Olympic trials, but narrowly missed making the 1980 U.S. Olympic Speed Skating Team. In 1980 and 1981, Blair trained while attending Champaign's (Illinois) Centennial High School and, in 1982, went to Europe to train on the Olympic-sized rinks and to compete on the European winter speed skating circuit.

Blair made the 1984 U.S. Olympic Speed Skating Team and competed in the 500 meters at the Sarajevo Winter Games, finishing eighth in the event. She returned from Sarajevo with a renewed dedication to her training. Blair's training regimen included skating sessions along with weight training, running, biking, and roller skating.

All the hard work paid off. At the 1986 World Sprint Championships, she tied for second place in the 500-meter competition. In the 1986-87 season, Blair lost only one other 500-meter race. She went on a whirlwind travel schedule in Europe, taking on the world's best. On her second trip to the Netherlands, Blair skated the 500 meters in 39.43 seconds, breaking the world record held by Karen Kania of East Germany.

Blair was the favorite to win the 500-meter event at the 1988 Olympic Winter Games in Calgary. When the gun sounded to start the race, she burst away from the starting line in her best start ever and zipped through the course in 39.10 seconds, setting a new world record and winning the gold medal. She also captured a bronze medal in the 1,000 meters, becoming the only athlete from the United States to win more than one medal at the Calgary Games.

In August 1988, Blair moved to Butte, Montana, where she enrolled at Montana College of Mineral Science and Technology. She cut back on her training and took up competitive bicycle racing for a brief period. Despite her scaled-down training, Blair finished second in the 1990 World Sprint Championships and third in the 1991 World Sprints.

Bonnie Blair
©Allsport USA/Jonathan Daniel

In the summer of 1991, Blair returned to full-time speed skating training and began working with U.S. Speed Skating Coach Peter Mueller. In the first two World Cup events of the 1991-92 season, Blair won two 500-meter races and two 1,000-meter races. She entered the 1992 Winter Olympics in Albertville, France, as the favorite in both races. Despite unfavorable weather conditions at the outdoor Albertville rink, Blair won the 500 meters with a time of 40.33 seconds, and four days later, she won the 1,000 meters in a time of 1:21.90 seconds, just two-hundredths of a second ahead of the second-place finisher. In winning the 500 meters, Blair became the first skater ever to win two consecutive gold medals in the 500-meter sprint. She received the 1992 Sullivan Award as the nation's outstanding amateur athlete, and the 1992 United States Olympic Committee (USOC) Sportswoman of the Year Award.

In 1992, the International Olympic Committee stopped staging both Winter and Summer Games in the same year and began a new schedule that called for the Games to alternate every two years. With the next Olympic Winter Games scheduled for 1994, Blair continued training after Albertville with her eyes on another chance to compete in the Olympics. When asked what motivated her to stay at the top after already proving she was the best, Blair replied, "I love the sport. When you're in a sport like speed skating where the clock gives you the results, there is always a faster goal or a personal best to beat."[14]

At the 1994 Lillehammer Olympics, Blair equaled her gold-medal-winning performances in both the 500- and 1,000-meter events. With five gold medals and one bronze medal, Blair became the most decorated female Winter Olympian in U.S. history. In 1994, she was named Associated Press Female Athlete of the Year, USOC Sportswoman of the Year, Women's Sports Foundation Individual Sportswoman of the Year, and the Babe Zaharias Female Amateur Athlete of the Year.

At the World Sprint Championships in February 1995, she skated to first-place finishes in both the 500- and the 1,000-meter events, enabling her to capture the gold medal for the overall world title. Leading up to the World Sprints, Blair placed first in both the 500- and the 1,000-meter events at the Calgary World Cup, the Hamar World Cup, and the Inzell World Cup. While in Calgary, Blair broke her own world record in the 500 meters with a time of 38.69 seconds. As a result of this fantastic year, she was named repeat winner of the Women's Sports Foundation Individual Sportswoman of the Year Award. She retired from competitive speed skating in March 1995 as the reigning World Sprint Champion.

Bonnie Blair was the heart of the U.S. Women's Speed Skating Team for more than a decade. Her incredible achievements at the Olympic Winter Games and World Sprint Championships set the standard for future female speed skaters around the world.

Further Reading

Breitenbucher, Cathy. *Bonnie Blair: Golden Streak.* New York: Lerner, 1994. 64 pp.

Daly, Wendy. *Bonnie Blair: Power on Ice.* New York: Bullseye Books, 1996. 64 pp.

Fanny Blankers-Koen (track and field star)

Born April 26, 1918, Amsterdam, Netherlands

Many people told Fanny Blankers-Koen that she was too old to be competing in the Olympics at the age of 30, and that she should be home caring for her two young children. But Blankers-Koen had been waiting 12 years to sprint for the gold, so she wasn't going to let a little thing like age get in her way. At the 1948 London Games, Blankers-Koen became the first and only woman to win four gold medals in track and field at a single Olympics. In London, she won the 100 meters, the 200 meters, and the 80-meter hurdles, and anchored Holland's 4x100-meter relay team to victory. She could have won six gold medals, but in 1948 athletes could only compete in four events so Blankers-Koen chose not to enter two events in which she held world records—the high jump and the long jump.

Blankers-Koen stands out as one of the most impressive Olympic athletes of her era. After her great success, the media played up her role as wife and mother, sometimes overshadowing her athletic achievements. However, the image they created of her as housewife/mother/athlete helped to dispel the myth that women would lose their femininity while competing in world-class track and field events.

Born Francina Elsje Koen, in Amsterdam, Netherlands, Fanny came from an athletic family who swam, skated, and played tennis. At age six, she joined the local sports club where she became an excellent swimmer and runner. In 1935, Blankers-Koen announced that "I've made up my mind to go in for sport."[15] She joined the Amsterdam Dames' Athletic Club and traveled to the city twice a week to train with Holland's best tracksters.

She ran in her first competition in 1935—a 200-meter race in Groningen—but did not do well in the meet. However, within one month she had defeated the Dutch national champion in the 800 meters. At that track meet, Blankers-Koen met track coach Jan Blankers who saw her potential as a jumper and a sprinter. Blankers was the coach of the Dutch team for the Berlin Olympics, and at his insistence Blankers-Koen was invited to join the Dutch Olympic team. At the 1936 Berlin Games, at age 18, Blankers-Koen finished in a tie for sixth in the high jump and fifth as a member of the Dutch 4x100-meter relay team.

Soon after the 1936 Olympics, Blankers-Koen began working with Coach Blankers to perfect her sprinting technique. Within a year, she had won every sprinting event in Holland as well as two competitions in Germany. In 1938, she finished third in the 100 meters at the European women's championships in Vienna. While working on the sprints, Blankers-Koen also became proficient at the long jump and hurdles.

In August 1940, Fanny married Jan Blankers. She continued to train through the Nazi occupation of Holland, only taking time out from training for the birth of her two children. During the war, she missed out on important international competi-

Fanny Blankers-Koen (far right)
© Allsport/Hulton Deutsch

tion, but managed to set two world records—in the high jump and the long jump—at national meets. With the Olympics cancelled in 1940 and 1944, Blankers-Koen did not get a chance to compete against an elite field for nearly a decade.

In 1946, the European championships resumed at Oslo. Blankers-Koen had quit training to give birth to her daughter Fanneke just seven months earlier so was not in perfect shape when she entered the events. Nonetheless, she won the 80-meter hurdles, anchored the Dutch women's team to a victory in the 4x100-meter relay, and placed fourth in the high jump.

Just before the start of the 1948 London Olympics, Blankers-Koen set a world record in the 100 meters at 11.5 seconds. Despite her record-setting performances, many believed that at 30 years old, Blankers-Koen was too old to win at the Olympics. But Blankers-Koen had waited 12 years to vie for the gold. At the 14th Olympiad, she won the 100 meters in 11.9 seconds, setting a new Olympic record. She followed with a victory in the 80-meter hurdles, just edging out British favorite Maureen Gardner and establishing another Olympic record. Two days later, Blankers-Koen ran the 200 meters, finishing nearly five meters ahead of the field. She ran her final event the next day as the anchor of Holland's gold-medal-winning 4x100-meter relay team. Of the nine women's track and field events contested in the 1948 London Olympics, Blankers-Koen won four of them. With her four gold medals, she became the only woman to win four golds in track and field in the same Olympics.

Nicknamed the "Flying Dutch Housewife," Blankers-Koen continued to compete after the Olympics. At the 1950 European championships, she duplicated her Olympic victories in the 100- and 200-meter dashes, and in the 80-meter hurdles, and ran with the Dutch relay team to second place. Blankers-Koen retired from competitive athletics in 1955 at the age of 37. She served as the manager of Holland's national team at the 1968 Mexico City Olympics.

During her illustrious career, Blankers-Koen set 13 world records, won four Olympic gold and five European gold medals, and between 1936 and 1955, won 58 Dutch national track and field titles in events ranging from the sprints, hurdles, high jump, and long jump to the shot put and the pentathlon. No woman in track history has won as many national titles.

Fanny Blankers-Koen was the most impressive Olympic athlete of her era. She played an important role in popularizing women's athletics after World War II. In 1948, the Associated Press selected her as their Female Athlete of the Year, and in 1980, she was inducted into the International Women's Sports Hall of Fame.

Susan Butcher (sled-dog racer)

Born December 26, 1954, Cambridge, Massachusetts

In the frozen tundra of Alaska, Susan Butcher has found peace, tranquility, and success as the world's foremost long-distance sled-dog racer and one of the greatest mushers (sled-dog driver) of all time. A four-time winner of the sport's most grueling event, the 1,157-mile Iditarod Trail Sled Dog Race from Anchorage to Nome, Alaska, she became a symbol of women's stamina and endurance in the toughest of sports—a sport that demands tactical race planning, the ability to train a sled-dog pack to achieve optimal performance, and the physical and mental strength to endure the isolation of the treacherous Alaskan terrain.

Susan Butcher
Courtesy of Jim Brown Photography

Raised in Cambridge, Massachusetts, Susan is the daughter of Charlie and Agnes Butcher. A very independent and determined child, Butcher was drawn to the wilderness at an early age. She wrote an essay when she was eight titled "I Hate the City" and preferred to spend time at her family's isolated home in Brooklin, Maine. As a teenager, Butcher learned to sail and later became a skilled carpenter. To combine the two skills, she applied to a boat-building school in Maine at age 16, but was rejected because she was a woman.

After graduating from Warehouse Cooperative School near Cambridge, Butcher moved to Boulder, Colorado, looking for the isolation of the Rocky Mountains. There she met a woman who bred and raced sled dogs. Butcher raced on the weekends and worked as a veterinarian's assistant during the week. In 1973, while browsing a mushing magazine, she read about the inaugural running of the Iditarod. She decided that was what she wanted to do.

Two years later, Butcher moved to Fairbanks, and within four months had settled in the southern Alaskan bush to train her first sled-dog team. She lived in virtual isolation in a small log cabin where she chopped firewood, hauled water, hunted for food, and mushed her dogs. In the summers, she traveled to Fairbanks to work as a midwife on a musk-ox farm.

In 1977, Butcher met Joe Redington, the founder and organizer of the Iditarod. She worked for Redington for two years, training and breeding champion sled dogs in return for dogs to complete her team for her first try at the Iditarod.

The Last Great Race on Earth, the Iditarod Trail Sled Dog Race begins in Anchorage, Alaska, and crosses the Alaska Range, veers west along the long and winding Yukon River, and dashes north up the Bering Sea coast to Nome. The race takes approximately 11 days to complete. Along the way, mushers must contend with sub-zero temperatures as they drive their dogs over icy tundra, across frozen rivers, and through dense forests and rugged mountain terrain. Mushers send dog food and supplies to checkpoints set up in small Eskimo villages along the way.

Butcher entered her first Iditarod race in 1978 and finished 19th. She placed ninth in 1979, and after the 1979 race, Butcher and Redington assembled a team of dogs and spent 44 days climbing to the top of Denali (Mt. McKinley), becoming the first people to mush to the summit of the highest peak in North America.

For the next six years, Butcher trained 6,000 to 7,000 miles every year in her attempt to win the Iditarod. She finished fifth in 1980 and 1981; second in 1982; and in 1983 and 1984, she finished ninth and second, respectively. In 1985, she was leading the race when a moose killed two of her dogs and injured 13 others. She dropped out of the race, only to watch Libby Riddles mush her way to the Iditarod title. In a 1987 interview in *Women's Sports and Fitness*, Butcher expressed her disappointment about losing her best team and the opportunity to be the first female winner of the grueling race, but she vowed to be the first woman who wins it more than once.

In 1986, Butcher won her first Iditarod, and she repeated the victory in 1987, 1988, and 1990. She has finished in the top 10 in 12 out of the 14 races she entered. In 1990, Butcher set the Iditarod speed record of 11 days, 1 hour, 53 minutes, and 23 seconds, which stood until 1994. She has held the records in four other races: the Norton Sound 250, the Kobuk 220, the Kusko 300, and the Beargrease. In 1995, Butcher retired her dogs after 16 years of mushing.

Many attribute her success to superior dog training and trail experience. "When I'm mushing, or caring for the dogs or picking up after them, I am in total contentment," she says. "I have found something that was made for me."[16] Living just 100 miles south of the Arctic Circle in Eureka, Alaska, Butcher operates Trail Breaker Kennels with her husband David Monson.

"My goal was never to be the first woman or the best woman," she said in an 1987 *Women's Sports and Fitness* interview. "It was to be the best sled dog racer."[17] She has twice been named the Women's Sports Foundation's Professional Sportswoman of the Year (1987, 1988); the *Anchorage Times* named her Sled Dog Racer of the Decade in 1989, and she was selected the Outstanding Female Athlete of the World by the International Academy of Sports in 1989. In 1990, the Amateur Athletic Foundation (AAF) honored her with one of the six regional World Trophy awards.

Susan Butcher's success in the Iditarod elevated the sport to a new level. Her total dedication to her dogs and her expertise in training and preparing for races propelled her to the top of her sport. A woman of remarkable courage and stamina, and with a tough, competitive spirit, Butcher helped to explode the lingering myth of women as the weaker sex. Her success attracted corporate sponsors that now underwrite many of the races, making sled-dog racing a viable and popular sport for men and women of the frozen North.

Further Reading

Dolan, Ellen M. *Susan Butcher and the Iditarod Trail*. New York: Walker and Co., 1993. 112 pp.

Connie Carpenter-Phinney (cyclist)

Born February 26, 1957, Madison, Wisconsin

At age 14, speed skater Connie Carpenter-Phinney placed seventh in the 1,500-meter event in the 1972 Olympic Winter Games in Sapporo, Japan. Four years later, in 1976, Carpenter-Phinney switched to cycling when an ankle injury forced her to retire from competitive speed skating. Eight years later, Carpenter-Phinney nipped teammate Rebecca Twigg at the finish line to win the inaugural Olympic women's cycling event at the 1984 Los Angeles Summer Olympics. One of America's best all-around cyclists, Carpenter-Phinney's success at the Olympics pushed women's cycling into the forefront and ushered in a new era of women's competitive cycling.

Born in Madison, Wisconsin, on February 26, 1957, Connie began speed skating on the frozen lakes and ponds of Wisconsin. When she was 14, she made the U.S. Olympic Speed Skating Team along with skaters Anne Henning, Dianne Holum, and Sheila Young. She finished seventh in the 1,500 meters at the 1972 Games, .88 seconds out of medal contention.

In 1976, she switched to cycling after her ankle injury, and although she had ridden a bike for summer training, she did not take up competitive racing until she was introduced to the sport by her older brother Chuck and by world champion speed skater and cyclist Sheila Young.

"In my first competitive season, I exceeded even my wildest expectations," she said.[18] In that first year, Carpenter-Phinney won the national championship in road race and pursuit, and won both titles again in 1977 and 1978. In 1977, she won a silver

Connie Carpenter-Phinney
© Allsport USA/P. Brouilet

medal at the world championship road race, her first international race, as well as winning the Coors International Classic, a premier cycling event.

Incredibly, Carpenter-Phinney took time off from cycling to compete in another sport at the elite level. While a student at the University of California, Berkeley, Carpenter-Phinney rowed on the 1979 and 1980 crew team helping them to a national title in 1980. After two years of rowing, she returned to cycling in 1981.

Carpenter-Phinney won the Coors International Classic in 1981 and again in 1982. She also won three national titles in 1981 and the bronze in the world championship road race. She continued to ride circles around her competitors in 1982. She won a silver medal at the world championships in the pursuit event, in which two cyclists start on opposite sides of the oval

track. If one cyclist catches the other, the race is over; otherwise, the winner is the first one to cross the finish line. Pursuit racing requires both tactical planning and sprinting strength.

A wrist injury forced her to bypass the 1983 Coors Classic, but she went on to successfully defend her national pursuit title that same year and followed it with the world championship in the sprint cycling event.

At the 1984 Los Angeles Olympics, Carpenter-Phinney faced stiff competition from teammate Rebecca Twigg in the first women's Olympic cycling event, the 79.2-kilometer road race. With 800 meters to go, five women remained in contention, but with 200 meters left, Twigg and Carpenter-Phinney broke away from the pack. Just three meters from the finish line, Carpenter-Phinney threw her bike forward to win the race by less than half a wheel length. She won the gold medal in 2:11:14, the first Olympic cycling medal for the United States since 1912.

Carpenter-Phinney retired from competitive cycling after her victory in the Olympic road race. She continued her education and earned a master of science degree from the University of Colorado in 1990. Each summer she and her husband, professional cyclist Davis Phinney, conduct cycling training camps at Copper Mountain, Colorado. She also works as a cycling consultant, television commentator, coach, and journalist, and is dedicated to advancing women's opportunities in amateur and professional cycling. She was named Colorado Sportswoman of the Year in 1983 and was inducted into the International Women's Sports Hall of Fame in 1990, and the U.S. Olympic Hall of Fame in 1992.

Her determined push at the finish line of the 1984 Olympic road race was one of the most dramatic events of the Los Angeles Games. Connie Carpenter-Phinney's world-class success moved women's cycling in the United States to a new, exciting level.

Florence Chadwick (long-distance swimmer)

Born November 9, 1918, San Diego, California; died March 15, 1995

Over her 40-year swimming career, Florence Chadwick became known for her long-distance swimming exploits, including numerous English Channel crossings. She loved to swim, especially long distances in rough waters. She began swimming as a youngster in San Diego and was inspired by Gertrude Ederle's record-breaking 20-mile swim across the English Channel in 1926. For the next 25 years, Chadwick trained and competed in numerous swimming events, with her sights always set on Ederle's record.

The daughter of Richard and Mary Chadwick, Florence learned to swim as a youngster near her home in San Diego Bay. She began swimming competitively when her uncle entered her in a race at age six. At 10, she won the six-mile San Diego Bay Channel race, the first child to do so. She continued to race, winning a number of regional contests. Despite her local success, she had trouble breaking into the national ranks. At age 13, she finished second to Eleanor Holm in the U.S. Nationals and failed to make the 1936 Olympic team.

Chadwick swam competitively for her school teams in San Diego. After graduating from high school in 1936, she attended San Diego State College, Southwestern University of Law in Los Angeles, and Balboa Law School before entering the workforce. During World War II, she directed and produced aquatic shows for the military and went to Hollywood to appear in a film with Esther Williams. After finishing the movie, she taught swimming at La Jolla Beach and Tennis Club and worked as a comptometer operator for the Arabian-American Oil Company.

During her early swimming career, Chadwick never lost sight of her main goal, to swim the English Channel. She took the job with the Arabian-American Oil Company in Saudi Arabia so she could train in the rough waters of the Persian Gulf. She swam before and after work, and as much as 10 hours a day on the weekends. In June 1950, Chadwick quit her job and headed for France for her first English Channel swim. She entered a London *Daily Mail* contest to swim across the Channel, but the newspaper rejected her application because she was an unknown. Undaunted, Chadwick

Florence Chadwick
Courtesy of the International Swimming Hall of Fame

took a practice swim in the Channel in July, and a month later, on August 8, 1950, she left Cape Gris-Nez on the French coast and reached Dover, England, 13 hours and 20 minutes later. She had broken Ederle's 24-year-old record by more than one hour.

Coming on shore on that cold August morning, she said: "I feel fine, I am quite prepared to swim back."[19] And she meant that literally. The following year, on September 11, 1951, she swam the Channel from England to France, a much more difficult task against the tide, in the record time of 16 hours, 22 minutes, becoming the only woman to swim the English Channel in both directions.

The English Channel had an unyielding grasp on Chadwick. She swam the 20-mile course four more times, breaking her own England-to-France record in September 1953 (in 14:42) and again in October 1955 (in 13:55).

After her 1950 swim, Chadwick returned to the United States to a hero's welcome. In New York, she made numerous radio and TV appearances, and San Diego welcomed her with a ticker-tape parade. She toured the country promoting sports and fitness and teaching children to swim. The lure of the sea continued to call her; in 1952, she swam the treacherous 21-mile Catalina Channel off the California coast in 13 hours, 47 minutes, the first woman to complete the swim. In a five-week period in the fall of 1953, at the age of 34, Chadwick swam the English Channel, the Straits of Gibraltar, a round-trip across the Bosporus between Europe and Asia, and the Turkish Dardanelles, all in world-record times.

After more than 30 years living the solitary life of a long-distance swimmer, Florence Chadwick retired from swimming in 1969. She became a stockbroker, but continued to coach young long-distance swimmers and to promote sports for women. She died in San Diego in March 1995 after a long illness. She was named to the International Swimming Hall of Fame in 1970, given the Living Legacy Award in 1984, and inducted into the San Diego Hall of Champions the same year; she was inducted into the International Women's Sports Hall of Fame in 1996.

Nadia Comaneci (gymnast)

Born November 12, 1961, Onesti, Romania

Just as the 1972 women's Olympic gymnastic competition belonged to Olga Korbut, the 1976 Games belonged to Nadia Comaneci of Romania. Comaneci recorded the first perfect score in Olympic gymnastics competition on her way to three gold medals, one silver, and one bronze. She earned seven perfect scores in the 1976 Olympics and dominated the world gymnastics scene for the next five years. Comaneci set the standard of perfection in women's gymnastics, and just as Korbut captured the imagination of the world with her charm, Comaneci captivated the world with her skill. At only 14, she gained respect as a hard-working, confident athlete, and confirmed that international gymnastics had abandoned its classical style, with an emphasis on maturity and ladylike grace, for a more physical style performed by powerful and agile teenagers capable of the most impossible routines. In the process, Comaneci helped to elevate the status of women's gymnastics around the world as a sport for the young and courageous.

Nadia Comaneci
Courtesy of International Gymnast

The daughter of Gheirghe and Alexandrina Comaneci, Nadia was born on November 12, 1961, in Onesti, Romania, a town of about 40,000 near the Carpathian Mountains. In 1967, Bela and Marta Karolyi, gymnastics coaches at the sports school in Onesti, spotted six-year-old Nadia running and jumping on the playground of the local kindergarten. After Nadia disappeared into her classroom when the bell rang, the Karolyis searched the school for her, asking the girls in each class, "Who loves gymnastics?" until they found Nadia who jumped up shouting "I do, I do!"[20]

Comaneci enrolled in the sports school where she began her training with the Karolyis. She took regular classes in the morning and had gymnastics training in the after-noons and evenings. From early on, Nadia showed special talent. Karolyi stated: "She is intelligent, dedicated, loves the sport, and has a strong spirit; she knows no fear."[21]

In 1969, Comaneci entered her first competition, the Romanian National Junior Championship, where she placed 13th. The following year, at age eight, she won the junior championship. Her success continued as she trained harder and harder to integrate more difficult moves into each of her routines. In 1971, she won the Romanian all-around title for her age group and successfully defended her title the following year.

By 1972, she was ready for international competition. In the Communist Bloc's Olympic hopefuls meet, Comaneci took three gold medals. At only 10, she was too young to compete in the Olympics despite her overwhelming success in the junior division of the international meets.

Comaneci became eligible for senior international competition in January 1975. In her first senior competition, the 1975 Champions All Tournament in London, she won a gold medal. Four months later, she entered the European championships at Skein, Norway, where she would meet the top Soviet gymnasts, including five-time European champion Lyudmilla Tourischeva. On the first day of the competition, Comaneci won the four-event all-around competition (vault, uneven parallel bars, balance beam, and floor exercise), and the next day she added individual gold medals in the vault, the uneven bars, and the balance beam. She finished second in the floor exercise to Soviet Nelli Kim. For her dominance in the European championship, Comaneci was voted the 1975 Sportswoman of the Year by European sportswriters and by the International Gymnastics Federation.

Comaneci and her teammates came to the United States in March 1976 to participate in several pre-Olympic events. While competing in the first American Cup, she performed the difficult Tsukahara vault— a full twist into a back somersault—to perfection, scoring a perfect 10. Hers was the first perfect 10 scored in gymnastics competition in the United States. She won the American Cup all-around championship with another perfect score in the floor exercise.

Just 14 years old, Comaneci had established herself as the top gymnast in the world by the start of the 1976 Montreal Olympics. She had developed unique and dangerous routines that she performed to perfection. But Comaneci still had to contend with the more experienced Soviet women, including Korbut and Tourischeva. Many predicted that the women's competition would be a battle between the three athletes. But Comaneci set the standard for the entire competition in her first routine by scoring a perfect 10 on the uneven parallel bars, the first perfect score in Olympic gymnastics' history. Over the three-day competition, Comaneci was awarded seven perfect 10s. She won a gold medal for the individual all-around, took the golds in the balance beam and the uneven parallel bars, and won a bronze in the floor exercise. She led Romania to a silver medal in the team competition.

After the Olympics, the confident Comaneci told reporters: "I was sure I would win. I knew that if I worked hard I would win."[22] Thousands of Romanians traveled to the Bucharest airport to welcome their champion home after the Games. For her performances, she received the Hero of Socialist Labor, the highest honor the country awarded. The Associated Press named her Female Athlete of the Year for 1976.

Comaneci continued to compete after the Montreal Olympics. In November 1976, she won the prestigious Chunichi Cup in Japan, and in early 1977, she won her second European all-around title. In 1978, she lost the world title to Soviet gymnast Elena Mukhina, but regained her European championship and won the World Cup in Tokyo the following year. She appeared to be set to defend her gold medals at the 1980 Moscow Olympics as the reigning queen of women's gymnastics. Comaneci performed brilliantly, winning gold medals in the balance beam and floor exercise, but lost her all-around title, finishing second to Elena Davidova of the Soviet Union after receiving questionably low scores from two judges in the balance beam event. Comaneci also took home a silver medal in the team competition. In two Olympics, Comaneci garnered five gold, three silver, and one bronze medals.

In her last major tournament, the World University Games in Bucharest in 1981, Comaneci won the all-around, uneven bars, and floor exercise competition. After the tournament, she performed exhibitions as a member of Romania's national team, but by that time her long-time coach Bela Karolyi had defected to the United States where he settled in Houston and established a gymnastics school for young girls. Comaneci retired from competition in 1984 and qualified to be an international gymnastics judge. She traveled to the 1984 Los Angeles Olympics as a coach of the Romanian team. In 1990, she defected from Romania to the United States with the goal to coach U.S. gymnasts. After several years of performing exhibitions, Comaneci is now based at the Bart Conner Gymnastics Academy, where she concentrates on her duties coaching and encouraging future stars.

The maneuvers that Comaneci perfected extended the limits of women's gymnastics. Her fearlessness and concentration combined with physical strength and agility led to the development of dangerous, athletic moves thought impossible by gymnastic experts. Moves like the twisting back-somersault dismount off the uneven parallel bars that now bears her name—the Salto Comaneci—and three back handsprings in a row on the balance beam are now expected moves for the world's elite gymnasts. Nadia Comaneci will be remembered for her athleticism, perfection, and steely determination.

Further Reading

Burchard, Sue H. *Sports Star, Nadia Comaneci*. New York: Harcourt Brace, 1977. 64 pp.

Grumeza, Ian. *Nadia*. New York: Hawthorn Books, 1977. 127 pp.

McMillan, Constance V. *Nadia Comaneci: Enchanted Sparrow*. St. Paul, MN: EMC Corp., 1977. 40 pp.

Miklowitz, Gloria D. *Nadia Comaneci*. New York: Grosset & Dunlap, 1977. 90 pp.

Sullivan, George. *The Picture Story of Nadia Comaneci*. New York: Julian Messner, 1977. 64 pp.

Maureen Connolly (tennis player)

Born September 17, 1934, San Diego, California; died June 21, 1969

In a spectacular international career that lasted just over four years, Maureen Connolly was the first woman to earn the Grand Slam of tennis—winning the U.S., British, French, and Australian championships—completing the task in 1953 at the age of 19.

Affectionately nicknamed "Little Mo" by the sports media, Connolly began her climb to the top of the tennis world on the municipal courts of San Diego, California. At age 10, she begged her parents, Marten and Jassamine, for a tennis racquet and lessons with the local pro. A fierce competitor from an early age, Connolly entered her first tournament shortly after taking up the game, finishing second. For the next few years, she practiced daily, often hitting a ball against her garage door into the wee hours of the night. In 1947, she became a student of the renowned tennis coach Eleanor "Teach" Tennant, who had coached several world champions including Helen Wills Moody and Alice Marble.

Under the watchful eye of her coach, Connolly practiced three hours a day, five days a week, the year round. Although a natural left-hander, she played right-handed, developing overpowering ground strokes, and was a formidable baseline player. Her quick feet, unwavering concentration, and pinpoint accuracy gave her the powerful tools she needed to win. Her delightful and refreshing personality off the court made her a favorite of the crowd and the media; yet when she appeared on the court with her game face on, she was no match for even the most experienced players.

At 13, Connolly won the national junior title and followed that victory with 56 straight matches without a loss. She won her first major title, the U.S. Championship, in 1951, just two weeks before her 17th birthday. She reached the finals without losing a set and defeated the favorite Doris Hart, 6-4, 6-4, in the final match.

After winning her first major senior title in 1951, Connolly lost only four matches during the rest of her career. From 1951 to 1953, Connolly was ranked number one among senior players. She won three consecutive U.S. National titles (1951-53), Wim-

Maureen Connolly
Courtesy of the Maureen Connolly Brinker Foundation

The hours of dedication involved in becoming number one in the world and staying on top required numerous sacrifices for Connolly. She had to juggle her studies at Cathedral High School in San Diego around her playing schedule. Horseback riding was always her first love, and when she was not playing tennis, she would return to her home to relax and take in a bit of riding.

Tragically, in 1954, just two weeks after winning her third straight Wimbledon crown, Connolly permanently injured her right leg in a serious horseback-riding accident, ending her illustrious competitive tennis career.

After her accident, Little Mo remained active in the sport as a sponsor and coach. She began the Maureen Connolly Brinker Foundation to benefit junior tennis and continued to coach the nation's young players before her death of cancer in 1969 at the age of 34. Connolly became a member of the International Tennis Hall of Fame in 1968 and the International Women's Sports Hall of Fame in 1987.

Little Mo dominated women's international tennis in her short career. She was the first of a long line of teenage tennis stars. Maureen Connolly worked diligently and tirelessly to perfect her all-around game. Her devotion to the game continued after her career-ending accident, helping other young players looking for those championships she cherished.

bledon three times (1952-54), the French Championship in 1953 and 1954, and the Australian and Italian Championships in 1953 and 1954, respectively. Connolly also played on the U.S. Wightman Cup Team, an international team competition between players from the United States and Great Britain, for four consecutive years, winning all of her matches. For her tremendous accomplishments, Connolly was named Associated Press Female Athlete of the Year in 1951, 1952, and 1953.

Donna de Varona (swimmer)

Born April 26, 1947, San Diego, California

One of the outspoken proponents of equal rights for women athletes in the twentieth century, champion swimmer Donna de Varona had a significant impact on promoting women's sports in the United States.

As a swimmer, de Varona won 37 individual national swimming titles and two Olympic gold medals. She excelled in all four of the basic swimming strokes—freestyle, butterfly, breaststroke, and backstroke. Swim-

Donna de Varona
Courtesy of the International Swimming Hall of Fame

ming experts called her the world's fastest as well as the world's best all-around swimmer of her day. After retiring from amateur competition in 1965, de Varona pursued a career in broadcasting, becoming the first female sports commentator on network television. In the mid-1970s, she became a spokesperson for women's sports, cofounded and served as president of the Women's Sports Foundation, and devoted her time to furthering amateur sports in the United States.

The daughter of Martha and Dave de Varona, Donna was born in San Diego, California. As she lived on the California coast, it was natural that de Varona would become involved in water sports at an early age. Paddling by age three and diving by age seven, she preferred freestyle swimming with her older brother in the ocean and public pools near her Lafayette, California, home.

At age 10, she entered the Far Western Amateur Athletic Union (AAU) meet held in San Francisco, where she finished 10th among 10 competitors. Undaunted by her last-place finish, de Varona practiced harder, swimming at the Berkeley YMCA, then training at the Santa Clara Swim Club. She swam five to six hours a day, strengthening her arms and legs and perfecting her technique. In 1960, at the age of 13, she broke her first world record in the 400-meter individual medley event at the AAU Outdoor National Championships. The medley, which is one lap each of the backstroke, breaststroke, butterfly, and freestyle, is considered the most difficult event in swimming competition because it requires expertise in all the strokes. De Varona had the versatility and athleticism to make the medley her best event.

Just after the outdoor nationals, de Varona qualified for the U.S. Women's Olympic Swimming Team, but her specialty, the 400-meter medley, was not an approved event for women in the 1960 Rome Summer Games. An alternate on the U.S. team, de Varona went to Rome as the youngest American in the Olympics.

When she returned to the United States, de Varona continued her rigorous training and competitive schedules. For the next four years, she became the standard-bearer in women's swimming. She dominated the four-stroke individual medley and also set world records in three individual events (the backstroke, the butterfly, and the freestyle).

In 1961, she defended her national AAU medley title, setting a world record of 5 minutes, 34.5 seconds. At the world championships in Lima, Peru, she won the medley title, beating her own world record by a full 18 seconds. At the 1964 Olympics in Tokyo, Japan, de Varona won the first gold medal awarded to a woman for the 400-

meter individual medley. She also won a gold medal in the 400-meter freestyle relay, and with her teammates set a world record in that event.

Nicknamed the "Queen of Swimming," de Varona dominated women's swimming in the early 1960s, winning 37 individual national championships and setting 18 national and world records. She became a member of the International Swimming Hall of Fame in 1969, the International Women's Sports Hall of Fame in 1983, and the U.S. Olympic Hall of Fame in 1987.

At age 18 in 1965, de Varona retired from amateur competition to attend college. She enrolled at the University of California at Los Angeles (UCLA), where she majored in political science. She joined ABC as a sports commentator, the first full-time female sportscaster in the United States, and the first female to cover the Olympics for U.S. network television. She covered the 1968, 1972, 1976, and 1984 Summer Olympics and the 1988 and 1994 Winter Olympics. She won an Emmy Award for her coverage and production of the 1991 Special Olympic Games. Many people agree that she helped advance the cause of women sports journalists with her knowledgeable analysis and insight on the current issues in sports.

As a cofounder and president of the Women's Sports Foundation, de Varona worked tirelessly to promote amateur and women's sports in the United States. She served on the President's Council on Physical Fitness, the Los Angeles Olympic Organizing Committee, President Ford's Commission on Olympic Sports, and President Carter's Advisory Committee for Women. As a special consultant to the U.S. Senate, de Varona played an important role in the passage of the Amateur Sports Act, which established a structure for conducting amateur sports in the United States, and then lobbied for the complete implementation of Title IX of the Education Amendments of 1972, designed to ensure equal opportunity for women in sports at the nation's schools and universities. For her efforts, the Women's Sports Foundation honored de Varona with the 1996 Flo Hyman Award.

Donna de Varona excelled in her sport at an early age and gained well-deserved fame as the dominant woman swimmer in the United States in the early 1960s. After 37 championship titles and two Olympic gold medals, she retired from competitive swimming to launch a successful sportscasting career, from which she actively promoted women's sports in the United States. She had a profound impact on increasing opportunities for women at all levels of sports. Through her efforts, women's sports, both amateur and professional, received more media coverage, career opportunities for women in sports began to open up, and female athletes gained access to better equipment, training, and coaching.

Gail Devers (track and field sprinter)

Born November 19, 1966, Seattle, Washington

In winning the 100 meters at the 1996 Atlanta Olympics, Devers became the first woman to win back-to-back Olympic 100-meter titles since Wyomia Tyus did so in 1964 and 1968. With personal bests of 10.82 in the 100 meters and 12.46 in the 100-meter hurdles, she is recognized as the fastest combination sprinter/hurdler in U.S. history. She also accomplished one of the greatest comebacks in track and field history. After being diagnosed with Graves' disease, a serious thyroid condition, in 1989, and being days from having her feet amputated, Devers recovered and went on to establish a U.S. record in the 100-meter hurdles. On surviving the disease, she said, "I'm a stronger, more determined person because of it. After conquering Graves' disease, I know there's no hurdle I can't get over."[23]

Born Yolanda Gail Devers on November 19, 1966, in Seattle, Washington, Gail grew up in San Diego, where her mother Alabe worked as a teacher's aide and her father Larry served as an associate minister of the Mount Erie Baptist Church. Devers had an active childhood, riding bikes and playing touch football with her younger brother. She began running track at National City (California) Sweetwater High School as a middle-distance runner. She switched to running sprints during her junior year. She won both the 100 meters and 100-meter hurdles and placed second in the long jump at the 1984 California State High School Championships as a senior.

Her success in high school caught the eye of Bob Kersee, the head track coach at University of California at Los Angeles (UCLA). Kersee told Devers she had the potential to be a world-class competitor and an Olympic gold medalist. She enrolled at UCLA in 1984, becoming the first female athlete from Sweetwater High School to earn an athletic scholarship from a major university. As a student at UCLA, Devers competed in the 100-meter dash, 100-meter hurdles, long jump, and triple jump. In 1987, she won the gold medal in the 100-meter dash at the Pan American Games. In May 1988, she set a U.S. record of 12.61 seconds for the 100-meter hurdles, winning the National Collegiate Athletic Association (NCAA) title in the event.

After graduating from UCLA with a degree in sociology, Devers qualified to compete in the 100-meter hurdles at the 1988 Seoul Olympics. But just prior to the Games, she began to suffer from muscle pain, headaches, and fatigue. At the Olympics, she failed to qualify for the finals, finishing last in her semifinal heat.

The symptoms of her mysterious illness began to get more serious. She experienced insomnia, fainting spells, muscle injuries, and fluctuations in body weight. She suffered for nearly two years before doctors recognized that she was suffering from an advanced case of Graves' disease, a hyperthyroid condition. The radiation used to treat the disease caused her feet to swell and bleed. They were so bad that doctors considered amputation, but instead changed her treatment, and she began to recover.

In March 1991, Devers resumed her track and field training. Two months later at the U.S. National Track and Field Championships, she won the 100-meter hurdles in

Gail Devers
Courtesy of UCLA Athletics

12.83 seconds, the fastest time turned in by a U.S. woman that season. The win qualified her for the world championship in Tokyo, Japan. At the 1991 world championships, Devers finished second in the 100-meter hurdles. "Six months ago I had no idea I would be here," she said. "It was just a matter of believing in myself."[24]

After the world championships, a healthy Devers set her sights on the 1992 Barcelona Olympics. She qualified for both the 100 meters and the 100-meter hurdles. She captured the gold medal for the 100 meters in Barcelona, running a personal-best time of 10.82 seconds. In the 100-meter hurdles event, she was leading the race until she struck the final hurdle and finished in fifth place.

At the 1993 world championships in Stuttgart, Germany, she won both the 100 meters and the 100-meter hurdles, becoming the first female to accomplish the rare double in international competition since Fanny Blankers-Koen accomplished the feat at the 1948 Olympic Games. Devers also anchored the United States' 4x100-meter relay team to the silver medal. *Track and Field News* and the United States Olympic Committee (USOC) named Devers the 1993 U.S. Female Athlete of the Year in track and field.

Devers missed most of 1994 with a hamstring injury and back problems result-ing from a car accident, but she returned to form for the 1995 world championships in Gothenburg, Sweden. She won the 100-meter hurdles with a time of 12.68 seconds, which still stands as the meet record. She continued training and rehabilitating the hamstring through 1995 in preparation for the 1996 Atlanta Games.

At the Centennial Olympics in Atlanta, Devers won the 100 meters in one of the closest races in Olympic history. She defeated Jamaican Merlene Ottey in a time of 10.94 seconds. In winning the 100 meters, Devers became the first woman to win back-to-back 100-meter titles since Wyomia Tyus accomplished the feat in 1964 and 1968. Devers added to her cache of Olympic medals when she ran the third leg of the gold-medal-winning U.S. team in the 4x100-meter relay.

Michael Janofsky wrote in the *New York Times* that Devers is "a beacon of hope, and example of fortitude to others who have suffered."[25] A three-time Olympic gold medalist, Gail Devers fought through illness, disappointment, and injury to become one of the fastest combination sprinter/hurdlers in U.S. track and field history. She credits part of her success to the lessons she learned from her illness. "I'm stronger as a person. There's nothing that can come up in my life that I can't get over after going through what I did."[26]

Jean Driscoll (wheelchair athlete)

Born November 18, 1966, Milwaukee, Wisconsin

"The first time I won Boston, I didn't think I even belonged in the race," said wheelchair athlete Jean Driscoll. "I couldn't help thinking it was a fluke."[27] Winning the women's wheelchair division of the Boston Marathon was no fluke for Driscoll. She won seven consecutive Boston Marathons (1990–96) and is the current world-record holder in the event. The racer has dominated women's wheelchair racing in the 1990s. Her success has helped changed the public's perception of athletes with disabilities

Jean Driscoll
Courtesy of B.A.A./Photo Run

and has opened the door for more female athletes with disabilities to follow their dreams.

Driscoll was born with spina bifida, an opening in the spinal column that caused interference in the nerve pathway to her lower body. Her parents were told that she would be unable to use her legs. Her determination and strength was first apparent at age two when, with the help of below-the-knee braces, she spent hours walking through her parents' home. At nine, she taught herself to ride a bike despite being unable to walk without dragging her legs. At age 14, she dislocated her hip, and her doctors confined her to a wheelchair.

Driscoll tried a variety of wheelchair sports growing up in Milwaukee, Wisconsin. "I did a different sport every night of the week and just loved it so much that I was hooked, and I became an athlete," she said.[28] She moved to Champaign, Illinois, in 1987, to play wheelchair basketball at the University of Illinois. She lettered four times in wheelchair basketball at the University of Illinois, leading her team to two consecu-

tive national championships (1990 and 1991).

While at Illinois, she got involved in wheelchair racing and was a dual-sport athlete during her undergraduate years. "My interest in racing came from a desire to go fast. It was a sport that I was curious about, and decided that I wanted to try it out."[29] Driscoll began working with coach Marty Morse, and in 1989, she won her first national-level race, a 12K in Spokane, Washington. Morse convinced her to try the marathon. Hesitantly, Driscoll entered the 1989 Chicago Marathon. "It was the only one I was ever going to do. I had no desire. I hated the training. I hated the distance. I didn't like the pain. And I wasn't even sure I would finish the whole 26 miles," recalled Driscoll.[30] She finished in second place and qualified for a spot in the Boston Marathon. Again Morse had to convince her to enter the race.

In 1990, Driscoll set a world record in her first Boston Marathon. She crossed the finished line in a time of 1:43:17, breaking the existing record by more than seven minutes. She was the first woman wheelchair racer to finish the marathon in less than 1 hour, 50 minutes. In 1991, Driscoll beat her previous record, winning the marathon in 1:42:42, and she beat it again in 1992 (1:36:52). The defending champion won the 1993 women's race in 1:34:50, shaving another 2:02 off her world mark from 1992. Driscoll's streak of winning each Boston Marathon in world-record time was in jeopardy before and after the starter's pistol fired in 1994. She came down with food poisoning just two days before the race and overcame a surprise early leader in the race, taking the lead on the grueling Heartbreak Hill and posting another world-record victory. Her time of 1:34:22 improved her existing mark by 28 seconds. In 1995, Driscoll faced difficult cross- and headwinds but outclimbed her competitors to win the race in a time of 1:40:41, just a few minutes off her world-record time.

In 1996, Driscoll captured her seventh consecutive Boston Marathon with a time of 1:52.54. She was in fourth place until the 11th mile but came from behind at the 17th mile and won the race almost four minutes ahead of the second-place finisher, Deanna Sodoma of Carlsbad, California.

Winner of 85 national and international track and field championships, Driscoll was a silver medalist in the 800-meter wheelchair race exhibition event at both the 1992 and 1996 Olympic Games. In 1992, she set world records in the women's wheelchair 800 and 1,500 meters at the Paralympic Test Meet in Barcelona, Spain. She was the female champion of the 1996 Paralympic Marathon and the Paralympic 10,000 meters. She placed second in the Paralympic 800-meter race and the Paralympic 5,000-meter race. She also took home gold medals at the 1996 Mobil World Challenge 10K, the 1996 Houston Marathon, and the 1996 Los An-geles Marathon (setting a course record). She is the current record holder in the 10K (road and track), the 10 miles (road), the marathon, and the 4x100-meter relay.

In 1991, Driscoll was voted the Women's Sports Foundation's Amateur Sportswoman of the Year, the Athletics Congress's Disabled Athlete of the Year, and the National Wheelchair Athletic Association's Female Athlete of the Year.

From 1990 to 1996, Jean Driscoll won seven consecutive Boston Marathons and is the current course and world-record holder in the women's wheelchair marathon. She has helped changed the public's perception of athletes with disabilities. "When I am out in the Boston Marathon, and doing 26.2 miles, I am not a wheelchair athlete. I am an athlete. The fact that my legs don't work doesn't matter because my legs are not required for my sport," she said.[31] Her success has opened doors for more female athletes with disabilities to follow their dreams.

Camille Duvall (water-skier)

Born July 11, 1960, Greenville, South Carolina

Camille Duvall is one of the greatest female water-skiers in the history of the sport. She garnered 14 U.S. national titles and 43 victories on the professional tour. She reigned as both the World Professional Slalom Champion and the U.S. Overall Champion five times, and was a member of the undefeated world champion U.S. Water Ski Team from 1975–78 and from 1983–87.

Duvall began waterskiing at the age of four, perched on one ski alongside her father. By age six, she had won her first tournament. Traditional waterskiing features slalom, trick, and jump skiing. Slalom skiing involves a slalom course. A skier must ski through entrance gates of the slalom course, around six buoys, and through the exit gates. Trick skiing involves complicated maneuvers on one or two trick skiis. Points are given for each trick. Jump skiing is a contest to see who can fly the farthest distance off of a jump ramp. Duvall excelled at slalom skiing. At 12, she was the junior national water-ski champion, and at 15, an alternate on the U.S. national team.

In 1979, Duvall injured her knee while competing in a jump competition in a tournament in Mexico City. She went into semi-retirement from the sport, but three years later returned to competitive skiing at the urging of her brother. "He said, 'Just for fun, why don't you drag out your dusty old skis from the closet and bring them with you?'" she recalled. "I hadn't been on a slalom course for all that time, and straight out of the box, I skied great."[32] She placed fourth in slalom at the U.S. nationals a few months later.

In 1985, Duvall simultaneously held waterskiing's triple crown: U.S. National Champion, World Slalom Champion, and Masters Champion. She became the first-ever water-skier honored by the Women's Sports Foundation when she was nominated as Professional Sportswoman of the Year in 1985, 1986, and 1987.

Duvall was the founder of the Professional Water Ski Tour and served as its president from 1988 to 1991. She retired from competitive waterskiing in 1994 after being diagnosed with a collapsed vertebral artery. Before her retirement, Duvall was ranked first in the world in jumping, fourth in slalom, and third overall.

Camille Duvall set the standard for amateur and professional water-skiers nationwide. She won 14 national titles and, in 1987, became the first woman to earn $100,000 a year in prize money and endorsements. She is considered by many to be the finest female water-skier in the history of the sport, and today's rising stars of the women's professional water-ski circuit are benefitting from her success.

Amelia Earhart (aviator)

Born July 24, 1897, Atchison, Kansas; died July 2, 1937

Amelia Earhart was the most famous female pilot of her time. In 1928, just one year after Charles Lindbergh flew across the Atlantic in the *Spirit of St. Louis*, Earhart became the first woman to fly the Atlantic. She quickly became a national hero and a symbol for women's increasing independence and physical capabilities. In 1932, she piloted her own plane from Newfoundland to Ireland, the first woman to fly solo across the Atlantic. In her last flying adventure, Earhart and her engineer Fred Noonan disappeared during their attempt to fly around the world. During her 16-year flying career, Earhart used her time in the limelight to encourage young women to follow their own path and to ensure that women had independence and equal economic opportunities.

Born to Edwin and Amy Otis Earhart, Amelia had quite an unsettled childhood. Her family moved around the country,

settling in Des Moines, Iowa; St. Paul, Minnesota; and finally in Chicago. Earhart spent most of her childhood visiting her grandparents in Atchison, Kansas. Earhart and her sister Muriel Grace led a vigorous outdoor life with horseback riding, bicycling, exploring caves, and playing football, tennis, and basketball.

In 1916, Earhart graduated from Hyde Park High School in Chicago and subsequently enrolled in the Ogontz School in Rydal, Pennsylvania. In December 1917, she visited her sister in Toronto where Earhart decided to remain as a volunteer aide at Spadina Military Hospital. Earhart's interest in flying emerged as she became captivated by the stories of the men of the Royal Flying Corps, whom she was helping at the hospital.

In 1920, Earhart moved to Los Angeles, and it was at the nearby Glendale airport that she took her first airplane ride, with

Amelia Earhart
Courtesy of The Ninety-Nines, Inc., Archives Department

renowned barnstorming pilot Frank Hawks. That night she told her parents that she'd like to learn to fly. She began taking lessons from pioneer woman pilot Neta Snook, and in June 1921, Earhart made her first solo flight, in a Kinner Airster plane, over the skies of Los Angeles.

Within weeks of her first solo flight in 1922, she set a women's altitude record of 14,000 feet, in a plane she purchased with money saved from her job at the local telephone company. In this 1920s era of barnstorming, daredevil aerobatics, and air shows, Earhart quickly became a familiar figure around the airports of southern California.

In 1924, Earhart moved to Medford, Massachusetts, where she taught English to immigrant factory workers and worked as a social worker at a Boston settlement house. She continued to fly as a Kinner demon-

stration pilot at nearby Denison Airport. Meanwhile, word came from across the ocean in England that Amy Phipps Guest, a U.S. flying enthusiast, had purchased a trimotor Fokker plane in hopes of becoming the first woman to cross the Atlantic by air. Because her family opposed such a flight, Guest asked U.S. publisher George Putnam to help her find another woman pilot to make the flight. Putnam suggested Earhart.

On June 17, 1928, Earhart left Newfoundland with pilot Wilmer Stultz and mechanic Lou Gordon in the airplane *Friendship*. Twenty hours and 40 minutes later the plane set down off Burry Port, Wales, in the United Kingdom. Although her role had been merely to keep a log, Earhart catapulted into fame overnight. The public fell in love with the daring young woman who looked so much like their hero Charles

Lindbergh. Throughout the country, Earhart received ticker-tape parades and events in her honor. She lectured about her experiences and wrote a book, *20 Hrs., 40 Min.*, about the flight.

Earhart continued her adventurous long-distance flying. In the fall of 1928, she became the first woman to fly from the Atlantic to the Pacific and back again. The following year, with 19 other female pilots, Earhart flew the course from Santa Monica, California, to Cleveland, Ohio, in the first Women's Air Derby. Fifteen of the 20 competitors completed the flight; Earhart finished third. She joined a newly formed passenger airline, Transcontinental Air Transport, that offered hourly service between New York City and Washington, DC, and overnight service from New York to California. Earhart traveled the country, speaking to women and encouraging them to travel by air. She also became a staff member of *Cosmopolitan* magazine, writing articles on women flying—both as passengers and as pilots.

During her time crisscrossing the country giving flying demonstrations and lecturing, Earhart harbored the desire to actually pilot a plane across the Atlantic herself. She reached her goal on May 22, 1932, when she became the first woman to fly the Atlantic alone. Setting off with only a leather flying suit, $15 in cash, and a toothbrush, she made the flight from Newfoundland to Ireland in slightly under 15 hours. The historic flight brought Earhart worldwide acclaim. President Hoover remarked that she demonstrated the new possibilities of the human spirit in overcoming the barriers of space.

Earhart continued to take on aeronautical challenges. In 1935, she made the first solo flight from Honolulu to the U.S. mainland, and also flew nonstop from Mexico City to Newark, New Jersey, the first person to accomplish this feat.

Earhart spent part of the 1935-36 school year counseling women students at Purdue University, encouraging them to seize their opportunities for independence and adventure. While Earhart worked at the university, the Purdue Research Foundation ordered a new plane, a Lockheed Electra, that she was to use as a flying laboratory. Her plan was to use the plane to study how flying affected people. But first she planned to use the plane to be the first person—male or female—to fly around the world at the equator.

She decided to fly an east-to-west route: Oakland to Hawaii to Howland Island in the Pacific, across to Australia, over to Africa and Brazil, and then home. Earhart, along with captain Harry Manning and navigator Fred Noonan, left Oakland on March 17, 1937, and landed safely in Hawaii 16 hours later. The plane experienced mechanical difficulties a few days later that required nearly two months to repair. After these delays, Earhart reversed her original flight plan, and on June 1, 1937, with Noonan as her navigator, left Miami heading west to resume her historic flight. The pair ran into rough weather, and on July 2, 1937, just two stops before completing her journey around the world, her plane disappeared into the Pacific without a trace.

Amelia Earhart loved to fly and to set goals and records in her airplane. She represented the hundreds of women pilots who took to the skies in the 1920s and 1930s. She flew on behalf of women, taking every opportunity to discuss women's issues of the time. In November 1929, she helped to found and served as president of the Ninety-Nines, an international organization of women pilots. For her achievements, she was awarded the Distinguished

Flying Cross from the U.S. Congress, the Cross of the French Legion of Honor, and the Gold Medal of the National Geographic Society, among others. She was inducted into the International Women's Hall of Fame and the International Women's Sports Hall of Fame in 1980. Her flights opened new frontiers in transportation and air safety, and showed the world the extent of women's physical capabilities, opening many doors for women and giving them the freedom to pursue all their endeavors.

Further Reading

Backus, Jean L. *Letters from Amelia*. Boston: Beacon Press, 1982. 253 pp.

Briand, Paul L. Jr. *Daughter of the Sky*. New York: Duell, Sloan and Pierce, 1960. 247 pp.

Burke, John. *Winged Legend*. New York: G.P. Putnam's Sons, 1970. 255 pp.

Earhart, Amelia. *Last Flight*. New York: Harcourt Brace, 1937. 224 pp.

Earhart, Amelia. *The Fun of It*. New York: Harcourt Brace, 1932; Chicago: Academy Chicago Publishers, 1984. 218 pp.

Earhart, Amelia. *20 Hrs., 40 Min.* New York: G.P. Putnam's Sons, 1928. 314 pp.

Morrissey, Muriel Earhart. *Courage Is the Price*. Wichita, KS: McCormick-Armstrong Publishing Division, 1963. 320 pp.

Putnam, George Palmer. *Soaring Wings*. New York: Harcourt Brace, 1939. 294 pp.

Gertrude Ederle (long-distance swimmer)

Born October 23, 1906, New York, New York

In 1925, Gertrude "Trudy" Ederle announced that she could and would swim the English Channel, a feat that only five men had accomplished and a challenge considered impossible for a woman. After one failed attempt in 1925, she took to the water on August 6, 1926, and completed the 20-mile swim in a record time of 14 hours, 31 minutes, faster than any man had ever done. Her long-distance swim captured the attention of the entire world. In a decade when women began to challenge the societal barriers against physical activity for women, Ederle's achievements inspired thousands of women to take up swimming for both competition and recreation, and helped pave the way for American women to enter the sports world.

Ederle grew up on the west side of New York City, the daughter of German immigrants Henry and Gertrude Ederle. She learned to swim at a young age, escaping the heat and dirt of city streets by diving into the invigorating waters of the neighborhood pool. Swimming soon became her passion. When she was 15, she joined the Women's Swimming Association on the

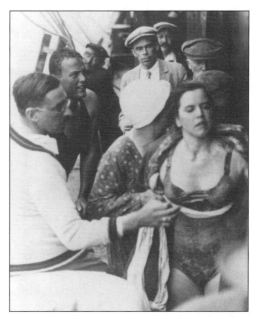

Gertrude Ederle
Courtesy of the International Swimming Hall of Fame

lower east side of Manhattan and began to take lessons that would improve her technique and increase her speed.

In 1921, Ederle entered her first competition, winning the Metropolitan New York junior 100-meter freestyle championship. She followed that victory with a record-setting performance in the 500-meter swim at Brighton Beach, New York. Attempting a longer distance, she won the 3½-mile international Joseph P. Day race the following year, defeating more than 50 world-class swimmers on her way to setting a course record.

She continued her winning ways, and by the time she was 17, she held 18 world distance records. At the 1924 Paris Olympics, Ederle represented the United States, winning three medals: bronze medals in the 100- and 400-meter freestyle events, and a gold medal as part of the 4x100-meter relay team.

Her win at the Joseph P. Day competition and her success at the Olympics pushed Ederle into international prominence. At age 17, she began to consider swimming longer, more challenging races. She announced that she would swim the English Channel. Publisher Captain Paterson of the *New York News* agreed to sponsor Ederle in her swim, supplied her with a coach, and sent along a reporter to cover the possible story of her swim across the Channel.

Ederle's first attempt came on August 18, 1925. She swam at a rapid pace, but after 8 hours, 46 minutes, she lost control of her stroke in the strong current, presumably from the fast pace she had set, and had to be rescued from the frigid waters.

One year later, Ederle returned to Cape Gris-Nez on the coast of France for her second try at conquering the Channel. She entered the water at 7:09 A.M. heading for England. For the next 14 plus hours, the 19-year-old battled high winds and rain, shifting tides, and a bout of seasickness, until she stepped on the sands of the British shore as the first woman to swim the English Channel. Her time, 14 hours, 31 minutes, was nearly two hours faster than the best male time.

Swimming the distance from France to England made Ederle an instant celebrity. New York City welcomed her back with a ticker-tape parade equalled only by the one staged for Charles Lindbergh a year later; the newspaper headlines heralded her as "Queen of the Waves" and "America's Best Girl." She received hundreds of movie, vaudeville, and commercial endorsement contracts estimated at more than $200,000. She toured Europe and the United States, giving swimming exhibitions at vaudeville houses along the way.

However, her celebrity status took its toll. In 1928, a nervous breakdown forced Ederle to cancel her touring commitments. The nervous condition, coupled with the years spent in the water, left her partially deaf. In 1933, she fell in her New York apartment, severely injuring her spine. After nearly four years of recovery, Ederle resumed her swimming exhibitions. When she retired from professional swimming, she went on to teach swimming to deaf children in New York. In 1965, 39 years after becoming the first woman to swim the English Channel, Ederle was inducted into the International Swimming Hall of Fame. She became a member of the International Women's Sports Hall of Fame in 1980.

Gertrude Ederle achieved greatness for her long-distance swimming prowess at a time when society believed that women could not endure such strenuous physical activity. Her accomplishments laid to rest the idea that women were not capable of achieving feats equal to those of men. She was the catalyst that took thousands of women to the beaches and pools of America, as swimming became one of the leading women's sports in the United States during the 1920s and 1930s.

Teresa Edwards (basketball player)

Born July 19, 1964, Cairo, Georgia

Playing in the 1996 Atlanta Olympics before her hometown crowd, Teresa Edwards became the first U.S. basketball player, male or female, to compete in four Olympiads (1984, 1988, 1992, 1996). She was selected by the U.S. delegation to take the Athlete Oath at the 1996 Centennial Olympics, only the third American so honored. As captain of the 1996 Olympic gold-medal-winning basketball team, she started all eight games and led the team with assists (averaging eight per game and setting a record against Australia with 15). One of the best to ever play women's basketball, Edwards is an exceptional point guard and leader on the floor, and has achieved success at every level of the game.

The only daughter of Mildred Edwards of Cairo, Georgia, Teresa was born on July 19, 1964. She grew up in a single-parent family, with four brothers. Teresa liked to "hang out" with the boys in her neighborhood, playing softball and tackle football, and shooting baskets through an old bicycle rim nailed to a pine tree in the front yard. Teresa played her first organized basketball at Washington Middle School as a seventh grader.

Edwards became a high school All-American and after graduating enrolled in the University of Georgia on an athletic scholarship. During her four seasons as point guard (1983-86), Edwards led Georgia to four National Collegiate Athletic Association (NCAA) tournaments, reaching the Final Four twice (1983, 1985). She was named consensus All-American in 1985

and 1986, and was selected to the All-SEC (South Eastern Conference) first team in 1984, 1985, and 1986. She ranks as Georgia's all-time career leader for assists (653) and steals (342). She graduated from the University of Georgia in 1989 with a degree in recreation. "I was the first in my family to graduate from college," Edwards told *Sports Illustrated*. "That's the biggest example I could make for my brothers. It means more than any shot I could ever take."[33]

Edwards made her first Olympic appearance as the youngest member of the 1984 U.S. Olympic Women's Basketball

Teresa Edwards
Courtesy of Sam Forencich/USA Basketball

Team. She averaged 2.5 points and 2.0 rebounds per game in limited playing time with the gold-medal-winning team. Her international experience continued as a member of the 1986 U.S. gold-medal-winning world championship and Goodwill Games teams. In 1987, she was a member of the 1987 gold-medal-winning U.S. Pan American Games team, averaging 16.8 points and 5.8 assists per game. USA Basketball named her Female Athlete of the Year in 1987.

In 1988, the outstanding point guard led the U.S. Olympic team to a gold medal, finishing as the team's second-leading scorer, averaging 16.6 points per game. She led the team in field goal percentage (.611), assists (3.4 per game), and steals (4.6 per game) at the Seoul Games. At the 1990 world championships and Goodwill Games, Edwards led the U.S. team to a pair of gold medals and averaged team highs of 21.9 points and 3.0 assists per game at the worlds and team highs of 16.4 points and 4.2 assists per game at the Goodwill Games.

Co-captain of the 1992 U.S. Olympic team that won the bronze medal, Edwards was the team's assist leader (27) and its third-leading scorer (12.6 points per game).

As a member of her fourth Olympic team in 1996, Edwards was selected for the prestigious honor of taking the Olympic Oath on behalf of all the Olympic athletes during the opening ceremonies of the Centennial Olympic Games in Atlanta.

The veteran leader of the women's basketball team, Edwards helped guide the U.S. women to an 8-0 record and the gold medal, her third Olympic gold medal. Starting all eight Olympic games, the 5'11" point guard led the U.S. team and the entire Olympic competition in assists, averaging 8.0 assists a game, while averaging 6.9 points, 3.8 rebounds, and 1.0 steals, and shooting 60 percent from the field. She was named the Women's Sports Foundation Team Sportswoman of the Year in 1996, and USA Basketball's Female Athlete of the Year in 1996.

In addition to her time playing with the U.S. national team, Edwards has played professionally overseas in France, Italy, Japan, and Spain. In 1991, as a member of the Mitsubishi Electric Corporation team in Nagoya, Japan, she led the league in scoring with an average of 31.8 points per game and in steals with 3.3 per game. She currently is player/coach of the Atlanta Glory of the American Basketball League (ABL). In her first year in the ABL (1996), she averaged 18.3 points, 7.1 rebounds, and 5.1 assists per game.

With three gold medals and one bronze in Olympic basketball competition, Teresa Edwards is USA Basketball's career leader for the Olympic Games in assists (116 total assists/4.8 assists per game) and steals (56 total/2.3 steals per game), and ranks second in points scored (216 total/9.0 points per game). She has been named USA Basketball Female Athlete of the Year three times (1987, 1990, 1996). "Teresa is fiercely competitive. On the court she found ways to help our team win," commented 1996 U.S. Olympic head coach Tara VanDerveer. "She was an excellent leader and led by example. Off the court she was a tireless promoter of women's basketball. She is an outstanding role model for young girls and boys. She gives back to the game she loves."[34]

Janet Evans (swimmer)

Born August 28, 1971, Placentia, California

"I think that I'd like to be remembered as a swimmer who stayed on top of her game for 10 years and broke a few world records and won a few gold medals along the way," remarked Janet Evans after appearing in her third consecutive Olympic Games.[35] One of the most decorated Olympic swimmers in U.S. history, Evans was the first U.S. woman to win four Olympic gold medals in swimming; she still owns two world records, and has won 45 national swimming titles. She is considered one of the best middle-distance swimmers in the history of the sport.

Born on August 28, 1971, in Placentia, California, the daughter of Barbara and Paul Evans, Janet learned to swim at the YMCA when she was just a year old. She could swim all four strokes by the time she was four. It was at this age that she joined the Fullerton Aquatics, a swim team near her home, and began competing in the six-and-under age group. At age 13, she swam in her first senior national championship meet.

In 1987, not yet 16, she set her first world record by finishing the 800 meters in a time of 8:22.44 at the U.S. Long-Course Championships. She also won the 400-meter individual medley and the 400-meter freestyle, and set another world record in winning the 1,500-meter freestyle. In December, at the United States Open, Evans toppled an eight-year-old world record in the 400-meter freestyle. She became the first woman swimmer to set world records in three different events in one year since Tracey Wickham of Australia did so in 1976.

Much of her success came as a result of a relentless training schedule. Her daily routine began when she awoke at 4:45 A.M. so she could swim more than four miles of freestyle before school. After school she went home to do her homework, then returned to the pool or the weight machines for two more hours of work. This routine continued for more than five years. Physiologically she had advantages as well. "Janet is the most energy-efficient machine in the water today, male or female," said John Troup, the director of sports medicine and science for U.S. Swimming, in 1988. "I've tested thousands of swimmers, and Janet uses less oxygen, or less energy, to swim at a fast pace than anybody I've ever seen."[36]

Janet Evans
Courtesy of Rod Searcey

Evans was a favorite to win three events at the 1988 Seoul Olympics. In the 400-meter individual medley, her first event, she used her strong backstroke and freestyle legs to surge ahead of the competition to win the event, finishing in 4:37.76 and giving the United States its first gold medal of the Games. In the 400-meter freestyle, Evans led the entire race and clipped 1.61 seconds off her own world record and finished in 4:03.85 to win the gold medal. In her final event, the 800-meter freestyle, she finished at 8:20.2, setting an Olympic record and taking home the gold. "She was the bright spot for the U.S. women swimmers," wrote Bruce Anderson in *Sports Illustrated*.[37] Evans won the 1989 Sullivan Award as the nation's top amateur athlete and was named the 1989 United States Olympic Committee (USOC) Sportswoman of the Year.

After the Olympics, Evans returned to the United States to a frenzy of publicity and appearances, yet she managed to continue with her school work and her training. She graduated from high school at the age of 17 and enrolled at Stanford University, a perennial power in women's swimming. At the 1990 National Collegiate Athletic Association (NCAA) championships, Evans broke the U.S. record in the 400-yard freestyle by almost two seconds, won the 400-yard individual medley, and anchored the 800-yard freestyle relay to victory. Evans was named NCAA Swimmer of the Year in 1990.

In 1991, Evans relinquished her collegiate eligibility and moved to Austin, Texas, to train with coach Mark Schubert. By that time she was ranked in the top three in the world in five events. She traveled to the 1992 Summer Games in Barcelona favored to win gold in two events, the 800-meter freestyle and the 400-meter freestyle. She won the gold in the 800-meter and the silver in the 400-meter freestyle, becoming the first U.S. woman swimmer to win four

Olympic gold medals and the first woman ever to repeat in the women's 800-meter freestyle in consecutive Olympics.

After the Olympics, Evans took a break from training for four months, but returned to the pool with a more positive attitude and more determination to prove she was still in top form. At the 1994 national championships, Evans won the 400-, 800-, and 1,500-meter events. The victory in the 800 gave her a record 12 national titles in one event. At the Olympic trials in March 1996, Evans won the 400-meter freestyle, qualifying for her third consecutive Olympic Games.

As a member of her third U.S. Olympic Swimming Team, Evans was given the honor of running the final leg of the torch relay during the opening ceremonies at the 1996 Atlanta Centennial Olympics. Although she failed to medal or even qualify for the finals in either of her middle-distance swimming events, she remained excited about the experience. "The fact that I could come to my third Olympics as a distance swimmer and compete for my home country was pretty much a great honor for me," she told ESPN.[38]

When Evans retired from competition after the 1996 Olympics, she still held two world records (in the 400 and 800 meters) and six national marks. One of the most decorated Olympic swimmers in U.S. history, Janet Evans was the first U.S. woman to win four Olympic gold medals in swimming. She is considered one of the best middle-distance swimmers in the history of the sport, and through her success, advanced the sport of women's swimming for future generations.

Chris Evert (tennis player)

Born December 21, 1954, Fort Lauderdale, Florida

In April 1985, the Women's Sports Foundation named Chris Evert the Greatest Woman Athlete of the last 25 years. In a remarkable tennis career that spanned two decades, Evert established herself as one of the premier female athletes of the twentieth century. She retired from competition in 1989, leaving a formidable record and a lasting legacy. New generations of players have imitated her baseline game and two-handed backhand, but no one is likely to duplicate her record of victories. Evert won 157 singles titles, has more than 1,300 career match wins, and owns the highest winning percentage in professional tennis history, .900. She won at least one Grand Slam (Australian, French, and U.S. Opens and Wimbledon) title per year for 13 years, 1974-86; and from 1972 to 1989 never ranked lower than the top four in women's tennis. She symbolized the best of women's athletics in the United States: drive, determination, skill, professionalism, and grace. Tennis great Billie Jean King wrote in her 1988 book, *We Have Come a Long Way: The Story of Women's Tennis,* about Evert: "Her unwavering focus, combined with her great, natural coordination, and her father's marvelous training, made Chris Evert one of the giants of the game."[39]

Christine Marie Evert was born in Fort Lauderdale, Florida, the second of James and Colette Evert's five children. The entire Evert family played tennis; James was the teaching professional at Fort Lauderdale's Holiday Park Tennis Center. Chris began hitting a tennis ball against the walls at the municipal courts at age six. When her father saw her hitting balls, he decided to give her lessons. Evert spent two to three hours a day and eight hours on the weekends on the courts, practicing her ground strokes and serves. Because she wasn't strong enough to hit the one-handed backhand, Evert learned to hit with the two-handed backhand, one of the first players to make it a weapon in their shot arsenal.

Chris Evert
Courtesy of Evert Enterprises/IMG

Evert won her first tournament at age 10 and began to make a name for herself by the time she was 15. Playing in the Carolinas Tournament in 1970, Evert upset the fourth-ranked player in the world, Francoise Durr, 6-1, 6-1, then defeated the top-ranked player, Margaret Court (who had just completed the Grand Slam—winning U.S., British, French, and Australian Championships—a few weeks before), 7-6, 7-6, in the semifinals. Evert lost to Nancy Richey in the finals, but her win over Court stunned the tennis world and marked her emergence into world-class tennis.

In April 1971, Evert won the $100,000 Virginia Slims Master's tournament in St. Petersburg, Florida, her first of 157 tournament victories. In August, she became the youngest woman ever to play for the U.S. Wightman Cup Team. (The Wightman Cup is an annual team competition between players from the United States and Great Britain). She won both her matches, beating Winnie Shaw, 6-0, 6-4, and Virginia Wade, 6-1, 6-1.

In September 1971, Evert traveled to the West Side Tennis Club in Forest Hills, New York, for her first U.S. Open. She had become so popular with spectators that the United States Lawn Tennis Association (USLTA) officials scheduled her first match on the stadium's center court. More than 9,000 spectators watched her first-round victory over Edda Buding of Germany. The next day, Evert played the most dramatic match of her young career by coming back from six match points in the second set to defeat American Mary Ann Eisel, 4-6, 7-6, 6-1. With grit, determination, and a barrage of passing shots, the 16-year-old battled back to capture the victory and the imagination of the spectators and the broadcast media. Evert faced the reigning queen of women's tennis, Billie Jean King, in the semifinals. More than 13,000 people watched King defeat Evert in straight sets, 6-3, 6-2.

Evert graduated from Fort Lauderdale's St. Thomas Aquinas High School in 1972 and turned professional on her 18th birthday. By 1974, she had reached the number one ranking and began her dominance of women's tennis. As a clay court specialist, Evert had a 125-match win streak on clay from August 1973 to May 1979. She reached the semifinals or better in 17 of 19 U.S. Open appearances, and the semifinals or better in 17 of 18 appearances at Wimbledon. She won the All-England Championships at Wimbledon in 1974, 1976, and 1981; the French Open singles title in 1974, 1975, 1979, 1980, 1983, 1985, and 1986;

and the U.S. Open women's singles title in 1975, 1976, 1977, 1978, 1980, and 1982.

Evert's excellence came from her many hours of practice and her mental toughness. She had tremendous endurance as a result of her long practice sessions and could outlast nearly any opponent. She played a calm, cool game, never letting her emotions get the best of her. "I don't show a lot of emotion on the court because I don't want to waste energy and I don't want my opponents to see how I really feel," she once explained.[40]

An extraordinary 15-year rivalry developed between Chris Evert and Martina Navratilova. Evert, with her mental tenacity and relentless baseline play, battled Navratilova's superior athleticism and serve-and-volley style in a match-up of two distinct talents and personalities. The rivalry, which began in 1973, vaulted women's tennis into one of the top sports attractions in the world.

Evert's tennis numbers are impressive, but she served women's tennis off the court as well. She was elected president of the Women's Tennis Association (WTA) a record nine times, including eight consecutive terms from 1983 to 1991. Evert said, "It wasn't like I was going to play the tournaments and collect the prize money and not be involved in the decision-making or take an interest in helping make changes for the better," she recalled. "[By serving the WTA] you feel like you're putting something back in the game."[41] Winner of the WTA Player Service Award in 1981, Evert was also selected by her peers to receive the WTA Karen Krantzcke Sportsmanship Award in 1979, and won the Player Service Award again in 1986 and 1987.

Evert represented her country in international matches as a member of the U.S. Federation Cup Team, 1977-80 and 1982; the U.S. Wightman Cup Team, 1971-73,

1975, and 1977-82; and the 1988 U.S. Olympic team. The Women's Sports Foundation presented Chris Evert with the 1990 Flo Hyman Award for commitment to excellence in supporting women's advancements in sports. The Associated Press named her Female Athlete of the Year four times (1974, 1975, 1977, 1980), and *Sports Illustrated* selected her as their Sportsman of the Year in 1976. In 1981, she was named the Women's Sports Foundation Sportswoman of the Year and was inducted into the International Women's Sports Hall of Fame. She was elected unanimously to the International Tennis Hall of Fame in 1995.

Since her retirement after the 1989 U.S. Open, Evert has remained active in the sport through her work and community service as a player and a sponsor. She hosts the annual Chris Evert/Phar-Mor Pro-Celebrity Tennis Classic to fight drug abuse and to help hurricane relief efforts. She also participates in the Virginia Slims Legends Tour to benefit the National AIDS Fund.

In January 1991, President George Bush appointed Evert to the President's Council on Physical Fitness and Sports. She also serves as special adviser to the United States Tennis Association (USTA) and is on the board of both the International Tennis Hall of Fame and the Women's Sports Foundation.

Chris Evert personified women's tennis for nearly two decades. Television brought Evert into American living rooms just as women's professional tennis was establishing itself in the sports world. Billie Jean King, Rosie Casals, and other tennis stars initiated, played, and promoted the fledgling women's professional tour, but it was Chris Evert, with her professionalism and unending dedication, who took the tour into the U.S. mainstream and stabilized its existence. Evert also helped lure thousands of youngsters into the game. She inspired a whole generation of girls who yearned to play tennis the way she did—with consistency, excellence, style, and grace.

Further Reading

Burchard, Sue H. *Chris Evert*. New York: Harcourt Brace Jovanovich, 1976. 64 pp.

Hahn, James, and Lynn Hahn. *Chris! The Sports Career of Chris Evert Lloyd*. Mankato, MN: Crestwood House, 1981. 41 pp.

Haney, Lynn. *Chris Evert, the Young Champion*. New York: G.P. Putnam's Sons, 1976. 127 pp.

Jacobs, Linda. *Chris Evert: Tennis Pro*. St. Paul, MN: EMC Corp., 1974. 40 pp.

Lloyd, Chris, and John Lloyd, with Carol Thatcher. *Lloyd on Lloyd*. New York: Beaufort Books, 1985. 215 pp.

Lloyd, Chris Evert, with Neil Amdur. *Chrissie, My Own Story*. New York: Simon & Schuster, 1982. 238 pp.

May, Julian. *Chris Evert: Princess of Tennis*. Mankato, MN: Crestwood House, 1975. 48 pp.

O'Shea, Mary Jo. *Winning Tennis Star: Chris Evert*. Mankato, MN: Creative Education Society, 1977. 31 pp.

Phillips, Betty Lou. *Chris Evert, First Lady of Tennis*. New York: G.P. Putnam's Sons, 1977. 189 pp.

Sabin, Francene. *Set Point, The Story of Chris Evert*. New York: G.P. Putnam's Sons, 1977. 127 pp.

Lisa Fernandez (softball player)

Born February 22, 1971, Long Beach, California

Considered by many to be the best all-around player in fast-pitch softball today and the most dominant pitcher in the history of collegiate softball, Lisa Fernandez compiled a four-year collegiate record of 93-7 (.93 winning percentage) with University of California at Los Angeles (UCLA) and led the Bruins to two National Collegiate Athletic Association (NCAA) national championships. In international competition, she has won two International Softball Federation (ISF) Women's World Championships gold medals (1990, 1994), two Pan American Games gold medals (1991, 1995), and the first-ever gold medal in Olympic softball competition as a member of the 1996 USA Women's Olympic Softball Team. A multi-talented athlete, Fernandez pitched and batted her way to the top of her sport with the intensity and confidence of a champion. "You have to have the mentality you are untouchable as a pitcher," she told *Olympian* magazine. "It might not always be true, but half the battle is believing you have the capabilities."[42]

Fernandez learned to played softball at an early age. "My dad [who played semipro baseball in Cuba] was my first coach," she recalled, "and my mom was my first catcher."[43] She was the batgirl for her mother's slow-pitch team until she was old enough to play herself. In her first game as a pitcher, at age seven, she lost 25-0. At age 11, she won her first Amateur Softball Association (ASA) Championship. Also an accomplished basketball player and cross-country runner, Fernandez settled on fast-pitch softball in high school. During her career at St. Joseph High School in Lakewood, California, she pitched 69 shutouts, 37 no-hitters, and 12 perfect games.

Fernandez enrolled at University of California at Los Angeles (UCLA) in 1989 and as a freshman in 1990 pitched the Bruins to an NCAA championship, and then to another in 1992. She was undefeated in 1992, posting a record of 29-0 for the Bruins. In 1993, Fernandez led UCLA to a second-place finish in the NCAA College Softball World Series. During the tournament, she became the first player ever to pitch two no-hitters. She finished the 1993 season number one in both batting average (.510) and earned run average (.25). During her college career at UCLA, Fernandez batted .382 and broke career records for singles (225), runs scored (142), walks (65),

Lisa Fernandez
Courtesy of USA Softball

hits (287), pitching wins (93), career winning percentage (.93), and no-hitters (11). She was a four-time NCAA All-America selection (1990–93). In 1993, Fernandez was named the Honda Broderick Award winner as the nation's outstanding female athlete.

The right-hander possesses an arsenal of pitches, from off-speed curve balls to the lethal "riseball," which rises in the strike zone as it crosses the plate. Some have called her "untouchable." When not pitching, Fernandez often plays third base in an intimidating fashion.

In ASA competition, Fernandez played for the world famous Raybestos Brakettes of Stratford, Connecticut, and the California Commotion of Woodland Hills, California. She was a four-time ASA All-American selection, and won the Bertha Tickey and MVP awards in the 1991 and 1992 Women's Major Fast Pitch National Championships.

Fernandez had success at every level of the sport. In international competition, she was a member of the USA team that won gold at the 1995 Superball Classic in Columbus, Georgia, and pitched a perfect game and a no-hitter with an ERA (earned run average) of 0.00 to help USA Softball win the gold medal at the 1995 Pan American Qualifier in Guatemala. She also batted .511 in the tournament. She recorded a .393 batting average and led the U.S. National Softball Team to a 10-0 record against a 20-nation field to win its third consecutive medal at the 1994 world championships. She was also a member of the gold-medal-winning U.S. team at both the 1991 Pan American Games in Cuba and the 1995 Pan American Games in Argentina. At the 1991 Games, Fernandez was forced to pitch five straight games after U.S. pitchers Debbie Doom and Michele Granger were injured.

With several solid innings of relief pitching, the right-hander closed out the final game to capture the Olympic gold medal at the 1996 Atlanta Olympic Games. She posted a 1-1 record and compiled a 0.33 ERA with 31 strikeouts in 21 innings pitched. Fernandez also batted .348 with eight hits, including one home run, and five RBIs (runs batted in) in the Olympic tournament. Also helping out at third base in the inaugural competition for women's softball at the Olympics, she posted a 1.000 fielding percentage (no errors). Fernandez was named United States Olympic Committee (USOC) Female Athlete of the Year in Softball in 1992 and 1993 and the Women's Sports Foundation Team Sportswoman of the Year in 1994.

As one of the most dominant pitchers in collegiate and international competition, Lisa Fernandez has earned a place in softball history. She and her teammates won the first-ever Olympic softball tournament, and their efforts ignited an interest in women's softball that will last for generations.

Peggy Fleming (figure skater)

Born July 27, 1948, San Jose, California

Called America's last true "ballerina on ice," Peggy Fleming took her graceful yet powerful style of skating to Grenoble, France, in 1968, where she wowed the audience and the judges on her way to an overwhelming victory in the Olympic figure skating competition. She outdistanced her nearest competitor, Gabriele Seyfert of East Germany, by 88.2 points to take the gold medal, the only gold medal that the

Peggy Fleming
Courtesy of the World Figure Skating Museum

United States would claim in the 1968 Winter Olympics. In her seven-year career of seniors skating, Fleming won an Olympic gold medal, three consecutive world titles, and five consecutive national titles.

The daughter of Albert and Doris Fleming, Peggy began skating at age nine after her family moved to Cleveland, Ohio, from San Jose, California. Two years later, the family moved back to California, settling in Pasadena. With her father's encouragement

to strive for excellence, Fleming began skating in earnest. She worked on both her skating and dance technique with long hours on the ice and on the dance floor. She entered her first skating competition in 1960, winning the Pacific Coast Juvenile Ladies' Championship, and proceeded up the levels of competition quickly. In 1961, she won the Pacific Coast Novice Ladies' Championship.

Fleming had been skating for just four years when her coach, Billy Kipp, was killed in a tragic airplane crash that also claimed the lives of the entire U.S. Figure Skating Team. Fleming was deeply affected by the loss of her coach and dedicated herself to honoring his memory through her hard work and determination. In 1962, she placed second in the National Novice Ladies' Championships, and a year later she won the Pacific Coast Senior Ladies' title. Although many observers predicted the decline of the U.S. figure skating program with the loss of so many great skaters, Fleming proved that the program would survive the 1961 tragedy. She nearly single-handedly brought the United States back to figure skating supremacy.

Her win at the Pacific Coast championships took Fleming back to Cleveland to compete in the national finals. At the age of 15, she captured the first of her five consecutive women's national senior championships, the youngest ever to win such a title at the time. As the nation's top woman figure skater, she represented the United States in the 1964 Olympics in Innsbruck, Austria. In her first major international competition, she finished in sixth place.

After the Olympics, Fleming went back to Pasadena to finish high school and to dedicate herself to both defending her national title and winning the world championships. She enrolled in the Hollywood Professional School in 1965, a school for students unable to attend regular school sessions, which enabled her to spend more time training. In February 1965, she successfully defended her national title, and a few weeks later won the bronze medal in the world championships held in Colorado Springs, Colorado.

Winning the bronze medal in the world championships was a great accomplishment for Fleming; yet despite her hours of practice and regimented training schedule, the high altitude and thin air of Colorado ultimately took its toll on her performance. With the 1966 worlds scheduled for Davos, Switzerland, another high-altitude town, the Flemings moved to Colorado Springs so Peggy could get accustomed to the thinner air, in addition to having access to the elaborate facilities at the Broadmoor Skating Club and the expert coaching of world-renowned figure skater Carlo Fassi.

In working with Fassi, Fleming spent hours on the ice building up her stamina and perfecting her technique, while also fine-tuning her dance and interpretative skills. Her unique combination of strength, grace, and poise showed as she took the ice in Davos. In February 1966, Fleming won the World Figure Skating Championship, the first American woman to do so in nearly a decade.

Fleming returned to Colorado, where she enrolled in Colorado College to pursue studies in dance and biology. She continued to train throughout 1967, successfully defending both her national and world titles. After nearly 20,000 hours of practice in 10 years of active competition, Fleming traveled to Grenoble, France, in 1968 as the clear-cut favorite for Olympic gold.

Stepping on the ice in the Stade de Glace to perform her free-skate program,

Fleming had already established a commanding lead in the competition. She glided across the ice to perform a program filled with inspiring and daring moves, including a spread-eagle, double-axel, spread-eagle combination that no other woman had done in international competition. Fleming won the gold medal in spectacular fashion. Her runner-up, Gabriele Seyfert of East Germany, observed: "Peggy has no weaknesses. She lands softly and everything she does is connected. It's pure ballerina."[44]

Shortly after defending her world singles title in Geneva in March 1968, Fleming announced her retirement from amateur skating. In April 1968, Fleming signed a long-term contract with NBC for an estimated $500,000. She appeared in numerous television specials, in addition to performing and starring in the Ice Follies and Holiday on Ice shows around the world.

Peggy Fleming was named the Associated Press Female Athlete of the Year in 1968 and the Woman of the Year by *Readers' Digest* in 1969. Inducted into the World Figure Skating Hall of Fame in 1976, Fleming also is a member of the U.S. Olympic Hall of Fame (1983) and the International Women's Sports Hall of Fame (1981).

She served as goodwill ambassador for UNICEF, on the President's Council on Physical Fitness, as a member of the Women's Sports Foundation advisory board, and as an Easter Seals national chair. She continues her work to actively promote the cause of women's sports in the United States.

Peggy Fleming's emergence in the early 1960s revitalized the U.S. skating program that had been decimated by a tragic plane crash over Belgium in 1961. Her success on the ice renewed the nation's interest in the graceful and powerful sport. America's ballerina on ice brought poise and dedication to her sport in capturing America's lone gold medal in the 1968 Winter Olympics. She inspired thousands of future skaters by exhibiting flawless performances that combined superior technical skill with a romantic, almost lyrical, style.

Further Reading

Morse, Charles, and Ann Morse. *Peggy Fleming*. Mankato, MN: Creative Education Society, 1974. 31 pp.

Van Steenwyk, Elizabeth. *Peggy Fleming: Cameo of a Champion*. New York: McGraw-Hill Book Co., 1978. 132 pp.

Juli Furtado (mountain bike racer)

Born April 4, 1967, New York, New York

Juli Furtado came to the new sport of mountain bike racing after retiring from an injury-shortened career as one of the United States' most promising Alpine ski racers. She is the most dominant mountain bike racer of the 1990s—a two-time world champion, a six-time U.S. World Mountain Bike Team member, a five-time Jeep Cross-Country Series national champion, and a three-time World Cup series champion. She was a member of the 1996 U.S. Olympic Cycling Team and a 1995 Pan American Games silver medalist. With her successes, she helped usher in women's mountain biking in the United States and helped advance the sport to a new level worldwide.

The daughter of Tommy Furtado and Nina Armaugh, Juliana Furtado was born in New York, New York, on April 4, 1967. She lived in New Jersey until age six, when she moved with her family to Londonderry, Vermont, at the foot of the Green Mountains. She played Little League baseball and learned to ski. In 1982, Furtado earned a spot on the U.S. National Ski Team at the age of 15. But the aggressive skiing took its toll on her knees. Over the next six years, she underwent six reconstructive surgeries to repair the damage. She made the difficult decision to retire at age 21. "I thought skiing would be my life," she told *Bicycling* magazine. "I think I was actually more gifted as a skier. I would like to know where I could have gone."[45]

In 1990, Furtado moved to Boulder, Colorado, and earned a marketing degree at the University of Colorado. Two years earlier, she had begun cycling as part of her physical therapy to rehabilitate her bad knees. In 1989, after only one year of cycling, Furtado won the U.S. National Road

Juli Furtado
Photo courtesy of GT Bicycles

Race Championship. Shortly thereafter, she switched from road racing to mountain biking and took to the dirt trails in the foothills of the Rocky Mountains.

Furtado experienced immediate and spectacular success. She won the 1990 World Mountain Bike Championship in the cross-country event. She followed her championship with a win at the National Off-Road Bicycle Association (NORBA) Championship. In 1991, she won five of six events in the Jeep Cross-Country Series (formerly the NORBA Championship) to claim the overall title, the first of her five consecutive titles (1991-1995).

With only three years of mountain biking experience, Furtado continued to improve her winning record. Her early skiing experience helped in her training, particularly in the downhill events. In 1992, she won her second world championship title when she finished ahead of the field in the downhill event at Bromont, Québec, Canada. In doing so, she became the first professional racer to win both a cross-country and a downhill championship.

In 1993, Furtado was nearly unbeatable. She won 17 out of 18 races she entered including nine of 10 events in the World Cup Series and all six in the Jeep Cross-Country Series. "Furtado's dominance forced all other competitors to get stronger to compete with her physiologically and technically," remarked fellow racer Susan DeMattei. "It's brought a lot of focus to the women's mountain biking scene."[46] *Velo News* magazine named Furtado the 1993 International Cyclist of the Year. She was the first female to receive the award.

In 1994, Furtado claimed the World Series and the Jeep Cross-Country Series Championships winning 11 of the 16 total events. The U.S. Cycling Federation selected her as 1994 Female Athlete of the Year, the first mountain biker, female or male, chosen for the prestigious award.

Furtado won a silver medal at the 1995 Pan American Games in Mar del Plata, Argentina, and then claimed her fifth consecutive Jeep Cross-Country overall title. *Velo News* selected her as 1995 Female Cyclist of the Year. She earned a spot on the 1996 U.S. Olympic Cycling team and represented the United States at the 1996 Olympic Summer Games in Atlanta. She finished 10th in the inaugural Olympic mountain biking competition.

"I'd like to be remembered as a great bike racer, she told *Bicycling* magazine, "but also a fair competitor, someone who could bring fun into it."[47] A popular champion, Juli Furtado ushered in the sport of mountain biking for women and gave it a new level of competition, visibility, and respectability. Her successes helped advance the sport for both men and women.

Althea Gibson (tennis player)

Born August 25, 1927, Silver, South Carolina

When Althea Gibson stepped onto Court 14 at the West Side Tennis Club in Forest Hills, New York, on August 28, 1950, she made tennis history by becoming the first Black person—female or male—to play in a major United States Lawn Tennis Association (USLTA) sanctioned event. Althea lost to former Wimbledon champion Louise Brough in the second round of the 1950 tournament, but became the first Black to win a Grand Slam tennis event when she captured the 1956 French Championships.

Althea Gibson
Courtesy of the International Tennis Hall of Fame

She went on to win both the Wimbledon and U.S. singles titles in 1957 and 1958. Gibson's success did not come easily. After years of training to play the major tournaments, she found the doors closed by racism. Until the 1950s, Blacks were excluded from the private country clubs where the world's best tennis players received their coaching and training, and Blacks were also barred from entry into major tournaments that, like the U.S. Championships and Wimbledon, were by invitation only. Gibson received the invitation to play in the USL-TA event only after proving herself as the number one player of the all-Black American Tennis Association (ATA). Her appearance at Forest Hills broke the color barrier in elite tennis and cleared the way for other Black competitors, both female and male, to enter world-class tennis events and other sports as well.

Born in Silver, South Carolina, the daughter of Daniel and Annie Gibson, Althea lived her first three years on a cotton farm in South Carolina where her father was a sharecropper. In 1930, during the throes of the Depression, the Gibson family moved to New York, to an apartment on West 143rd Street in Harlem. Gibson was a "mischievous" girl, roaming the streets of Harlem, skipping school, and staying out all night. She spent her time bowling or playing basketball, baseball, or paddle tennis.

Gibson played paddle tennis on one of the courts that the Police Athletic League (PAL) had set up on West 143rd Street. She excelled at the game, claiming the championship of the block. In the summer of 1941, the PAL supervisor, Buddy Walker, suggested that Gibson take up regular tennis and bought her two secondhand rackets. He took her to nearby Mount Morris Park to hit tennis balls against the wall of the handball court, and a few days later, the two went to the Harlem River Tennis Courts where Gibson played and won several matches against local male players.

Her success at the Harlem River courts led to an invitation to join the Cosmopolitan Club, New York's most prestigious Black tennis club. At the Cosmopolitan, Gibson's game developed quickly; and a year after she started lessons, she entered her first tournament, the ATA's New York State Open Championship, which she won. In 1944 and 1945, Gibson won the ATA girls' division title; and in 1946, at the age of 18, she moved from the girls' division to the women's division of ATA competition.

In her first women's division championship match, Gibson lost to Roumania Peters, but her potential caught the eye of two ATA officials interested in promoting Black tennis players. Dr. Hubert Eaton and Dr. Robert Johnson offered to help Gibson with her college education, only to find out she had dropped out of high school. They struck a deal with her that resulted in her move to Wilmington, North Carolina, to live with the Eatons. During the school year she attended high school and practiced on Eaton's private court; during the summer she lived with the Johnsons in Lynchburg, Virginia, and traveled the ATA circuit.

In 1947, Gibson won the first of her 10 consecutive women's ATA national championship titles. During 1947, she won all nine of the ATA tournaments, including eight mixed doubles titles with Johnson as her partner. She repeated this achievement in 1948. The towering right-hander intimidated and overpowered her opponents with her serve, her volleys, and her smashing overhead.

While Gibson dominated the ATA circuit, ATA officials were working to get her entered into USLTA events. Her first opportunity came in 1949 when she received an entry for the USLTA-sponsored Eastern Indoor Championships. She reached the quarterfinals in her first USLTA event, and a week later she competed in the National Indoor Championships and again reached the quarterfinals. Her fine performance assured an invitation for 1950, and in the winter of 1950 she entered both the Eastern Indoor and National Indoor Championships. This time she won the Eastern Indoor and finished second in the National Indoor.

Despite her triumphs in indoor competition, Gibson still could not get an invitation to play in the USLTA national tournament. The help she needed finally came from former champion Alice Marble, who wrote a lengthy editorial in the July 1950 issue of *American Lawn Tennis* against racial discrimination in tennis. She wrote: "If Althea Gibson represents a challenge to the present crop of women players, it's only fair that they should meet that challenge on the courts, where tennis is played. . . . If she is

refused a chance to succeed or to fail, then there is an ineradicable mark against a game to which I have devoted most of my life, and I would be bitterly ashamed."[48]

Marble's remarks shocked the tennis establishment into inviting Gibson to more USLTA events. Finally, in August 1950, Gibson received an invitation from the USLTA to play in the national championships at Forest Hills. On August 28, 1950, she defeated Barbara Knapp of England, 6-2, 6-2, in the first round of play at the 1950 U.S. Championships. In the second round, Wimbledon champion Louise Brough defeated Gibson in a hard-fought match, 6-1, 3-6, 9-7.

In 1951, Gibson became the first Black to play in the All-England Tennis Championships at the All-England Club in Wimbledon. She played on Centre Court in her first match and advanced to the quarterfinals before losing. By 1952, Gibson ranked ninth in USLTA standings.

She won the ATA championship each summer from 1951 through 1955, but for some unknown reason, her play on the USLTA tour began to decline. By 1954, her ranking had fallen to 13th. However, she went on an extended exhibition tour of Asia for the U.S. State Department in 1955, which seemed to revitalize her game.

During the 1956 season, Gibson won 16 out of 18 tournaments, winning in such places as Cannes, France; Monte Carlo, Monaco; and Florence, Italy. On May 20, 1956, Gibson won the French Championships, defeating Angela Mortimer of England, 6-3, 11-9. With the victory, she became the first Black person to win a major tennis singles title. From 13th in 1954, Gibson's ranking shot up to number two in 1956.

Despite a disappointing loss in the 1956 Wimbledon quarterfinals, Gibson remained confident of her ability to reach the top ranking in women's tennis in 1957. At the beginning of the season, she toured Australia and Asia with great success as she prepared for the 1957 All-England Championships.

The 30-year-old breezed through the early rounds of the 1957 Wimbledon, defeating Zsuzsi Kormoczy of Hungary and Christine Truman of Great Britain on her way to a finals match against Californian Darlene Hard. Gibson controlled the match from the outset, taking less than an hour to defeat Hard, 6-3, 6-2, for the Wimbledon Ladies' Singles Championship.

The new champion returned to the United States and was treated to a ticker-tape parade and received congratulations from New York Governor W. Averell Harriman and President Dwight D. Eisenhower. In an emotional homecoming to Harlem, she commented that returning home to Harlem and seeing all her neighbors who came out to greet her and tell her they were glad she had gone out into the world and done something big was more moving than meeting Queen Elizabeth.

Gibson captured her first U.S. Championship in 1957, when she defeated her earlier nemesis Louise Brough, 6-3, 6-2, in the finals of the Forest Hills tournament. In 1957, she also won the National Clay Court Championships and represented the United States on its Wightman Cup Team in the annual tournament against players from England. She became the number one ranked female tennis player in the world and the Associated Press named her the 1957 Female Athlete of the Year. In 1958, she successfully defended both her Wimbledon and U.S. titles, retained the number one ranking, and repeated as the Associated Press Female Athlete of the Year.

After winning her second U.S. title, Gibson retired from amateur competition. In the early 1960s, Gibson took up golf and set out to break another color barrier by becoming the first Black woman to hold a Ladies Professional Golf Association (LPGA) player's card. She earned her LPGA player's card in 1964 by finishing in the top 80 percent in three tournaments. Once again, she had helped pave the way for other Black athletes in a sport that had long been open only to Whites. She played seven more years before retiring from full-time touring.

Gibson began a career as a professional tennis teacher in 1971 and served as a tennis coach and mentor until she retired in 1992. In 1971, she was inducted into the International Tennis Hall of Fame, and in 1980, the International Women's Sports Hall of Fame.

From the street life in Harlem to Centre Court at Wimbledon, Althea Gibson changed tennis forever with her appearance at the 1950 U.S. Championships and her success at the Wimbledon and U.S. Championships seven years later. She removed the barrier to Black participation in top-level tennis. She was a powerful tennis player; and by her example and athletic skills, she opened doors for thousands of future athletes—Black and White, female and male.

Further Reading

Biracree, Tom. *Althea Gibson*. New York: Chelsea House Publishers, 1989. 109 pp.

Davidson, Sue. *Changing the Game: The Stories of Tennis Champions Alice Marble and Althea Gibson*. Seattle, WA: Seal Press, 1997. 160 pp.

Gibson, Althea. *I Always Wanted to Be Somebody*. New York: Harper & Brothers, 1958. 186 pp.

Gibson, Althea, and Richard Curtis. *So Much to Live For*. New York: G.P. Putnam's Sons, 1968. 160 pp.

Lucy Giovinco (bowler)

Born March 15, 1957, Tampa, Florida

One of the finest amateur bowlers in the United States, Lucy Giovinco is a six-time member of TEAM USA, the U.S. National Women's Bowling Team, and has won four gold medals and one silver medal in Federation Internationale des Quilleurs (FIQ) competitions. In an international career that spans three decades, Giovinco has remained at the top of her sport, dominating women's amateur bowling in the 1990s. She is the epitome of what it takes to be a team player in an individual sport.

Born in Tampa, Florida, to Julio and Susan Giovinco, Lucy started bowling on her sixth birthday. "Since both my parents bowled, I grew up in the bowling center and couldn't wait until my dad let me get on the lanes and roll that big bowling ball down the lane," she remembered.[49] She was active in a number of sports. In high school, she played softball and basketball, and bowled. At Tampa Catholic High School, she bowled in a weekly league and competed in tournaments against other high schools.

Giovinco enrolled in Hillsborough Community College, where she was a member of the women's bowling team in 1976. Coached by Delores Alvarez, Giovinco learned how to be a fierce competitor while maintaining focus and composure. "She inspired me to bowl competitively while still being a good person and a good sport," she recalled.[50] Giovinco won the 1976 Women's Intercollegiate All-Events title with a total score of 1,734 for nine games. She led Hillsborough Community College to the National Junior College Athletic Association (NJCAA) Team Championship in 1977, winning the all-events title at the competition.

In international competition, Giovinco won the 1976 AMF World Cup Championship in Teheran, Iran. As a member of the U.S. national team, she won three gold medals—in the women's six-player, women's five-player, and women's doubles events—at the 1977 FIQ American Zone Championships in Panama City, Panama.

Giovinco continued to bowl throughout the 1980s in local amateur competition but regained her championship form. She rejoined TEAM USA in 1990 and has dominated women's amateur bowling in the 1990s. She led the team to championships at the 1992 Africa Cup, the 1992 LPBT Team Tournament, and the 1994 World Tenpin Team Cup. In 1996, she led the team to a gold medal at the Challenge of the Hemispheres II in Sydney, Australia, a second-place finish in the Brunswick World Team Challenge Grand Championships in New Orleans, Louisiana, and second in the

Lucy Giovinco
Courtesy of Lucy Giovinco

FIQ World Tenpin Team Cup in Calgary, Alberta, Canada. In 1997, Giovinco captured two gold medals at the 12th FIQ American Zone Championships in Santo Domingo, Dominican Republic.

Giovinco's additional individual achievements include the 1991 and 1994 Women's International Bowling Congress (WIBC) Open Division Doubles Championships. She was the 1994 AMF World Cup Runner-up, falling just 22 pins short of winning her second World Cup championship. She captured the National Amateur Champion title in 1996.

Giovinco also served as USA Bowling's Athlete Advisory Council representative in 1992 and 1993, and is the United States Olympic Committee (USOC) Athlete Advisory Council representative for the sport of bowling. She works tirelessly to promote the sport of bowling in the international community with the hopes of getting bowling accepted as an Olympic sport. She was the athletes' representative during the FIQ Atlanta Bowling Challenge held in Atlanta just prior to the 1996 Centennial Games to showcase the sport to International Olympic Committee officials.

Her awards from the bowling world are numerous. She is a member of the Florida Women's Bowling Hall of Fame. She was twice named the USOC Female Athlete of the Year in Bowling (1992, 1996), and was selected the 1994 Bowling Writer's Association of America (BWAA) Amateur Bowler of the Year. In 1995, Giovinco was nominated for the Women's Sports Foundation Team Sportswoman of the Year Award.

A six-time member of the U.S. National Women's Bowling Team and a five-time medalist in FIQ competition, Lucy Giovinco is a leader on and off the lanes. In an international career that has spanned three decades, she has remained at the top of her sport, promoting it to the international community. Her consistency and longevity in the sport have made Giovinco a role model for young bowlers around the world.

Diana Golden (disabled ski racer)

Born March 20, 1963, Cambridge, Massachusetts

Diana Golden is one of the best ski racers—male or female—that the United States has ever produced. But she is known for more than her success on the ski slopes. She will undoubtedly be remembered as "the sportswoman who brought crossover credibility to the disabled-sports movement."[51] An avid skier as a youngster, Golden lost her right leg to cancer when she was 12, but that did not deter her from pursuing excellence in her favorite sport. In a decade-long ski racing career, she won 19 U.S. and 10 world disabled-skiing titles, including a gold medal in the women's disabled giant slalom, a demonstration event at the 1988 Winter Olympics in Calgary, Alberta, Canada.

Growing up in Lincoln, Massachusetts, an affluent suburb of Boston, Golden was on skis by age five. She made regular outings with her parents to their vacation home in Franconia, New Hampshire, and the nearby Cannon Mountain ski resort.

One day in 1975 when she was 12, Golden was walking through the snow on her way home from a day of skiing when her right leg collapsed beneath her. Doctors diagnosed bone cancer and determined that they had to amputate the leg above the knee to stop the spread of the disease. Of that time, she remembered: "Even before surgery, my first question was, 'Will I still be able to ski?' When the doctors said yes, I figured it wouldn't be too bad."[52]

After leaving the hospital, Golden was fitted with a prosthetic device, learned to walk again, and within seven months was back on the slopes. Regarding her skiing career, she said: "Losing a limb was not something I had to overcome. I always skied, and I intended to keep on skiing. There was never any question in my mind about that."[53]

One winter as Golden was practicing on the slopes of Cannon Mountain, Sudbury Regional High School ski-team coach David Livermore sought her out and invited her to try out for the team. She soon became one of the best skiers on the squad. With her training as part of the high school team, she soon got involved in competitive disabled racing. By the time she was 17, she had made the national U.S. Disabled Ski Team (USDST).

After graduating from high school, Golden enrolled in Dartmouth College to study literature and continue her ski racing. She raced with the nondisabled racers at Burke Mountain Academy in Vermont; and in 1982, she traveled to her first international competition, the World Handicapped Championships in Norway, where she placed first in the downhill and second in the giant slalom.

Despite her success, Golden quickly became disillusioned with the sport and the expectations put upon her as "the inspirational girl who overcame cancer," and retired from ski racing. She completed her degree in English at Dartmouth in 1984 and began selling computer software for a local company. Then one weekend she went skiing in Connecticut with a friend and was drawn to the resort's race course. The excitement and passion for racing returned as she stood in the starting gate. After a day of

Diana Golden
Courtesy of Diana Golden

racing through the slalom gates, Golden decided to rededicate herself to becoming the best ski racer in the world.

In March 1985, she rejoined the USDST. She received a scholarship from the Women's Sports Foundation to help with her training and travel expenses, and she actively wrote letters to ski companies and other sponsors asking for financial support for her return to full-time training. Rossignol Ski Company, the first ski company in the world to financially support a ski racer with a disability, agreed to sponsor Golden in her training efforts. Marker and Unex ski companies also agreed to sponsor her, and other sponsors quickly came to her side.

With the help of Rossignol and the other sponsors, and the National Handicapped Sports and Recreation Association (NHSRA), Golden returned to racing with full force. "I wanted to be recognized as a top-notch athlete, as the best in the world," she recalled.[54] Within a year, she established herself as a major presence on the ski circuit, winning four gold medals in international competition.

Always challenging herself, she quickly gave up using outriggers for ski poles (poles with small skis attached), opting for standard ski poles. To do so, she had to increase her sense of balance and strengthen her stomach, arms, and leg, which required hours of weight training.

Golden pioneered the idea that racers with disabilities should be allowed to compete on an equal basis in nondisabled events. Her initiative led, in 1985, to the passage of the United States Ski Association's (USSA) "Golden Rule," which specifies preferential seeding of disabled skiers in sanctioned USSA races. Under the Golden Rule, places are reserved at the end of the top seed—after the first 15 racers—for the top disabled skiers (based on international rankings) so that they can race on the course before it becomes too rough from overuse. The USDST, which, until the rule was adopted, had just encouraged its athletes to participate in USSA-sanctioned races, now requires its racers to ski in at least five nondisabled races a year.

In 1987, Golden finished 10th in a USSA midseries race, where all 39 of her competitors had two legs and no handicaps. The same year, she was ranked the 10th-best three-track skier in the world—men and women combined. "Diana went into territory where no one had been before," said USDST assistant head-coach Jennifer Kennedy. "It just isn't possible to be as good on one leg as the best in the world on two. But Diana asked herself, How good can I be? How far can I go?"[55] And by her example, she made other skiers with disabilities ask the same questions of themselves.

Golden was rewarded for her athletic success. In 1986, she won the USSA Beck Award, given to the best U.S. racer in international skiing. *Ski Racing* magazine named her the 1988 U.S. Female Alpine Skier of the Year, and the same year the United States Olympic Committee named her the Female Skier of the Year over all other racers.

At the 1990 world championships in Winter Park, Colorado, Golden won three golds, putting an exclamation mark and finishing touch on an outstanding ski racing career. During one downhill race, she was clocked skiing at nearly 65 miles per hour—on one ski with standard ski poles.

Golden retired from ski racing competition after the 1990 worlds but continues to work with the USDST and the NHSRA in promoting sports for people with disabilities. She spearheaded efforts for other disabled athletes, working to attract sponsors for USDST training centers across the country. Affiliated with the Professional Ski Instructors of America Demonstration Team, she said, "I'd like to bring credibility to disabled skiers as instructors—not just as teachers of other disabled people, but of anyone."[56] She also worked with the NHSRA in their campaign to recruit more disabled girls and women into sports. In 1991, the Women's Sports Foundation awarded Golden the prestigious Flo Hyman award, presented to an athlete who exhibits "dignity, spirit, and commitment to excellence."

The increased acceptance of disabled skiing in the world of sports was spurred in part by Diana Golden's exemplary career. She was among the first athletes to persuade sponsors and the public to accept athletes with disabilities as *athletes*; and since her retirement from ski racing in 1990, she has worked tirelessly to promote sports for people with disabilities in the United States. She inspired hundreds of athletes with disabilities to become involved in competitive sports.

Michelle Gould (racquetball player)

Born December 22, 1970, Ontario, Oregon

Michelle Gould is the most accomplished player in the history of racquetball. She has won 37 national, 50 international, and 42 professional titles. She is an eight-time American Amateur Racquetball Association (AARA) Athlete of the Year (1989-96), and a six-time Sullivan Award Athlete of the Year nominee.

Born on December 22, 1970, the daughter of Larry and Brenda Gilman, Gould began playing racquetball in 1980. Her parents gave her a membership to a health and racquetball club for her 10th birthday. "I was awful," Gould said. "I spent hour upon hour upon hour in the court. I just wanted to be as good as my brother John and at least get some credit in that regard."[57]

By the time she turned 12, she was nationally ranked. At 14, she became the youngest-ever player named to the U.S. National Racquetball Team. Before she turned 15, Gould had accumulated four regional championships, three international titles, and one national crown. Between 1986 and 1989, Gould won four AARA junior national titles, two Olympic Festival gold medals, and seven International Racquetball Federation (IRF) gold medals. In 1990, she won the AARA U.S. national singles, doubles, and mixed doubles crowns; IRF Tournament of the Americas gold medals in the individual and women's team events; a U.S. Olympic Festival gold medal in the women's singles event; and a gold at the IRF World Championships. "I won everything that I could have possibly won in one year," she told *Olympian* magazine.[58]

Gould also won her first professional title, the Women's Professional Racquet-ball Association's (WPRA) National Championship, in 1990. This title was the first of six consecutive WPRA National Championships. She has been ranked number one on the women's professional tour every year since 1990 and has been the player of the year four times (1991, 1993, 1995, 1996).

Gould's style of play is aggressive, relentless, and powerful. With a serve that has been clocked at over 150 miles per hour, she dominates her opponents. In 1995, Gould won the singles competition at the AARA U.S. Nationals, Pan American Games, and three other WPRA tour events. In the 1995-96 season, Gould won every Women's International Racquetball Tour-

Michelle Gould
Courtesy of the Women's International Racquetball Tour

nament (WIRT) event of the season (nine). During her incredible undefeated season, her games record was 105-4 and her winning percentage was over 96 percent. She ended the season with the top ranking and was awarded the most valuable player honors on the WPRA tour.

Considered the best racquetball player in the history of the sport, Michelle Gould has won more national, international, and professional tournaments than any other player. She was a three-time finalist as the Women's Sports Foundation Sportswoman of the Year, and is a member of the United States Racquetball Association (USRA) Hall of Fame. Her success brought recognition to the sport on a national and international level and has opened up more amateur and professional opportunities for women in the sport.

Steffi Graf (tennis player)

Born June 14, 1969, Mannheim, West Germany

On October 1, 1988, 19-year-old Steffi Graf stepped up onto the winner's podium in Seoul, South Korea, to accept her Olympic gold medal for tennis. Winning the gold medal capped one of the most extraordinary years for a player in the history of women's tennis. In 1988, Graf won 72 out of the 75 matches she played and became only the third woman in tennis history to win the Grand Slam—the Australian Open, the French Open, Wimbledon, and the U.S. Open women's singles championships—in a calendar year. Graf began her professional career at age 13. Six years later, she claimed the number one ranking in the world, and she reigned as the number one ranked player for a record 186 weeks consecutively (August 17, 1987-March 10, 1991), more than any man or woman. To gain the top ranking, Graf dethroned the reigning queens of tennis, Chris Evert and Martina Navratilova, signaling a "passing of the torch" in women's tennis. Graf's powerful forehand, overwhelming serves, and blazing quickness, combined with her unwavering dedication to be the best, propelled her to the "Golden Grand Slam."

Stephanie Maria Graf was born in Mannheim, West Germany, on June 14, 1969, the daughter of Peter and Heidi Graf. Steffi's parents were avid tennis players and often worked with children at the local club. At four years old, Steffi begged her father to teach her how to play, and so Peter sawed off an old racket so that she could hold it in her little hands. Father and daughter played in the house, over a string stretched between two chairs in the living room. They played on their makeshift court every day, until Steffi started breaking lamps from hitting the ball so hard.

Steffi Graf
© Allsport USA/Gary M. Prior

At age five, Graf graduated to real tennis courts. She started playing against kids her own age and some even older. She won her first tennis tournament when she was six, a junior event in Munich. She took lessons at the local club and with the German Tennis Federation program in Liemen. When Graf was eight, her father sold his business and moved the family to Bruhl, where he opened the Graf Tennis Club. It was there that he began coaching Graf on a full-time basis. Her father has been her only coach.

Graf won her age-group championship in West Germany when she was eight, and after that, won her age group championship every year until she was 12. She won the German 14-and-unders *and* the 18-and-unders in 1981. In the fall of 1982, at the age of 13 years, 4 months, Steffi turned professional. Within weeks of joining the international women's tour, she became the second-youngest player to be given a computer ranking—number 124—by the Women's Tennis Association (WTA).

In her first two years on tour, the teenager had a tough time in the major events, making it through the early rounds in only a few tournaments. In 1984, Graf traveled to Los Angeles to represent West Germany in Olympic tennis competition. Tennis had been reinstated as a demonstration sport, but the competition was only open to players age 21 and under. At age 15, Graf was the youngest of the 32 players participating in the event. She defeated Sabrina Goles of Yugoslavia in the finals to win her first international tournament and an honorary gold medal.

In 1985, Graf began to make her presence felt in women's tennis. She started the year ranked 22nd in the world; and although she did not win a major tournament in 1985, her computer ranking inched up steadily. By the end of 1985, she was ranked

sixth in the world. In April 1986, Graf defeated Chris Evert in the *Family Circle* Magazine Cup in Hilton Head, South Carolina, to claim her first major tournament victory as a professional. In 1986, she won 8 of the 14 tournaments she had entered and came in second in 3 more. She finished third in the 1986 computer rankings.

Returning to the women's tour in February 1987, Graf won the Virginia Slims tournament in Boca Raton, Florida, and a week later defeated Evert, then Navratilova, in back-to-back victories to capture the Lipton Players International Championships in Key Biscayne, Florida. Graf won her first Grand Slam tournament in 1987, when she defeated Navratilova, 6-4, 4-6, 8-6, in the 1987 French Open. Navratilova returned the favor at both Wimbledon and the U.S. Open later that year. Those were the only two losses for Graf in a remarkable year in which she won 11 of the 13 tournaments she entered and jumped firmly into the number one ranking.

As incredible as 1987 was, Graf had an even better year in 1988. She defeated Evert, 6-1, 7-6, in the Australian Open in Melbourne in January; handily defeated Soviet Natalia Zvereva, 6-0, 6-0, in the French Open finals; won a hard-fought victory over Navratilova, 5-7, 6-2, 6-1, at the All-England Championships at Wimbledon; and outlasted Argentine teenager Gabriela Sabatini, 6-3, 3-6, 6-1, in the finals of the U.S. Open to take the women's title and the Grand Slam of tennis.

Within a few days of her last Grand Slam victory, Graf was whisked off to Seoul, South Korea, where she competed in the 1988 Olympic Games and won the gold for West Germany, rounding out her remarkable "Golden Grand Slam."

Graf remained the number one player in the world until March 1991, when she dropped to the number two slot behind

Monica Seles;. she has traded the number one ranking with Arantxa Sanchez Vicario, Monica Seles, and Martina Hingis through 1997. Graf defended three of her four Grand Slam titles in 1989, losing only the French Open title to Spain's Arantxa Sanchez Vicario. In 1990, Graf won 10 tournaments, including repeating as Australian Open winner; was a finalist in the French, U.S., and German Opens; and a Wimbledon semifinalist. The following year she won her third Wimbledon singles title; and on October 3, 1991, she became the youngest female tennis player to amass more than 500 victories—at the ripe old age of 22 years, 3 months. She also won 10 singles titles in 1993, nine in 1995, and seven in 1996. Throughout her career, she has won 102 singles titles, including 21 Grand Slam titles.

The Associated Press named Graf the 1989 Female Athlete of the Year and the Women's Sports Foundation selected her as the Professional Sportswoman of the Year. She was the Women's Tennis Association (WTA) Player of the Year for 1987-90 and 1993-95, UPI International Athlete of the Year in 1987 and 1989, and *Tennis* magazine named her Player of the Year in 1995 and 1996.

Combined with her pure athletic ability, Graf's sincere love of the game is what made her a champion. When not competing, she practices hours every day. Her intimidating topspin forehand is widely considered to be the best in the history of women's tennis. She has developed an all-court game and has had success on every surface; she won the Grand Slam on four different surfaces: rubberized hardcourt in Australia, slow red clay in France, fast grass in England, and hard DecoTurf in the United States.

Steffi Graf became the standard-bearer for women's tennis in the 1990s. Stronger, taller, and faster than any of her predecessors, Graf dominates her opponents with overpowering ground strokes, overheads, and serves. With her all-court game, she has elevated the women's game to yet another level.

Further Reading

Heady, Sue. *Steffi: Public Power, Private Pain.* London: Virgin Books, 1996. 256 pp.

Hilgers, Laura. *Steffi Graf.* New York: The Time Inc. Magazine Company, 1990. 124 pp.

Knapp, Ron. *Sports Great Steffi Graf.* Springfield, NJ: Enslow, 1995. 64 pp.

Monroe, Judy. *Steffi Graf.* Mankato, MN: Crestwood House, 1988. 48 pp.

Janet Guthrie (auto racer)
Born March 7, 1938, Iowa City, Iowa

On May 29, 1977, the owner of the Indianapolis Motor Speedway made his historic call to the competitors: "In company with the first lady ever to qualify at Indianapolis—gentlemen, start your engines." Janet Guthrie had broken the gender barrier in championship auto racing, becoming the first woman to qualify for and race in the Indianapolis 500, auto racing's premier event. She was a pioneer in auto racing, working her way through the ranks to gain national recognition on several levels. Her road to Indianapolis was not an easy one. The male-dominated auto racing establishment was reluctant to open its doors to a woman, yet only through her intelligence, tenacity, and dedication did Guthrie achieve what no woman had ever achieved—suc-

Janet Guthrie
Courtesy of Janet Guthrie

cessfully competing against male drivers to qualify for and finish in the top 10 of an Indianapolis 500.

Janet is the oldest daughter of W. Lain and Jean Ruth Guthrie. Born in Iowa City, Iowa, Janet moved with her family to Miami when her father took a job as an Eastern Airlines pilot. She attended Miss Harris's Florida School, a private girls' prep school in Miami. Her adventurous spirit surfaced at a young age; flying became her passion. She flew her first plane at 13, soloed at 16, made her first parachute jump at 16, and had earned her pilot's license by age 17.

After graduating from high school, Guthrie enrolled in the University of Michigan, where she earned a degree in physics in 1960. For the next seven years, she worked as an aerospace engineer in Long Island, New York. During that time, she

passed the National Aeronautics and Space Administration's (NASA) first tests for its new scientist-astronaut program. She was one of only four women to pass the tests. But she lacked the necessary Ph.D. degree to qualify for further participation in the program.

In 1960, Guthrie bought her first sports car, a used Jaguar XK 120, a beautiful car she had admired since she was a teenager. To test the car's performance, she joined a local car club and entered several of its gymkhana competitions—low-speed, precision-driving events on zigzag courses. In her first season of competition, she garnered trophies in most of the events she entered.

The challenge of reaching high speeds combined with driving performance intrigued Guthrie so much that she enrolled in a driving school in Connecticut. In 1962, she bought a used Jaguar XK 140, taught herself the mechanics of the car, then rebuilt it herself for racing.

With her Jaguar XK 140, Guthrie entered several races in 1964, including the six-hour, 500-mile Watkins Glen (New York) race, where she finished second in her class and sixth overall. She finished the year with a victory in a Long Island Sports Car Association race, placing second in two more.

For the next seven years, Guthrie raced several different cars, moving from one level of racing to another. In 1967, she quit her job to concentrate on auto racing full-time. That same year, Guthrie finished second in her class at the 12-hour Sebring race, and the following year she won the Governor of Florida's Award at Sebring. By 1971, she had logged nine straight finishes in the nation's top endurance events.

Guthrie established an outstanding record and was eager to move to the top levels of professional racing. But the male racing establishment was reluctant to let her in. She searched for sponsors and owners with cars for her to race, but few were willing to accept a woman driver.

In late 1971, Guthrie decided that there was only one way out of her dilemma—to build her own race car. She bought a Toyota Celica, took it apart bit-by-bit and began to rebuild the car to race in the 1972 Toyota 2.5 Challenge Series racing program. It took a year to rebuild the car, and by the time she was finished, the Sports Car Club of America (SCCA) had cancelled the series. Despite this enormous setback, Guthrie stuck with the sport, and for the next three years she worked part-time and raced her Toyota in amateur events while looking for that ever-elusive sponsor. She won the North Atlantic Road Racing Championship in 1973, but by the end of 1975, she was deep in debt, and the Celica was obsolete.

Then, finally, her persistence and dedication paid off.

In 1976, car designer and builder Rolla Vollstedt offered Guthrie one of his cars to race in the Indianapolis 500. She secretly tested the car at the Ontario (California) Motor Speedway, reaching a top average speed of more than 172 miles per hour. At Indianapolis that year she passed the rookie test with a top speed of 171.429, but mechanical problems forced the withdrawal of the Vollstedt machine. On the last day of qualifying, A.J. Foyt let Guthrie take his backup car out in practice. She easily surpassed 181 mph, the speed necessary to qualify, but Foyt declined her further use of his machine.

Disappointed yet undeterred, Guthrie became the first woman ever to race in a National Association for Stock Car Auto Racing (NASCAR) Winston Cup event when, instead of competing in Indianapolis on Memorial Day of 1976, she raced in the Charlotte World 600, finishing 15th after starting in 27th place. She drove the entire 600 miles without a relief driver. She drove in four other NASCAR events in 1976, as well as four United States Auto Club (USAC) races in Rolla Vollstedt's Indy car.

In 1977, Vollstedt offered Guthrie a newer, faster car for Indianapolis. Averaging 188.403 miles per hour in the time trials, Guthrie became the first woman to qualify for the Indianapolis 500. Although her engine broke down after only 27 laps, Guthrie had made history.

She also competed for Rookie of the Year in NASCAR in 1977, taking the top rookie position at the Daytona 500 and in four other races. In Vollstedt's car, she competed in USAC's other two 500-mile races, running as high as 8th at Ontario. Cale Yarborough, the reigning NASCAR champion, said: "There is no question about her ability to race with us. She has made it in what is the most competitive racing circuit in the world."[59]

Over the winter of 1977-78, she sought access to better equipment for Indianapolis. Just one month before the 1978 race, Texaco agreed to sponsor her. Guthrie formed her own team and qualified for the race in 15th place, with a four-lap average of 190.325. Two days before the race, she fractured her right wrist—a mishap that she zealously concealed. More than 400,000 fans saw Guthrie drive an intelligent, well-planned race, finish ninth, and become the first woman to complete the Indianapolis 500, defeating some of the world's best drivers in the process.

Guthrie's 1978 Indianapolis 500 driver's suit and helmet are in the Smithsonian Institution in Washington, DC. She is a member of the International Women's Sports Hall of Fame.

During her racing career, Janet Guthrie faced many triumphs, yet through her many disappointments and setbacks her desire and determination to succeed kept her on the road to Indianapolis. The male racing establishment fought to keep her off the track, but her record behind the wheel was indisputable. As one of the top 10 racers at the 1978 Indianapolis 500, Guthrie quieted the skeptics who believed that women didn't have the physical or mental strength to handle the fast cars. By breaking another myth about women's abilities, Guthrie had a profound impact on future generations of sportswomen in the United States.

Further Reading

Fox, Mary Virginia. *Janet Guthrie: Foot to the Floor.* Minneapolis, MN: Dillon Press, 1981. 46 pp.

Hahn, James, and Lynn Hahn. *Janet Guthrie: Champion Racer.* St. Paul, MN: EMC Corp., 1978. 40 pp.

Olney, Ross R. *Janet Guthrie, First Woman to Race at Indy.* New York: Harvey House, 1978. 54 pp.

Robison, Nancy. *Janet Guthrie: Race Car Driver.* Chicago: Children's Press, 1979. 44 pp.

Dorothy Hamill (figure skater)

Born July 26, 1956, Riverside, Connecticut

America knew little about its reigning figure skating queen when Dorothy Hamill went to Innsbruck, Austria, to compete in the 1976 Winter Olympics. Although she had won three straight U.S. national seniors titles, Hamill was not considered a favorite to win the gold medal because she had been the runner-up two years in a row at the world championships. But after she scored two perfect 6.0s in the two-minute short program and went into the final part of the competition leading the field in the 1976 Olympic figure skating competition, the media began to take notice. Hamill went on to win Olympic gold and followed it with a world title just one month later. Her bubbly personality and approachable manner endeared her to the media and the public. She became a symbol of athletic success for thousands of young girls in America in a sport that combined power, athleticism, and grace of movement.

Born in Riverside, Connecticut, the daughter of Chalmers and Carol Hamill, Dorothy began skating after receiving a pair of skates for Christmas when she was eight years old. She skated on the local pond that first winter and quickly mastered forward skating. But Hamill had trouble skating in reverse so she asked her mother for lessons so she could learn to skate backward. Her first coach was former national ladies' singles champion, Sonya (Klopfer) Dunfield. Hamill worked with Coach Dun-

Dorothy Hamill
Courtesy of the World Figure Skating Museum

field for the next three years, and at age 12, Hamill won the U.S. National Ladies' Novice Singles Championship.

The dedication and self-discipline required for achieving world-class level in skating led Hamill to leave school at age 14 to devote more time to training. She was privately tutored until she obtained her high school diploma. While training with Gustave Lussi in Lake Placid, New York, the 14-year-old invented the famous "Hamill camel" move, a spiral spin to a sit spin. In 1970, Hamill won the Eastern Junior Ladies' Singles title and placed second in the national competition.

Hamill's lightning-quick development caught the attention of famous skating coach Carlo Fassi, who had coached Peggy Flem-

ing to a gold medal in the 1968 Olympics. He invited Hamill to Colorado to train. She moved to Denver to work with Fassi, often training seven hours a day, six days a week under Fassi's watchful eye. Fassi helped Hamill with her compulsory figures and brought in former Olympic gold medalist Bob Paul to help choreograph her short and long programs.

In 1973, Hamill finished fourth in the world championships, and in February 1974, she won her first of three U.S. National senior titles. At the 1974 world championships in Munich, West Germany, Hamill skated to a silver medal behind one of her rivals, Christine Errath of East Germany. The following year, she defended her U.S. title but again was runner-up in the worlds, this time to Dutch skater Dianne de Leeuw.

Because of these losses, Hamill was not favored to win the gold medal in the 1976 Innsbruck Olympics. However, she took an early lead in the compulsory figures and the following day skated a brilliant short program that garnered her a perfect 6.0 score for both technical merit and artistic expression. The final part of the skating competition, the free-skating program, proved to be just as flawless. With millions watching on television and a supportive crowd in the arena, Hamill executed another dazzling performance in her finely choreographed program filled with jumps and spins. Her array of 5.9 (out of a possible 6.0) scores earned her the gold medal.

After the Olympics, Hamill went to Göteborg, Sweden, in early March 1976 to compete in the world championships. Her momentum and confidence from the Olympic victory carried her through the world competition, where she won both the compulsories and the free-skate to become the first U.S. world figure skating titleholder since Peggy Fleming in 1968.

The Olympic and world champion returned to the United States a popular hero. Upon her return, Hamill retired from amateur competition, signing contracts for television commercials, endorsements, and a two-year deal to tour with the Ice Capades. She also competed in and won the women's NutraSweet Professional World Title in 1986 and 1987. Hamill became a member of the U.S. Olympic Hall of Fame and the U.S. Figure Skating Hall of Fame in 1991.

Hamill's quick rise to athletic excellence and her ensuing popularity with the nation's media had a far-reaching effect on women's skating in the United States. Thousands of young girls cut their hair in the wedge style that Hamill favored and signed up for ice skating lessons hoping to emulate the skating champion. Her performance contracts introduced her and her sport to millions of fans, who learned to appreciate not only her gracious manner but also her athletic ability. With one Olympic medal, one world title, and three national titles, Dorothy Hamill did not dominate the sport like her predecessors, Tenley Albright, Carol Heiss, and Peggy Fleming. Yet in the mid-1970s, when doors were just beginning to open for women in sports, Hamill was one of the many female athletes who came to symbolize athletic excellence to America's youth, helping to spur more young women into sports in America.

Further Reading

Burchard, Sue H. *Sports Star, Dorothy Hamill.* New York: Harcourt Brace Jovanovich, 1978. 63 pp.

Dolan, Edward F., Jr., and Richard B. Lyttle. *Dorothy Hamill, Olympic Skating Champion.* Garden City, NY: Doubleday & Co., 1979. 95 pp.

Hamill, Dorothy, with Elva Clairmont. *Dorothy Hamill, On and Off the Ice.* New York: Alfred A. Knopf, 1983. 189 pp.

Schmitz, Dorothy Childers. *Dorothy Hamill, Skate to Victory.* Mankato, MN: Crestwood House, 1977. 47 pp.

Smith, Miranda A. *Dorothy Hamill.* Mankato, MN: Creative Education Society, 1977. 31 pp.

Alison Hargreaves (mountain climber)

Born February 17, 1962, Derbyshire, England; died August 13, 1995

"It is better to have lived one day as a tiger than a thousand years as a sheep." Alison Hargreaves lived her life by these words of her favorite Tibetan saying. Considered by many to be the finest woman alpinist in history, Hargreaves firmly established herself as an elite mountain climber before her untimely death in 1995. She became the first person—man or woman—ever to solo the six classic north faces of the Alps in one season, and the second to climb Mount Everest unassisted by supplementary oxygen or partners. She was one of the top mountain climbers in the world.

Born in rural Derbyshire, England, the daughter of John and Joyce Hargreaves, Alison often went on hiking expeditions as a youngster. She began climbing at age 13. At age 18, she left school and home and moved in with fellow climber and future husband, Jim Ballard. Climbing became her passion and her career. In 1988, she scaled the treacherous north face of Switzerland's Eiger while six months pregnant, becoming the first British woman to ascend the north wall of the Eiger. "I think I was being quite conservative. I had planned a trip up Denali (Mount McKinley), but my physician said it wouldn't be wise to go above 12,000 [feet above sea level], so I went to the Alps instead,"[60] Hargreaves said about her controversial climb.

In 1993, Hargreaves became the first person to scale the six classic north faces of the Alps—the Eiger, Matterhorn, Grandes Jorasses, Dru, Badille, and Cima Grande—in one season. In May 1995, Hargreaves became the first woman—and only the second human being—ever to reach the 29,028-foot summit of Mount Everest, the world's highest peak, alone and without oxygen tanks. "I was on the summit for 40 minutes," she told reporters. "It was the best moment in my life."[61]

Hargreaves died on August 13, 1995, after ascending the summit of Karakoram 2 (K2) in Pakistan. She was climbing K2, a more difficult climb than Everest, in an attempt to scale her second of the three highest peaks in the world—Mount Everest, K2, and Kanchenjunga—without supplemental oxygen. She and six others were struck down on their descent by hurricane-force winds, subzero temperatures, and an avalanche that left them stranded. Hargreaves was 33 and is survived by her husband and two children.

Lydia Brady, the only other woman to have reached the summit of Everest without oxygen, summed up Hargreaves's career when she told *Women's Sports and Fitness*, "Alison made great strides in alpinism, breaking barriers and setting new standards for women as well as men. Not only did she establish herself as a barometer for female alpinists, but she proved herself equal to, or better than, contemporary male alpinists—and on her own terms."[62]

Carol Heiss (figure skater)

Born January 20, 1940, New York, New York

At age 13, Carol Heiss went to Davos, Switzerland, to compete in the 1953 World Figure Skating Championships. She finished fourth in the competition but established herself as a formidable presence in the figure skating world. For the next four years, Heiss competed against rival Tenley Albright for U.S. and world skating titles, finishing second in nearly all major competitions. In 1956, Heiss finally broke through by defeating Albright to win the first of her five consecutive world championships. She also won four U.S. titles in the late 1950s. At 19, Heiss ranked as the top women's figure skater in the world. Her youth and unbridled enthusiasm helped her through a tough training regimen, numerous second-place finishes, and personal tragedy. The teenager was world champion longer than anyone but Sonja Henie and earned more international titles than any other North American woman in skating history.

The eldest daughter of German immigrants Edward and Marie Heiss, Carol was born in New York City in 1940. When she was four, she received a pair of roller skates and started skating in the basement of her New York home. She did so well with the roller skates that her parents thought she should try ice skating as well. Heiss and her mother took the subway to the Brooklyn Ice Palace for her skating practice. The entertainer in Heiss surfaced when, at age six, she made her first public appearance in an amateur ice show.

In 1948, Heiss began taking private lessons from former Olympic and world champions Pierre and Andrée Brunet. For the next three years, she practiced her figures and free-skating for five to eight hours a day. Her family made many sacrifices to finance her training sessions. "My parents were never well off financially," she recalled. "My training was expensive with skates, costumes, and rink fees. . . . Without their help, understanding, and encouragement I never could have gotten started."[63]

The sacrifices and training paid off when Heiss won her first championship in 1951, the National Ladies' Novice Singles title, and the following year progressed to the next level, winning the National Ladies' Junior Singles title. The 13-year-old earned a spot on the world team and traveled to the world championships, where she finished fourth.

Heiss met with an unfortunate accident in 1954, when she collided with her sister during a practice session. Her sister's skate severed the tendon below the calf on her left leg. The career-threatening injury sidelined Heiss for a few months, but she returned to competitive skating within the year, placing second to Albright in the 1955 World Ladies' Singles Championships in Vienna, Austria. In a three-year period (1953-55), the two U.S. skaters met in competition six times; Heiss finished second to Albright in every event.

In 1956, Heiss went to Cortina d'Ampezzo, Italy, to participate in her first Winter Olympics. The youngest girl ever to skate for the United States at that time, Heiss gained valuable experience in winning the silver medal, finishing second in world-class competition for the last time. Two weeks after the Olympics, Heiss met Albright one more time in the world championships in Garmisch-Partenkirchen, West Germany. Heiss finally outscored Albright in the compulsory skating program and finished the competition scoring 5.9s (out of a perfect 6.0) from all nine judges to win her first world title.

Carol Heiss
Courtesy of the World Figure Skating Museum

After her breakthrough against Albright, Heiss won four straight U.S. National Ladies' Singles titles (1957-60), two North American crowns (1958 and 1959), and five consecutive world titles (1956-1960). With this record, Heiss became the favorite to win the gold at the 1960 Squaw Valley Olympics. The crowd favorite, Heiss earned first-place votes from all nine judges to easily win the women's figure skating title.

Recognized for her achievements, Heiss was inducted into the World Figure Skating Hall of Fame in 1976 and the International Women's Sports Hall of Fame in 1992.

Heiss retired from amateur competition shortly after the 1960 Olympics. She continues to be active in the sport, teaching and coaching future world stars and working as a television commentator at skating events.

Carol Heiss was the top women's figure skater in the world for the last half of the

1950s, and her tenacity and dedication to reach Olympic gold played an important role in setting a positive example for young skaters—U.S. skaters like Peggy Fleming and Dorothy Hamill—who would dream of U.S., world, and Olympic titles of their own.

Further Reading

Parker, Robert. *Carol Heiss, Olympic Queen.* Garden City, NY: Doubleday & Co., 1961. 128 pp.

Sonja Henie (figure skater)

Born April 8, 1912, Oslo, Norway; died October 12, 1969

One of the true pioneers in women's sports, Sonja Henie made her first appearance on the international figure skating scene at the Olympics at Chamonix, France, in 1924. Just 11 years old at the time, Henie finished last in the competition, but her display of agility and strength left a lasting impression on the spectators and the skating world. Henie revolutionized competitive figure skating by incorporating a wide variety of spins, jumps, and turns within a well-choreographed, complete program. Her technical skill and artistic impression set the standard in women's figure skating as she won 10 straight world titles and three consecutive Olympic gold medals. Upon retiring from amateur competition, Henie toured the world with her ice shows and established a movie career unparalleled for the time. She was enormously popular, attracting huge crowds and inspiring thousands of women to take up the sport of figure skating.

Born in Oslo, Norway, on April 8, 1912, Sonja was the daughter of Hans Wilhelm and Selma Henie. Her father encouraged both his children to become active in the winter sports of Oslo. At age five, Henie received her first pair of skates and followed her older brother Leif to the local outdoor skating rink. With informal lessons from the skating regulars, Henie quickly mastered the basics, showing the balance, agility, and grace she had developed through earlier ballet and dance lessons. Within two years, Henie won the children's figure skating championship of Oslo, and a year later the nine-year-old captured the Junior Class C national title.

The young skater began to take private skating lessons to develop her skills and continued with her dance lessons to better her free-skating performances. In 1923, 10-year-old Sonja won the national figure skat-

Sonja Henie
Courtesy of the World Figure Skating Museum

ing championship of Norway. Early the next year, she entered the first Winter Olympics at Chamonix, France. Although she finished last, her free-skating wowed the judges, who placed her third in that portion of the event.

Henie maintained an intensive training schedule over the next three years. During that time, she began to introduce choreography as a part of her free-skating program, something the other competitive skaters had not yet tried. She wanted to achieve a graceful, total effect in her performances, instead of a series of difficult yet disconnected technical moves, which was the norm. In 1927, Henie took her innovative program of spins, jumps, and dance to the world championships, and at age 15, she won the first of 10 consecutive figure skating titles (1927-36).

She won the ladies' figure skating gold medal at the 1928 Olympics in St. Moritz, Switzerland. As Olympic gold medalist and world champion, Henie made her first visit to the United States in 1929 on an exhibition tour that took her across the country. The trip ended with a victory at the 1930 world championships held in New York City.

Her popularity soared around the world as a result of her skating exhibitions that introduced her to new audiences in this pretelevision era. When she returned to the United States in 1932 and successfully defended her title in the Lake Placid Winter Games, she received rave reviews and offers for thousands of dollars to give up amateur skating and turn professional.

By 1936, Henie was so popular that police were needed to control the crowds wherever she performed. She traveled to Garmisch-Partenkirchen, West Germany, to compete in her fourth Olympics. She defeated Cecilia Colledge of Great Britain for her third gold medal and a week later captured her 10th world title in Paris. Announcing her retirement from competition, Henie signed a contract to make a series of professional exhibition appearances in the United States.

Her tour consisted of 17 performances in nine cities. One of the stops was Los Angeles, where she attracted the attention of movie studio executive Darryl F. Zanuck, who signed Henie to a five-year film contract for a series of skating films. Between 1936 and 1939, Henie made six films for 20th Century Fox. Her first, *One in a Million,* released during the 1936 Christmas season, was a huge box-office success. She followed with *Thin Ice* (1937), *Happy Landing* and *My Lucky Star* (1938), and *Second Fiddle* and *Everything Happens at Night* (1939). By 1939, she ranked only behind Clark Gable and Shirley Temple in box-office popularity.

In 1940, Henie began the first tour of her *Hollywood Ice Revue,* which featured the ballet *Les Sylphides* on ice. She played to sold-out crowds around the country as her movie fans flocked to see her skate. The success of the show led Henie to establish the Center Theatre in New York City as a year-round home for the ice revues; and although she did not appear there, she provided financial and advisory support to bring the ice skating shows to the public.

Her movie career continued with the enormously popular *Sun Valley Serenade* (1941) and *Wintertime* and *Iceland* (1942). During World War II, Henie made an eight-week tour of U.S. army hospitals in Europe as a USO entertainer. She became a U.S. citizen in 1941; and after two failed marriages, she wed her childhood sweetheart, Norwegian shipowner Niels Onstad, in 1956. At the time of her death of leukemia at the age of 57, Henie had amassed more than $47 million from her films and ice shows.

During her competitive career, Henie accumulated 1,473 cups, medals, and trophies for figure skating, but skating was not her only talent. An all-around athlete, Henie also won Norwegian championships in tennis and skiing, and excelled in running, swimming, horseback riding, and auto racing.

Henie combined her athletic skill with her creative talent to revolutionize the sport of figure skating. It was her fusion of dance and skating that had the most profound effect on the development of figure skating. Going beyond the technical routine to add style and grace, Henie gave the sport life and made it entertaining to watch.

Sonja Henie will be remembered for her success as a professional skater and for the impact she had on popularizing the sport for the masses. At the height of the economic Depression, Henie's movies and ice revues provided entertainment for thousands of people searching for relief from the tensions of the time. Her influence was far-reaching during the 1930s. Artificial ice rinks sprung up everywhere as young skaters flocked to the arenas to try the twists, turns, and spins they watched her perform.

Further Reading

Henie, Sonja. *Wings on My Feet*. New York: Prentice-Hall, 1940. 184 pp.

Lynn Hill (rock climber)

Born January 3, 1961, Detroit, Michigan

"Achievement is not about what you've *done,* but what you've gained from your experience,"[64] Lynn Hill told *Women Sports and Fitness* in 1997. But what Hill has done is to define rock climbing for women, and she is credited with helping to guide the sport into mainstream public acceptance. Hill's climbing achievements—from being the first female to climb the grade of 5.14 (a very difficult climb) to being the first person, male or female, to free climb the 3,000-foot Nose of El Capitán in Yosemite in a single day—set the women's standard for extreme rock climbing routes and opened many doors, professional and recreational, for women in rock climbing

Born on January 3, 1961, in Detroit, Michigan, Lynn moved with her family to Fullerton, California, where she grew up. "I was extremely active when I was young," she said. "I climbed trees. I climbed light poles. I just liked climbing."[65] Hill competed in swimming, gymnastics, and track and field in high school, but it was rock climbing that captured her attention.

Hill began rock climbing at age 14 after traveling to Joshua Tree National Monument in California on a climbing trip with her sister. She was drawn to the sport immediately. "I remember the light hitting the granite, the colors on the rock's face, and thinking what a privilege it was to be climbing and not in school like the other kids my age. I didn't know then that I'd be a climber for the rest of my life, but I realized right away that it was a bonus that somehow made me different."[66]

She quickly progressed to tougher and tougher climbs and soon was free climbing 5.10, which at the time was at the top of the grade scale. (The American system rates free climbs from 5.0 to 5.14d; free climbing is to climb using hands and feet only; the rope is used only for protection in case of a fall.) Within two years, she was leading 5.11 climbs and undertaking a number of big-wall routes, including the Nose and the Shield on El Capitán in Yosemite National Park. (Leading a climb is much more difficult than just climbing it. The lead climber is the first on the climb and sets all the rope anchors, determining the course up the wall.) At age 18, she made the first ascent of Ophir Broke, a 5.12d/13a climb in Telluride, Colorado, the hardest route ever done by a woman at the time.

In 1980, she appeared on the televised sports program *Survival of the Fittest*, which ran competitors through a series of obstacle courses. She won the grand prize four years in a row. In 1983, Hill moved to New Paltz, New York, where she attended the State University of New York at New Paltz. She graduated in 1985 with a degree in biology and considered a career in physical therapy, but was drawn to a life of climbing.

New Paltz is near the Shawangunk Mountains, considered by many to be the best rock climbing region east of the Rockies. She climbed the Vandals (5.13a), the most difficult route on the East Coast at the time. Hill's reputation for climbing the tough routes opened opportunities for her to compete against the finest female climbers in the world for prize money in the growing sport of competitive climbing.

In 1986, Hill was invited to compete at the International Sport Climbing Competition in Arco, Italy. Although she lost the competition to Catherine Destivelle in a disputed ruling, Hill returned to the contest the next year and climbed away the winner. Throughout the late 1980s, Hill dominated rock climbing competitions around the world. She won the 1987 World Indoor Rock Climbing Premier at Grenoble, France; the 1988 International Climbing Championships at Marseilles, France; the 1988 and 1989 Masters Competition in Paris; the 1989 German Free Climbing Championships; the International Sport

Climbing Competition in 1989 and 1990; and the World Cup competition in Lyon, France, in 1989 and 1990.

In addition to dominating women's competitive climbing, Hill also set the women's standard for extreme rock routes. In 1990, she ascended Masse Critique at Cimai, France, the first 5.14 ever climbed by a woman.

In 1994, Hill took on the challenge of her 20-year climbing career when she began training to complete a one-day, all-free ascent of the 3,000-foot Nose on Yosemite's El Capitán. Hill had climbed the Nose when she was 18, but it had not been a free climb, and it had taken her four days to complete. (The first person to climb the Nose of El Capitán took 45 days to finish the route.) In September 1994, Hill began her climb at 3:30 A.M. under a full moon and reached the summit 23 hours later. She is

Lynn Hill
© Allsport USA/Tony Duffy

still the only person to free climb the Nose in a day. French climbing legend Yvon Chouinard called it "the biggest thing that has ever been done on rock."[67]

Hill used her early gymnastics training to develop much of her expert technique. She is small in stature but not in strength. Her strength-to-weight ratio, which is crucial to climbing, is excellent, but many contend that her best attribute is her focus. "She sometimes struggles with difficult moves, but she can just about always reach inside and pull out whatever it takes to make the move," noted Alison Osius, a former member of the U.S. Climbing Team.[68]

Lynn Hill retired from full-time competitive climbing in 1993, but she continues to push the limits for other women. She told *Women's Sport and Fitness*, "For the past decade, I've tried to break ground in the sport, pushing the level of difficulty for women to be equal to that of men. . . . Climbing can teach females things about themselves that aren't generally stressed by society—such as perseverance, problem-solving, and self confidence. Climbing is a matter of capitalizing on one's own particular strengths and realizing that there is usually a solution for anything, however insurmountable it may seem at the moment."[69]

Flo Hyman (volleyball player)

Born July 29, 1954, Inglewood, California; died January 24, 1986

About Flo Hyman, one journalist wrote: "She was women's volleyball in the United States—its biggest star and most dedicated proponent."[70] The best female volleyball

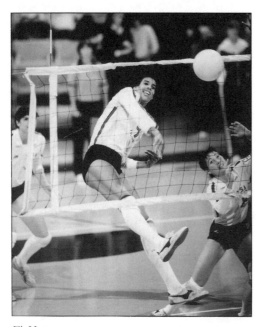

Flo Hyman
Courtesy of United States Volleyball Association

player the United States ever produced, Hyman led the U.S. Women's Olympic Volleyball Team to a silver medal in the 1984 Los Angeles Olympics. A 10-year member of the U.S. national team, she moved women's volleyball in the United States from obscurity to international acclaim. Her style of play and leadership ability on the court brought a new image and a new breed of player to the game. At 6 feet, 5 inches tall, she used her height and natural athletic ability to dominate as a power hitter (spiker) and server, intimidating the best players in the world.

Born in Inglewood, California, Flora "Flo" Hyman began playing volleyball after her older sister encouraged her to join the high school team. Already over 6 feet tall as a teenager, Hyman immediately took to the sport, and it did not take her long to become one of the nation's top players.

Hyman joined the U.S. national team in 1974. She also played collegiate volleyball at the University of Houston, where she was a three-time All-American and named the outstanding collegiate player in 1976. She chose to forgo her final year of collegiate competition to train full-time with the national team. The United States Volleyball Association (USVBA) established a training center in 1974 to train its men's and women's teams on a full-time, year-round basis. Although the women's team failed to qualify for the 1976 Olympics, by 1978 the U.S. team was ranked fifth in the world, and the following year the team was ranked second. Hyman played an important part in the team's seemingly meteoric rise to the world-class level. She used her height to tremendous advantage and became one of the world's best hitters. Under the tutelage of coach Arie Selinger, Hyman worked hard to become an all-around player, pushing her team to greater heights with her own talent and spirit.

Hyman provided maturity, leadership, and motivation for the relatively inexperienced U.S. team at the 1978 and 1982 world championships. In 1979, she was named most valuable player at the North/Central and Caribbean American (NORCECA) Championship, leading the U.S. team to a second-place finish.

The "old lady" of the team, as she liked to call herself, Hyman was one of seven players who stayed with the U.S. national team after America's 1980 boycott of the Moscow Olympics. By that time, she was widely regarded as one of the world's best female players. At the 1981 World Cup, international volleyball coaches and officials judged Hyman the best hitter in the world and chose her as one of only six members of the All-World Cup Team at the Tokyo tournament.

At the 1984 Los Angeles Olympics, the exciting volleyball matches received some of the highest television ratings of all the Olympic events. Millions of Americans watched Hyman and her teammates battle and beat the best teams in the world. Thirty-year-old Hyman led the U.S. women's team to a silver-medal finish, losing to the powerful Chinese team in the final. She said of her Olympic performance: "We accomplished a lot. We're proud of our silver medal."[71]

After the Olympics, Hyman retired from the U.S. national team, and with no professional volleyball opportunities in the United States, she signed to play on the professional circuit in Japan. While playing a match in Matsue on January 24, 1986, Hyman collapsed and died suddenly from a ruptured aorta. (Hyman suffered from Marfan's Syndrome—a genetic heart disorder that is extremely difficult to diagnose.) Hyman, who was 31 at the time of her death, had planned to rejoin the U.S. team to participate in the 1988 Olympics.

The high-caliber play of the U.S. team in the 1984 Olympic tournament brought volleyball into the limelight and contributed to making it one of the most popular high school sports for girls in the United States; their success helped promote the outdoor sport of professional beach volleyball for women as well. In her 10 years on the U.S. team, Hyman helped establish the United States' presence in international volleyball. She showed that in volleyball a woman's height was a definite advantage, and using her height and strength, she became one of the world's best outside power hitters. As a woman of color, Flo Hyman introduced more Black women to a game traditionally reserved for White, middle-class YMCA players. Since 1987, the Women's Sports Foundation has honored her memory by awarding the "Flo Hyman Award" to the woman athlete "who captures Flo's dignity, spirit, and commitment to excellence." Winners have included Martina Navratilova, Jackie Joyner-Kersee,

Evelyn Ashford, Chris Evert, Diana Golden, Nancy Lopez, Lynette Woodard, Patty Sheehan, Mary Lou Retton, Donna de Varona, and Billie Jean King.

Charmayne James (barrel racer)

Born June 23, 1970, Clayton, New Mexico

Charmayne James is the most successful barrel racer in professional rodeo history. Barrel racing is the only sport open to women in professional rodeo. The world's top cowgirl, James won 10 consecutive world championships (1984–93) and became barrel racing's first million dollar winner in 1994. James and her horse Scamper have shattered every barrel racing record known to rodeo.

The daughter of Charlie and Gloria James, Charmayne began riding when she was four years old on the James's ranch in New Mexico. In 1982, her father paid $1,100 for Scamper, a bad-tempered bay American Quarter Horse who had bucked one owner right into the hospital. "My dad said, 'There's a little bay horse down there in the pen. Go get on him and ride. But be careful, 'cause he bucks.' So I get on and start loping him. He wanted to buck, and I'm just laughing. I think Scamper sensed right away that I was no threat to him, that I was just a kid. He kinda liked me," she told *Horse & Rider*.[72] Although barrel racing may look less harrowing than some other rodeo events, it certainly is not for the faint-hearted. The event is fast and furious. In barrel racing, the contestant enters the arena at full speed on her horse. The racer rides a cloverleaf pattern around three barrels positioned in the arena, and sprints back out of the arena. The contestant can touch or move the barrels, but receives a five-second penalty for each barrel overturned. The fastest time wins. Success in barrel racing requires great horsemanship skills and competitive drive, which James possessed at an early age.

James and Scamper are the most successful barrel racing team in rodeo history. Soon after James got Scamper, they began taking home the top prizes from local jackpots and small rodeos throughout New Mexico. In 1983, when James was 13, she was issued a permit to compete on the professional rodeo circuit. She won at Dodge City, Kansas, in only her second pro-rodeo competition.

In 1984, James obtained her full-fledged pro card, and began a whirlwind tour across the country, competing in more than 70 rodeos. The 14-year-old won the

Charmayne James
Courtesy of Kenneth Springer

Women's Pro Rodeo Association (WPRA) World Championship, the National Finals Rodeo Championship (only the top 15 money winners are invited to participate), and the WPRA Rookie of the Year award. She earned more than $50,000 that year. This began a streak unequalled in women's professional rodeo history.

In 1994, James surpassed $1 million in total earnings, becoming the first million dollar cowgirl. She began to cut Scamper's races and in 1995 began competing on a younger barrel horse, Magic. James finished 12th in the rankings and earned more than $50,345. In 1996, her total earnings were $49,995. By 1997, she had moved back up in the standings, ranked sixth in the Crown Royal World Standings.

James was inducted into the National Cowgirl Hall of Fame in 1992 and the Texas Cowgirl Hall of Fame in 1995, and she was selected in 1995 for induction into the Pro Rodeo Hall of Fame in Colorado Springs, Colorado, under the heading of timed-event horse.

Charmayne James is the all-time leading money winner in barrel racing history. She rode to 10 consecutive world championships and has competed in 14 consecutive National Finals Rodeo events. Her superb horsemanship skills in handling one of the best barrel horses elevated her sport to a new level and opened many doors for future riders.

Lynn Jennings (distance runner)
Born July 1, 1960, Harvard, Massachusetts

The greatest cross-country runner in U.S. history, Lynn Jennings has been on the forefront of women's running in the United States for more than two decades. She has won eight national titles and three world championship titles in cross-country. "Cross-country provides the basis of excellence for track success," she told *Runner's World*. "And most kids get their start as runners in high school cross-country. I'd like to think that my success with cross-country could serve as a kind of beacon to them."[73]

Born in Harvard, Massachusetts, on July 1, 1960, Jennings began running at a young age and quickly showed championship form. In 1976, she won the U.S. Junior National Cross-Country Championships and competed in the 1976 Olympic 1,500-meter trials. As a 17-year-old, she ran the Boston Marathon against the advice of her coach and finished an unofficial (at 17, she was too young to officially enter the race) third in 2 hours, 46 minutes. As a senior, she ran the 1,500 meters in a high school indoor record time of 4:18.9, a mark that still stands.

In 1985, Jennings won the first of eight The Athletic Congress (TAC) National Cross-Country Championships (1985, 1987-1993). Equally at home on track and trail, Jennings finished second to Zola Budd Pieterse at the World Cross-Country Championships in 1987, and won the 10,000 meters at the U.S. nationals. In 1988, she won the TAC 3,000 meters and qualified for the U.S. Olympic team in the 10,000-meter run. She finished sixth in the event at the 1988 Seoul Olympics.

Many consider the World Cross-Country Championships to be the most competitive foot race in the world, drawing mara-

Lynn Jennings
© Allsport USA/Mike Powell

Summer Olympics in Barcelona, finishing third in the women's 10,000-meter race, behind Derartu Tulu of Ethiopia and Elana Meyer of South Africa. Jennings set a U.S. record of 31:19.89 in winning the bronze. "I ran the greatest race of my life in the Olympics," she told *Runner's World.* "I did everything right in preparation and racing. I did everything right in getting the bronze, but I didn't run a perfect race. Only Tulu ran a perfect race."[74] Jennings was the only U.S. runner, male or female, to medal at a distance of more than 800 meters at the 1992 Summer Olympics.

In 1993, Jennings won the USA indoor 3,000 meters and the outdoor 10,000 meters, a Bud Lite Couples 5 K, the Tufts Women's 10 K, the Tulsa Run 15 K, and her eighth national cross-country championship. She won the national titles in the indoor 3,000 meters and the outdoor 10,000 meters in 1995. At age 38, Jennings won the 10,000-meter race in the time of 32:26.41 at the 1997 U.S. Outdoor National Championships.

All told, Lynn Jennings has won more than 20 national track and cross-country national titles, three world cross-country titles, and an Olympic medal in the 10,000 meters. "I feel like I've been on this steady, relentlessly paced journey," she told *Runner's World* in 1993. "There hasn't been one defining moment in my career—there have been many defining moments, each one feeding into the next."[75] The greatest cross-country runner in U.S. history, Jennings has been on the forefront of women's running in the United States for more than two decades and continues to set the pace for the advancement of women's cross-country and track and field in the United States into the next century.

thoners and milers, road runners, and cross-country specialists. In March 1990, at Aix-les-Bains, France, Jennings became the first American in 15 years to win the title. She also set a world indoor track record of 15:22.64 in the 5,000 meters, as well as a U.S. indoor record of 8:40.45 in the 3,000 meters that year. With her victory at the world championship, the United States Olympic Committee (USOC) voted Jennings the Sportswoman of the Year for 1990. She also won the 1990 Jesse Owens Award as the outstanding U.S. female track and field performer of the year.

By 1992, Jennings had won three back-to-back World Cross-Country Championships (1991, 1992, 1993) and had been named *Runner's World* American Female Runner of the Year all three years. Adding to her cache of championship medals, Jennings won the bronze medal at the 1992

Joan Joyce (softball player)

Born August 1, 1940, Waterbury, Connecticut

An accomplished all-around athlete, Joan Joyce was introduced to sports by her father at a young age. Joyce played basketball and volleyball, but gained her fame as the most dominant softball pitcher in the world. Her level of play set a new standard in fast-pitch softball in the 1960s, and her ability to excel at several sports garnered her comparisons to the great Babe Didrikson Zaharias.

Born in Waterbury, Connecticut, on August 1, 1940, Joyce participated in many sports and games with her brother at the local level. In 1953, at the age of 13, she joined the Raybestos Brakettes, an amateur women's fast-pitch softball team in Stratford, Connecticut. Her pitching career was launched during the 1958 Amateur Softball Association's (ASA) National Championships when the team's nationally recognized pitcher, Bertha Tickey, hurt her arm, forcing Joyce to move from first base to starting pitcher. The 18-year-old Joyce finished pitching a no-hitter to win the national championship for the Brakettes. Joyce played 20 years as an amateur with the Brakettes and the Orange Lionettes of Orange, California.

In her combined 22 pitching seasons, Joyce compiled 509 wins and 33 losses. She used a slingshot style of pitching, throwing screwballs, rises, drops, curves, and knuckleballs and had a fastball clocked at over 115 miles per hour. She pitched 105 no-hit games and 33 perfect games, struck out 6,648 batters in 3,972 innings, and recorded a lifetime earned run average (ERA) of 0.21. She holds or shares the ASA national championship records for most total strikeouts in a national championship tournament (134), most strikeouts in a seven-inning game (19), most innings pitched in

one tournament (70), and the most no-hitters in a national tournament (2).

When not pitching, Joyce contributed to the team effort with her hitting and fielding expertise. She had a lifetime batting average of .327, knocked in 534 runs, and led the Brakettes in batting six times. Joyce was a member of 15 national championship

Joan Joyce
Courtesy of the National Softball Hall of Fame, Oklahoma City

and 6 runner-up softball teams. ASA named her to All-American teams 18 consecutive years, and she was the MVP of the league eight times.

Her impressive amateur career led to a short but successful professional career. In 1975, with the help of tennis star Billie Jean King and entrepreneur Dennis Murphy, Joyce established the International Women's Professional Softball Association (IWPSA). As the star player, manager, and part-owner of the Connecticut Falcons, Joyce led her team to the World Series Championship all four years the IWPSA existed. Although the IWPSA folded in September 1979 because of a lack of financial support, Joyce drew crowds wherever she played. Her team played exhibitions before crowds of nearly 7,000 at stadiums around the country. Her record in the IWPSA was 101-15.

Joan Joyce was inducted into the National Softball Hall of Fame in 1983 and the International Women's Sports Hall of Fame in 1990. A complete athlete, she earned Amateur Athletic Union (AAU) All-American basketball honors three times while at Chapman College, compiled an impressive 180 average in bowling, and starred on a leading amateur volleyball team. Upon retiring from softball in 1978, Joyce joined the women's professional golf tour at the age of 37. Her athletic career spanned three decades, and she excelled in a variety of sports, but her legacy is her excellence on the softball field. She set the standard for future generations of female players.

Further Reading

Joyce, Joan, and John Anquillare. *Winning Softball.* Chicago: Henry Regnery Co., 1975. 109 pp.

Florence Griffith Joyner (track and field sprinter)

Born December 21, 1959, Los Angeles, California

At the U.S. Olympic trials in July 1988, Florence "FloJo" Griffith Joyner flashed onto the world track and field scene by shattering the world record in the women's 100-meter dash, earning the unofficial title of the "world's fastest woman." Her striking appearance and her amazing performances on the track captured the attention of the media and sports fans who watched her live up to the "fastest woman" title in the 1988 Seoul Olympics. FloJo, as she came to be called, won three golds and a silver in the women's sprint events in Seoul. She had an enormous influence on women's track and field in 1988, bringing a certain style and flair to women's track with her dramatic racing outfits and outrageous makeup and fingernails, but it is her world-record time of 10.49 in the 100 meters that

will keep her in track and field record books for years to come.

Delorez Florence Griffith, the daughter of Robert and Florence Griffith, was born on December 21, 1959. The seventh of 11 children, Florence grew up in the Jordan Downs housing project in the Watts section of Los Angeles. Her mother had moved the family there when Griffith Joyner was four. Griffith Joyner picked up the nickname Dee Dee as a youngster, a name she still answers to when among family and friends.

Griffith Joyner began running track at age seven and competed in the 50- and 70-meter dashes with the Sugar Ray Robinson Youth Foundation, a program for underprivileged youngsters in Watts. When she was 14, she won the Jesse Owens National

Youth Games and repeated the victory a year later. She competed on the track team at Jordan High School in Los Angeles, where she set school records in sprinting and the long jump. After graduating from Jordan High in 1978, Griffith Joyner enrolled in California State University at Northridge, but financial constraints forced her to quit school after just one year to take a job as a bank teller.

She returned to college at the insistence of Bob Kersee, the assistant track coach at Northridge. Griffith Joyner began training with Kersee, and in 1980, she transferred to the University of California at Los Angeles (UCLA), where Kersee had taken a full-time coaching position. While at UCLA, Griffith Joyner specialized in the 200-meter race and barely missed making the 1980 U.S. Olympic team in the event. In 1982, she won the National Collegiate Athletic Association (NCAA) 200-meter title with a time of 22.29 seconds. The following year, Griffith Joyner won the 400-meter title and finished second in the 200 meters.

To prepare for the 1984 Olympics, Griffith Joyner trained with Kersee at the World Class Track Club in Los Angeles. A member of the 1984 U.S. Olympic team, Griffith Joyner earned a silver medal in the 200 meters with a personal best of 22.04 seconds. Griffith Joyner semiretired from competition after the Olympics.

In 1987, Griffith Joyner began training with her sights on the 1988 Olympic trials. She rejoined the World Class Track Club and set up a rigorous training regimen that included midnight workouts and an exhaustive weightlifting program. "It was time to run better or move on," she decided.[76] Also during this time, she met and married Al Joyner, former Olympic triple-jump gold medalist and brother of her World Class Track Club teammate Jackie Joyner-Kersee. Griffith Joyner's training paid off with

Florence Griffith Joyner
Courtesy of UCLA Athletics

a silver medal in the 200 meters and a gold medal as a part of the victorious 4x100-meter relay team at the 1987 World Track and Field Championships in Rome.

For the 1988 Olympic trials, Griffith Joyner worked on the 200 meters and also had her sights set on the 400 meters. But after running a personal best in the 100 meters at the Michelob Invitational just two weeks before the trials, she decided to focus on that event as well. In the second 100-meter preliminary at the U.S. Olympic team trials in Indianapolis, Griffith Joyner ran the distance in 10.49 seconds, shattering Evelyn Ashford's four-year-old record by more than a quarter of a second, an enormous amount of time in sprinting events. Griffith Joyner also set a U.S. record in the 200-meter sprint, beating reigning Olympic champion and long-time nemesis Valerie Brisco-Hooks.

At the Summer Olympics in Seoul, Griffith Joyner set a new Olympic record in the 100 meters and a world record in the 200 meters (21.34 seconds), winning golds in both events. She ran the third leg of the 4x100-meter relay, which garnered her another gold medal, and she earned a silver medal as a member of the 4x400-meter relay. For her Olympic success, Griffith Joyner won the 1988 Jesse Owens Award as the year's outstanding track and field athlete, the 1988 Sullivan Award as the top amateur athlete in the United States, and the 1988 Associated Press Female Athlete of the Year Award. She was inducted into the National Track and Field Hall of Fame in 1995.

Griffith Joyner retired from competition in 1989 but continues to work on behalf of youth sports through the Florence Griffith Joyner Youth Foundation. In 1993, President Bill Clinton named her to the President's Council on Physical Fitness and Sports.

Florence Griffith Joyner was the media star of the 1988 Seoul Olympics. Her flamboyant style and meteoric rise to sprinting excellence put women's track and field in the spotlight. Her intensive training effort after a two-year layoff led to astonishing world records that may never be equaled. Surviving the hardships of the Los Angeles ghetto to become the "fastest woman in the world," Griffith Joyner became an important role model for young women, once stating, "Chasing records and giving the young kids coming up something to chase, that's what the sport is all about."[77]

Further Reading

Aaseng, Nathan. *Florence Griffith Joyner: Dazzling Olympian*. Minneapolis, MN: Lerner Publications, 1989. 60 pp.

Jackie Joyner-Kersee (track and field heptathlete)

Born March 3, 1962, East St. Louis, Illinois

Jackie Joyner-Kersee holds the world record in track and field's most grueling discipline, the heptathlon. "I like the heptathlon," Joyner-Kersee once said, "because it shows you what you're made of."[78] The heptathlon consists of seven events—the 200-meter dash, 100-meter hurdles, high jump, shot put, long jump, javelin throw, and 800-meter run—held over a two-day period. Heptathletes are awarded points based on individual performances in each event. In the 1988 Seoul Olympics, Joyner-Kersee outdistanced her closest competitor by nearly 500 points, setting a new world record with 7,291 points to win the gold medal. She successfully defended her title at the 1992 Olympics in Barcelona, becoming the only woman to win back-to-back heptathlon titles. A member of four U.S. Olympic teams, Joyner-Kersee won three gold medals, one silver, and two bronzes. She also won two world heptathlon titles (1987, 1993) and two world long jump titles (1987, 1991). Many regard her as the world's greatest female athlete.

Born to Alfred and Mary Joyner of East St. Louis, Illinois, on March 3, 1962, Jacqueline Joyner was named for then First Lady Jacqueline Kennedy. The first lady of track and field, Joyner-Kersee began running and jumping at the Mayor Brown Youth Center near her home in an economically depressed area of East St. Louis. At age nine, she entered her first track competition, finishing last. With the support of her parents and brother Al (husband of 100-meter world-record holder Florence Griffith Joyner), Joyner-Kersee continued to compete, specializing in the long jump. By the time she was 12, she could leap distances over 17 feet. Her chief competitor at this time was her older brother Al. Her achievements inspired him to compete in track and field himself; he went on to win a gold medal in the triple jump at the 1984 Olympics.

When Joyner-Kersee was 14, she took up the five-event pentathlon and announced to family and friends that she would one day compete in the Olympics. In 1978, she won the first of four consecutive National Junior Pentathlon Championships. Joyner-Kersee won the long jump at the Pan American Junior Games in 1979 and placed eighth in the long jump at the 1980 U.S. Olympic trials, with a personal best jump of 20 feet, 3¼ inches.

A three-sport athlete at Lincoln High School in East St. Louis, she played volleyball and basketball and set a state high school record in the long jump. Joyner-Kersee also excelled in academics, and after graduating from Lincoln High School in 1980 in the top 10 percent of her class, she went to the University of California at Los Angeles (UCLA) on a basketball scholarship. She competed in basketball and track while at UCLA. A four-year starter on the Bruins basketball team, Joyner-Kersee ranked among the top 10 all-time Bruins in assists, rebounding, and scoring.

In 1981, Joyner-Kersee began working with coach Bob Kersee on the seven-event heptathlon and the long jump. Within a year, she established a collegiate record in the heptathlon and won the National Collegiate Athletic Association (NCAA) title. As a sophomore, Joyner-Kersee led the Bruins to the 1982 NCAA Track and Field

Jackie Joyner-Kersee
Courtesy of UCLA Athletics

Championship, scoring 32 of the Bruins' 153 points. In 1983, she won the Broderick Award as the nation's top female track and field athlete.

In 1984, Joyner-Kersee took a year off from collegiate basketball to focus her attention on the Los Angeles Olympics. She qualified for the U.S. team in both the long jump and the heptathlon. Hampered by a recurring hamstring injury she first sustained during the 1983 world championships in Helsinki, Finland, Jackie placed fifth in the 1984 Olympic long jump and finished second in the heptathlon, just five points behind Australia's Glynis Nunn.

Throughout 1985, Joyner-Kersee's performances continued to improve. One of the nation's top student-athletes, she graduated from UCLA after establishing a collegiate long jump record of 22 feet, 11¼ inches and a collegiate heptathlon record of 6,718 points. For those accomplishments, she garnered the Honda Broderick Cup as the nation's outstanding collegiate sportswoman.

In January 1986, she set a new U.S. record in the heptathlon at Gotzis, Austria. In July 1986 at the Goodwill Games in Moscow, USSR, she became the first woman to score more than 7,000 points in the grueling event. She set personal bests in almost every event, and her 7,148-point mark shattered the world record by 200 points. Just 26 days later, at the U.S. Olympic Festival, Joyner-Kersee won every event in the heptathlon and broke her world record with 7,161 points. In 1986, she was named *Track & Field News*'s Athlete of the Year, won the Jesse Owens Award as the top track and field athlete, and received the Sullivan Memorial Trophy as America's top amateur athlete.

She continued to astound the athletic world with her amazing performances in both the heptathlon and in individual events as well. During the 1987 indoor season, Joyner-Kersee won five of eight high-hurdles races, improved her marks in the long jump, and mastered the 400-meter run. In the outdoor season, she won the national heptathlon title at the U.S. championships and leapt 23 feet, 4½ inches to set a new U.S. women's long jump record. At the Pan American Games in Indianapolis in August 1987, she tied the world long jump record at 24 feet, 5½ inches, becoming the first woman in 22 years to hold both individual and multievent world track and field records simultaneously. The following month, she won both events at the World Track and Field Championships in Rome, Italy, becoming the first person, male or female, since 1924 to capture gold medals in multisport and individual events at a world-class competition. That year, Joyner-Kersee was named Amateur Sportswoman of the Year by the Women's Sports Foundation, won

her second consecutive Jesse Owens Award as the best U.S. track and field athlete, and received the Associated Press Female Athlete of the Year Award.

To avenge her disappointing second-place finish in 1984, Joyner-Kersee entered the 1988 Olympics with an overwhelming drive to set a new Olympic and world record in her specialty. As the outright favorite in the heptathlon, she took a commanding lead in the first day's events, setting a personal best in the 100-meter hurdles. On the second day, she set a heptathlon world record in the long jump and set a personal best in the 800 meters. Her total for the seven events set a new heptathlon world record with 7,291 points and surpassed the old Olympic mark by nearly 1,000 points. Five days later, Joyner-Kersee defeated world-record holder Galina Tchistiakova of the Soviet Union and Heiki Drechsler of East Germany to capture the long jump title and her second gold medal of the 1988 Seoul Olympics.

At the 1991 world championships in Tokyo, Joyner-Kersee won the gold medal in the long jump but injured a hamstring during the heptathlon event and was unable to defend her title. But she was fit and ready for the 1992 Olympics in Barcelona. She won the gold in the heptathlon and the bronze in the long jump. Four years later, she returned to the Olympics to attempt a "three-peat" in the heptathlon but was forced to withdraw from the contest after one event with a sore leg; she went on to win a bronze in the long jump despite her injury.

Her honors and awards are many. She was selected the Associated Press Female Athlete of the Year in 1987, and won the Sullivan Award in 1986, the United States Olympic Committee (USOC) Sportswoman of the Year in 1986 and 1987, and *Track & Field News*'s Athlete of the Year in 1986,

1987, and 1994. She became the first athlete to win the Jesse Owens Award twice (1986, 1987). The Women's Sports Foundation honored her with the 1988 Flo Hyman Award, presented to the female athlete who exemplifies Hyman's dignity, spirit, and commitment to excellence. The Women's Sports Foundation also named Joyner-Kersee its Amateur Sportswoman of the Year for 1992.

If Babe Didrikson was the "female athlete of the first half century," then Jackie Joyner-Kersee may well be the "female athlete of the second half century." Her courage and stamina as a multisport athlete will be her lasting legacy. She clearly understands her place in history and the influence she has on the next generation of female track stars. Raised in the ghetto of East St. Louis, Joyner-Kersee is a role model for young women striving to escape the hardships brought on by poverty and lack of opportunity. "I remember where I came from," she says, "and I keep that in mind . . . . If a young female sees the environment I grew up in and sees my dreams and goals come true, they will realize their dreams and goals might also come true."[79]

Further Reading

Cohen, Neil. *Jackie Joyner-Kersee*. New York: Sports Illustrated for Kids, 1992. 124 pp.

Goldstein, Margaret J., and Jennifer Larson. *Jackie Joyner-Kersee: Superwoman*. Minneapolis, MN: Lerner, 1994. 56 pp.

Joyner-Kersee, Jackie, with Sonja Steptoe. *A Kind of Grace: The Autobiography of the World's Greatest Female Athlete*. New York: Warner Books, 1997. 340 pp.

Billie Jean King (tennis player)

Born November 22, 1943, Long Beach, California

In 1990, *Life* magazine named Billie Jean King one of the 100 Most Important Americans of the 20th Century. Only three other athletes—Babe Ruth, Jackie Robinson, and Muhammad Ali—made the list. *Life* cited King's efforts in promoting and supporting the women's sports movement in America as the "winningest woman for equal rights." In 1995, she placed fifth on *Sports Illustrated*'s Top 40 Athletes list for "significantly altering or elevating sports in the previous four decades."

An outspoken advocate of equal rights for women, King created a forum for her views as one of the top female tennis players of the 1960s and 1970s. In that time, she won 67 Women's Tennis Association (WTA) singles titles, including 39 Grand Slam (Australian, French, British, and U.S. championships) singles titles and ranks fifth on the all-time victory list with 695. She holds a record 20 Wimbledon titles and is the only woman to win U.S. Open singles titles on all four of the surfaces on which it has been played: grass, clay, carpet, and hard court.

A true sports pioneer, King was the first woman in any sport to earn more than $100,000 in a single season of competition ($117,000 in 1971); the first woman to coach a coed professional sports team, the Philadelphia Freedoms of the World TeamTennis league in 1974; and in 1984, became the first female commissioner in professional sports history—governing TeamTennis, the first professional sports league in which women compete on a completely equal basis with men.

King was the driving force behind the creation of a women's professional tennis tour in 1971, a tour that in 1997 paid out more than $38 million in prize money. Through her efforts to promote women's professional sports and opportunities for female athletes, King became one of the most important symbols for women's sports and the women's movement in the 1970s and 1980s.

Born Billie Jean Moffitt in Long Beach, California, the daughter of Bill and Betty Moffitt, Billie Jean got involved in sports as a youngster. She played baseball with her father and brother, and played football with her neighborhood friends. At age 10, she played on a championship girls' softball team. When King was 11, her parents decided that football and baseball were not the best sports for their little girl. Her father suggested tennis.

King enrolled in the free tennis lessons offered by city recreation coach Clyde

Billie Jean King
Courtesy of Sharon Hoogstraten

Walker on the municipal courts at Houghton Park in Long Beach. "That first day I really fell in love with tennis. . . . I stayed out there a couple of hours and I was completely enthralled," she wrote in her autobiography *Billie Jean*. That day she told her mother, "I want to play tennis forever. I'm going to be the Number One tennis player in the whole world." "That's fine, dear," her mother replied.[80]

For the next five years, King worked diligently to learn tennis fundamentals and to improve her game. She practiced for hours after school and on the weekends, never losing sight of her goal to be the best. She won her first title in 1958, the Southern California Championship. When she was 16, King began taking lessons from tennis great Alice Marble. After lessons with Marble, King's national ranking jumped from 19th to fourth. "She taught me a flat serve and how to get behind the ball, but most important, she showed me what it was to be a champion—to believe in myself."[81]

In 1960, King reached the finals of the U.S. National Girls' 18-and-under Championship but lost to Karen Hantze. The following year, she and Hantze, both 17-year-olds, became the youngest pair ever to win the women's doubles title at Wimbledon. In 1962, King returned to Wimbledon, and before 18,000 spectators on Centre Court, she defeated top-ranked Margaret Smith of Australia, 1-6, 6-3, 7-5, in the second round. This victory vaulted King into the realm of world-class singles tennis.

In December 1965, King received her first number one ranking. She was ranked number one in the world five times between 1966 and 1972, and was in the top 10 a total of 17 years (beginning in 1960). King also ranked number one in U.S. doubles for a record 12 years, 8 of those years with partner Rosie Casals. Her aggressive serve-and-volley style of play served her well on the fast grass courts of Wimbledon, and as a doubles player where her quick reflexes and creative shot making made her a formidable foe.

After defending her Wimbledon doubles title with Hantze in 1962, King teamed with Maria Bueno (1965), Rosie Casals (1967-68, 1970-71, 1973), Betty Stove (1972), and Martina Navratilova (1979) to win 10 women's doubles titles at Wimbledon. She won the ladies' singles title at the All-England Championships (Wimbledon) six times (1966-68, 1972-73, 1975) and captured four mixed doubles championships with Owen Davidson (1967, 1971, 1973, 1974). In 1973, King scored the triple at Wimbledon—winning the singles, doubles, and mixed-doubles championships.

King found an equal amount of success on her home soil. She won 30 U.S. singles and doubles championships, both amateur and professional, including the U.S. Open singles title four times (1969, 1971, 1972, 1974), doubles five times (1964, 1967, 1974, 1978, 1980), and mixed doubles four times (1967, 1971, 1973, 1976). In eight years of Federation Cup play for the United States, King won all 27 of her doubles matches. (The Federation Cup is an international team competition.)

From her position as the top female tennis player in the world, King worked to promote a professional women's tennis tour. In 1970, she spearheaded a group of women players to form the Virginia Slims women's professional tennis circuit. Just as the new women's professional circuit was getting off the ground, 55-year-old former tennis champion Bobby Riggs challenged her to a five-set match. King accepted the challenge, and before 30,472 spectators at the Houston Astrodome, the largest paid attendance in tennis history, King easily won what the media billed as the "Battle of the Sexes," 6-4, 6-3, 6-3.

Not only did the match against Riggs help tennis, but King's victory also became symbolic of a woman's right to participate in sports and to test her athletic and physical potential. Many who had earlier criticized women's sports soon began to acknowledge women's abilities as athletes and their rightful place in the sport world. One male sportswriter noted:

> Seldom has there been a more classic example of a skilled athlete performing at peak efficiency in the most important moment of her life. Because of Billie Jean alone, who was representing a sex supposedly unequipped for such things, what began as a huckster's hustle in defiance of serious athleticism ended up not mocking the game of tennis but honoring it. This night King was both a shining piece of show biz and the essence of what sport is all about.[82]

Billie Jean King founded the Women's Tennis Association (WTA), the players' association, in 1973, and served as its president from June 1973 to September 1975 and from September 1980 to September 1981. The same year, she began a new magazine, *womenSports* (forerunner to *Women's Sports and Fitness*), to give women athletes more visibility and a forum for discussing issues in women's sports; and in 1974, she was one of the founding members of the Women's Sports Foundation. A lifelong proponent of team sports for women, King helped establish the International Women's Professional Softball Association (IWPSA), along with star softball pitcher Joan Joyce. King retired from competitive tennis in 1984 to focus her time and energy as the chief executive officer of World TeamTennis. However, she returned to the courts as a participant of the 1995 and 1996 Virginia Slims Legends Tour to benefit the National AIDS Fund, and she captained the U.S. team for the 1995 and 1996 Federation Cup and the 1996 U.S. Olympic Tennis Team.

Her awards include being named the *Sports Illustrated* Sportsman of the Year in 1972, and the Associated Press Female Athlete of the Year in 1967 and 1973. She was inducted into the International Women's Sports Hall of Fame in 1980 and the International Tennis Hall of Fame in 1987. She was given the 1995 Sarah Palfrey Danzig Award, U.S. tennis's highest honor for sportsmanship and contributions to the game, and the 1997 Women's Sports Foundation's Flo Hyman Award.

Billie Jean King's efforts to establish professional tennis for women spilled over into the women's rights movement in the 1970s. As a public figure, King was outspoken in her beliefs of equal opportunity and successfully used her outstanding athletic ability on the tennis court to draw attention to the issues of the era. *Life* magazine, recognizing King as one of the most influential and important women of the twentieth century, wrote: "She embodied the cause of women's sports and did more than show women of America they could win—she put them in the game."[83]

Further Reading

Baker, Jim. *Billie Jean King.* New York: Grosset & Dunlap Publishers, 1974. 90 pp.

Burchard, Marshall, and Sue H. Burchard. *Sports Hero, Billie Jean King.* New York: G.P. Putnam's Sons, 1975. 95 pp.

King, Billie Jean, with Cynthia Starr. *We Have Come a Long Way: The Story of Women's Tennis.* New York: McGraw-Hill Book Co., 1988. 208 pp.

King, Billie Jean, with Frank Deford. *The Autobiography of Billie Jean King.* New York: Granada Publishing, 1982. 214 pp.

King, Billie Jean, with Kim Chapin. *Billie Jean.* London: W.H. Allen, 1975. 208 pp.

King, Billie Jean, and Joe Hyams. *Billie Jean King's Secrets of Winning Tennis.* New York: Holt, Rinehart & Winston, 1974. 126 pp.

Micki King (diver)

Born July 26, 1944, Pontiac, Michigan

In 1968, Micki King went to the Mexico City Olympics as America's top female diver and favorite to take home the gold medal. Going into the next to last dive in the springboard event, King held a clear lead over her competition when disaster struck. She hit her arm on the board during the dive, breaking a bone in her left forearm. She returned to complete her last dive, broken arm and all, but dropped to fourth place. After the disastrous Olympics, King retired from competition to let her arm heal, but returned to diving soon after to train for the next Olympics. Displaying the courage of a seasoned, confident champion, the 28-year-old diver re-

turned to the Olympics in 1972, now a captain in the U.S. Air Force, to claim the gold she lost on that one tragic dive. Her

Micki King
Courtesy of the International Swimming Hall of Fame

success in Olympic diving led to a career in coaching where she broke the gender barrier as the first woman to coach at a U.S. military academy.

Born and raised in Pontiac, Michigan, Maxine "Micki" King took swimming lessons as a toddler. Active in numerous sports as a youngster, King particularly felt at home in the water. Her mother enrolled her in figure skating lessons, but to King skating the tedious figures was not nearly as exciting as inventing new ways to dive into the water off an elevated platform. At age 10, King joined the local YMCA and began to concentrate on learning the technique of diving. Later, she joined the high school swim team and loved the rough and tumble of water polo.

King entered her first diving competition at age 15, which she won. A year later, her coach encouraged her to compete in the 1960 Olympic diving trials; she finished 29th out of 30 divers. She continued to enter local competitions until 1962, when she enrolled at the University of Michigan, majoring in journalism. She joined the women's water polo team her freshman year as the goalie and earned All-American honors as one of the best in the country. As a sophomore, King began to take diving more seriously. Despite the fact that she was just starting to learn the basics of the sport at an age when some of the greatest divers were at the height of their careers, University of Michigan diving coach Dick Kimball saw her potential and determination to be a champion. She became the leader of the university diving team for the next three years, winning several Big 10 Conference diving titles. In 1964, she competed in the Olympic tryouts, finishing a respectable fifth place.

After graduating from the University of Michigan in 1966, King found herself in the precarious situation typical of many amateur athletes of the time—unable to afford the training expenses involved in preparing for international competition. She wanted to compete in the Olympic Games in 1968, but needed to fill the two years between graduation and the Games with training and work. The military offered her the solution.

King enlisted in the U.S. Air Force in the fall of 1966 as an officer candidate and received her commission as a second lieutenant. She returned to her alma mater to work with the University of Michigan Reserve Officer Training Corp. During her assignment, she continued to train with Coach Kimball. A true innovator, King worked on her technique while developing new and daring dives. In the two years leading up to the 1968 Olympics, she spent hours on the board perfecting her twists and turns.

She went to the 1968 Olympics with high hopes of winning the gold for the United States. The inward reverse 1½ layout was one of her best dives, but on that day in Mexico City, she jumped too high, and her attempt to correct the mistake caused her left arm to hit the board. As a result of this mistake, she dropped from first to fourth place in the springboard event. With her arm in a cast, King returned to the United States and announced her retirement from competitive diving; but after watching the national indoor championships in Los Angeles in the spring of 1969, her desire to compete returned. She began intensive training, determined to win the gold at the 1972 Munich Olympics.

In 1969, she entered the World Military Games held in Pescara, Italy. The only woman in the Games, King competed directly against men in the international competition, completing dives that no other woman had done in competition. She finished fourth in the platform event and third overall in the springboard contest.

For the next three years, King dominated American women's diving. Between 1969 and 1972, she claimed 10 national springboard and platform diving championships. Before the 1972 Olympics, she represented the United States in the Pan American Games, the World University Games, and the International Invitational. With this valuable experience behind her, King readied herself for her second chance at an Olympic gold medal.

She went to Munich in 1972, again the heavy favorite in the women's diving events. She had been diving in international competition for nearly 10 years, and in Munich, all the years of training and experience finally paid off. She swept through the competition, successfully completing all of her dives to near perfection to win the gold medal in the springboard event.

In 1973, King became the diving coach at the Air Force Academy, the first woman to hold a faculty position at a U.S. military academy. She coached there until 1977, when she moved to Tacoma, Washington, to train young divers in the local school system from 1978 to 1980; she then returned to the Air Force Academy in 1983 after a tour of duty in Germany to coach female and male cadets.

King, a retired Air Force colonel, was president of U.S. Diving from 1990–94.

She has spent countless hours in the promotion of sports and fitness for the nation's youth. She is one of the founding members of the Women's Sports Foundation and served on the United States Olympic Committee's (USOC) Board of Directors from 1968–72. An outspoken advocate of amateur sports, she played an instrumental role in the passage of the Amateur Sports Act of 1978, which established a structure for conducting amateur sports in the United States.

Her efforts have not gone unnoticed. She became a member of the International Swimming Hall of Fame in 1978, the International Women's Sports Hall of Fame in 1983, and the U.S. Olympic Hall of Fame in 1992.

Micki King's achievements are remarkable considering that she began her athletic career relatively late and that she was one of the very few prominent athletes, including males, to pursue a career in the military. Military life gave her the chance to pursue national and Olympic titles while she served her country. After the disappointing Olympics in 1968, her success in the 1972 Olympics is a tribute to her courage and tenacity as well as to her skill. Her success continued a long tradition of American women diving champions and led to a career as an advocate for amateur sports.

Olga Korbut (gymnast)

Born May 16, 1955, Grodno, Soviet Union

As gymnast Olga Korbut walked onto the mat at the Munich arena during the 1972 Olympics, she was about to change the future of women's gymnastics in the world forever. A member of the strong Soviet team, Korbut captured the public's eye with a spectacular routine on the uneven parallel bars during the team competition.

Over the three-day gymnastics competition, she won three gold medals and one silver medal, and in the process won the admiration of the world's sports fans. A sharp contrast to her stoic and more experienced teammates, Korbut had a dazzling smile and a playful attitude that enticed the worldwide television audience. She successfully completed daring and innovative moves never before attempted in international competition. Her popularity during the Olympics resulted in a huge surge in interest in gymnastics in the United States. Her performance inspired thousands of girls to become involved in sports, contributing to the women's sports revolution of the early 1970s.

Born in Grodno, in the Soviet republic of Byelorussia near the Polish border, Olga was an energetic child often prone to mischief. Her running and jumping ability was spotted by her physical education teacher who suggested she may have potential as a gymnast. Gymnastics had always been a very popular sport throughout the Soviet Union, and youngsters who showed unusual promise were sent to special sports schools. As there was a sports school in Grodno, Olga did not have to go far for her gymnastics training.

At age 11, Korbut began to study with Renald Knysh, a coach known for his innovative and revolutionary ideas. As one of Knysh's students, Korbut quickly learned the most difficult stunts on the gymnastic apparatus, including a back flip on the 4½-inch balance beam. In 1969, Korbut demonstrated her treacherous moves for the first time at the USSR championship meet, where she placed fifth. The following year she won a gold medal in the vault at a national meet and earned a spot as an alternate to the 1970 world championships in Yugoslavia. Although not allowed to compete because her coach thought she was too young and inexperienced for international competition, she did perform a demonstration of her extraordinary stunts that impressed the audience and the judges.

After an injury and a short illness that kept her from training for a few months, Korbut returned to competition with a third-place finish in the all-around event at the USSR national championships in 1972, and then won the USSR Cup just prior to the Munich Olympics.

Korbut went to the 1972 Olympics as an alternate on the strong Soviet women's gymnastic team but later replaced an injured teammate as a regular member. On the first day of the competition, Korbut performed flawlessly, leading her team to its sixth consecutive team gold medal. A

Olga Korbut
© Allsport

worldwide television audience watched her execute a backward somersault on the uneven parallel bars, the first person to successfully complete the move in competition.

With scores compiled during the team competition, Korbut had accumulated enough points to lead the race for the all-around title. But as she started her performance on the uneven parallel bars, she scuffed her feet on the mat as she mounted, then slipped off the bars during the routine. The judges gave her a 7.5, which eliminated her from the race for the all-around title; she finished in seventh place.

Korbut rebounded from this setback the next day during the individual apparatus competition. To the delight of her fans, she completed the "Korbut loop" on the uneven bars and the "Korbut somersault" on the balance beam, winning a silver medal on the uneven parallel bars and two gold medals for the balance beam and floor exercise.

In the United States, Korbut's dramatic cycle of success, failure, and success as well as her ability to perform daring moves captured national attention. Girls signed up for gymnastics by the thousands. The Associated Press named her the 1972 Female Athlete of the Year, the first athlete from a Communist nation to receive the award, and ABC's *Wide World of Sports* selected her as their Athlete of the Year.

Korbut continued to compete after the Munich Olympics. Her popularity overshadowed the fact that she was not the number one gymnast on the Soviet team. The Soviet women's team made a U.S. tour in 1973 and played to sold-out crowds. At Madison Square Garden in New York, 19,694 people—the largest crowd ever to see a gymnastics event—watched Korbut and her teammates perform.

She competed in the 1976 Montreal Olympics and came away with a gold in the team competition and a gold in the balance beam. Korbut retired from international competition in 1976 and went to work for the Byelorussian State Sport Committee as a coach at the sports school where she had learned her daring moves. In 1982, she was named to the International Women's Sports Hall of Fame.

In 1991, Korbut immigrated to Atlanta, Georgia, where she continued her coaching career. She also established the Olga Korbut Foundation to raise money for medical supplies, equipment, and training to aid victims of the Chernobyl disaster, which occurred quite near her hometown.

Olga Korbut introduced a new brand of daring gymnastics that changed the face of the sport. Her moves, once considered dangerous and still considered difficult, are now commonplace for young gymnasts worldwide to perform. The small, agile body needed to execute her moves also contributed to changing the sport from one for long, lean experienced dancers to a sport for young, petite tumblers. Her appearance at the 1972 Games inspired thousands of youngsters to take up gymnastics at a time when women's sports in the United States was undergoing its own revolution.

Further Reading

Beecham, Justin. *Olga, Her Life and Her Gymnastics*. New York: Two Continents Publishing Groups, 1974. 128 pp.

Coffey, Wayne R. *Olga Korbut*. Woodbridge, CT: Blackbirch Press, 1992. 64 pp.

Jacobs, Linda. *Olga Korbut, Tears and Triumph*. St. Paul, MN: EMC Corp., 1974. 40 pp.

Suponev, Michael. *Olga Korbut: A Biographical Portrait*. Garden City, NY: Doubleday & Co., 1975. 87 pp.

Julie Krone (jockey)
Born July 24, 1963, Benton Harbor, Michigan

Thoroughbred horse racing is now the premier sport where women jockeys and trainers compete directly against men, but until 1968, the sport was closed to women riders. In the 1970s, a few women made their living at local racetracks, but no one made an impact like Julie Krone when she rode her first winner in February 1980. Krone was the first woman to win five races in one day at a New York track; the first woman to win a riding title at a major track; one of only four jockeys to win six races in one day; and the first woman to compete in the prestigious Breeders' Cup race. In 1993, Krone rode Colonial Affair to victory in the Belmont Stakes, the first woman ever to win a leg of the Triple Crown (Kentucky Derby, Preakness, and Belmont Stakes). Julie Krone is the winningest female jockey in the history of horse racing. She proved to the racing world that women are tough enough both physically and mentally to be a part of the "sport of kings."

Julieann Louise Krone was born in Benton Harbor, Michigan, the daughter of Don and Judi Krone. Raised on a 10-acre farm near Eau Claire, Michigan, Julie inherited her love of horses from her mother, an accomplished equestrian. Krone learned to ride before she could walk. When she was two, her mother placed her atop a horse that trotted off; instinctively, Krone picked up the reigns and tugged them, guiding the horse back to her mother.

As a youngster, Krone raced horses around the family farm, jumping fences and riding while standing up. She won numerous county fair horse show ribbons around Michigan, including the Berrien County Youth Fair horse show, 21-and-under division, when she was five years old. But her real love was racing. "I was always going to

be a jockey, and a great one, too," Krone said.[84]

In 1979, when she was 15, Krone persuaded her mother to take her to Churchill Downs, the home of the Kentucky Derby. Julie got a summer job as a morning workout rider at the racetrack, her first job in the world of thoroughbred horse racing. In the fall, Krone returned to Michigan and began

Julie Krone
Photo by Patricia Osmon

racing at local fairground tracks. With her mind set on becoming a winning jockey, she left high school and moved to Tampa, Florida, to live with her grandparents and ride at Tampa Bay Downs racetrack.

Krone got her first ride on January 30, 1980, and just five weeks after arriving in Tampa, she won her first race. In only 48 races at Tampa, Krone won nine, finished second four times, and third 10 times. She met agent Chick Lang, who took her to Baltimore to race at Pimlico, the home of the Preakness. Despite the success early in her career, Krone had a difficult time getting rides because she was a female rider. Many trainers and owners still felt that women didn't belong at the racetrack. Julie traveled to different racetracks along the Atlantic seaboard to get rides and to prove that she was a good jockey.

In 1982, Krone won the riding title at Atlantic City, winning 155 races and more than $1 million in prize money (Krone got 10 percent of the winnings), becoming the first female jockey to win a racing title at a major thoroughbred track.

Krone recaptured the riding title in Atlantic City in 1983, but late in the year she fell from her horse during a race, breaking her back. She spent the next four months in rehabilitation.

In 1986, Krone moved from Atlantic City to three other New Jersey racetracks: Garden State Park, the Meadowlands, and Monmouth Park. She won 199 races and earned more than $2.3 million in prize money at those tracks. On August 19, 1987, she rode six winners at Monmouth Park, equaling the track's single-day record. In December 1987, she began racing at Aqueduct racetrack in New York City, one of the country's premier thoroughbred racetracks. She won four races on opening day. As one reporter wrote: "She [Krone] has demonstrated she will have impact anywhere she rides, that she is an athlete who must be compared not to other female riders, but in the context of her performance against men."[85]

Krone placed sixth among the nation's top jockeys in 1987 with 324 total wins. On March 6, 1988, she became the leading female jockey in history when she won her 1,205th race, surpassing the record held by P.J. Cooksey. In October, she defeated legendary jockey Willie Shoemaker in a $30,000 match race; and in November, she rode in the annual Breeders' Cup races at Churchill Downs, the first woman ever to participate in the event. She rode Forty Niner to a fourth-place finish in the $3 million race.

Krone claimed the riding titles at both Monmouth Park and the Meadowlands in 1988, and finished as the fourth-leading rider in the United States. In 1989, she was the leading jockey at Monmouth Park for the third consecutive year, but a fall in a late November race left her arm badly injured, causing her to miss the next eight months of racing. Recovered from her injuries, she finished in the top 10 among the nation's riders in 1990. On June 8, 1991, Krone became the first woman to ride in the Belmont Stakes—the third leg of the triple crown—in its 123-year history.

In 1992, Krone's horses won $9.2 million in purses, and she ranked ninth among all jockeys in the nation. Her most dramatic victory was the 1993 Belmont Stakes, where she guided her horse, a long shot named Colonial Affair, to a first-place finish and sealed her rightful place in horse racing history.

Two months after winning the Belmont, Krone was seriously injured again when she fell from her mount at Saratoga racetrack, fracturing her right ankle so severely it required two plates and 14 screws to repair. She returned to the track in May 1994 and finished 1994 with 101 victories. Krone took another fall in January 1995 and fractured her left hand but after several months of rehabilitation regained her strength and finished the year with 147 victories and more than $8 million in purse earnings.

With more than 3,000 wins and more than $70 million in purse earnings, Julie

Krone is the winningest female jockey of all time, and many experts suggest one of the best jockeys overall, which has always been her goal. As Krone would say: "I don't want to be the best female jockey in the world, I want to be the best jockey."[86] Her tenacity and determination guided her into the winner's circle on thousands of occasions, and she has proven that women have the phys-

ical and mental capability to succeed in thoroughbred horse racing.

Further Reading

Callahan, Dorothy M. *Julie Krone: A Winning Jockey*. Minneapolis, MN: Dillon Press, Inc., 1990. 64 pp.

Krone, Julie. *Riding for My Life*. New York: Little, Brown and Co., 1995. 212 pp.

Marion Ladewig (bowler)

Born October 30, 1914, Grand Rapids, Michigan

Considered by many to be the greatest woman bowler of all time, Marion Ladewig earned that title by virtue of the numerous national bowling titles she won throughout her more than 30-year career. Because of the extensive media coverage given bowling in the 1950s and 1960s, she emerged as bowling's first female superstar and helped elevate women's bowling to a more competitive level.

Born Marion Van Oosten on October 30, 1914, in Grand Rapids, Michigan, Marion was the youngest daughter of a retired police officer. Ladewig became involved in numerous sports activities at an early age. In her teens, this self-described "tomboy" ran track and played shortstop on her brother's baseball team. From baseball, Ladewig moved on to playing softball on a local women's team, and by the time she was 22, she had established herself as an excellent player.

At a softball game in 1935, William T. Morrissey, Sr., a Grand Rapids bowling proprietor and sponsor of the Fanatorium women's softball team, watched Ladewig play shortstop and was impressed with her strong throwing arm. Convinced that she would make a good bowler, Morrissey invited her to his Fanatorium bowling center

for a free game or two, and she accepted the invitation. "After bowling one game, that was it—I was hooked on the sport. I simply enjoyed the game itself and the challenge it presented," she stated.[87]

Ladewig left softball in 1937 to devote all her time to bowling. As her coach, Morrissey insisted that she practice every day. She later recalled that "with Mr. Morrissey around, I made sure that I bowled every day from 1940 through 1962."[88]

Ladewig averaged 149 in her first season and within three years had brought her average up to 182. She began to dominate tournament competition in Grand Rapids and around the state of Michigan. Her first big title came in 1941, when she won the singles event in the Western Michigan Gold Pin Classic, a prestigious Midwestern tournament. Two years later, she went on to win the all-events title in the Grand Rapids city tournament, Western Michigan and Central States tournaments, and the prestigious *Chicago American* event.

On December 8, 1949, Ladewig won the first National All-Star Match Games tournament open to women. This victory began a long reign for Ladewig, who dominated the event for a decade. She won five consecutive titles (1950-54), finished third

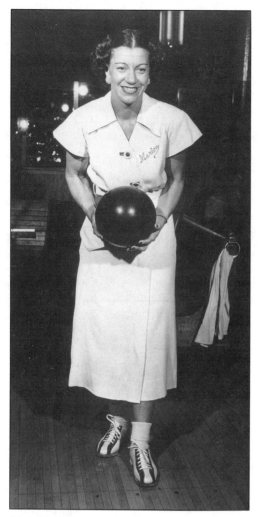

Marion Ladewig
Courtesy of the International Bowling Museum and Hall of Fame

events title, while leading her Fanatorium team to the team title. In 1955, she again won the all-events crown along with the doubles title. Ladewig bowled in a total of 31 annual WIBC championship tournaments in her career, averaging 187.07, placing her third on the average list for women who have bowled in 30 or more WIBC championship tournaments.

Ladewig credited much of her success to determination and years of practice. She recalled: "There was nothing outstanding about my style but my biggest asset was my accuracy. If there was any other reason for the success I had, it was simply the fact that the game never became easy for me, and I always had to keep working at it."[89]

After Ladewig won her first National All-Star tournament in 1950, the Brunswick-Balke-Collender Company hired her as part of their advisory staff of bowling champions. This job included traveling 8,000 to 10,000 miles a year doing exhibitions, conducting instructional clinics for local bowlers, and making numerous television appearances. She worked for the Brunswick Corporation for 30 years; traveled to all 50 states; went on two European tours; ventured to North Africa to instruct U.S. servicemen during World War II; and represented the Brunswick Corporation in September 1988 in Seoul, South Korea, where bowling debuted as an Olympic demonstration sport.

The Bowling Writers Association of America named her Woman Bowler of the Year nine times: 1950-54, 1957-59, and 1963. In 1952, she received four first-place votes for the Associated Press Female Athlete of the Year (she finished seventh); and in 1963, she finished third in the same balloting, the closest any bowler has come to receiving the honor.

Ladewig was voted the greatest woman athlete in Michigan history by the Helms

in the 1955 event, and went on to win the All-Star title in 1957, 1959, and 1963. In the 1951 event, Ladewig set a record on the first day by bowling an eight-game block of 1,981 pins—255, 279, 247, 227, 247, 224, 255, and 247—for an average of 247.6 in the qualifying round. Not only did she beat the other 63 women entered in the event, she also outscored all 160 men who were competing for the men's title.

Ladewig also had great success in the Women's International Bowling Congress (WIBC) national championship tournaments. In 1950, she won the WIBC all-

Athletic Foundation and is a member of their Sports Hall of Fame. In 1956, the National Women Bowling Writers' Association awarded Ladewig the Jo Ettien Trophy for distinguished service to women's bowling. She was elected to the Michigan Sports Hall of Fame in 1959 and was the first woman inducted into the Superior Performance category of the WIBC Hall of Fame in 1964. Ladewig was also inducted into the International Women's Sports Hall of Fame in 1984.

Ladewig helped organize the first professional women's bowling organization, the Professional Women's Bowling Association (PWBA), then won its first event in 1960. She retired from professional competition in 1965 but continued to do exhibitions and to bowl in the local, state, and national WIBC tournaments. She is proprietor of her own bowling center in Grand Rapids.

Marion Ladewig was a champion in both ability and attitude. Her gracious demeanor impressed the bowling community as much as her bowling skill. She achieved fame because her accomplishments came in the era when the mass media began covering the new professional bowling league for women, but her record of outstanding achievements alone made her a champion. She raised bowling to a new competitive level in the professional ranks. For women's organized bowling, she came to represent what could be achieved in the world of sports, and thus inspired a significant number of women to take up bowling as both a recreational activity and a competitive sport.

Andrea Mead Lawrence (Alpine skier)

Born April 19, 1932, Rutland, Vermont

Alpine skiing was a relatively young sport in America when the International Olympic Committee (IOC) added the sport to its schedule of events in the 1936 Winter Games. About this time in Vermont, Andrea Mead Lawrence, just four years old, was donning her first pair of skis to glide down the slopes of her parents' ski resort. Lawrence would become one of the most successful members of the U.S. women's Alpine ski team, dominating international skiing in 1951 on her way to winning two gold medals in the 1952 Olympics in Oslo, Norway. Her preeminence on the slopes set a standard of excellence for future generations of U.S. Alpine skiers. She remains the only U.S. skier, woman or man, to win two gold medals in one Winter Olympic Games.

Raised in the backyard of Vermont's Pico Peak ski resort, Andy began skiing almost before she could walk. As a youngster, she watched and followed her parents, Bradford and Janet Mead, and participated in Pico's instructional skiing program. Ski racing came naturally to Andy. She loved to fly down the mountain making quick, sharp turns with reckless abandon. She had no formal instruction on racing technique, yet her career blossomed.

At age 8, she entered local races; by age 11, she competed in her first major event, finishing second in the Women's Eastern Slalom Championships. At age 14, she qualified for the U.S. Olympic team by winning the slalom event. When the Olympics resumed in 1948, she traveled to St. Moritz, Switzerland, as the youngest member of the

Andrea Mead Lawrence
Courtesy of the U.S. National Ski Hall of Fame Archives

U.S. Women's Alpine Skiing Olympic Team. In her first international competition, Lawrence finished a respectable eighth place in the slalom event, missing the bronze medal by just over one tenth of a second. She also finished 21st in the combined and 35th in the downhill.

Lawrence went to Whitefish, Montana, for the 1949 nationals and the Federation International de Ski tryouts. She won all the women's events held at the meet— the slalom, the downhill, and the combined—making her eligible to represent the United States on the international team. Although she skied poorly during the 1950 season, she returned to championship form in 1951, skiing in 16 races, winning 10, and finishing second in four others, including gliding past the competition in the Arlberg-

Kandahar downhill, skiing's most prestigious international event.

Facing less than ideal snow conditions at the Oslo Olympics in 1952, Lawrence entered the gate for the giant slalom as hundreds of Norwegian soldiers shoveled snow onto the course. She flew down the course to win the event by nearly three seconds over Dagmar Rom of Austria. In the slalom event, Lawrence fell on her first run but, showing her determination and extraordinary ability, recovered to finish the run with the fourth-best time. Her second run was flawless, and the combined time of the two put her in first place to capture her second gold medal of the 1952 Winter Olympics.

Lawrence continued to compete in national and international ski events after the Olympics. She married fellow skier Dave Lawrence just prior to the Oslo Olympics and gave birth to the third of their five children just four months before competing in the 1956 Games. In her third Olympiad, she tied for fourth in the giant slalom, finishing less than one tenth of a second behind the bronze medalist.

For her achievements in women's Alpine skiing, Lawrence was awarded the White Stag Trophy in 1949 for the Best Ladies' Combined Downhill and the Beck International Trophy in 1952 as the outstanding U.S. skier in international competition. In 1958, she was inducted into the National Ski Hall of Fame. Two years later, the United States Olympic Committee (USOC) selected Lawrence to ski the Olympic flame into the stadium for the opening of the 1960 Winter Olympics at Squaw Valley, California. She was named to the International Women's Sports Hall of Fame in 1983.

Andrea Mead Lawrence forged her way to the top of women's Alpine skiing in the early 1950s and became the preeminent skier in the world. Her success in the Winter Olympics is unequalled by other U.S. skiers, and her example of excellence advanced the sport for all future Olympic skiers.

Further Reading

Lawrence, Andrea Mead, and Sara Burnaby. *A Practice of Mountains.* New York: Seaview Books, 1980. 230 pp.

Nancy Lieberman-Cline (basketball player)

Born July 1, 1958, Brooklyn, New York

One of the premier women's basketball players of all time, Nancy Lieberman-Cline led her college team to two national titles, qualified for two U.S. Olympic teams, and was the first woman to play in a professional men's basketball league when she joined the Springfield Fame of the U.S. Basketball League in 1986. She played for the Washington Generals against the Harlem Globetrotters and toured with Athletes in Action. Her competitive career has spanned more than two decades. She forged her own way and made professional basketball a career at a time when there were no real professional opportunities for women in basketball in the United States, earning more than $1 million as a basketball star. She has been a constant crusader for women's professional basketball, and her pioneering efforts in the men's leagues helped to change perceptions about women's abilities to play high-quality, entertaining basketball.

The daughter of Jerome and Renee Lieberman, Nancy was born in Brooklyn, New York, and later moved to nearby Far Rockaway, where she became obsessed with sports at an early age. Even though her mother constantly told her that sports were not for little girls, Lieberman-Cline spent most of her childhood on the playgrounds of New York, shooting baskets with the neighborhood boys. Because females were not allowed to play in New York's Public School Athletic League, she would go anywhere to play—the local YMCA, the beach, the playground—anywhere there was a pickup game going on. "I must have spent a million hours on basketball," she wrote in her first book, *Basketball My Way.* "I thought about it, I played it, and I dreamed of making history in it. I was an oddity for many—a girl playing in what has always been a male-dominated sport."[90]

Nancy Lieberman-Cline
Courtesy of Nancy Lieberman-Cline

Lieberman-Cline played for the Far Rockaway High School basketball team and in the summer would travel to Harlem to play for an Amateur Athletic Union (AAU) team, the New York Chuckles. Her skills and dedication did not go unnoticed. In 1975, she earned a spot on the U.S. Pan American team, and the following year she qualified for the U.S. Olympic team. At 17, Lieberman-Cline was the youngest person to make the 1976 Olympic Women's Basketball Team and, as a top reserve, contributed to the team's silver-medal-winning performance.

After graduating from high school and being recruited by the top colleges and universities in the country, Lieberman-Cline enrolled at Old Dominion University (ODU) in Norfolk, Virginia. As a Lady Monarch, she earned All-American honors three times and led her team to national titles in 1979 and 1980. Those same years Lieberman-Cline won the Wade Trophy, awarded to the outstanding female college basketball player. In her four-year college career, Lieber-

man-Cline averaged 18.1 points and 9 rebounds per game, and had a total of 286 steals and 961 assists. She had an enormous influence on the interest in women's basketball at Old Dominion. In her freshman year at ODU, the team was drawing about 350 people to its games; in her senior year, they drew nearly 10,000 at a game against the Soviet Union.

Her amateur career continued with the 1979 U.S. national team that won the World Women's Basketball Championship in Seoul, South Korea. The next year, she earned a spot on her second U.S. Olympic team but did not get to play because of the U.S. boycott of the Moscow Games.

Lieberman-Cline turned professional in 1981, signing a three-year, $100,000 contract with the Dallas Diamonds of the Women's Basketball League (WBL). She was the first woman in professional basketball to sign a contract for more than $100,000. In her first year, she averaged 26.3 points, led the team to the Coastal Division title, and was named All-Pro and Rookie of the Year. The league folded the next year because of financial difficulties, and so Lieberman worked in various sports-related ventures, including being a trainer and motivator for tennis star Martina Navratilova and a television sports commentator. When the Women's American Basketball Association (WABA) formed in 1984, Lieberman-Cline was again the first-draft pick of the Dallas Diamonds. She signed another three-year contract, this time for $250,000. The Diamonds won the WABA Championship, but the league folded after only one year.

In 1986, Lieberman-Cline became the first woman to play in a men's professional basketball league when she joined the Springfield, Massachusetts, Fame of the summer U.S. Basketball League. In 1988, she completed a year-long European tour playing with the Washington Generals against the Harlem Globetrotters. In 1989, after a nine-year layoff from international competition, Lieberman-Cline rejoined the U.S. national team.

Lieberman-Cline retired from basketball in 1992, only to pick up the game again in 1996 as she toured with Athletes in Action, averaging 15.7 points and 6.4 rebounds per game. Her career came full circle when, in 1997, the Phoenix Mercury of the Women's National Basketball Association (WNBA) drafted Lieberman-Cline in the second round of its elite draft. "I know I can play at this level," said 38-year-old Lieberman-Cline.[91]

In addition to the Wade Trophy, Lieberman-Cline has received other basketball honors. In 1980, she was awarded the Broderick Cup as the top female college athlete. In 1996, she was inducted into the Naismith Memorial Basketball Hall of Fame.

Committed to making basketball a career, Nancy Lieberman-Cline has played the game on a world-class level for more than two decades. She is considered by many to be one of the greatest to ever play the game. With no stable professional women's league in the 1970s and 1980s, she created her own opportunities. Her participation in the men's league helped change perceptions about women's basketball, and her activities, including writing about and broadcasting women's collegiate games in the off-season, have kept women's basketball at the forefront, paving the way for more amateur and professional opportunities for women.

Further Reading

Lieberman, Nancy. *Basketball My Way*. New York: Charles Scribner's Sons, 1982. 193 pp.

Lieberman-Cline, Nancy, with Robin Roberts. *Basketball for Women: Becoming a Complete Player*, Champaign, IL: Human Kinetics Publishing, 1995. 283 pp.

Lieberman-Cline, Nancy. *Lady Magic: The Autobiography of Nancy Lieberman-Cline*. New York: Sagamore Publishing, 1991. 270 pp.

Nancy Lopez (golfer)

Born January 6, 1957, Torrance, California

At age 21 in 1978, Nancy Lopez charged onto the women's professional golf scene and nearly single-handedly catapulted the Ladies Professional Golf Association (LPGA) into the mainstream of American sports. Lopez joined the LPGA in July 1977; and in 1978, her first full season on the women's tour, she broke the LPGA prize money record, winning more than $189,000. She won nine tournaments in her first year, including a record five in a row. She is the only female golfer to be named both Rookie of the Year and Player of the Year *in the same year*. Not since Babe Didrikson Zaharias in the 1950s had a female golfer attracted more media attention and spectator support than Lopez. A consistent winner on the LPGA tour, Lopez dominated women's golf in 1978 and 1979 and again in 1985, winning Player of the Year honors in each of those years. Through 1997, she had 48 LPGA tournament victories to her credit and had won more than $4.6 million. Her popularity helped attract new corporate sponsorships and television contracts for the LPGA. Lopez embodied the new generation of professional women golfers and epitomized the professional female athlete of the 1980s.

The daughter of Domingo and Marina Lopez, Nancy was born in Torrance, California, on January 6, 1957. When Nancy

Nancy Lopez
Courtesy of the Ladies Professional Golf Association

was three years old, her family moved to Roswell, New Mexico. Nancy was an active child while growing up in Roswell. She took dancing and gymnastic classes and liked to play basketball, volleyball, and touch football. But golf was her first love. At age seven, she often followed her parents as they played on the Roswell public golf course. When she was eight, her father pulled a golf club out of her mother's bag, a sawed-off four wood, and told her to hit the ball until she got it in the hole. And hit it she did.

When Lopez was nine, she played in her first tournament, which she won by 110 strokes. At the age of 12, Lopez won the New Mexico State Women's Amateur Championship. By the time she was 16, Lopez was the top-ranked amateur golfer

in the world. She played on the all-male Godard High School golf team and led the team to a state championship.

After high school, Lopez enrolled at the University of Tulsa on an athletic scholarship. In 1975, she entered the U.S. Women's Open as an amateur and finished second. The next year, Lopez won the Association of Intercollegiate Athletics for Women (AIAW) national championship. She also played on the U.S. Curtis Cup and World Amateur Teams.

Lopez joined the LPGA tour on July 29, 1977, and played in six tournaments that year. She finished second at the Colgate European Open in only her second tournament as an LPGA member. In 1978, she joined the tour full-time. Her first victory on the LPGA tour came at the Bent Tree Classic at Sarasota, Florida, on February 27, 1978. Later that year, she recorded five consecutive wins (Greater Baltimore Classic, May 12-14; Coca-Cola Classic, May 19-21; Golden Lights Championship, May 26-29; LPGA Championship, June 8-11; Bankers Trust Classic, June 16-18). In 1978, she won a total of nine LPGA events, and the following year she won eight of the 19 events she entered.

Although she cut back on her tournament appearances in the 1980s, Lopez continued to post victories on the LPGA tour. She won 12 tournaments between 1980 and 1984, and topped the million-dollar mark in career earnings on April 3, 1983, at the Nabisco Dinah Shore Classic. In 1985, Lopez came back to the tour full-time and captured five tournaments, including her second LPGA Championship. That same year, at the Willow Creek Golf Club in High Point, North Carolina, during the Henredon Classic, Lopez set a record with her 20-under-par score of 268 (66, 67, 69, 66) for 72 holes.

On July 20, 1987, she became the 11th member inducted into the LPGA Hall of Fame after collecting her 35th career victory at the Sarasota Classic. In 1989, Lopez was inducted into the PGA/World Golf Hall of Fame.

Between 1988 and 1993, Lopez won 12 more tournaments including another major, the Mazda LPGA Championship, in 1989. She also represented the victorious U.S. team in the 1990 inaugural Solheim Cup, the international match play competition similar to the men's Ryder Cup. She won the 1993 Youngstown-Warren LPGA Classic for her 47th career victory, and crossed the $4 million mark in career earnings in 1994. Lopez scored her 48th career victory in the rain-shortened Chick-fil-A Charity Championship in Stockbridge, Georgia, on April 26, 1997, her first victory in nearly four years.

The Associated Press selected Lopez as the Female Athlete of the Year in 1978 and 1985. *Golf Magazine* named Lopez the "Golfer of the Decade" for the years 1978 to 1987. She was the LPGA Player of the Year in 1978, 1979, 1985, and 1988; and she won the Vare Trophy for lowest scoring average in 1978, 1979, and 1985. In 1987, LPGA members chose Lopez to receive the Powell Award, "given annually to a member, who, in the opinion of her playing peers, by her behavior and deeds best exemplifies the spirit, ideals, and values of the LPGA" (*LPGA Player Guide*). She received the 1991 LPGA Samaritan Award for her humanitarian and charitable efforts, and in 1992, she was given the Flo Hyman Award by the Women's Sports Foundation, which is given to the woman athlete who captures Hyman's dignity, spirit, and commitment to excellence.

Her game is characterized by great strength for long drives, unbelievable poise in pressure situations, and impeccable putting. As a Latina, Nancy Lopez is a role model and sports hero for young Latinas nationwide. Her athletic skill and personable nature made her a tremendous draw for the LPGA tour. Lopez's emergence onto the golf scene brought women's professional golf into the mainstream of American sports, and with it came a new level of acceptance for women in other sports.

Further Reading

Lopez, Nancy, and Peter Schwed. *The Education of a Woman Golfer.* New York: Simon & Schuster, 1979. 191 pp.

Lopez, Nancy, with Don Wade. *Nancy Lopez's The Complete Golfer.* Chicago: Contemporary Books, 1987. 228 pp.

Phillips, Betty Lou. *The Picture Story of Nancy Lopez.* New York: Julian Messner, 1980. 64 pp.

Alice Marble (tennis player)

Born September 28, 1913, Beckworth, California; died December 13, 1990

As part of a group of successful and talented California players, San Francisco's Alice Marble reigned as the best women's tennis player in the late 1930s. She developed a style of play, the serve-and-volley, that revolutionized women's tennis. With this new power game, Marble became a tenacious doubles player and won numerous major doubles and singles titles throughout an amateur career that spanned nearly a decade.

As a young girl growing up in San Francisco, Alice Marble took a keen interest in baseball. She would spend hours

Alice Marble
Courtesy of the International Tennis Hall of Fame

watching the local teams play and often would play catch with some of the players. To get her away from this "masculine" sport, Marble's parents, Harry and Jessie, encouraged her to take up a more "ladylike" sport like tennis. At the age of 15, she began playing on the courts at Golden Gate Park. Marble picked up the game quickly; she had natural athletic ability and a quick aptitude for the game, but without a coach to teach her the fundamentals, she opted to rush the net to avoid having to use long ground strokes to return the ball.

Her quick feet allowed her to intercept her opponents' passing shots with ease, making her a formidable doubles player. In 1930, Eleanor "Teach" Tennant, a former nationally ranked player turned coach, began to coach Marble on the fundamentals she had been missing. Within two years, Marble had won both the California Junior Tennis Singles Championship and the U.S. National Girls' Doubles Championship, and had emerged as number seven on the national rankings for senior players by 1932.

Marble continued to progress with her serve-and-volley game. Her career took an unexpected turn when she developed health problems during the 1934 French Champi-

onships. During the Paris tournament, she collapsed on the court and was rushed to the hospital where doctors diagnosed her condition as tuberculosis and told her she would never play tennis again.

Despite the prognosis, Marble fought back to regain her strength and tennis skills. She began a program of diet and exercise that included hours of practice on the tennis court. Within two years, Marble had regained her championship form. She began her comeback with the U.S. Championships in 1936, winning both the singles and mixed doubles (with Gene Mako). She captured the U.S. singles title three more times (1938-40); the women's doubles title with Sarah Palfrey Fabyan four consecutive years (1937-40); and the mixed doubles title in 1938, 1939, and 1940 with three different partners.

She was equally impressive in international competition, claiming the Wimbledon singles title in 1939 and controlling the doubles play with wins in the ladies' doubles (1938, 1939) and the mixed doubles for three consecutive years (1937–39); her wins in 1939 gave her an unusual All-England tennis triple crown. Marble also played on winning Wightman Cup Teams (international team competition between players from the United States and Great Britain) in 1933, 1937, 1938, 1939, and 1940.

Marble was ranked number one among women tennis players in the world between 1936 and 1940, and the Associated Press honored her accomplishments by naming her Female Athlete of the Year in 1939 and 1940. She also had the distinction of being the first woman to wear shorts in international competition, a trend that caught on immediately among women players. In 1964, she was inducted into the International Tennis Hall of Fame.

In 1941, at the height of her career, Marble wanted to continue playing, but personal financial obligations and the halt in international amateur competition due to the onset of World War II compelled her to sign a professional contract with U.S. promoter Charles C. Pyle, ending her amateur career and the opportunity to vie for the major international titles. (Competitions such as the French, American, Australian, and British Championships were amateur events until 1968.) Marble toured the country playing exhibition matches against Britain's Mary Hardwick; these matches provided the foundation for the formation of a professional women's tennis circuit two decades later.

Marble was a tenacious competitor on the court and an outspoken advocate off the court as well. In 1950, when the all-White USLTA was considering an invitation to Black tennis star Althea Gibson to play in their championship, Alice wrote an editorial in *American Lawn Tennis* that garnered much attention. She wrote, "To me, she is a fellow tennis player and, as such, deserving of the same chance I had to prove myself . . . she is a fellow human being to whom equal privileges ought to be extended."[92]

Alice Marble stormed onto the tennis scene in 1934 with a revolutionary style of play that moved women's tennis away from the standard, often tedious, baseline play to an aggressive power game. She also challenged the traditions of women's tennis and influenced changes in restrictive clothing, which contributed to the advancement of the sport. Her determination and fortitude to play the game she loved on her own terms is her legacy to the sport of tennis.

Further Reading

Davidson, Sue. *Changing the Game: The Stories of Tennis Champions Alice Marble and Althea Gibson.* Seattle, WA: Seal Press, 1997. 160 pp.

Marble, Alice. *Courting Danger: My Adventure in World-Class Tennis, Golden-Age Hollywood, and High Stakes.* New York: St. Martin's Press, 1991. 255pp.

Marble, Alice. *The Road to Wimbledon.* New York: Charles Scribner's Sons, 1943. 167 pp.

Christy Martin (boxer)

Born June 12, 1968, Mullens, West Virginia

Christy Martin is the most successful and prominent female boxer in the United States. With a record of 38-2-2 (28 knockouts—KOs) through mid-1997, she has not lost a fight in nearly a decade. Her victory before 1.1 million pay-per-view fans on the undercard of the 1996 Tyson-Bruno fight showed the world that female boxers are skillful, aggressive athletes. Martin's accomplishments in the ring have knocked down barriers for women in this male-dominated sport and have legitimized women's efforts to be full participants in boxing.

Born Christy Salter, in Mullens, West Virginia, Martin was a catcher in Little League and an all-state basketball player in high school. She won a basketball scholarship to attend Concord College in Athens, West Virginia. Her introduction to boxing came when she accepted a dare to enter a local "Toughwoman" contest. She won three consecutive Toughwoman titles, and a few other fights in her area. Her success in these contests encouraged her to seek out a boxing trainer. She found Jim Martin in Bristol, Tennessee. (She married trainer and coach Martin in 1991.)

Martin recorded her first career win in a three-round decision over Sue McNamara in October 1, 1987. From 1987 until 1993, Martin posted a record of 23-2-1. Fourteen of her victories came by knockout, eight of them in the first round. A turning point in her career came in 1993 when Martin signed with boxing promoter Don King. She has appeared in several undercards of King-sponsored events, which has given

Christy Martin
Courtesy of Don King Productions

her well-deserved recognition and more prize money. Richard Hoffer wrote in *CNNSI*, "Anybody who knows how hard it is to become a good boxer has been impressed with the level of Martin's skill and her determination."[93]

On the undercard of the March 16, 1996, Mike Tyson-Frank Bruno pay-per-view bout in Las Vegas, Martin displayed her relentless, aggressive style and technically correct boxing skills to more than 1.1 million television viewers. She defeated Ireland's Deirdre Gogarty in a unanimous six-round decision to retain the honorary World Boxing Council (WBC) Women's Lightweight Championship. As one reporter noted, "The women's bout had more action and better boxing than the main event."[94]

On the undercard of the infamous Tyson-Holyfield fight in Las Vegas on June 28, 1997, Martin survived a broken nose in the first round to defeat Andrea DeShong of Ohio with a technical knockout in the seventh round. She earned $150,000 for the victory.

With a record of 38-2-2, Christy Martin hasn't lost a fight since 1989 and has become the first woman to be taken seriously for her considerable skills in the ring. Her legitimacy knocked down stereotypes and opened doors for other female boxers around the world. As she told the *Fort Worth Star Telegram:* "I try to prepare myself well, try to go and put on the best show I possibly can for the people. I don't look at it as [being a female] in a male-dominated sport, because I'm not trying to fight a man. I'm just competing against a woman."[95]

Helene Mayer (fencer)

Born May 1910, Konigstein, Germany; died October 1953

Considered by many to be the greatest woman fencer in the history of the sport, Helene Mayer was the 1928 Olympic gold medalist, the 1937 world champion, a two-time European champion (1929, 1931), and an eight-time U.S. national champion (1934-46). She was a formidable competitor capable of holding her own against the best fencers of her generation.

Born in Germany in 1910, Mayer won her first national championship at age 13. A few days before her 18th birthday, she won the women's foil event at the 1928 Olympics in Amsterdam. The 17-year-old swept through the Olympic tournament with remarkable ease, winning 18 bouts and losing two.

A year later, Mayer captured the European (now called the world's) championship, and repeated in 1931. She traveled to Los Angeles in the summer of 1932 to compete in the Olympic Summer Games; she finished fifth in the women's foil competition. She remained in the United States after the Games, attending Scripps College in California as an exchange student. In 1933, she had been expelled from the Offenbach Fencing Club in Germany as part of a Nazi purge of Jewish athletes. Because of the political and social upheaval caused by the rise of Nazism in Germany, Mayer decided to make the United States her permanent home.

The daughter of a Jewish father and a Christian mother, Mayer became embroiled in the politics surrounding the 1936 Olympics. As a condition for hosting the 1936 Olympics, the German Organizing Committee assured the International Olympic Committee (IOC) that German Jews would not be excluded from the German teams, and so the German government invited Mayer to compete as a member of the German team. Mayer accepted the invitation as an opportunity to recapture the gold medal and to see the family she had left behind. In an electrifying duel, Mayer finished second to Hungarian Ilona Schacherer-Elek (who was also Jewish) in the foil competition at the Berlin Games. After the Olympics, Mayer returned to California. In 1937, she made the trip from California to Paris for the 1937 world championship, and defeated all her opponents, including Schacherer-Elek. It was her final international event; she never returned to Germany.

During her 20-year residence in the United States, Mayer competed in nine national fencing championships. She won eight national foil titles (1934-35, 1937-39, 1941-42, 1946). Her only loss came in 1947, her last national championship tournament, when she was defeated by Helena Mroczkowska Dow.

Mayer retired from competition in 1947 but continued to coach young fencers. An accomplished linguist, she taught German, French, and Italian at Mills College while working on a master's degree at the University of California at Berkeley. She later became a political science professor at the City College of San Francisco. Mayer became a naturalized citizen of the United States just prior to the outbreak of World War II. She died of cancer in October 1953.

A classical stylist and a tremendous competitor, Helene Mayer is regarded by many to be the greatest woman fencer in the history of her sport. She was a national, world, and Olympic champion, and her accomplishments advanced the sport of fencing for women around the world.

Patricia McCormick (diver)

Born May 12, 1930, Seal Beach, California

When diving was added as an Olympic event for women, platform in 1912 and springboard in 1920, U.S. women took a stranglehold on the events and nearly swept the Olympic medals for more than four decades. One of America's greatest divers, Patricia McCormick, continued the tradition of U.S. domination by winning a total of four gold medals in two successive Olympic Games, the only woman in Olympic diving history to achieve the "double double." Her victories came in Helsinki in 1952 and Melbourne in 1956. In addition to her Olympic success, McCormick won a total of 27 national championships, and three gold and two silver medals at the Pan American Games. Her grace and daring on the diving board, combined with intense dedication, led to a career that became the standard by which other diving careers are judged.

The daughter of Robert and Harriet Keller, McCormick grew up on the California coast, spending all her free time in the waters off Seal and Muscle Beach. As a teenager, McCormick went to the Los Angeles Aquatics Club to refine her skills and diving technique. At age 14, she won her first title, the Long Beach City women's one-meter diving Gold Cup. She trained long hours at the aquatics club, practicing twisting and turning dives rarely even attempted by men.

In 1949, McCormick won the national platform title and successfully defended the title the following year, winning the springboard event as well. In 1951, she became the first woman to sweep all the national

Pat McCormick
Courtesy of the International Swimming Hall of Fame

Amateur Athletic Union (AAU) indoor and outdoor diving championships.

She practiced eight hours a day, six days a week, performing 80 to 100 dives a day to perfect her technique. McCormick focused on executing the most difficult dives. This intense training would prove to be her edge against international competition.

McCormick traveled to the 1952 Helsinki Olympics as the leader of the U.S. swimming and diving team. The 22-year-old outdistanced the field by performing nearly flawless dives with a degree of difficulty not previously seen in women's diving. She won gold medals in both the platform and springboard events.

She returned to the United States with little fanfare, ready to retire to raise her family. But the burning desire to compete remained, and McCormick continued to train at the Los Angeles Aquatics Club for the 1956 Olympics in Melbourne. McCormick dove to perfection in the Games, successfully defending her Olympic titles in both the platform and springboard events.

When she finally retired from competitive diving, she had accumulated an unprecedented four Olympic gold medals, five Pan American Games medals, and 27 national championships. Recognized for her outstanding achievements, she was the 1956 Associated Press Female Athlete of the Year and was awarded the 1956 James E. Sullivan Award as the Amateur Athlete of the Year, only the second woman to be so honored. (Swimmer Ann Curtis won in

1944.) In 1965, she became the first woman to be inducted into the International Swimming Hall of Fame. She also was named to the International Women's Sports Hall of Fame in 1984 and the U.S. Olympic Hall of Fame in 1985.

McCormick remained active in diving, opening up a diving camp to teach future U.S. divers. One of her students, daughter Kelly, won the silver medal at the 1984 Los Angeles Olympics and a bronze medal at the 1988 Seoul Olympics.

McCormick was a member of the U.S. Olympic Committee and the 1984 Los Angeles Olympic Organizing Committee, and was one of several American Olympic heroes to escort the Olympic flag into the Los Angeles Memorial Coliseum during the opening ceremonies of the 1984 Summer Olympics.

In a sport that requires the grace of a ballet star, the daring of a parachutist, and the agility of a high jumper, Patricia McCormick combined her talents to become one of the greats in her sport. The degree of difficulty she attained on her dives set a new standard for future female divers, and her determination to achieve perfection took her to new heights as an athlete. She gave back to her sport by actively promoting Olympic competition in the United States and training the next generation of American divers. Her record "double double" has stood through 10 Olympiads; and with the increasing specialization in sports, it may never be equaled.

Floretta Doty McCutcheon (bowler)

Born July 22, 1888, Ottumwa, Iowa; died February 2, 1967

Floretta Doty McCutcheon reigned as the queen of women's bowling in the 1920s and 1930s. She brought recognition to women's bowling as an accomplished bowler, but she was perhaps most influential as a bowling instructor. She became a role model for women who otherwise would not have become involved in the "masculine" sport of bowling. McCutcheon is credited with teaching nearly 300,000 women to bowl in her 26 years as a teacher.

Born in Ottumwa, Iowa, on July 22, 1888, Floretta Doty moved with her family to Denver, Colorado, in 1901. She attended public schools there and subsequently met and married Robert J. McCutcheon. In 1921, the McCutcheons moved to Pueblo, Colorado.

For recreation, McCutcheon joined the women's volleyball team at the local YMCA while her husband bowled in a weekly industrial league. Her husband and her friends encouraged her to take up bowling, but she was reluctant to do so because of family and church obligations. In November 1923, her husband formed a new league and put McCutcheon on one of the teams (without her knowledge). "I was literally forced into bowling," she explained later.[96] At the age of 35, McCutcheon bowled her first game, knocking down 69 pins. McCutcheon joined two leagues during 1924. Her scores increased with practice, but her delivery style was anything but polished. She commented later: "I often wonder why I didn't break my neck running the way I did. . . . I stood as far back as I could, ran to the foul line, swinging the 16-pound ball. My impression of the way to bowl was to throw as hard as possible."[97]

At the end of the season, McCutcheon quit bowling for three years because of ill health but picked it up again in 1926. Adopting a more controlled delivery, McCutcheon's scores increased dramatically. Within a year, she had rolled her first perfect game and several three-game series of 700 or better. By the fall of 1927, she had become a sensation in local bowling circles and began doing exhibitions around the state. In one exhibition, she bowled three 800 series (an average of more than 266 per game).

In 1927, McCutcheon challenged world champion bowler Jimmy Smith to a three-game set. The crowd packed into the Denver Bowling Company alleys on December 18 to watch McCutcheon defeat Smith 704 to 697. After the match, Smith commented: "She is simply the greatest bowler I have ever seen."[98]

Floretta Doty McCutcheon
Courtesy of the International Bowling Museum and Hall of Fame

McCutcheon's victory made headlines in sports pages around the country. On the heels of the exploits of such heroines as Gertrude Ederle and Amelia Earhart, Mc-Cutcheon gained national recognition as an exceptional sportswoman in her own right. But she did not fit the mold of her predecessors. At the age of 39, she presented an interesting image on the lanes. Reporters characterized her as "a quiet, studious, smiling, [prematurely] gray-haired little woman who might have just dropped her knitting."[99] Because of her quiet demeanor, McCutcheon became an excellent role model for future women bowlers of all ages.

In 1928, Brunswick Corporation offered McCutcheon a job as a traveling instructor. She took the job to raise money for her daughter's college education. In her first tour in 1928, she bowled 788 games in 66 cities; the next season took her on a tour of 44 West Coast cities.

In her first two years as a teacher, McCutcheon primarily staged exhibition matches against local bowlers, with some time set aside for instruction. Her manager began setting up newspaper-sponsored bowling schools patterned after the popular cooking schools of the day. The *Peoria Star* of Illinois sponsored the first Mrs. McCutcheon School of Bowling in 1931. The same year the *Chicago Herald Examiner* sponsored a school that more than 3,500 women attended. At the new bowling schools, McCutcheon gave personal instruction by day and bowled exhibitions at night. Financed by bowling center owners and operators, the schools provided free instruction to all women bowlers attending. At this time, McCutcheon was the only bowling teacher in the country giving instructions specifically to women.

From 1930 to 1938, McCutcheon toured the United States setting up schools and organizing leagues. In addition to her public instructional sessions, she conducted classes for high school girls and for blind bowlers, and she gave special instruction to female students at Vassar College and New York University. She often told her students that "bowling is one of the few sports at which women and men can have such hilarious fun while participating as equals . . . . Since bowling depends on rhythm and timing rather than on strength, women often make more rapid progress than men."[100]

McCutcheon retired from touring in 1938 after 10 years on the road. She averaged a remarkable 201 for 8,076 games. She bowled eleven 800 series and 10 perfect games in her career. McCutcheon settled in New York, then later moved to Chicago where she continued to teach and organize women's leagues. In 1954, she retired from teaching and moved to Pasadena, California, where she remained active in local bowling circles until her death in 1967.

For her "ability in both field performance and organization," McCutcheon was inducted into the Women's International Bowling Congress Hall of Fame in 1956; she was also inducted into the Colorado Sports Hall of Fame in 1973 and the Pueblo, Colorado, Sports Association Hall of Fame in 1974.

Floretta Doty McCutcheon remains a legend in many bowling circles. She is credited with single-handedly thrusting women's bowling into the limelight. She drew other women into the game with a gracious manner and a genuine love of people and the game. Her enthusiasm was infectious as she taught thousands of women to enjoy the game.

Early in her career, McCutcheon established herself as a woman of enormous energy and a role model for future women bowlers. To start the game at age 35 proved to many women (and men) that it really was "never too late." In her years as bowling's "Pied Piper," she made organized bowling more accessible to women who otherwise would have stayed away from the game.

Ann Meyers (basketball player)

Born March 26, 1955, San Diego, California

A woman whose life is full of firsts, Ann Meyers is a true pioneer in women's basketball. Meyers was the first high school player to make the U.S. Women's National Basketball Team (1974), a member of the first women's Olympic basketball team (1976), the first female recipient of a full athletic scholarship at the University of California at Los Angeles (UCLA) (1974), and the first woman to sign a contract with a National Basketball Association (NBA) team (1979). Meyers's pioneering efforts proved to the nation that women's basketball was a healthy and viable sport for girls and women around the country.

Meyers came from a basketball-playing family, and so it was natural that she would pick up the game, too. Her father, Bob, played guard for Marquette University and later played with the American Basketball Association (ABA) Milwaukee Shooting Stars. Her brother, Dave, also played basketball at UCLA and was a starting forward for the Milwaukee Bucks of the NBA.

Meyers got involved in sports at a young age, initially more interested in track and field than in basketball. She excelled at the high jump, and at age 15, finished third in the event at the California State Junior Olympics. One of the great all-around women athletes, Meyers lettered in seven sports in high school. Basketball became her passion, though, and while a senior at Sonora High School, she became the first high school player to make a U.S. national team that played against international teams, including the Soviet Union.

Meyers entered UCLA in 1974. As a freshman for the Bruins, she had an immediate impact on the team. She was a hardworking, inspirational leader, motivating her teammates to strive for greatness. She was an excellent shooter and passer and played intense defense as well. Meyers was named All-American all four years she played for UCLA. She led the team to postseason tournament play in each of those years including a national championship in 1978.

In response to her remarkable 1978 season, the university honored her as their Athlete of the Year, she won the Broderick Award as the outstanding women's college basketball player of the year, and she was chosen Collegiate Woman Athlete of the Year by the National Association for Girls and Women in Sports. At a school that dominated men's collegiate basketball in the 1960s and 1970s and that sent numerous players to the NBA, Meyers scored more points than any other player in UCLA's history—male or female. Her college jersey was retired in the Naismith Memorial Basketball Hall of Fame in 1978.

While Meyers's collegiate career soared, she gained extensive international experience. She played on the U.S. team at the 1975 Pan American Games, taking home a gold medal. At the 1976 Olympics in Montreal, Meyers teamed with other stars such as Nancy Lieberman(-Cline) and Patricia

Ann Meyers
Courtesy of UCLA Athletics

Head (Summitt) to win the silver medal in the first women's basketball tournament at the Olympics. She also participated in the 1977 World University Games, finishing second, and captained the gold-medal-winning teams at the 1979 Pan American Games and world championships.

In 1979, she became the first—and only—woman to be drafted by the NBA. She signed with the Indiana Pacers of the league. She participated in a three-day, twice-a-day tryout. "My sole purpose was to make the ball club as a player," Meyers said. "I feel very proud and grateful to have been a part of that experience."[101]

After not making the Indiana Pacers team, Meyers signed a contract with the New Jersey Gems of the Women's Professional Basketball League (WPBL). She averaged 22.2 points a game, led the league in steals, and was voted co-MVP in the 1979-80 season. She left the Gems in 1981 over a contract dispute; the league folded a year later because of financial difficulties.

Exhibiting her all-around athletic ability, Meyers finished fourth in the first Women's Superstar competition, an event sponsored by *Ladies Home Journal* and *womenSports* magazine that pitted notable women athletes against one another in several different sports including softball throwing, cycling, rowing, swimming, and the 60- and 440-yard dashes. She went on to win the annual competition for the next three years until a rule change forced her to retire from the competition.

Meyers started a broadcasting career while playing for the Gems. She provided game analysis at the 1984 Los Angeles Olympics and continues to do commentary for women's basketball on ESPN, NBC, and local stations around the country. For her efforts as a player, Meyers was inducted into the International Women's Sports Hall of Fame in 1985 and the Naismith Memorial Basketball Hall of Fame in 1993.

Ann Meyers's outstanding career as a collegiate and international player had a significant impact on women's basketball and women's sports in general. Her All-American efforts in college transferred to international competition, providing talent and leadership abilities that resulted in gold and silver medals for the United States. Her contract with the Indiana Pacers brought attention to the women's game, giving the team sport a place in the sports world and inspiring younger players to reach for goals previously unattainable in women's sports.

Cheryl Miller (basketball player)

Born January 3, 1964, Riverside, California

As one of the nation's top female basketball players of the 1980s, Cheryl Miller of Riverside, California, set innumerable scoring records during her four years at the University of Southern California (USC). She led her USC teams to two consecutive National Collegiate Athletic Association (NCAA) championship titles and was the leading scorer on the gold-medal-winning 1984 U.S. women's basketball team. She played an aggressive game and was an inspiring leader on the court. In the Los Angeles media spotlight, Miller showed fans that women could play with the quickness and speed most often associated with the men's game. As a result, she was influential in ushering in a new, more exciting brand of women's collegiate basketball in the 1980s.

The daughter of Saul and Carrie Miller, Cheryl began playing basketball with her

Cheryl Miller
USC Sports Information

brothers, including future NBA star Reggie, on the courts of Riverside, California, at age seven. Her father, a former high school and college player, taught her the basics, emphasizing the importance of developing an all-around game. When she was 10, she played on the fifth-grade boys' basketball team. Miller said of her early playing days, "The boys on the other teams laughed at me in the beginning, but then they'd see the score at the end of the game and they weren't laughing anymore."[102]

During her four years at Riverside Poly High School (1979-82), Miller played in 90 games, averaged 32.8 points per game, and led the team to a 132-4 record. She holds the California Interscholastic Federation records for most career points (3,405) and most points scored in one season (1,156). In a game against Norte Vista High School on January 26, 1983, Miller became the first woman to dunk a basketball in regulation play. In that game she scored 105 points, leading Riverside Poly to a 179-15 victory.

Parade magazine named Miller to its High School All-American Team four consecutive years (1979–82); she was a consensus All-American four times (1979–82); and she was selected *Street and Smith*'s top high school basketball player (1981–82). By the end of her senior year, Miller was the most sought-after female college basketball player in the country. She had scholarship offers from nearly 250 colleges and universities.

In 1983, Miller enrolled at USC to study communications and broadcasting and to play for the Women of Troy. She made the transition from high school to college basketball with ease. In her freshman year, Miller led USC in scoring, blocking, and steals and helped the Women of

Troy win the 1983 NCAA championship over defending champion Louisiana Tech. In the title game, she scored 27 of USC's 69 points and had nine rebounds. In the 1983-84 season, the 6' 3'' inch sophomore led the team to a 24-4 regular season record and another NCAA championship. In both appearances, Miller was voted the tournament's most valuable player.

In international competition, Miller was a member of the U.S. national team that won the gold medal at the 1983 Pan American Games. The following year she won another gold medal as the leading scorer of the U.S. Women's Olympic Basketball Team at the 1984 Los Angeles Olympics.

Miller's best college season came in 1984-85, after the Olympics, when she averaged 26.8 points per game for the Women of Troy. More than an offensive powerhouse, Miller also averaged 15.8 rebounds per game and is the all-time NCAA rebounding leader at 10.6 rebounds per game. In her senior year, she finished fourth in scoring average (25.4 points per game), leading USC to a 31-5 record and an appearance in the NCAA championship game. (USC lost to the University of Texas, 97-81.)

In one of the most illustrious collegiate basketball careers, Miller won nearly every major basketball award. She won the Broderick Award as the college player of the year (1984, 1985); the Wade Trophy, voted on by the National Association for Girls and Women in Sports (1985); the Naismith Trophy (1984, 1985, 1986); the Women's Basketball Coaches' Association Player of the Year (1985, 1986); and the Female College Athlete of the Year (1984). In addition to winning these national awards, Miller was chosen to numerous all-conference and all-tournament teams. In March 1986,

USC retired her number, 31, making her the first USC basketball player to be so honored. She was inducted into the International Women's Sports Hall of Fame in 1991 and the Naismith Memorial Basketball Hall of Fame in 1995.

After graduating from USC in 1986, Miller played on the U.S. national team, winning a gold medal at the Goodwill Games in Moscow in July 1986 and at the World Basketball Championships the following month. A severe knee injury caused her to miss both the 1987 Pan American Games and the 1988 Olympics.

After retiring from competition in 1988 and armed with a degree in communications from USC, Miller took up broadcasting, working as a color commentator for ABC and ESPN. She joined the coaching staff at USC as an assistant coach from 1986-91. In 1993, she took over the head coaching job at USC, guiding her team to a 44-14 record, a Pac-10 title in 1994, and two NCAA tournament berths. She returned to broadcasting in 1995 for the Turner Sports Network. In 1997, the Phoenix Mercury of the Women's National Basketball Association (WNBA) hired Miller as their head coach and general manager. In her first year as coach and GM, she led the Mercury to a 16–12 record, the Western Conference title, and a trip to the WNBA finals.

During her high school, collegiate, and international basketball careers, Cheryl Miller demonstrated incredible athletic talent. With the majority of her games played under the spotlight in one of the country's media centers, her superior skills attracted attention to women's collegiate basketball. She electrified audiences all over the country and helped to transform women's basketball into an exciting spectator sport.

Shannon Miller (gymnast)

Born March 10, 1977, Rolla, Missouri

Shannon Miller is the most decorated gymnast in U.S. history, winning more Olympic and world championship medals than any other American gymnast. Miller is the only American to win two consecutive world championship all-around titles. She helped the United States win its first women's Olympic team title at the 1996 Atlanta Olympics. An Olympic gold medalist at age 19, Miller helped reclaim the sport of gymnastics for older, more artistic athletes by contributing grace and athleticism to every performance. "She's a goal achiever," said her coach Steve Nunno, "and she's setting the pace for the rest of the youth of America. They'll see that all the hard work and dedication you put in to something is worth it."[103]

Born on March 10, 1977, in Rolla, Missouri, the daughter of Ron and Claudia Miller, Shannon was introduced to gymnastics at age five when her parents bought a trampoline. She like to bounce all day on her new trampoline. Within two weeks, she could do a front flip. Impressed with her enthusiasm and acrobatic skills, Miller's parents enrolled her at a local gymnastics center called Adventures in Gymnastics.

In 1986, at age nine, Miller made the United States Association of Independent Gymnastics Clubs' (USAIGC) junior elite team. As a member of the team, she traveled to the Soviet Union to attend a gymnastics training camp. It was in Moscow that she met coach Steve Nunno of Dynamo Gymnastics in Oklahoma City, Oklahoma. Once Miller started training at Dynamo, her gymnastics skills progressed dramatically. Miller's first national competition was the 1987 USAIGC National Gymnastics Championship at the University of Delaware in Newark, a team competition in

which her team placed third. At her next big event, the 1988 U.S. Classic, she won the vault, balance beam, and all-around events in her age group.

Throughout 1990 and 1991, Miller continued to perform well as she prepared for her first Olympic Games. She won the vault, balance beam, floor exercise, and all-around events at the 1990 Catania Cup in Catania, Italy. She also won the all-around title at the Swiss Cup in St. Gallen, Switzerland, and the balance beam at the U.S. Gymnastics Championships in Indianapolis, Indiana, in 1991.

Miller won the all-around title at the Olympic trials to earn a spot on the 1992 U.S. Women's Olympic Gymnastic Team. At the Games in Barcelona, Spain, Miller led the Americans to a bronze medal in the team event. In the individual events, she won bronze in the uneven bars, silver in the balance beam, and bronze in the floor exercise. Miller also won the silver in the all-around, losing the gold by just .012 points to Tatyana Gutsu of the Unified Team. Her five medals were the most won by a U.S. athlete in the Barcelona Games.

Miller followed up her Olympic medals with a first-place finish in the 1993 American Cup. She added new, more difficult moves to her routines as she headed into the 1993 world championships. With strong performances in the balance beam, uneven bars, and floor exercise, Miller won the all-around competition at the 1993 World Gymnastics Championships in Birmingham, England. She added golds in the individual uneven bars and floor exercise. Her total of three gold medals was the most ever won by a U.S. gymnast at a world or Olympic competition. She concluded the 1993 season at the U.S. National Gymnas-

Shannon Miller
© Allsport USA/Mike Powell

tics Championships, where she won her first national all-around title and completed the competition by winning both the uneven bars and the floor exercise. She successfully defended her world title when she won the all-around title and a gold medal on the balance beam at the 1994 World Gymnastics Championships in Brisbane, Australia—the first athlete ever to win two consecutive all-around gymnastics titles in world championship competition.

As Miller prepared for the 1996 Olympics, critics began to question her abilities because of her age. (She would be 19, ancient by contemporary gymnastics standards.) These comments made her more determined. "When the media started to write that I was too old for the sport, it was then I decided I would show myself and a lot of other people that I wasn't too old, that I could still learn the skills, and that I had what it takes to win," she said.[104]

Miller led the U.S. team to America's first-ever gold medal in Olympic team gymnastics competition at the 1996 Centennial Olympics. She finished her Olympic career before a crowd of more than 30,000 at the Georgia Dome with a near perfect performance on the balance beam, scoring 9.862 to earn the gold medal. It was her first individual gold medal in Olympic competition. "It was a fantastic note on which to end my Olympic competition," she said.[105]

Miller was nominated for the Women's Sports Foundation Sportswoman of the Year in 1992, 1993, and 1994 and was selected the 1994 Female (Artistic) Athlete of the Year by USA Gymnastics and the United States Olympic Committee (USOC). She also won the 1994 Dial Award as the top female high school athlete in the nation.

America's most decorated gymnast, Miller has earned seven Olympic medals and nine world championships medals and back-to-back all-around world championships. "I'd like to tell young athletes that gymnastics is a great sport, because it helps you with the coordination, strength, and discipline you need for any sport. It teaches you the value of hard work and about goal setting. Your goal doesn't have to be to make the Olympics. There are other goals to pursue: college scholarships, national and international competitions, but most important, you can get an education and prepare yourself for the world," she told writer Nancy Kleinbaum in *The Magnificent Seven: The Authorized Story of American Gold*.[106]

Combining artistic talent with an incredibly high skill level, Shannon Miller claimed a place in gymnastics for older and more graceful athletes. The two-time Olympian and world champion set a new standard for women's gymnastics in the United States in the 1990s, and helped ensure a strong future for women's gymnastics in the twenty-first century.

Further Reading

Green, Septima. *Going for the Gold: Shannon Miller.* New York: Avon Books, 1996. 86 pp.

Quiner, Krista. *Shannon Miller: America's Most Decorated Gymnast.* East Hanover, NJ: The Bradford Book Company, 1996. 220 pp.

Helen Wills Moody (tennis player)

Born October 6, 1905, Centerville, California; died January 1, 1998

When Martina Navratilova won her ninth singles title at Wimbledon in July 1990, she beat Helen Wills Moody's record that had stood for more than half a century. Between 1923 and 1938, Moody won a total of eight Wimbledon singles titles; in addition, she won the U.S. women's singles title seven times, the French Championship four times, and the gold medal at the 1924 Paris Olympics. As a top female player for nearly two decades, she became a sports hero and a darling of the media and the American public; her pioneering efforts in promoting dress emancipation for women contributed to improving women's tennis.

Born in Centerville, California, in 1905, the daughter of Dr. Clarence Wills, Helen first played tennis with her father at the Berkeley Tennis Club. In 1919, she won her first championship, the Pacific Coast Juniors, and when she was 15, she captured the national junior girls' title. In 1922, she made it to the finals of the U.S. Championships, where she lost to eight-time winner Molla Mallory in straight sets.

In 1923, Moody began her campaign to become the top female tennis player in the world. She won the first of her seven U.S. singles titles (1923-25, 1927-29, 1931) at Forest Hills, New York. She won the Wimbledon women's singles title eight times (1927-30, 1932-33, 1935, 1938) and the French Championship four times (1928-30, 1932). She competed on nine Wightman Cup Teams (international team competition between players from the United States and Great Britain)—1923, 1925, 1927-32, 1938—and won an Olympic gold medal in singles play at the 1924 Paris Games. Although not a strong net player, Moody also won numerous doubles crowns, including the U.S. women's title (with Marian Jessup in 1922, Hazel Hotchkiss Wightman in 1924 and 1928, and Mary K. Browne in 1925), the Wimbledon doubles three times (with Wightman in 1924 and with Elizabeth Ryan in 1927 and 1930), and the Olympic gold medal at the 1924 Games (with Wightman).

A formidable baseline player, Moody had a powerful serve and strong ground strokes. Her remarkable consistency and

Helen Wills Moody
Courtesy of International Tennis Hall of Fame

steadfast concentration demoralized most opponents. She could hit the ball with power and made very few unforced errors.

Her steely expressions and tenacity on the court showed only one side of Moody. Articulate and outspoken, Moody became a champion of women's dress reform in tennis. The tennis establishment had set strict standards of dress and expected women players to wear the "acceptable" tennis dress of the time—long skirts, long sleeves, and stockings—which hindered movement on the court. By 1920, however, Moody and several other players began to challenge the dress code. Her standard attire of a knee-length, pleated skirt and a white visor became her trademark.

A multitalented woman, Moody graduated Phi Beta Kappa from the University of California in 1928 with a degree in fine arts. As an illustrator and author, she wrote several novels and published an instructional book, *Tennis,* in 1928. She also published her memoirs, *Fifteen-Thirty,* in 1937. In 1935, the Associated Press selected Moody as the Female Athlete of the Year; and in 1959, she became a member of the International Tennis Hall of Fame.

Winning more U.S. Championship singles titles (seven) than any other woman in international tennis history, Helen Wills Moody dominated women's tennis for nearly two decades. She became an authentic heroine, idolized by the thousands who followed her career during the 1920s and 1930s, America's "Golden Age of Sports." Moody brought women's international tennis to the public eye and helped to convince critics that tennis was an "acceptable" sport for women. Although she will be remembered for her outstanding accomplishments on the court, perhaps she played a more important role in changing women's tennis attire, which had a direct impact on improving the standard of international play.

Further Reading

Engelmann, Larry. *The Goddess and the American Girl: The Story of Suzanne Lenglen and Helen Wills.* New York: Oxford University Press, 1988. 478 pp.

Wills, Helen. *Fifteen-Thirty: The Story of a Tennis Player.* New York: Charles Scribner's Sons, 1937.

Shirley Muldowney (drag racer)

Born June 19, 1940, Schenectady, New York

In the world of drag racing, no woman has been more successful than Shirley Muldowney, and very few men can claim the predominance on the drag strip that Muldowney established in the late 1970s and early 1980s. Not only did Muldowney break down gender barriers in auto racing, she also totally dominated the sport of drag racing, a sport that requires direct competition with men. In 1975, at age 35, Muldowney became the first woman licensed in

the United States to drive top fuel dragsters, and two years later, she won the first of three world championship titles. Early in her career, Muldowney had to overcome discrimination from sponsors, drivers, and racing fans. She earned their respect and admiration with her determination and expert driving skills.

Born Shirley Roques on June 19, 1940, in Schenectady, New York, Shirley's fascination with cars and racing began when she

Shirley Muldowney
© Allsport USA/Tim DeFrisco

was 14. Growing up in suburban New York, she would sneak away with her boyfriend Jack Muldowney to late-night drag races on the secluded back roads and deserted streets. Jack was an avid street racer, and Muldowney picked up her love of the sport from him. He let her drive his 1951 Mercury and she quickly experienced success in the late-night races.

When Shirley turned 16, she left high school to marry Jack. (She returned to get her diploma eight years later.) The couple continued to race cars, Shirley as driver and Jack as her mechanic. She bought her first car—a 1940 Ford Coupe—for $40, rebuilt it, and began racing it as a funny car dragster at local track competitions. She won her first major race in Rockingham, North Carolina, in 1971. As Muldowney became more successful, she immersed herself in full-time racing.

In 1972, Muldowney hired top fuel racer Connie Kalitta as her crew chief. She

raced in the funny car class for two years. After surviving three fiery crashes, Muldowney switched to the safer and faster top fuel dragsters. (In the funny car, the engine is mounted in front, while in the top fuel racer, the engine is in a safer position behind the driver.)

Muldowney became the first woman to qualify for a national event in top fuel (1974); the first woman to win a National Hot Rod Association (NHRA) event title—the Springnationals in Columbus, Ohio (1976); and the first woman to break the six-second barrier on the quarter-mile track (1980). In 1977, Muldowney won three consecutive national events that gave her the 1977 NHRA World Championship title.

Despite her success as the leading top fuel driver in the country, Muldowney could not secure a sponsor to finance her driving. The racing world credited her success to the work of Kalitta rather than to her driving skill; and after Muldowney ended her partnership with him, she had to prove herself all over again. By 1980, the determined driver and her young crew had come of age.

At the season's first race, the Winternationals in Pomona, California, Muldowney set a record, speeding down the quarter-mile track at 255 miles per hour. In her trademark pink dragster, she became the first woman to break the six-second barrier when she clocked 5.705 seconds to win the Gatornationals in Gainesville, Florida. Muldowney and her crew won 11 races in 1980 to claim her second NHRA Top Fuel World Championship, the first driver to win the world title more than once.

In 1981, Muldowney won two national events, and in 1982, she defeated her former crew chief Connie Kalitta at the U.S. Nationals in Indianapolis and set a new drag racing record in blasting down the quarter-mile track in 5.57 seconds. The win gave Muldowney her first U.S. Nationals title and her third world championship. The following year, Hollywood made a movie about her amazing career, *Heart Like a Wheel*, in which Muldowney served as creative consultant.

Disaster struck in 1984 when Muldowney's car blew a front tire doing 250 miles per hour down the Sanair Speedway near Montreal. The car broke into pieces and flew nearly 600 feet before coming to a stop in an embankment. Muldowney's legs were shattered; her pelvis, right hand, and five fingers were broken; and her right thumb and left foot were nearly severed. She spent seven and a half weeks in a Montreal hospital and had five more operations in the next year. Through it all, she never considered quitting racing: "I started racing in 1958, before women's lib, before anything like that. I was just doing what I wanted to do. The accident took a lot out of me physically, but it really didn't kill my will to win."[107]

Muldowney returned to racing in January 1986 at Firebird International Raceway in Phoenix, Arizona. More than 20,000 spectators came to welcome back the world-champion drag racer. Her first run was just .03 second slower than her all-time best. In her comeback season, she had her career-best time (5.42 seconds) and raced over 267 miles per hour. She finished 10th overall in the national standings in 1986, ranked ninth in 1989, and 10th in 1990, and continued to race on a limited basis through 1997.

Racing for more than a quarter of a century, Shirley Muldowney survived discrimination and fiery crashes to carve her place in auto racing history. Her career is a tribute to her strength, commitment, and perseverance. A pioneer sportswoman, Muldowney opened doors for women and broke down the barriers of a male-controlled sport. She didn't just compete; she excelled in a sport that requires skill, stamina, and courage. As one of the most successful women athletes in U.S. history to compete directly against men, Muldowney set the standard for future female racers.

Further Reading

Duden, Jane. *Shirley Muldowney*. Mankato, MN: Crestwood House, 1988. 48 pp.

Martina Navratilova (tennis player)

Born October 18, 1956, Prague, Czechoslovakia

The National Sports Review, the Associated Press, and the United Press International named Martina Navratilova their Female Athlete of the Decade for the 1980s for her dominance in women's tennis. And Navratilova began the 1990s by winning her ninth Wimbledon singles title, breaking Helen Wills Moody's record of eight wins, which had existed since 1938. When she retired from singles play in 1994, Navratilova had won 167 titles and 1,438 singles matches, and earned more than $20 million in career prize money. Navratilova took women's tennis to a new level in the 1980s, bringing speed, power, and strength to the game. She revolutionized the way women trained for matches by establishing a daily weight training, running, and nutrition program. Her physical conditioning, combined with mental toughness, allowed her to overpower her opponents with a serve-and-volley game unseen in the history of women's tennis. Some consider her the best tennis player, if not the best female athlete, of all time.

Born Martina Subertova in Prague, Czechoslovakia, to Miroslav and Jana Subert on October 18, 1956, Martina grew up in the foothills of the Krkonose Mountains in rural Czechoslovakia. Martina's parents were divorced when she was three. Her mother subsequently met and married Mirek Navratil (Navratilova is the feminine form of Navratil), a tennis instructor in Revnice near Prague.

Navratilova's mother was an accomplished gymnast, tennis player, and ski instructor at the local ski resort; and her grandmother, Agnes Semanska, was a tennis champion, ranking as high as number two among Czech women during her amateur career. "I learned a lesson from my mother at an early age: sports are good for young women," she wrote in her autobiography, *Martina*. "It's good to compete, good to run, good to sweat, good to get dirty, good to feel tired and healthy and refreshed. Women played sports and had families and jobs. That simple. My mother was my role model."[108]

With female role models to support her endeavors, it was very likely that Navratilova would become an excellent athlete. Skiing was her first sport; she began gliding

Martina Navratilova
Courtesy of International Tennis Hall of Fame

down the slopes at age two. At four and a half, Navratilova got her first tennis racket, a hand-me-down from her grandmother, and often hit an old tennis ball against the practice wall while her parents played on the regulation courts. When Navratilova was six, her stepfather began to give her lessons. "The moment I stepped onto that crunchy red clay, felt the grit under my sneakers, felt the joy of smacking the ball over the net, I knew I was in the right place," she remembered.[109]

Navratilova entered her first tournament at age eight and reached the semifinals in the 12-and-under division. When she was nine, she began taking lessons from Czechoslovakian Tennis Federation Coach George Parma, who taught her the mechanics of the game and encouraged her aggressive net play. However, just two years later in 1968, the Soviet Union invaded Czechoslovakia and Coach Parma defected to the West.

Despite the loss of her coach and the political unrest around her, Navratilova continued to improve as a tennis player. At 14, she won the girls' 14-and-under national title, and a year later she won the national women's title. As the country's top player, Navratilova was sent to the United States in 1973 by the Czechoslovakian Tennis Federation to play the eight-week USLTA tournament circuit. In April 1973, Navratilova lost to Chris Evert in the first round of the Akron, Ohio, tournament, marking the beginning of a 15-year rivalry unmatched in professional sports. Navratilova returned to Czechoslovakia after her summer tour, but the United States and the freedom it offered left an indelible mark on the 16-year-old.

In 1974, Navratilova finished second in the Italian and German Opens, and again traveled to the United States to join the new Virginia Slims women's professional tennis circuit. She won her first professional title in Orlando, Florida, on September 22, 1974. That year, she won 13 of her 22 matches on the circuit and garnered Rookie of the Year honors from *Tennis* magazine. In December 1974, Martina defeated Margaret Court in the quarterfinals of the Australian Open, and a month later she defeated Chris Evert in a Virginia Slims tournament in Washington, DC. The victories over two top-ranked players launched Navratilova's career into world-class tennis.

The most pivotal year in Navratilova's young life came in 1975, when she led Czechoslovakia to its first Federation Cup Championship in May. Later that year, just hours after losing to Chris Evert in the semifinals of the U.S. Open, Navratilova announced her defection from Czechoslovakia to the United States. She became a naturalized citizen of the United States in 1981.

As the number three player in the world in 1977, Navratilova embarked on a mission to become the number one women's tennis player. She earned her first number one ranking in July 1978, and for 14 consecutive years (1977-90), she ranked among the top three players in the world.

In the early 1980s, Navratilova began to run, lift weights, and play basketball to improve her physical conditioning. With the help of basketball star Nancy Lieberman (-Cline), Navratilova began a program of weightlifting on the Nautilus machines and with free weights. She worked with Renee Richards on game tactics and with coach Mike Estep on technical aspects of her game.

The hard work and the planning paid off for Navratilova as she began a decade of athletic excellence nearly unmatched in professional sports. Navratilova won 55 Grand Slam (Australian, French, and U.S. Opens and Wimbledon) titles, second only to Margaret Smith Court in total Grand Slam victories. The tennis phenom won nine Wimbledon (1978–79, 1982–87, 1990), four U.S. Open (1983–84, 1986, 1987), three Australian Open (1981, 1983, 1985), and two French Open (1982, 1984) singles championships.

In 1982, Navratilova lost only three of 93 singles matches; in 1983, she lost only one of 87 matches; and between January 15 and December 6, 1984, she won 74 consecutive matches. Within that stretch, she won

13 tournaments, including the French Open, Wimbledon, and the U.S. Open. In 1989, Navratilova won eight singles titles, second only to Steffi Graf who won 14, and was a finalist in three others. The following year, she won five singles titles and five doubles titles. Navratilova won her final singles title at the Paris Indoor Championship in 1994. She won the mixed doubles title at the 1995 All-England Championship at Wimbledon, for her 19th title at the grass-court championship.

As an aggressive serve-and-volley player who loved to play at the net, Navratilova also excelled at doubles. She and partner Pam Shriver formed one of the greatest doubles teams in tennis history. The dynamic duo set a record by winning 109 consecutive matches between April 24, 1983, and July 6, 1985, including 18 Grand Slam ladies doubles titles. Navratilova has won a total of 165 doubles titles over her 20-year career. At the 1987 U.S. Open, she scored the rare triple crown, winning mixed doubles with Emilio Sanchez, women's doubles with Pam Shriver, and the women's singles title.

In international competition, Navratilova played for the U.S. Federation Cup Team (1982–86), an international team competition, and the U.S. Wightman Cup, an international team competition between players from the United States and Great Britain (1983). In an emotional homecoming, she returned to Prague in 1986, the first time she had returned to her homeland in 11 years, to lead the U.S. Federation Cup Team to victory over the Czechoslovakian team.

Off the court, Navratilova has devoted time and money to the promotion of women's tennis and women's sports. She served as the Women's Tennis Association (WTA) president in 1979-80, 1983-84, and 1994-95, and served 11 years on the WTA Board of Directors. She has worked diligently in supporting and promoting sports for women. In 1987, the Women's Sports Foundation recognized her efforts by awarding her the first Flo Hyman Award for commitment to excellence in supporting women's advancements in sports. In recent years, Navratilova has been active in promoting lesbian and gay rights in professional sports.

Navratilova has won numerous awards. The Associated Press named her the Female Athlete of the Year in 1983 and 1986; she was the WTA Player of the Year in 1978, 1979, and from 1982 to 1986; and the Women's Sports Foundation chose her Sportswoman of the Year each year from 1982 to 1984. She was inducted into the International Women's Sports Hall of Fame in 1984.

With lightning reflexes, an arsenal of shots including sharp and deep-angled volleys, a 90-mile-an-hour serve, and "an overhead that makes teeth chatter," Martina Navratilova set the standard for women's tennis in the 1980s and forever changed the look and style of the women's game. She is considered by many to be the best ever to play the game.

Further Reading

Blue, Adrianne. *Martina: The Lives and Times of Martina Navratilova.* New York: Birch Lane Press, 1995. 228 pp.

Navratilova, Martina, with George Vecsey. *Martina.* New York: Alfred A. Knopf, 1985. 287 pp.

Cindy Nelson (Alpine skier)

Born August 19, 1955, Lutsen, Minnesota

Endurance is a characteristic of championship athletes—the ability to persevere through arduous training regimens, grueling travel schedules, and nerve-racking competition. Cindy Nelson's career as a member of the U.S. Alpine Ski Team epitomizes endurance. A 14-year member of the U.S. team, Nelson qualified for four U.S. Olympic teams (1972, 1976, 1980, 1984). One of the best U.S. downhill racers ever, Nelson struggled through severe injuries early in her career; but rather than quit, she fought back to regain championship form. She skied to a bronze medal in the 1976 Winter Olympic downhill and has four World Cup victories to her credit. Her longevity is a testament to her commitment to bring fame and recognition to the U.S. Alpine Ski Team.

Nelson began skiing at age two on the slopes of her family's ski resort overlooking beautiful Lake Superior in Lutsen, Minnesota. Both her parents taught skiing at the resort, so by the time Nelson was 11, she had developed expert technique. That skill, combined with her extraordinary daring, led to victory at numerous local and regional races. The self-described "little demon" practiced up to 60 runs a day with her brothers and sisters under the watchful eye of Lutsen's ski coach.

In 1971, at age 15, Nelson qualified for the U.S. World Cup team, and three months after her 16th birthday, she was on her way to Europe for a season of World Cup racing. Racing against great European veteran skiers in her first international competition, she recorded 12th- and 13th-place

Cindy Nelson
Courtesy of U.S. National Ski Hall of Fame Archives

finishes in her first two World Cup downhills.

Later that year, Nelson qualified for the 1972 U.S. Olympic team. But just a few days after being named to the team, she fell while racing and dislocated her hip. She remembered: "I was in a total panic. I flew 30 feet up in the air and as I was flying I knew it would be a flat landing. And the ground hits you like you're driving into a brick wall."[110]

Nelson was out of the hospital in time to watch the 1972 Games on television. She considered retiring, but after her hip had healed, she was back on the slopes training for the 1973 racing season. She won the national downhill title in 1973 and the slalom title in 1975 and 1976. At the 1976 Innsbruck Winter Olympic Games, Nelson finished third in the downhill, 0.66 second behind gold-medal-winner Rosi Mittermaier of West Germany.

For the next four years, Nelson continued to train and travel, competing in more than 40 races each winter season. She regained her national downhill title in 1978 and added the combined championship to her list of U.S. victories. She won a bronze in the combined at the 1978 world championship. A superb technical skier, she had to adapt her style to the changing nature of downhill courses in the late 1970s. The courses changed from steep slopes with difficult turns and sharp terrain that required a skier to be technically strong, to much straighter and faster courses requiring a looser, gliding skiing style.

In 1980, at the Lake Placid Olympics, Nelson competed in all three Alpine events—the slalom, the giant slalom, and the downhill—with her best finish being a tie for seventh in the downhill. Later that year, she won the silver medal for the world combined championship, and in 1982, she won a silver in the downhill at the world championships and led the U.S. women's ski team to its first Nations Cup, given to the national team with the most World Cup points at season's end.

Nelson finished the 1983 season seventh overall in World Cup standings and second in giant slalom points. In 1984, at age 28, she qualified for her fourth Olympic team. Two months before the Games, she injured her right knee and had to withdraw from the downhill event. Despite the injury, she skied with a brace in the slalom, finishing 19th.

During her 14-year career with the U.S. Alpine Ski Team, Nelson traveled thousands of miles and spent hours on the slopes training for her next race. She is one of the best downhill racers the United States ever produced. In 1974, she won the Beck International Award, presented to the nation's outstanding skier of the year, and she was inducted into the U.S. National Ski Hall of Fame in 1976.

Despite the independent nature of most skiers, Nelson always felt she was part of a team. She would encourage her younger teammates: "When they have a bad race, I try to tell them it's just one race in 300 in a couple of years times and that's not too bad. The important thing is that you have to keep going."[111] This commitment to the team and her teammates is the legacy of skier Cindy Nelson.

Further Reading

Jacobs, Linda. *Cindy Nelson: North Country Skier*. St. Paul, MN: EMC Corp., 1976. 40 pp.

Paula Newby-Fraser (triathlete)

Born June 2, 1962, Harare, Zimbabwe

The *Los Angeles Times* and ABC Sports have called Paula Newby-Fraser "The Greatest All-Around Female Athlete in the World." The eight-time Ironman Triathlon World Champion holds the Ironman world record—8:55:28—a time she set in 1992. Her total domination of ultradistance events has made her one of the greatest female endurance athletes in history. She has been a barrier breaker and an outstanding spokesperson for the sport of triathlon. Her success has advanced her sport to new levels of participation for women and revolutionized ideas about women's endurance capabilities.

Born in Harare, Zimbabwe, on June 2, 1962, Paula moved with her family to Durban, South Africa, when she was two. She had an active childhood. At age four, she began ballet lessons. She participated in many sports, swimming competitively throughout junior high school and becoming a national-level swimmer in South Africa as a teenager. She also participated in field hockey, netball, riding, karate, and gymnastics.

Newby-Fraser enrolled at the local university after graduating from high school. While at college, "I pretty much gave up physical activity altogether and gained a lot of weight," she admitted to *Women's Sports and Fitness*. "I just had such an overdose of physical activity as a young child, that it was almost a relief when I got to college."[112] After graduating in 1984 with a degree in social science from the University of Natal, in Durban, South Africa, she began to work out to lose the extra pounds she picked up in college. Aerobics classes, jogging, and weightlifting became part of her daily routine. She noticed the triathlon when she accompanied a triathlete friend to a short-course event in 1984.

In January 1985, Newby-Fraser entered her first triathlon and led the women's field the whole way, setting a new women's course record. In April 1985, she won the women's division of the Ironman distance race in South Africa, which earned her a free trip to the Hawaii Ironman Triathlon the following October.

Paula Newby-Fraser
Lois Schwartz

Newby-Fraser traveled to Hawaii, where she finished third in the 1985 Ironman Triathlon, an event that includes a 2.4-mile swim, 112.0-mile bike ride, and 26.2-mile run. "I found I'd renewed my connection to physical activity, competition, and personal challenge," she says.[113] She returned in 1986 to claim her first Hawaii Ironman title. She would win again in 1988, 1989, 1991, 1992, 1993, 1994, and 1996. In the 1988 Ironman, she made an unbelievable performance breakthrough for women in endurance sports, destroying the Ironman women's record by more than 30 minutes, finishing in 9:01:01. She placed an incredible 11th overall (men and women). Newby-Fraser broke the nine-hour barrier and set the world record in 1992, finishing the race in 8:55:28.

Besides holding the Hawaii Ironman titles, she is also a four-time Ironman Japan Champion (1988, 1990, 1991, 1992), four-time Nice International Triathlon Champion (1989, 1990, 1991, 1992), two-time Ironman Lanzarote Champion (1994, 1995), three-time Germany Ironman Champion (1992, 1994, 1995), and two-time Escape from Alcatraz winner (1991, 1992).

Triathlete magazine named Newby-Fraser Triathlete of the Year in 1988 and 1991. In 1990, the Women's Sports Foundation gave Newby-Fraser the most prestigious international award given to female athletes by naming her Professional Sportswoman of the Year. The *Los Angeles Times* named her Professional Female Athlete of the decade in 1990.

Paula Newby-Fraser is one of the best triathletes in the world and has been a trendsetter in the women's sports world. "All I want from the sport is the respect from my competitors and to make a living. I love doing what I'm doing—training, working out—and I love the people I'm with. That's the way I want it," she says.[114] She is a role model for active women worldwide. Her success in the triathlon, the world's most grueling sport, helped changed perceptions about women's physical capabilities.

Mary Lou Retton (gymnast)
Born January 24, 1968, Fairmont, West Virginia

Mary Lou Retton ignited the world during the 1984 Los Angeles Olympics with a perfect performance on the vault that earned her the Olympic gold medal in the women's all-around event at the gymnastics competition. Retton's powerful approach to gymnastics furthered the gymnastics revolution started by Olga Korbut and Nadia Comaneci a decade earlier—changing women's gymnastics from a ballet-style, graceful sport of long, thin athletes to an explosive sport requiring strength, power, speed, and daring.

Born in Fairmont, West Virginia, the youngest daughter of Ronnie and Lois Jean Retton, Mary Lou began taking dance lessons when she was four, learning the basics of ballet, tap, jazz, and acrobatics. Three years later, Retton enrolled in gymnastics classes for youngsters at West Virginia University. She progressed so rapidly that her mother took her to the Aerial-Port Gymnastics Center in Fairmont run by Pete Longdon. At Aerial-Port, Retton began working with coach Gary Rafaloski on the specific gymnastics skills needed for competing on the separate gymnastics apparatus. "From the beginning I never had any trouble relating to the equipment," she recalled. "I just got up and it felt natural."[115]

In 1976, when she was eight years old, Retton won the beginners' title at a statewide meet in West Virginia. She continued to progress so rapidly that at age 12 she entered the 1980 Class I nationals. Competing against girls much older and more experienced, she won the vault event, was second in the floor exercise, and finished seventh in the all-around competition. The same year, she won the West Virginia state gymnastics title; and in 1981, she was named to the U.S. Junior National Team. She

Mary Lou Retton
Courtesy of Mary Lou Retton

traveled to Canada to compete in her first international competition and won the all-around title. Over the next two years, she traveled to meets around the world, winning events in the United States, Japan, China, and South Africa. She made her first real mark on the international gymnastics scene when she won every individual event in the South African Cup competition in 1982.

At a competition in Las Vegas in 1982, Retton met world-renowned gymnastics coach Bela Karolyi, who invited her to Houston to train at his U.S. Gymnastics Center. She moved to Houston in December 1982 to study with Karolyi. Retton sharpened her skills while in Houston, adding power and difficulty to each of her events. After only two weeks with Karolyi, Retton received her first perfect 10 on the vault, and two months later she defeated America's top gymnasts at a meet in Las

Vegas. At the premier U.S. international meet, the McDonald's American Cup, she won the all-around, vault, and floor exercise, and tied for first on the uneven parallel bars.

Retton made a real breakthrough in international gymnastics in 1983 when she became the first woman in the world to successfully complete a variation of the Tsukahara vault—a layout 1½ back somersault with a double twist.

At the 1983 U.S. championships in Chicago, Retton suffered a stress fracture of the left wrist, which forced her to skip the world championships that year. However, in December 1983, she returned to competition with a victory in the Chunichi Cup in Japan, the first American to win the all-around title. After this victory, she set out to defend her American Cup all-around title, where she scored 39.50 points out of a possible 40.00. At the 1984 U.S. championships, she won the vault, the floor exercise, and the all-around.

Preparing for the upcoming Olympics, Retton undertook a strenuous training schedule, working eight- to 10-hour days in the gym. Her hard work paid off; she won the U.S. Olympic trials and a place on the eight-member U.S. women's team. Just before the competition in Los Angeles, she tore cartilage in her right knee and had to have arthroscopic surgery. Two days after the surgery, she returned to the gym to resume her hectic training schedule.

With her knee fully recovered, Retton led the U.S. women's gymnastics team to a silver medal in the team competition at the 1984 Olympic Summer Games. It was the first Olympic medal captured by U.S. women gymnasts since the U.S. squad won a bronze in 1948. In dramatic fashion, she executed her twisting, layout Tsukahara vault to perfection to capture the Olympic all-around title, the first American woman to win an individual medal in gymnastics. Retton also qualified for the individual finals in three events, and finished her Olympic competition with a silver medal in the vault and bronze medals in both the floor exercise and the uneven bars. Her five medals were the most won by any athlete at the 1984 Games.

The youngest winning gymnast and most decorated U.S. athlete at the 1984 Los Angeles Olympics, Retton became an instant celebrity. She appeared on the covers of national magazines and made appearances on several television specials. Her perky personality and enthusiasm endeared her to the American public. For her achievements, the Associated Press selected her the 1984 Female Athlete of the Year; *Sports Illustrated* named her 1984 Sportsman of the Year; and in 1985, she became the first gymnast and the youngest athlete inducted into the U.S. Olympic Hall of Fame. She joined other pioneering athletes as a member of the International Women's Sports Hall of Fame in 1993. One of her most unique honors came when she signed a contract with Wheaties which made her the first official female spokesperson for the product and the first sportswoman pictured on the prestigious Wheaties cereal boxes.

Although she signed several endorsement contracts after her Olympic victory, Retton was allowed to retain her amateur status, and she continued to compete through 1985. She won the American Cup all-around title for the third time before announcing her retirement from full-time gymnastics in the fall of 1986. In 1994, the United States Olympic Committee (USOC) established in her honor the annual "Mary Lou Retton Award" for athletic excellence, and in 1995, she received the Flo Hyman Award from the Women's Sports Foundation, given to the athlete who captures Hyman's dignity, spirit, and commitment to excellence.

About Mary Lou Retton, Bela Karolyi remarked: "I have been teaching gymnastics 25 years, and had many world and Olympic champions, but I have never coached anybody more positive and dedicated than this little girl."[116] At 4' 9", and 92 pounds, Retton represented a new generation of world-class gymnasts. With her speed and powerful movements, she followed in the footsteps of Olga Korbut and Nadia Comaneci and helped revolutionize her sport, changing it from traditional balletic movements to those dependent on power, speed, and agility. As a national hero, Retton inspired thousands of youngsters to enroll in gymnastics classes around the country, ensuring a strong future for women's gymnastics in the United States.

Further Reading

Retton, Mary Lou, and Bela Karolyi. *Mary Lou: Creating an Olympic Champion.* New York: McGraw-Hill Book Co., 1986. 189 pp.

Silverstein, Herman. *Mary Lou Retton and the New Gymnasts.* New York: Franklin Watts, 1985. 83 pp.

Washington, Rosemary G. *Mary Lou Retton, Power Gymnast.* Minneapolis, MN: Lerner Publishing Co., 1985. 55 pp.

Manon Rheaume (ice hockey goalie)

Born February 24, 1972, Lac Beauport, Québec, Canada

According to USA Hockey, 5,533 female ice hockey players registered to play organized hockey in the United States during the 1990-91 season. Since then, the number has increased four-fold with more than 20,000 registered girls and women playing ice hockey across the United States. Ice hockey is one of the fastest-growing sports for women in America. This tremendous growth is due in part to the efforts of Canadian goalie Manon Rheaume, who, on September 23, 1992, played in an exhibition game between the Tampa Bay Lightning and the St. Louis Blues, becoming the first woman to play in the National Hockey League (NHL). She broke a gender barrier in one of the roughest of the men's big four sports (football, baseball, basketball, and hockey) and shattered another misconception about the physical limitations of female athletes.

The daughter of Pierre and Nicole Rheaume, Manon was born on February 24, 1972, in Lac Beauport, Québec, Canada. She started skating when she was three. Her father made a rink in the yard so Rheaume and her brothers could skate there. Her father also ran a local outdoor rink and coached a boys' hockey team. At the home rink, her brothers would take shots while Manon guarded the net. Manon developed into quite a good skater, and so one day, when she was five, Manon volunteered to be the goalie for one of her father's teams at a local tournament. From that moment on, hockey became her passion.

Rheaume played on the boys' teams all through school and the youth leagues. After high school, she made Canada's Junior B league, and in 1991, she played briefly at the Junior A level—the level just below the NHL—for Trois-Rivières of the Québec

Major Junior Hockey League (QMJHL). Rheaume was the first woman to play in the QMJHL.

Besides her experience in men's leagues, Rheaume has played on some of the best international women's teams. She was the goaltender for the women's Canadian team at the 1992 International Ice Hockey Federation (IIHF) Women's World Championship in Tampere, Finland. She gave up just two goals in three games in the world championship tournament as Canada won the gold medal. She also was goaltender for the Canadian women's team that won the 1994 IIHF Women's World Championship in Lake Placid, New York.

Rheaume made her professional hockey debut when she was signed as a free agent by the Tampa Bay Lightning on August 8,

Manon Rheaume
Courtesy of Jonathan Hayt

1992; she played in an exhibition game on September 23, 1992. Minding the nets for the Lightning, she gave up two goals and made seven saves in the first period of an exhibition contest against the St. Louis Blues. Afterward, Tampa Bay General Manager Phil Esposito signed her to a three-year contract with the club's minor-league affiliate, the Atlanta Knights. On December 13, 1992, she guarded the nets for Atlanta during the Knights' home game against the Salt Lake City Golden Eagles of the International Hockey League (IHL), the first woman to play in a regular season IHL game. "I was nervous, but I think any goalie playing in their very first game would be a little nervous," she told *The Arizona Republic*.[117]

In the 1993-94 season, Rheaume played in four games with the Knoxville Cherokees of the East Coast Hockey League (ECHL). Her first win in a professional hockey game came in a start with the Cherokees against Johnstown (PA) chiefs, a 9-6 win. The following season, Rheaume played for the Las Vegas Aces of the IHL and the Tallahassee Tiger Sharks of the ECHL. She played a total of 73 minutes in three games, allowing seven goals. During the summer of 1994, she played in the Roller Hockey International (RHI) league for the New Jersey Rock N' Rollers.

During the 1995–96 season, Rheaume divided her play between the roller hockey league, minor league ice hockey teams, and Team Canada's women's ice hockey team. She played goaltender for the Ottawa Roll-erbladers and the Sacramento River Rats of the RHI. Rheaume also guarded the nets for the gold-medal-winning Canadian women's team at the 1996 Pacific Rim Three Nations Cup. In November 1996, she returned to the ice after a summer on the hardwood in the roller hockey league to play for the Reno Renegades of the West Coast Hockey League. She played the first period of a game for Reno against the Alaska Gold Kings (in Fairbanks) stopping eight shots out of 12, giving up four goals. She was goaltender for Team Canada at the 1998 Olympics in Nagano, Japan, as women's ice hockey made its debut as a full-medal sport in the Olympic Winter Games.

"It's all about hard work, and where hard work and dedication can take you," said Rheaume. "It's never been easy. But I've always wanted to play hockey. I love hockey. I'd rather play hockey than do anything else. If you have that kind of desire, I think you can achieve what you want to achieve."[118] Rheaume continues to pursue her dream to be a full-time professional hockey player. By breaking down the gender barrier in one of the world's toughest sports, Manon Rheaume is a role model for all young girls and women pursuing opportunities in nontraditional sports.

Cathy Rigby (gymnast)

Born December 12, 1952, Los Alamitos, California

When Cathy Rigby won the silver medal at the 1970 World Gymnastics Championships, she served notice to the rest of the world that U.S. women could compete in international gymnastics. Historically, gymnastics had been a minor sport in America, often practiced only in high school and college physical education classes. With the lack of adequate training and resources, U.S. women gymnasts could not successfully compete against the strong European and Soviet women in international compe-

Cathy Rigby
© Allsport USA/Tony Duffy

Over the next five years, Rigby devoted her time and energy to becoming a world-class competitor. She practiced every night after school, and during her vacations, eight hours a day, seven days a week, to learn the basic compulsory moves and to develop more difficult maneuvers on the separate gymnastics apparatus. She learned quickly, her drive and determination guiding her through the strenuous routines and numerous falls. Her hard work paid off in 1967, when she entered her first major national meet in Chicago, Illinois, and finished second overall in her age group.

At age 15, Rigby competed for the United States in the 1968 Mexico City Olympics, finishing seventh in the balance beam and placing sixteenth in the all-around scoring, the highest Olympic finish ever achieved by a U.S. gymnast at the time.

Rigby came home from the Olympics with renewed enthusiasm and an eye toward the 1972 Games. She continued her intensive training, progressively adding more difficult stunts. The balance beam became her best event; her fearlessness allowed her to develop innovative jumps, flips, and turns on the 4½-inch bar. In 1970, she took her new daring routine to the world championships in Lyubljava, Yugoslavia. With the world watching, she executed her moves with near perfection, flowing across the beam with grace and ease. Her scores, 9.9 and 9.8 (out of a perfect 10.0), were enough to capture the silver medal in the event. She proudly accepted the medal as the first U.S. woman to win an individual medal in international competition.

tition. When Rigby arrived on the scene in 1970, however, the media broadcast her outstanding performances, and American audiences began to sit up and take notice of the sport. With her silver medal in the balance beam at the world championship meet, Rigby became the first U.S. woman to medal in international competition.

Cathy weighed less than four pounds at her birth in 1952 in Los Alamitos, California. The daughter of Paul and Anita Rigby, Cathy developed an enthusiastic interest in sports and ballet. She showed unusual daring and independence at a very young age; she taught herself to roller skate soon after she learned to walk, and to ride a bike at age five. When her father took her to a trampoline class, she mastered the backflip before the night was over. In 1963, she joined Bud Marquette's Southern California Acrobatic Team (SCAT), a newly formed girls' gymnastics club.

In 1971, she earned a gold medal in the all-around at the Miami World Cup Gymnastics Championships. In 1972, she won the Amateur Athletic Union (AAU) women's gymnastics all-around title and ascended to the top of American women's gymnastics by defeating reigning U.S. women's all-around champion Linda Metheny at the U.S. Olympic semi-trials. Disaster struck in the U.S. Olympic trials, when Rigby, leading the competition, fell during her uneven parallel bar routine and fractured a toe. The following day, with a taped-up toe and an iron will, she struggled through the floor exercise, only to injure her ankle on a difficult flip combination. After X-rays showed torn ligaments, Rigby had to withdraw from the remainder of the competition. Despite her mishap, the U.S. Olympic Committee elected her to be a member of the team without finishing the trials. At the 1972 Munich Games, Rigby led the U.S. women's team to a fourth-place finish in the team competition, and individually, she placed 10th overall and seventh on the balance beam.

In 1973, Rigby retired from competition to open two gymnastic clubs in Ana-heim and Mission Viejo, California, and she went on to a career on Broadway, starring in Wizard of Oz, Paint Your Wagon, and Meet Me in St. Louis. She also produced her own national tour of Peter Pan.

Cathy Rigby's efforts at the 1970 world championships and the 1972 Olympics excited the imagination of girls throughout the nation. Her success, and that of other world-class gymnasts like Olga Korbut, started a groundswell of gymnastic activity in the United States. She proved that with hard work and determination, Americans could challenge the European and Soviet women for world-class stature in women's gymnastics.

Further Reading

Jacobs, Linda. *Cathy Rigby: On the Beam*. St. Paul, MN: EMC Corp., 1975. 40 pp.

Wilma Rudolph (track and field sprinter)
Born June 23, 1940, Bethlehem, Tennessee; died November 12, 1994

The first U.S. woman to win three track and field gold medals in one Olympic Games, Wilma Rudolph captivated the world at the 1960 Rome Olympics. More than any other athlete, Rudolph is credited with increasing the interest among female athletes in track events. Her accomplishments opened up the door for women in track because sports fans the world over appreciated her grace, beauty, and athleticism.

To achieve her success, Rudolph had to overcome severe childhood illnesses that threatened to limit her physical abilities. Born in rural Tennessee to Edward and Blanche Rudolph, Wilma contracted double pneumonia, scarlet fever, and polio at age four, which left her left leg partially paralyzed. For two years, her mother drove her 45 miles to Nashville for therapy, and every night her family of 10 brothers and sisters took turns massaging her leg until she was able to walk without a brace. At age eight, Rudolph was fitted with an orthopedic shoe to help her walk; by the time she was 11, however, she had discarded the shoe to play basketball with her brothers.

Rudolph played basketball and ran track while attending segregated Burt High School in Clarksville, Tennessee. She earned All-State honors for basketball all four years and set a single-season scoring record her sophomore year, scoring 803 points in 25 games (an average of 32.12 points per game). During track season, Rudolph specialized

Wilma Rudolph
© Allsport/Hulton Deutsch

in the sprint events, winning the Tennessee state high school titles in the 50-, 75-, and 100-yard dashes.

In 1955, Tennessee State University track coach Ed Temple discovered Rudolph playing in a basketball tournament and convinced her high school coach Clinton Gray to have Rudolph focus on track. That summer, Gray drove Rudolph to Tennessee State University to practice with Coach Temple's Tigerbelles track team. She ran as a junior Tigerbelle and the following year, at age 16, earned a spot on the 1956 U.S. Olympic team. At the Melbourne Olympics, Rudolph ran the third leg of the 4x100-meter relay and, along with teammates Mae Faggs, Margaret Matthews, and Isabelle Daniels, captured the bronze medal.

After graduating from Burt High School in 1957, Rudolph enrolled at Tennessee State University to continue training with Coach Temple. An injury in 1958

forced her off the track for most of the year, but she returned in 1959 to win the first of her four consecutive Amateur Athletic Union (AAU) 100-meter titles. She pulled her hamstring in a dual meet between the United States and the Soviet Union, which forced another layoff; then in early 1960, she became violently ill after a tonsillectomy. Nevertheless, Rudolph fought through these injuries and illnesses to prepare for the 1960 Rome Olympics. Two months before she traveled to Rome, Rudolph set a world record in the 200 meters, and won both the 100- and 200-meter AAU titles.

The heart of the U.S. Women's Track and Field Team at the Rome Olympics came from the Tennessee State University Tigerbelles. Rudolph and six of her teammates made the team that year and won a total of nine gold medals. At the Stadio Olimpico in Rome, Rudolph electrified the crowd with three spectacular performances as she became the first U.S. woman to win three track and field gold medals in the same Olympic Games. She tied the world record of 11.3 in her 100-meter semifinal and won the finals in a wind-aided 11.0 time. She also won the 200-meter final in the rain, breaking the existing Olympic record in a qualifying heat. The sprinter won her third gold medal by anchoring the 4x100-meter relay team to a victory over the German team. The U.S. relay team had set a world record of 44.4 in the semifinals.

Rudolph toured Europe after the Olympics, competing in various invitational track meets and drawing crowds of admirers wherever she went. Italian and French journalists described her as "La Gazelle" and "La Perle Noire" (the Black Pearl). She returned to the United States and received the same adulation. In February 1961, Rudolph competed in the prestigious Millrose Games at Madison Square Garden. She won the 60-yard dash in 6.9 seconds, tying her own world record, and two weeks later, she set a world record in the event, running it in 6.8 seconds. The same year, Rudolph broke Stella Walsh's 25-year-old record in the 70-yard dash by nearly half a second, and that summer she established a women's world record of 11.2 seconds in the 100 meters to ensure her place as the finest female sprinter of her time.

This graceful sprinter was named the Associated Press Female Athlete of the Year in 1960 and 1961, and won the 1961 Sullivan Memorial Trophy as the nation's top amateur athlete. In 1974, Rudolph was inducted into the National Track and Field Hall of Fame; in 1980, she became a member of the International Women's Sports Hall of Fame; and in 1983, she was selected to the United States Olympic Hall of Fame.

Rudolph retired from competition in 1962 and became the U.S. Goodwill Ambassador to French West Africa. She founded the Wilma Rudolph Foundation in Indianapolis to help disadvantaged youngsters through sports and education. The organization works with thousands of young people each year, teaching them discipline, hard work, and dedication in athletics and life. "I wanted to leave behind a legacy, and I thought this would be ideal," she said.[119] Rudolph died of brain cancer in 1994.

Women's athletics in the United States was at the crossroads when Rudolph stepped onto the track at the 1960 Rome Olympics. As one of the greatest female track stars of the twentieth century, Wilma Rudolph epitomized hard work and athletic grace. Her outstanding performances, viewed by a television audience of millions, inspired thousands of girls to join their local track clubs or to demand competitive opportunities in their schools. Her talent caught the imagination of the world media, which resulted in the promotion of the sport among women worldwide.

Further Reading

Biracree, Tom. *Wilma Rudolph*. New York: Chelsea House Publishers, 1989. 112 pp.

Coffey, Wayne R. *Wilma Rudolph*. Woodbirch, CT: Blackbirch Press, 1993. 64 pp.

Sherrow, Victoria. *Wilma Rudolph*. New York: Chelsea House Publishers, 1995. 79 pp.

Joan Benoit Samuelson (marathon runner)

Born May 16, 1957, Cape Elizabeth, Maine

Joan Benoit Samuelson said to herself upon approaching the entrance to the tunnel of the Los Angeles Coliseum on that hot August day in 1984: "When you come out from underneath the tunnel, you're going to be a different person."[120] Benoit Samuelson emerged from the tunnel ahead of the field to run the last yards of the first women's Olympic marathon, to win an Olympic gold, and to catapult herself into women's sports history as America's best female long-distance runner. In winning the marathon, Benoit Samuelson came to symbolize the end of the long struggle to achieve worldwide recognition of women's long-distance running and endurance capabilities.

Joan, the daughter of Andre and Nancy Benoit, was born and raised in Cape Elizabeth, Maine. An all-around athlete, she learned to snow ski about the time she learned to walk. Skiing was her first love, but she also participated in other sports like tennis, basketball, lacrosse, and field hockey. She began running during her senior year in high school to get back in shape after suffering a broken leg in a skiing accident. Within a year, she qualified for Junior Olympics track competition in North Carolina.

In 1976, she enrolled in Bowdoin College in Brunswick, Maine, to study history and environmental studies. Although she continued to participate in other sports, Benoit Samuelson began concentrating on running during her sophomore year. She also spent three semesters at North Carolina State University, where she had an opportunity to train in a high-powered running program.

She burst onto the world marathon scene in 1979. In only her second try at that distance (26 miles, 385 yards), she won the prestigious Boston Marathon in 2:35:15, setting a new U.S. record in the process. Shunning publicity for the isolation and serenity of her Maine home, she trained alone, slowly improving her times, but her enthusiasm for distance running took its toll. In 1981, she had surgery on her Achilles tendon and was out of racing for nearly 10 weeks. During her recuperation, she lifted weights and rode a stationary bicycle, which enabled her to come back to road racing stronger than before her surgery.

Between 1981 and 1983, Benoit Samuelson coached track and field and cross-country at Boston University. She trained alongside her students until she decided to devote herself full-time to her running career. In 1983, Benoit Samuelson won her second Boston Marathon. Her time of 2:22:43 established a world record that last-

Joan Benoit Samuelson
Courtesy of Maine Sports Hall of Fame

ed for nearly two years and a Boston Marathon course record that stood for more than a decade.

With her sights on the 1984 Los Angeles Olympics, Benoit Samuelson ran more than 100 miles a week from May to November 1983. One day she experienced pain in her right knee during a morning run, and just 17 days before the U.S. Olympic marathon trials, Benoit Samuelson had arthroscopic surgery on her knee to remove an inflamed mass that was inhibiting the movement of the joint. Determined to make the Olympic team, she returned to training within the week and pushed so hard that she pulled her left hamstring.

Nursing both a sore right knee and a pulled left hamstring, Benoit Samuelson still won the Olympic trials in Olympia, Washington, in a time of 2:31:04. Three months later, nearly recuperated from the injuries, Benoit Samuelson captured the first women's Olympic marathon, soundly defeating the world's top marathon runner, Grete Waitz of Norway. Benoit Samuelson took the lead from the former world-record holder Waitz just 14 minutes into the race and finished more than a minute ahead of the field. In 1984, Benoit Samuelson received the Sullivan Memorial Trophy as the nation's best amateur athlete, and she shared the 1984 Women's Sports Foundation Sportswoman of the Year award with gymnast Mary Lou Retton.

Two months after the Olympics, Benoit Samuelson won the Philadelphia Distance Run (a 13.1-mile half marathon) with a personal best time of 1:08:34. In 1985, she won a 12-kilometer race in San Francisco and a 7-mile race in Davenport, Iowa, and set a U.S. record of 2:21:21 in the Chicago Marathon.

Benoit Samuelson retired from running after the Chicago Marathon to give birth to her daughter Abigail. She returned to running after the birth of her second child, but chose not to attempt to qualify for the 1988 and 1992 Olympic teams. She returned to competitive running to try out for the 1996 Olympic team but did not finish among the top three finishers. Benoit Samuelson continues to run and is an active participant in a number of community organizations devoted to public service.

In winning the first women's Olympic marathon, America's best long-distance runner became a symbol for the success and abilities of women athletes in all sports. Joan Benoit Samuelson's efforts contributed to the increased participation in women's distance running around the world.

Further Reading

Benoit, Joan, with Sally Baker. *Running Tide.* New York: Alfred A. Knopf, 1987. 213 pp.

Cristina Sánchez (bullfighter)

Born February 20, 1972, Villaverde, Spain

Spanish women have tried for decades to win the coveted title of matador de toros—a bullfighter of first rank, but have faced many barriers in one of the most traditionally male domains in the sports world. On May 25, 1996, Cristina Sánchez became

Spain's first female *matador de toros*. A bullfighter of classic elegance, Sánchez won praise from even the most hard-line aficionados. "I want to be the woman who changes men's thinking," Sánchez said. "I like that role. Why? Because I have the capacity.

Bullfighting makes me feel very big inside. Bullfighting is to dream awake."[121]

Cristina Sánchez de Pablos was born in Villaverde, in the province of Madrid, Spain, on February 20, 1972, the daughter of Antonio and María Carmen Sánchez. Sánchez grew up traveling with her father across Spain on the bullfighting circuit and listening to the men talk of styles and tactics. At 14, she began making trips to the plaza de toros in Parla, her hometown about 40 miles north of Madrid, joining the young matadors who practiced there with her father. At age 16, she enrolled in the Tauromaquia de Madrid bullfighting school, where she worked on her technique, including hours with the cape and swords.

Sánchez appeared in her first fight in 1990 at age 18, and she made her debut in her first novillada (bullfight with small bulls) with picadors (assistants) in Ecuador on November 1992. She toured Central and South America fighting young bulls, then returned to Spain, where she appeared in a novillada in Valdemorillo on February 13, 1993, a "mixed" corrida (bullfighting event) with matadors Luis Sesena and Francisco Javier Martinez Paquiro. In July 1995, she appeared in Madrid, and her fine performance assured her return to that plaza. She followed her successes in Valdemorillo and Madrid with widely praised fights in Seville and other Spanish cities. She quickly became a sensation in the bullfighting arenas of Spain, earning hundreds of fights. Through 1996, she had dispatched more than 400 bulls and had been gored three times in the process.

On May 25, 1996, at the ancient Roman arena in Nîmes, France, Sánchez met Pocobarbas, the biggest and strongest animal she had ever faced in her *alternativa,* a ceremonial rite of passage, to become a *matador de toros.* The sellout crowd was so thrilled by her performance that they de-

Cristina Sánchez
© Allsport/Pascal Bowdeau

manded she be presented with *una oreja*—one of the bull's ears.

In 1996, Sánchez had more than 100 fights, which vaulted her into the top 10 of Spanish bullfighters. She has reached superstar status in the bullfighting towns of Spain and South America. In this same year, bullfight attendance was up and applications to the Madrid bullfighting school she attended increased, especially for girls.

By reaching the status of *matador de toros,* Cristina Sánchez has broken down one of the most impenetrable gender barriers in sports. Other women before her have fought little bulls, but Sánchez is the first woman to have taken her *alternativa* in Europe and to have made her debut as a matador in Spain. She told *Sports Illustrated:* "[I want] to demonstrate that women, just as men, deserve an opportunity, and to put an end to all those centuries of discrimination."[122]

Eleonora Sears (all-around athlete)

Born September 28, 1881, Boston, Massachusetts; died March 26, 1968

Often called America's first true "sportswoman," Eleonora Sears delighted in trying the unusual and the unexpected, and that generally meant the challenge of any new sports being introduced to America at the turn of the century. Born into Boston's elite society, Sears had the opportunity to participate in the sports of the wealthy. Over the years, she became proficient at several diverse sports including tennis, golf, swimming, polo, squash, and long-distance walking. Horses were her passion, however; she was an expert rider and jumper. A true pioneer in women's sports, Sears was the first woman to challenge many of the conventions of society regarding appropriate feminine behavior. She won the first women's national squash championship and was the first woman to play the rough-and-tumble sport of polo. Although she did not see herself as a crusader for women's sports—she participated strictly for the love of sport and the challenge it offered—her independent and outspoken ways opened the doors for twentieth-century sportswomen in America.

Eleonora was the only daughter of Frederick Richard and Eleonora Randolph Sears. The great-great granddaughter of Thomas Jefferson, she was raised in an atmosphere where young girls were educated by private tutors and were expected to attend social teas and debutante balls. At a young age, she shocked her fellow socialites with her independence and pursuit of the challenges of sports and the outdoors, preferring an aggressive game of tennis to the more gentle game of croquet, and comfortable trousers to tight-fitted corsets. Although she participated in the social night life of Boston and New York, dancing into the early hours dressed in elegant gowns,

Sears lived for her days on the tennis and squash courts chasing balls in her breeches and riding her horses at full gallop.

Sears's family took to the game of tennis soon after Mary Outerbridge introduced the sport in 1874. Her father was one of the first to play the game in America, and her uncle, Richard, won the first U.S. Cham-

Eleonora Sears
Courtesy of the Sears Chapel Endowment

pionship in 1881 and held the title until 1887. Eleonora Sears became a champion herself, winning numerous club championships in Newport, Rhode Island. In tennis, as in other sports, she adopted an aggressive style of play. Often rushing the net to attack her opponent's passing shots, she became a formidable doubles player with quick feet and precise ground strokes. Her success with this style of play led to capturing the national doubles championship four times (1911 and 1915 with Hazel Hotchkiss

Wightman, and 1916 and 1917 with Molla Bjurstedt Mallory). Sears also captured two other doubles titles, the 1916 mixed doubles championship with Willis Davis and the 1939 women's veteran's doubles title with Sylvia Henrotin.

In 1918, Sears took up squash, a fast-paced indoor court game similar to racquetball using a badminton racquet and a rubber ball smaller than a tennis ball. Her experience and daring from the tennis courts followed Sears onto the squash courts. Undaunted by the fact that women were forbidden from entering the building, she invaded the courts of the Harvard Club of Boston because there were no courts open to women at that time (not until a decade later did the Harvard Club open its courts to women). Sears was instrumental in founding the U.S. Women's Squash Racquets Association in 1928, and then won its first singles championship the same year. Her participation attracted many followers, and she is credited with popularizing the sport for women in the 1920s and 1930s. She served as president of the association and captained the U.S. international team, while remaining an active competitor. In 1954, at the age of 72, Sears competed in the women's veteran's division of the national championships.

As with tennis, Sears inherited a love of walking from her father. She often strolled the 20 miles from her home in Boston to her summer home in Prides Crossing, Massachusetts. She excelled at long-distance walking, annually trekking the 47 miles from Boston to Providence, Rhode Island, in record time. In 1926, she recorded her best time, covering the distance in 9:53:00. She also once walked the 108 miles from Burlingame to Del Monte, California, in 19:50:00. These exploits attracted widespread publicity, as much for her attire as for her endurance. She wore a short skirt

and waistcoat, with socks rolled down to sturdy hiking boots, and a felt hat to cover her from the summer sun. With a chauffeur-driven car following her, she presented an imposing figure on the roads of New England and California.

Although she excelled at tennis, squash, and marathon walks, Sears's real passion was horses. She maintained stables of racing thoroughbreds and show horses, and spent nearly every day on horseback, becoming quite an accomplished equestrian. In 1912, she shocked the Burlingame, California, society set by charging onto the all-male polo field wearing trousers instead of a long skirt, riding astride instead of the traditional sidesaddle, and asking to join the men's team. Of course, the request was denied, and her outrageous behavior led to the local Mother's Club issuing a statement denouncing her appearance and demanding that she "restrict herself to the usual feminine attire in the future." That request also was denied.

Her extraordinary exploits on the playing field were matched only by her generosity off the field. She gave extensive financial support to the U.S. equestrian team for several years, often lending the team horses for international and Olympic competition. She sponsored the National Horse Show to ensure that it remained an annual event, and in the early 1960s, she even offered some of her horses to the Boston Police Department so that they could retain their mounted police division. Additionally, as a long-time member of the Boston Skating Club and a fan of figure skating, Sears contributed time and money to rebuilding the U.S. Olympic Figure Skating Team after the tragic plane crash in 1961 that killed 18 members of the national team.

An avid and active sportswoman until her death in 1968, Eleanora Sears was a true pioneer in the sporting world. Her outrageous behavior shocked the social set, yet her unabashed enjoyment of participating and excelling in several sports opened the door for other women to challenge the turn-of-the-century mores of feminine behavior and fashion. Her independent ways set an example for future sportswomen carrying on the battle to break down the barriers of the all-male sports world.

Monica Seles (tennis player)

Born December 2, 1973, Novi Sad, Yugoslavia

One of the top tennis stars in the 1990s, Monica Seles dominates opponents with her powerful two-handed backhand and forehand baseline strokes and mental toughness. Seles soared to the number one ranking on March 19, 1991, after just two years on the professional tour. She has won nine Grand Slam titles (Australian, French, and U.S. Opens and Wimbledon), including three consecutive French Open titles (1991–93). In April 1993, while at the top of her game, Seles was stabbed in the back by a crazed fan during a match in Germany. The injury forced her off the professional circuit for more than two years. She made a successful return to the women's tour in 1995 and showed enormous courage and strength in attempting to regain championship form.

Born on December 2, 1973, in Novi Sad, Yugoslavia, Monica is the daughter of Karolj and Esther Seles. She began playing tennis at age six and was only nine years old when she won the Yugoslavian 12-and-under championship. She won the 12-and-under European championship again the following year, and in 1985, as an 11-year-old, she repeated as 12-and-under European champion and was named Yugoslavia's Sportswoman of the Year.

In 1985, Seles caught the attention of instructor Nick Bollettieri who ran a tennis school in Bradenton, Florida. He offered Seles a scholarship to attend his tennis academy. So at the age of 12, Seles moved to Florida to begin her journey to become the best female tennis player in the world.

Seles turned professional on February 12, 1989, when she was just 15. She reached the semifinals of her first professional tournament, and in her second tournament, the 1989 Houston Open, she defeated top-seeded Chris Evert to win her first professional title. Seles also reached the semifinals of the 1989 French Open, where she lost in three sets to top-ranked Steffi Graf.

Monica Seles
© Michael Baz

Her career took off in 1990. Seles won the Italian Open, the German Open, and her first Grand Slam title, the 1990 French Open. She surpassed the million dollar mark in career earnings at the 1990 Wimbledon tournament. The teenage phenom moved to the top of the world rankings on March 11, 1991, at age 17 years, 3 months, 9 days, the youngest player (male or female) to reach the number one ranking in tennis. (Tracy Austin was 17 years, 3 months, 26 days when she earned the number one ranking on April 7, 1980.)

From October 1990 to March 1992, Seles reached the finals of 21 straight tournaments. She won three consecutive French Opens (1991, 1992, 1993), two Australian Opens (1991, 1992), and two U.S. Opens (1991, 1992). At Wimbledon, the only Grand Slam title she has never won, she was a quarterfinalist in 1990 and finalist in 1992. By winning $2.457 million in 1991, Seles set a record for single-season earnings, a record she broke in 1992 with $2.622 million. In 1993, she also won her third consecutive Australian Open.

Seles was named the Women's Tennis Association (WTA) Player of the Year in 1991 and 1992, the Associated Press Female Athlete of the Year in 1991 and 1992, and the United Press International (UPI) International Athlete of the Year in 1991 and 1992.

On April 30, 1993, during a changeover while competing in a quarterfinal match against Magdalena Maleeva in Hamburg, Germany, Seles was stabbed in the back, just below her left shoulder blade, by a crazed fan. Her recovery from the injury was slow as she had to overcome both physical and psychological pain.

Seles won the 1995 Canadian Open, her first event back on the WTA tour after a 27-and-a-half-month absence. She defeated Amanda Coetzer, 6-0, 6-1, for the championship. The left-hander set a tournament record for the least number of games played by the champion through the tournament (74). The title was the 33rd of her career. Continuing her comeback, Seles won the 1996 Australian Open, her ninth Grand Slam title, and won tournaments at Tokyo, Sydney, and on the grass at Eastbourne, England. She won her 300th career singles match over Dally Randriantefy in the third round of the 1996 U.S. Open. Seles reached the finals of the 1996 U.S. Open before losing to Steffi Graf, 7-5, 6-4.

Becoming a naturalized citizen of the United States in 1994, Seles competed for the winning U.S. Federation Cup Team (international competition) in 1996 and was a member of the 1996 U.S. Olympic Tennis Team.

Monica Seles ranks eighth in career singles titles in the Open era with 40. Her overall career record through November 1997 was 353 wins, 48 losses. One of the rising stars in women's tennis until her unfortunate assault, Seles showed enormous courage and strength in her comeback, the marks of a true champion. She is one of America's most inspiring talents.

Further Reading

Layden, Joe. *Return of a Champion: The Monica Seles Story.* New York: St. Martin's Press, 1996. 278 pp.

Seles, Monica, with Nancy Richardson. Monica: *From Fear to Victory.* New York: Harper Collins, 1996. 320 pp.

Mary Decker Slaney (middle-distance runner)

Born August 4, 1958, Bunnvale, New Jersey

In the highly successful U.S. women's track and field program that has produced world-champion sprinters and marathoners, one runner established herself as America's premier female middle-distance runner. In a long career (20+ years) interrupted by numerous injuries and long layoffs, Mary Decker Slaney set innumerable U.S. and world records at 800 meters, 1,500 meters, and 3,000 meters on both indoor and outdoor tracks.

Born in Bunnvale, New Jersey, the daughter of John and Jacqueline Decker, Mary moved with her family to southern

Mary Decker Slaney
© Allsport USA/Gray Mortimore

California in 1968. She began running at age 10, shortly after moving to California. At age 11, she entered a parks board cross-country race, which she won easily. Her racing career continued with victories in

several junior and open competitions. She ran for the Long Beach Comets running club, racing three or four times a weekend.

By the time she was 14, Decker Slaney was a world-class runner but was too young to try out for the 1972 Olympic team. At 15, Decker Slaney set three world records—in the outdoor 800 meters, indoor 880 yards, and indoor 1,000 yards. In 1973, she toured Europe and Africa as the best U.S. middle-distance runner.

Her obsession with running and hard training and her rigorous racing schedule took its toll on her body. She suffered an ankle injury then developed severe shin splits, so severe that sometimes she could barely walk. For nearly three years, Decker Slaney took treatments on her legs to relieve the pain. Unable to compete in the 1976 Olympics, Decker Slaney watched runners she had beaten two years earlier take home Olympic medals.

In January 1977, Decker Slaney enrolled in the University of Colorado on an athletic scholarship. There she met distance runner Dick Quax, who immediately diagnosed her physical problem as compartment syndrome, in which her muscles had grown too large for the surrounding sheaths. An operation relieved her calf pain, but injuries continued to plague her. Two auto accidents and an Achilles tendon operation later, Decker Slaney's running began to improve by 1980. She ran 13 miles a day, training in the morning and late afternoon. She moved to Eugene, Oregon, to train with members of Athletics West—the only female member allowed to train with the elite male runners' club.

In 1980, Decker Slaney set a U.S. record in the 800-meter race and world records in the 880-yard and 1,500-meter races. At the top of her form after more than five years of injuries, Decker Slaney was primed for her try at Olympic gold when the United States announced its intentions to boycott the Moscow Olympics.

Despite the disappointment of missing the Olympics, Decker Slaney dominated women's middle-distance running for the next four years. From 1980 to 1984, she won every middle-distance race she entered. In 1982, she set seven world records and was given the Jesse Owens Award as the outstanding U.S. track and field athlete, the first woman to be so honored; was named Associated Press Female Athlete of the Year; and she received the Sullivan Award as America's outstanding amateur athlete in 1983.

At the inaugural World Track and Field Championships in 1983, Decker Slaney won both the 1,500- and 3,000-meter races. By the spring of 1984, she held every U.S. distance record from 800 to 10,000 meters. For her astounding achievements, she was selected the Women's Sports Foundation Sportswoman of the Year in 1983.

Her reputation as the world's best made Decker Slaney the favorite going into the 1984 Los Angeles Olympics. She qualified for both the 1,500 and 3,000 meters at the U.S. Olympic trials, but because the two events overlapped on the Olympic schedule, Decker Slaney chose to run in only the 3,000 meters. In the finals of the race, with three laps to go, Decker Slaney became entangled with Zola Budd, her chief rival; lost her balance; and fell into the infield, dashing her hopes for Olympic gold.

The fall damaged Decker Slaney's pride and her hip; she was unable to run again in 1984. But she returned to racing in January 1985 in top form, setting a world indoor record in the 2,000 meters. She re-established her U.S. records during the 1985 outdoor season with records in the 800, 1,000, 3,000, and 5,000 meters.

Decker Slaney missed the 1986 indoor and outdoor seasons because of the birth of her daughter Ashley, and the entire 1987 outdoor and 1988 indoor season because of injuries. She qualified for the 1988 U.S. Olympic team in the 3,000 meters but failed to finish in the medal standings at the Seoul Summer Games. She failed to qualify for the 1992 Games and suffered through another surgery (she has had more than 20) to repair her Achilles tendon in 1994, and through three stress fractures in her left foot in 1995.

Rebounding from these injuries, Decker Slaney returned to competitive running in 1996 with an attempt to win a place on her fourth Olympic team. She captured the third spot on the U.S. Olympic team in the women's 5,000 meters, but finished out of medal contention in the Atlanta Games.

In 1997, at age 38 and in her first appearance at the U.S. Indoor Championships in 23 years, Decker Slaney won the women's 1,500-meter run in 4:03.08 seconds, the fastest time in the world since 1990. Decker Slaney holds the U.S. 1,500 meters record, 4:00.8, set in 1980. Her time at the indoor championships was the second-fastest ever by an American and the eighth fastest in history.

Mary Decker Slaney epitomized women's middle-distance running in the United States for nearly two decades. Despite her injury-ridden career and Olympic disappointments, she set numerous world and U.S. records and inspired thousands of women to challenge their physical abilities in middle-distance running.

Further Reading

Jacobs, Linda. *Mary Decker: Speed Records and Spaghetti.* St. Paul, MN: EMC Corp., 1975. 40 pp.

Newman, Matthew. *Mary Decker Slaney.* Mankato, MN: Crestwood House, 1986. 48 pp.

Francie Larrieu Smith (middle-distance runner)

Born November 23, 1952, Palo Alto, California

Francie Larrieu-Smith carried the American flag for the U.S. delegation at the opening ceremonies of the 1992 Summer Olympic Games. The five-time Olympian (1972, 1976, 1980, 1988, 1992) received the honor via a vote by team captains and representatives of the 25 American teams in Barcelona. Larrieu-Smith began running as a teenager, and her career has spanned more than three decades of world-class running. She has won 19 national titles and set 48 world or U.S. records in road, track, and cross-country racing. Over her career, Larrieu-Smith has progressively increased her racing distances—from 1,500 meters to the marathon—and has continued racing at a world-class level well into her 40s. Her longevity in the sport is an inspiration for all women runners. Her coach, Robert Vaughan, called her "a national treasure."

Born Frances Larrieu on November 23, 1952, in Palo Alto, California, Francie began racing at age 13 and won the first competition she ever entered, a 660-yard race for junior high girls. She ran for the Santa Clara Club, then was invited to take part in the boys' track practices at her high school. With special permission, she was allowed to compete in the boys' meets.

After graduating from Fremont High School in Sunnyvale, California, in 1970, Larrieu-Smith won the first of seven 1,500-meter national championships. For the next 10 years, Larrieu-Smith was the dominant U.S. female miler. She set 12 world indoor records and 36 American records, indoor and outdoor, in the 1,500 meters, the mile, the 3,000 meters, and two miles.

During those years, Larrieu-Smith also attended college. After graduating from DeAnza Community College in 1973, she enrolled in the University of California at Los Angeles (UCLA), but there were no track scholarships for women in those days; she also had to train with the men. Despite these difficulties, she won Association of Intercollegiate Athletics for Women (AIAW) titles in the 800, 1,500, and 3,000 meters in 1974.

In 1972, at age 19, Larrieu-Smith was the youngest member of the U.S. Olympic Track and Field Team at the Olympic Games in Munich. She competed in the women's 1,500 meters, making it to the semifinals with a personal best time of 4:11.2. Running the 1,500 meters again in 1976 at the Montreal Olympics, Larrieu-Smith ran a time of 4:09.07 but did not qualify for the finals. She also made the 1980 U.S. Olympic Track and Field Team, finishing fourth in the 1,500 meters at the Olympic trials but

Francie Larrieu Smith
Courtesy of Francie Larrieu Smith

stayed home because of the U.S.-led boycott of the Games in Moscow.

In the 1980s, Larrieu-Smith began to run longer distances. She captured the 10,000 meters at the The Athletics Congress (TAC) Championships in 1985. She returned to the Olympics in 1988, qualifying for the 10,000 meters—the first time this distance was an Olympic event for women. At these games, Larrieu-Smith turned in her best Olympic performance ever, reaching the finals for the first time and placing fifth, running 31:35.52 seconds, missing the U.S. record by three tenths of a second. In April 1991, Larrieu-Smith erased Mary Decker Slaney's nine-year-old U.S. record in the 10,000 meters, running it in 31:28.92 at the Texas Relays in Austin.

Never one to rest on her laurels, Larrieu-Smith ran her first marathon in January 1986, in Houston, Texas, and finished second in 2:33:36. At age 39, Larrieu-Smith qualified for her fifth U.S. Olympic team after she finished third in the 1992 Women's Olympic trials marathon in the time of 2:30:39. "Each team is special," said Larrieu-Smith. "I never dreamed I'd be competing at this age or in the marathon. It's especially exciting at nearly 40 to be able to pursue the goal I set for myself at 13—an Olympic medal."[123] She finished 12th in the marathon at the 1992 Summer Olympic Games in Barcelona, Spain.

In her forties, Larrieu-Smith continues to run distance races in master's level (over age 40) competitions as a member of Team New Balance. Busy off the track, she is a national spokesperson for the Susan G. Komen Foundation and Race for the Cure, a national series of road race benefits to combat breast cancer.

Francie Larrieu-Smith set her first national record and won her first U.S. title in 1969. She set her most recent U.S. record in 1991. She is one of the greatest distance runners of all time, not only because of the time period she has spanned, but also because of her range of distances and diversity of surfaces—the track, the roads, and the cross-country paths. "Although I look in the mirror, and I see that I'm aging," she admitted to *Runner's World* in 1991, "I do not in any way think of myself any differently than when I was 24 years old and chasing around Europe."[124] This durable runner is an inspiration for women athletes of all ages.

Vivian Stringer (basketball coach)

Born March 16, 1948, Edenborn, Pennsylvania

Vivian Stringer has been a women's basketball coach for more than a quarter of a century, and ranks third among active women's collegiate coaches in winning percentage (.765). Through the 1996-97 season, she has compiled a record of 544-167. She is the only women's coach to take two different teams to the National Collegiate Athletic Association (NCAA) Final Four (Cheyney State College in 1982 and the University of Iowa in 1993). Her career has been marked with great triumph and personal tragedy, yet she has persevered and established herself as one of the great coaches in the women's game.

Born Charlene Vivian Stoner, on March 16, 1948, in Edenborn, Pennsylvania, the daughter of Charles and Thelma Stoner, Vivian loved sports at an early age. In her small town high school, no athletic teams

Vivian Stringer
© Allsport USA/Ken White

were open to girls, and so she played football, basketball, and baseball with the boys on the weekends. In 1966, she enrolled at Slippery Rock University, where she studied physical education and met her future husband William Stringer. While at Slippery Rock, Stringer played for nationally ranked basketball, tennis, field hockey, and softball teams. She graduated from Slippery Rock with a degree in health and physical education in 1970.

In 1971, Stringer joined Cheyney State College as an assistant professor of recreation, health, and physical education. She volunteered to coach all the women's teams. The young coach, without the advantage of scholarships to offer the nation's top players, built a winning women's basketball team at Cheyney State. In the 1981-82 season, her team posted a 28-3 record and made the first-ever NCAA Women's Final Four, losing the championship game, 82-

76, to Louisiana Tech University. In her 11 seasons at Cheyney State, Stringer compiled a 251-51 record.

Stringer left Cheyney State in 1983 to coach at the University of Iowa in the Big 10 Conference. She coached 12 seasons at Iowa, posting a record of 269 wins and 84 losses. Under her guidance, the Hawkeyes made nine consecutive NCAA tournament appearances and won six Big 10 championships. In 1993, the team made the NCAA Women's Final Four, but lost to The Ohio State University by one point in the semifinals. Stringer became the third woman coach in the United States to win at least 500 college games, reaching that milestone at the University of Iowa on January 28, 1994. In July 1995, Rutgers University hired Stringer to rebuild their women's program. Rutgers's offer of a base salary of $225,000 made her the highest-paid women's coach in the country.

Stringer has significant international coaching credentials as well. She coached the 1985 World University Games team and the 1989 U.S. world championship zone qualification team, and her team won a bronze medal at the 1991 Pan American Games in Havana, Cuba.

Many of her peers regard Stringer as possessing one of basketball's most creative minds. Her careful analysis of opponents' game plans, meticulously planned practices, and brilliant game plans are her trademark. She was voted Women's Basketball Coaches Association National Coach of the Year in 1982, 1988, and 1993, and named *Sports Illustrated*'s National Coach of the Year in 1993. In 1993, she also received the Carol Eckman Award, given annually to the women's basketball coach who demonstrates spirit, courage, commitment, leadership, and service to women's basketball.

Stringer's impact on women's basketball reaches beyond her remarkable won-loss record. Her personal courage has been an inspiration to all her peers and players. In 1971, Stringer married William Stringer, an exercise physiologist, and has three children: David, Janine, and Justin. In 1982, four months before Stringer's first appearance at the NCAA Final Four, 14-month-old Janine was struck with spinal meningitis and was left brain damaged and physically disabled, confined to a wheelchair. In November 1992, just four months before her second appearance at the Final Four, her husband of 21 years died suddenly of a heart attack.

One of the great leaders in the history of women's basketball, Vivian Stringer has made a success of balancing family and work, handling the pressures of winning basketball, and raising a disabled child. "She's always talked to us about coming back, about getting back up and not letting anything keep you down," said Iowa player Toni Foster in 1994. "Every day she shows us how to do it."[125]

Patricia Head Summitt (basketball coach)

Born June 14, 1952, Clarksville, Tennessee

Coach Patricia Head Summitt watched the final seconds of the clock tick off as her Lady Volunteers from the University of Tennessee claimed the 1997 National Collegiate Athletic Association (NCAA) Women's Basketball Championship. This victory sealed the fifth championship for Summitt, highlighting an illustrious coaching career that began in 1974. In that time, she has established a career record of 625-143 through the 1996-97 season. In international competition, her teams have won gold in the 1979 world championships and the 1984 Olympics.

Before becoming a coach, Summitt was an outstanding player. As a player, she set multiple scoring records while at the University of Tennessee at Martin (UTM) and won a silver medal as a member of the U.S. national team at the 1973 World University Games, a gold in the 1975 Pan American Games, and a silver in the 1976 Olympics. Her time as a player helped her develop knowledge and a playing philosophy that she transferred to coaching. In making one of the most successful transitions from player to coach in the history of

Pat Summitt
Courtesy of the University of Tennessee

basketball, Summitt has become a role model for females aspiring to become major college coaches, and her success as a coach has helped elevate the women's game into a popular spectator sport.

Patricia Sue Head, the daughter of James and Hazel Head, was born in Clarksville, Tennessee, on June 14, 1952. She began her basketball career as a child playing two-on-two with her three brothers on a makeshift court in the hayloft of the family's barn. Her passion for the game developed through elementary and junior high school; but when Summitt reached high school, Clarksville High did not have a girls' basketball team. Thus, the Head family moved to nearby Montgomery so she could play basketball at Cheatham County High School in Ashland City, Tennessee. The 5' 10" freshman played forward on the varsity squad. (The girls' team still played a six-player format with three forwards and three guards on a split court.)

In the fall of 1970, Summitt enrolled in the University of Tennessee at Martin (UTM) because it was one of the few colleges that had a women's intercollegiate basketball program. In 1972, Summitt led the UTM team to a spot in the first Association of Intercollegiate Athletics for Women (AIAW) National Basketball Championships. In 1973, Summitt captained the U.S. team to a silver medal at the World University Games in Moscow. In 1976, she was selected as a member of the U.S. Olympic team that played in the inaugural Olympic women's basketball tournament. The U.S. team lost to the Soviet Union in the finals, finishing in second place and taking home the silver medal.

While playing at UTM, Summitt suffered a knee injury and had to sit out her senior year, but in her previous three years as a player, she set several UTM records that have yet to be broken, including most career points (1,405), most career free throws (361), most points in a season (530 in 1971–72), and most free throws in a season (132 in 1971–72).

During the two-year layoff to rehabilitate her knee, Summitt earned her bachelor's degree in physical education in 1974

from UTM and enrolled in the master's degree program at the University of Tennessee at Knoxville (UTK). She received a graduate assistantship that year, which made her coach of the women's basketball team, beginning her legacy as one of the finest coaches in the game of women's basketball.

In her first season as coach, Summitt finished with a record of 16 wins and 8 losses. She had only 12 players, many of whom had never played a five-woman, full-court game. She taught them basketball fundamentals, conditioning, and teamwork and had an uncanny understanding of the game as well as an ability to motivate her players, both on and off the court. Her success as a coach proceeded rapidly. In 1977, UTK placed third in the national championships, and repeated the feat two years later. In her 23-year career as head coach of the University of Tennessee Lady Volunteers, Summitt has compiled a record of 625 wins and 143 losses, and has led her teams to five national championships (1987, 1989, 1991, 1996, 1997).

Summitt also established herself as an elite international coach. In 1977, she coached the U.S. Junior National Team to a gold medal in their first international competition; the same squad traveled to Mexico City to compete in the Pan American Games, where they also won gold. Her U.S. squad won the world championships and finished second in the Pan American Games in 1979. One year later, Summitt was selected as assistant coach of the 1980 U.S. Olympic team, which did not get to play because of the U.S.-led boycott of those Games.

In 1984, Summitt was named head coach of the U.S. Olympic team. Her team included All-Americans Teresa Edwards of Georgia, Lynette Woodard of Kansas, Anne Donovan of Old Dominion, and Cheryl Miller of the University of Southern California. She directed the team to a silver medal in the 1983 world championship as a tune-up for the Olympics. At the 1984 Los Angeles Games, Summitt was the only woman among all the head basketball coaches. The U.S. team went undefeated in the tournament, beating South Korea in the gold-medal game, 85-55. Summitt's international coaching record is a phenomenal 63-4.

For her achievements as a coach, the Women's Basketball Coaches Association named Summitt the Coach of the Year in 1983 and 1995; she was named the 1987, 1989, and 1994 Naismith Coach of the Year. In 1989, she was given the most prestigious award by the Basketball Hall of Fame, the John Bunn Award for excellence in coaching, the first female coach to receive the award in its 18-year history; and

she was inducted into the International Women's Sports Hall of Fame in 1990.

With 625 wins, Patricia Head Summitt is the third-winningest active coach—male or female—(behind only Bobby Knight and Jody Conradt) in the NCAA, and she is considered one of the very best college basketball coaches in the nation. Her career has spanned a time of tremendous growth and change for women's basketball, and she has managed to keep up with all of it. Her success at the college level helped turn women's college basketball into a popular spectator sport. Summitt is an important role model for girls and women aspiring to hold leadership positions in women's sports.

Further Reading

Lay, Nancy. *The Summitt Season.* Champaign, IL: Leisure Press, 1989.

Wyomia Tyus (track and field sprinter)
Born August 29, 1945, Griffin, Georgia

In women's track and field, the 1960s belonged to the Tigerbelles, the Tennessee State University (TSU) track team. Out of that program came a number of national and Olympic champions. One of the Tigerbelles, Wyomia Tyus, ascended to the top of women's sprinting in the United States in the 1960s. In her amateur career, Tyus captured three Olympic gold medals and one silver, and was the first person, woman or man, to successfully defend a 100-meter Olympic title. She set numerous world records in the 100 meters and 200 meters, and as a member of 4x100-meter relay teams. One of the first female professional track and field stars, Tyus was unbeatable in 60- and 100-meter dashes. A sincere athlete who loved to run, she represented a generation of Black female athletes who faced

racial and sexual discrimination but remained dedicated to achieving world-class distinction in track and field.

The fourth child of Willie and Maria Tyus, Wyomia was born in Griffin, Georgia, in 1945. Her father encouraged her to participate in competitive sports. She played basketball, her favorite sport, until she went out for the Griffin High School girls' track team with the intention of high jumping. She soon realized that running, not jumping, was her forte.

Despite strong opposition from her female relatives, who told her that competing was "unladylike," Tyus practiced hard at her high school track. In 1961, at the Georgia High School State Track Championships, Ed Temple, legendary coach of the TSU Tigerbelles, watched Tyus run and

Wyomia Tyus
© Allsport/(USOC)

invited her to participate in his summer track and field camp. At the camp, she undertook an intensive conditioning program and benefited from additional coaching on her sprinting technique. The following year, she traveled to Los Angeles to compete in the 1962 Girls' Amateur Athletic Union (AAU) Championships. The 17-year-old won the 100-yard dash, setting a U.S. record for her age group. She also won the 50- and 75-yard dashes in the track meet. The next year she defended her girls' title in the 100-yard dash, and a month later competed in her first AAU senior women's meet, where she finished second in the 100-yard dash to Edith McGuire.

Tyus went to TSU in 1963 to continue training with Coach Temple. She worked out with other Tigerbelles, including AAU champion McGuire. With the Tokyo Olympics one year away, the top athletes at the

university pushed their training schedules to the limit. For Tyus, the increased training had a positive effect. In 1964, she won the AAU 100-meter title, defeating McGuire, and two weeks later earned a place on the U.S. Olympic team.

Tyus went to the 1964 Tokyo Games still considered second-best to the likes of McGuire and other world-class sprinters. But she gained immediate respect when, in the second heat of the 100-meter dash, the former Griffin High School track star tied the world-record time of 11.2 seconds. She sped to first place and a gold medal in the event and finished her first Olympics by anchoring the U.S. women's 4x100-meter relay team's silver-medal run.

After the Olympics, Tyus returned to TSU to continue running and studying. Her family urged her to quit training because they felt it was unfeminine, but she kept going, wanting another shot at Olympic gold. On her way to the 1968 Olympics, Tyus captured the 1965 and 1966 AAU 100-yard dash titles and also added the AAU 220-yard dash title to her list of accomplishments. In 1967, she traveled to Winnipeg, Canada, to win the 200-meter crown at the Pan American Games.

In her second Olympics, Tyus faced the constant warning about the "repeat jinx"—no one had won the 100 meters in two consecutive Olympics. The added pressure to defend her title, combined with the racially tense atmosphere surrounding the Mexico City Games, had little effect on Tyus's performance. She soundly defeated her opponents, winning the 100 meters in a world record of 11.0 seconds. She went on to collect another gold in the 4x100-meter relay, establishing a second world record with her team.

After the tumultuous events of the 1968 Mexico City Olympics, Tyus retired from amateur sports. She was lured out of retirement in 1973 by the newly formed Professional International Track Association (PITA), which invited her to participate in the sole women's event, the 60-yard dash. After a five-year layoff from competitive running, Tyus began training in earnest. In her first year as a professional trackster, she won eight of 18 races and was the women's leading money maker. The next year, she won all 22 events she entered and became one of the circuit's most popular performers. Many agreed that her efforts helped give professional track respectability, but she saw her role in a much broader context—as a way of helping to promote women's participation in the sport. "I've always felt that women's track and field in the United States has been on the bottom of the totem pole. People hardly realize women run other than every four years. I believe we should get just as much recognition as the men do."[126]

Supporting and promoting women in all sports, especially track, became a lifelong goal of this sports pioneer. She coached female tracksters at Beverly Hills High School, encouraging her athletes "to be competitive but maintain a balanced outlook on sports because it is just one part of life."[127]

A founding member of the Women's Sports Foundation, Tyus served on the Foundation's advisory board for several years; she also served as an official Goodwill Ambassador to Africa and as a consultant to the Olympic Experience Group, where top competitors use their athletic backgrounds to show others how to cope with everyday life.

In 1980, Tyus was elected to the National Track and Field Hall of Fame and became a member of the International Women's Sports Hall of Fame in 1981. This Tigerbelle flew her way to the title of the world's fastest woman; yet her success as a professional track star, and her later role as an outspoken proponent of civil rights in America, opened the door for the next generation of minority women in sports.

Glenna Collett Vare (golfer)

Born June 20, 1903, Providence, Rhode Island; died February 10, 1989

The 1920s are often called the "Golden Age of Sports" for the exploits of a gallery of stars such as Babe Ruth, Bobby Jones, and Helen Wills Moody. Not only did Americans swarm to see these sports stars, but they also became participants in the sports their heroes played. The popularity of golf contributed to the decade's obsession with sports. During this time, women began playing the game in greater numbers, in part because of the emergence of Glenna Collett Vare, the leading female golfer of the era. Vare won more amateur golf championships than any other golfer. With her superior skills, she convinced the skeptics of the time that there was a place for women on the golf course.

The daughter of George and Ada Collett of Providence, Rhode Island, Glenna was born into an athletic family. She was an active girl, playing numerous sports with her brother, including baseball and tennis, and she was an outstanding swimmer and diver. When she was 13, her father took her to the Metacomet Golf Course in East Providence to hit a few balls. She "rather liked it," she recalled; and about two years later, after watching an exhibition match with Bobby Jones, Glenna decided to take up the game more seriously.

She practiced daily and with the help of Scottish golfer Alex Smith developed a powerful swing. In 1921, she won her first tournament by beating British champion Cecil Leitch for the Berthellyn Cup in Philadelphia. For the next 10 years, Vare was nearly unbeatable as she began to amass amateur victories.

At age 19, she won the North, the South, and the Eastern Amateur Championships. At that time, women were not known for their power and accuracy, but Vare changed all that. She once drove the ball 307 yards off the tee. Her long drives caught the attention of golf writers, who began to publicize her exploits around the country.

Glenna Collett Vare
Courtesy of the Ralph W. Miller Golf Library/Museum

Vare won the first of her record six U.S. Women's Amateur Championships in 1922, and the following year she claimed the Canadian Women's Amateur title. In perhaps her best year, 1924, the 21-year-old won 59 of the 60 events she entered, including a second Canadian championship. She added the French championship to her array of trophies in 1925, but despite her gallant attempts, she was never able to capture the most prestigious title of the time, the British Ladies Amateur Championship.

She represented the United States on six Curtis Cup Teams, serving as captain four of those years. The idea of the Curtis Cup, a biennial international match play competition between the United States and the Great Britain, originated in 1905; but it was not until 1930, when Vare arranged for a group of American women amateurs to play in Great Britain, that the United States Golf Association (USGA) agreed to make it a regular amateur event.

In 1931, Glenna married Edward Vare of Philadelphia. Her playing dropped off until 1935, when she came back to win her sixth U.S. Women's Amateur Championship. On the final day of the tournament, 15,000 people came to watch Vare compete against some of the best young American players, including 17-year-old Minnesotan Patty Berg. Vare defeated the teenager to recapture the title.

Although her level of play dropped in the 1930s, Vare remained an active player. Over a 39-year period (1919-58), Vare played in the national amateur tournament 26 times. At 56 years old, she captured the Rhode Island State Championship, 37 years after winning it for the first time; and in 1986, at the age of 83, she played in her 62nd straight Point Judith, Rhode Island, Invitational Tournament.

For her outstanding achievements and contributions to women's golf, Vare was inducted into the World Golf Hall of Fame in 1975 and the International Women's Sports Hall of Fame in 1981. In 1952, the Ladies Professional Golf Association (LPGA) initiated the Vare Trophy in her honor, presented annually to the player with the lowest scoring average. (Interestingly, the first Vare Trophy went to Patty Berg, whom Vare had beaten in 1935 when Berg was 17.) Vare also was awarded golf's Bobby Jones Award in 1965 for her sporting conduct on and off the golf course.

In the 1920s and 1930s, women golfers had no professional tour to jump to after their amateur careers. With no prize money on the line, these women became fierce competitors vying for national amateur titles. Vare said, "It wasn't at all difficult to be accepted as a woman golfer because there just weren't that many women playing, and among those who played everything was congenial."[128] Her skill made it easy for her to succeed around the golf links as she accumulated admirers like men's champion Bobby Jones. But for those not so skilled, she opened doors to the golf world that had previously been closed to women. When the sportswriters began to follow her game, they began to notice other women players as well. She helped establish golf as a pastime for both women and men.

Grete Andersen Waitz (marathon runner)

Born October 1, 1953, Oslo, Norway

In October 1978, Grete Andersen Waitz of Norway entered her first marathon, the New York City Marathon, and won the event in world-record time. Her victory in front of thousands of spectators and millions of television viewers left an indelible mark on women's distance running. With her subsequent victories, Waitz put the women's marathon on the map of world track, and her accomplishments helped win approval for the first women's Olympic marathon in 1984.

Born Grete Andersen in Oslo, Norway, the youngest of John and Reidun Andersen's three children, Grete became involved in sports at a young age, starting with handball and moving on to gymnastics and track. At age 12, she began running in an old pair of spikes she found. After two months, she joined Vidar, a local sports

club. By age 16, Waitz had won the Norwegian junior titles in the 800 and 1,500 meters. In 1971, she set a European junior record in the 1,500 meters with a time of 4:17.

In 1972, Waitz competed in her first Olympics, traveling to Munich to run in the 1,500 meters, the longest race for women at the time. She failed to medal in the event, but she continued to train at the middle distances. At the 1974 European Championships, Waitz placed third in the 1,500 meters; and the following year, she set a record in the 3,000 meters. Despite a first-place ranking going into the 1976 Olympics, Waitz did not run her best race and was eliminated in the semifinals of the 1,500 meters at Montreal. In 1977, the Norwegian won the inaugural World Cup 3,000-meter race and finished fifth in the 1,500 meters in the European Championships. In March 1978, she won the first of her five world cross-country titles.

By age 25, Waitz had established herself as the top 3,000-meter runner in the world. Recognizing her accomplishments at distance running, the New York Road Runners Club invited her to compete in the 1978 New York City Marathon. Her husband, Jack Waitz, convinced her to run the race, saying it was their one and only chance to see America.

In her first New York City Marathon, Waitz ran the first nine miles alongside the women's favorite, Christa Vahlensieck of Germany, but pulled out in front of Vahlensieck and was the first woman across the finish line. Waitz completed her first marathon in 2:32:30, taking two minutes off the world record. After years of running the 1,500 and 3,000 meters, Waitz had found her distance.

With her success in future marathons, Waitz almost single-handedly changed the image of women's distance running. She won an astounding nine out of 11 New York City Marathons (1978-80, 1982-86, 1988). In the 1979 marathon, she shaved nearly five minutes off her record, finishing with a time of 2:27:33, becoming the first woman to run a marathon under two and a half hours. In June 1979, she set a world record in the 10,000-meter L'Eggs Mini-Marathon in Central Park, a race she would win five times.

Perhaps her best year as a distance runner was 1980. Waitz won her third world cross-country championship; set new world records for 5 miles, 10 miles, 15,000 meters, and 20,000 meters; and won the New York City Marathon for the third straight year. For her acments, she was selected Sportswoman of the Year by *Women's Sports and Fitness* magazine.

In 1983, Waitz won the London Marathon, and later that summer, she won the marathon at the first World Track and Field Championships in Helsinki, Finland. She traveled to Los Angeles in 1984 to compete in her third Olympic Games as the favorite in the first-ever women's marathon. An expected battle between the three top marathoners—Waitz, her Norwegian teammate Ingrid Kristiansen, and American Joan Benoit—never materialized. Benoit broke away from the field after three miles and held onto the lead throughout. Waitz ran a conservative race because of the heat and held onto second place to win the silver medal.

Twelve weeks after the Olympics, Waitz captured her sixth New York City Marathon; and in 1985, she ran only in New York, winning the race again. At age 33, she won the two marathons she ran in 1986, the London and New York City Marathons, putting her on top of the world rankings for the sixth time. In 1988, she repeated as New York champion, and in her final New York Marathon in 1991, she finished third.

Grete Waitz
© Nancy Coplon

Through the 1980s, Waitz epitomized women's distance running. In 1991, *Runner's World* magazine named her the best female distance runner of the past 25 years. She was inducted into the International Women's Sports Hall of Fame in 1995.

Grete Andersen Waitz's success in the New York races spotlighted women's endurance running, and her intense drive and dedication brought acclaim to the sport. She became an international celebrity, running in road races around the world, holding clinics, and making personal appearances. Her accomplishments and efforts to promote women's distance running worldwide transformed running for women from recreation to competition. As one woman told her before the running of one L'Eggs Mini-Marathon: "Before you came along, people used to come to watch the women. Now they come to watch the competition. Thank you."[129]

Further Reading

Waitz, Grete, with Gloria Averbuch. *World Class: A Champion Runner Reveals What Makes Her Run, with Advice and Inspiration for All Athletes.* New York: Warner Books, 1986 259 pp.

Kathy Whitworth (golfer)

Born September 27, 1939, Monahans, Texas

In 1984, Kathy Whitworth captured the Rochester International golf tournament, claiming her 85th career title and surpassing Sam Snead's record for the most professional golf tournament victories. In a career that has lasted more than 30 years, Whitworth won her first tournament in 1962 and followed that victory with 17 consecutive years (1962-78) of posting at least one tournament win (88 total titles). In her illustrious career, she has won every major tournament except the U.S. Women's Open. When Mickey Wright retired from full-time touring in 1965, Whitworth took the reigns as the Ladies Professional Golf Association's (LPGA) number one player, a position she held for more than a decade. Her immense popularity, overall athletic ability, and total dedication to the game resulted in increased acceptance of women's golf as a legitimate and acceptable professional sport. Through her quiet demeanor and leadership abilities, she has become an important role model for generations of female golfers.

Kathrynne Ann Whitworth was born in Monahans, Texas, the youngest daughter of Morris and Dama Ann Whitworth. When Kathy was a toddler, her family moved to

Kathy Whitworth
Courtesy of the Ladies Professional Golf Association

Jal, New Mexico, just north of El Paso, Texas. Like many great sportswomen, Whitworth participated in several activities as a youngster. She played football, softball, and basketball, but as she grew older, the number of opportunities that she had to participate began to dwindle. In the 1950s, only a few sports were deemed acceptable for adolescent females. At age 15, Whitworth searched for a sport that would allow her to compete and develop as an athlete. She found golf.

While sports had always come easy to Whitworth, golf presented a real challenge to the 15-year-old. She went to the Jal Country Club every day to practice. She began taking lessons from a golf pro in 1955, and by 1956, she had improved so much that he suggested she work with another pro in Austin, Texas. For two years, Whitworth traveled to Austin by bus during the summers to take lessons from well-known golf pro Harvey Penick.

In 1957, Whitworth won her first title, the New Mexico State Amateur Championship, and successfully defended her crown the following year. With her confidence level at an all-time high in December 1958, three months after her 19th birthday, Whitworth announced that she wanted to try the professional tour. She traveled two days by bus to Augusta, Georgia, for her first LPGA Titleholders tournament. She recalled: "I had a little Sunday bag, and I didn't even have a complete set of clubs. My caddie was almost too embarrassed to carry the bag."[130]

For the next three years, Whitworth struggled to make it on the professional circuit. Although she was not making much money, her game continued to improve as did her concentration and confidence. She finally broke through with her first victory at Baltimore's Kelly Girl Open in 1962. Twenty years later, Whitworth recorded her 83rd LPGA victory to break Mickey Wright's long-standing mark. She passed the million-dollar career earnings mark, the first woman to do so, with a third-place finish in the 1981 U.S. Open.

As a pro, she dominated the circuit in the 1960s. She won eight tournaments in 1963, 1965, and 1967; nine in 1966; and 10 in 1968. She was the leading money earner eight times (1965-68, 1970-73) and won the Vare Trophy for low scoring average seven times (1965-67, 1969-72).

When the LPGA initiated its Player of the Year award in 1966, Whitworth was the first recipient; she won the honor six more times (1967-69, 1971-73). The Associated Press sportswriters chose Whitworth as the Female Athlete of the Year in 1965 and 1966, and the honors continued. She was inducted into the LPGA Hall of Fame in 1975, the World Golf Hall of Fame and the Texas Sports Hall of Fame in 1982, and the International Women's Sports Hall of Fame in 1984.

She was a champion of women's golf on and off the course, working to increase the number of sponsorships and tournaments as an LPGA officer for seven years. As president of the LPGA, Whitworth worked to raise the purses at women's pro events, and the LPGA benefited from her leadership. She captained two U.S. teams in the international Solheim Cup competition (1990, 1992), and has written numerous instructional articles in *Golf for Women Magazine*.

Women's golf came into its own as a major sport in the 1970s because of the hard work of its veteran players. When Whitworth went over the million-dollar earnings mark, she commented: "It will be very good for the LPGA. People will read about it and realize that women's golf now has a very legitimate place in professional sports."[131]

Throughout her 30-year career, Whitworth demonstrated what a top-level female athlete could accomplish with quiet determination and dedication. Because she chose to stay out of the limelight, her accomplishments are often overlooked, but her achievements speak for themselves. She was a role model for the younger, more flamboyant players who arrived on the scene in the late 1970s. Rightfully so, Whitworth is considered one of the all-time great female golfers of the twentieth century.

Further Reading

Eldred, Patricia Mulrooney. *Kathy Whitworth*. Mankato, MN: Creative Education Society, 1975. 31 pp.

Hazel Hotchkiss Wightman (tennis player)

Born December 20, 1886, Healdsburg, California; died December 5, 1974

The "Queen Mother of Tennis," Hazel Hotchkiss Wightman, an accomplished player and tennis instructor, helped shape the future of women's tennis in America by introducing net play to the women's game, by supporting dress reform, by initiating the idea of international tennis matches, and by devoting her life to teaching thousands of youngsters the game. She taught future champions—such as Sarah Palfrey, Helen Wills Moody, and Helen Hull Jacobs—who in turn left their marks on the game. Wightman had an active role in transforming the game in its early years, from a "genteel" activity to a competitive sport, and inspired women of all ages to play the game.

The only daughter of William and Emma Hotchkiss, Hazel was born in Healdsburg, California, in 1886, just 12 years after Mary Outerbridge introduced tennis to the United States. The Hotchkiss family lived on a 1,500-acre ranch in a remote area of California, where the children played games in the wide open spaces around them. Although Wightman suffered from poor health as a child, she

Hazel Hotchkiss Wightman
Courtesy of the International Tennis Hall of Fame

actively participated in football and base-ball with her brothers. When Wightman was 14, her family moved to Berkeley, California. At that time, the family encouraged her to give up the rough sports she had played and to replace them with the new sport of tennis. After watching the 1902 Pacific Coast Championship tournament, Wightman embraced the sport with enthusiasm, working to become a champion.

The graveled backyard of the family home became a practice court. Wightman often practiced by herself, hitting the ball up against the side of the house or playing with her brothers over a rope strung across the yard. She worked hard to hit the ball before it bounced in the gravel, all the while skillfully developing the art of volleying. To play on Berkeley's only asphalt court, Wightman had to go at five o'clock in the morning because girls were not allowed to play after eight o'clock.

After six months, Wightman entered her first tournament, the Bay Counties Women's Doubles in San Francisco, which she and partner Mary Radcliffe won. At that tournament, Wightman introduced her volley and net play for the first time. The women's game, until that time, had been played from the baseline without much movement. Her style of play made women's tennis a much more dynamic sport to play and to watch. With her movement at the net, Wightman challenged the restrictive style of tennis attire. She wanted more freedom to hit the ball on her serve, volleys, and overhead smashes, and often wore sleeveless dresses, a revolutionary fashion statement for a turn-of-the-century American woman.

In 1909, Wightman won the national triple—the singles, doubles, and mixed doubles. She repeated the feat in 1910 and in 1911. In the 1911 tournament, she won the finals of all three events on the same day. After graduating from the University of California in 1911, Wightman played tennis during the summer on the East Coast, where she met her future husband, George. She married the following year and settled in Boston, where she began to limit her tennis to raise a family. The couple had five children.

Within months after George, Jr., was born in 1913, Wightman defeated the national champion at the Longwood Cricket Club in Chestnut Hill, Massachusetts. In 1919, after two more children, she recaptured the national singles title. In a career that spanned nearly 60 years, she won a total of 44 national titles, including two Olympic gold medals in the doubles and mixed doubles tennis at the 1924 Paris Games.

In 1919, Wightman introduced the idea of international matches to promote competition between women players from different countries. She donated a silver vase to the United States Lawn Tennis Association (USLTA) for such a competition, which quickly became known as the "Hazel Hotchkiss Wightman Trophy," now the Wightman Cup. After four years of delays, the first Wightman Cup match inaugurated the new West Side Tennis Club at Forest Hills, New York. Representatives from Great Britain and the United States initiated the competition in 1923. From that first match, the Wightman Cup evolved into a prestigious contest between U.S. and British teams, with the best players from each country vying for the Cup. Wightman represented the United States as a player five times (1923, 1924, 1927, 1929, 1931) and as a coach for 13 years.

In the 1920s, Wightman began her career as a teacher of tennis. She held free clinics, open to everyone, at the Longwood Cricket Club and ran tournaments for all skill levels for nearly half a century. In 1933, she wrote *Better Tennis,* offering advice about basic strokes, conditioning, and strategy. During the large tournaments, the coach often opened her sprawling Chestnut Hill home to visiting female players, providing them with a place to stay and a chance to socialize with other players off the court.

Wightman retired from competitive tennis in 1960, playing in her last national tournament at the age of 73. Until her death in 1974, she continued to teach tennis to the stars of the future. She received numerous honors for her long career as both a player and a teacher. She received the USLTA Service Bowl in 1940 and became a member of the International Tennis Hall of Fame in 1957. Upon the 50th anniversary of the Wightman Cup in 1973, Queen Elizabeth II made Wightman an honorary Commander of the British Empire.

Hazel Hotchkiss Wightman left a permanent and positive mark on the game of tennis. One of the most influential women the game has known, she helped shape the future of women's tennis, both in the United States and internationally. As a player, she revolutionized the style of play, inspired women to play a more aggressive game, and influenced dress reform on the court, which had a resounding impact off the court. Her development of the Wightman Cup matches was important for promoting international competition for women, but it also signified women's growing independence in determining their own scheduling and competitive match play.

Early in her career, Wightman established herself as a formidable player and a role model for women tennis players. As the "Queen Mother of Tennis," she introduced hundreds of young girls to the game, and coached champions and future role models. Her enthusiasm inspired females of all ages to participate and turned the "genteel" game of tennis into one of the most popular individual sports for women in twentieth-century America.

Lynette Woodard (basketball player)

Born August 12, 1959, Wichita, Kansas

In October 1985, Lynette Woodard signed a contract as the first female member of the Harlem Globetrotters, basketball's traveling ambassadors of goodwill. Woodard joined the Globetrotters after an illustrious collegiate basketball career at the University of Kansas. She used her experience as one of the Globetrotters to bring recognition to women's basketball and to help expand women's opportunities in the sport.

The daughter of Lugene and Dorothy Woodard, Lynette was born and raised in Wichita, Kansas. As a youngster, she played pick-up games with her older brother Darrell but didn't start playing organized basketball until her sophomore year in high school. She played for the Wichita North High School team, where she developed basic ball-handling and shooting skills. Woodard graduated from Wichita North in 1977 and enrolled in the University of Kansas the following fall term.

As a freshman member of the Jayhawk women's basketball team, 5' 11" Woodard led the nation in rebounds with a 14.8 average and was second in scoring with an average of 25.2 points per game. She was named the Freshman Player of the Year by both *Street and Smith's* and *Basketball Weekly.*

In her second year at the University of Kansas, she led the nation in scoring average (31 points per game) and set a single-season scoring record (1,177 points). She also set a single-game rebound mark with 33. A four-time collegiate All-American (1978-81), Woodard set the women's career college scoring mark with 3,649 points. She scored 35 or more points in 20 collegiate games and grabbed at least 16 rebounds on 16 separate occasions. In 1981, she won the Wade Trophy and the Broderick Award as the nation's outstanding women's collegiate basketball player.

The last two years of her collegiate career, Woodard earned Academic All-American honors with her 3.04 grade-point average. She graduated from the University of Kansas in 1981 with a bachelor's degree in speech communications and human relations and went to work on her master's degree.

In international competition, Woodard played on the gold-medal-winning U.S. Women's Basketball Team at the 1979 World University Games. The following year, she was chosen for the 1980 Olympic team but did not play because of the boycott. After graduating from the University of Kansas in 1981, Woodard played basketball in Italy for one year but returned to the United States to join the coaching staff at her alma mater.

She captained the U.S. national team to a victory over the Soviet Union in 1982, scoring 21 points in the winning effort. In 1983, she played on the U.S. team that won the gold medal at the Pan American Games and the silver medal at the World University Games. Named captain of the Olympic team in 1984 because of her extensive international experience, Woodard provided consistency and leadership to guide the team to America's first women's basketball Olympic gold medal.

In October 1985, she became the first woman to play for the Harlem Globetrotters. She quickly earned the respect of her teammates with her ball-handling skills and entertaining personality. "This is a dream come true," she stated. "We're bringing joy to people's lives through our basketball talent, and we're having fun."[132]

Lynette Woodard
Courtesy of the Harlem Globetrotters

Woodard played for the Globetrotters for two years before leaving the team over a contractual dispute. While on the team, this star player worked to increase women's playing opportunities outside of collegiate competition. "I hope the publicity from my playing on the Globetrotters helps a women's professional basketball league become viable and stable," she said in 1986. "There are a lot of other women who had the same dream I had, but they don't have any place to go after their college days."[133]

After her stint with the Globetrotters, Woodard played three seasons in Japan and four in Italy. In 1994, she retired from professional basketball and returned to the

United States. After three years away from the game, Woodard joined the Cleveland Rockers of the Women's National Basketball Association (WNBA) as a starting forward in 1997. She averaged 7.8 points and 4.1 rebounds a game for the Rockers in the inaugural season.

In 1986, the Women's Sports Foundation selected Woodard the Professional Sportswoman of the Year, and in 1993 honored her with the Hyman Award, which is given to the athlete who captures Flo Hyman's "dignity, spirit, and commitment to excellence."

As a member of the Harlem Globetrotters, Lynette Woodard broke a gender barrier on one of the world's most respected sports teams. Her ball-handling and shooting skills showed audiences around the world that women were competitive and graceful athletes. She is a true pioneer in twentieth-century women's sports.

Further Reading

Newman, Matthew. *Lynette Woodard.* Mankato, MN: Crestwood House, 1986. 48 pp.

Rosenthal, Bert. *Lynette Woodard, The First Female Globetrotter.* Chicago: Children's Press, 1986. 45 pp.

Mickey Wright (golfer)

Born February 14, 1935, San Diego, California

When her father bought her a set of golf clubs, Wright had found her niche. "Golf is my means of expression," she said.[134] One of the greatest woman golfers ever, Wright dominated the Ladies Professional Golf Association (LPGA) tour in the mid-1950s and 1960s. She changed the face of women's golf with her enormous drives off the tee and superior all-around game. Golf legend Ben Hogan once declared, "[Wright] has the finest golf swing I ever saw, man or woman."[135]

Born Mary Kathryn Wright on Valentine's Day, 1935, in San Diego, California, Mickey began swinging the golf club at the practice range at La Jolla Country Club when she was nine. On her 11th birthday, her father gave her a set of clubs—one wood, two irons, and a putter. Mickey headed to the course for her first full 18 holes of golf, where she scored approximately 145. By the time she was 13, she had improved her score to the high 80s.

Wright won her first tournament, the Southern California Girls' Championship, at age 14; and the following year, at an Invitational Tournament at La Jolla, she made her first hole-in-one and won the event. In 1952, the 17-year-old won the national United States Golf Association (USGA) Junior Girls' Championship.

Mickey Wright
Courtesy of the Ladies Professional Golf Association

After graduating from high school, Wright enrolled at Stanford University. In the summer following her freshman year, she was the low amateur (best finisher) at the U.S. Women's Open and runner-up in the U.S. Amateur Championship. Her low scores compared to those of the country's top female professionals, leading Wright to leave college to play the professional tour as an amateur for the 1954-55 season. At the 1954 U.S. Women's Open, she was paired with her idol, Babe Didrikson Zaharias. After Wright outdrove her on several holes, Zaharias commented, "What are you doing. Copying my swing?"[136] Zaharias went on to win the tournament; Wright finished as the low amateur.

Wright turned professional the following year, beginning a career that produced 82 tournament victories. In her rookie year, she earned $6,325, $8,253 the next, and more than $11,000 the next two years. By 1963, her yearly earnings reached nearly $32,000, the highest of any woman golfer. Wright led the tour in money earned four straight years (1961-64).

Equipped with what some described as a "perfect swing," Wright won the Vare Trophy for low scoring average for five consecutive seasons (1960-64). The 18-hole score of 62 she shot in the 1964 Midland, Texas, tournament set an LPGA scoring record. She could outdrive most men and often hit fairway shots 225 to 270 yards. Once, in a Dallas tournament, she overdrove a green on a 385-yard hole with help from a strong wind.

Between 1959 and 1968, Wright averaged 7.9 victories per year, and her 82 victories are second only to Kathy Whitworth's 88 total career wins. She won at least one LPGA tournament for 14 straight years (1956-69); her last tournament victory came at the Colgate-Dinah Shore Winner's Circle in 1973. Her list of victories includes four LPGA Championships and four U.S. Women's Open titles. In 1961, she won the Grand Slam of women's golf: the Titleholders (Masters), the U.S. Women's Open, and the LPGA Championship. She was the only woman to win the Open and the LPGA Championship in the same year—a feat she repeated in 1963—until Meg Mallon equalled the effort in 1991. She won an unprecedented 13 tournaments in 1961, averaging 72.81 strokes per 18 holes. The Associated Press named Wright the Female Athlete of the Year in 1963 and again in 1964.

In 1965, Wright suffered a wrist ailment that forced her to cut back her tournament schedule. In 1970, at age 35, she decided to retire from full-time touring. She said, "I felt I had accomplished what I set out to do, which was to become the best woman golfer in the world."[137]

Wright came out of retirement in 1993 to play in the Sprint Senior Challenge, where she tied for fifth place. In 1994, she finished second in the Challenge and earned $30,000—the biggest paycheck of her career.

Many would agree that Wright was the best woman golfer in the world. In 1964, she was inducted into the LPGA Hall of Fame, and in 1976, she became a member of the World Golf Hall of Fame. She joined a list of great sportswomen with her induction into the International Women's Sports Hall of Fame in 1981.

Mickey Wright played with power off the tee and developed one of the most perfect golf swings in the game. Her long drives wowed the crowds that came to see her play; she often outdistanced her competitors by as much as 50 yards off the tee. She exemplified a new breed of exciting personalities in the sport, and as one female golfer noted, "Mickey got the outside world to take a second hard look at women golfers, and when they looked they saw the rest of us."[138]

Kristi Yamaguchi (figure skater)

Born July 12, 1971, Hayward, California

Kristi Yamaguchi captured the gold medal in figure skating for the United States in the 1992 Winter Olympic Games, the first American woman to win the Olympic championship title in figure skating since Dorothy Hamill in 1976. Yamaguchi's mastery of both the technical and the artistic aspects of skating put her a level above the competition. Her success at world-class competition set a standard of excellence for female skaters in the 1990s. More than just a figure skating icon, the fourth-generation Japanese American became a role model for Asian American female athletes in all sports.

The daughter of Carole and Jim Yamaguchi, Kristi was born in Hayward, California, on July 12, 1971. She had a foot deformity that required her to wear corrective shoes for the first few years of her life. Her parents enrolled her in ballet lessons at age four as a way to get her legs and feet moving as part of the corrective process. She also took up ice skating and immediately liked the sport. She watched Dorothy Hamill win the gold medal at the 1976 Olympics and fell in love with the Olympic champion and her sport. As a result, Yamaguchi was determined to become an Olympic champion one day. At age five, she began to take her skating lessons very seriously and often practiced for up to four hours a day. She entered her first competition at age eight.

In 1983, Yamaguchi began skating with Rudy Galindo in the pairs competition. They were coached by Jim Hulick. The pair finished fifth in the U.S. National Junior Figure Skating Championships in 1985 and won the competition the following year. Yamaguchi and Galindo finished first in the 1988 world junior pairs, and Yamaguchi, beginning to emerge as an equally strong singles competitor, won the world junior singles title.

In 1989, the pair won the gold medal at the U.S. National Championships, and Yamaguchi finished second in the singles event, the first woman to win two medals at the nationals since Margaret Graham accomplished the feat in 1954. The free-skate part of her singles program was one of the most technically difficult programs being performed in world competition at the time. She achieved success by blending this technical ability with great artistry and elegance on the ice.

Kristi Yamaguchi
© Allsport USA/Rick Stewart

Yamaguchi continued to skate with Galindo in pairs competition. They placed fifth in the 1989 and 1990 world pairs championships, but changes in Yamaguchi's skating career were imminent. In the spring of 1989, her long-time coach Christy Kjarsgaard-Ness moved to Edmonton, Alberta. Yamaguchi decided to leave the San Francisco area and follow her coach to Canada. Galindo also relocated, but Coach Hulick remained in California. The skaters and their coach divided their time between Canada and California, and it appeared to work for a while. But in December 1989, Coach Hulick died of colon cancer. Unable to find a new coach, and with the failure of the team to improve on their fifth-place finish at the worlds, Yamaguchi decided to withdraw from pairs competition to concentrate solely on singles competition. "I figured we accomplished as much as we could together. To improve in one or the other, I had to choose. It was a difficult decision but I knew something would have to change."[139]

Figure skating itself was changing—to Yamaguchi's favor. The compulsory figures were eliminated from major competitions after July 1990. This rule change allowed Yamaguchi to concentrate on the strongest part of her skating, her creative and artistic free-skate programs. She quickly became one of the world's best. She won the 1990 Goodwill Games, the 1990 Nations Cup match, and the 1990 Skate America contest, defeating European and world champions. But at the 1991 U.S. Nationals, Yamaguchi finished second to Tonya Harding, the first U.S. woman to complete a triple axel in competition. Although "a little disappointed," Yamaguchi set her sights on the upcoming world championships.

In addition to skating a nearly perfect short program, Yamaguchi gave one of the best free-skate performances of her career at the 1991 world championships in Munich, Germany. She completed six triple jumps in her program, and scored eight 5.9s (out of 6.0) for technical merit and seven

5.9s and one perfect 6.0 for artistic competition to claim her first world championship title. (The United States swept the medals at the 1991 world championships with Yamaguchi, Harding, and Nancy Kerrigan finishing 1-2-3.) A few months later, Yamaguchi won the 1992 U.S. National Championship ladies' singles title.

As the reigning national and world champion, Yamaguchi was the favorite going into the 1992 Winter Olympics at Albertville, France. Skating to Strauss's *Blue Danube Waltz*, Yamaguchi skated a flawless short program and won the highest scores from all nine judges. With a convincing lead going into the long program two days later, she displayed her artistic and athletic ability and despite one fall in the long program, finished ahead of the other skaters to win Olympic gold.

One month later, Yamaguchi won her second consecutive world championship in front of a hometown crowd in Oakland, California, and became the first U.S. woman to successfully defend her world title since Peggy Fleming did it in 1968. The win gave Yamaguchi a rare triple in 1992, winning the national, world, and Olympic championships.

Yamaguchi turned professional in 1993 and joined the Discover Card "Stars on Ice" tour. She skates over 50 performances a year and is one of the most popular figure skaters on the professional circuit. "Ever since I started skating, I just knew I wanted to be touring as a professional figure skater," she told *International Figure Skating*. "I think living out that dream and being able to perform every night in all these different cities and hopefully touching these people with my skating—that's what Stars on Ice has provided me."[140] But Yamaguchi has not given up skating competitions altogether. She continues to compete in professional figure skating events. In 1997, she won her fourth World Professional Figure Skating Championship.

At the 1992 Albertville Olympics, Kristi Yamaguchi demonstrated her artistry in a spectacular, near-flawless performance that evoked memories of her role model, Dorothy Hamill, the 1976 Olympic gold medalist. The torch was passed to Yamaguchi in 1992, and the fourth-generation Japanese American has become a role model for young figure skaters who strive for that rare combination of artistry and athleticism in their skating.

Sheila Young (speed skater and cyclist)

Born October 14, 1950, Birmingham, Michigan

In this era of sports specialization, it is rare that one person could successfully compete at a world-class level in more than one sport. Sheila Young is the first athlete—male or female—to hold world titles in two sports, speed skating and cycling, in the same year, and she did it twice. Her remarkable career on the ice and on the bicycle makes her one of the great female athletes of the twentieth century. Her success in cycling inspired a generation of women cyclists to go beyond recreational biking to competitive sprint and road racing.

The daughter of Clair and Georgia Young, Sheila was born in Birmingham, Michigan, on October 14, 1950. Her mother and father, both competitive skaters and cyclists, encouraged their children to become active in sports. Sheila received her first pair of ice skates at age two, and by age four, she was soloing on a two-wheel bicycle. Sports was a real family event in the Young household, and it was the enthusiastic competition with her siblings that got her interested in speed skating. The whole family would train at Quarton Lake in Birmingham in preparation for weekend races. Cycling is part of most skaters' summer training regimen, so it was natural that Young would take up cycling during the off-season to build up the leg strength she needed for skating. Skating in the winter and cycling in the summer became Young's

Sheila Young
© Allsport USA/Tony Duffy

life for nearly a decade. She set her sights on the 1968 Winter Olympics but failed to make the U.S. Speed Skating Team. Rather than give up, she dedicated herself to four more years of rigorous training in preparation for the 1972 Olympics.

In 1970, Young won her first of many speed skating titles, the U.S. national outdoor competition and the North American outdoor championship. The same year, she began to see cycling as more than just a conditioning exercise. She worked as hard on her cycling techniques as on her skating techniques and eventually reached world-class form in both. In 1971, soon after successfully defending her national outdoor speed skating championship, she won her first major cycling championship, the Amateur Bicycle League of America's women's national sprint title. With these titles, Young began her journey as a two-sport athlete, applying the same discipline and determination to both sports.

In 1972, at age 22, Young qualified for the U.S. Olympic Speed Skating Team. She finished fourth in the women's 500-meter competition, missing the bronze medal by just eight one-hundredths of a second. She said afterward: "To lose by such a narrow margin was a disappointment, but at the same time it encouraged me. That was the first year I had really trained seriously, and I could see the improvement."[141] Less than a month after the Olympics, Young traveled to Sweden, where she won two 500-meter races in the World Sprint Championships.

Young's arduous training schedule continued throughout 1972. She progressively lowered her times in both cycling and speed skating while increasing her endurance and refining her technique. In January 1973, she took to the ice to capture all three women's events—the 500-, 1,000-, and 3,000-meter competitions—at the U.S. Olympic-style Speed Skating Championships in West Allis, Wisconsin. Later that month, she traveled to Europe to begin her quest for more championship wins. She raced to a gold medal in the 500 meters at the 1973 World Speed Skating Championships at Davos, Switzerland, setting a new world record in the process. In February 1973, she traveled to Oslo, Norway, for the World Sprint Championships, where she won three more events. She finished her

European tour in Stromsund, Sweden, with a win in the 500 meters at the Women's World Speed Skating Championships.

With just enough time to pack up her skates and dust off her bicycle, Young returned to the United States to begin her quest for cycling championship wins. In August 1973, she won the U.S. sprint title, and then was off to Europe again to compete in the World Cycling Championships. Facing tough competition from seasoned veterans, Young recorded a remarkable and courageous performance. Crashing twice while jockeying for position, she had lacerations on her arms and legs and a deep gash on her forehead that required a clamp to close the wound, but her will to win sped her across the finish line ahead of her rivals to capture the 1973 women's sprint title. Her victory marked the first time an American had won a world sprint cycling title in more than 50 years. As one journalist wrote: "Sheila's dramatic victory will undoubtedly stand as one of the most memorable of all time—and as a tribute to her courage as well as her skill."[142]

To capture the world titles in two strenuous and perilous events would be enough for anyone, but this extraordinary woman continued to pursue that elusive Olympic gold. Between 1974 and 1976, Young skated and cycled internationally, setting new records and winning more titles. Her victory at the World Sprint Championships in 1975 made her the favorite speed skater going into the Innsbruck Winter Games in 1976. That year, she entered three events and became the first American in the history of the Winter Olympics to bring home three medals, earning the gold in the 500-meter, the silver in the 1,500-meter, and the bronze in the 1,000-meter speed skating events. Later that winter, she established a new world record in the 500 meters at the 1976 women's all-around

World Speed Skating Championships. And to cap off her best year of athletic competition in 1976, she wheeled her way to both the U.S. and world sprint cycling titles.

In 1976, Young married cyclist Jim Ochowicz, who competed for the U.S. Olympic team. She retired from competition in 1976 to have her first child but began training again in both sports after the 1980 Winter Olympics. She placed seventh in the 1981 World Speed Skating competition in Grenoble, France; won the World Cycling Championships the same year; and placed second in 1982. She retired from skating and cycling in 1983.

Young was a founding member of the Women's Sports Foundation, and she served on the board of the U.S. Olympic Committee, the U.S. Cycling Federation, and the Special Olympics International. In 1981, she was named the U.S. Olympic Committee's Sportswoman of the Year;

she is also a member of the International Women's Sports Hall of Fame, the U.S. Cycling Federation Hall of Fame, and the Speed Skating Hall of Fame.

As a two-sport world champion, Sheila Young is one of America's greatest female athletes. She competed in speed skating and cycling because, as she once said: "I love the feeling of going fast."[143] Her courage and grit surfaced more than once on the international circuit. Her participation in three Olympiads produced three medals; and if cycling had been an Olympic event for women at the time, she undoubtedly would have brought home more. Her unquestionable athleticism combined with unmatched dedication and drive led to one of the most remarkable sports careers.

Further Reading

Soucheray, Joe. *Sheila Young.* Mankato, MN: Creative Education Society, 1977. 31 pp.

Mildred "Babe" Didrikson Zaharias (all-around athlete)

Born June 26, 1911, Port Arthur, Texas; died September 27, 1956

"I was always determined to be the greatest athlete that ever lived," Babe Didrikson Zaharias wrote in her autobiography, *This Life I've Led.*[144] In 1950, the Associated Press named her the Female Athlete of the Half Century. This honor came not for her performance in one sport, but for her remarkable succession of athletic achievements in many sports. Zaharias was an All-American basketball player, an Olympic gold medalist in track and field, and a ladies' golf champion.

Perhaps the greatest woman athlete in American history, Zaharias loved sports from an early age and had an obsession to be the best in whatever she tried—and in the sports world, that was nearly every-

thing. Flamboyant and provocative, she propelled women's sports into society's mainstream, becoming a media favorite and a bona fide sports hero at a time in America's history when women were discouraged from participating in competitive sports. At the 1932 Los Angeles Olympics, she won a silver medal in the high jump, and golds in the 80-meter hurdles and the javelin throw, to become the only person to win individual medals in running, throwing, and jumping events. In 1934, she took up golfing in earnest and went on to become a founding member of the Ladies Professional Golf Association (LPGA) in 1949, winning 31 of its major tournaments in the next 10 years. As much an entertainer as an

Mildred Babe Didrikson Zaharias
Courtesy of the Ladies Professional Golf Association

athlete, Zaharias drew crowds wherever she went, happy to exhibit her athletic abilities. She set new standards for sports in a career unprecedented in its breadth and success.

Born Mildred Ella Didriksen (she changed the spelling to Didrikson in 1932) in Port Arthur, Texas, the sixth of seven children of Norwegian immigrants Ole and Hannah Didriksen, Zaharias earned her nickname, "Babe," from her exploits in the parks of Beaumont, Texas. She could kick a football farther and throw a baseball harder than any of the boys in the neighborhood. She could hit home runs like their idol Babe Ruth, and so her playmates began to call her "Babe"; the nickname stayed with her all her life.

Babe learned to play basketball in elementary school and made the girls' team at South End Junior High and at Beaumont High School. In fact, in high school she played on every girls' team: volleyball, basketball, baseball, tennis, swimming, and golf.

In February 1930, Colonel M.J. McCombs of the Employers Casualty Company in Dallas recruited Zaharias to play on the company's Amateur Athletic Union (AAU)–sanctioned basketball team, the Golden Cyclones. With few opportunities for competitive sports for women in the nation's colleges, she jumped at the chance to play for the Cyclones. She left high school and moved to Dallas, where she took a job in the company's typing pool. She was paid to type, but her real job was to play basketball. A three-time AAU All-American for the Golden Cyclones, she led the company's team to two finals (1930, 1932) and one national championship (1931).

McCombs also introduced Zaharias to track and field. In June 1930, she entered her first meet, and just one month later, won two national titles at the national AAU meet. At the AAU nationals, she hurled the javelin 133 feet, 5 inches to set a new U.S. record and duplicated the feat in the baseball throw with a 268-foot, 10-inch toss that also set an U.S. record. Between 1930 and 1932, she entered AAU track meets, competing in the shot put, discus, javelin, high jump, long jump, hurdles, and baseball throw.

The 1932 AAU nationals doubled as the Olympic qualifying meet. Zaharias went to the nationals as the only member of the Employers Casualty team. She entered eight of the 10 events. In one day, within a span of three hours, she won five events (shot put, baseball throw, long jump, 80-meter hurdles, and javelin throw), tied one (high jump), and finished fourth in another (discus). She single-handedly won the team title for Employers Casualty with 30 points. In second place with 22 points was the University of Illinois, which had sent a 22-woman team.

Olympic rules limited Zaharias to only three individual events, so she chose the three in which she had set world records—the high jump, 80-meter hurdles, and javelin. At the 1932 Los Angeles Olympics, she won gold medals in the javelin throw and the hurdles, and finished second in the high jump when officials ruled her jumping style illegal because she dove over the bar. (She used the new western roll style rather than the then-normal scissor-kick.)

Olympic champion Zaharias became an instant celebrity. She returned to Dallas to continue working for Employers Casualty, but before the year was out, the AAU barred her from further amateur competition because she allowed an automobile company to use a photo of her in their advertisements. Zaharias turned professional in December 1932. She formed and played on the Babe Didrikson All-American Basketball Team. In 1934, she pitched at Major League Baseball spring training games and traveled with the bearded House of David baseball team. People bought tickets by the thousands to her exhibitions, wanting to see a real live folk hero, while many others considered her more of a freak than a celebrity. Amid her successes, she bore the brunt of the stereotypes and prejudices many women athletes faced during this era of American women's sports.

In 1932, Zaharias took up golf in earnest, determined to become a champion. She had learned the basic golf shots from her Beaumont High School coach and could already drive a golf ball more than 250 yards. She entered her first tournament in October 1934, the Fort Worth Women's Invitational; she qualified for match play but lost in the first round. In April 1935, she won the Texas Women's Golf Association Amateur Championship, but the United States Golf Association (USGA) declared her a professional athlete because of her

years of exhibition touring. Once again, Zaharias was forced to give up amateur competition.

Because there were no professional opportunities for women in golf at this time, she signed a contract for $1,000 a week in 1936 to do an exhibition tour with leading male golfer Gene Sarazen. In 1938, she met professional wrestler George Zaharias while playing as the only female contestant in the 1938 Los Angeles Open Golf Tournament. They were married on December 23, 1938; they had no children.

From 1940 to 1943, Zaharias played in professional golf tournaments but refused the cash prizes. She wanted to regain her amateur status so she could participate in the major women's tournaments, such as the U.S. Women's Amateur and the British Amateur. In 1944, the USGA reinstated Zaharias to amateur status, reviving one of the most illustrious golf careers the game had known. She won the 1945 Western Open, Texas Open, and Broadmoor Invitational. During the 1946-47 season, she won 17 amateur tournaments in a row, including the 1946 U.S. Amateur and the 1947 British Amateur, the first American woman to capture the British title in its 54-year history.

In August 1947, after her victory at the British Amateur, Zaharias announced that she would again turn professional; she joined the Women's Professional Golf Association (WPGA) and helped found the Ladies Professional Golf Association in 1949. As a professional golfer, she had 31 LPGA victories. She was the leading money earner in women's professional golf four consecutive years (1948–51) and captured the Vare Trophy for low scoring average in 1954. She won three U.S. Women's Open titles (1948, 1950, 1954) and three women's Titleholders tournaments (1947, 1950, 1952).

In 1953, at the height of her golf career, Zaharias was diagnosed with colon cancer and underwent an emergency colostomy. Three and a half months after the surgery, she returned to the LPGA tour, finishing 15th in the All-American tournament. The USGA honored her with the Ben Hogan Trophy for the greatest comeback of the year. The following year, 1954, she won the U.S. Women's Open by a record 12 strokes. She competed in several other tournaments and finished her autobiography before the cancer returned and claimed her life on September 27, 1956.

Babe Didrikson Zaharias was the nation's leading female sports star for more than three decades. The Associated Press named her Female Athlete of the Year six times (1932, 1945, 1946, 1947, 1950, 1954). She was elected to the LPGA Hall of Fame in 1951; the PGA/World Golf Hall of Fame and National Track and Field Hall of Fame in 1974; the International Women's Sports Hall of Fame in 1980; and the U.S. Olympic Hall of Fame in 1983.

Zaharias's athletic accomplishments left an indelible mark on women's sports in America. At a time when the nation's col-lege faculties worked to suppress competitive athletics for women, her successes in the Olympics helped solidify women's presence in this premier sporting event. She converted women's golf to an exciting power game with her towering drives and aggressive shot-making. In addition to being an excellent athlete, she also made women's professional golf an entertaining game to watch. One of the greatest women athletes in the history of American sports, Zaharias had a tremendous influence on American women and symbolized what women could achieve in sports.

Further Reading

Cayleff, Susan E. *Babe: The Life and Legend of Babe Didrikson Zaharias.* Chicago: University of Illinois Press, 1996. 327 pp.

Johnson, William D., and Nancy Williamson. *Whatta Gal! The Babe Didrikson Story.* Boston: Little, Brown, 1977. 224 pp.

Knudson, R.R. *Babe Didrikson: Athlete of the Century.* New York: Viking Press, 1985. 57 pp.

Lynn, Elizabeth A. *Babe Didrikson Zaharias.* New York: Chelsea House Publishers, 1988. 111 pp.

Zaharias, Babe Didrikson. *This Life I've Led.* New York: A.S. Barnes & Co., 1955. 255 pp.

NOTES TO CHAPTER 3

1. "My Life Story," Michelle Akers' WWW home page, <http://www.michelleakers.com/story.html>, Retrieved from the World Wide Web on November 4, 1996.

2. Quoted in Kelly Whiteside, "World Beater," *Sports Illustrated,* June 5, 1995, p. 74.

3. Quoted in Anne Johnson, *Great Women in Sports* (Detroit: Visible Ink Press, 1996), p. 3.

4. Quoted in *Current Biography 1956,* p. 4.

5. *Current Biography 1956,* p. 4.

6. Tracy Austin with Christine Brennan, *Beyond Center Court: My Story* (New York: William Morrow & Company, 1992), p. 3.

7. Austin, p. 89.

8. Quoted in Betty Spears, "Senda Berenson Abbott: New Woman, New Sport," in *A Century of Women's Basketball: From Frailty to Final Four,* Joan S. Hult & Marianna Trekell, eds. (Reston, VA: American Alliance for Health, Physical Education, Recreation, and Dance, 1991), p. 23.

9. Quoted in *Current Biography 1940,* p. 75.

10. Rhonda Glenn, "Interview: Patty Berg," *Golf Yearbook 1989,* p. 131.

11. Quoted in Rhonda Glenn, *The Illustrated History of Women's Golf* (Dallas, TX: The Taylor Publishing Company, 1991), p. 126.

12. Glenn, "Interview," p. 129.

13. Glenn, "Interview," p. 130.

14. "Bonnie Blair Speaks Out," *Women's Sports and Fitness,* May/June 1994, p. 18.

15. Quoted in Ernest O. Hauser, "Look at That Girl Go," *Saturday Evening Post,* January 22, 1949, p. 100.

16. Quoted in Sonja Steptoe, "The Dogged Pursuit of Excellence," *Sports Illustrated,* February 11, 1991, p. 194.

17. Quoted in Kathleen McCoy, "Susan Butcher and Libby Riddles Face Each Other and 60 Men—In the Coldest Race on Earth," *Women's Sports and Fitness,* February 1987, p. 25.

18. Connie Carpenter-Phinney, "Just a Girl on a Bike," *Bicycling,* August 1987, p. 53.

19. Quoted in *Current Biography 1950,* p. 89.

20. Karolyi quoted in *Current Biography 1977,* p. 113.

21. *Current Biography 1977,* p. 113.

22. Quoted in *Current Biography 1977,* p. 114.

23. Gail Devers, "Running for My Life," *Family Circle,* May 18, 1993, p. 21.

24. Quoted in Jeff Hollobaugh, *100 Stars of American Track & Field* (Indianapolis, IN: U.S. Track & Field, 1996), p. 208.

25. Michael Janofsky, "Devers Conquers All and Captures the 100," *New York Times,* August 2, 1992, p. 1.

26. Quoted in Anne Johnson, *Great Women in Sports* (Detroit: Visible Ink Press, 1996), p. 125.

27. Dave Kuehls, "Wheels of Fortune," *Runner's World,* April 1, 1996, p. 70.

28. "Jean Driscoll, How She Got Started in Wheelchair Racing," Interview on Boston Marathon World Wide Web site <http://www.bostonmarathon.org/101/audio7_driscoll.html>, retrieved from the World Wide Web on June 4, 1997.

29. "Jean Driscoll"

30. "Jean Driscoll"

31. "Jean Driscoll"

32. Quoted in Melissa Isaacson, "Splash Dancer!" *Women's Sports and Fitness,* June 1986, p. 23.

33. Quoted in Jill Lieber, "Going for Three," *Sports Illustrated,* July 22, 1992, p. 129.

34. Quoted in "Edwards and Pippen Named 1996 USA Basketball Athletes of the Year," *USA Basketball News,* December 1996, p. 10.

35. Quoted in "Zone Users Q&A with Janet Evans, ESPN Sports Zone World Wide Web site <http://ESPNET.SportsZone.com/editors/talk/transcripts/0730evans.html>, retrieved from the World Wide Web on June 13, 1997.

36. Quoted in *Current Biography,* July 1996, p. 19.

37. Quoted in Bruce Anderson, "Of Gold and Glee," *Sports Illustrated,* October 3, 1988, p. 56.

38. Quoted in "Zone Users," June 13, 1997.

39. Billie Jean King, *We Have Come a Long Way: The Story of Women's Tennis* (New York: McGraw Hill Company, 1988), p. 135.

40. King, p. 150.

41. Quoted in Barry Lorge, "The Legacy of Chris Evert," *Tennis Magazine,* November 1989, p. 33.

42. Quoted in Barry Wilner, "The Untouchable," *Olympian,* May 1993, p. 15.

43. Quoted in "Lisa Fernandez," *Women's Sports and Fitness,* October 1996, p. 24.

44. Quoted in *Current Biography 1968,* p. 129.

45. Quoted in Geoff Drake, "The Reluctant Hero," *Bicycling,* May 1994, p. 60.

46. Quoted in Scott Martin, "Cycling Sisters: Meet Four Women Who Shape the Sport," *Bicycling,* May 1996, p. 62.

47. Martin, p. 62.

48. Alice Marble, "A Vital Issue," *American Lawn Tennis,* July 1, 1950, p. 14.

49. Letter to Author, May 13, 1997.

50. Letter to Author, May 13, 1997.

51. Quoted in Meg Lukens, "Skiing a Formidable Course," *Sports Illustrated,* January 7, 1991, p. 4.

52. Lukens, p. 5.

53. Quoted in Peter Miller, "Golden Girl," *Skiing,* November 1987, p. 63.

54. Lukens, p. 5.

55. Lukens, pp. 5-6.

56. Lukens, p. 6.

57. Quoted in Larry Hurrle, "Michelle: The Belle of Racquetball," *Olympian,* May 1993, p. 41.

58. Hurrle, p. 41.

59. Quoted in *Rochester (New York) Times-Union,* December 2, 1977.

60. Quoted in Nancy Prichard, "Mountaineering: Alison Hargreaves Wants to Know..." *Outside Magazine,* May 1995.

61. Quoted in David Ellis, "Final Ascent," *People Magazine,* September 4, 1995, p. 69.

62. Nancy Prichard, "On Her Own Terms," *Women's Sports and Fitness,* November/December 1995, p. 43.

63. Quoted in *Current Biography 1959,* p. 182.

64. Quoted in Nancy Prichard, "The Climb of Her Life," *Women's Sports and Fitness,* May 1997, p. 66.

65. Nicholas O'Connell, "Lynn Hill," in *Beyond Risk: Conversations with Climbers* (Seattle, WA: The Mountaineers, 1993), p. 253.

66. Prichard, "The Climb of Her Life," p. 65.

67. Quoted in "Rock Steady," *Women's Sports and Fitness,* January/February 1995, p. 23.

68. Quoted in Elizabeth Kaufmann, "Lynn Hill Knows How to Challenge Herself to the Extreme," *Women's Sports and Fitness,* July/August 1991, p. 34.

69. Quoted in Prichard, "The Climb of Her Life," p. 65.

70. Quoted in Michele Kort, "Remembering Flo," Women's Sports and Fitness, April 1986, p. 76.

71. Quoted in Michele Kort, "Flo Hyman: Variety is the Spike of Life," *Women's Sports and Fitness,* December 1985, p. 14.

72. Quoted in Anne Lang, "Scamper," *Horse & Rider,* November 1994, p. 22.

73. Quoted in John Brant, "A Clear Vision," *Runner's World,* February 1993, p. 39.

74. Brant, p. 39.

75. Brant, p. 39.

76. Quoted in *Current Biography 1989,* p. 221.

77. *Current Biography,* 1989.

78. Quoted in *Current Biography 1987,* p. 293.

79. Quoted in *Current Biography 1987,* p. 296.

80. Billie Jean King, *Billie Jean* (London: W.H. Allen, 1975), p. 15.

81. Quoted in Barry Lorge, "Billie Jean King: The Pied Piper of Tennis," *Tennis Magazine,* July 1991, p. 64.

82. Curry Kirkpatrick, "There She Is, Ms. America," *Sports Illustrated,* October 1, 1973, p. 30.

83. "100 Most Important Americans of the 20th Century," *Life,* Fall 1990, p. 28.

84. Quoted in *Current Biography 1989,* p. 315.

85. Paul Moran, *New York Newsday,* December 17, 1987.

86. "Julie Krone," *Sports Illustrated,* May 22, 1989, p. 96.

87. Quoted in Herman Weiskopf, *The Perfect Game* (Englewood Cliffs, NJ: Prentice-Hall, Inc., 1978), p. 215.

88. Weiskopf, p. 216.

89. Weiskopf, p. 216.

90. Nancy Lieberman-Cline, *Basketball My Way* (New York: Charles Scribner's Sons, 1982), p. 4.

91. Quoted in Jeff Metcalfe, "Mercury Pleased to Add Hall of Famer; Shooting Guard," *Arizona Republic,* February 28, 1997, p. C5.

92. Alice Marble, "A Vital Issue," *American Lawn Tennis,* July 1, 1950, p. 14.

93. Quoted in Richard Hoffer, "Christy Martin is Knocking Down Stereotypes even as She Refuses to Champion the Cause of Women in the Ring," SIOnline: Sports Illustrated Web Site <http://www.sionline.com/si/1996/960415/index.html>, retrieved from World Wide Web on July 7, 1997.

94. Hoffer, July 7, 1997.

95. Quoted in Tasha Zemke, "Boxer Pulling All the Punches at Leader in Her Field," *Fort Worth Star Telegram,* July 1, 1996.

96. Quoted in Herman Weiskopf, *The Perfect Game* (Englewood Cliffs, NJ: Prentice-Hall, Inc., 1978), p. 222.

97. Quoted in Phyllis Raybin Emert, "Foremothers: Floretta McCutcheon," *womenSports,* October 1976, p. 61.

98. Smith quoted in Emert, p. 61.

99. Weiskopf, p. 223.

100. Quoted in Weiskopf, p. 223.

101. Quoted in Jeannie Roberts, "Setting the Pace," *Women's SportsPages,* January/February 1992, p. 9.

102. Quoted in Terry Mulgannon. "It's Miller Time," *Women's Sports,* May 1982, p. 24.

103. Quoted in "Miller Gets Her Golden Reward," *USA Today,* July 23, 1996.

104. Nancy Kleinbaum, *The Magnificent Seven: The Authorized Story of American Gold* (New York, Bantam Books, 1996), p. 54.

105. Quoted in "Miller Comes Back to Win Beam Gold," Reuters, July 29, 1997.

106. Kleinbaum, p. 55.

107. Quoted in Stan Sutton, "A Street Lady of Another Sort," *The Sporting News,* January 28, 1987, p. 47.

108. Martina Navratilova, with George Vecsey, *Martina* (New York: Alfred A. Knopf, 1985), pp. 18-19.

109. Navratilova, p. 24.

110. Quoted in "Cindy Nelson," *Women's Sports,* March 1983, p. 25.

111. "Cindy Nelson," p. 26.

112. Quoted in Julie Ridge, "Enduring Greatness," *Women's Sports,* June 1989, p. 26.

113. Quoted in Elisa Kinder, "Woman of Iron: Turning Both Struggles and Victories into Triumph," *Fitness Plus,* June 1997, p. 5.

114. Ridge, p. 29.

115. Quoted in *Current Biography Yearbook 1986,* p. 462.

116. *Current Biography Yearbook 1986*, p. 464.

117. Quoted in Bob McManaman, "Lady-in-Waiting," *Arizona Republic,* February 2, 1993.

118. Quoted in Bob Cunningham, "Manon Rheaume: Insisting She's Just 'One of the Guys,'" Hockey Player Magazine Web site <http://www.hockeyplayer.com/manon.html>, retrieved from the World Wide Web on November 26, 1996.

119. Quoted in "Wilma Rudolph," *Women's Sports,* October 1984, p. 45.

120. Quoted in Jacqueline Hanson, "Joan Benoit: Here Runs the Bride," *Women's Sports and Fitness,* January/February 1985, p. 49.

121. Quoted in Gary Smith, "A Woman's Place," *Sports Illustrated,* March 9, 1992, p. 124.

122. Smith, p. 134.

123. Quoted in Dick Patrick, "Smith, 39, Makes 5th Olympic Team," *USA Today,* January 30, 1992.

124. Quoted in "Fabulous Francie," *Runner's World,* October 1991, p. 87.

125. Quoted in Phil Taylor, "Vivian Stringer," *Sports Illustrated,* March 22, 1993, p. 72.

126. Quoted in Irwin Stambler, *Women in Sports* (New York: Doubleday and Company, 1975), p. 83.

127. Quoted in "Running Proud: Wyomia Tyus," *Women's Sports,* October 1981, p. 29.

128. Quoted in Jim Dodson, "Talking Golf: A Conversation with Glenna Collett Vare," *Golf Magazine,* March 1989, p. 41.

129. Quoted in Gloria Averbuch, "The New Grete Waitz," *Women's Sports and Fitness,* October 1985, p. 22.

130. Quoted in Betty Hicks, "Kathy Whitworth: Out of the Shadows," *Women's Sports,* p. 33.

131. Hicks, p. 57.

132. Quoted in Bert Rosenthal, *Lynette Woodard, The First Female Globetrotter* (Chicago: Children's Press, 1986), p. 38.

133. Rosenthal, p. 44.

134. Quoted in "The Wright Stuff: Mickey Wright," *Women's Sports,* October 1981, p. 30.

135. Quoted in Rhonda Glenn, *The Illustrated History of Women's Golf* (Dallas, TX: Taylor Publishing Company, 1991), p. 202.

136. Glenn, p. 208.

137. Quoted in Rhonda Glenn, "Mickey Wright," *Golf Magazine,* January 1988, p. 42.

138. Quoted in Robert Markel, *For the Record: Women in Sports* (New York: World Almanac Publishers, 1985), p. 49.

139. Quoted in *Current Biography Yearbook 1992,* p. 618.

140. Quoted in Lois Elfman and Mark A. Lund, "Living the Dream," *International Figure Skating,* March/April 1997, p. 47.

141. Quoted in *Current Biography 1977,* p. 456.

142. *Current Biography 1977,* p. 457.

143. *Current Biography 1977,* p. 456.

144. Zaharias, Babe Didrikson. *This Life I've Led* (New York: A.S. Barnes & Co., 1955), p. 27.

Chapter 4
Outstanding Women's Teams

"Being a member of a team is part of the bigger picture of life. People always have to work together to succeed and success alone is not too fun."

—Jennifer Azzi[1]
1996 U.S. Olympic Women's Basketball Team gold medalist

Over the last one hundred years, women have banded together to wage battles, overcome defeat, and share victory in the name of equality on and off the sports field. But female athletes faced enormous obstacles in their efforts to get women's team sports accepted into the sports world. Since the turn of the century, individual sports like swimming, badminton, golf, tennis, and bowling were emphasized for women and considered more acceptable than team sports like volleyball, basketball, and softball. These attitudes limited women's opportunities in team sports, despite the message from America's physical educators that while they did not believe in taking competition out of activity, they believed the ultimate role of women in society was for cooperation rather than competition. Physical educators encouraged women to play team sports for fun, but not to compete seriously.

But women found ways to compete outside educational institutions, and their numbers began to grow in the 1920s and 1930s. The Amateur Athletic Union (AAU) sponsored a number of national champi-

onships in a variety of team sports beginning in the 1920s. By the end of the 1930s, softball had become the top women's sport in the United States, and in the 1950s, the Raybestos Brakettes of Stratford, Connecticut, started their three-decade reign as the dominant women's fast-pitch softball team. During World War II, more than 500 women played baseball in the All-American Girls Professional Baseball League (AAGPBL), and in the 1960s, members of the Tennessee State University Tigerbelles excelled in women's track and field in AAU and Olympic competition.

After the passage of Title IX in 1972, which mandated that schools receiving federal funds provide equal programs, facilities, and opportunities for girls and women, interest in sports for girls grew dramatically in individual and teams sports. Girls' soccer leagues were born and Little League teams were integrated. The Amateur Sports Act of 1978 created a structure for the development of Olympic sports that ensured support for both men's and women's programs. Women's team sports were added to the Olympic roster, and the United

States Olympic Committee (USOC) began training coaches of girls' team sports. In just a few years, the athletic skill level of women rose dramatically. The Association of Intercollegiate Athletics for Women (AIAW) formed in 1971 and took over the governance of women's sports teams at the nation's colleges and universities and began offering scholarships, coaching, training, and national championships.

Throughout this time, women continued to challenge gender barriers in male-dominated sports. In 1994, the Colorado Silver Bullets, an all-female professional baseball team, made its debut playing against men's professional teams, and America[3] was the first all-women's team to compete for the America's Cup sailing competition.

Powerful women's teams made up of strong individual players began to emerge in the quarter of a century after Title IX was enacted. At the 1996 Olympics, U.S. women worked together, winning all three swimming relays; both track relays; and team golds in basketball, soccer, softball, gymnastics, and synchronized swimming. These Olympics provided the world with a view of the culmination of a hundred years of women's efforts to develop outstanding women athletes on a number of women's teams. This chapter contains the stories of 10 of the most successful and influential teams/organizations and their key players. The chapter includes brief histories of the teams, how and when they were formed, lists of their accomplishments, followed by brief biographical profiles of selected team members.

All-American Girls Professional Baseball League

One of the first professional sports leagues for women, the All-American Girls Professional Baseball League (AAGPBL) debuted during World War II. Chicago Cubs owner and chewing gum magnate Philip K. Wrigley, concerned that fans would lose interest in the national pastime while the men were at war, organized the league in 1943 to attract fans to the major league ballparks until the men returned. The league lasted from 1943 to 1954. During its 12-year existence, the league went through many changes—in name, in the game itself, in organizational structure, in location, and in players. More than 500 women played for teams from Wisconsin, Indiana, Minnesota, Michigan, and Illinois. The women who played in the league were talented athletes and offered a high caliber of play to the millions of fans who came to see them.

Wrigley initially called the league the All-American Girls Softball League. Softball was a tremendously popular sport in the United States at the time, and Wrigley wanted to get the top stars to play in his league. In 1943, Wrigley and other team sponsors sent scouts to scour softball fields around the country for the best players. The owners invited more than 250 of the top women softball players to try out for their teams. The All-American Girls Softball League began play in 1943 in four Midwestern cities: Kenosha and Racine, Wisconsin; South Bend, Indiana; and Rockford, Illinois. Teams played a regulation form of softball, except that stealing bases was allowed.

Despite the popularity of softball, team owners who favored a major league style of play quickly pushed a change toward base-

All-American Girls Baseball League, 1945 Rockford Peaches
National Baseball Hall of Fame Library, Cooperstown, NY

ball. By 1948, the league had adopted a regulation nine-inch baseball, replaced the underhand throw with the overhand pitch, and increased the distance of the base paths to 85 feet. The league also changed its name to the All-American Girls Ball League, then to the All-American Girls Baseball League, and finally to the All-American Girls Professional Baseball League (AAGPBL). The women, all former softball players, had to learn how to adjust to this new game.

Most of the players signing with the league were single and young, with ages ranging from about 15 to 28. The league offered some players their first opportunity to travel; many of the women had never been outside their own hometowns. In 1943, the average salary was between $45 and $75 a week for a regular season that lasted about four months.

Great pains were taken to ensure that the players retained their femininity. In preseason training, players learned game fundamentals during the day and went to charm school at night to learn etiquette and makeup techniques. During regular season games, players wore uniforms—one-piece, tunic-like dresses with the skirt above the knee. Players could not wear slacks, shorts, or jeans in public; they could not cut their hair; and each team had a chaperon for the players. The league strove to give the public the image of complete femininity of all the players.

The league was a huge success in its early years. In the first season of play, the AAGPBL drew more than 200,000 spectators. Nearly one million fans flocked to the games in 1948.

The Racine Belles won the first league championship in 1943. The Milwaukee

Chicks topped the league in 1944, and the Rockford Peaches, portrayed in the popular 1992 movie *A League of Their Own*, won three championships (1945, 1949, 1950). The Grand Rapids Chicks won in 1947 and 1953; the South Bend Blue Sox claimed two consecutive league championships in 1951 and 1952; and the Kalamazoo Lassies won the final league championship in 1954. Top players in the league included Helen Callaghan, who led the league in batting in 1945 with a .299 average; Sophie Kurys, whose 201 stolen bases in a single season still stands as a professional record (71 more than Rickey Henderson's 1982 record); and Jean Faut, who pitched two perfect games (no hits, no walks, no runs) and had a career record of 132 wins and 61 losses.

Despite the league's early popularity, by 1950 it began to experience decreasing attendance and gate receipts. The men had returned from the war and Major League Baseball was back in full swing. Also, recruiting new players became a problem as many AAGPBL players began to retire, get married, and have families.

The league folded in 1954 because of financial troubles brought on by the return of men's baseball and the subsequent popularity of television and televised Major League games. Nonetheless, for more than 10 years, the nation had a successful professional women's team sport that entertained millions. The players forever changed the notion that women could not play an aggressive style of baseball. "We played tough, even when we were hurt. Back then we had no trainers like today. We'd have strawberries on our legs from sliding in skirts, huge bruises, and the chaperons would just tape us up and out we'd go," remembered Helen (Callaghan) St. Aubin. She added: "I was just a little girl, miles from home, and this experience allowed

me to be independent, to have my own money, and make my own decisions at a time when few women did that, let alone girls. Women were supposed to be in the kitchen, taking care of kids. They weren't supposed to be considered independent people. That's what was so great about it. We got to make choices."[2] The women of the AAGPBL were true sports pioneers.

Selected All-American Girls Professional Baseball League Players

Isabel Alvarez

Growing up in Cuba, Alvarez learned to play baseball from a neighbor. When she was 13, she joined *Estrellas Cubanas* ("Cuban Stars"), a Cuban baseball league modeled after the AAGPBL. *Cubanas* were recruited to play in the AAGPBL, and five made their way to the United States. Alvarez came to the United States in 1949 and for two years traveled around the country on an AAGPBL-sponsored tour with other young players hoping to make it on an established team. In 1951, Alvarez joined the Fort Wayne Daisies. She played 13 games with the Daisies in 1951, pitching 39 innings, earning two wins and no losses. Alvarez moved around the league, playing for the Kalamazoo Lassies, the Grand Rapids Chicks, and the Battle Creek Belles.

Helen Callaghan

In her first year in the AAGPBL, 1944, Callaghan played left field for the Minneapolis Millerettes. She was the lead-off batter and finished second in batting in the league with a .287 average. That season, she had 114 hits, including three home runs, five doubles, and four triples. In 1945, she was traded to the Fort Wayne Daisies and won the league batting title with a .299 average. She had 122 hits in 111 games and scored 77 runs. Callaghan played with the Daisies until she retired from professional baseball in 1947.

Jean Faut

Regarded by many as the best overhand pitcher in the AAGPBL, Faut played for the South Bend Blue Sox from 1946 to 1953. She joined the Blue Sox in 1946 as a third baseman but was switched to pitcher late in the season. She started 12 games, winning eight and losing three. The following year, Faut pitched in 44 games, posting a 19-13 record with a 1.15 earned run average (ERA). In 1948, the league went to overhand pitching, and Faut was one of the few pitchers to make the successful transition from underhand to overhand. Faut played only part of the 1948 season because of her pregnancy, but she still compiled a 16-11 record. In 1949, she started 34 games, won 24 and lost 8 and recorded a 1.10 ERA. She had great control and could throw a variety of pitches. On July 21, 1951, she pitched a perfect game (no hits, no runs, no walks) against the Rockford Peaches, retiring 27 batters in a row. On September 3, 1953, she pitched her second perfect game, this time against the Kalamazoo Lassies. Faut was named Player of the Year in 1951 and 1953. Her career statistics are 140 wins and 64 losses—a .686 winning percentage—and a 1.23 ERA.

Betty Foss

Foss began her playing career in 1950 with the Fort Wayne Daisies. In her first year, she won the league batting title with a .346 average and was nominated for Rookie of the Year. She won the batting title again in 1951 (.368) and 1952 (.334). In 1952, she led the league in runs (79), hits (135), total bases (207), doubles (26), triples (17), and runs batted in (RBIs) (74). For her outstanding offensive achievements, she was named 1952 Player of the Year. Foss was also an outstanding infielder, playing first or third base. She was selected to three All-Star teams. Her lifetime batting average was .342, with 649 hits, 32 home runs, and 312 RBIs in 498 games played.

Rose Gacioch

Gacioch joined the AAGPBL in 1944 with the South Bend Blue Sox. She played right field for the Blue Sox for one season then was traded to the Rockford Peaches in 1945. She set an all-time AAGPBL record with 31 assists (throws for outs) from the outfield in her first year with the Peaches. She also hit nine triples and batted in 44 runs—in 1945, she led the league in triples and RBIs. In 1948, Gacioch switched from outfield to pitcher. In 1951, she posted a 20-7 record and a 1.68 ERA; she was the league's only 20-game winner that season. In 1953, she hurled a no-hitter against South Bend. She was a three-time All-Star (1952, 1953, 1954).

Dorothy Kamenshek

Regarded as the best all-around player in the history of the AAGPBL, Kamenshek played for the Rockford Peaches from 1943 to 1951 and in 1953. Selected for seven All-Star teams, she was consistently one of the top batters in the league and won the batting crown in 1946 (.316) and 1947 (.306). In 1950, she batted .334, and in 1951, .345. She had the highest lifetime batting average of all long-time players—.292. Also regarded as the best first baseman in the league, Kamenshek's defensive abilities set her apart from other players in the league. She committed only 192 errors in 1,005 games. Her lifetime fielding percentage was .982.

Sophie Kurys

An eight-year starter for the Racine Belles (1943-50), Kurys led the league in base stealing for five straight years, averaging more than 100 stolen bases per season. In 1944, she reached first base 172 times and stole 166 bases, seven in just one game, and the following year she stole 115 bases. In 1946, Kurys set a league record. She reached first base 215 times, attempted 203 steals, and was successful 201 times, a phenomenal 99 percent success rate. Her base-stealing record of 201 in one season is unequaled in baseball history. Kurys was blessed with lightning speed, an ability to judge pitchers' moves, and an unusual aggressiveness on the base paths. As the lead-off hitter for the Belles, Kurys had an uncanny ability to reach first base. In her record-setting year, she played in 113 games, got 112 hits, drew 93 walks, and was hit by 10 pitches. For her outstanding base stealing and run-scoring, Kurys was named Player of the Year in 1946. She also was an outstanding fielder, selected to All-Star teams four consecutive years (1946-49) as second baseman. In 1950, Kurys stole 120 bases and hit a season-high seven home runs. Kurys finished her career with the Battle Creek Belles in 1952. Her career record for stolen bases stands at 1,114.

Dorothy Schroeder

The only player to have played all 12 seasons in the AAGPBL, Schroeder joined the South Bend Blue Sox in 1943 at age 15. In her first year, she batted .188 and hit one home run. By 1954, her batting average had improved to .304, and she hit 17 home runs that year. In 1951, she led the league in home runs. One of the league's most outstanding shortstops, Schroeder was selected to the All-Star team in 1952, 1953, and 1954. Her overall career fielding percent-

age was .913. She finished her career in 1954 with the Kalamazoo Lassies.

Joanne Weaver

Weaver was an outstanding outfielder for the Fort Wayne Daisies and a powerhouse hitter. She led the league in batting average three consecutive years, 1952, 1953, and 1954, with averages of .344, .346, and .429. In 1954, the final year of the AAGPBL, she led the league in batting average (.429), runs scored (109), base hits (143), and stolen bases (79). She was chosen 1954 Player of the Year. Her lifetime batting average was .359, with 438 hits, 38 home runs, and 234 RBIs in 329 games played.

Connie Wisniewski

An outstanding pitcher for the Milwaukee Chicks, Wisniewski joined the team in 1944, where she compiled a record of 23 wins and 10 losses, the highest winning percentage in the league. In 1945, the Chicks moved their franchise to Grand Rapids, Michigan. That year in Grand Rapids, Wisniewski started 46 games, ending the season with a 32-11 record and a 0.81 ERA. She was chosen the first-ever AAGPBL Player of the Year. She outdid herself the following year with a 33-9 record. Wisniewski earned the nickname "Iron Woman" after twice pitching both ends of a double-header (16 consecutive innings). In 1948, when the league switched to overhand pitching, Wisniewski moved to the outfield and became an outstanding right fielder. She was chosen as an All-Star outfielder in 1948 and 1949, and again in 1951 and 1952.

Further Reading

Berlage, Gai Ingham. *Women in Baseball: The Forgotten History*. Westport, CT: Praeger Publishers, 1994. 208 pp.

Brown, Lois. *Girls of Summer: The Real Story of the All-American Girls Professional Baseball League.* Toronto: Harper Collins, 1992. 224 pp.

Gregorich, Barbara. *Women at Play: The Story of Women in Baseball.* San Diego: Harcourt, Brace & Company, 1993. 224 pp.

Helmer, Diana Star. *Belles of the Ballpark.* Brookfield, CT: The Millbrook Press, 1993. 96 pp.

Johnson, Susan E. *When Women Played Hardball.* Seattle, WA: Seal Press, 1994. 292 pp.

Macy, Sue. *A Whole New Ball Game: The Story of the All-American Girls Professional Baseball League.* New York: Henry Holt & Co., 1993. 140 pp.

America³

The America's Cup is modern sports' oldest international trophy. Since its first defense over one hundred years ago, only seven women had sailed in the America's Cup competition. After winning the 1992 America's Cup as skipper of *America³*, Bill Koch decided to take a revolutionary tack: For his 1995 title defense, the yachtsman would recruit and train an all-female crew. When it came time to defend the Cup in 1995, Koch thought that a women's team could greatly enhance the sport. Koch had been particularly impressed by Dawn Riley, a member of his 1992 crew: "She did her job better than any of the men, demonstrating that women could do it," claimed Koch in Anna Seaton Huntington's *Making Waves: The Inside Story of Managing and Motivating the First Women's Team to Compete for the America's Cup.*[3] His America³ philosophy was simple: With the right focus, commitment, and teamwork, ordinary people—men or women—can do extraordinary things. Koch was offering the world's top female sailors a chance to show what they could do when given one of the world's best boats.

Koch published an 800 number in newspapers across the country soliciting applications from female sailors and women accomplished in other sports. Six hundred and eighty-seven women responded to the announcement. Forty-four women were invited to San Diego for three, one-week-long, on-the-water tryouts. The women were judged by a small panel of coaches according to certain criteria: attitude, teamwork, ability, sailing experience, and physical fitness. Every evening the coaches rated each woman on a scale of one to 10 in each category.

Twenty-four women were selected to be crew members on America³. The team roster was officially announced in early

America3
© Daniel Forster

June 1994, and training in San Diego began about 10 days later. Training included weightlifting in the morning and work on the boat in the afternoon.

The 1995 America's Cup Defenders Selection Series pitted the women's team against two other American crews, Team Dennis Conner and PACT '95, in a round-robin competition with points awarded on place of finish. The winner would defend the Cup against the winner of the Challenger Selection Series, which would be held simultaneously, also off the San Diego coast.

In November 1994, the women showed their mettle at the International World Championships off San Diego, a warm-up for the Cup, finishing second only to the team from Australia. Team Dennis Conner and PACT '95 finished far behind *America³*.

After nearly six months of intensive training in San Diego, the all-women's team left San Diego Bay on January 13, 1995, for the first race in the series. With J.J. Isler at the helm, *America³* established a lead right off the starting line and crossed the finish line more than one minute and nine seconds ahead of the next competitor. The race was only the first in the four-month-long trials leading up to the Cup, but the win boosted the confidence of the crew and coaches.

For the first six months of training and racing, the crew raced the three-year-old *America³* that had won the 1992 Cup. Prior to the fourth round, Koch brought in a "new and improved" boat, *Mighty Mary*. (Koch named the yacht after his mother, who was an avid hunter and tennis player. Her athletic prowess, he said, never brought her the recognition she had deserved.)

After four months and nearly 60 races among the three teams in early 1995, the race for the America's Cup came down to one final three-boat race. Team Dennis Conner managed to squeeze past *Mighty Mary* just two boat lengths—or 52 seconds—ahead of the women to win the final of the Defender's Series and earn the right to represent the United States in the defense of America's Cup.

Despite the loss, *America³* was a great success. "The women's team fell short of winning, but even so, we achieved much more than most people predicted," wrote Huntington. "When we started the campaign, few believed we could match the physical strength of the men's team, but once the racing began, the strength issue was never raised again . . . . We proved to pose a serious competitive threat [to Team Dennis Conner and PACT '95]."[4]

"Through all my years of competitive sailing, I never thought the America's Cup would be within my reach—or that of any group of women," said Linda Lindquist. "Now I'm convinced that women can compete with men at this level. I hope that this will prompt more people to support athletics as a healthy part of women's lives. Athletic role models are just as important to little girls and grown women as they are to boys and men."[5] One of the most visible teams in the history of women's sports, *America³* made the sport of sailing more visible and because of the efforts of the *America³* women's team, more female sailors, as well as women athletes in other sports, will be included at higher levels of competition, judged by their ability, not by their gender.

For the readers who are not familiar with sailing terms, the following definitions may be helpful:

Sailing Terms

Grinder—cranks the handles of the big winches on command from person trimming those sails.

Sewer—stays below decks mostly, repacking spinnakers and getting sails ready for sail changes; also may be the number two person on the bow, helping hook up spinnaker, clearing lines, and sometimes going aloft (to top of the mast).

Pitman—hauls in, tails and releases halyards; adjusts boom vang and cunningham; tails running backs; works in area from mast to back of boat.

Helmsman—drives (steers) the boat.

Foredeck pitman—responsible for lines from mast to bow of boat; assisting with spinnaker sets (topping lift, downhaul), helps with changing headsails.

Tactician—calls the shots, advises helmsman when to change course, watches competition and feeds information back to helmsman and crew.

Sail trimmer—responsible for easing out or trimming in the sheets (lines) that are attached to the mainsail, genoas, and spinnaker.

Source: Women's Sailing Association

Mainsail trimmer—specifically responsible for handling the mainsheet, and when possible, the boom vang and traveler, which all determine the efficiency of the biggest sail on the boat.

Starboard genoa trimmer—handles the tail of the jib sheet wrapped around the genoa winch on the right-hand side of the boat, specifically responsible for easing out and trimming in the genoa when the boat is on port tack. (The genoa is set on the starboard side).

Port genoa trimmer—handles the tail of the jib sheet wrapped around the genoa winch on the left side of the boat, specifically responsible for easing out and trimming in the genoa when the boat is on starboard tack. (The genoa is set on the port side).

Bow crew—hooks up the spinnaker, changes headsails, cleans up lines after sail changes, and acts as a lookout on the bow when in close quarters with other boats.

Mast crew—hoists and releases halyards, handles the inboard end of the spinnaker pole, jumps in to help wherever necessary after job is done.

America³ Crew

Stephanie Armitage-Johnson

When she joined the America³ syndicate at the 1995 America's Cup Defenders Selection Series as a grinder, Armitage-Johnson was the assistant strength and conditioning coach for the University of Washington Huskies football team. Also a world-class weightlifter, she was among the top 10 in the world in super-heavy and heavyweight classes for five years (1989-1993). She was on the U.S. Weightlifting Federation Women's Team, and won gold and several silver medals at the Olympic Sports Festival.

Amy Baltzell

Grinder for the America³ syndicate at the 1995 America's Cup Defenders Selection Series, Baltzell was a member of the 1992 U.S. Olympic Rowing Team. She won a gold medal in the 1991 women's eight races in Lucerne, Switzerland. A seven-time medalist at the U.S. National Rowing Championships, Baltzell won gold and silver medals in 1991; two silver medals in 1990; silver and bronze medals in 1989; and a gold medal in 1987. She is a graduate of Wesleyan University in Middletown, Connecticut, where she was a member of the varsity rowing and basketball teams.

Shelley Beattie

Grinder for the America[3] syndicate at the 1995 America's Cup Defenders Selection Series, Beattie attended Western Oregon State College in Monmouth. A versatile and accomplished all-around athlete, she began weightlifting at age 14 and became a professional bodybuilder at age 22 after winning the 1990 U.S. Bodybuilding Championship. She placed third in the 1992 Ms. Olympia competition. Prior to joining the America[3] sailing team, she spent three seasons as "Siren" on the weekly television show, *American Gladiators.*

Courtenay Becker-Dey

Becker-Dey was navigator of the *Mighty Mary* of the America[3] syndicate in the 1995 America's Cup Defenders Selection Series. An accomplished sailor, she won a bronze medal at the 1996 Olympic Games in the European dinghy class. Before joining the America[3] team, Becker-Day, a seasoned veteran of U.S. and international sailboat racing circuits, captured more than 17 championships. She was ranked number one on the U.S. Sailing Team for six consecutive years from 1989 to 1994 and was number five in world sailing rankings from 1990 through 1993. Her sailing achievements include Rolex Yachtswoman of the Year, United States Olympic Committee (USOC) Athlete of the Year for Yachting, and gold medalist in the 1990 Women's Sailing Pre-Olympics.

Sarah Bergeron

Grinder for the America[3] syndicate in the 1995 America's Cup Defenders Selection Series, Bergeron graduated from George Washington University (GWU) in May 1994 with a degree in international business and was a four-year member of the GWU crew team. She was the strongest rower on her collegiate team for two and a half years. Her 2,000m erg (a test of strength, endurance, and mental toughness) score ranked her number four in United States and number one among all collegiate rowers in 1994.

Merritt Carey

Carey, the sewer for the America[3] syndicate in the 1995 America's Cup Defenders Selection Series, has extensive experience racing big boats, including the Caribbean Gold Cup Transatlantic Fastnet race. Carey served as foredeck/rigger for Dawn Riley on *Heineken,* the only all-women's crew in the grueling nine-month 1993-94 Whitbread 'Round the World Race.

Sarah Cavanagh

Cavanagh grew up in a New England sailing family and has been sailing since the age of three. Prior to joining the America[3] syndicate in the 1995 America's Cup Defenders Selection Series, she had extensive racing experience including several all-women's teams in competitions such as the Rolex International Regatta, the Fort Lauderdale to Jamaica race, the La Rochelle (France) to New Orleans race, and the Southern Ocean Racing Circuit (SORC). Cavanagh also has a degree in yacht design from The Landing School in Kennebunkport, Maine.

Lisa Charles

Pitman for the America[3] syndicate for the 1995 America's Cup Defender Selection Series, Charles began sailing seriously in 1990. Her sailing, racing, and cruising experience includes the 1993 European and the 1991 and 1993 Caribbean circuits (both big boats); the 1994 Southern Ocean Racing Circuit (SORC) in England; and running a 40 foot boat in Maine in 1992. She received her RYA Yachtmasters Offshore License in 1993 (equivalent to a U.S. Coast Guard license).

Leslie Egnot

A 1992 Olympic silver medalist in women's sailing, Egnot joined the America[3] syndicate in the 1995 America's Cup Defenders Selection Series as a helmsman. A native of South Carolina, Egnot has lived in New Zealand since 1973, where she is considered one of the country's top sailors. Her other sailing accomplishments include New Zealand's Women's 470 (470 is a class of boat) Champion every year since 1985; New Zealand Women's Keelboat Champion in 1990, 1991, and 1993; second place in the 1989 470 Women's World Championships in Japan; 1990 Women's World Keelboat Championship; and 1991 Women's North American 470s Championship.

Christy Evans

With extensive experience in sailboat racing and worldwide offshore cruising, Evans joined the America[3] syndicate in the 1995 America's Cup Defenders Selection Series as a foredeck pitman. She participated in the U.S. Rolex International Women's Keelboat Championships as tactician and sail trimmer in 1989 and 1991. Evans sails regularly on *Jazz Sensation,* a Nelson/Mareck 40, out of Marblehead, Massachusetts.

Amy Fuller

A silver medalist in rowing in the 1992 Olympics, Fuller spent five years on the U.S. National Rowing Team before joining the America[3] syndicate as a grinder. In addition to her Olympic silver medal, she holds 25 other national and international rowing titles, including the gold medal in women's eights at the 1995 world championship, and was on the 1996 Olympic team, finishing fourth in the coxed eights competition. She was also 1993 U.S. Rowing Female Athlete of the Year. She graduated

with a degree in biology from the University of California at Santa Barbara in 1990, where she also spent two years coaching rowing.

Susan Hemond-Dent

Hemond-Dent is an accomplished endurance athlete and experienced racing and cruising sailor. A volunteer sailing team assistant for America[3] during the 1992 campaign, Dent first began working with the 1995 America[3] all-women's team in March 1994 as sailing team assistant on the boat and in the training room. She was a member of the San Diego State University Track and Field Team from 1979-82, competing in the 800-meter race in the 1982 U.S. Track and Field Nationals.

Anna Seaton Huntington

A bronze medalist in women's pair rowing (with Stephanie Maxwell-Pierson) in the 1992 Olympics, Seaton Huntington was a grinder on the America[3] syndicate at the 1995 America's Cup Defenders Selection Series. Also on the 1988 U.S. Olympic Rowing Team that went to Seoul, she has won 14 national championships and four world championship silver medals during her nine-year rowing career. In 1990, the U.S. Rowing Association named her Female Athlete of the Year.

J. J. Isler

A world-class sailor, Isler joined the America[3] syndicate in the 1995 America's Cup Defenders Selection Series as its tactician. Isler won the 1992 Olympic bronze medal in Barcelona in the women's 470 class (with teammate Pam Healy). She and Healy were the only Americans to win medals at the prestigious 1991 Women's 470 World Championship. Her many other national and international titles include first in the 1987 Rolex International Women's Keelboat Championship, and first in the 1986 Women's World and European Championships in 470s. She was selected 1986 and 1991 Rolex Yachtswoman of the Year. The first woman to skipper on the International Match Racing and Formula One circuits, Isler is a graduate of Yale University, where she was the first female captain of the varsity sailing team and one of the few women to be named collegiate All-American in sailing.

Diana Klybert

Klybert began sailing and racing in 1982 in Portland, Oregon, on 30- to 40-foot boats. Her sailing experience prior to joining the 1995 America³ syndicate included the 1992 Newport-Bermuda race, the 1993 Marblehead-Halifax race, and the 1992 New Zealand Women's Keelboat Championships. Klybert holds a 100-ton U.S. Coast Guard captain's license and is a certified diver.

Linda Lindquist

Lindquist served joint roles as both 1995 America³ sailing team member and co-director of development for the America³ Foundation, which was responsible for raising money for the all-women's team efforts. During her 25 years of racing experience, Lindquist has sailed a wide variety of boats (470s, Lasers, Lightnings, National One Designs). She was part of the first all-women's crew to compete in the Newport-Bermuda race in 1992 and has held various crew positions on winning boats, including those competing in the 1990 Great Lakes Championships, the 1991 Queen's Cup, and the 1993 Verve Cup. Lindquist is a founding member of Sail America, Sail Expo (the largest sail show in United States), International Women in Boating, and the U.S. Women's Match Race Union.

Stephanie Maxwell-Pierson

Before joining the America³ syndicate in the 1995 America's Cup Defenders Selection Series as a grinder, Maxwell-Pierson was an accomplished rower. She won the bronze medal in the women's pairs rowing competition (with Anna Seaton) at the 1992 Barcelona Olympics. She has won more than 18 international and national titles and was twice named the U.S. Rowing Association's Female Athlete of the Year (1990, 1991). Her more notable wins include 12 first-place finishes in U.S. National Rowing Women's Championships from 1988–91; silver medals in the World Rowing Championships in 1987, 1990, and 1991; and a silver medal in the 1990 Goodwill Games in Seattle, Washington.

Susie Leech Nairn

Nairn joined the America³ syndicate in the 1995 America's Cup Defenders Selection Series as a member of the bow crew. An aerospace engineer with 17 years of racing and sailing experience, Nairn spent two years sailing around the world and has dozens of races to her credit, including the 1994 Southern Ocean Racing Circuit (SORC), the 1993 China Coast Cup, and the 1993 Santa Maria Cup.

Annie Nelson

A world-class sailor, Nelson has been racing for more than 25 years and has more than 15 national and international sailing titles to her credit. Nelson joined the America³ syndicate in the 1995 America's Cup Defenders Selection Series as a navigator. She was a member of the U.S. Women's World Sailing Team in 1982, 1983, and 1984. Nelson was the first and only woman skipper of two all-female crews in the Southern Ocean Racing Circuit (SORC) in 1981 and 1982. Also a world-class board sailor,

Nelson won the silver medal in the 1984 Olympic Board Sailing Exhibition in Los Angeles.

Merritt Palm

A sail trimmer for the America³ syndicate in the 1995 America's Cup Defenders Selection Series, Palm is a veteran of a number of races, including the Adams Cup in 1988. She is ranked among the top 10 U.S. sailors in the European dinghy class. A certified U.S. Sailing Association instructor and trainer, Palm received a bachelor's degree in English and political science in 1990 from the University of Miami, where she was captain of the sailing team for two years.

Debbie Pettibone

A mainsail trimmer for the America³ syndicate for the 1995 America's Cup Defenders Selection Series, Pettibone began sailing at age 14. Her mother taught her to sail and Pettibone learned to tie nautical knots from her grandmother. She was a skipper in the Women's Yacht Racing Association (WYRA) of Miami. Before joining the America's Cup all-women's team, she was a sail maker at Shore Sails Miami in Florida.

Katie Pettibone

A master of a number of crew positions in boats ranging from 19 to 50 feet, Pettibone was a starboard genoa trimmer for the America³ syndicate in the 1995 America's Cup Defenders Selection Series. Prior to joining America³, she was a student at the University of Miami, where she was studying marine biology. She is the sister of Debbie Pettibone, also a member of the America³ crew.

Marci Porter

Before joining the 1995 America³ syndicate as a grinder, Porter was on the U.S. National Rowing Team from 1991 to 1993. Her rowing credits include alternate for the 1992 Olympic team and a second-place finish in the alternates' race in Barcelona; first in the 1993 U.S. national women's pairs; first in women's eights, fours, and pairs in the 1992 U.S. national championships; and first in the 1989 and 1990 Olympic Festival women's eights and fours. Porter's international titles include first in women's pairs at the 1991 Pan American Games and first in senior women's eights at the 1990 Royal Canadian Henley.

Melissa Purdy

Purdy has numerous sailing titles to her credit since she began racing in 1986. She joined the America³ syndicate in the 1995 America's Cup Defenders Selection Series as a mainsail trimmer. Her other sailing career highlights include first in the 1993 J/24 District Championships in Seattle, second in the J/22 class of the 1993 Santa Maria Cup Women's Match Racing, and second in the J/24 class of the 1992 Women's West Coast Championships.

Dawn Riley

A superb big-boat and match-racing sailor, Riley was team captain and helmsman of America³ at the 1995 America's Cup Defenders Selection Series. She was the skipper of *Heineken,* the all women's team in the 1993-94 Whitbread 'Round the World Race. Riley was pitman on Koch's *America³* for the defender series of the 1992 America's Cup. Her sailing accomplishments include first place in both the 1992 Santa Maria Cup in Baltimore, Maryland, and the 1992 Women's Cup in Portofino, Italy. A graduate of Michigan State University, Riley served as captain of the sailing team and division "A" skipper. She was a nominee for the Women's Sports Foundation 1995 Team Sportswoman of the Year Award.

Suzette Hau'oli Smith

Smith actively raced yachts ranging from 18 to 70 feet in a variety of regattas, including the Kenwood Cup, San Francisco Big Boat Series, and Mexorc, before joining the America[3] syndicate in the 1995 America's Cup Defenders Selection Series. In 1992, the Hawaii Yacht Club named her Yachtswoman of the Year. A native Hawaiian, Smith has raced outrigger canoes for 15 years, steering her crew to a 1993 Hawaii state championship.

Hannah Swett

Swett, a port genoa trimmer on the America[3] syndicate in the 1995 America's Cup Defenders Selection Series, has experience sailing all size boats from dinghies to J/24. She has won many U.S. and international races including the 1991 Fastnet, the J/24 class in the 1993 Rolex Regatta, the 1993 Lightning Atlantic Coast, the 1993 Women's Lightning Championships, and the 1993 Antigua Race Week. Swett was named All-American woman sailor in 1989 and 1991 while at Brown University, where she led the sailing team to the collegiate national championship in 1989.

Joan Lee Touchette

Touchette had extensive racing experience in a variety of crew positions before joining the America[3] syndicate on the mast crew in the 1995 America's Cup Defenders Selection Series. Her many accomplishments include winning the Adams Cup in 1993 and the Laser Women's World Championships in 1990, finishing fifth in 1993 and third in 1991 in the Women's Rolex competition. Touchette attended the U.S. Coast Guard Academy from 1988 to 1990, where she was captain of the women's sailing team.

Source: America[3] Foundation

Further Reading

Larsen, Paul C., and Daniel Forster. *America[3], the Women's Team.* Hatboro, PA: Legacy Books, 1997.

Huntington, Anna Seaton. *Making Waves: The Inside Story of Managing and Motivating the First Women's Team to Compete for the America's Cup.* Arlington, TX: The Summit Publishing Group, 1996. 176 pp.

1994 Colorado Silver Bullets

In the summer of 1993, former Atlanta Braves executive Bob Hope approached the Coors Brewing Company with the idea of creating a women's professional baseball team that would play high-caliber baseball against professional men's teams. Coors immediately endorsed the team and committed nearly $3 million to the effort. On Mother's Day, May 8, 1994, the Colorado Silver Bullets began their inaugural season as the first and only all-female professional baseball team to be officially recognized by the National Association of Professional Baseball Leagues.

Hope hired former major-league pitcher Phil Niekro as the team's manager. "Women should have opportunity to play competitive professional ball," Niekro said. "I think we are going to surprise quite a few people with the ability of these athletes and the caliber of ball they can play."[6]

Colorado Silver Bullets—(1st row, l–r) Pam Schaffrath, Julie Croteau, Stacy Sunny, Phil Niekro, Michele McAnany, Michelle Delloso, Charlotte Wiley; (2nd row, l–r) Tommy Jones, Joe Niekro, Rachelle McCann, Gina Satriano, Keri Kropke, Allison Geatches, Bridget Venturi, Elizabeth Burnham, Ann Williams, KC Clark, Kim Braatz, John Niekro; (3rd row, l–r) Jeanette Amado, Laurie Gouthro, Lee Anne Ketcham, Lisa Martinez, Shae Sloan, Toni Heisler, Missy Cress, Shannan Mitchem, Melissa Coombes
Gregg Wagner

After hiring Niekro, the Silver Bullets immediately began the process of selecting the country's top athletes to fill the team's roster. In the spring of 1994, more than 1,300 women showed up at 11 sites around the country to try out for the team. Most were softball players in high school and college who had a dream of playing professional ball. Fifty-five of the players were invited to spring training at Tinker Field, in Orlando, Florida, from which 24 players were picked to join the Silver Bullets for the inaugural season.

The athletes worked out seven days a week for over a month under the guidance of Coach Niekro. Finally, on April 3, 1994, the 24-player squad was introduced to the public.

After only five weeks of spring training, the first Silver Bullets team embarked on a season that would offer many challenges and opportunities. The team played 12 games in the Northern League (a minor league system) and 30 exhibition games against other minor-league and semi-pro teams around the country. Led by Gina Satriano, Stacy Sunny, Julie Croteau, and Melissa Coombes, the inaugural Silver Bullets won six of 42 games in their first season of play. Their first win came against the Richfield Rockets on May 27, 1994, at Municipal Stadium in St. Paul, Minnesota. The Bullets defeated the Rockets 7-2 behind the strong pitching of Lee Anne Ketcham. Michele McAnany got the first hit on May 8, 1994, against the Northern League All-Stars at Knights Castle Stadium in Charlotte, North Carolina, and Shannan Mitchem drove in Charlotte Wiley in the second inning versus the Red Mountain Bandits in Tucson, Arizona, on May 18, 1994, for the team's first run batted-in (RBI) and run scored.

The 1995 season proved to be more successful as the players gained more experience. The Bullets won 11 games and lost

33. Team batting average and pitching also improved.

The Colorado Silver Bullets' success has had a far-reaching effect on women's baseball in the United States. In 1996, USA Baseball and the American Amateur Baseball Congress initiated a pilot program to develop a six-team women's baseball league in the Midwest.

"I feel that the Silver Bullets will give every girl in America a chance to have a female role model and reason to try anything she wants in life,"[7] said Silver Bullet second baseman Michelle Delloso in 1994. The first women's professional baseball team to play against men's teams has raised public awareness of women's athletics and provides thousands of young girls hope for a future in professional sports.

1994 Colorado Silver Bullets Team

Jeanette Amado

In her first season with the Silver Bullets, outfielder Amado batted .200, with seven hits and four runs scored, and led the team in on-base percentage at .404. Prior to joining the Silver Bullets, she played women's slow-pitch softball. In 1990, she led Coors of Midland, Texas, to the Women's Major Slow Pitch World Series, where she was named best defensive player of the tournament. In 1991, she participated in the Women's Nationals and was named the best offensive player. Amado played softball at the University of Arizona and recorded a career batting average of .310.

Kim Braatz

In her first season with the Silver Bullets, outfielder Braatz played in 13 games before sustaining a back injury that required surgery. In those 13 games, she batted .088, with three hits and three runs scored. Prior to joining the Silver Bullets, Braatz hit .466 for a professional softball team in Novara, Italy. She played softball for two years for the University of New Mexico (1990, 1991), where she was a National Collegiate Athletic Association (NCAA) Division I Second-Team All-American.

Elizabeth Burnham

In her first season as a catcher with the Silver Bullets, Burnham batted .122, with nine hits and six RBIs. Prior to joining the Silver Bullets, she played softball for the University of Connecticut (1988-89) and for Lyndon State College, Lyndonville, Vermont (1992-93). While at Lyndon, she hit .444 and led the National Association of Intercollegiate Athletics (NAIA) Division III in RBIs (31) in 1993. She also played Babe Ruth baseball for four years (1984-87).

K.C. Clark

In her first season with the Silver Bullets, center fielder Clark batted .058, with three hits, two RBIs, and five runs scored, and was one for one in stolen bases. Prior to joining the Silver Bullets, she played outfield for the women's softball teams at Sacramento City College (1988-90) and at California State-Fullerton (1991-92). She also played Little League baseball for seven years.

Melissa Coombes

In her first season as a pitcher with the Silver Bullets, Coombes finished second on the team in both games started (10) and games completed (2). She struck out 21 in 47.2 innings and finished the season with a 5.92 earned run average (ERA). The only left-hander on the pitching staff in 1994,

Coombes was the top fielder on the pitching staff with a 1.00 fielding percentage (no errors). The ace of the Silver Bullets pitching staff also had the best win-loss record in 1995 (5-8), when she led the team in strikeouts (48), ERA (3.90), complete games (7), and wins (5). Prior to joining the Silver Bullets, Coombes played softball for California State-Fullerton, where she batted .359 in 1990. She also played Little League, and in 1983 made the Pony League All-Star team as a pitcher.

Missy Cress

In her first season with the Silver Bullets, Cress played only three games. In 1995, she played in 20 games and batted .114 with four hits. She came to the Silver Bullets from California State-Northridge, where she led the Matadors to an appearance at the 1993 NCAA Women's Softball World Series. She was also an American Softball Association (ASA) All-American with the Southern California Jazz.

Julie Croteau

In her first season with the Silver Bullets, first baseman Croteau batted .078, with four hits and two RBIs. An outstanding infielder, she posted a .989 fielding percentage at first base, committing only two errors in 27 games. Prior to joining the Silver Bullets, she played on the male semi-pro Fredericksburg (Virginia) Giants, where she has a lifetime batting average of .261. In 1989, Croteau became the first woman to play on an NCAA Division III men's team when she took the field with the St. Mary's (Maryland) College Seahawks. She played for the Seahawks for three years.

Michelle Delloso

In her first season with the Silver Bullets, second baseman Delloso batted .129, with

eight hits and two RBIs, and was one for one in stolen bases. Prior to joining the Silver Bullets, she played softball for four years at the University of South Carolina (USC). She was a three-time NCAA All-American at second base. Her lifetime statistics with USC were .320 batting average, 22 doubles, 12 triples, and 121 RBIs. Delloso also played Little League baseball until the age of 12.

Allison Geatches

In her first season with the Silver Bullets as an outfielder and first baseman, Geatches batted .034, with two hits and four RBIs. She also registered a .942 fielding percentage in 32 games played. Playing for the Crusaders tournament softball team prior to joining the Silver Bullets, she was recognized for her play in various summer-league team tournaments. An all-around athlete, Geatches also played for Team Belgium, a semi-pro basketball team, and was a *Parade* magazine high school All-American selection in basketball.

Laurie Gouthro

Gouthro played outfield for the Silver Bullets after being selected for a spot on the roster at the New York tryout camp. With no at-bats in 1994, Gouthro played 21 games in 1995, with 13 at-bats. Prior to joining the Silver Bullets, she played softball at the University of South Florida, where she set a school record for on-base percentage. She also played softball at Florida Community College.

Toni Heisler

As a shortstop for the Silver Bullets, Heisler batted .141, with 12 hits and four RBIs in the inaugural season. Prior to joining the Silver Bullets, she played professional softball for Marcoli Novara in Italy. She hit .448

with five home runs and 18 RBIs and led the Italian Softball Federation in slugging percentage (.792), runs scored (42), and total bases (76). During her college career at California State-Sacramento, Heisler batted .327 and set a school record with 14 doubles. She also stole 14 of 14 bases in 1989.

Lee Anne Ketcham

Ketcham won five of the team's six victories in the Silver Bullets' inaugural season and led the pitching staff in ERA (4.80). She struck out 62 batters and walked only 21 in 77.1 innings. In her best game of the season, Ketcham struck out 14 batters in seven innings against the Richfield Rockets in St. Paul, Minnesota, to lead the team to its first victory. Prior to joining the Silver Bullets, she led the Oklahoma State University (OSU) Cowgirls softball team to four Big Eight championships. While at OSU, Ketcham was a three-time Academic All–Big Eight. She played baseball for the boys' varsity at Vestavia Hills (Alabama) High School where she posted a 12-5 career record.

Keri Kropke

In her first season with the Silver Bullets, outfielder Kropke batted .098, with eight hits and two RBIs, and stole two bases in two attempts. She hit the team's first double in the first inning of the May 21, 1994, contest against the Setting Suns, at Wolfson Park in Jacksonville, Florida. Playing in 32 games, she posted a 1.000 fielding percentage (no errors). Prior to joining the Silver Bullets, Kropke played for the University of California, Berkeley (Cal), women's softball team. While at Cal, she set career records for stolen bases (74) and triples (17), and was named NCAA All-American in 1993.

Lisa Martinez

In her first season with the Silver Bullets, pitcher Martinez finished the season with a 5.50 ERA and 24 strikeouts in 42 innings pitched. The right-hander played softball for the University of California, Berkeley, in 1986, where she was a 24-game winner. She also played for Team Puerto Rico in the Central American Games and the Pan American Games. In 1981, Martinez posted a .39 ERA while pitching for Texas A&M women's softball team.

Michele McAnany

Second baseman McAnany led the team in walks (31), plate appearances (136), and tied with two others for the leading batting average (.200) in the Silver Bullets' inaugural season. She got the first hit in Silver Bullet history on May 8, 1994, off of former Boston Red Sox pitcher "Oil Can" Boyd. During her college career, McAnany played softball for California State-Northridge, where she was a two-time All-American (1984, 1985), and helped lead the team to NCAA Division II championships in 1983, 1984, and 1985.

Rachelle McCann

In her first season with the Silver Bullets, third baseman McCann did not see any action. She was selected for the team at the Sacramento tryout camp. Prior to joining the Silver Bullets, McCann played softball with the Golden State Royals of the ASA summer league. She was an ASA All-American in 1991 and 1992. Playing for San Francisco State University in 1992, McCann led the NCAA Division II in RBIs (44). She also played basketball at San Francisco State.

Shannan Mitchem

In her first season with the Silver Bullets, third baseman Mitchem finished the year ranked fourth on the team in batting average (.194) and third in on-base percentage (.333). Mitchem drove home the Silver Bullets' first run of the season with an RBI single against the Red Mountain Bandits at Hi Corbett Field in Tucson, Arizona. Prior to joining the Silver Bullets, Mitchem was a four-year starter at third base for the Florida State University women's softball team (1989–92). She played in the NCAA Women's Softball College World Series in 1990, 1991, and 1992.

Gina Satriano

Right-hand pitcher Satriano posted a 5.05 ERA and struck out 15 batters in 34.2 innings pitched in her first season with the Silver Bullets. At age 28, Satriano had considerable baseball experience. In 1973, she became the first female to play Little League in California. For six years (1973–78), she played for Malibu and Canoga Park National Little League boys' teams. In 1981, she pitched an undefeated season in the Santa Monica Colt League, and she pitched for the NY Heartbreakers, an El Segundo, California, men's semi-pro team, from 1984 to 1986.

Pam Schaffrath

In her first season with the Silver Bullets, catcher Schaffrath tied for the team lead in both doubles (4) and stolen bases (2). She finished the season batting .162 with 18 hits and four RBIs. Prior to joining the Silver Bullets, Schaffrath led Drake University to a Missouri Valley Conference softball title in 1993. She played five years of Little League baseball and was an All-Star in 1984.

Shae Sloan

In her first season with the Silver Bullets, pitcher Sloan completed one game in eight starts. She struck out 19 batters in 33.2 innings pitched. During her college career, Sloan started all four years at shortstop for the University of Nebraska women's softball team. She was team captain in 1993 and hit .319 with 31 RBIs. From 1986 through 1989, the right-hander played for the Splendora High School (Texas) boys' baseball team and made first-team all district in 1988-89. She was the first female to play in the Boys' All-Star State Tourney in Texarkana, Texas.

Stacy Sunny

Sunny played catcher and third base for the Silver Bullets' 1994 inaugural season, and led the team in games played (43), runs (11), hits (22), doubles (4), triples (1), RBIs (11), and total bases (28). She played center field for the University of Nebraska Cornhuskers softball team (1983-85), and in 1985, she was named NCAA All-American. In 1988, by then at University of California at Los Angeles (UCLA), she led the Bruins to victory in the NCAA College Softball World Series with a .311 batting average. Sunny played baseball in Little League and was an All-Star in 1977 and 1978. In 1975, she was the only girl in the league.

Bridget Venturi

In her first season with the Silver Bullets, pitcher Venturi made 11 appearances and struck out nine in 14.2 innings pitched. Prior to joining the Silver Bullets, she played softball for Spirit of Chicago, which won the Cavigal Gerland Cup in Nice, France, in 1992. During her college career, Venturi played right field for the University of Michigan women's softball team in 1988, where she batted .262 and posted a 1.000 fielding percentage (no errors).

Charlotte Wiley

Wiley did not see any action in the Silver Bullets' inaugural regular season, but did hit the first home run at the Silver Bullets' training camp. While in college, she batted .400 for the California State-Hayward women's softball team and made the NCAA Division II All-American team. In 1986, she pitched and played second base for the Richmond (California) High School boys' baseball team.

Ann Williams

Right-handed pitcher Williams posted a 5.87 ERA and struck out 23 batters in 22.2 innings in her first season with the Silver Bullets. Prior to joining the Silver Bullets, she played softball for Nicholls State University (Louisiana) for three years (1990-92). She led the team in hitting as a sophomore, was captain in her junior year, and was named an All-Southland Conference selection in her final year.

Source: *Colorado Silver Bullets 1994 Media Guide*

Further Reading

Kindred, Dave. *The Colorado Silver Bullets for the Love of the Game: Women Who Go Toe-to-Toe With the Men*, Atlanta, GA: Longstreet Press. 1995. 112 pp.

Raybestos Brakettes

In 1996, the Raybestos Brakettes celebrated their 50th year in women's major league fast-pitch softball. The greatest dynasty in the history of women's major league fast-pitch softball, the Brakettes have won 23 national championships and three world titles since their formation in 1947.

The Raybestos Girl All-Stars of Stratford, Connecticut, made their first appearance in 1947. The team was founded by Bill Simpson, the personnel director of the Raybestos Division of Raybestos-Manhattan. One of the company's leading products was brake linings, and so in 1948, the team became the Brakettes.

The Brakettes won their first national championship in 1958. From 1966 to 1978, the team took 10 out of 13 championships. By virtue of their national titles, the Brakettes had the honor of representing the United States in five International Softball Federation (ISF) World Championships (1965, 1974, 1978, 1986, 1990), where they won four gold medals and one silver, compiling a record of 49 wins and 3 losses. In the 1974 ISF Championships, the Brakettes outscored their opponents 75-0. Joan Joyce set records for most strikeouts (76); lowest earned run average (ERA) (0.00); most consecutive scoreless innings (36); most no-hit, no-run games (3); and most perfect games (2). The team's batting average was .356. In the 1978 tournament, pitchers Kathy Arendsen and Barbara Reinalda won eight of nine games by shutout.

Pitching, speed, and defense were the foundations of the Brakettes' success. Throughout the years, several star players emerged to help the Brakettes to their 23 championships, including Kathy Arendsen, Joan Joyce, Donna Lopiano, Mickey Stratton, and Bertha Tickey. Fifteen members of the Brakettes have been inducted into the National Softball Hall of Fame. U.S. Olympic gold medalists Dot Richardson, Sheila Cornell, Lisa Fernandez, and Michele Granger also have played for the Brakettes.

In 1996, Raybestos Products dropped its long-time sponsorship of the team, and many of the veteran Brakettes opted to play in California in preparation for the 1996 Olympics. Now called the Stratford Brakettes, the team has a legacy of great players and great championships and defined women's major league fast-pitch softball for five decades.

Raybestos Brakettes American Softball Association (ASA) Hall of Famers

Rosie Adams

Adams joined the Brakettes in 1971 and was a member of four consecutive national championship teams. In 1974, she competed in the ISF World Championships when the Brakettes, representing the United States, won the gold medal. She was named first-team All-American in 1971, 1972, and 1973. In four years with the Brakettes, Adams batted .279 in national championship play, having 19 hits in 68 at-bats. She also played seven years with the Orange, California, Lionettes. She had a .209 batting average during her 11-year career, with 340 hits in 1,624 at-bats and 133 runs batted in (RBIs). Adams was inducted into the National Softball Hall of Fame in 1987.

Louise Albrecht

Starring as a pitcher and outfielder during a 24-year career, Albrecht played for the Raybestos Brakettes as well as for other top women's teams. She compiled a career record of 304 wins and 83 losses for a .785

winning percentage. In eight ASA National Championships, she won 17 games, lost seven, with an earned run average (ERA) of .700. She was an ASA All-American six times. She was inducted into the National Softball Hall of Fame in 1985.

Kathy Arendsen

During her 15-year career as a pitcher for the Brakettes, Arendsen won 334 games and lost only 25. In 2,362 innings, she fanned 4,308 batters and hurled 79 no-hitters and 42 perfect games. Arendsen was a member of nine ASA National Championship teams, three Pan American teams (1979, 1983, 1987), and three ISF World Championship teams (1978, 1986, 1990). Thirteen times she was named an ASA All-American and four times she won the Bertha Tickey Award as the outstanding pitcher in the ASA Women's Major Fast Pitch National Championship. Arendsen played for the Texas Women's University team that defeated University of California at Los Angeles (UCLA) for the Women's College Softball World Series in 1979. She was inducted into the National Softball Hall of Fame in 1996.

Sharron Backus

Backus played with the Brakettes for seven years (1969–75) and was a member of five national championship teams (1971–75). She earned ASA All-American honors three times (1970, 1971, 1974). Backus had a .292 batting average with the Brakettes. She also played with the Whittier, California, Gold Sox and Orange, California, Lionettes. In 1975, Backus was named head softball coach at UCLA and coached the Lady Bruins for 21 years before retiring in June 1997. During her 21 years as head coach, Backus compiled a record of 847-167-3. She led the Bruins to nine national championships, compiling a postseason record of 118-32. She was inducted into the National Softball Hall of Fame in 1985 and the International Women's Sports Hall of Fame in 1993.

Pat Harrison

Harrison played fast-pitch softball for 20 years, nine with the Brakettes (1964–72). She was a member of five Brakette National Championship teams. She had a cumulative .303 batting average during this time, with 430 hits in 1,421 at-bats, including 66 doubles, 42 triples, and 18 homers. She drove in 189 runs in 482 games. Twice she led the Brakettes in batting, 1966 (.301) and 1971 (.340). Harrison played in 11 national championships, nine with the Brakettes and two with the Erv Linds Florists of Portland, Oregon. Harrison was inducted into the National Softball Hall of Fame in 1976.

Joan Joyce

Joyce joined the Brakettes in 1953 at the age of 13. She played first base for five years, but was moved into the pitcher's spot during the 1958 ASA National Championships. That year, the 18-year-old pitched a no-hitter to win the national championship for the Brakettes. Joyce played 20 years as an amateur with the Brakettes and the Orange Lionettes of Orange, California. In her combined 22 pitching seasons, Joyce compiled a record of 509 wins and 33 losses. She pitched 105 no-hit games and 33 perfect games, struck out 6,648 batters in 3,972 innings, and recorded a lifetime ERA of 0.21. More than a great pitcher, she had a lifetime batting average of .327, knocked in 534 runs, and led the Brakettes in hitting six times. Joyce was a member of 15 national championship and six runner-up softball teams. ASA named her to All-Ameri-

Raybestos Brakettes, 1971 National Champions
Amateur Softball Association

can teams 18 consecutive years, and she was the MVP of the national championships eight times. Joyce was inducted into the National Softball Hall of Fame in 1983 and the International Women's Sports Hall of Fame in 1990. (See more complete biographical information on p. 155.)

Peggy Kellers

Except for one season, Kellers spent all of her amateur softball career with the Brakettes (1964–74). She earned ASA All-American honors six times as a catcher. Kellers played on 11 ASA National Championship teams with the Brakettes, and she compiled an aggregate batting average of .238 in national championship play. A starting catcher nine of the 11 years she played for the Brakettes, Kellers compiled a .218 batting average in 529 games with 280 hits in 1,287 at-bats, including 29 doubles, 21 triples, seven homers, and 121 RBIs. She was inducted into the National Softball Hall of Fame in 1986.

Kathryn (Sis) King

In three years with the Brakettes, King had a .322 batting average. She led the Brakettes with a .352 batting average and a team-high 12 hits, including four triples, in the 1965 ISF Women's World Fast Pitch Championship in Melbourne, Australia. She also played for the Brakettes in the 1967 Pan American Games, winning a gold medal. King was the first woman to hit a home run over the scoreboard at Raybestos Memorial Field. She was inducted into the National Softball Hall of Fame in 1975.

Donna Lopiano

Lopiano played 10 years for the Brakettes, and twice led the Brakettes in batting, in 1970 (.316) and 1972 (.367); she still shares the team record for homers in a season (8).

She was an ASA All-American nine times and won the MVP award in the ASA National Championships three times. Lopiano has a .295 lifetime batting average playing for the Brakettes, with 518 hits in 1,756 at-bats; scoring 285 runs; batting in 281 runs; and hitting 23 homers, 67 doubles, and 54 triples. As a pitcher, Lopiano had a .910 winning percentage, winning 183 games and losing 18. In 10 years, she pitched 817 innings, struck out 1,633 batters, walked only 384, and hurled 16 no-hitters. She was inducted into the National Softball Hall of Fame in 1983. Lopiano served as women's athletic director at the University of Texas for more than a decade before taking over as executive director of the Women's Sports Foundation in 1992.

Willie Roze

Roze played 10 years for the Brakettes (1966–75) and earned All-American honors eight times in helping them win eight ASA Women's Major Fast Pitch National Championships. She was a first-team All-American five times (1967, 1969, 1971, 1973, 1974) and second-team All-American three times (1968, 1969, 1973). In the 10 years with the Brakettes, Roze compiled a .281 batting average with 526 hits in 629 games. Besides the eight ASA National Championship teams (1966–68, 1971–75), she also played on the 1974 ISF Women's World Fast Pitch Championship Team. She was inducted into the National Softball Hall of Fame in 1985.

Diane Schumacher

Schumacher played with the Brakettes from 1976–86. During that time, she led the team in batting five times while compiling a .329 lifetime batting average. She was a member of eight ASA National Championship teams (1976, 1977, 1978, 1980, 1982, 1983, 1984,

1985) and one ISF World Championship team (1978). She earned All-American honors four times (1976, 1977, 1978, 1984). Schumacher was inducted into the National Softball Hall of Fame in 1992 and the International Softball Federation Hall of Fame in 1993, the only American player enshrined there.

Mickey Stratton

Catcher for the Raybestos Brakettes, Stratton batted .300 or better in seven of her 10 seasons with the team (1956–65). Three times she led the team in batting (with .320 in 1959, .324 in 1961, and .370 in 1965); her lifetime batting average is .314. She played in four national championships, including 1958, the year the Brakettes won the first of their 18 national titles (in 1983, they defeated the California Blazers for their 18th title.) Retiring after the 1965 season, Stratton was named to the National Softball Hall of Fame in 1969, the first Brakette to receive that honor.

Bertha Tickey

Tickey pitched for the Raybestos Brakettes for 13 years (1956–68) and compiled a record of 285 wins and 26 losses with the Brakettes. She was a member of seven national championship teams with the Brakettes. The right-hander had a 23-year career in which she pitched 757 winning games and lost 88. Eighteen times she was named an ASA All-American and eight times she was named the MVP in the ASA Women's Major Fast Pitch National Championship. Included in her lifetime record

are 162 no-hitters, one of them a 13-inning game against Fresno in 1967—the year she retired. She was inducted into the National Softball Hall of Fame in 1972. The award for outstanding pitching at the ASA National Championships is named in her honor.

Shirley Topley

Topley played for the Brakettes in 1963-64, helping her team to the national championship in 1963. Twice she led the team in hitting, with averages of .372 in 1963 and .340 in 1964. In a career that spanned 19 years, she participated in 16 ASA National Championships, and she was named an ASA All-American 11 times. She was inducted into the National Softball Hall of Fame in 1981.

Gina Vecchione

Vecchione played with the Brakettes for 12 years (1978–89). During her 12-year career, she earned ASA All-American honors seven times, and twice led the Women's Major Fast Pitch National Championship tournament in batting. Vecchione was a member of six national championship teams, four ISF World Championship teams, and the 1983 USA Pan American team. She had a .322 batting average with the Brakettes, .242 in national championship play. In 1988, she batted .444 to win her second ASA batting title. She had a .328 lifetime batting average. Vecchione was inducted into the National Softball Hall of Fame in 1997.

Source: American Softball Association National Softball Hall of Fame

Tennessee State University Tigerbelles

In the 1950s and 1960s, Tennessee State University (TSU) had America's premier collegiate track program for women. Considered by many to be the most successful women's teams in U.S. track and field history, members of the TSU Tigerbelles won 34 Amateur Athletic Union (AAU) titles, 30 Pan American Games medals, and 23 Olympics medals, 15 of which were gold. Forty Tigerbelles have participated in the Olympic Games since 1952.

In the 1950s, interest in women's track and field waned in the United States, brought on in part by the continued efforts by physical educators to discourage women from competing on the elite level. But interest in women's track and field was beginning to grow at the nation's all-Black universities, such as Tuskegee Institute and TSU.

At TSU, Tom Harris coached women's track and field from 1947 to 1950, when Edward Temple, a professor of sociology at the university, took over the program. With only two members on the women's track team in 1952, Temple needed to recruit athletes or the university would cancel the program altogether. To find the most promising athletes for his program, Temple scouted state and local track meets in and around Nashville. In 1952, the TSU program got a boost when Mae Faggs, already an Olympic gold medalist, enrolled in TSU with hopes of getting an education and

Tennessee State University Tigerbelles, 1956—Front row (l–r) Darlene Scott, unknown, unknown, Willye B. White; Back row (l–r) Coach Edward S. Temple, Martha Hudson, Yvonne Macon, Lucinda Williams, Isabelle Daniels, Wilma Rudolph, Charlesetta Reddick, Margaret Matthews, Lorraine Holmes, Ella Ree Turner, Mae Faggs
Courtesy of Tennessee State University

continuing her athletic training. She was determined to keep the track and field program going and her efforts laid the foundation for much of the Tigerbelles' future success.

In addition to running the women's track team during the academic year, Temple developed an invitation-only summer track and field program for talented high school students. The most outstanding students from the summer program were offered work aid scholarships to the university. Tigerbelle standouts Lucinda Williams, Isabelle Daniels, and Willye White first came to the summer training program while they were still high school students. Wilma Rudolph and Martha Hudson were still high school students when they ran on the TSU junior team at the 1955 AAU Outdoor Nationals. The summer programs provided the wellspring that built and strengthened the Tigerbelle teams for decades.

The TSU women's team practiced year-around, competing in both outdoor and indoor meets. The key to the Tigerbelles' success was the emphasis placed on track and field fundamentals. Coach Temple spent hours teaching the sprinters such techniques as how to lean toward the tape at the finish line to get that extra edge, and how to properly and safely pass the baton, which is crucial for successful relay teams.

In addition to their rigorous training schedule, the Tigerbelles were expected to maintain high standards in their coursework and personal conduct. Academics always came first. Of the 40 Olympians from the TSU track program, 39 completed college degrees, 28 earned their master's, and 6 earned Ph.D.s. There was more to these women than just athletic ability.

Six members of the Tigerbelles made the 1956 U.S. Olympic team. The all–Tennessee State team of Mae Faggs, Margaret Matthews, Wilma Rudolph, and Isabelle Daniels won the bronze medal in the 4x100-meter relay, and Willye White won the silver in the long jump. The heart of the U.S. Women's Track and Field Team at the 1960 Rome Olympics also came from the Tigerbelles. Rudolph and six of her teammates made the team that year and won a total of nine gold medals. After the Olympics, *Sports Illustrated* called them "the Notre Dame of women's track and field." The Tigerbelles were most proficient in the relays, track and field's only "team" competition. Members of their teams were on medal-winning relays in five straight Olympics (1952–68).

The team's success continued into the 1970s with Olympic medalists Chandra Cheeseborough and Kathy McMillan. When Coach Temple retired in 1994 after 36 years, he handed the coaching reigns over to his protégé, Cheeseborough.

Many of the members of the Tigerbelles considered their time at TSU a life-changing experience: "Athletics was my flight to freedom," Willye White told *Runner's World* in 1993. "Freedom from prejudice. Freedom from illiteracy. Freedom from bias. It was my acceptance in the world. My athletic ability, my God-given talent, was a gift to me to enable me to leave from a very unkind situation."[8] Wyomia Tyus added: "Sports really changed my life. To be African-American in Georgia at that time, there was nothing to do. And if you were poor, you could do even less. Track gave me opportunities."[9]

The internationally famous Tigerbelles are regarded as the most successful women's track team in U.S. history. With their achievements in the 1956, 1960, and 1964 Olympics, the Tigerbelles became an Olympic force. With their summer programs for high school students, they established a tradition of offering opportunities in education and athletics for African American women and kept women's track and field in the United States on the path to future glory.

Tennessee State University Tigerbelle Olympians

Chandra Cheeseborough

A member of the Tennessee State University Tigerbelles from 1975-78, Cheeseborough was the first female to win gold medals as a member of both sprint relay teams (4x100-meters and 4x400-meters) in the same Olympics—the Los Angeles Games in 1984. She also claimed a silver in the 400 meters in the 1984 Games. The three-time Olympian (1976, 1980, 1984) attended the summer track program at TSU when she was in high school. At age 16, she won a gold medal in the 200-meters at the 1975 Pan American Games in Mexico City. She also won the national indoor 220-yard dash in 1979 and from 1981 to 1983. Cheeseborough now coaches the TSU women's track team.

Isabelle Daniels

A Tennessee State University Tigerbelle from 1954 to 1959, Daniels won the bronze medal at the 1956 Melbourne Olympic Games as a member of the 4x400-meter relay team. She also won a silver medal in the 60-meter dash at the 1955 Pan American Games.

In 1990, she was named National Coach of the Year by the National High School Athletic Coaches Association. Currently, she works as a physical education teacher at Ronald E. McNair Junior High School in Georgia.

Edith McGuire Duvall

A Tennessee State University Tigerbelle from 1961 to 1965, Duvall won the gold medal in the 200 meters at the 1964 Tokyo Olympics, running it in 23.0 seconds and breaking Wilma Rudolph's world record. She also won silver medals in the 100 meters and as a member of the 4x100-meter relay team. In 1963, Duvall won the 100 meters at the Pan American Games and at the Amateur Athletic Union (AAU) nationals. She also was the 200-meter champion in 1964 and 1965. Duvall was inducted into the U.S. National Track and Field Hall of Fame in 1979.

Martha Hudson

A Tennessee State University Tigerbelle from 1957 to 1960, Hudson ran the first leg for the U.S. team that won the gold medal and set the world record in the 4x100-meter relay at the 1960 Rome Olympics. She also won the 100-yard dash at the 1959 AAU Indoor Nationals. Hudson was inducted into the Tennessee Sports Hall of Fame in 1983 and the Georgia Sports Hall of Fame in 1986.

Barbara Jones

A Tennessee State University Tigerbelle from 1957 to 1961, Jones was the youngest woman (15) ever to win a gold medal in track and field in the Olympics. At the 1952 Helsinki Olympics, she won the gold and broke the world record in the 4x100-meter relay with her teammates. She struck gold again at the Pan American Games in 1955, and at the 1960 Rome Olympics, she was a member of the winning 4x100-meter relay team.

Margaret Matthews

A Tennessee State University Tigerbelle from 1955 to 1959, Matthews was the first American woman to leap 20 feet in the broad jump. At the 1956 Olympic trials in Washington, DC, she set a American record of 19 feet, 9 1/2 inches. In 1958, she set a new American record in the broad jump: 20 feet, 1 inch. Also a runner, Matthews was the captain of the U.S. team that captured the bronze in the 4x100-meter relay at the 1956 Melbourne Olympics.

Kathy McMillan

A Tennessee State University Tigerbelle from 1976 to 1980, McMillan was a silver medalist in the long-jump competition at the 1976 Montreal Olympics. She was also a member of the 1980 U.S. Olympic team that stayed home because of the U.S.-led boycott. As a student at TSU, she won the 1977 AAU Indoor Championship and the 1979 AAU Indoor and Outdoor Championships in the long jump. McMillan also won the gold medal in the 1979 Pan American Games in the long jump.

Madeline Manning Mims

A Tennessee State University Tigerbelle from 1968 to 1972, Mims was a four-time Olympic track team member (1968, 1972, 1976, 1980) and served as captain in 1972, 1976, and 1980. She is the only U.S. woman to win an Olympic gold medal in the 800 meters. She won the event at the 1968 Mexico City Olympics. Mims won a silver medal as part of the 4x400-meter relay team at the 1972 Olympics in Munich. She also won seven national outdoor championships and four Olympic trials. Mims was

inducted into the U.S. National Track and Field Hall of Fame in 1984 and the International Women's Sports Hall of Fame in 1987.

Wilma Rudolph

A Tennessee State University Tigerbelle from 1958 to 1962, Rudolph was the first U.S. woman to win three track and field gold medals in one Olympic Games. At the 1960 Rome Olympics, she won the gold medal in the 100 meters, 200 meters, and as a member of the 4x100-meter relay team. She also won a bronze medal at the 1956 Melbourne Olympics as a member of the 4x100-meter relay team. In 1959, Rudolph won the first of her four consecutive AAU 100-meter titles. She was named the Associated Press Female Athlete of the Year in 1960 and 1961 and won the 1961 Sullivan Memorial Trophy as the nation's top amateur athlete. In 1974, Rudolph was inducted into the U.S. National Track and Field Hall of Fame; in 1980, she became a member of the International Women's Sports Hall of Fame; and in 1983, she was selected to the United States Olympic Hall of Fame. (See more complete biographical information on p. 210.)

Mae Faggs Starr

A Tennessee State University Tigerbelle from 1952 to 1956, Starr was first U.S. female track athlete to participate in three Olympics (1948, 1952, 1956). She won a gold medal in the 4x100-meter relay at the 1952 Olympics in Helsinki and a bronze medal in the same event at the 1956 Olympics in Melbourne. An AAU All-American from 1954 to 1956, Starr won the AAU 200 meters in 1954, 1955, and 1956. In addition, she won the indoor 100-yard dash in 1952 and recorded six victories in the 200-meter outdoor event from 1949–56. Starr was inducted into the U.S. National Track and Field Hall of Fame in 1976 and the International Women's Sports Hall of Fame in 1996.

Wyomia Tyus

A Tennessee State University Tigerbelle from 1963 to 1968, Tyus captured three Olympic gold medals and one silver, and was the first person, woman or man, to successfully defend a 100-meter Olympic title. She set numerous world records in the 100 meters and 200 meters, and as a member of 4x100-meter relay teams. She won the three consecutive AAU outdoor 100-meter titles (1964, 1965, 1966). A founding member of the Women's Sports Foundation, Tyus became a member of the International Women's Sports Hall of Fame in 1981 and was elected to the U.S. National Track and Field Hall of Fame in 1980. (See more complete biographical information on p. 227.)

Willye B. White

A Tennessee State University Tigerbelle from 1956 to 1959, White was a member of five Olympic teams (1956, 1960, 1964, 1968, 1972). Her Olympic experience began in 1956, when she won the silver medal in the long jump. White also won a silver medal at the 1964 Olympic Games in Tokyo as a member of the U.S. 4x100-meter relay team. She won the AAU outdoor long jump 10 times between 1960 and 1972, adding the indoor championship in 1962. She was inducted into the U.S. National Track and Field Hall of Fame in 1981 and the International Women's Sports Hall of Fame in 1988.

Lucinda Williams

A member of the Tennessee State University Tigerbelles from 1954 to 1959, Williams ran the third leg of the 4x100-meter relay that won the gold at the 1960 Olympics Games in Rome. At the 1958 Pan American Games in Chicago, Williams captured three gold medals and posted a U.S. record for the women's 200-meter dash. She represented TSU at the indoor and outdoor national championships, helping her teams win five consecutive outdoor 440-yard relay championships (1955–59).

U.S. Olympic Synchronized Swimming Team

"Synchronized for Gold" was the motto of the 1996 U.S. Olympic Synchronized Swimming (USSS) Team as they prepared to compete in the Atlanta Games. The United States had assembled the finest group of synchronized swimmers in the sport's history. U.S. Coach Gail Emery told *Women's Sports and Fitness*, "We have so much talent on this team that I believe we're creating moves no one else in the world would even consider trying."[10] The U.S. team— Suzannah Bianco, Tammy Cleland, Becky Dyroen-Lancer, Emily Porter LeSueur, Heather Pease, Jill Savery, Nathalie Schneyder, Heather Simmons-Carrasco, Jill Sudduth, and Margot Thien—won the gold medal at the Atlanta Games with a perfect score of 100, the first time in Olympic synchronized swimming history that a routine had earned a perfect score from all judges.

Of all the modern Olympic sports, synchronized swimming is the only all-female discipline. It requires grace, skill, and pure athleticism. *Inside Sports* magazine named it one of the five toughest Olympic events: "[Synchronized swimmers] will be among the most dedicated, aerobically fit, and technically skilled performers in Atlanta."[11] The team competition features eight women in the water at one time. Performing in nine feet of water and without touching the bottom, teams incorporate acrobatic elements, lifts raising swimmers above the water, and precise movements into routines synchronized to music. They are judged on required technical elements as well as on difficult moves and artistic choreography. The sport made its debut in the 1984 Olympics with solo and duet competitions. At the Centennial Games, the team event, the sport's premier competition, replaced the solo and duet events.

USSS, the national governing body of synchronized swimming, held the U.S. Olympic trials in Indianapolis in October 1995. Thirty-one athletes from around the country tried out for the 10 spots on the 1996 squad. Athletes first had to learn, then swim, two routines (technical and free routines) individually and in groups. Judges selected the team based on overall points awarded in the competition.

The 10 team members earning spots on the Olympic team had significant international experience in solo, duet, and team competition, having participated in a number of World Cup, world championship, and Pan American Games competitions. The average numbers of years each athlete spent on the national team was 8.5. Dyroen-Lancer, Savery, Simmons-Carrasco, and Sudduth all had 10 years of experience competing on the national team and in international competition, but Atlanta

U.S. Olympic Sychronized Swimming Team—1st row (l–r) Heather Pease, Margot Thien, Becky Dyroen-Lancer; 2nd row (l–r) Emily Porter LeSuer, Jill Sudduth; 3rd row (l–r) Nathalie Schneyder, Tammy Cleland, Jill Savery; 4th row (l–r) Suzannah Bianco, Heather Simmons-Carrasco
Courtesy of Synchro Swimming USA

would be their first chance at Olympic gold.

The team began training together on October 31, 1995. The athletes hit the water six to eight hours a day, six days a week, swimming laps and practicing routines. Training also included three weekly sessions of plyometrics, exercises designed to increase explosive strength, and individual cross-training exercises, including running, cycling, and weight training three to four times a week. Schneyder even incorporated rock climbing into her cross-training regimen. Ten-time U.S national team member Sudduth commented, "You have to be a very strong athlete to even come close to doing the things we do. But on top of that, we have to know how to interpret music. It's a real test."[12]

Prior to their selection as Olympic teammates, all 10 members of the U.S. team made synchronized swimming history at the 1995 NationsBank Synchronized Swimming World Cup held at the Georgia Tech Aquatics Center in August 1995. Swimming together in the team technical routine program, the U.S. team scored 99.133 (out of 100). For their free routine, which featured a risky pyramid lift where three swimmers were lifted out of the water standing on top of each other's shoulders, the judges awarded straight 10s in artistic impression and three 10s and two 9.9s in technical merit for a total of 99.800. It was the highest score ever awarded in World Cup history.

The U.S. team's momentum continued at the Olympic qualifying event with another record-setting performance. Team USA dominated the field in the technical routine and performed a free routine that earned them straight 10s in both technical and artistic impression, the first perfect score in international competition. Eight countries qualified for the Olympic Games at the qualifying event—Canada, China, France, Italy, Japan, Mexico, Russia, and the United States.

Returning to the Georgia Tech Aquatics Center for Olympic competition, the U.S team was the heavy favorite to the win the gold. Team USA had a nearly flawless swim in the two-minute, 50-second technical round, performing all the required elements to the music from "When the Saints Go Marching In" and the "Hallelujah Chorus" to near perfection. For their efforts, they earned a score of 99.2, which included three 9.9s and two 10s in technical merit, and three 9.9s, a 9.8, and a 10 in artistic

impression. Swimming in the technical routine for the USA were Cleland, Dyroen-Lancer, Pease, LeSueur, Savery, Schneyder, Sudduth, and Thien. For the free routine, Bianco and Simmons-Carrasco replaced LeSueur and Thien.

More than 15,000 spectators filled the stands at the aquatics center to see the free swim portion of the competition. Swimming to "Fantasia on an Orchestra," Team USA performed an exciting five-minute free routine filled with captivating lifts and intricate precision moves. The judges awarded Team USA straight 10s in technical merit and four out of five 10s in artistic impression. Dropping the high and low scores, it was a perfect score of 100, the first time in Olympic synchronized swimming history that a routine had earned a perfect score.

After the victory, co-captain Emily Porter LeSueur reflected on the team's accomplishments. She told *Synchro Swimming USA*, "I think for us tonight, it was a perfect swim and we'll always remember this moment as being a perfect moment."[13]

During the years 1991–96, the United States Synchronized Swimming Team was ranked number one in the world. This remarkable team was composed of highly talented individuals with dozens of individual awards among them. For example, at the 1994 World Aquatic Championships in Rome, Dyroen-Lancer won three gold medals, more gold medals than any other American at the championships (events included swimming, diving, synchronized swimming, and water polo). She had nine consecutive "grand slams" (winning solo, duet, and team medals in the same competition) 1992–96, and with partner Jill Sudduth, reigned as World Cup duet champion, 1983–96. In 1995, Dyroen-Lancer received the Federation Internationale de Natation Amateur (FINA) Prize—the highest award given to a member of the aquatics community—the first U.S. female athlete (swimmers and divers included) to receive the award.

A combination of individual conditioning, strength, hard work, and dedication to winning the gold was what set the U.S. squad apart from the rest of the field in the athletic and graceful sport of Olympic synchronized swimming. Strength and conditioning consultant Dr. Donald A. Chu told the *Wall Street Journal*, "These women have taken the sport to an absolutely new level."[14] The success of the 1996 U.S. Olympic Synchronized Swimming Team will ensure that the sport will continue to grow and gain its duly earned respect as a sport that requires skill, grace, and pure athleticism.

1996 U.S. Olympic Synchronized Swimming Team

Suzannah Bianco

Bianco was on the national team eight of her 14 years in synchronized swimming. Her career highlights include the 1995 NationsBank World Cup and Pan American Games team champion, Jantzen Nationals team champion, and duet silver medalist; 1994 world team champion, French Open team champion, and Jantzen Nationals team champion and duet silver medalist; 1993 World Cup team champion; 1992 U.S. Olympic trials duet silver medalist and Swiss Open team champion; and 1991 FINA World Cup team champion and French Open team champion. She was named USSS All-American five consecutive years (1991–95).

Tammy Cleland

Cleland was on the national team seven of her 15 years in synchronized swimming.

She was selected USSS All-American four times (1992–95) and was the 1993 captain of the U.S national team. Her career highlights include the 1995 NationsBank World Cup and Pan American Games team champion, and Jantzen National team silver medalist; 1994 world team champion, French Open team champion, and Jantzen Nationals team silver medalist; 1993 World Cup team champion, and Scottish Open solo and duet champion; 1992 American Cup solo and duet champion; and 1991 junior world championships team silver medalist.

Becky Dyroen-Lancer

Dyroen-Lancer was a member of the national team for 10 of her 15 years in synchronized swimming. She is considered one of the greatest swimmers in synchronized swimming history. Her career highlights include the 1995 NationsBank World Cup, Pan American Games, and Jantzen Nationals solo, duet, team, and figures (combined scores) champion; 1994 world championships, French Open, and Jantzen Nationals solo, duet, team, and figures champion; 1993 World Cup solo, duet, team, and figures, and U.S. Nationals solo, duet, and team champion; 1992 Swiss Open solo, duet, figures, and team champion; 1991 Pan American Games solo champion, and FINA World Cup and world championships team champion.

Emily Porter LeSueur

LeSueur was on the national team seven of her 12 years in synchronized swimming. She was co-captain of the 1996 Olympic gold-medal-winning team. Her career highlights include the 1995 NationsBank World Cup team champion and Pan American Games team champion; 1994 world and French Open team champion; and 1991

Pan American Games team champion. USSS named her All-American for the years 1991–95.

Heather Pease

Pease was on the national team seven of her 11 years in synchronized swimming. Her career highlights include the 1995 NationsBank World Cup team champion and Pan American Games team champion; 1994 world and French Open team champion; and 1993 World Cup team champion. She was selected USSS All-American four consecutive years (1992–95).

Jill Savery

Savery was on the national team 10 of her 14 years in synchronized swimming. She was the U.S. national team captain (1989, 1991, 1994), USSS All-American (1990–95), and the 1994 Collegiate Synchronized Swimmer of the Year. Her career highlights include the 1995 NationsBank World Cup and Pan American Games team champion; 1994 world championships and French Open team champion; 1993 World Cup and Swiss Open team champion; 1992 Swiss Open team champion; and 1991 FINA World Cup, Rome Open, and world championships team champion.

Nathalie Schneyder

Schneyder was on the national team nine of her 19 years in synchronized swimming. Her career highlights include the 1995 NationsBank World Cup team champion and Pan American Games team champion; 1994 world championships and French Open team champion; 1993 World Cup team champion; 1992 Swiss Open team champion; and 1991 FINA World Cup, Rome Open, and world championships team champion. She was a USSS All-Ameri-

can selection seven consecutive years (1989–95).

Heather Simmons-Carrasco

Simmons-Carrasco was on the national team 10 of her 18 years in synchronized swimming. In 1994, she won the Esther Williams Creative Achievement Award and has been selected USSS All-American seven times (1989–95). Her career highlights include the 1995 NationsBank World Cup, Pan American Games, and Jantzen Nationals team champion; 1994 world championships, French Open, and Jantzen Nationals team champion; 1993 World Cup team champion; 1992 Swiss Open team champion; and 1991 FINA World Cup, French Open, and world championships team champion.

Jill Sudduth

Sudduth was on the national team 10 of her 18 years in synchronized swimming. Her career highlights include the 1995 Nations-Bank World Cup and Jantzen Nationals duet and team champion; 1994 world championships, French Open, and Jantzen Nationals duet and team champion; 1993 World Cup and U.S. Nationals duet and team champion; 1992 Swiss Open duet and team champion; and 1991 FINA World Cup and world championships team champion. She was selected *Swimming World*'s World Synchronized Swimmer of the Year in 1993, and was named a USSS All-American six consecutive years (1990–95).

Margot Thien

Thien was on the national team eight of her 15 years in synchronized swimming. Her career highlights include the 1995 Nations-Bank World Cup and Pan American Games team champion; 1994 world championships and French Open team champion; 1993 World Cup team champion; and 1992 Swiss Open and U.S. Nationals team champion. She was selected a USSS All-American 1991–95.

Source: *U.S. Synchronized Swimming 1996 Media Guide*

U.S. Women's Gymnastics Team

The 1996 Centennial Olympic Games in Atlanta found their defining moment in the women's gymnastics competition. Kerri Strug's heroic final vault capped the end of the Olympic reign of the Russian women's team as the U.S. women defeated the world gymnastics power for the USA's first team gold medal in Olympic history. "The Magnificent Seven"—Amanda Borden, Amy Chow, Dominique Dawes, Shannon Miller, Dominique Moceanu, Jaycie Phelps, and Kerri Strug—defeated Russia by less than a point; the final score in the team competition was USA 389.225, Russia 388.404. The most talented team ever to represent the United States in international gymnastics competition, the Magnificent Seven will be remembered for their skill, teamwork, and heroics in the 1996 Olympic Games. "This was a total team effort," said Steve Nunno, Miller's coach. "All of our pieces had to fit together in order to win the gold medal. We don't have just one star, we have seven."[15]

Nearly a generation of gymnasts had grown up since Mary Lou Retton sparked an enormous growth in gymnastics in the United States with her victorious vault to win the all-around gold medal in the 1984 Los Angeles Olympics. With more opportunities and better coaching, America's gymnasts began to emerge as serious challengers in international competitions. The bronze-

U.S. Women's Gymnastics Team—(l–r) Amanda Borden, Dominique Dawes, Amy Chow, Jaycie Phelps, Dominique Moceanu, Kerri Strug, Shannon Miller
© Dave Black

medal finish of the U.S. team at the 1992 Barcelona Olympics served notice to the gymnastic powerhouses, such as Russia and Romania, that the U.S. team had come of age and was on the verge of something big.

USA Gymnastics, the national governing body of women's gymnastics, invited the nation's top gymnasts from around the country to compete for a spot on the 1996 Olympic team.

Fourteen competitors came to the 1996 Olympic Qualifying Trials in Boston on June 27, 1996, with the dream of making the Olympic team and of competing in front of a hometown crowd in Atlanta, Georgia. Two of American's top gymnasts, Miller and Moceanu, were nursing injuries and unable to compete in the trials, but were given spots on the Olympic team based on their scores at the national championships. Miller, a five-time Olympic medalist, was suffering from tendinitis in her wrist, and Moceanu, the youngest member of the squad, had a stress fracture in her right shin. With two spots already taken, the Olympic team had room for only five more. The top five finishers in the all-around would make the team. Dawes emerged as the top performer, followed by Strug, Phelps, Chow, and Borden. Chow made a spectacular recovery on the balance beam after she fell and hit her head on the beam. Despite a wide scratch and a growing welt next to her eye, Chow hopped back on and completed the routine. She turned in scores impressive enough to make the U.S. team.

By the time the trials were over, it was clear that the United States had put together its most experienced and talented Olympic team ever. Three of the seven members—Dawes, Miller, and Strug—had been on the 1992 Olympic team, and the remaining four had been to at least one world championship. They had won more than 15 Olympic and world championship medals among them.

The Magnificent Seven were united in their goal to win the gold. An ethnically and culturally diverse team, the women seemed to truly appreciate the value of teamwork. "We work as a team," Strug told *USA Today*. "We set the bars and boards for each other. If anyone is stressed, then the team helps. We just help each other out."[16]

The U.S. Olympic team was not the favored team going into the Atlanta Summer Games, but Nunno said, "They're at the top of their game, every single one of them."[17] After the compulsory round of competition, the United States emerged in second place, just .127 points behind Russia going into the optional finals.

The crowd of more than 32,000 packed the Georgia Dome to cheer on the U.S. squad in the optional finals. In the finals, the U.S. team hit solid routines during the first three rotations—balance beam, floor exercise, and uneven bars—with no scores lower than 9.6. But they developed problems in the vault, their final event. Moceanu had fallen on her two tries and scored only 9.2. When Strug stepped up to the apparatus, she was the last American with a chance to bring home the team gold for the United States. But on her first vault, she landed awkwardly, twisted her left ankle, fell, and scored just 9.162. In obvious pain, but thinking she needed to complete her second vault for the victory, Strug walked back to the end of the vault runway. She bravely ran down the runway, throwing herself into the air up and over the vaulting horse, and landing on her injured ankle to score a 9.712. Her vault score was enough for the U.S. victory. The final scoreboard read USA 389.225, Russia 388.404. The margin of victory was less than a point, 0.821. World champion Romania was third with a 388.246 score. The crowed chanted

USA! USA! and gave the team a standing ovation as they mounted the podium to receive their medals.

It was a historic moment for the U.S. women's team when they defeated world gymnastics powers Russia and Romania for the USA's first team gold medal in Olympic history. The Soviet Union had won every Olympic team gold medal since 1952, except for the boycotted 1984 Games (Romania won the gold). In 1992, the Unified Team, a team from the former Soviet Union, also won the gold—its tenth in Olympic history.

Three of the seven members of the U.S. team advanced to the all-around and individual event finals. Strug had qualified for the individual all-around and floor exercise and vault, but could not compete because of her injury. Dawes, who replaced Strug in the floor exercise, won the bronze medal in the event, while Chow scored a 9.837 on the uneven bars to earn the silver medal in the individual event finals. Miller capped her Olympic career with a gold medal on the balance beam, scoring a 9.862 and becoming the first U.S. female gymnast to win a gold medal on an individual apparatus. "It was a fantastic note on which to end my Olympic competition," she said.[18]

The Magnificent Seven vaulted to Olympic glory by becoming the first U.S. Gymnastics Team to win team gold. They worked together as a team and called upon their experience, talent, and enthusiasm to carry them to the champions' platform at the 1996 Atlanta Olympic Summer Games. "Competing as a team definitely helped all of us," said Phelps. "We were all pushing for each other. It's a lot of fun to be a member of a team. If each member does her best, the team is going to do well and everyone will benefit together. A team wins because of a team effort."[19]

1996 U.S. Olympic Gymnastics Team

Amanda Borden

A six-year member of the U.S. National Gymnastics Team. Borden was a member of the U.S. team that won the gold medal at the 1996 Atlanta Olympics. She was a three-time world championship team member and won a gold medal as a member of the winning U.S. team at the 1995 Pan American Games and a silver medal at the 1994 World Championships. In individual events, Borden won a gold medal in the beam and a silver in the all-around and floor exercise competitions at the 1995 Pan American Games. She also won the beam event and the floor exercise at the 1995 McDonald's American Cup. Borden trains at the Cincinnati Gymnastics Academy and is coached by Mary Lee Tracy.

Amy Chow

A six-year member of the U.S. National Gymnastics Team, Chow was the first Asian American on the U.S. national team. In addition to a gold medal in the team competition, she earned a silver medal in the uneven bars in the individual apparatus finals at the 1996 Olympics. At the 1995 Pan American Games, she won the vault, placed second on bars, and came in third in the all-around, helping her team clinch the gold medal. She was a member of the U.S. team that won the 1994 world championship silver medal. Chow trains at the West Valley Gymnastics School and is coached by Mark Young and Diane Amos.

Dominique Dawes

A six-year member of the U.S. National Gymnastics Team, Dawes was a member of the U.S. team that won the gold medal at the 1996 Atlanta Olympics. In addition, she won an individual bronze medal in the floor exercise. She was first in the all-around at the 1996 U.S. Olympic trials. In 1994, she swept the U.S. National Gymnastics Championship, winning the gold medal in the all-around and all four event finals, the first gymnast to accomplish this feat since 1969. Dawes was also a member of the U.S. team that captured the bronze medal at the 1992 Olympic Games. She was named USA Gymnastics' Sportsperson of the Year and was a finalist for the Sullivan Award in 1994 and a nominee for the 1995 Women's Sports Foundation Individual Sportswoman of the Year Award. Dawes trains at Hill's Gymnastics and is coached by Kelli Hill.

Shannon Miller

A seven-year member of the U.S. National Gymnastics Team, Miller was a member of the U.S. team that won the gold medal at the 1996 Atlanta Olympics. She also earned the gold medal in the balance beam in the individual apparatus final. Miller is the most decorated U.S. gymnast in history, winning more Olympic and world championship medals than any other U.S. gymnast, male or female. She has earned seven Olympic medals—two gold, two silver, and three bronze—and nine world championship medals—five gold, three silver, and one bronze. Miller also won gold medals in the team event and the individual event finals in the all-around, uneven bars, and floor exercise at the 1995 Pan American Games. In national competitions, she has won more than 15 individual national championships. She was named 1994 USA Gymnastics' Athlete of the Year and is a three-time Sullivan Award nominee (1993-95). Miller trains at Dynamo Gymnastics and is coached by Steve Nunno and Peggy Liddick. (See more complete biographical information on p. 192.)

Dominique Moceanu

A five-year member of the U.S. National Gymnastics Team, Moceanu, at 14, was the youngest member of the U.S. team that won the gold medal at the 1996 Atlanta Olympics. She was a silver and bronze medalist at the 1995 world championships in Sabae, Japan. In national competition, she won the all-around at the 1995 Coca-Cola National Championships, the youngest to ever win the national all-around title. She began participating in competitive gymnastics at age three. At age 10, she qualified for the U.S. Junior National Team, and won her first international all-around title at the 1995 Visa Challenge in Fairfax, Virginia. Moceanu is coached by Arthur Akopyan.

Jaycie Phelps

A three-year member of the U.S. National Gymnastics Team, Phelps was a member of the U.S. team that won the gold medal at the 1996 Atlanta Olympics. She is a three-time world championships team member and helped her team to the bronze medal at the 1995 world championships. Phelps also won a silver medal in the team event at the 1994 team world championships in Dortmund, Germany. In national competition, she earned the individual all-around title at the 1996 American Classic/world championships trials and was second in the all-around at the 1996 Coca-Cola National Championships. Phelps trains at the Cincinnati Gymnastics Academy and is coached by Mary Lee Tracy.

Kerri Strug

A six-year member of the U.S. National Gymnastics Team, Strug was a member of the U.S. team that won the gold medal at the 1996 Atlanta Olympics. Her dramatic vault on an injured ankle led her to win the Olympic Spirit Award. Strug has been a member of five world championships teams, winning a team bronze at the 1995 world championships, and a team silver at the 1991 world championships and the 1994 team world championship. In 1996, she won the all-around title at the 1996 McDonald's America Cup. In national competition, she won the all-around, uneven bars, balance beam, and floor exercise at the 1993 American Classic/world championships trials. She trains at Karolyi's Gymnastics and is coached by Bela and Marta Karolyi.

Source: *USA Gymnastics 1996 Media Guide*

Further Reading

Cohen, Daniel and Susan Cohen. *Gold Medal Glory: The Story of America's 1996 Women's Gymnastics Team.* New York: Pocket Books, 1996. 117 pp.

Kleinbaum, Nancy H. *The Magnificent Seven: The Authorized Story of American Gold.* New York: Bantam Books, 1996. 108 pp.

U.S. Women's National Soccer Team

"Judging by the adoring gazes of the girls who watched the U.S. team make history on a steamy night in Georgia, the indelible mark of the Olympic soccer tournament was left not only on the players but also on another generation," wrote *Sports Illustrated*'s Michael Farber of the U.S. Women's National Soccer Team's gold-medal-winning performance.[20] A collection of the best soccer players—Michelle Akers, Brandi Chastain, Joy Fawcett, Julie Foudy, Carin Gabarra, Mia Hamm, Mary Harvey, Kristine Lilly, Shannon MacMillan, Tiffeny Milbrett, Carla Overbeck, Cindy Parlow, Tiffany Roberts, Briana Scurry, Tisha Venturini, and Staci Wilson—in the history of U.S. women's soccer, the U.S. team captured the first-ever women's Olympic gold medal by defeating China 2-1 on August 1, 1996, before a crowd of 76,481 at Sanford Stadium in Athens, Georgia. Winning the gold medal reestablished the United States as the top women's soccer program in the world, and Mia Hamm, one of the top players in the world, suggested a more important impact. "[Olympic soccer] was another step, bigger than most," said Hamm. "Maybe it will help start a [professional] league, give

girls who want to play soccer something to look forward to."[21]

Women's soccer at an international level is a relatively young sport. The movement for women's international soccer began in Europe with national teams forming in Sweden in 1973, Denmark in 1974, and Norway in 1978. Women's national teams in Germany, Italy, and England soon followed. The first European championship for women was held in 1984.

In the United States, the groundswell of support for international soccer began to build after the United States hosted the men's World Cup in 1994, but soccer has been played extensively at the grassroots level since the late 1960s. The United States Soccer Federation (USSF), the governing body of soccer in the United States, formed the women's national soccer team program in July 1985 at the Olympic Festival in Baton Rouge, Louisiana. Two months later, the U.S. women made their international debut in a 1-0 loss to Italy in Jesolo, Italy. On July 7, 1986, the U.S. team played its first international competition in the United States, defeating Canada 2-0 in Blaine, Minnesota.

U.S. Women's National Soccer Team—(1st row, l–r) Michelle Akers, Carin Gabarra, Mia Hamm, Carla Overbeck, Cindy Parlow (2nd row, l–r) Tisha Venturini, Joy Fawcett, Brianna Scurry, Mary Harvey, Brandi Chastain, Julie Foudy (3rd row, l–r) Shannon MacMillan, Tiffeny Milbrett, Kristine Lilly, Staci Wilson, Tiffany Roberts
© J. Brett Whitesell/ISI

The Federation Internationale de Football Association (FIFA), the world governing body of soccer, sanctioned its first world championship for women in 1991. Teams entered in the inaugural event included Brazil, China, Denmark, Germany, Italy, Japan, New Zealand, Nigeria, Norway, Sweden, Taiwan, and the United States. Playing in Guangzhou, China, the U.S. Women's National Soccer Team went undefeated in the tournament with a record of 6-0, and won the first-ever FIFA Women's World Championship, defeating Norway in the final game, 2-1. The U.S. women gave up only five goals in the entire competition. U.S. player Carin Jennings (Gabarra) was named most valuable player in the tournament.

The first Women's World Championship did more than establish the United States as the best team in the world and showcase the talents of American athletes Michelle Akers, Julie Foudy, Mia Hamm, and their teammates. The tournament paved the way for women's soccer to gain entrance into the 1996 Summer Olympic Games. (Men's soccer has been a part of the Olympics since 1900.)

With the Olympics on the horizon, many of the U.S. team members stayed in training with hopes of getting the opportunity to play in the Centennial Games. The U.S. team won the silver medal at the 1993 World University Games then qualified for the 1995 world championship by sweeping the competition at the Confederation of North Central and Carribean American Football (CONCACAF) Qualifying Championship in Montreal in the summer of 1994. The U.S. team finished the tournament with a 4-0 mark, recording wins over Mexico, 9-0; Trinidad & Tobago, 11-1; Jamaica, 10-0; and Canada, 6-0.

In January 1995, USA Soccer held a training camp for prospective players to prepare for the 1995 world championships and the 1996 Olympics. Twenty-four players were invited to the camp, including the core of the 1991 world championship team. "The old training routine of 10 days a month would not prepare us sufficiently," said Coach Tony DiCicco. "We know it's going to be harder to win the championship this time."[22]

The United States placed third at the 1995 world championship in Sweden. They lost to Norway, 1-0, in the semifinal match. Norway went on to win the championship. The United States avenged the loss when they defeated Norway, 2-1, in overtime in the 1995 U.S. Women's Cup.

The women's team opened their bid for Olympic gold on July 23, 1996, in Orlando, Florida, with a 3-0 win over Denmark. Venturini, Hamm, and Milbrett scored goals in front of a crowd of more than 25,000. Two days later, the U.S. team won 2-1 over Sweden, and followed that with a 0-0 tie in the game against China. On July 28, the women's Olympic soccer tournament moved to Athens, Georgia, where the United States defeated world champion Norway, 2-1, for a spot in the gold-medal game.

On August 1, 1996, more than 76,000 fans packed Sanford Stadium in Athens, Georgia—the largest crowd ever to watch an Olympic soccer match and the largest crowd ever to see a women's sporting event in the United States—to watch the United States defeat China, 2-1, to win the first-ever gold medal in women's Olympic soccer.

U.S. team member Joy Fawcett had an eye on the future for her daughter Katelyn and her sport as a result of the U.S. Olympic victory. "I hope [Katelyn] can do the same thing," Fawcett told *Sports Illustrated*.

"I hope she has more opportunities and finds it a lot easier than I did. If she chooses this sport and gets to this level, there should be much more recognition."[23] Defender Brandi Chastain added: "People are going to see our gold medal and say, 'We want a piece of that. We want to see them play.'"[24] And people will get their chance to see the players as the United States prepares to host the FIFA Women's World Championship in 1999.

1996 U.S. Women's National Soccer Team

Michelle Akers

A member of the U.S Women's National Soccer Team since 1985, Akers played forward for the 1996 gold-medal-winning soccer team at the 1996 Olympic Summer Games. She was the MVP of the 1994 CONCACAF Qualifying Championship in Montreal and the leading goal scorer in the first FIFA Women's World Championship in 1991. Akers was selected U.S. Soccer's Female Athlete of the Year in 1990 and 1991. She played collegiate soccer at the University of Central Florida in Orlando, where she was a four-time All-American, and played professionally overseas for three seasons (1990, 1992, 1994) in Sweden with the Tyreso Football Club. (See more complete biographical information on p. 77.)

Brandi Chastain

Chastain played forward for the gold-medal-winning team at the 1996 Atlanta Olympics and was a member of the U.S. national team that won the inaugural FIFA Women's World Championship held in China in 1991. She also played with the 1993 U.S. women's team that won the CONCACAF Championship. In 1986, she attended University of California at Berkeley, where she earned

Freshman Player of the Year honors. She was forced to sit out two years due to knee surgery, but she completed her collegiate career at Santa Clara University, where she earned First-Team All-American honors in 1990. Chastain traveled overseas to play professionally in Japan for one season (1993).

Joy Fawcett

As a member of the 1996 U.S. Women's National Soccer Team, Fawcett made the assist in the game-winning goal in the final game that clinched the gold medal at the Atlanta Olympics. She played every minute of the six games that the United States played in the 1995 FIFA Women's World Championship in Sweden and was a member of the U.S. team that won the 1994 CONCACAF Qualifying Championship in Montreal. She also played with the U.S. team that won both the 1993 CONCACAF Championship in New York and the 1991 FIFA World Championship. U.S. Soccer named her the 1988 Female Athlete of the Year. A three-time All-American from the University of California at Berkeley, Fawcett helped her team to a third-place finish in the National Collegiate Athletic Association (NCAA) tournament in 1987 and 1988. Presently, she is the head coach of the women's soccer team at the University of California at Los Angeles (UCLA).

Julie Foudy

A nine-year member of the U.S. Women's National Soccer Team, midfielder Foudy was co-captain of the 1996 U.S. team that won the gold medal at the Atlanta Olympics. She was a member of the U.S. national team that won the 1994 CONCACAF Qualifying Championship and that placed third at the 1995 FIFA Women's World Championship. Foudy also helped the U.S.

team clinch the gold medal at the 1991 FIFA Women's World Championship. Foudy played collegiate soccer at Stanford University, where she earned All-American honors four consecutive years (1989-92). She played professionally for the Tyreso Football Club in Sweden in 1994.

Carin Gabarra

Gabarra played forward for the gold-medal-winning U.S. Women's National Soccer Team at the Atlantic Olympics and participated on the U.S. national team that finished third at the 1995 FIFA World Championship in Sweden. She was also a member of the U.S. team that won the 1994 CONCACAF Qualifying Championship in Montreal. She was named U.S. Soccer's Female Athlete of the Year in 1987 and 1992. At the 1991 FIFA World Championship, she scored six goals in leading the U.S. team to the first-ever world title and won the Golden Ball Award as the tournament's outstanding player. A four-time All-American from the University of California at Santa Barbara (UCSB), she was voted the school's Female Athlete of the Decade in 1987.

Mia Hamm

Generally recognized as the best all-around female soccer player in the world, Hamm was key in clinching the U.S. soccer team's gold medal at the Atlanta Olympic Games. She started all 19 games played by the national team prior to the Olympics and led the team in total points. Hamm led the team to the 1995 U.S. Cup Championship win and was named that tournament's Most Valuable Player. U.S. Soccer Federation named Hamm Female Athlete of the Year three consecutive years (1994–96). A three-time All-American, Hamm led the University of North Carolina women's soccer team to four NCAA championship titles (1989, 1990, 1992, 1993). Hamm won the 1993-94 Honda Award for academic success, and she became the first soccer player to win the Honda Broderick Cup, which recognizes the outstanding collegiate woman athlete of the year.

Mary Harvey

Back-up goalkeeper for the U.S. team that won the gold medal at the Atlanta Olympic Games, Harvey also was a member of the U.S. Women's National Soccer Team that placed third at the 1995 FIFA Women's World Championship and that won the 1994 CONCACAF Qualifying Championship in Montreal. Harvey played every minute in goal and recorded three shutouts for the United States in the 1991 FIFA Women's World Championship. She played for the University of California at Berkeley from 1983-86. In 1986, she was named National Goalkeeper of the Year. She played professionally in Sweden and Germany.

Kristine Lilly

A midfielder for the U.S. team that won the gold medal at the Atlanta Olympic Games, Lilly played for the 1993 U.S. team that won the CONCACAF Championship in New York and the U.S. Women's National Soccer Team that won the inaugural FIFA Women's World Championship in China in 1991. She was named U.S. Soccer's 1993 Female Athlete of the Year. The four-time All-American from the University of North Carolina helped her team to four NCAA championships from 1989–92. She played professionally in Sweden in 1994.

Shannon MacMillan

A midfielder for the U.S. team that won the gold medal at the Atlanta Olympic Games, MacMillan scored the winning goals in matches against Sweden and Norway in the Olympic tournament. MacMillan also was a member of the U.S. Women's National Soccer Team that won the silver medal at the 1993 World University Games in Buffalo, New York. A four-time All-American at the University of Portland (Oregon), MacMillan was named the 1995 Hermann Award winner as the outstanding collegiate soccer player.

Tiffeny Milbrett

A forward for the U.S. team that won the gold medal at the 1996 Atlanta Olympic Games, Milbrett scored the winning goal in the final match against China. She was a member of the U.S. team that finished third at the 1995 FIFA World Championship in Sweden and that won the 1994 CONCACAF Qualifying Championship in Montreal. During her collegiate career at the University of Portland (Oregon), she became the school's all-time leading scorer and led the nation in scoring and assists in 1994. That year, she helped her team to the Final Four of the NCAA Division I Women's Soccer Championship, where she was named to the All-Tournament team. Milbrett played professionally with Shiroki Serena of the women's league in Japan in 1995.

Carla Overbeck

Captain of the U.S. Women's National Soccer Team that won the gold medal at the 1996 Atlanta Games, Overbeck also played for the United States in its victory in the 1991 FIFA World Championship in China and on the 1993 U.S. team that won the CONCACAF Championship in New York. The defender played every minute of the U.S. team's five matches at the 1996 Olympic Games. She was a finalist for the 1995 Women's Sports Foundation Team Sportswoman of the Year award. While attending the University of North Carolina, the three-time All-American helped her team to four NCAA championships (1987–90).

Cindy Parlow

Parlow, at 18 years of age, was the youngest member of the U.S. Women's National Soccer Team that won the gold medal at the 1996 Atlanta Games. She joined the national team in March 1995. She played collegiate soccer at the University of North Carolina and finished third in scoring her freshman year. Parlow was named MVP at the 1995 U.S. Youth Soccer national tournament.

Tiffany Roberts

A midfielder for the U.S. Women's National Soccer Team that won the gold medal at the 1996 Atlanta Games, Roberts also played for the U.S. team that finished third at the 1995 FIFA Women's World Championship in Sweden and for the U.S. team that won the CONCACAF Qualifying Championship in 1994. She played midfield for the University of North Carolina in 1995. In 1994, she was named California Soccer Player of the Year. A star in track and field in high school, Roberts was ranked in the top 20 in the United States in the 400-meter dash while at Carondelet High School in San Ramon, California.

Briana Scurry

Goalkeeper for the U.S. Women's National Soccer Team that won the gold medal at the 1996 Atlanta Games, Scurry played every minute of the U.S. team's five matches in the Olympic tournament. She also played for the U.S. women's team that finished third at the 1995 FIFA Women's World Championship in Sweden and for the team that won the 1994 CONCACAF Qualifying Championship in Montreal. In her first year as goalkeeper for the U.S. national team, she recorded seven shutouts in 12 starts. Scurry completed her collegiate career at the University of Massachusetts with 37 shutouts in 65 starts and a 0.56 goals-against average.

Tisha Venturini

A midfielder for the 1996 Olympic gold-medal-winning team, Venturini scored the game-winning goal against Denmark in the 1996 Olympic tournament. She was one of only two athletes to play in all 23 games for the 1995 U.S. national team. She finished in a tie for the leading goal-scorer of the U.S. team at the 1995 Women's World Championship in Sweden and was a member of the U.S. Women's National Soccer Team that won the 1994 CONCACAF Qualifying Championship in Montreal. A four-time All-American, Venturini helped the University of North Carolina to four consecutive national championships (1991–94). She was named the NCAA Tournament's Most Valuable Defensive Player in 1991 and the Most Valuable Offensive Player in 1994.

Staci Wilson

A defender for the U.S. Women's National Soccer Team that won the gold medal at the 1996 Atlanta Games, Wilson made her first start for the U.S. national team in March 1995. She was a member of the 1994 NCAA Division I Women's Soccer Championship team at the University of North Carolina, where she was named first-team All-Atlantic Coast Conference (ACC) in 1994.

Source: *USA Soccer 1996 Media Guide*

1995–96 USA Basketball Women's National Team
1996 U.S. Olympic Women's Basketball Team

"The Women's National Team captured the imagination of millions of fans and elevated the game to levels never before seen around the world," proclaimed USA Basketball President Russ Granik after naming the 1996 U.S. Olympic Women's Basketball Team as USA Basketball's 1996 Team of the Year.[25] The women's "Dream Team" consisted of 12 of the United States' most talented female players. Eleven members of the 1996 U.S. Olympic Women's Basketball Team—Jennifer Azzi, Ruthie Bolton, Teresa Edwards, Lisa Leslie, Rebecca Lobo, Katrina McClain, Nikki McCray, Carla McGhee, Dawn Staley, Katy Steding, and Sheryl Swoopes—began training on October 2, 1995, as the U.S. national team, and over the course of 10 months traveled more than 100,000 miles in seven countries over a 52-game schedule, posting an average victory margin of 30.8 points per game. All 11 members of the national team were selected to the 1996 Olympic team (Venus Lacey joined the team in May 1996 to round out the 12-member Olympic roster), and they continued their winning ways, culminating in an 8-0 record in Olympic tournament play to claim the gold medal for the United States at the 1996 Olympic Games in Atlanta.

While the national team kept a constant eye on the gold, they also worked toward raising the popularity of women's basketball throughout the United States. "We can go down in history as one of the best teams ever put together," Bolton told *USA Basketball News*. "We hold the key to the future of the women's game. We have a responsibility. We have a chance to make history."[26]

During its 10-month schedule, the national team amassed an impressive 60-0 record. They had the opportunity to showcase their amazing talents and to introduce

USA Basketball Women's National Team—(1st row, l–r) Tara VanDerveer, Nikki McCray, Katrina McClain, Katy Steding, Carla McGhee, Sheryl Swoopes, Nancy Darsch; (2nd row, l–r) Ceal Barry, Ruthie Bolton, Jennifer Azzi, Venus Lacey, Rebecca Lobo, Lisa Leslie, Teresa Edwards, Dawn Staley, Marcia Washington
Courtesy of Steven Freeman/USA Basketball

America to the highest level of women's basketball in the world.

The "Road to the Olympics" began with the idea of putting together a national team to provide an opportunity for America's best female basketball players to train and compete in their own country. The process began in April 1995 when Tara VanDerveer, Stanford University women's basketball coach and veteran international coach, was named the U.S. national team coach and the 1996 U.S. Olympic head coach. VanDerveer championed the national team concept from the beginning: "We've never had a team train together for a year or really had the opportunity to develop a team strategy. We've always taken great players and put them together in a short amount of time. The National Team is the best way for the United States to prepare its players to win a gold medal at the Olympic Games. It will also provide an opportunity to accentuate the athleticism and the individual skills of the players while assembling the best team possible."[27]

In May 1995, USA Basketball's Women's Player Selection Committee invited an elite group of 27 candidates to the week-long national team trials held at the U.S. Olympic Training Center in Colorado Springs, Colorado. Reading like a who's who of American women's basketball, invitees included former Olympians, such as Edwards and McClain; top Americans playing professionally in Europe, such as Azzi, Leslie, and McGhee; and several of the nation's top collegiate players, such as Lobo and McCray. The women competed in grueling two-a-day workouts staged by VanDerveer and her assistant coaches Reneé Brown and Nell Fortner.

After the team members were named, VanDerveer complimented the selection committee on their choices: "This is a very talented team that the Selection Committee has put together. We have an excellent balance of experienced international players and younger players. We have the makings of a great team here, but we also have a lot of work ahead of us."[28]

The national team began competition in November 1995 with a 20-game tour against top collegiate women's teams. In January 1996, the team started an international tour that included competition against teams from the Ukraine, China, Cuba, South Korea, Canada, and Australia. Along the way, they amassed a 52-0 record in the two tours.

Following the international tour, USA Basketball named all 11 members of the national team to the 1996 U.S. Olympic team. Venus Lacey, who had been playing with the national team since May, rounded out the 12-member Olympic roster. Alternates included Shanda Berry, Edna Campbell, Sylvia Crawley, Katie Smith, Teresa Weatherspoon, and Kara Wolters, and Coach VanDerveer named Ceal Barry, Nancy Darsch, and Marian Washington assistant coaches.

Led by team captain Teresa Edwards, appearing in her fourth Olympic Games, the U.S. team won the gold medal at the Centennial Olympics in dominating fashion. They posted victories over Cuba (101-84), Ukraine (98-65), Zaire (107-47), Australia (96-79), and South Korea (105-64) in preliminary-round play, and defeated Japan 108-93 to advance to the medal round semifinals. The U.S. defeated Australia 93-71 in the semifinal game, and dominated current world champion Brazil in the gold-medal game, winning in overwhelming fashion 111-87. Team USA outscored their opponents by an average of 28.6 points a game, and outrebounded their opponents by 15.1 boards per game. Defensively, the U.S. team allowed its opponents an average of just 73.8 points a game in the Olympic tournament.

Leslie led all scorers with an average of 19.5 points per game in the Olympic tournament. Three-time Olympian McClain followed with an average of 14.1 points per game; Swoopes averaged 13.0 points per game; and Bolton added 12.8 points per game. The gold-medal effort by the U.S. women was the United States' third in five Olympic competitions. The United States, which won the bronze medal in 1992, captured back-to-back gold medals at the 1984 and 1988 Summer Olympic Games.

The U.S. women drew crowds of over 30,000 in all six of its games played at the Georgia Dome, including a women's basketball world record attendance figure of 33,952 in the game versus Australia on July 27. The increased popularity of the game during their national tour and Olympic play made the team members definite role models for young players. "Little girls need big girls to look up to," explained Edwards. "I want little girls and even little boys to have someone to model their game after. I'm sure a little girl would like to dribble like Dawn (Staley), or shoot like Sheryl (Swoopes), or be an intimidating force like Rebecca (Lobo). That excites me incredibly."[29]

The success of the national and Olympic teams resulted in an unparalleled interest in women's basketball in the United States. Two new professional basketball leagues formed, the American Basketball League (ABL) and the Women's National Basketball Association (WNBA). No longer do U.S. players have to go overseas to play professional basketball. All 12 members of the U.S. team play in the new leagues. Young women now can look forward to a career of playing basketball in their own country, due in part to the success of the 1995-96 USA Basketball Women's National Team/1996 U.S. Olympic Women's Basketball Team.

1996 USA Olympic Women's Basketball Team

Jennifer Azzi

Azzi averaged 7.5 points per game, while shooting .510 from the field and .441 from three-point range as member of the 1995-96 USA Basketball Women's National Team. At the 1996 Atlanta Games, the 5'8" guard averaged 5.9 points per game, while shooting .667 from three-point range. At the 1994 USA Goodwill Games, she averaged 7.3 points and 2.0 rebounds per game, helping her team clinch the gold. At the 1994 Women's World Championship, she and her teammates won the bronze medal. A 1993 USA Basketball Women's National Team trials participant, she was an alternate for the 1992 U.S. Olympic Basketball Team. As a member of the 1991 Pan American Games team, she averaged 6.7 points and 1.7 assists per game, helping her team earn a bronze medal. During her four seasons (1987-90) at Stanford University, Azzi helped Stanford compile a 101-23 record, make three National Collegiate Athletic Association (NCAA) tournament appearances, and win the 1990 NCAA title. She was the 1990 recipient of the Wade Trophy and the Naismith National Player of the Year Award, and was named Kodak All-American in 1989 and 1990. She played the 1994 and 1995 seasons in Sweden and also played professionally in Italy and France. Azzi currently plays for the San Jose Lasers of the ABL.

Ruthie Bolton

As a member of the 1995-96 USA Basketball Women's National Team, 5'8" guard Bolton averaged a team second-best 13.0

points per game, while shooting .494 from the field and .380 from three-point range. At the 1996 Atlanta Games, she started all eight games and averaged 12.8 points per game while shooting .444 from the field. She also had 16 assists and 23 steals. The versatile guard won a gold medal as a member of the 1994 Goodwill Games team and a bronze medal in the 1994 world championships. She captured a gold medal as a member of the 1991 World University Games team and was selected the 1991 USA Basketball Female Athlete of the Year. She played collegiate basketball at Auburn University in Alabama. During her four years at Auburn (1986-89), she helped her team compile a 119-13 record, make four NCAA tournament appearances, and finish as the NCAA runner-up twice (1988, 1989). Bolton played professionally in Italy for three seasons. In 1991-92, she became the first U.S. woman to play professionally in Hungary. She plays for the Sacramento Monarchs of the WNBA.

Teresa Edwards

As a member of the 1995-96 USA Basketball Women's National Team, 5'11" guard Edwards averaged 6.4 points and a team-best 5.1 assists per game. By playing in Atlanta, she became the first U.S. basketball player to compete in four Olympics. She was elected by the U.S. athlete delegation to take the Athlete Oath at the 1996 Centennial Olympics. As captain of the 1996 Olympic gold-medal team, she started all eight games and led the team with assists (averaging eight per game and setting an Olympic record against Australia with 15). The standout point guard and All-American from the University of Georgia scored a total of 55 points, made 64 assists, and led the national team to its 8-0 record. Edwards was a co-captain of the 1992 Olympic team, where she was the third-leading scorer and

assist leader with 27. As a member of the 1994 world championship bronze medal team, she was named to the All-World Championship team. She also led the 1988 U.S. Olympic team to a gold medal with a field goal percentage of .611, an average of 3.4 assists and 4.6 steals per game. Edwards has also won gold medals as a member of the 1990 world championship and Goodwill Games teams, 1987 Pan American Games team, and the 1986 world championship team. She was named USA Basketball's Female Athlete of the Year in 1987 and 1990. Edwards played professionally overseas in Italy, Japan, and Spain. She is currently player/coach of the Atlanta Glory of the ABL (See more complete biographical information on p. 115.)

Venus Lacey

A resident of Ruston, Louisiana, Lacey played with the USA Basketball Women's National Team during its June 1996 three-game series against Canada, and its May 26 game versus Cuba, and the June 15 game against Russia. At the 1996 Atlanta Olympics, the 6'4" center averaged 6.6 points and 4.4 rebounds per game, while shooting .643 from the field. She was a member of the 1991 Pan American Games Team that earned a bronze medal. During her three seasons on the college level (1988–90), she helped Louisiana Tech compile a 96-7 record, make three NCAA Tournament Final Four appearances, and win the NCAA National Championship in 1988. She played professionally overseas in Japan, Italy, and Greece. She plays for the Long Beach Sting Rays of the ABL.

Lisa Leslie

As a member of the 1995-96 USA Basketball Women's National Team, 6'5" center Leslie was the team's leading scorer, averaging 17.3 points and 7.0 rebounds per game, while shooting .574 from the field. At the 1996 Atlanta Olympics, she led the team in scoring with 19.5 points per game. She was a member of the 1993 USA Women's World Championship Qualifying Team and was named the 1993 USA Basketball Female Athlete of the Year. She helped lead the U.S. Women's Basketball Team to a bronze medal at the 1994 world championships. During her four seasons (1991–94) at the University of Southern California (USC), she helped the Women of Troy compile an 89-31 record, make four NCAA tournament appearances, and win one Pac-10 conference title. She won the 1994 Broderick Award as the National Female College Basketball Player of the Year, and earned All-American honors in 1992, 1993, and 1994. Leslie played in Italy for one season (1994-95), and currently plays for the Los Angeles Sparks of the WNBA.

Rebecca Lobo

As a member of the 1995-96 USA Basketball Women's National Team, 6'4" center Lobo averaged 5.8 points and 3.7 rebounds per game. At the 1996 Olympics, she averaged 3.9 points and 2.0 rebounds per game, while shooting .579 from the field. At the University of Connecticut, she led her team to a national championship with a perfect 35-0 record for the 1994-95 season. Named the NCAA's 1995 Final Four Most Outstanding Player, Lobo led the Huskies in scoring (17.1 points per game), rebounding (9.8 per game), and blocks (3.5 per game). During her four college seasons (1992-95), Connecticut compiled a 106-25 record, made four NCAA tournament appearances, and won two Big East conference titles. She received the 1995 Wade Trophy, the 1995 and 1996 Broderick Award, and was named the U.S. Basketball Writers' Association's 1995 National Player of the Year. Her other honors include the 1994–95 Kodak All-

American first team, the 1994–95 Big East Conference Player of the Year, and the 1994-95 Big East Conference Tournament Most Outstanding Player. For all of her efforts, Lobo was named the Women's Sports Foundation 1995 Team Sportswoman of the Year and Associated Press 1995 Female Athlete of the Year. She plays for the New York Liberty of the WNBA.

Katrina McClain

As a member of the 1995-96 USA Basketball Women's National Team, 6'2" forward McClain averaged 12.5 points per game and a team-best 9.3 rebounds per game, while shooting a team-leading .635 from the field. During the 1996 Atlanta Olympics, she averaged 14.1 points and 8.3 rebounds per game, while shooting a team-high .739 from the field. McClain is one of only three three-time U.S. Olympic basketball players. She was a member of the 1992 U.S. Olympic bronze-medal-winning team and the 1988 U.S. Olympic gold-medal-winning team. She was named USA Basketball Female Athlete of the Year in 1988 and 1992. During her four seasons (1984-87) at the University of Georgia, McClain helped Georgia compile a 116-15 record, and make four NCAA tournament appearances. She was named consensus All-American in 1986 and 1987. She played professionally overseas for eight years—five seasons in Japan, one in Italy, and two in Spain. She plays for the Atlanta Glory of the ABL.

Nikki McCray

As a member of the 1995-96 USA Basketball Women's National Team, 5'11" guard McCray averaged 6.2 points and 2.3 rebounds per game. During the 1996 Atlanta Olympics, she averaged 9.4 points and 3.5 rebounds per game, while shooting 65 percent from the field. She also played for the 1993 USA Women's World Championship

Qualifying Tournament Team, averaging 4.4 points and 3.3 rebounds per game. During her four seasons (1992-95) at the University of Tennessee, McCray helped the Lady Vols compile a 122-11 record, make four NCAA tournament appearances, and win three Southeastern Conference (SEC) regular season titles. She plays for the Columbus Quest of the ABL.

Carla McGhee

As a member of the 1995-96 USA Basketball Women's National Team, 6'2" center/forward McGhee averaged 5.8 points and 4.1 rebounds per game. At the 1996 Atlanta Olympics, she averaged 3.1 points and 1.8 rebounds per game. She won a gold medal as a member of the 1994 Goodwill Games team and a bronze medal at the 1994 world championships. During her three seasons (1987, 1989-90) at the University of Tennessee, McGhee helped the Lady Vols win two NCAA national titles (1987, 1989). She played professionally overseas in Germany, Italy, Spain, and France. She plays for the Columbus Quest of the ABL.

Dawn Staley

As a member of the 1995-96 USA Basketball Women's National Team, 5'6" guard Staley averaged 5.0 points and 3.7 assists per game. She captured a gold medal with the 1994 Goodwill Games team, and a bronze medal as a member of the 1994 world championship team. USA Basketball named her the 1994 Female Athlete of the Year. During her four seasons (1989–92) at the University of Virginia, she helped Virginia to four NCAA tournament appearances, and three NCAA Final Fours (1990, 1991, 1992). A 1992 graduate of the University of Virginia, she won the Broderick Award as female collegiate basketball player of the year in 1991 and 1992, was a three-time Kodak All-American, and was a two-time U.S. Basketball Writers Association All-American. She played professionally overseas in Tarbes, France, and Segovia, Spain. She plays for the Richmond Rage of the ABL.

Katy Steding

As a member of the 1995-96 USA Basketball Women's National Team, 6'0" forward Steding averaged 6.8 points and 3.8 rebounds per game. During the 1996 Atlanta Olympics, she averaged 3.1 points and 2.4 rebounds per game. She earned a gold medal with the 1993 world championship qualifying team, and the 1991 World University Games team. During her four seasons (1987–90) at Stanford, she led the team to a NCAA title (1990) and a 101-23 overall record. She played professionally overseas in Spain and Japan. She plays for the Portland Power of the ABL.

Sheryl Swoopes

As a member of the 1995-96 USA Basketball Women's National Team, 6'0" guard/forward Swoopes averaged 12.0 points, 4.4 rebounds, and 2.4 steals per game. During the 1996 Atlanta Games, she averaged 13.0 points and 3.5 rebounds per game, while shooting .547 from the field. She earned a gold medal with the 1994 Goodwill Games team, and a bronze medal as a member of the 1994 world championship team. While at Texas Tech University, she led her team to the NCAA tournament both years she played and to the championship in 1993, scoring a record 47 points in the championship game. She won the 1993 Broderick Award and was named 1993 Player of the Year by *USA Today* and *Sports Illustrated,* and was voted the Associated Press Female Athlete of the Year. She played professionally with Basket Bari in the Italian League in

1993-94. She plays for the Houston Comets of the WNBA.

Source: *USA Basketball's 1996 Media Guide*

Further Reading

Corbett, Sara. *Venus to the Hoop: A Gold-Medal Year in Women's Basketball.* New York: Doubleday, 1997. 342 pp.

USA Softball Women's National Team

Women's fast-pitch softball made its debut at the 1996 Olympic Summer Games, and it hit an immediate home run. The Olympic dream began back in 1965 when representatives from five countries, including the United States, established the first women's world championship to be held in Melbourne, Australia. In that first world championship, the United States team won the silver medal. The U.S. team won the 1974 world championship and since that time, the USA Softball Women's National Team has been one of the most successful sports dynasties in modern history. A collection of some of the best players to ever play the game, the 1996 USA Softball Women's National Team—Laura Berg, Gillian Boxx, Sheila Cornell, Lisa Fernandez, Michele Granger, Lori Harrigan, Dionna Harris, Kim Maher, Leah O'Brien, Dot Richardson, Julie Smith, Michele Smith, Shelley Stokes, Dani Tyler, and Christa Williams—brought home the first-ever Olympic softball gold medal. "We did it for all the people who played before and are playing now," Richardson told *USA Today.* "And for those who are going to play in the future."[30]

In 1965, representatives from Canada, Japan, Australia, and the United States met

USA Softball Women's National Team—(1st row, l–r) Julie Smith, Dot Richardson, Laura Berg, Dani Tyler, Shelly Stokes, Kim Maher; (2nd row, l–r) Michele Smith, Leah O'Brien, Christa Williams, Dionna Harris, Lisa Fernandez, Gillian Boxx, Michele Granger, Lori Harrigan; (3rd row, l–r) Ronnie Isham, Ralph Raymond, Sheila Cornell, Margie Wright, Ralph Weekly
Long Photography

in Stratford, Connecticut, in an effort to create a strong international presence for women's fast-pitch softball in order to convince then Olympic Committee President Avery Brundage to add softball to the Olympic program. These representatives organized the first women's world championship tournament, but it would be 31 years before their Olympic dreams would be realized. In those 31 years, the United States established itself as the most dominant team in international competition. The United States has participated in eight world championships and five Pan American Games competitions and have brought home five gold and two silver world championship medals and four gold and silver medals from the Pan American Games. In world championship play, the United States has amassed an overall record of 74-9. Since 1986, the United States has not lost a single world championship or Pan American Games contest. Their record stands at 63-0 for this period.

The 15 players chosen for the 1996 Olympic team had the monumental task of maintaining this tradition of winning. When the International Olympic Committee (IOC) announced that softball would make its first appearance at the 1996 Summer Games, the American Softball Association (ASA) began a three-year search to find the best players to represent the United States. Over several intense months of competition, including the 1995 Pan American Games and the 1995 Olympic Festival, a select few made their way onto an elite list of finalists. In September 1995, 67 athletes met in Oklahoma City for a three-day tryout in front of a seven-member national selection committee that judged their every play. On September 4, 1995, the selection committee introduced the sport's first-ever Olympic team. "We're on the brink of becoming part of history. It's been a dream of all of us since we were little girls to play

in the Olympics for the U.S.," said Richardson. "This is a dream. We are living our dreams."[31]

The U.S. team practiced together for four months in Columbus, Georgia, then embarked on a 21-city exhibition tour to give the players a chance to play together as a unit and to give the fans around the country an opportunity to see the team in action. Team USA won 63 of the 64 exhibition games it played against various regional All-Star teams. The five-member pitching staff that included Lisa Fernandez, Michele Granger, Lori Harrigan, Michele Smith, and Christa Williams, amassed a 0.08 earned run average (ERA) over 356 innings on the pre-Olympic tour.

With the most outstanding international record over the past 10 years (110-1) coming into the Olympics, the U.S. team was favored to win the gold. Contestants in the Olympic tournament included Australia, Canada, China, Chinese Taipei, Japan, the Netherlands, Puerto Rico, and the United States. In round-robin competition, the United States went 6-1, losing only to Australia. In the semifinal game, the United States defeated China 1-0 in 10 innings, behind strong pitching from Fernandez, to earn a spot in the gold-medal game.

The U.S. team defeated China 3-1 to capture the first-ever gold medal in women's Olympic softball. A crowd of over 8,500 watched the United States win behind the strong pitching of Granger and then Fernandez, who came in relief in the sixth inning. Richardson hit a two-run home run over the right field fence and Cornell brought Maher home with a drive to centerfield in the third inning for the third and final run of the game. That was all the United States needed to win the gold medal.

It took more than 30 years to get softball into the Olympics, and its appearance was celebrated by the victorious U.S. team and fans alike. With sellout crowds of

8,500 for nearly every game, softball earned a permanent place on the Olympic roster, and the victorious 1996 USA Softball Women's National Team helped to ensure a bright outlook for their sport in future Olympics.

About the young female fans that crowded around the fences and in the stands at the Olympic softball field, Richardson told *Sports Illustrated*, "I see a look in their eyes that they will never be the same . . . that they now know they can be an Olympian and that through softball they can receive an education and actually achieve a lot of their dreams."[32]

1996 USA Softball Women's National Team

Laura Berg

Outfielder for the 1996 USA Softball Women's National Team that won the gold medal at the 1996 Atlanta Summer Olympics, Berg batted .273 with six hits and two runs scored in the Olympic tournament. A strong defensive player, she is considered one of the best outfielders in the world. She won a gold medal at the 1994 International Softball Federation (ISF) World Championships and at the 1995 Superball Classic in Columbus, Georgia. Berg was a two-time All-American at Fresno State University (1994, 1995) and won the 1994 Golden Glove Award. She hit .425 for the 1995 season and was named to the All-West, All-WAC, and All-American teams.

Gillian Boxx

Catcher for the 1996 USA Softball Women's National Team that won the gold medal at the 1996 Atlanta Summer Olympics, Boxx batted .250 with four hits and three runs batted in (RBIs) in the Olympic tournament. Boxx's debut in international com-

petition came in 1994 at the ISF World Championship, where she won a gold medal as a member of the U.S. team. A four-time National Collegiate Athletic Association (NCAA) All-American at the University of California at Berkeley, Boxx ended her college career in 1995 with a .369 batting average. She was named to the All-Pac 10 first team in 1993, 1994, and 1995.

Sheila Cornell

Starting first baseman for the 1996 USA Softball Women's National Team that won the gold medal at the 1996 Atlanta Summer Olympics, Cornell batted .393 with 11 hits, including three home runs and nine RBIs in the Olympic tournament. At the 1995 Pan American Games, Cornell led all hitters with a .581 batting average and 18 hits, including three doubles and three singles. She also played for the U.S. teams that won gold at the 1995 Superball Classic and at the 1994 South Pacific Classic in Sydney, Australia. Cornell added more gold medals to her collection when she played for the U.S. team that won the 1993 Intercontinental Cup in Holland and the 1987 and 1991 teams that won the Pan American Games. While at the University of California at Los Angeles (UCLA), she won two NCAA national titles in 1982 and 1984.

Lisa Fernandez

Pitcher for the 1996 USA Softball Women's National Team that won the gold medal at the 1996 Atlanta Summer Olympics, Fernandez posted a 0.33 ERA with 31 strikeouts in 21 innings pitched. She also batted .348 with eight hits, including one home run and five RBIs, in the Olympic tournament. She was a gold medalist at the 1990 world championships in Normal, Illinois; the 1991 Pan American Games in Cuba; the 1994 ISF World Championship in Canada; and 1995 Superball Classic in Columbus, Georgia. Named the 1993 NCAA Player of the Year, Fernandez led the University of California at Los Angeles (UCLA) to a second-place finish in the NCAA College Softball World Series. She became the first player ever to pitch two no-hitters in the tournament as well as the first to finish the season number one in both batting average and ERA. The four-time NCAA All-American led the Bruins to two NCAA titles. During her college career at UCLA, Fernandez batted .382 and broke career records for singles (225), runs scored (142), walks (65), hits (287), pitching wins (93), career winning percentage (.93), and no-hitters (11). Fernandez was named the 1994 Women's Sports Foundation's Team Sportswoman of the Year and the 1993 Honda Broderick Cup winner as the nation's top female college athlete. (See more complete biographical information on p. 122.)

Michele Granger

Pitcher for the 1996 USA Softball Women's National Team that won the gold medal at the 1996 Atlanta Summer Olympics, Granger posted a 0.87 ERA with 25 strikeouts in 16 innings pitched. In the gold-medal game against China, she struck out eight and allowed three hits in five and two-thirds innings. Granger also pitched the U.S. team to a gold medal at the 1986 and 1994 ISF World Championships, the 1991 and 1995 Pan American Games, and Superball Classic in 1995. While at the University of California at Berkeley, Granger set 20 of 22 school pitching records and six NCAA records, and was an NCAA All-American four times. She also won the Bertha Tickey Award as the most valuable pitcher at the 1986, 1987, and the 1988 American Softball Association (ASA) Women's Major Fast Pitch National Championships.

Lori Harrigan

Pitcher for the 1996 USA Softball Women's National Team that won the gold medal at the 1996 Atlanta Summer Olympics, Harrigan posted a 0.00 ERA with five strikeouts in seven innings pitched. In 1994, she led the USA Softball Women's National Team to their third consecutive ISF World Championship title by shutting out China 6-0 in the gold-medal final. She also won gold at the 1995 Pan American Games in Argentina. Harrigan played softball for the University of Nevada-Las Vegas, where she led the team to two appearances in the NCAA Women's College Softball World Series.

Dionna Harris

Outfielder for the 1996 USA Softball Women's National Team that won the gold medal at the 1996 Atlanta Summer Olympics, Harris led the team in batting with a .409 average, including nine hits and one RBI, in the Olympic tournament. She was a gold medalist at the 1993 Intercontinental Cup in Holland. She led the 1995 Women's Major Fast Pitch National Championship in batting with a .611 average and is a four-time ASA All-American. Harris played her collegiate softball at Delaware Technical and Community College and Temple University. She was the 1990 Temple University Player of the Year.

Kim Maher

Infielder for the 1996 USA Softball Women's National Team that won the gold medal at the 1996 Atlanta Summer Olympics, Maher batted .219 with seven hits, including one home run and three RBIs, in the Olympic tournament. In other international competition, she won gold medals at the 1995 Pan American Games in Argentina and the 1995 Superball Classic in Columbus, Georgia. Maher also played for the 1993, 1994, and 1995 ASA Women's Major Fast Pitch National Champions, the Redding Rebels. During her collegiate career, she played for Fresno State University, where she led the team to three NCAA Women's College Softball World Series appearances. She was named NCAA All-American in 1994.

Leah O'Brien

Outfielder for the 1996 USA Softball Women's National Team that won the gold medal at the 1996 Atlanta Summer Olympics, O'Brien batted .300 with three hits and one run scored in the Olympic tournament. She made her international debut by winning a gold medal in the 1995 Pan American Games Qualifier in Guatemala, leading the team in hitting with a .513 batting average. She also won a gold medal at the 1995 Superball Classic in Columbus, Georgia. Collegiately, she played for the three-time NCAA champion University of Arizona. She is a two-time NCAA All-American and was selected the 1996 Arizona Athlete of the Year.

Dot Richardson

Starting shortstop for the 1996 USA Softball Women's National Team that won the gold medal at the 1996 Atlanta Summer Olympics, Richardson hit the game-winning home run in the gold-medal game against China. Richardson batted .273 with nine hits, including three home runs and seven RBIs, in the Olympic tournament. Widely regarded as the best shortstop to have ever played the game, Richardson has been named to 14 ASA All-American teams and is a seven-time Erv Lind Award winner as the best defensive player in the ASA Women's Major Fast Pitch National Cham-

pionship. In international competition, Richardson has won seven gold medals, her first at the 1979 Pan American Games in San Juan, Puerto Rico. She has won gold medals at four Pan American Games (1979, 1983, 1987, 1995), and at two ISF World Championships (1986, 1994). In college, Richardson played for the University of California at Los Angeles (UCLA), where she led the team in hitting three consecutive years (1981–83). She was a four-time NCAA All-American and was selected NCAA Player of the Decade for the 1980s.

Julie Smith

Infielder for the 1996 USA Softball Women's National Team that won the gold medal at the 1996 Atlanta Summer Olympics, Smith batted .238 with five hits and one RBI in the Olympic tournament. At the 1995 Pan American Games, she batted .276 and scored eight runs, helping her team win the gold. Smith also won gold at the 1994 South Pacific Classic, the 1991 Pan American Games, and the 1987 Junior Girls' World Championship. While attending Fresno State University, Smith was named NCAA First Team All-American in 1990 and 1991, and was named to the NCAA Women's College Softball World Series All-Decade Team in 1991. In 1990–91, she was named Fresno State's Female Athlete of the Year.

Michele Smith

Pitcher for the 1996 USA Softball Women's National Team that won the gold medal at the 1996 Atlanta Summer Olympics, Smith recorded a 1.50 ERA with 23 strike outs in 14 innings pitched in the Olympic tournament. Smith also served as the designated hitter in the gold-medal game against China and finished the tournament with four hits and two RBIs. On the pre-Olympic Softball Tour she had a 12-0 pitching record, including four perfect games and three no-hitters. She is a six-time gold medalist in international competition in her six years with the USA Softball Women's National Team, including wins at the 1994 ISF World Championships, the 1995 Pan American Games, and the 1995 Superball Classic. She has never lost in international competition and has a career USA Softball ERA of 0.00. The United States Olympic Committee (USOC) honored her as its Softball Sportswoman of the Year Award three times. She was a two-time NCAA All-American while playing for Oklahoma State University, where she compiled an 82-20 pitching record with 46 shutouts and a .804 winning percentage.

Shelley Stokes

Catcher for the 1996 USA Softball Women's National Team that won the gold medal at the 1996 Atlanta Summer Olympics, Stokes batted .167 with one hit and one RBI in the Olympic tournament. One of the best defensive catchers in the game, Stokes posted a 1.000 fielding average (no errors) at the Centennial Games. She made her USA Softball debut at the 1995 Pan American Games in Argentina, where she batted .308 with four hits and four runs scored to help the U.S. team win the gold. She also won a gold medal at the 1995 Superball Classic in Columbus, Georgia. During her collegiate career, Stokes led Fresno State University to four NCAA Women's College Softball World Series appearances (1987–90).

Dani Tyler

Infielder for the 1996 USA Softball Women's National Team that won the gold medal at the 1996 Atlanta Summer Olympics, Tyler batted .167 with three hits, including a double and a triple, in the Olympic tournament. In other international competition, she won a gold medal at the 1994 Pan American Qualifier in Guatemala and at the 1995 Superball Classic in Columbus, Georgia. In her collegiate career, Tyler played for Drake University, where she batted .395 in her first three seasons. In 1994, she led the team in seven offensive categories, including hitting (.384), slugging percentage (.647), at-bats (190), hits (73), RBIs (50), doubles (16), and home runs (9).

Christa Williams

Pitcher for the 1996 USA Softball Women's National Team that won the gold medal at the 1996 Atlanta Summer Olympics, Williams posted a 0.00 ERA with 15 strikeouts in 9 2/3 innings pitched. The youngest member of the U.S. national team at age 18, Williams made her international debut at the 1995 Pan American Games Qualifier, winning a gold medal. Williams finished her Guatemala debut with a 0.00 ERA, three shutouts, and 45 strikeouts. Williams played in the 1995 ISF Junior Girls' World Championships in Normal, Illinois, where she went 6-0 and led the tournament with 86 strikeouts.

Source: *USA Softball's 1996 Media Guide*

Further Reading

Babb, Ron. *Etched in Gold: The Story of America's First Ever Olympic Gold Medal Winning Softball Team.* Grand Rapids, MI: Master's Press, 1997. 240 pp.

NOTES TO CHAPTER 4

1. Jennifer Azzi, *1995-96 USA Basketball Women's National Team Commemorative Guide,* p. 14.

2. Helen St. Aubin, "This Mother Could Hit," *People Magazine,* August 17, 1987, p. 79.

3. Anna Seaton Huntington, *Making Waves: The Inside Story of Managing and Motivating the First Women's Team to Compete for the America's Cup* (Arlington, TX: The Summit Publishing Group, 1996), p. x.

4. Huntington, p. 145.

5. "America³," Special Advertising Section, *Sports Illustrated,* p. A1.

6. Quoted in Kathleen Christie, "Silver Bullets Shoot for History," Lifetime Online Web site <http://www.lifetimetv.com/sports/SilverBullets/History/sbhist.html>, retrieved from the World Wide Web on December 23, 1996.

7. Colorado Silver Bullets 1994 Souvenir Program, p. 16.

8. Quoted in Lyn Votava, "Ahead of Their Time," *Runner's World,* June 1993, p. 54.

9. Votava, p. 52

10. Quoted in Sarah Henry, "Hey! A Little Respect, Please," *Women's Sports and Fitness,* July/August 1996, p. 75.

11. Mark McDonald, "Only the Strong Survive," *Inside Sports,* June 1996, p. 74.

12. Henry, p. 75.

13. Quoted in Laura LaMarca, "The Perfect Olympic Moment," *Synchro Swimming USA,* Summer/Fall 1996, p. 14.

14. Glenn Ruffenach, "Pumping Iron to Tread Water: Artistic Swimmers Get Tough," *Wall Street Journal,* July 25, 1996.

15. Mark Fainaru-Wada, "Americans Find Gold in Vault," ESPNET Sports Zone Web site <http://ESPNET.SportsZone.com/editors/atlanta96/sports/gym/0723women.html>, retrieved from the World Wide Web on June 13, 1997.

16. "USA Women Gymnasts After First-Ever Team Gold," *USA Today,* July 22, 1996.

17. "Coaches Say US Women's Team Strongest They've Ever Seen," *USA Today,* July 18, 1996.

18. "Miller Comes Back to Win Beam Gold," *Reuters,* July 29, 1997.

19. Nancy Kleinbaum, *The Magnificent Seven: The Authorized Story of American Gold* (New York: Bantam Books, 1996), p. 72.

20. Michael Farber, "Score One for Women," *Sports Illustrated,* August 12, 1996, p. 72.

21. Quoted in " '96 Games Were 'Women's Games,' " *USA Today,* August 4, 1997.

22. Quoted in Priscilla Williams, "Sweden '95: U.S. Women Get Ready," *Sports Illustrated for Kids,* May/June 1995, p. 23.

23. Farber, p. 72.

24. Farber, p. 75.

25. Quoted in "Women's National Team/U.S. Olympic Women's Basketball Team Named 1996 USA Basketball Team of the Year," *USA Basketball News,* December 1996, p. 12.

26. Adrian Wojnarowski, "Women's National Team Travels Globe to Sell Dream," *USA Basketball News, Pre-Olympic Issue,* 1996, pp. 8-9.

27. "A Team of Our Own," *1995-96 USA Basketball Women's National Team Commemorative Guide,* USA Basketball, pp. 9-10.

28. Quoted in "11 Named to Historic 1995-96 USA Women's National Team, *USA Basketball News,* July 1995, p. 12.

29. "A Team of Our Own," p. 11.

30. Quoted in " '96 Games Were 'Women's Games,' " *USA Today,* August 4, 1997.

31. Quoted in "Overview: Softball," NBC Sports Olympic Web site <http://www.olympics.nbc.com/sports/softball/overview.html>, retrieved from the World Wide Web on November 26, 1996.

32. Quoted in Steve Rushin, "Playing with Heart," *Sports Illustrated,* July 29, 1996, p. 56.

Part III

Basic Resources

Chapter 5
Selected Bibliography

Basketball

Beran, Janice A. *From Six-on-Six to Full Court Press: A Century of Iowa Girls' Basketball.* Ames, IA: Iowa State University Press, 1993. 227 pp.

A history of girls' basketball in Iowa including college, business, and industry teams, as well as Iowa high school teams, including six-player and five-player teams, and a listing of season scoring records.

Blais, Madeleine. *In These Girls, Hope Is a Muscle.* New York: The Atlantic Monthly Press, 1995. 264 pp.

Follows one season in the history of a high school girls' basketball team, the Lady Hurricanes of Amherst, Massachusetts, capturing the complexities of girls' experiences in high school, in sports, and in society.

Hult, Joan S., and Marianna Trekell, eds. *A Century of Women's Basketball: From Frailty to Final Four.* Reston, VA: American Alliance for Health, Physical Education, Recreation and Dance, 1991. 430 pp.

A collection of essays on the history of women's basketball in the United States, including "The Domestication of Basketball," the "Early Years of Basketball in Kentucky," and "The Legacy of AIAW."

Kelly, J. *Superstars of Women's Basketball.* New York: Chelsea House Publishers, 1997. 64 pp.

Profiles the lives and basketball careers of Ann Meyers, Nancy Lieberman-Cline, Cheryl Miller, Sheryl Swoopes, and Rebecca Lobo.

Kessler, Lauren. *Full Court Press: A Season in the Life of a Winning Basketball Team and the Women Who Made It Happen.* New York: EP Dutton, 1997. 288 pp.

A year in the life of the women's basketball team at the University of Oregon. Follows the efforts of the new head coach to mold a winning team while battling the school over noncompliance with Title IX.

Lobo, Ruthann, and Rebecca Lobo. *The Home Team: Of Mothers, Daughters, and American Champions.* New York: Kodansha, 1996. 192 pp.

Recounts collegiate basketball star Rebecca Lobo's life from her childhood to her place on the 1996 Olympic team, and tells the story of her mother's struggle with breast cancer.

Swoopes, Sheryl. *Bounce Back.* New York: Taylor Publishing Co., 1996. 48 pp.

Chronicles Swoopes's extraordinary rise to her current status as one of the best female basketball players in the world.

VanDerveer, Tara, with Joan Ryan. *Shooting from the Outside: How a Coach and Her Olympic Team Transformed Women's Basketball.* New York: Avon Books, 1997. 276 pp.

The autobiography of Tara VanDerveer, the head coach of the 1996 gold-medal-winning U.S. Women's Basketball Team. VanDerveer chronicles her life in basketball and the year-long effort to win Olympic gold.

Bodybuilding

Gaines, Charles. *Pumping Iron II: The Unprecedented Woman.* New York: Simon & Schuster, 1984. 224 pp.

A look at women's bodybuilding competition at the prestigious Caesars Cup, and the careers of athletes like Lisa Lyons, Rachel McLish, and Bev Francis.

Weider, Ben, and Robert Kennedy. *Superpump! Hardcore Women's Bodybuilding.* New York: Sterling Publishing Co., 1986. 192 pp.

Provides brief biographical sketches of 18 female bodybuilders, including how they became involved in the sport, their training regimens, and other tips for success.

Canoeing, Kayaking, and Rowing

Lewis, Linda. *Water's Edge: Women Who Push the Limits in Rowing, Kayaking & Canoeing.* Seattle, WA: Seal Press, 1992. 300 pp.

Takes the reader inside the world of competitive rowing, kayaking, and wilderness canoeing through 10 candid profiles of women who have made their mark in these sports—from pioneering rower Ernestine Bayer to Arctic distance canoer Valerie Fons.

Niemi, Judith and Barbara Wieser, eds. *Rivers Running Free: A Century of Women's Canoeing Adventures.* Seattle, WA: Seal Press, 1997. 304 pp.

An anthology of women's journals, stories, and essays in which the writers record the influence canoeing has had on their lives and the boundaries it has inspired them to push beyond. Spanning more than a century and several continents, the book includes trips through backcountry wilderness and urban wilds.

Teal, Louise. *Breaking into the Current: Boatwomen of the Grand Canyon.* Tucson: University of Arizona Press, 1994. 178 pp.

Profiles 11 of the first full-season Grand Canyon boatwomen, and includes their stories of guiding passengers down the Colorado River.

Collective Biographies

Johnson, Anne Janette. *Great Women in Sports.* Detroit, MI: Visible Ink Press, 1996. 576 pp.

Profiles the lives and achievements of 150 women athletes, with facts about the athletes, anecdotes of their childhoods, early training, and later successes in their sports.

Jones, Betty Millsaps. *Wonder Women of Sports.* New York: Random House, 1981. 69 pp.

Profiles the lives and careers of 12 athletes who have accomplished unusual feats in women's sports, such as Diana Nyad's 66-mile swim, Kitty O'Neil's role as a Hollywood stuntwoman, and Roberta Gibb Bengay's entry as the first woman in the Boston Marathon in 1966. Other athletes profiled include mountain climber Annie Peck, golfer Mickey Wright, golf and track star Babe Didrikson, tennis players Althea Gibson and Billie Jean King, gymnast Nadia Comaneci, track star Wilma Rudolph, softball player Joan Joyce, and figure skater Sonja Henie.

Layden, Joe. *Women in Sports: The Complete Book on the World's Greatest Female Athletes.* Los Angeles: General Publishing Group, 1997. 272 pp.

Offers an introduction to 250 famous female athletes, including Babe Didrikson Zaharias, Althea Gibson, Martina Navratilova, and Jackie Joyner-Kersee, who all have advanced the popularity of women's sports.

Markel, Robert, and Nancy Brooks Markel. *For the Record: Women in Sports.* New York: World Almanac Publishers, 1985. 204 pp.

Offers brief biographical sketches of more than 100 women athletes in sports from badminton to volleyball. Also presents records and a list of champions for most sports.

McMane, Fred. *Winning Women: Eight Great Athletes and Their Unbeatable Stories.* New York: Demco Media, 1995. 109 pp.

Profiles the lives and careers of Oksana Baiul, Shannon Miller, Bonnie Blair, Steffi Graf, Julie Krone, Nancy Lopez, Teresa Edwards, and Gail Devers.

Cycling

Willard, Frances Elizabeth. *Wheel Within a Wheel.* Reprint Edition. New York: Applewood Books, 1997. 96 pp.

A reprint of Willard's 1895 book in which she describes her efforts to learn to ride a bicycle and extols its benefits for other women.

Dog Sledding

Nielsen, Nicki J. *The Iditarod: Women on the Trail.* Anchorage: Wolfdog Publishers, 1986. 73 pp.

Offers a historical look at the Iditarod Sled Dog Trail race and the women who have participated in the treacherous competition.

Riddles, Libby, and Tim Jones. *Race across Alaska: First Woman to Win the Iditarod Tells Her Story.* Harrisburg, PA: Stackpole Books, 1989. 239 pp.

A day-by-day account of Libby Riddles's 18-day trek across Alaska in 1985, when she became the first woman to win the Iditarod Race. Includes numerous stories about the Iditarod Race and sled-dog racing in general.

Encyclopedias and Bibliographies

Markel, Robert, Susan Waggoner, and Marcella Smith, eds. *The Women's Sports Encyclopedia.* New York: Henry, Holt & Co., 1997. 354 pp.

One-stop reference containing a history of women's participation in over 30 sports, more than 650 biographies of international athletes, and a chronological timeline of women's sports from 500 B.C. to the present.

Oglesby, Carole, ed., with Doreen L. Greenberg, Ruth Louise Hall, Karen L. Hill, Frances Johnston, and Sheila Easterby Ridley. *Encyclopedia of Women and Sport in America.* Phoenix, AZ: The Oryx Press, 1998. 384 pp.

Focuses on the challenges and achievements of female athletes in the United States. It is an extensive collection of nearly 300 articles and biographies written by prominent experts in the field of women's sports as well as by the athletes themselves.

Remley, Mary L. *Women in Sport: An Annotated Bibliography and Resource Guide, 1900-1990.* Boston: G.K. Hall & Co., 1991. 224 pp.

A year-by-year annotated bibliography on women's sports, fitness, and physical education. Includes other sources of information, such as periodicals, sports organizations, and halls of fame.

Sherrow, Victoria. *Encyclopedia of Women and Sports.* San Diego: ABC-CLIO, Inc., 1996. 382 pp.

An alphabetical listing containing brief descriptions of more than 300 events, athletes, and organizations related to women and sports.

Shoebridge, Michele. *Women in Sport: A Select Bibliography.* New York: Mansell, 1988.

An annotated bibliography on women's sports, with citations from monographs, conference proceedings, journal articles, and books. Topics include sociological and physiological aspects of women in sport; the disabled; the aged; sports equipment; and sports medicine.

Figure Skating

Baiul, Oksana, with Heather Alexander. *Oksana: My Own Story.* New York: Random House, 1997. 46 pp.

A portrait of Olympic gold-medal-winning figure skater Oksana Baiul. Chronicles her youth as a Ukrainian orphan, the tragedies and obstacles she overcame to achieve her dreams, and her victorious accomplishments in the ice skating world.

Bezic, Sandra, with David Hayes. *The Passion to Skate: An Intimate View of Figure Skating.* Atlanta: Turner Publishing, 1996.

A view of the world of figure skating, with essays on the sport, profiles of some of the world's leading skaters, and a collection of images from top photographers.

Cohen, Joel H. *Superstars of Women's Figure Skating.* New York: Chelsea House Publishers, 1997. 64 pp.

Profiles such stars in the world of figure skating as Peggy Fleming, Dorothy Hamill, Katarina Witt, Kristi Yamaguchi, and Oksana Baiul.

Kerrigan, Nancy, with Steve Woodward. *Nancy Kerrigan: In My Own Words.* Los Angeles: Hyperion, 1996. 68 pp.

An autobiography of Kerrigan that chronicles her childhood determination, support of her family, and revelations about her skating techniques. Also includes information about the Detroit attack that left her injured and propelled her into the media spotlight.

Lipinski, Tara, with Emily Costello. *Triumph on Ice: An Autobiography.* New York: Bantam Doubleday, 1997. 128 pp.

Profiles the career of Tara Lipinski, the youngest U.S., World, and Olympic Figure Skating Champion ever.

Ryan, Joan. *Little Girls in Pretty Boxes: The Making and Breaking of Elite Gymnasts and Figure Skaters.* New York: Warner Books, 1996. 244 pp.

Documents the preponderance of abuse, eating disorders, weakened bones, and damaged psyches that are often the result of intensive training. Reveals stories of the physical and psychological abuse suffered by young girls driven to achieve Olympic medals.

Shaughnessy, Linda. *Michelle Kwan: Skating Like the Wind.* New York: Crestwood House, 1997. 64 pp.

A biography of American figure skater Michelle Kwan, who, at the age of 15, won the 1996 world championships.

Fishing

Morris, Holly. *A Different Angle: Fly Fishing Stories by Women.* Seattle, WA: Seal Press, 1995. 270 pp.

An anthology of fly-fishing memoirs with essays by women, including E. Annie Proulx, Pam Houston, Lorian Hemingway, Joan Wulff, Margot Paige, and Jennifer Smith.

General Studies

Blue, Adrianne. *Grace under Pressure: The Emergence of Women in Sport.* London: Sidgwick & Jackson, 1987. 228 pp.

An informal social history of women in sports. Includes discussions of the issues facing women in sports, including drug use and sex testing. Describes the successful careers of several well-known athletes.

Boutelier, Mary A., and Lucinda San Giovanni. *The Sporting Woman.* Champaign, IL: Human Kinetics, 1983. 306 pp.

Provides a historical, psychological, and social perspective on the role of women in sport. Focuses on theoretical as well as practical issues of women's sports experiences.

Burton, Mariah Nelson. *Are We Winning Yet? How Women Are Changing Sports and Sports Are Changing Women.* New York: Random House, 1991. 321 pp.

Explores issues in women's sports that range from the personal to the social and physiological. The author looks at how women's values are redefining sports and interviews several top female athletes, such as dog sledder Susan Butcher, auto racer Lyn St. James, and triathlete Paula Newby-Fraser.

Burton, Mariah Nelson. *The Stronger Women Get, The More Men Love Football: Sexism and the American Culture and Sports.* New York: Avon Books, 1994. 320 pp.

An in-depth look at America's male-dominated sports mania, and at the dangerous attitudes fostered behind the closed locker room door.

Cahn, Susan K. *Coming on Strong: Gender and Sexuality in Twentieth-Century Sports.* New York: Free Press, 1994. 368 pp.

Chronicles the history of women athletes who have persisted and succeeded in fashioning alternative, more positive meanings from their athletic experience.

Festle, Nancy Jo. *Playing Nice: Politics and Apologies in Women's Sports.* New York: Columbia University Press, 1996. 400 pp.

Reveals the story of public attitudes and private ambitions surrounding women's athletics in the post–World War II era, including the politics of equality, difference, identity, and self-determination that have shaped women's participation in sports.

Gerber, Ellen W., Jan Felshin, Pearl Berlin, and Waneen Wyrick. *The American Woman in Sport.* Reading, MA: Addison-Wesley Publishing Co., 1974. 573 pp.

A historical, sociological, and physiological analysis of the American woman in sports. Discusses the sportswoman in society and the biological factors of the female related to her participation in sports.

Green, Tina Sloan, Carole A. Oglesby, Alpha Alexander, and Nikki Franke. *Black Women in Sport.* Reston, VA: American Alliance for Health, Physical Education, Recreation, and Dance, 1981. 80 pp.

Focuses on Black women in sports and the problems and discrimination they have faced. Includes brief biographical sketches of 17 Black women who have achieved success in the sports world.

Hargreaves, Jennifer. *Sporting Females: Critical Issues in the History and Sociology of Women's Sport.* New York: Routledge, 1994. 332 pp.

A collection of essays on sports feminism including issues such as women in the Olympics, female exercise, and recreation and competitive sports.

Lenskyj, Helen. *Women, Sport and Sexuality.* Toronto: The Women's Press, 1986. 179 pp.

Explores the historical relationship between sport, femininity, and sexuality.

Oglesby, Carole A. *Women and Sport: From Myth to Reality.* Philadelphia: Lea and Febiger, 1978. 268 pp.

A collection of research papers that discusses a variety of subjects concerned with women and sports. A brief history of women's participation in sports is followed by chapters on sports and the female body, sports and involvement, and sports achievement.

Salter, David F. *Crashing the Old Boys' Network: The Tragedies and Triumphs of Girls and Women in Sport.* Westport, CT: Praeger Publishers, 1996. 180 pp.

An analysis of the status of women's sports in the United States from a father's point of view.

Twin, Stephanie L. *Out of the Bleachers.* Old Westbury, NY: Feminist Press, 1979. 229 pp.

An anthology of both contemporary and historical articles on women's involvement in sports. Selections include articles related to physiological aspects and social attitudes, reflections on the lives of selected sportswomen, and essays on the structure of women's sports.

Wade, Paul, and Tony Duffy. *Winning Women.* New York: Times Books, 1983. 156 pp.

A collection of colorful action photographs depicting outstanding women athletes involved in a range of sports from basketball and golf to waterskiing and windsurfing.

Golf

Blalock, Jane, and Dwayne Netland. *The Guts to Win.* New York: Simon & Schuster, 1977. 158 pp.

The autobiography of professional golfer Jane Blalock. Includes insights into life as a member of the Ladies Professional Golf Association in the 1970s and offers some helpful instructional techniques for women golfers.

Burnett, Jim. *Tee Times: On the Road with the Ladies' Professional Golf Tour.* New York: Scribner, 1997. 400 pp.

A first-hand account of life on the Ladies Professional Golf Association tour during the 1996 season, complete with competition results and details of the high-drama successes and slip-ups. Includes personal accounts of legendary golfers Nancy Lopez and JoAnne Carner.

Chambers, Marcia. *The Unplayable Lie: The Untold Story of Women and Discrimination in American Golf.* New York: Pocket Books, 1995. 228 pp.

An exposé of the extraordinary injustices that are par for the course for women at private golf clubs throughout America. Describes how the male-dominated country clubs restrict female membership, charge higher membership fees for women, limit playing times, and otherwise discriminate against women.

Crosset, Todd W. *Outsiders in the Clubhouse: The World of Women's Professional Golf.* Albany: State University of New York Press, 1995. 276 pp.

Examines the social and historical context of the Ladies Professional Golf Association. Includes player profiles.

Glenn, Rhonda. *The Illustrated History of Women's Golf.* Dallas: Taylor Publishing Co., 1991. 348 pp.

Chronicles the history of women's golf, including discussion of the battle for recognition and the hard-fought advances of women athletes. Contains more than 200 photos.

Horn, Jane. *Golf Is a Woman's Game.* New York: Adams Publishing, 1997. 256 pp.

Contends that women have a strong natural ability for golf, and identifies more than 40 myths that women have been taught about their golf swings.

Nickerson, Elinor. *Golf: A Women's History.* Jefferson, NC: McFarland & Co., Inc., 1987. 166 pp.

A general history of the role of women in the development of golf. Focuses on the evolution of the Ladies Professional Golf Association and offers brief biographical sketches of numerous influential players including Babe Didrikson, Patty Berg, Mickey Wright, and Kathy Whitworth.

Penick, Harvey. *For All Who Love the Game: Lessons and Teachings for Women.* New York: Simon & Schuster, 1995. 188 pp.

Famous golf instructor Harvey Penick blends commonsense advice with delightful storytelling designed especially for woman golfers. Offers advice for women on how they can hit the ball further, save crucial strokes around the green, and avoid the advice of well-intentioned men.

Wilner, Barry. *Superstars of Women's Golf.* New York: Chelsea House Publishers, 1997. 64 pp.

Discusses the history of women in professional golf and profiles such players as Babe Didrikson Zaharias, Nancy Lopez, Betsy King, Pat Bradley, and Patty Sheehan.

Gymnastics

Goodbody, John. *The Illustrated History of Gymnastics.* London: Stanley Paul, 1982. 144 pp.

Records the history of gymnastics with graphic descriptions and pictures. Traces the origins of the sport and its popularity in Europe and in the Olympics.

Kelly, J. *Superstars of Women's Gymnastics.* New York: Chelsea House Publishers, 1997. 64 pp.

Discusses the evolution of gymnastics competition and the role of women in the sport, highlighting the careers of Olga Korbut, Nadia Comaneci, Mary Lou Retton, and Shannon Miller.

Quiner, Krista. *Dominique Moceanu: A Gymnastics Sensation.* East Hanover, NJ: Bradford Book Co., 1997. 200 pp.

A biography of Dominique Moceanu, a member of the gold-medal-winning 1996 U.S. Olympic gymnastics team.

Quiner, Krista. *Kim Zmeskal: Determination to Win: A Biography.* East Hanover, NJ: Bradford Book Co., 1995. 200 pp.

A biography of Kim Zmeskal, the first American to win the all-around title at the world championships.

Ryan, Joan. *Little Girls in Pretty Boxes: The Making and Breaking of Elite Gymnasts and Figure Skaters.* New York: Warner Books, 1996. 244 pp.

Documents the preponderance of abuse, eating disorders, weakened bones, and damaged psyches that are often the result of intensive training. Reveals stories of the physical and psychological abuse suffered by young girls driven to achieve Olympic medals.

Simons, Minot. *Women's Gymnastics: A History 1966 to 1974.* Carmel, CA: Welwyn Publishing Co., 1995. 432 pp.

A worldwide history of gymnastics that includes all major competitions between 1966 and 1974, emphasizing the Olympics of 1968 and 1972. Includes biographies and behind-the-scenes stories.

Strug, Kerri, with John P. Lopez. *Landing on My Feet: A Diary of Dreams.* New York: Andrews and McMeel, 1997. 224 pp.

The autobiography of Kerri Strug, gold-medal winning gymnast and star of the 1996 U.S. women's gymnastics team, who captured the world's attention with her success under fire at the Atlanta Olympics.

History

Guttmann, Allen. *Women's Sports: A History.* New York: Columbia University Press, 1991. 339 pp.

A monograph that traces the history of women's sports from antiquity to the present, focusing on the role of women's athletics in a social and cultural context.

Howell, Reet, ed. *Her Story in Sport: A Historical Anthology of Women in Sports.* West Point, NY: Leisure Press, 1982. 612 pp.

A collection of 42 essays that explores the historical development of sports for women. The book is divided into three time periods: prior to 1860, 1860 to 1920, and 1920 to 1982. Other sections include essays on sports for women in higher education and articles that explore specific developments in selected sports such as basketball, baseball, rodeo, and tennis.

Macy, Sue. *Winning Ways: A Photohistory of American Women in Sports.* New York: Henry Holt & Co., 1996. 217 pp.

Chronicles the changes in the women's sports world over the past 150 years through narrative and photographs. Athletes who changed their sports and the nation's perception of female competitors are highlighted.

Mangan, J. A., and Roberta J. Park., eds. *From "Fair Sex" to Feminism: Sport & the Socialization of Women in the Industrial & Post-Industrial Eras.* London: Frank Cass, 1987. 312 pp.

A collection of essays on women, sport, and society from a cross-cultural perspective. Papers discuss Victorianism in America, England, and other Commonwealth countries.

McCrone, Kathleen E. *Playing the Game: Sport & the Physical Emancipation of English Women, 1870-1914.* Lexington, KY: University of Kentucky Press, 1988. 336 pp.

Relates the historical development of women's sports in England between 1870 and 1914. Focuses on middle-class women and their participation in sports in public schools and at private schools such as Oxbridge Women's College. Also offers a historical look at medical and scientific debate about women's sports, sports and dress reform, and literature of women in sports.

Peiss, Kathy. *Cheap Amusements: Working Women and Leisure in Turn-of-the-Century New York.* Philadelphia: Temple University Press, 1986. 255 pp.

Describes the lives and culture of young working women in New York City between 1880 and 1920. Explores the recreational habits of the working-class women and concludes with case studies on the commercialization of working-class amusements, dance halls, and amusement parks.

Sparhawk, Ruth M., Mary E. Leslie, Phyllis Turbow, and Zina Rose. *American Women in Sports, 1887-1987.* Metuchen, NJ: The Scarecrow Press, 1989. 165 pp.

Presents a year-by-year chronology of the important milestones for women in sports, both major individual achievements by women in sports over the past century and the major events that shaped women's sporting experiences.

Stanley, Gregory Kent. *The Rise and Fall of the Sportswoman: Women's Health, Fitness, and Athletics, 1860-1940.* New York: Peter Lang Publishing, 1996. 168 pp.

Examines health and fitness advice for American women in the years 1860 to 1940. Describes the factors that propelled the sportswoman to the current level of a highly visible cultural symbol.

Horseracing, Rodeo, and Equestrian

Burke, Jackie C. *Equal to the Challenge: Pioneering Women of Horse Sports.* New York: Howell Book House, 1997. 208 pp.

Chronicles the history of women in riding, and their struggle to get acceptance into the sport, including efforts to get full participation in Olympic equestrian competition.

Lecompte, Mary Lou. *Cowgirls of the Rodeo: Pioneer Professional Athletes.* Champaign, IL: University of Illinois Press, 1993. 252 pp.

Explores the lives of cowgirls of the rodeo, detailing their struggles and triumphs in this study of America's first successful professional women athletes.

Van Steenwyk, Elizabeth. *Women in Sports: Rodeo.* New York: Harvey House, 1978. 78 pp.

Presents a brief history of the development of rodeo for women; describes the events in which women compete, and profiles the lives of several young competitors involved in competitive rodeo.

Mountaineering

Allison, Stacy, with Peter Carlin. *Beyond the Limits: A Woman's Triumph on Everest.* New York: Little, Brown & Company, 1993. 282 pp.

The true story of Stacy Allison, the first American woman to reach the summit of Mount Everest.

Blum, Arlene. *Annapurna, A Woman's Place.* San Francisco: Sierra Club Books, 1980. 268 pp.

Chronicles the 1978 ascent of Annapurna by a team of American women. Includes excerpts from the diaries of the climbers.

da Silva, Rachel. *Leading Out: Women Climbers Reaching for the Top.* Seattle, WA: Seal Press, 1992. 358 pp.

An anthology of essays from more than 25 women involved in the world of climbing and mountaineering. Contains personal accounts of high ascents.

Mazel, David. *Mountaineering Women: Story by Early Climbers.* College Station, TX: Texas A&M University Press, 1994. 184 pp.

A compilation of 16 stories by female mountaineers from the 200-year history of women's climbing.

Robertson, Janet. *The Magnificent Mountain Women.* Lincoln, NE: University of Nebraska Press, 1990. 237 pp.

Describes the exploits of women mountain climbers and other recreational mountaineers in the Colorado Rockies.

Williams, Cicely. *Women on the Rope.* London: George Allan & Unwin, 1973. 240 pp.

Describes the history of women's participation in mountain climbing from the colorful accounts of nineteenth-century women climbers and the "petticoat pioneers" who climbed in long dresses and petticoats to the rugged adventures of twentieth-century climbers.

Olympics

Blue, Adrianne. *Faster, Higher, Further: Women's Triumphs and Disasters at the Olympics.* London: Virago Press, 1988. 192 pp.

Focuses on stories about women's successes in the Olympic Games, including the Benoit vs. Waitz rivalry in the 1984 women's marathon; the introduction of "killer gymnastics" by Olga Korbut, Nadia Comaneci, and Mary Lou Retton; and the influence of Babe Didrikson at the 1932 Los Angeles Games.

Connolly, Olga. *The Rings of Destiny.* New York: David McKay Co., 1968. 311 pp.

The story of the romance of Czechoslovakian discus thrower Olga Fikotova and U.S. hammer thrower Harold Connolly during the 1956 Melbourne Olympics, which culminated in their marriage after Fikotova was granted special permission by the Czechoslovakian government.

Davis, Michael. *Black American Women in Olympic Track and Field: A Complete Illustrated Reference.* Jefferson, NC: McFarland and Company, 1992. 170 pp.

A comprehensive listing of every female African American Olympic track athlete through 1992. Includes a biographical sketch of each woman.

Laklan, Carli. *Golden Girls.* New York: McGraw-Hill Book Co., 1980. 164 pp.

Presents the stories of a variety of Olympic athletes, including figure skaters Sonja Henie, Tenley Albright, Carol Heiss, Peggy Fleming, Barbara Ann Scott, and Dorothy Hamill; track stars Babe Didrikson, Fanny Blankers-Koen, Wyomia Tyus, and Willye B. White; swimmers Gertrude Ederle and Donna de Varona; gymnasts Cathy Rigby and Olga Korbut; and tennis star Helen Wills Moody.

Leder, Jane. *Grace and Glory: A Century of Women in the Olympics.* Chicago, IL: Triumph Books, 1996. 102 pp.

Arranged chronologically, this book reveals women's struggles and victories in the Olympics through profiles of outstanding Olympic athletes in both the Summer and Winter Games.

Pieroth, Doris H. *Their Day in the Sun: Women of the 1932 Olympics.* Seattle, WA: University of Washington Press, 1996. 186 pp.

A compendium of stories of female Olympic athletes of 1932, including track star Babe Didrikson, swimmer Helene Madison, and Black sprinters Tidye Pickett and Louise Stokes.

Plowden, Martha Ward. *Olympic Black Women.* New York: Pelican Publishing Co., 1995. 160 pp.

A tribute to the accomplishment of Olympic women throughout the years. Highlights the accomplishments of female Black Olympic medalists with a brief biographical outline and listing of each award won.

Sheafer, Silvia Ann. *Olympic Women, The Best in the World.* Mariposa, CA: Journal Publications, 1984. 118 pp.

Describes women's experiences in the Olympic Games from 1900 to the 1984 Winter Games in Sarajevo, Yugoslavia. Contains brief biographical sketches of many Olympic competitors and lists the gold medalists for all women's events.

Physical Education

Lee, Mabel. *Memories beyond Bloomers, 1924-1955.* Washington, DC: American Alliance for Health, Physical Education, and Recreation, 1978. 474 pp.

The second volume of Mabel Lee's memoirs, which continues the story of her professional career in physical education up to the time of her retirement in 1954. She discusses her work in various professional organizations, offers insights into the political workings of these groups and the ongoing controversies surrounding women's athletics, and relates her experiences as the first woman president of the American Physical Education Association.

Lee, Mabel. *Memories of a Bloomer Girl, 1894-1924.* Washington, DC: American Alliance for Health, Physical Education, and Recreation, 1977. 384 pp.

The first volume of Mabel Lee's memoirs, which details her early school days and entry into a career in physical education up to 1924. She discusses her experiences in promoting sports and physical education for women in the United States.

Spears, Betty. *Leading the Way: Amy Morris Homans and the Beginnings of Professional Physical Education for Women.* New York: Greenwood Press, 1986. 193 pp.

Focuses on Amy Morris Homans's work to establish one of the first physical education teacher training schools in the United States.

Skiing

Valens, E. G. *The Other Side of the Mountain.* New York: Warner Books, 1975. 285 pp.

The story of Alpine skier Jill Kinmont, an aspiring Olympic athlete whose career ended after a skiing accident left her paralyzed from the shoulders down. Focuses on her life before the accident and then on her rehabilitation and determination to become a successful teacher.

Walter, Claire. *Women in Sports: Skiing.* New York: Harvey House, 1977. 66 pp.

Presents the highlights in the ski racing careers of Barbara Ann Cochran, Annemarie Moser-Pröll, Cindy Nelson, and cross-country racer Jana Hlavaty. Introduces the new competitive event of freestyle skiing and the accomplishments of its early aficionados Suzy Chaffee, Judy Nagel, and Genia Fuller.

Soccer

Hanna, S. S. *Beyond Winning: Memoir of a Women's Soccer Coach.* Denver: University Press of Colorado, 1996.

A look at contemporary women's college sports and college life through the eyes of a women's soccer coach. Follows the formation of a women's soccer team from its early practice sessions to its last game, and comments on issues such as recruiting and participation at the varsity level.

Softball

Richardson, Dot, and Don Yaeger. *Living the Dream.* New York: Kensington Publishing, 1997. 180 pp.

Tells the life story of Dot Richardson, orthopedic surgeon and member of the 1996 USA Softball Women's National Team that won the first-ever gold medal in Olympic softball competition.

Sportswriting

Nauen, Elinor. *Diamonds Are a Girl's Best Friend: Women Writers on Baseball.* New York: Faber and Faber, 1995. 276 pp.

This collection contains essays, poems, short stories, and excerpts from novels and memoirs written by women on the subject of baseball, both as a game played by men and watched by women, and as a game played by women themselves.

Rapoport, Ron. *A Kind of Grace: A Treasury of Sportswriting by Women.* Berkeley, CA: Zenobia Press, 1994. 386 pp.

A collection of 73 articles from some of the top female sportswriters in the United States and Canada.

Sandoz, Joli, ed. *A Whole Other Ball Game: Women's Literature on Women's Sport.* New York: Noonday Press, 1997. 288 pp.

This collection contains contemporary stories, poems, novel excerpts, and essays by women athletes that explore the liberating possibilities of sports for women as well as detail the struggles of women to accept the notion that it is possible to be both a woman and an athlete without slighting either.

Tennis

Aaseng, Nathan. *Winning Women of Tennis.* Minneapolis, MN: Lerner Publishers Co., 1981. 80 pp.

Profiles the lives and careers of tennis greats Helen Wills Moody, Althea Gibson, Margaret Smith Court, Billie Jean King, Chris Evert, Evonne Goolagong, Martina Navratilova, and Tracy Austin.

Court, Margaret Smith, and George McGann. *Court on Court: A Life of Tennis.* New York: Dodd, Mead & Co., 1975. 211 pp.

The autobiography of Australian tennis great Margaret Smith Court. Describes her introduction to tennis and early years as an amateur, and then her transition to the professional tour.

Frayne, Trent. *Famous Women Tennis Players.* New York: Dodd, Mead & Co., 1979. 223 pp.

Profiles the lives and careers of tennis greats Suzanne Lenglen, Helen Wills Moody, Helen Hull Jacobs, Alice Marble, Maureen Connolly, Margaret Smith Court, Althea Gibson, Virginia Wade, Evonne Goolagong, Billie Jean King, Chris Evert, and Martina Navratilova.

Goolagong, Evonne, and Bud Collins. *Evonne! On the Move.* New York: E.P. Dutton & Co., 1975. 190 pp.

The autobiography of tennis star Evonne Goolagong. Chronicles her life as an aborigine in the Australian outback, her introduction to the sport, her early years as an amateur, and her move into the professional ranks.

Hart, Doris. *Tennis with Hart.* Philadelphia: J.B. Lippincott Co., 1955. 192 pp.

The autobiography of tennis player Doris Hart. Includes anecdotes from many of her world travels related to tennis and provides an insider's view of the Wimbledon tournament, which she won in 1951.

King, Billie Jean, with Cynthia Starr. *We Have Come a Long Way: The Story of Women's Tennis.* New York: McGraw-Hill Book Co., 1988. 208 pp.

A detailed history of the evolution of women's tennis, from the nineteenth century when Mary Outerbridge introduced the game to the United States through the 1987 women's professional season. Includes profiles of several of the game's most illustrious stars.

Lumpkin, Angela. *Women's Tennis: A Historical Documentary of the Players and Their Game.* New York: The Whitson Publishing Company, 1981. 194 pp.

Analyzes the contributions of women to the game of tennis in the United States. Describes the careers of several American players as well as the significant events in women's competitive tennis.

Schwabacher, Martin. *Superstars of Women's Tennis.* New York: Chelsea House Publishers, 1997. 64 pp.

Profiles some of the stars in the world of women's tennis, including Billie Jean King, Chris Evert, Martina Navratilova, Steffi Graf, and Monica Seles.

Shriver, Pam, Frank DeFord, and Susan B. Adams. *Passing Shots: Pam Shriver on Tour.* New York: McGraw-Hill Book Co., 1987. 223 pp.

A diary of Pam Shriver's experiences on the tennis circuit from December 1984 to December 1985. Provides insights into life as a top-ranked player in women's professional tennis.

Smith, Margaret. *The Margaret Smith Story.* London: Stanley Paul, 1965. 192 pp.

The autobiography of Australian tennis player Margaret Smith, with a description of Smith's early introduction to tennis as a child and her climb to the top of women's tennis. Also offers instructional tips for women players.

Spain, Nancy. *"Teach" Tennant.* London: Werner Laurie, 1953. 112 pp.

Describes the life and career of tennis player and coach Eleanor "Teach" Tennant. Discusses her experience as coach of tennis greats Maureen Connolly, Alice Marble, and Pauline Betz. Also offers some of her coaching techniques.

Wade, Virginia, with Jean Rafferty. *Ladies of the Court: A Century of Women at Wimbledon.* New York: Atheneum, 1984. 192 pp.

A historical overview of the women's participation in the All-England Championships at Wimbledon; highlights the most notable matches and provides biographical data for many of its winners.

Track and Field

Averbuch, Gloria. *The Woman Runner.* New York: Simon & Schuster, 1984. 223 pp.

Includes interviews with top female runners and offers tips on training for competition.

Drinkwater, Barbara L., ed. *Female Endurance Athletes.* Champaign, IL: Human Kinetics Publishers, 1986. 176 pp.

A historical overview of women's distance running along with a discussion of the psychological, nutritional, and physical issues related to long-distance running.

Henderschott, Jon. *Track's Greatest Women.* Los Altos, CA: Tafnews Press, 1987. 254 pp.

Chronicles the lives and careers of 15 superstars: from Babe Didrikson and Fanny Blankers-Koen in earlier days, to Evelyn Ashford and Heike Drechsler in the 1980s. Also presents capsule profiles of more than 100 additional greats, worldwide and American.

Sullivan, George. *Superstars of Women's Track.* New York: Dodd, Mead & Co., 1981. 129 pp.

Introduces the careers of six top female track and field athletes: Evelyn Ashford, Mary Decker, Madeline Manning, Julie Shea, Grete Waitz, and Candy Young.

Tricard, Louise Mead. *American Women's Track and Field: A History 1895 through 1980.* Jefferson, NC: MacFarland and Company, 1996. 746 pp.

A compendium of records and personality profiles of women in track and field, including the results of each of the Amateur Athletic Union (AAU) women's indoor and outdoor track and field championships from 1923–80, each Pan American Games 1955–80, and each Olympic Games 1928–80.

Wickham, Martha. *Superstars of Women's Track and Field.* New York: Chelsea House Publishers, 1997. 64 pp.

Traces the achievements of some of the top women in track and field, including Florence Griffith Joyner, Jackie Joyner-Kersee, Wilma Rudolph, Joan Benoit Samuelson, and Grete Waitz.

Volleyball

Reece, Gabrielle, with Karen Karbo. *Big Girl in the Middle.* New York: Crown Publishers, 1997. 256 pp.

The autobiography of professional beach volleyball player and TV commentator Gabrielle Reece.

Water Sports

Nyad, Diana. *Other Shores.* New York: Random House, 1978. 174 pp.

An autobiographical account of Diana Nyad's achievements as a long-distance swimmer. Details her training regimen and the preparation for her swim from Havana, Cuba, to Marathon, Florida.

Chapter 6
Directory of Organizations

The following is a directory of organizations that promote and support women's participation in a variety of sports, from archery to waterskiing. Addresses, founding dates, and descriptions of the organizations have been provided.

Archery

National Archery Association of the United States, Inc., One Olympic Plaza, Colorado Springs, CO 80909.

Founded in 1879. Promotes the sport of archery in the United States. Sanctions and conducts tournaments, and selects U.S. representatives for international competitions such as the Olympics, Pan American Games, and world championships.

National Field Archery Association, 31407 Outer I-10, Redlands, CA 92373.

Founded in 1939. Promotes national competition and educational programs in field archery events for women and men.

Badminton

United States Badminton Association, One Olympic Plaza, Colorado Springs, CO 80909.

Founded in 1936 as the American Badminton Association. Promotes national and international amateur badminton competition in the United States. Holds clinics and tournaments, and encourages development of the sport of badminton as a lifetime, recreational endeavor.

Baseball

Colorado Silver Bullets, 1575 Sheridan Rd., NE, Atlanta, GA 30324.

Formed in 1994 as the first all-women's professional baseball team to compete against men.

Ladies League Baseball, 600 W. Broadway, San Diego, CA 92101.

Founded in 1997. Established to provide women athletes access to baseball at the professional level.

National Women's Baseball Association, 4730 E. Indian School Rd., Ste. 120, Phoenix, AZ 85018.

Founded in 1985. Promotes women's baseball at the grassroots, amateur level by giving females of all ages the opportunity to play in national and regional tournaments.

Basketball

American Basketball League, 1900 Embarcadero Rd., Ste. 110, Palo Alto, CA 94303.

Founded in 1996. Organized to provide women the opportunity to play basketball at a professional level.

USA Basketball, 5465 Mark Dabling Blvd., Colorado Springs, CO 80918.

Founded in 1974 as the Amateur Basketball Association, it changed its name in 1989. Serves as the national governing body for basketball in the United States, responsible for selecting and training national teams that represent the United States in international competitions, including the

Olympics, world championships, and Pan American Games.

Women's Basketball Coaches Association,
4646 Lawrenceville Hwy., Lilburn, GA 30247.

Founded in 1981. Promotes the game of basketball by unifying coaches and interested individuals at all levels of competition. Bestows awards, offers coaching seminars, and sponsors clinics for players.

Women's National Basketball Association,
645 Fifth Ave., Olympic Tower, New York, NY 10022.

Founded in 1997. Established to provide women the opportunity to play basketball at a professional level.

Biathlon

United States Biathlon Association, 29 Church St., P.O. Box 297, Burlington, VT 05402-0297.

Founded in 1979. Acts as a governing body for the Olympic sport of biathlon in the United States. Established to recruit, train, and support athletes to compete in the Olympic Games.

Billiards

Women's Professional Billiards Association, 1411 Pierce St., Sioux City, IA 51105.

Founded in 1976. Sponsors championship professional billiards tournaments for women.

Bowling

Ladies Professional Bowlers Tour, 717 Cherryvale Blvd., Rockford, IL 61112.

Founded in 1981. Sponsors championship professional bowling tournaments for women.

USA Bowling, 5301 S. 76th St., Greendale, WI 53129.

Founded in 1986. Promotes the sport of amateur bowling in the United States. Responsible for selecting and training bowlers for international competition.

Women's All-Star Association, 29 Garey Dr., Chappaqua, NY 10514.

Founded in 1971. Sponsors and sanctions amateur bowling tournaments for women ages 17 and older.

Women's International Bowling Congress, 5301 S. 76th St., Greendale, WI 53129.

Founded in 1916. Acts as a governing body for women's bowling in the United States, Canada, and several other countries. Determines rules for league and tournament competition; develops programs to increase interest and bowling skills among women; and conducts the WIBC Championship Tournament.

Boxing

Women's International Boxing Federation, 2640 Hollywood Blvd., Ste. 101, Hollywood, FL 33020.

Founded in 1993. Sponsors and sanctions boxing tournaments for women.

Camping, Fishing, and Mountaineering

Bass'n Gal, P.O. Box 13925, 2007 Roosevelt, Arlington, TX 76013.

Founded in 1976. Promotes fishing for women and encourages the preservation of the environment. Sponsors tournaments and educational programs to introduce the youth of America to the wonders of fishing.

Camping Women, 625 W. Cornell Ave., Fresno, CA 93705.

Founded in 1976. Promotes outdoor activities to develop camping abilities and a comfortable feeling for women in the out-of-doors.

International Women's Fishing Association, P.O. Drawer 3125, Palm Beach, FL 33480.

Founded in 1955. Promotes women's participation in angling competition of all kinds.

Woodswomen, 25 W. Diamond Lake Rd., Minneapolis, MN 55419.

Founded in 1977. Promotes a variety of outdoor activities for women, including mountaineering, backpacking, and canoeing. Sponsors educational programs, conducts wilderness trips, and offers supportive and challenging learning opportunities for women within the context of safe, enjoyable outdoor and wilderness travel experiences.

Canoeing and Kayaking

United States Canoe and Kayak Team, Inc., Pan American Plaza, 201 S. Capitol Ave., Indianapolis, IN 46225.

Founded in 1979. Acts as a governing body for canoeing and kayaking in the United States. Established to recruit, train, and support athletes to compete in the Olympic Games in flatwater sprint and whitewater slalom canoe/kayak racing. Also sponsors educational programs that promote water safety.

Croquet

United States Croquet Association, 500 Avenue of Champions, Palm Beach Gardens, FL 33418.

Founded in 1976. Promotes the sport of croquet in the United States. Sponsors district, regional, state, and national championships.

Curling

United States Curling Association, 1100 Centerpoint Dr., Stevens Point, WI 54481.

Founded in 1958. Promotes and organizes curling activities in the United States. Sanctions local, state, and national competitions, and trains curling coaches, officials, and instructors.

United States Women's Curling Association, N25 W27798 Highway SS, Pewaukee, WI 53072.

Founded in 1947. Promotes the game of curling among women throughout the United States by cultivating friendly relations among its member clubs; preserving the traditions and literature of the game; conducting the annual USWCA national bonspiel and the USWCA senior bonspiel; and providing the rules and regulations of the game of curling.

Cycling

United States Cycling Federation, One Olympic Plaza, Colorado Springs, CO 80909.

Founded in 1921. Governs amateur cycling in the United States and sanctions all bicycling competition, including road, track, and mountain bike races. Sponsors national championships.

Women's Mountain Bike & Tea Society (WOMBATS), P.O. Box 757, Fairfax, CA 94978.

Founded in 1984. Promotes the sport of mountain biking for women by offering a women's off-road cycling network so members can find riding partners, encouraging women to try cycling for the fun of it, and improving their cycling skills.

Disabled in Sports

American Athletic Association for the Deaf, 1134 Davenport Dr., Burton, MI 48529.

Founded in 1945. Promotes athletic competition and recreational sports for the deaf and sponsors the World Games for the Deaf.

National Foundation of Wheelchair Tennis, 940 Calle Amanecer, Ste. B, San Clemente, CA 92672.

Founded in 1980. Sponsors clinics and wheelchair tennis tournaments; promotes wheelchair tennis for the disabled.

National Handicapped Sports, 451 Hungerford Dr., Ste. 100, Rockville, MD 20850.

Founded in 1967. Promotes sports and recreational opportunities for individuals with visual and mobility handicaps. Conducts national clinics for teaching adaptive sports activities.

National Wheelchair Athletic Association, 3595 E. Fountain Blvd., Ste. 2-1, Colorado Springs, CO 80910.

Founded in 1957. Promotes the participation of individuals with impaired mobility in team and individual sports. Conducts regional competitions for women and men in wheelchair sports, and sponsors the annual National Wheelchair Games.

Special Olympics International, 1350 New York Ave., N.W., Ste. 500, Washington, DC 20005.

Founded in 1968. Promotes athletic competition, physical fitness, and sports participation for mentally retarded persons. Conducts Special Olympics competitions all over the world.

United States Association for Blind Athletes, 33 N. Institute, Brown Hall #015, Colorado Springs, CO 80903.

Founded in 1976. Promotes independence for the visually impaired through athletic participation; sponsors regional and national competition in a variety of sports.

Wheelchair Sports, USA, 3595 E. Fountain Blvd., Ste. L-1, Colorado Springs, CO 80910.

Founded in 1955. Provides opportunities for individuals with impaired mobility as a result of a permanent, lower extremity disability to compete in team and individual sports at local, regional, national, and international levels. WSUSA governs 12 sports: archery, athletics (track & field), basketball, fencing, quad rugby, racquetball, shooting, sled hockey, swimming, table tennis, waterskiing, and weightlifting.

Fencing

United States Fencing Association, One Olympic Plaza, Colorado Springs, CO 80909.

Founded in 1893. Promotes growth and development of fencing in the United States. Selects members of the U.S. Olympic Fencing Team.

Field Hockey

United States Field Hockey Association, One Olympic Plaza, Colorado Springs, CO 80909.

Founded in 1921. Governs women's field hockey in the United States and sponsors national tournaments.

Figure Skating

United States Figure Skating Association, 20 First St., Colorado Springs, CO 80906.

Founded in 1921. Governs the sport of amateur figure skating in the United States.

Golf

Ladies Professional Golf Association, 100 International Golf Dr., Daytona Beach, FL 32124.

Founded in 1949. Chartered in 1950. Sponsors championship professional golf tournaments for women. Maintains members' statistics on money winnings and tournament championships.

Gymnastics

USA Gymnastics, Pan American Plaza, 201 S. Capitol Ave., Ste. 300, Indianapolis, IN 46225.

Founded in 1963. Governs amateur gymnastics in the United States; conducts and sanctions national competitions.

Horseracing, Rodeo, and Equestrian

Professional Rodeo Cowboys Association, 101 Pro Rodeo Dr., Colorado Springs, CO 80919.

Founded in 1945 as the Cowboy's Turtle Association; became the Professional Rodeo Cowboys Association in 1975. Sanctions professional rodeos including the National Finals Rodeo.

United States Equestrian Team, Inc., Pottersville Rd., Gladstone, NJ 07934.

Founded in 1950. Responsible for selecting and training equestrians for international competition.

Women's Professional Rodeo Association, 1235 Lake Plaza Dr., Ste. 134, Colorado Springs, CO 80906.

Founded in 1948. Promotes the participation of women in rodeo events. Sanctions rodeo events for women and sponsors clinics on horseback-riding skills.

Lacrosse

The Lacrosse Foundation and Hall of Fame Museum, 113 W. University Pkwy., Baltimore, MD 21210.

Founded in 1959. Dedicated to the promotion and development of lacrosse throughout the United States and abroad. Maintains the world's most complete resource center of lacrosse information and memorabilia.

United States Women's Lacrosse Association, P.O. Box 2178, Amherst, MA 01004.

Founded in 1931. Promotes women's participation in lacrosse. Establishes rules for competition and sponsors an annual national tournament.

Luge

United States Luge Association, P.O. Box 651, Lake Placid, NY 12946.

Founded in 1979. Promotes the development of the sport of luge in the United States. Selects, prepares, and trains the U.S. National Luge Team for international and Olympic competition.

Martial Arts

National Women's Martial Arts Federation, 1377 Studer Ave., Columbus, OH 43206.

Founded in 1972. Encourages women's participation in the martial arts; sponsors competitions and conducts workshops and training camps to develop skills.

United States Judo Association, P.O. Box 10013, El Paso, TX 79991.

Founded in 1954. Promotes participation in competitive and recreational judo. Responsible for selecting and training athletes for international competitions including the Olympics.

United States Taekwondo Union, One Olympic Plaza, Colorado Springs, CO 80909.

Founded in 1974. Responsible for selecting and training athletes for international competitions including the Olympics.

Motor Sports

Motormaids, Inc., P.O. Box 443, Chardon, OH 44204.

Founded in 1941. Promotes motorcycling activities for women.

Women's International Motorcycle Association, 360 E. Main St., Waterloo, NY 13165.

Founded in 1950. Promotes women's motorcycle racing.

National Multisports Organizations

Amateur Athletic Foundation of Los Angeles, 2141 W. Adams Blvd., Los Angeles, CA 90018.

Founded in 1984. Sponsors youth athletic programs in Los Angeles and around the country.

Amateur Athletic Union (AAU), P.O. Box 10000, Lake Buena Vista, FL 32821.

Founded in 1888. Sponsors Junior Olympics, Chrysler Fund/AAU Physical Fitness Program, and senior sports programs.

National Association for Girls and Women in Sport (NAGWS), 1900 Association Dr., Reston, VA 22091.

Founded in 1899. Supports and promotes quality sports programs for girls and women.

National Association of Intercollegiate Athletics (NAIA), 6120 S. Yale, Ste. 1450, Tulsa, OK 74136.

Founded in 1940. Develops rules and standards for intercollegiate competition and sponsors national women's and men's championships for member schools.

National Collegiate Athletic Association (NCAA), 6201 College Blvd., Overland Park, KS 66211.

Founded in 1905. Establishes rules governing all sports competition for college women and men, and sanctions national championships for member schools.

Women's Sports Foundation (WSF), Eisenhower Park, East Meadow, NY 11554.

Founded in 1974. Promotes women's participation in all sports activities, conducts educational seminars, and presents awards for outstanding achievements in women's sports.

Racquetball

United States Racquetball Association, One Olympic Plaza, Colorado Springs, CO 80909.

Founded in 1968. Promotes the development of competitive and recreational racquetball in the United States.

Women's Professional Racquetball Association, 6586 Ambrosia Dr., #5303, San Diego, CA 92124.

Founded in 1979. Provides opportunities for women to compete at the elite level in racquetball. Sponsors professional racquetball tournaments for women and supervises all sanctioned tournaments in the United States.

Roller Skating

United States Amateur Confederation of Roller Skating, 4730 South St., P.O. Box 6579, Lincoln, NE 68506.

Founded in 1937. Serves as the national governing body for the sport of roller skating. Sponsors training camps; sanctions artistic, hockey, and speed competitions in the United States.

Rowing

United States Rowing Association, Pan American Plaza, 201 S. Capitol Ave., Ste. 400, Indianapolis, IN 46225.

Founded in 1872. Promotes amateur rowing in the United States; establishes rules and regulations; and sanctions women's, men's, and master's championship regattas. Selects U.S. representatives to the world championships and the Olympic and Pan American Games.

Sailing

International Women's Boardsailing Association, P.O. Box 44549, Washington, DC 20026.

Founded in 1982. Promotes competitive boardsailing for women at both the amateur and the professional ranks.

National Women's Sailing Association, 16731 McGregor Blvd., Ft. Myers, FL 33908.

Founded in 1994. Promotes and encourages women of all ages to participate in sailing by developing educational programs, acting as a clearinghouse of information for women who sail, and supporting individuals and organizations that involve women in sailing.

United States Sailing Association, P.O. Box 1260, Portsmouth, RI 02871.

Founded in 1974 as the United States Yacht Racing Union. Changed name to the United States Sailing Association in 1991. Promotes the sport of sailing and yachting in the United States.

Shooting

United States Shooting Team, One Olympic Plaza, Colorado Springs, CO 80909.

Founded in 1979. Governs the sport of Olympic-style shooting and is responsible for training and selecting athletes to represent the United States at the Olympics, World Shooting Championships, and Pan American Games.

Skiing and Snowboarding

United States Ski and Snowboard Association, 1500 Kearns Blvd., Highway 248, Bldg. E/F, Ste. F200, Park City, UT 84060.

Founded in 1904. Governs skiing and snowboarding in the United States. Sponsors competition at regional, national, and international levels in Nordic, Alpine, and freestyle skiing, and snowboarding.

Skydiving and Hang Gliding

United States Hang Gliding Association, P.O. Box 1330, Colorado Springs, CO 80901.

Founded in 1971. Promotes the sport of hang gliding. Sanctions competitions and conducts training and safety clinics.

United States Parachute Association, 1440 Duke St., Alexandria, VA 22314.

Founded in 1957. Promotes the sport of skydiving by encouraging competition and by conducting training and safety clinics.

Soccer

United States Soccer Federation, US Soccer House, 1801-1811 S. Prairie Ave., Chicago, IL 60616.

Founded in 1913. Establishes rules and regulations, and governs the sport of soccer in the United States. Conducts clinics and competitions including the National Women's Amateur Cup.

Softball

Amateur Softball Association, 2801 N.E. 50th St., Oklahoma City, OK 73111.

Founded in 1933. Develops and promotes amateur softball throughout the United States.

Speed Skating

Amateur Skating Union of the United States, 1033 Shady Ln., Glen Ellyn, IL 60137.

Founded in 1928. Promotes amateur ice skating—long and short track speed skating—in the United States.

United States Speed Skating Association, P.O. Box 16157, Rocky River, OH 44116.

Founded in 1966. Responsible for selecting and preparing teams that represent the United States in international competition.

Swimming and Diving

United States Diving, Pan American Plaza, 201 S. Capitol Ave., Ste. 430, Indianapolis, IN 46225.

Founded in 1977. Promotes the growth and development of diving in the United States.

United States Swimming, One Olympic Plaza, Colorado Springs, CO 80909.

Founded in 1978. Promotes the development of the sport of swimming in the United States.

Synchronized Swimming

United States Synchronized Swimming, Inc., Pan American Plaza, 201 S. Capitol Ave., Ste. 510, Indianapolis, IN 46225.

Founded in 1980. Sanctions synchronized swimming competition and conducts educational programs for officials, swimmers, and coaches. Selects U.S. representatives for international competitions such as the Olympics, Pan American Games, and world championships.

Table Tennis

United States Table Tennis Association, One Olympic Plaza, Colorado Springs, CO 80909.

Founded in 1933. Promotes the development of table tennis in the United States. Establishes rules and regulations and sponsors national championships.

Team Handball

United States Team Handball Federation, One Olympic Plaza, Colorado Springs, CO 80909.

Founded in 1959. Promotes team handball in the United States by sponsoring competition, training, and participation at the state and local levels.

Tennis and Squash

American Platform Tennis Association, P.O. Box 901, Upper Montclair, NY 07043.

Founded in 1931. Promotes the game of platform tennis in the United States.

Black Tennis and Sports Foundation, 1893 Amsterdam Ave., New York, NY 10032.

Founded in 1977. Provides support and resources for Black and minority youth through organized tennis teams, including the annual Arthur Ashe/Althea Gibson Tennis Classic.

Maureen Connolly Brinker Tennis Foundation, P.O. Box 7065, Dallas, TX 75209.

Founded in 1968. Promotes the development and training of young people with talent and the desire to become outstanding players by sponsoring tournaments, bestowing awards, and providing financial support.

United States Squash Racquets Association Inc., P.O. Box 1216, Bala-Cynwyd, PA 19004.

Founded in 1928. Acts as the national governing body of the sport of squash in the United States. Establishes rules and regulations and sponsors national championships.

United States Tennis Association, 70 West Oak Ln., White Plains, NY 10604.

Founded in 1881. Promotes amateur tennis, establishes and maintains the rules of play, and sanctions tournaments.

Women's Tennis Association, 1266 East Main St., Stamford, CT 06902.

Founded in 1973. The organization of female tennis professionals formed to negotiate for better prize money and sponsorship.

Track & Field

American Running and Fitness Association, 4405 E. West Hwy., Ste. 405, Bethesda, MD 20814.

Founded in 1968. Encourages running and other aerobic fitness activities, and provides information about fitness and running.

Road Runners Club of America, 1150 S. Washington St., Alexandria, VA 22314.

Founded in 1958. Promotes grassroots running through more than 400 chapter clubs around the United States. Provides coordinated national communication, education programs, and services for its clubs.

USA Track & Field, Pan American Plaza, 201 S. Capitol Ave., Ste. 140, Indianapolis, IN 46225.

Founded in 1979. Governs track and field, road racing, and race walking in the United States. Conducts training and development programs and sanctions amateur competitions.

Triathlon

USA Triathlon, 3595 E. Fountain Blvd., Ste. F-1, Colorado Springs, CO 80910.

Founded in 1982 as the United States Triathlon Association. It changed its name in January 1996. Acts as the national governing body for the sports of triathlon and duathlon.

Volleyball

United States Volleyball Association, 3595 E. Fountain Blvd., Colorado Springs, CO 80910-1740.

Founded in 1928. Sanctions and conducts amateur volleyball competitions throughout the United States. Serves as the national governing body for U.S. volleyball.

Women's Professional Volleyball Association, 840 Apollo, Ste. 205, El Segundo, CA 90245.

Founded in 1986. Promotes professional beach volleyball for women and sanctions tournaments around the United States.

Waterskiing

American Water Ski Association, P.O. Box 191, Winter Haven, FL 33882.

Founded in 1939. Promotes recreational and competitive waterskiing in the United States, and establishes rules for competition.

Part IV

Appendixes

Appendix A
Olympic Gold Medalists*

Olympic Summer Games

Archery, Individual

1972	Doreen Wilbur, USA
1976	Luann Ryon, USA
1980	Keto Losaberidze, SOV
1984	Hyang-Soon Seo, KOR
1988	Seo-Nyung Kim, KOR
1992	Cho Youn-jeon, KOR
1996	Kim Kyung-wook, KOR

Archery, Team

1988	South Korea
1992	South Korea
1996	South Korea

Archery, Double Columbia Round (discontinued)

1904	Lida Howell, USA

Archery, Double National Round (discontinued)

1904	Lida Howell, USA

Archery, National Round (discontinued)

1908	Sybil Newall, GBR

Badminton, Singles

1992	Susi Susanti, ITA
1996	Bang Soo Hyun, KOR

Badminton, Doubles

1992	Hwang Hye-young, Chung So-young, KOR
1996	Ge Fei, Gu Jun, CHN

Badminton, Mixed Doubles

1996	Kim Dong-mon, Gil Young-ah, KOR

Basketball

1976	Soviet Union
1980	Soviet Union
1984	United States
1988	United States
1992	Soviet Union
1996	United States

Beach Volleyball

1996	Sandra Pires, Jackie Silva, BRA

Canoeing, Kayak Singles, 500 Meters

1948	Karen Hoff, DEN
1952	Sylvi Saimo, FIN
1956	Yelisaveta Dementyeva, SOV
1960	Antonina Seredina, SOV
1964	Lyudmila Khvedosyuk, SOV
1968	Lyudmila Khvedosyuk Pinayeva, SOV
1972	Yulia Ryabchinskaya, SOV
1976	Carola Zirzow, GDR
1980	Birgit Fischer, GDR
1984	Agneta Andersson, SWE
1988	Vania Guecheva, BUL

*A list of nation abbreviations follows this section.

1992 Birgit Schmidt, GER
1996 Rita Koban, HUN

Canoeing, Kayak Pairs, 500 Meters

1960 Maria Chubina, Antonina Seredina, SOV
1964 Roswitha Esser, Annemarie Zimmermann, GER
1968 Roswitha Esser, Annemarie Zimmermann, FRG
1972 Lyudmila Pinayeva, Ekaterina Kuryshko, SOV
1976 Nina Gopova, Galina Kreft, SOV
1980 Carsta Genauss, Martina Bischof, GDR
1984 Agneta Andersson, Anna Olsson, SWE
1988 Birgit Schmidt, Anke Nothnagel, GDR
1992 Ramona Portwich, Anke von Seck, GER
1996 Agneta Andersson, Susanne Gunnarsson, SWE

Canoeing, Kayak Fours, 500 Meters

1984 Romania
1988 East Germany
1992 Hungary
1996 Germany

Canoeing, Kayak Slalom Singles

1972 Angelika Bahmann, GDR
1996 Stepanka Hilgertova, CZE

Cycling, 1,000-Meter Sprint

1988 Erika Saloumae, SOV
1992 Erika Saloumae, EST
1996 Felicia Ballanger, FRA

Cycling, 3,000-Meter Individual Pursuit

1992 Petra Rossner, GER
1996 Antonella Bellutti, ITA

Cycling, Cross-Country Race

1996 Paola Pezzo, ITA

Cycling, Points Race

1996 Nathalie Lancien, FRA

Cycling, Road Race

1984 Connie Carpenter-Phinney, USA
1988 Monique Knol, HOL
1992 Kathryn Witt, AUS
1996 Jeannie Longo-Ciprelli, FRA

Cycling, Road Time Trial

1996 Zulfiya Zabirova, RUS

Diving, Platform

1912 Greta Johansson, SWE
1920 Stefani Fryland-Clausen, DEN
1924 Caroline Smith, USA
1928 Elizabeth Becker Pinkston, USA
1932 Dorothy Poynton, USA
1936 Dorothy Poynton Hill, USA
1948 Victoria Draves, USA
1952 Patricia McCormick, USA
1956 Patricia McCormick, USA
1960 Ingrid Krämer, GER
1964 Lesley Bush, USA
1968 Milena Duchková, CZE
1972 Ulrika Knape, SWE
1976 Elena Vaytsekhovskaya, SOV
1980 Martina Jäschke, GDR
1984 Zhou Jihong, CHN
1988 Xu Yanmei, CHN
1992 Fu Mingxia, CHN
1996 Fu Mingxia, CHN

Diving, Springboard

1920 Aileen Riggin, USA
1924 Elizabeth Becker, USA
1928 Helen Meany, USA
1932 Georgia Coleman, USA
1936 Marjorie Gestring, USA
1948 Victoria Draves, USA
1952 Patricia McCormick, USA
1956 Patricia McCormick, USA
1960 Ingrid Krämer, GER
1964 Ingrid Engel-Krämer, GER
1968 Sue Gossick, USA
1972 Micki King, USA
1976 Jennifer Chandler, USA
1980 Irina Kalinina, SOV
1984 Sylvie Bernier, CAN
1988 Gao Min, CHN
1992 Gao Min, CHN
1996 Fu Mingxia, CHN

Fencing, Épée, Individual

1996 Laura Flessel, FRA

Fencing, Épée, Team

1996 France

Fencing, Foil, Individual

1924 Ellen Osiier, DEN
1928 Helene Mayer, GER
1932 Ellen Preis, AUT
1936 Ilona Schacherer-Elek, HUN
1948 Ilona Elek, HUN
1952 Irene Camber, ITA
1956 Gillian Sheen, GBR
1960 Heidi Schmid, GER
1964 Ildikó Ujlaki-Rejtö, HUN

1968	Yelena Novikova, SOV
1972	Antonella Ragno-Lonzi, ITA
1976	Ildikó Schwarczenberger, HUN
1980	Pascale Trinquet, FRA
1984	Luan Jujie, CHN
1988	Anja Fichtel, FRG
1992	Giovanna Trillini, ITA
1996	Laura Badea, ROM

Fencing, Foil, Team

1960	Soviet Union
1964	Hungary
1968	Soviet Union
1972	Soviet Union
1976	Soviet Union
1980	France
1984	West Germany
1988	West Germany
1992	Italy
1996	Italy

Field Hockey

1980	Zimbabwe
1984	Holland
1988	Australia
1992	Spain
1996	Australia

Golf (discontinued)

1900	Margaret Abbott, USA

Gymnastics, All-Around

1952	Maria Gorokhovskaya, SOV
1956	Larissa Latynina, SOV
1960	Larissa Latynina, SOV
1964	Vera Cáslavská, CZE
1968	Vera Cáslavská, CZE
1972	Lyudmila Tourischeva, SOV
1976	Nadia Comaneci, ROM
1980	Yelena Davydova, SOV
1984	Mary Lou Retton, USA
1988	Elena Chouchounova, SOV
1992	Tatyana Gutsu, UKR
1996	Lilia Podkopayeva, UKR

Gymnastics, Balance Beam

1952	Nina Bocharova, SOV
1956	Ágnes Keleti, HUN
1960	Eva Bosáková, CZE
1964	Vera Cáslavská, CZE
1968	Natalya Kuchinskaya, SOV
1972	Olga Korbut, SOV
1976	Nadia Comaneci, ROM
1980	Nadia Comaneci, ROM
1984	Simona Pauca, ROM
1988	Daniela Silivas, ROM

1992	Tatyana Lysenko, UKR
1996	Shannon Miller, USA

Gymnastics, Floor Exercises

1952	Ágnes Keleti, HUN
1956	Ágnes Keleti, HUN
1960	Larissa Latynina, SOV
1964	Larissa Latynina, SOV
1968	Vera Cáslavská, CZE
1972	Olga Korbut, SOV
1976	Nelli Kim, SOV
1980	Nadia Comaneci, ROM
1984	Ecaterina Szabó, ROM
1988	Daniela Silivas, ROM
1992	Lavinia Milosovici, ROM
1996	Lilia Podkopayeva, UKR

Gymnastics, Team Combined

1928	Holland
1936	Germany
1948	Czechoslovakia
1952	Soviet Union
1956	Soviet Union
1960	Soviet Union
1964	Soviet Union
1968	Soviet Union
1972	Soviet Union
1976	Soviet Union
1980	Soviet Union
1984	Romania
1988	Soviet Union
1992	Unified Team
1996	United States

Gymnastics, Uneven Parallel Bars

1952	Margit Korondi, HUN
1956	Ágnes Keleti, HUN
1960	Polina Astakhova, SOV
1964	Polina Astakhova, SOV
1968	Vera Cáslavská, CZE
1972	Karin Janz, GDR
1976	Nadia Comaneci, ROM
1980	Maxi Gnauck, GDR
1984	Ma Yanhong, CHN
1988	Daniela Silivas, ROM
1992	Lu Li, CHN
1996	Svetlana Chorkina, RUS

Gymnastics, Vault

1952	Yekaterina Kalinchuk, SOV
1956	Larissa Latynina, SOV
1960	Margaita Nikolayeva, SOV
1964	Vera Cáslavská, CZE
1968	Vera Cáslavská, CZE
1972	Karin Janz, GDR
1976	Nelli Kim, SOV
1980	Natalya Shaposhnikova, SOV

1984	Ecaterina Szabó, ROM
1988	Svetlana Boguinskaia, SOV
1992	Lavinia Milosovici, ROM
1996	Simona Amanar, ROM

Gymnastics, Rhythmic, All-Around

1984	Lori Fung, CAN
1988	Marina Lobatch, SOV
1992	Oleksandra Tymoshenko, UKR
1996	Ekaterina Serebryanskaya, UKR

Gymnastics, Rhythmic, Team

1996	Spain

Handball, Team

1976	Soviet Union
1980	Soviet Union
1984	Yugoslavia
1988	South Korea
1992	South Korea
1996	Denmark

Judo, Extra Lightweight

1992	Cecile Nowak, FRA
1996	Kye Sun, PRK

Judo, Half Lightweight

1992	Almudena Muñoz Martinez, SPA
1996	Marie-Claire Restoux, FRA

Judo, Lightweight

1992	Miriam Blasco Soto, SPA
1996	Driulis Gonzalez, CUB

Judo, Half Middleweight

1992	Catherine Fleury, FRA
1996	Yuko Emoto, JPN

Judo, Middleweight

1992	Odalys Reve Jimenez, CUB
1996	Cho Min-sun, KOR

Judo, Half Heavyweight

1992	Kim Mi-jung, KOR
1996	Ulla Werbrouck, BEL

Judo, Heavyweight

1992	Zhuang Xiaoyan, CHN
1996	Sun Fuming, CHN

Rowing, Single Sculls

1976	Christine Scheiblich, GDR
1980	Sanda Toma, ROM
1984	Valeria Racila, ROM
1988	Jutta Behrendt, GDR
1992	Elisabeth Lipa, ROM
1996	Yekaterina Khodotovich, BLR

Rowing, Lightweight Double Sculls

1996	Constanta Burcica, Camelia Macoviciuc, ROM

Rowing, Double Sculls

1976	Svetla Otsetova, Zdravka Yordanova, BUL
1980	Yelena Khloptseva, Larissa Popova, SOV
1984	Marioara Popescu, Elisabeta Oleniuc, ROM
1988	Birgit Peter, Martina Schroeter, GDR
1992	Kerstin Koppen, Kathrin Boron, GER
1996	Marnie McBean, Kathleen Heddle, CAN

Rowing, Quadruple Sculls with Coxswain

1976	East Germany
1980	East Germany
1984	Romania
1988	East Germany
1992	Germany
1996	Germany

Rowing, Pairs without Coxswain

1976	Siika Kelbecheva, Stoyanka Grouicheva, BUL
1980	Ute Steindorf, Cornelia Klier, GDR
1984	Rodica Arba, Elena Horvat, ROM
1988	Rodica Arba, Olga Homeghi, ROM
1992	Marnie McBean, Kathleen Heddle, CAN
1996	Megan Still, Kate Slatter, AUS

Rowing, Fours with Coxswain

1976	East Germany
1980	East Germany
1984	Romania
1988	East Germany

Rowing, Eights

1976	East Germany
1980	East Germany
1984	United States
1988	East Germany
1992	Canada
1996	Romania

Shooting, Air Pistol

1988	Jasna Sekaric, YUG
1992	Marina Logvinenko, RUS
1996	Olga Klochneva, RUS

Shooting, Air Rifle

1984	Pat Spurgin, USA
1988	Irina Chilova, SOV
1992	Yeo Kab-soon, KOR
1996	Renata Mauer, POL

Shooting, Small-Bore Rifle, Three Positions

1984	Wu Xiaoxuan, CHN
1988	Silvia Sperber, FRG
1992	Launi Meili, USA
1996	Aleksandra Ivosev, YUG

Shooting, Sport Pistol

1984	Linda Thom, CAN
1988	Nino Saloukvadze, SOV
1992	Marina Longvinenko, RUS
1996	Li Duihong, CHN

Soccer

1996	United States

Softball

1996	United States

Swimming, 50-Meter Freestyle

1988	Kristin Otto, GDR
1992	Yang Wenyi, CHN
1996	Amy Van Dyken, USA

Swimming, 100-Meter Freestyle

1912	Fanny Durack, AUS
1920	Ethelda Bleibtrey, USA
1924	Ethel Lackie, USA
1928	Albina Osipowich, USA
1932	Helene Madison, USA
1936	Rie Mastenbroek, HOL
1948	Greta Andersen, DEN
1952	Katalin Szöke, HUN
1956	Dawn Fraser, AUS
1960	Dawn Fraser, AUS
1964	Dawn Fraser, AUS
1968	Jan Henne, USA
1972	Sandra Neilson, USA
1976	Kornelia Ender, GDR
1980	Barbara Krause, GDR
1984	Nancy Hogshead, USA & Carrie Steinseifer, USA (tied)
1988	Kristin Otto, GDR
1992	Zhuang Yong, CHN
1996	Le Jingyi, CHN

Swimming, 200-Meter Freestyle

1968	Debbie Meyer, USA
1972	Shane Gould, AUS
1976	Kornelia Ender, GDR
1980	Barbara Krause, GDR
1984	Mary Wayte, USA
1988	Heike Friedrich, GDR
1992	Nicole Haislett, USA
1996	Claudia Poll, CRC

Swimming, 400-Meter Freestyle

1920	Ethelda Bleibtrey, USA
1924	Martha Norelius, USA
1928	Martha Norelius, USA
1932	Helene Madison, USA
1936	Rie Mastenbroek, HOL
1948	Ann Curtis, USA
1952	Valéria Gyenge, HUN
1956	Lorraine Crapp, AUS
1960	Christine Von Saltza, USA
1964	Virginia Duenkel, USA
1968	Debbie Meyer, USA
1972	Shane Gould, AUS
1976	Petra Thümer, GDR
1980	Ines Diers, GDR
1984	Tiffany Cohen, USA
1988	Janet Evans, USA
1992	Dagmar Hase, GER
1996	Michelle Smith, IRE

Swimming, 800-Meter Freestyle

1968	Debbie Meyer, USA
1972	Keena Rothhammer, USA
1976	Petra Thümer, GDR
1980	Michelle Ford, AUS
1984	Tiffany Cohen, USA
1988	Janet Evans, USA
1992	Janet Evans, USA
1996	Brooke Bennett, USA

Swimming, 100-Meter Backstroke

1924	Sybil Bauer, USA
1928	Maria Braun, HOL
1932	Eleanor Holm, USA
1936	Nida Senff, HOL
1948	Karen-Margrete Harup, DEN
1952	Joan Harrison, SAF
1956	Judith Grinham, GBR
1960	Lynn Burke, USA
1964	Cathy Ferguson, USA
1968	Kaye Hall, USA
1972	Melissa Belote, USA
1976	Ulrike Richter, GDR
1980	Rica Reinisch, GDR
1984	Theresa Andrews, USA
1988	Kristin Otto, GDR
1992	Krisztina Egerszegi, HUN
1996	Beth Botsford, USA

Swimming, 200-Meter Backstroke

1968	Lillian Watson, USA
1972	Melissa Belote, USA
1976	Ulrike Richter, GDR
1980	Rica Reinisch, GDR
1984	Jolanda de Rover, HOL
1988	Krisztina Egerszegi, HUN
1992	Krisztina Egerszegi, HUN
1996	Krisztina Egerszegi, HUN

Swimming, 100-Meter Breaststroke

1968	Djurdjica Bjedov, YUG
1972	Cathy Carr, USA
1976	Hannelore Anke, GDR
1980	Ute Geweniger, GDR
1984	Petra van Staveren, HOL
1988	Tania Dangalakova, BUL
1992	Yelena Rudkovskaya, UT
1996	Penny Heyns, SAF

Swimming, 200-Meter Breaststroke

1924	Lucy Morton, GBR
1928	Hildegard Schrader, GER
1932	Clare Dennis, AUS
1936	Hideko Maehata, JPN
1948	Petronella van Vliet, HOL
1952	Éva Székely, HUN
1956	Ursula Happe, GER
1960	Anita Lonsbrough, GBR
1964	Galina Prozumenshikova, SOV
1968	Sharon Wichman, USA
1972	Beverley Whitfield, AUS
1976	Marina Koshevaia, SOV
1980	Lina Kaciusyté, SOV
1984	Anne Ottenbrite, CAN
1988	Silke Hörner, GDR
1992	Kyoko Iwasaki, JPN
1996	Penny Heyns, SAF

Swimming, 100-Meter Butterfly

1956	Shelly Mann, USA
1960	Carolyn Schuler, USA
1964	Sharon Stouder, USA
1968	Lynette McClements, AUS
1972	Mayumi Aoki, JPN
1976	Kornelia Ender, GDR
1980	Caren Metschuck, GDR
1984	Mary T. Meagher, USA
1988	Kristin Otto, GDR
1992	Qian Hong, CHN
1996	Amy Van Dyken, USA

Swimming, 200-Meter Butterfly

1968	Ada Kok, HOL
1972	Karen Moe, USA
1976	Andrea Pollack, GDR
1980	Ines Geissler, GDR
1984	Mary T. Meagher, USA
1988	Kathleen Nord, GDR
1992	Summer Sanders, USA
1996	Susan O'Neill, AUS

Swimming, 200-Meter Individual Medley

1968	Claudia Kolb, USA
1972	Shane Gould, AUS
1984	Tracy Caulkins, USA
1988	Daniela Hunger, GDR
1992	Lin Li, CHN
1996	Michelle Smith, IRE

Swimming, 400-Meter Individual Medley

1964	Donna de Varona, USA
1968	Claudia Kolb, USA
1972	Gail Neall, AUS
1976	Ulrike Tauber, GDR
1980	Petra Schneider, GDR
1984	Tracy Caulkins, USA
1988	Janet Evans, USA
1992	Krisztina Egerszegi, HUN
1996	Michelle Smith, IRE

Swimming, 4x100-Meter Freestyle Relay

1912	Great Britain
1920	United States
1924	United States
1928	United States
1932	United States
1936	Holland
1948	United States
1952	Hungary
1956	Australia
1960	United States
1964	United States
1968	United States
1972	United States
1976	United States
1980	East Germany
1984	United States
1988	East Germany
1992	United States
1996	United States

Swimming, 4x100-Meter Medley Relay

1960	United States
1964	United States
1968	United States
1972	United States
1976	East Germany
1980	East Germany
1984	United States

1988	East Germany
1992	United States
1996	United States

Swimming 4x200-Meter Freestyle Relay

1996	United States

Synchronized Swimming, Solo

1984	Tracie Ruiz, USA
1988	Carolyn Waldo, CAN
1992	Kristen Babb-Sprague, USA

Synchronized Swimming, Duet

1984	Tracie Ruiz, Candy Costie, USA
1988	Carolyn Waldo, Michelle Cameron, CAN
1992	Karen Josephson, Sarah Josephson, USA

Synchronized Swimming, Team

1996	United States

Table Tennis, Singles

1988	Jing Chen, CHN
1992	Deng Yaping, CHN
1996	Deng Yaping, CHN

Table Tennis, Doubles

1988	Jung-Hwa Hyun, Young-Ja Yang, KOR
1992	Deng Yaping, Qiao Hong, CHN
1996	Deng Yaping, Qiao Hong, CHN

Tennis, Singles

1900	Charlotte Cooper, GBR
1906	Esmee Simiriotou, GRE
1908	Dorothy Chambers, GBR
1908	Gwendoline Eastlake-Smith, GBR (Indoor Courts)
1912	Marguerite Broquedis, FRA
1912	Edith Hannam, GBR (Indoor Courts)
1920	Suzanne Lenglen, FRA
1924	Helen Wills, USA
1988	Steffi Graf, FRG
1992	Jennifer Capriati, USA
1996	Lindsay Davenport, USA

Tennis, Doubles

1920	Winifred McNair, Kitty McKane, GBR
1924	Hazel Hotchkiss Wightman, Helen Wills, USA
1988	Pam Shriver, Zina Garrison, USA
1992	Gigi Fernandez, Mary Joe Fernandez, USA
1996	Gigi Fernandez, Mary Joe Fernandez, USA

Tennis, Mixed Doubles

1900	Charlotte Cooper & Reginald Doherty, GBR
1906	Marie Decugis & Max Decugis, FRA
1912	Dora Köring & Heinrich Schomburgk, GER
1912	Edith Hannam & Charles Percy Dixon, GBR (Indoor Courts)
1920	Suzanne Lenglen & Max Decugis, FRA
1924	Hazel Hotchkiss Wightman & R. Norris Williams, USA

Track & Field, 100 Meters

1928	Elizabeth Robinson, USA
1932	Stanislawa Walasiewicz [Stella Walsh], POL
1936	Helen Stephens, USA
1948	Fanny Blankers-Koen, HOL
1952	Marjorie Jackson, AUS
1956	Betty Cuthbert, AUS
1960	Wilma Rudolph, USA
1964	Wyomia Tyus, USA
1968	Wyomia Tyus, USA
1972	Renate Stecher, GDR
1976	Annegret Richter, FRG
1980	Lyudmila Kondratyeva, SOV
1984	Evelyn Ashford, USA
1988	Florence Griffith Joyner, USA
1992	Gail Devers, USA
1996	Gail Devers, USA

Track & Field, 200 Meters

1948	Fanny Blankers-Koen, HOL
1952	Marjorie Jackson, AUS
1956	Betty Cuthbert, AUS
1960	Wilma Rudolph, USA
1964	Edith McGuire, USA
1968	Irena Kirszenstein Szewinska, POL
1972	Renate Stecher, GDR
1976	Barbel Eckert, GDR
1980	Barbel Eckert Wockel, GDR
1984	Valerie Brisco-Hooks, USA
1988	Florence Griffith Joyner, USA
1992	Gwen Torrence, USA
1996	Marie-Jose Perec, FRA

Track & Field, 400 Meters

1964	Betty Cuthbert, AUS
1968	Colette Besson, FRA
1972	Monika Zehrt, GDR
1976	Irena Kirszenstein Szewinska, POL
1980	Marita Koch, GDR
1984	Valerie Brisco-Hooks, USA
1988	Olga Bryzguina, SOV
1992	Marie-Jose Perec, FRA
1996	Marie-Jose Perec, FRA

Track & Field, 800 Meters

1928	Lina Radke, GER
1960	Lyudmila Shevtsova, SOV
1964	Ann Packer, GBR
1968	Madeline Manning, USA
1972	Hildegard Falck, FRG
1976	Tatyana Kazankina, SOV
1980	Nadezhda Olizarenko, SOV
1984	Doina Melinte, ROM
1988	Sigrun Wodars, GDR
1992	Ellen van Langen, HOL
1996	Svetlana Masterkova, RUS

Track & Field, 1,500 Meters

1972	Lyudmila Bragina, SOV
1976	Tatyana Kazankina, SOV
1980	Tatyana Kazankina, SOV
1984	Gabriella Dorio, ITA
1988	Paula Ivan, ROM
1992	Hassiba Boulmerka, ALG
1996	Svetlana Masterkova, RUS

Track & Field, 3,000 Meters

1984	Maricica Puica, ROM
1988	Tatiana Samolenko, SOV
1992	Yelena Romanova, RUS

Track & Field, 5,000 Meters

1996	Wang Junxia, CHN

Track & Field, 10,000 Meters

1988	Olga Bondarenko, SOV
1992	Derartu Tulu, ETH
1996	Fernanda Ribeiro, POR

Track & Field, Marathon

1984	Joan Benoit, USA
1988	Rosa Mota, POR
1992	Valentina Yegorova, UT
1996	Fatuma Roba, ETH

Track & Field, 80-Meter Hurdles

1932	Babe Didrikson, USA
1936	Trebisonda Valla, ITA
1948	Fanny Blankers-Koen, HOL
1952	Shirley Strickland, AUS
1956	Shirley Strickland, AUS
1960	Irina Press, SOV
1964	Karin Balzer, GDR
1968	Maureen Caird, AUS

Track & Field, 100-Meter Hurdles

1972	Annelie Ehrhardt, GDR
1976	Johanna Schaller, GDR
1980	Vera Komisova, SOV
1984	Benita Fitzgerald-Brown, USA
1988	Jordanka Donkova, BUL
1992	Paraskevi Patoulidou, GRE
1996	Ludmila Enqist, SWE

Track & Field, 400-Meter Hurdles

1984	Nawal El Moutawakel, MOR
1988	Debra Flintoff-King, AUS
1992	Sally Gunnell, GBR
1996	Deon Hemmings, JAM

Track & Field, 10-Kilometer Walk

1992	Chen Yueling, CHN
1996	Yelena Ninikolayeva, RUS

Track & Field, 4x100-Meter Relay

1928	Canada
1932	United States
1936	United States
1948	Holland
1952	United States
1956	Australia
1960	United States
1964	Poland
1968	United States
1972	West Germany
1976	East Germany
1980	East Germany
1984	United States
1988	United States
1992	United States
1996	United States

Track & Field, 4x400-Meter Relay

1972	East Germany
1976	East Germany
1980	Soviet Union
1984	United States
1988	Soviet Union
1992	Unified Team
1996	United States

Track & Field, Discus Throw

1928	Halina Konopacka, POL
1932	Lillian Copeland, USA
1936	Gisela Mauermayer, GER
1948	Micheline Ostermeyer, FRA
1952	Nina Romaschkova, SOV
1956	Olga Fikotová, CZE
1960	Nina Ponomaryeva, SOV
1964	Tamara Press, SOV
1968	Lia Manoliu, ROM
1972	Faina Melnik, SOV
1976	Evelin Schlaak, GDR
1980	Evelin Schlaak Jahl, GDR

1984	Ria Stalman, HOL
1988	Martina Hellmann, GDR
1992	Maritza Marten, CUB
1996	Ilke Wyludda, GER

Track & Field, Heptathlon

The seven-event heptathlon replaced the five-event pentathlon in 1984.)

1964	Irina Press, SOV
1968	Ingrid Becker, FRG
1972	Mary Peters, GBR
1976	Siegrun Siegl, GDR
1980	Nadezhda Tkachenko, SOV
1984	Glynis Nunn, AUS
1988	Jackie Joyner-Kersee, USA
1992	Jackie Joyner-Kersee, USA
1996	Ghada Shouaa, SYR

Track & Field, High Jump

1928	Ethel Catherwood, CAN
1932	Jean Shiley, USA
1936	Ibolya Csák, HUN
1948	Alice Coachman, USA
1952	Esther Brand, SAF
1956	Mildred McDaniel, USA
1960	Iolanda Balas, ROM
1964	Iolanda Balas, ROM
1968	Miloslava Rezková, CZE
1972	Ulrike Meyfarth, FRG
1976	Rosemarie Ackermann, GDR
1980	Sara Simeoni, ITA
1984	Ulrike Meyfarth, FRG
1988	Louise Ritter, USA
1992	Heiki Henkel, GER
1996	Stefka Kostadinova, BUL

Track & Field, Javelin Throw

1932	Babe Didrikson, USA
1936	Tilly Fleischer, GER
1948	Herma Bauma, AUT
1952	Dana Zátopková, CZE
1956	Inese Jaunzeme, SOV
1960	Elvira Ozolina, SOV
1964	Mihaela Penes, ROM
1968	Angéla Németh, HUN
1972	Ruth Fuchs, GDR
1976	Ruth Fuchs, GDR
1980	Maria Colon Rueñes, CUB
1984	Tessa Sanderson, GBR
1988	Petra Felke, GDR
1992	Silke Renk, GER
1996	Heli Rantanen, FIN

Track & Field, Long Jump

1948	Olga Gyarmati, HUN
1952	Yvette Williams, NZE
1956	Elzbieta Krzesinska, POL
1960	Vyera Krepkina, SOV
1964	Mary Rand, GBR
1968	Viorica Viscopoleanu, ROM
1972	Heidemarie Rosendahl, FRG
1976	Angela Voigt, GDR
1980	Tatiana Kolpakova, SOV
1984	Anisoara Cusmir-Stanciu, ROM
1988	Jackie Joyner-Kersee, USA
1992	Heiki Drechsler, GER
1996	Chioma Ajunwa, NGR

Track & Field, Triple Jump

| 1996 | Iness Kravets, UKR |

Track & Field, Shot Put

1948	Micheline Ostermeyer, FRA
1952	Galina Zybina, SOV
1956	Tamara Tyshkevich, SOV
1960	Tamara Press, SOV
1964	Tamara Press, SOV
1968	Margitta Gummel, GDR
1972	Nadezhda Chizhova, SOV
1976	Ivanka Hristova, BUL
1980	Ilona Slupianek, GDR
1984	Claudia Losch, FRG
1988	Natalia Lisovskaya, SOV
1992	Svetlana Krivaleva, UT
1996	Astrid Kumbernuss, GER

Track & Field, 800-Meter Wheelchair

| 1988 | Sharon Hedrick, USA |

Volleyball

1964	Japan
1968	Soviet Union
1972	Soviet Union
1976	Japan
1980	Soviet Union
1984	China
1988	Soviet Union
1992	Cuba
1996	Cuba

Yachting, 470 Class

1988	Allison Jolly, Lynne Jewell, USA
1992	Theresa Zabell Lucas, Patricia Guerra Cabrera, SPA
1996	Begona Via Dufresne, Theresa Zabell, SPA

Yachting, Europe Class

| 1992 | Linda Andersen, NOR |
| 1996 | Kristine Roug, DEN |

Yachting, Mistral Class

1996   Lee Lai-Shan, HKG

Yachting, Sailboard

1992   Barbara Kendall, NZE

Olympic Winter Games

Alpine Skiing, Downhill

1948	Hedy Schlunegger, SWI
1952	Trude Jochum-Beiser, AUT
1956	Madeleine Berthod, SWI
1960	Heidi Biebl, GER
1964	Christl Haas, AUT
1968	Olga Pall, AUT
1972	Marie-Theres Nadig, SWI
1976	Rosi Mittermaier, FRG
1980	Annemarie Moser-Pröll, AUT
1984	Michela Figini, SWI
1988	Marina Kiehl, FRG
1992	Kerrin Lee-Gartner, CAN
1994	Katja Seizinger, GER
1998	Katja Seizinger, GER

Alpine Skiing, Slalom

1948	Gretchen Fraser, USA
1952	Andrea Mead Lawrence, USA
1956	Renée Colliard, SWI
1960	Anne Heggtveit, CAN
1964	Christine Goitschel, FRA
1968	Marielle Goitschel, FRA
1972	Barbara Cochran, USA
1976	Rosi Mittermaier, FRG
1980	Hanni Wenzel, LIE
1984	Paoletta Magoni, ITA
1988	Vreni Schneider, SWI
1992	Petra Kronberger, AUT
1994	Vreni Schneider, SWI
1998	Hilde Gerg, GER

Alpine Skiing, Giant Slalom

1952	Andrea Mead Lawrence, USA
1956	Ossi Reichert, GER
1960	Yvonne Rüegg, SWI
1964	Marielle Goitschel, FRA
1968	Nancy Greene, CAN
1972	Marie-Theres Nadig, SWI
1976	Kathy Kreiner, CAN
1980	Hanni Wenzel, LIE
1984	Debbie Armstrong, USA
1988	Vreni Schneider, SWI
1992	Pernilla Wiberg, SWE
1994	Deborah Compagnoni, ITA
1998	Deborah Compagnoni, ITA

Alpine Skiing, Super Giant Slalom

1988	Sigrid Wolf, AUT
1992	Deborah Compagnoni, ITA
1994	Diann Roffe-Steinrotter, USA
1998	Picabo Street, USA

Alpine Skiing, Alpine Combined

1936	Christl Cranz, GER
1948	Trude Beiser, AUT
1988	Anita Wachter, AUT
1992	Petra Kronberger, AUT
1994	Pernilla Wiberg, SWE
1998	Katja Seizinger, GER

Biathlon, 7.5 Kilometers

1992	Anfisa Reztsova, UT
1994	Myriam Bedard, CAN
1998	Galina Kukleva, RUS

Biathlon, 15 Kilometers

1992	Antje Misersky, GER
1994	Myriam Bedard, CAN
1998	Yekaterina Dafovska, BUL

Biathlon, 4x7.5-Kilometer Relay

1992	France
1994	Russia
1998	Germany

Cross-Country Skiing, 5 Kilometers

1964	Claudia Boyarskikh, SOV
1968	Toini Gustafsson, SWE
1972	Galina Kulakova, SOV
1976	Helena Takalo, FIN
1980	Raisa Smetanina, SOV
1984	Marja-Liisa Hämäläinen, FIN
1988	Marjo Matikainen, FIN
1992	Marjut Lakkarinen, FIN
1994	Lyubov Egarova, RUS
1998	Larissa Lazutina, RUS

Cross-Country Skiing, 10 Kilometers

| 1952 | Lydia Wideman, FIN |
| 1956 | Lyubov Kosyreva, SOV |

1960   Maria Gusakova, SOV
1964   Claudia Boyarskikh, SOV
1968   Toini Gustafsson, SWE
1972   Galina Kulakova, SOV
1976   Raisa Smetanina, SOV
1980   Barbara Petzold, GDR
1984   Marja-Liisa Hämäläinen, FIN
1988   Vida Venciene, SOV

Cross-Country Skiing, 10-Kilometer Freestyle Pursuit

1992   Lyubov Egorova, UT
1994   Lyubov Egorova, RUS
1998   Larissa Lazutina, RUS

Cross-Country Skiing, 15-Kilometer Freestyle

1992   Lyubov Egorova, UT
1994   Manuela Di Centa, ITA
1998   Olga Danilova, RUS

Cross-Country Skiing, 20 Kilometers

1984   Marja-Liisa Hämäläinen, FIN
1988   Tamara Tikhonova, SOV

Cross-Country Skiing, 30 Kilometers

1992   Stefania Belmondo, ITA
1994   Manuela Di Centa, ITA
1998   Yulia Tchepalova, RUS

Cross-Country Skiing, 4x5-Kilometer Relay

1956   Finland
1960   Sweden
1964   Soviet Union
1968   Norway
1972   Soviet Union
1976   Soviet Union
1980   East Germany
1984   Norway
1988   Soviet Union
1992   Unified Team
1994   Russia
1998   Russia

Curling

1998   Canada

Freestyle Skiing, Moguls

1992   Donna Weinbrecht, USA
1994   Stine Lisa Hattestad, NOR
1998   Tae Satoya, JPN

Freestyle Skiing , Aerials

1994   Lina Cherjazona, UZB
1998   Nikki Stone, USA

Figure Skating

1908   Madge Syers, GBR
1920   Madga Julin, SWE
1924   Herma Planck-Szabó, AUT
1928   Sonja Henie, NOR
1932   Sonja Henie, NOR
1936   Sonja Henie, NOR
1948   Barbara Ann Scott, CAN
1952   Jeanette Altwegg, GBR
1956   Tenley Albright, USA
1960   Carol Heiss, USA
1964   Sjoukje Dijkstra, HOL
1968   Peggy Fleming, USA
1972   Beatrix Schuba, AUT
1976   Dorothy Hamill, USA
1980   Anett Pötzsch, GDR
1984   Katarina Witt, GDR
1988   Katarina Witt, GDR
1992   Kristi Yamaguchi, USA
1994   Oskana Baiul, UKR
1998   Tara Lipinski, USA

Figure Skating, Ice Dance

1976   Lyudmila Pakhomova & Aleksandr Gorshkov, SOV
1980   Natalia Linichuk & Gennady Karponosov, SOV
1984   Jayne Torvill & Christopher Dean, GBR
1988   Natalia Bestemianova & Andrei Bukin, SOV
1992   Marina Klimova & Sergei Ponomarenko, UT
1994   Oksana Gritschuk & Yevgeny Platov, RUS
1998   Oksana Gritschuk & Yevgeny Platov, RUS

Figure Skating, Pairs

1908   Anna Hübler & Heinrich Burger, GER
1920   Ludovika Jakobsson & Walter Jakobsson, FIN
1924   Helene Engelmann & Alfred Berger, AUT
1928   Andrée Joly & Pierre Brunet, FRA
1932   Andrée Joly Brunet & Pierre Brunet, FRA
1936   Maxi Herber & Ernst Baier, GER
1948   Micheline Lannoy & Pierre Baugniet, BEL
1952   Ria Falk & Paul Falk, GER
1956   Elisabeth Schwartz & Kurt Oppelt, AUT
1960   Barbara Wagner & Robert Paul, CAN
1964   Lyudmila Belousova & Oleg Protopopov, SOV
1968   Lyudmila Belousova & Oleg Protopopov, SOV
1972   Irina Rodnina & Aleksei Ulanov, SOV
1976   Irina Rodnina & Aleksandr Zaitsev, SOV
1980   Irina Rodnina & Aleksandr Zaitsev, SOV
1984   Elena Valova & Oleg Vasiliev, SOV
1988   Ekaterina Gordeeva & Sergei Grinkov, SOV
1992   Natalya Mishkutienak & Artur Dmitriev, UT
1994   Ekaterina Gordeeva & Sergei Grinkov, RUS
1998   Oksana Kazakova & Artur Dmitriev, RUS

Ice Hockey

1998	United States

Luge, Singles

1964	Ortrun Enderlein, GER
1968	Erica Lechner, ITA
1972	Anna-Maria Müller, GDR
1976	Margit Schumann, GDR
1980	Vera Zozulia, SOV
1984	Steffi Martin, GDR
1988	Steffi Martin Walter, GDR
1992	Doris Neuner, AUT
1994	Gerda Weissensteiner, ITA
1998	Silke Kraushaar, GER

Snowboarding, Giant Slalom

1998	Karine Ruby, FRA

Snowboarding, Halfpipe

1998	Nicola Thost, GER

Speed Skating, 500 Meters

1960	Helga Haase, GER
1964	Lydia Skoblikova, SOV
1968	Lyudmila Titova, SOV
1972	Anne Henning, USA
1976	Sheila Young, USA
1980	Karin Enke, GDR
1984	Christa Rothenburger, GDR
1988	Bonnie Blair, USA
1992	Bonnie Blair, USA
1994	Bonnie Blair, USA
1998	Catriona LeMay Doan, CAN

Speed Skating, 1,000 Meters

1960	Klara Guseva, SOV
1964	Lydia Skoblikova, SOV
1968	Carolina Geijssen, HOL
1972	Monika Pflug, FRG
1976	Tatiana Averina, SOV
1980	Natalia Petruseva, SOV
1984	Karin Enke, GDR
1988	Christa Rothenburger, GDR
1992	Bonnie Blair, USA
1994	Bonnie Blair, USA
1998	Marianne Timmer, HOL

Speed Skating, 1,500 Meters

1960	Lydia Skoblikova, SOV
1964	Lydia Skoblikova, SOV
1968	Kaija Mustonen, FIN
1972	Dianne Holum, USA
1976	Galina Stepanskaya, SOV
1980	Annie Borckink, HOL
1984	Karin Enke, GDR
1988	Yvonne Van Gennip, HOL
1992	Jacqueline Borner, GER
1994	Emese Hunyady, AUT
1998	Marianne Timmer, HOL

Speed Skating, 3,000 Meters

1960	Lydia Skoblikova, SOV
1964	Lydia Skoblikova, SOV
1968	Johanna Schut, HOL
1972	Christina Baas-Kaiser, HOL
1976	Tatiana Averina, SOV
1980	Bjorg Eva Jensen, NOR
1984	Andrea Mitscherlich Schone, GDR
1988	Yvonne Van Gennip, HOL
1992	Gunda Niemann, GER
1994	Svetlana Bazhanova, RUS
1998	Gunda Niemann-Stirnemann, GER

Speed Skating, 5,000 Meters

1988	Yvonne Van Gennip, HOL
1992	Gunda Niemann, GER
1994	Claudia Pechstein, GER
1998	Claudia Pechstein, GER

Speed Skating, Short Track, 500 Meters

1992	Cathy Turner, USA
1994	Cathy Turner, USA
1998	Annie Perreault, CAN

Speed Skating, Short Track, 1,000 Meters

1994	Chun Lee-Kyung, KOR
1998	Chun Lee-Kyung, KOR

Speed Skating, Short Track, 3,000-Meter Relay

1992	Canada
1994	South Korea
1998	South Korea

Nation Abbreviations

ALG	Algeria
ARG	Argentina
AUS	Australia
AUT	Austria
BEL	Belgium
BLR	Belarus
BOH	Bohemia
BRA	Brazil
BUL	Bulgaria
CAN	Canada
CHI	Chile
CHN	China
CRC	Costa Rica
CUB	Cuba
CZE	Czechoslovakia
DEN	Denmark
EST	Estonia
ETH	Ethiopia
FIN	Finland
FRA	France
FRG	West Germany (Federal Republic of Germany) 1968-88
GBR	Great Britain and Northern Ireland
GDR	East Germany (German Democratic Republic) 1968-88
GER	Germany (1896-1964; in 1956, 1960, and 1964 East Germany and West Germany entered combined teams; 1992-)
GRE	Greece
HKG	Hong Kong
HOL	Holland (Netherlands)
HUN	Hungary
IRE	Ireland
ITA	Italy
JAM	Jamaica
JPN	Japan
KOR	South Korea
LIE	Liechtenstein
MEX	Mexico
MOR	Morocco
NGR	Nigeria
NOR	Norway
NZE	New Zealand
PER	Peru
POL	Poland
POR	Portugal
PRK	North Korea (People's Republic of Korea)
ROM	Romania
RUS	Russia
SAF	South Africa
SOV	Soviet Union
SPA	Spain
SWE	Sweden
SWI	Switzerland
SYR	Syria
TAI	Taiwan
UKR	Ukraine
USA	United States of America
UT	Unified Team
UZB	Uzbekistan
YUG	Yugoslavia

Appendix B
Selected National Award Winners and Champions

Associated Press Female Athlete of the Year

Selected annually by Associated Press newspaper sports editors.

1931	Helene Madison, swimming
1932	Babe Didrikson, track
1933	Helen Jacobs, tennis
1934	Virginia Van Wie, golf
1935	Helen Wills Moody, tennis
1936	Helen Stephens, track
1937	Katherine Rawls, swimming
1938	Patty Berg, golf
1939	Alice Marble, tennis
1940	Alice Marble, tennis
1941	Betty Hicks Newell, golf
1942	Gloria Callen, swimming
1943	Patty Berg, golf
1944	Ann Curtis, swimming
1945	Babe Didrikson Zaharias, golf
1946	Babe Didrikson Zaharias, golf
1947	Babe Didrikson Zaharias, golf
1948	Fanny Blankers-Koen, track
1949	Marlene Bauer, golf
1950	Babe Didrikson Zaharias, golf
1951	Maureen Connolly, tennis
1952	Maureen Connolly, tennis
1953	Maureen Connolly, tennis
1954	Babe Didrikson Zaharias, golf
1955	Patty Berg, golf
1956	Patricia McCormick, diving
1957	Althea Gibson, tennis
1958	Althea Gibson, tennis
1959	Maria Bueno, tennis

1960	Wilma Rudolph, track
1961	Wilma Rudolph, track
1962	Dawn Fraser, swimming
1963	Mickey Wright, golf
1964	Mickey Wright, golf
1965	Kathy Whitworth, golf
1966	Kathy Whitworth, golf
1967	Billie Jean King, tennis
1968	Peggy Fleming, skating
1969	Debbie Meyer, swimming
1970	Chi Cheng, track
1971	Evonne Goolagong, tennis
1972	Olga Korbut, gymnastics
1973	Billie Jean King, tennis
1974	Chris Evert, tennis
1975	Chris Evert, tennis
1976	Nadia Comaneci, gymnastics
1977	Chris Evert, tennis
1978	Nancy Lopez, golf
1979	Tracy Austin, tennis
1980	Chris Evert Lloyd, tennis
1981	Tracy Austin, tennis
1982	Mary Decker Tabb, track
1983	Martina Navratilova, tennis
1984	Mary Lou Retton, gymnastics
1985	Nancy Lopez, golf
1986	Martina Navratilova, tennis
1987	Jackie Joyner-Kersee, track
1988	Florence Griffith Joyner, track
1989	Steffi Graf, tennis
1990	Beth Daniel, golf
1991	Monica Seles, tennis
1992	Monica Seles, tennis
1993	Sheryl Swoopes, basketball
1994	Bonnie Blair, speed skating
1995	Rebecca Lobo, basketball
1996	Amy Van Dyken, swimming
1997	Martina Hingis, tennis

United States Olympic Committee (USOC) Sportswomen of the Year

1974	Shirley Babashoff, swimming
1975	Kathy Heddy, swimming
1976	Sheila Young, speed skating
1977	Linda Fratianne, figure skating
1978	Tracy Caulkins, swimming
1979	Cynthia Woodhead, swimming
1980	Beth Heiden, speed skating
1981	Sheila Young Ochowicz, speed skating and cycling
1982	Melanie Smith, equestrian
1983	Tamara McKinney, skiing
1984	Tracy Caulkins, swimming
1985	Mary Decker Slaney, track
1986	Jackie Joyner-Kersee, track
1987	Jackie Joyner-Kersee, track
1988	Florence Griffith Joyner, track
1989	Janet Evans, swimming
1990	Lynn Jennings, track
1991	Kim Zmeskal, gymnastics
1992	Bonnie Blair, speed skating
1993	Gail Devers, track
1994	Bonnie Blair, speed skating
1995	Picabo Street, skiing
1996	Amy Van Dyken, swimming
1997	Tara Lipinski, figure skating

Flo Hyman Award Winners

Presented annually since 1987 by the Women's Sports Foundation for the athlete "exemplifying dignity, spirit, and commitment to excellence," and named in honor of the late captain of the 1984 U.S. Women's Volleyball Team.

1987	Martina Navratilova, tennis
1988	Jackie Joyner-Kersee, track
1989	Evelyn Ashford, track
1990	Chris Evert, tennis
1991	Diana Golden, skiing
1992	Nancy Lopez, golf
1993	Lynette Woodard, basketball
1994	Patty Sheehan, golf
1995	Mary Lou Retton, gymnastics
1996	Donna de Varona, swimming
1997	Billie Jean King, tennis

Honda Broderick Cup

Presented to the outstanding collegiate woman athlete of the year in NCAA competition.

1977	Luisa (Lucy) Harris, Delta State, basketball
1978	Ann Meyers, UCLA, basketball
1979	Nancy Lieberman, Old Dominion, basketball
1980	Julie Shea, NC State, track
1981	Jill Sterkel, Texas, swimming

1982	Tracy Caulkins, Florida, swimming
1983	Deitre Collins, Hawaii, volleyball
1984	Tracy Caulkins, Florida, swimming
	Cheryl Miller, USC, basketball
1985	Jackie Joyner, UCLA, track
1986	Kamie Ethridge, Texas, basketball
1987	Mary T. Meagher, California, swimming
1988	Teresa Weatherspoon, Louisiana Tech, basketball
1989	Vicki Huber, Villanova, track
1990	Suzy Favor, Wisconsin, track
1991	Dawn Staley, Virginia, basketball
1992	Missy Marlowe, Utah, gymnastics
1993	Lisa Fernandez, UCLA, softball
1994	Mia Hamm, North Carolina, soccer
1995	Rebecca Lobo, Connecticut, basketball
1996	Jennifer Rizzotti, Connecticut, basketball

Alpine Skiing
U.S. National Champions

Downhill

1933	Marian McKean
1934	Elizabeth Woolsey
1935-39	No race held
1940	G.C. Lindley
1941	Nancy Reynolds
1942	Shirley McDonald
1943	No race held
1944	No race held
1945	No race held
1946	Paula Kahn
1947	Rhoda Wurtele
1948	Janette Burr
1949	Andrea Mead
1950	Janette Burr
1951	Katy Rodolph
1952	Andrea Mead Lawrence
1953	Katy Rodolph
1954	Nancy Banks
1955	Andrea Mead Lawrence
1956	Katherine Cox
1957	Linda Meyers
1958	Beverly Anderson
1959	Beverly Anderson
1960	Nancy Greene
1961	No race held
1962	Sharon Pecjak
1963	Jean Saubert
1964	Jean Saubert
1965	Nancy Greene
1966	Madeleine Wuilloud
1967	Nancy Greene
1968	Ann Black
1969	Ann Black
1970	Ann Black
1971	Cheryl Bechdolt
1972	Stephanie Forrest
1973	Cindy Nelson
1974	No race held

1975	Gail Blackburn	1974	Susie Patterson
1976	Susie Patterson	1975	Cindy Nelson
1977	No race held	1976	Cindy Nelson
1978	Cindy Nelson	1977	Christin Cooper
1979	Irene Epple	1978	Becky Dorsey
1980	Cindy Nelson	1979	Cindy Nelson
1981	Holly Flanders	1980	Christin Cooper
1982	Cindy Oak	1981	Cindy Nelson
1983	Pam Fletcher	1982	Tamara McKinney
1984	Lisa Wilcox	1983	Tamara McKinney
1985	Holly Flanders	1984	Tamara McKinney
1986	Hilary Lindh	1985	Ann Melander
1987	Pam Fletcher	1986	Tamara McKinney
1988	Pam Fletcher	1987	Tamara McKinney
1989	Hilary Lindh	1988	Tamara McKinney
1990	Lucie LaRoche	1989	Tamara McKinney, Diann Roffe
1991	Megan Gerety	1990	Monique Pelletier
1992	Kate Pace	1991	Eva Twardokens
1993	Lindsey Roberts	1992	Diann Roffe-Steinrotter
1994	Picabo Street	1993	Kristi Terzian
1995	Megan Gerety	1994	Kristi Terzian
1996	Picabo Street	1995	Kristina Koznick
		1996	Kristina Koznick

Slalom

1938	G.C. Lindley
1939	Doris Friedrich
1940	Nancy Reynolds
1941	Marilyn Shaw
1942	Gretchen Fraser
1943	No race held
1944	No race held
1945	No race held
1946	Rhoda Wurtele
1947	Olivia Ausoni
1948	Anne Winn
1949	Andrea Mead
1950	Norma Godden
1951	Katy Rodolph
1952	Andrea Mead Lawrence
1953	Katy Rodolph
1954	Jill Kinmont
1955	Andrea Mead Lawrence
1956	Sally Deaver
1957	Sally Deaver
1958	Beverly Anderson
1959	Linda Meyers
1960	Anne Heggtveit, Nancy Holland
1961	Linda Meyers
1962	Linda Meyers
1963	Sandra Shellworth
1964	Jean Saubert
1965	Nancy Greene
1966	Marielle Goitschel
1967	Penny McCoy
1968	Judy Nagel
1969	No race held
1970	Patty Boydstun
1971	Barbara Cochran
1972	Marilyn Cochran
1973	Lindy Cochran

Giant Slalom

1952	Rhona W. Gillis
1953	Andrea Mead Lawrence
1954	No record of event
1955	Janette Burr Bray
1956	Sally Deaver
1957	Noni Foley
1958	Beverly Anderson
1959	Beverly Anderson
1960	Anne Heggtveit
1961	Nancy Holland
1962	Tammy Dix
1963	Jean Saubert
1964	Jean Saubert
1965	Nancy Greene
1966	Florence Steurer
1967	Sandra Shellworth
1968	Marilyn Greene
1969	Barbara Cochran
1970	Susie Corrock
1971	Laurie Kreiner
1972	Sandra Poulsen
1973	Debi Handley
1974	Marilyn Cochran
1975	Becky Dorsey
1976	Lindy Cochran
1977	Becky Dorsey
1978	Becky Dorsey
1979	Vicki Fleckenstein
1980	Christin Cooper
1981	Tamara McKinney
1982	No race held
1983	Tamara McKinney
1984	Christin Cooper
1985	Eva Twardokens
1986	Beth Madsen

1987	Debbie Armstrong
1988	Monique Pelletier
1989	Diann Roffe
1990	Kristi Terzian
1991	Eva Twardokens
1992	Diann Roffe-Steinrotter
1993	Diann Roffe-Steinrotter
1994	Eva Twardokens
1995	Heidi Voelker
1996	Jennifer Collins

Super G

1987	Pam Fletcher
1988	Pam Fletcher
1989	Kristin Krone
1990	Krista Schmidinger
1991	Julie Parisien
1992	Diann Roffe-Steinrotter
1993	Picabo Street
1994	Shannon Nobis
1995	No race held
1996	Picabo Street

Combined

1938	Marian McKean
1939	Erna Steuri
1940	Marilyn Shaw
1941	Nancy Reynolds, Gretchen Fraser
1942	Clarity Heath
1943	No race held
1944	No race held
1945	No race held
1946	Rhoda Wurtele
1947	Rhoda Wurtele
1948	Suzanne Harris
1949	Andrea Mead
1950	Lois Woodworth
1951	Katy Rodolph
1952	Andrea Mead Lawrence
1953	Katy Rodolph, Sally Neidlinger
1954	Nancy Banks
1955	Andrea Mead Lawrence
1956	Katherine Cox
1957	Madi S. Miller
1958	Beverly Anderson
1959	Linda Meyers
1960	Elizabeth Greene
1961	Nancy Holland
1962	Linda Meyers
1963	Starr Walton
1964	Jean Saubert
1965	Nancy Greene
1966	Florence Steurer
1967	Karen Budge
1968	Judy Nagel
1969	No race held
1970	Rosie Fortna
1971	Judy Crawford
1972	Stephanie Forrest

1973	Marilyn Cochran
1974-83	No races held
1984	Eva Twardokens
1985	Eva Twardokens
1986	Beth Madsen
1987	Pam Fletcher
1988	Monique Pelletier
1989	Kristin Krone
1990	Julie Parisien
1991	Wendy Fisher
1992	Hilary Lindh
1993	Julie Parisien
1994	Melanie Turgeon
1995	Carrie Sheinberg
1996	Kirsten Clark

Archery
National Target Champions

1879	Mrs. Spaulding Brown
1880	Mrs. T. Davies
1881	Mrs. A.H. Gibbes
1882	Mrs. A.H. Gibbes
1883	Mrs. M.C. Howell
1884	Mrs. H. Hall
1885	Mrs. M.C. Howell
1886	Mrs. M.C. Howell
1887	Mrs. M.C. Howell
1888	Mrs. A.M. Phillips
1889	Mrs. A.M. Phillips
1890	Mrs. M.C. Howell
1891	Mrs. M.C. Howell
1892	Mrs. M.C. Howell
1893	Mrs. M.C. Howell
1894	Mrs. Albert Kern
1895	Mrs. M.C. Howell
1896	Mrs. M.C. Howell
1897	Mrs. J.S. Barker
1898	Mrs. M.C. Howell
1899	Mrs. M.C. Howell
1900	Mrs. M.C. Howell
1901	Mrs. C.E. Woodruff
1902	Mrs. M.C. Howell
1903	Mrs. M.C. Howell
1904	Mrs. M.C. Howell
1905	Mrs. M.C. Howell
1906	Mrs. E.C. Cook
1907	Mrs. M.C. Howell
1908	Harriet Case
1909	Harriet Case
1910	J.V. Sullivan
1911	Mrs. J.S. Taylor
1912	Mrs. Witwer Tayler
1913	Mrs. P. Fletcher
1914	Mrs. B.P. Gray
1915	Cynthia Wesson
1916	Cynthia Wesson
1917	No contest held
1918	No contest held
1919	Dorothy Smith

1920	Cynthia Wesson	1981	Debra Metzger
1921	Mrs. L.C. Smith	1982	Luann Ryon
1922	Dorothy Smith	1983	Nancy Myrick
1923	Norma Pierce	1984	Ruth Rowe
1924	Dorothy Smith	1985	Terri Pesho
1925	Dorothy Smith	1986	Debra Ochs
1926	Dorothy Smith	1987	Terry Quinn
1927	Mrs. Robert Johnson	1988	Debra Ochs
1928	Beatrice Hodgson	1989	Debra Ochs
1929	Audrey Grubbs	1990	Denise Parker
1930	Audrey Grubbs	1991	Denise Parker
1931	Dorothy Cummings	1992	Sherry Block
1932	Ilda Hanchette	1993	Denise Parker
1933	Madelaine Taylor	1994	Judi Adams
1934	Mrs. Desales Mudd	1995	Jessica Carlson
1935	Ruth Hodgert	1996	Janet Dykman
1936	Gladys Hammer	1997	Janet Dykman
1937	Gladys Hammer		
1938	Jean Tenney		

Badminton
U.S. Women's National Champions

1939	Belvia Carter		
1940	Ann Weber		
1941	Ree Dillinger		
1942	No contest held	1937	Mrs. Del Barkhuff
1943	No contest held	1938	Mrs. Del Barkhuff
1944	No contest held	1939	Mary E. Whitemore
1945	No contest held	1940	Evelyn Boldrick
1946	Ann Weber	1941	Thelma Kingsbury
1947	Ann Weber	1942	Evelyn Boldrick
1948	Jean Lee	1943	No contest held
1949	Jean Lee	1944	No contest held
1950	Jean Lee	1945	No contest held
1951	Jean Lee	1946	No contest held
1952	Ann Weber	1947	Ethel Marshall
1953	Ann Weber	1948	Ethel Marshall
1954	Laurette Young	1949	Ethel Marshall
1955	Ann Clark	1950	Ethel Marshall
1956	Carole Meinhart	1951	Ethel Marshall
1957	Carole Meinhart	1952	Ethel Marshall
1958	Carole Meinhart	1953	Ethel Marshall
1959	Carole Meinhart	1954	Judy Devlin
1960	Ann Clark	1955	Margaret Varner
1961	Victoria Cook	1956	Judy Devlin
1962	Nancy Vonderheide	1957	Judy Devlin
1963	Nancy Vonderheide	1958	Judy Devlin
1964	Victoria Cook	1959	Judy Devlin
1965	Nancy Pfeiffer	1960	Judy Devlin
1966	Helen Thornton	1961	Judy (Devlin) Hashman
1967	Ardelle Mills	1962	Judy Hashman
1968	Victoria Cook	1963	Judy Hashman
1969	Doreen Wilbur	1964	Dorothy O'Neil
1970	Nancy Myrick	1965	Judy Hashman
1971	Doreen Wilbur	1966	Judy Hashman
1972	Ruth Rowe	1967	Judy Hashman
1973	Doreen Wilbur	1968	Tyna Barinaga
1974	Doreen Wilbur	1969	Tyna Barinaga
1975	Irene Lorenson	1970	Tyna Barinaga
1976	Luann Ryon	1971	Diane Hales
1977	Luann Ryon	1972	Pam Brady
1978	Luann Ryon	1973	Eva Twedberg
1979	Lynette Johnson	1974	Cindy Baker
1980	Judi Adams		

1975	Judianne Kelly
1976	Pam Stockton
1977	Pam Brady
1978	Cheryl Carton
1979	Pam Brady
1980	Cheryl Carton
1981	Utami Kinard
1982	Cheryl Carton
1983	Cheryl Carton
1984	Cheryl Carton
1985	Judianne Kelly
1986	Nina Lolk
1987	Joy Kitzmiller
1988	Joy Kitzmiller
1989	Linda Safarik-Tong
1990	Linda Safarik-Tong
1991	Liz Aronsohn
1992	Joy Kitzmiller
1993	Andrea Anderson
1994	Joy Kitzmiller
1995	Andrea Anderson
1996	Yeping Tang
1997	Cindy Shi

Biathlon
U.S. National Champions

Individual Women

In the individual competition, the skiing course measures 15k for women. Skiers complete five loops and shoot five shots at each of four stages. A one-minute penalty for every missed shot is added to the competitor's ski time.

1982	Pam Weiss
1983	Not held
1984	Kari Swenson
1985	Julie Newman
1986	Anna Sonnerup
1987	Anna Sonnerup
1988	Peggy Hunter
1989	Anna Sonnerup
1990	Pam Nordheim
1991	Anna Sonnerup
1992	Angie Stevenson
1993	Beth Coats
1994	Joan Smith
1995	Beth Coats
1996	Ntala Skinner
1997	Ntala Skinner

Sprint Women

In the sprint competition, the women ski a total of 7.5K. The athletes start individually at one-minute intervals. The competitors ski a total of three loops. They shoot five rounds in the prone position, and five rounds in the standing position. The competitor must ski a 150m penalty loop for each missed shot.

1982	Patrice Jankowski
1983	No contest held
1984	Holly Beatie
1985	Kari Swenson
1986	Pam Nordheim
1987	Pam Nordheim
1988	Mary Ostergren
1989	Anna Sonnerup
1990	Mary Ostergren
1991	Patrice J. Anderson
1992	Joan Guetschow
1993	Angie Stevenson
1994	Joan Smith
1995	Beth Coats
1996	Kris Sebasteanski
1997	Ntala Skinner

Billiards

Women's Professional Billiards Association National 9-Ball Champions

1977	Jean Balukas
1978	Jean Balukas
1979	Jean Balukas
1980	Gloria Walker
1983	Jean Balukas
1984	Jean Balukas
1985	Belinda Bearden
1986	Jean Balukas
1987	Mary Guarino
1988	Loree Jon Jones
1989	Robin Bell
1990	Loree Jon Jones
1991	Ewa Mataya
1992	Vivian Villarreal
1993	Loree Jon Jones
1994	Jeanette Lee
1995	Allison Fisher
1996	Allison Fisher
1997	Gerda Hofstatter

Bowling—Major Champions

BPAA U.S. Open

The BPAA U.S. Open was started by the Bowling Proprietors' Association of America in 1949, 11 years before the founding of the Professional Women's Bowling Association. Originally the BPAA Women's All-Star Tournament, it became the U.S. Open in 1971. There were two BPAA All-Star tournaments in 1955, in January and December.

a—denotes amateur

Year	Winner
1949	Marion Ladewig
1950	Marion Ladewig
1951	Marion Ladewig
1952	Marion Ladewig
1953	No contest held
1954	Marion Ladewig
1955	(January) Sylvia Wene
1955	(December) Anita Cantaline
1956	Marion Ladewig
1957	No contest held
1958	Merle Matthews
1959	Marion Ladewig
1960	Sylvia Wene
1961	Phyllis Notaro
1962	Shirley Garms
1963	Marion Ladewig
1964	LaVerne Carter
1965	Ann Slattery
1966	Joy Abel
1967	Gloria Bouvia
1968	Dotty Fothergill
1969	Dotty Fothergill
1970	Mary Baker
1971	a-Paula Sperber
1972	a-Lorrie Koch
1973	Millie Martorella
1974	Pat Costello
1975	Paula Sperber Carter
1976	Patty Costello
1977	Betty Morris
1978	Donna Adamek
1979	Diana Silva
1980	Pat Costello
1981	Donna Adamek
1982	Shinobu Saitoh
1983	Dana Miller
1984	Karen Ellingsworth
1985	Pat Mercatanti
1986	a-Wendy Macpherson
1987	Carol Norman
1988	Lisa Wagner
1989	Robin Romeo
1990	Dana Miller-Mackie
1991	Anne Marie Duggan
1992	Tish Johnson
1993	Dede Davidson
1994	Aleta Sill
1995	Cheryl Daniels
1996	Liz Johnson
1997	No contest held

WIBC Queens

Sponsored by the Women's International Bowling Congress, the Queens is a double-elimination, match-play tournament open to qualified professionals and amateurs.

a—denotes amateur

Year	Winner
1961	Janet Harman
1962	Dorothy Wilkinson
1963	Irene Monterosso
1964	D.D. Jacobsen
1965	Betty Kuczynski
1966	Judy Lee
1967	Millie Martorella
1968	Phyllis Massey
1969	Ann Feigel
1970	Millie Martorella
1971	Millie Martorella
1972	Dotty Fothergill
1973	Dotty Fothergill
1974	Judy Soutar
1975	Cindy Powell
1976	Pam Buckner
1977	Dana Stewart
1978	Loa Boxberger
1979	Donna Adamek
1980	Donna Adamek
1981	Katsuko Sugimoto
1982	Katsuko Sugimoto
1983	Aleta Sill
1984	Kazue Inahashi
1985	Aleta Sill
1986	Cora Fiebig
1987	Cathy Almeida
1988	Wendy Macpherson
1989	Carol Gianotti
1990	a-Patty Ann
1991	Dede Davidson
1992	Cindy Coburn-Carroll
1993	Jan Schmidt
1994	Anne Marie Duggan
1995	Sandra Postma
1996	Lisa Wagner
1997	Sandra Jo Odom

Sam Town's Invitational

Year	Winner
1981	Cindy Coburn
1982	No contest held
1983	No contest held
1984	Aleta Sill
1985	Patty Costello
1986	Aleta Sill
1987	Debbie Bennett
1988	Donna Adamek
1989	Tish Johnson
1990	Wendy Macpherson
1991	Lorrie Nichols
1992	Tish Johnson
1993	Robin Romeo
1994	Tish Johnson
1995	Michelle Mullen
1996	Carol Gjanotti-Black
1997	Kim Adler

U.S. National Amateur Champions

Year	Winner
1986	Cora Fiebig
1987	Heather Nelson

1988	Patty Ann
1989	Linda Graham
1990	Julie Gardner
1991	Julie Gardner
1992	Joey Simpson
1993	Liz Johnson
1994	Liz Johnson
1995	Linda Norry
1996	Lucy Giovinco
1997	Janette Pieseynski

Cycling
U.S. National Champions

Individual Road Race

1967	Nancy Burghart
1968	Nancy Burghart
1969	Donna Tobias
1970	Audrey McElmury
1971	Mary Jane Reoch
1972	Debbie Bradley
1973	Eileen Brennan
1974	Jane Robinson
1975	Linda Stein
1976	Connie Carpenter
1977	Connie Carpenter
1978	Barbara Hintzen
1979	Connie Carpenter
1980	Beth Heiden
1981	Connie Carpenter
1982	Sue Novara
1983	Rebecca Twigg
1984	Rebecca Daughton
1985	Rebecca Daughton
1986	Katrin Tobin
1987	Janelle Parks
1988	Inga Benedict
1989	Juli Furtado
1990	Ruthie Matthes
1991	Inga Thompson
1992	Jeanne Golay
1993	Inga Thompson
1994	Jeanne Golay
1995	Jeanne Golay
1996	Dede Demet
1997	Louisa Jenkins

Time Trial

1975	Mary Jane Reoch
1976	Lyn Lemaire
1977	Lyn Lemaire
1978	Esther Salmi
1979	Beth Heiden
1980	Beth Heiden
1981	Connie Carpenter
1982	Rebecca Twigg
1983	Cindy Olavarri
1984	Patti Cashman
1985	Elizabeth Larsen

1986	Jane Marshall
1987	Inga Benedict
1988	Phyllis Hines
1989	Jeanne Golay
1990	Inga Thompson
1991	Inga Thompson
1992	Jeanne Golay
1993	Rebecca Twigg
1994	Rebecca Twigg
1995	Mari Paulsen
1996	Mari Holden
1997	Elizabeth Emery

Criterium

1981	Connie Paraskevin
1982	Connie Carpenter
1983	Connie Carpenter
1984	Betsy Davis
1985	Betsy Davis
1986	Peggy Maass
1987	Sally Zack
1988	Sally Zack
1989	Ruthie Matthes
1990	Karen Bliss
1991	Shari Rodgers
1992	Laura Charameda
1993	Rebecca Twigg
1994	Karen Bliss Livingston
1995	Laura Charameda
1996	Carmen Richardson
1997	Karen Bliss Livingston

National Track Champions

Match Sprint

1967	Nancy Burghart
1968	Nancy Burghart
1969	no contest held
1970	Jeanne Kloska
1971	Sheila Young
1972	Sue Novara
1973	Sheila Young
1974	Sue Novara
1975	Sue Novara
1976	Sheila Young
1977	Sue Novara
1978	Sue Novara
1979	Sue Novara
1980	Sue Novara
1981	Sheila Young
1982	Connie Paraskevin
1983	Connie Paraskevin
1984	Rebecca Twigg
1985	Connie Paraskevin
1986	Maria Wisser
1987	Connie Paraskevin-Young
1988	Connie Paraskevin-Young
1989	Connie Paraskevin-Young

1990	Renee Duprel
1991	Renee Duprel
1992	Connie Paraskevin-Young
1993	Lucy Tyler
1994	Connie Paraskevin-Young
1995	Connie Paraskevin-Young
1996	Connie Paraskevin-Young
1997	Nicole Reinhart

Kilometer Time Trial

1984	Rebecca Twigg
1985	Ellen Braun
1986	Rebecca Twigg
1987	Ellen Braun
1988	Peggy Maass
1989	Janie Eickhoff
1990	Sharon Penn
1991	Lucy Vinnicombe
1992	Amanda Henry
1993	Lucy Tyler
1994	Karen Dunne
1995	Rebecca Twigg

500 Meters (replaced Kilometer time trial)

| 1996 | Chris Witty |
| 1997 | Nicole Reinhart |

Individual Pursuit

1967	Nancy Burghart
1968	Nancy Burghart
1969	No contest held
1970	Audrey McElmury
1971	Kathy Ecroth
1972	Clara Teyssier
1973	Mary Jane Reoch
1974	Mary Jane Reoch
1975	Mary Jane Reoch
1976	Connie Carpenter
1977	Connie Carpenter
1978	Mary Jane Reoch
1979	Connie Carpenter
1980	Betsy Davis
1981	Rebecca Twigg
1982	Rebecca Twigg
1983	Cindy Olavarri
1984	Rebecca Twigg
1985	Betsy Davis
1986	Rebecca Twigg
1987	Mindee Mayfield
1988	Mindee Mayfield
1989	Mindee Mayfield
1990	Janie Eickhoff
1991	Janie Eickhoff
1992	Rebecca Twigg
1993	Janie Eickhoff
1994	Janie Eickhoff
1995	Rebecca Twigg
1996	Rebecca Twigg
1997	Rebecca Twigg

Points Race

1978	Mary Jane Reoch
1979	Mary Jane Reoch
1980	Mary Jane Reoch
1981	Connie Carpenter
1982	Connie Carpenter
1983	Betsy Davis
1984	Rebecca Twigg
1985	Collette Gernay
1986	Karen Bliss
1987	Karen Bliss
1988	Janie Eickhoff
1989	Karen Bliss
1990	Janie Eickhoff
1991	Karen Bliss
1992	Janie Eickhoff
1993	Janie Eickhoff
1994	Janie Eickhoff
1995	Jessica Grieco
1996	Jane Quigley
1997	Karen Dunne

Diving
Women's Outdoor National Champions

Springboard—Three Foot/One Meter

1948	Zoe Ann Olsen
1949	Zoe Ann Olsen
1950	Patricia McCormick
1951	Patricia McCormick
1952	No contest held
1953	Patricia McCormick
1954	Patricia McCormick
1955	Patricia McCormick
1956	Patricia McCormick
1957	Paula Jean Myers
1958	Paula Jean Myers
1959	Irene MacDonald
1960	No contest held
1961	No contest held
1962	No contest held
1963	No contest held
1964	Patsy Willard
1965	Joel O'Connell
1966	Joel O'Connell
1967	Micki King
1968	Cynthia Potter
1969	Cynthia Potter
1970	Cynthia Potter
1971	Cynthia Potter
1972	Cynthia Potter
1973	Cynthia Potter
1974	Cynthia Potter
1975	Cynthia Potter-McIngvale
1976	Cynthia Potter-McIngvale
1977	Jennifer Chandler
1978	Cynthia Potter
1979	Kelly McCormick

1980	Kelly McCormick		1961	Joel Lenzi
1981	Kelly McCormick		1962	Barbara McAlister
1982	Megan Neyer		1963	Jeanne Collier
1983	Megan Neyer		1964	Barbara Talmage
1984	Wendy Lucero		1965	Micki King
1985	Wendy Lucero		1966	Sue Gossick
1986	Megan Neyer		1967	Micki King
1987	Megan Neyer		1968	Jerrie Adair
1988	Megan Neyer		1969	Micki King
1989	Wendy Lucero		1970	Micki King
1990	Krista Wilson		1971	Cynthia Potter
1991	Wendy Lucero		1972	Cynthia Potter
1992	Kristen Kane		1973	Carrie Irish
1993	Carrie Zarse		1974	Christine Loock
1994	Melisa Moses		1975	Cynthia Potter-McIngvale
1995	Doris Glenn Easterly		1976	Cynthia Potter-McIngvale
1996	Doris Glenn Easterly		1977	Christine Loock
1997	Erica Sorgi		1978	Jennifer Chandler
			1979	Michele Hain

Springboard—Ten Foot/Three Meter

1921	Helen Meany		1980	Chris Suefert
1922	Helen Meany		1981	Megan Neyer
1923	Aileen Riggin		1982	Kelly McCormick
1924	Aileen Riggin		1983	Chris Suefert
1925	Aileen Riggin		1984	Wendy Lian Williams
1926	Helen Meany		1985	Kelly McCormick
1927	Helen Meany		1986	Megan Neyer
1928	Lillian Fergus		1987	Kelly McCormick
1929	Georgia Coleman		1988	Tristan Baker-Schultz
1930	Georgia Coleman		1989	Wendy Lucero
1931	Georgia Coleman		1990	Wendy Lucero
1932	Katherine Rawls		1991	Krista Klein
1933	Katherine Rawls		1992	Veronica Ribot-Canales
1934	Katherine Rawls		1993	Eileen Richetelli
1935	Mary Hoerger		1994	Melisa Moses
1936	Claudia Eckert		1995	Eileen Richetelli
1937	Marjorie Gestring		1996	Erica Sorgi
1938	Marjorie Gestring		1997	Laura Wilkinson
1939	Helen Crienkovich			
1940	Marjorie Gestring			
1941	Helen Crienkovich		## Platform (10 Meter)	
1942	Ann Ross			
1943	Ann Ross		1916	Evelyn Burnett
1944	Ann Ross		1917	Aileen Allen
1945	Helen C. Morgan		1918	Josephine Bartlett
1946	Zoe Ann Olsen		1919	Betty Grimes
1947	Zoe Ann Olsen		1920	No contest held
1948	Zoe Ann Olsen		1921	Helen Meany
1949	Zoe Ann Olsen		1922	Helen Meany
1950	Patricia McCormick		1923	Helen Meany
1951	Patricia McCormick		1924	No contest held
1952	No contest held		1925	Helen Meany
1953	Patricia McCormick		1926	Esther Foley
1954	Patricia McCormick		1927	No contest held
1955	Patricia McCormick		1928	Helen Meany
1956	Patricia McCormick		1929	Georgia Coleman
1957	Paula Jean Myers		1930	Georgia Coleman
1958	Paula Jean Myers		1931	Georgia Coleman
1959	Irene MacDonald		1932	No contest held
1960	Patsy Willard		1933	Dorothy Poynton
			1934	Dorothy Poynton Hill
			1935	Dorothy Poynton Hill
			1936	Ruth Jump

1937	Ruth Jump
1938	Ruth Jump
1939	Marjorie Gestring
1940	Marjorie Gestring
1941	Helen Crienkovich
1942	Marjorie Reinholdt
1943	Jeanne Kessler
1944	No contest held
1945	Helen Crienkovich
1946	Victoria Draves
1947	Victoria Draves
1948	Victoria Draves
1949	Patricia McCormick
1950	Patricia McCormick
1951	Patricia McCormick
1952	No contest held
1953	Paula Jean Myers
1954	Patricia McCormick
1955	Juno Irwin
1956	Patricia McCormick
1957	Paula Jean Myers
1958	Paula Jean Myers
1959	Paula Jean Myers
1960	Juno Stover Irwin
1961	Barbara McAlister
1962	Linda Cooper
1963	Barbara Talmage
1964	Patsy Willard
1965	Lesley Bush
1966	Shirley Teeples
1967	Lesley Bush
1968	Ann Peterson
1969	Micki King
1970	Cynthia Potter
1971	Cynthia Potter
1972	Janet Ely
1973	Deborah Keplar
1974	Teri York
1975	Janet Ely
1976	Barbe Weinstein
1977	Christine Loock
1978	Melissa Briley
1979	Kit Salness
1980	Barb Weinstein
1981	Debbie Rush
1982	Wendy Wyland
1983	Michele Mitchell
1984	Michele Mitchell
1985	Michele Mitchell
1986	Michele Mitchell
1987	Mary Ellen Clark
1988	Wendy Lian Williams
1989	Wendy Wyland
1990	Wendy Lian Williams
1991	Ellen McGrath
1992	Mary Ellen Clark
1993	Mary Ellen Clark
1994	Becky Ruehl
1995	Becky Ruehl
1996	Becky Ruehl
1997	Laura Wilkinson

Fencing
U.S. National Champions

Women's Foil

The foil has a flexible, rectangular blade, approximately 35 inches in length, weighing less than one pound. Points are scored with the tip of the blade, which must land within the torso of the body.

1912	A. Baylis
1913	W.H. Dewar
1914	M. Stimson
1915	J. Pyle
1916	A. Voorhees
1917	F. Walton
1918	No contest held
1919	No contest held
1920	A. Gehring
1921	A. Gehring
1922	A. Gehring
1923	A. Gehring
1924	I. Hopper
1925	F. Schoonmaker
1926	F. Schoonmaker
1927	S. Stern
1928	M. Lloyd
1929	F. Schoonmaker
1930	E. Van Buskirk
1931	M. Lloyd
1932	D. Locke
1933	D. Locke
1934	H. Mayer
1935	H. Mayer
1936	J. De Tuscan
1937	H. Mayer
1938	H. Mayer
1939	H. Mayer
1940	H. Mroczkowska
1941	H. Mayer
1942	H. Mayer
1943	H. Mroczkowska
1944	M. Dalton
1945	M. Cerra
1946	H. Mayer
1947	H. Mroczkowska Dow
1948	H. Mroczkowska Dow
1949	P. Craus
1950	J. York
1951	J. York
1952	M. Mitchell
1953	P. Sweeney
1954	M. Mitchell
1955	M. Mitchell
1956	J. York-Romary
1957	J. York-Romary
1958	M. Mitchell
1959	P. Roldan
1960	J. York-Romary

1961	J. York-Romary
1962	E. Takeuchi
1963	H. King
1964	J. York-Romary
1965	J. York-Romary
1966	J. York-Romary
1967	H. King
1968	J. York-Romary
1969	R. White
1970	H. King
1971	H. King
1972	R. White
1973	T. Adamovich
1974	G. Jacobsen (D'Asaro)
1975	N. Tomlinson (Franke)
1976	A. O'Donnell (Russell)
1977	S. Armstrong
1978	G. Jacobsen D'Asaro
1979	J. Angelakis
1980	N. Tomlinson Franke
1981	J. Angelakis
1982	J. Angelakis
1983	D. Waples
1984	V. Bradford
1985	M. Sullivan
1986	C. Bilodeaux (Banos)
1987	C. Bilodeaux (Banos)
1988	S. Monplaisir
1989	C. Bilodeaux (Banos)
1990	Jen. Yu
1991	M.J. O'Neill
1992	C. Bilodeaux (Banos)
1993	F. Zimmermann
1994	A. Marsh
1995	A. Marsh
1996	F. Zimmermann
1997	I. Zimmermann

Women's Épée

The épée is similar in length to the foil, but is heavier, weighing approximately 27 ounces, with a larger guard (to protect the hand from a valid hit) and a much stiffer blade. Touches are scored only with the point of the blade. The entire body is the valid target area.

1981	S. Badders
1982	V. Bradford
1983	V. Bradford
1984	V. Bradford
1985	C. McClellan
1986	V. Bradford
1987	D. Stone
1988	X. Brown
1989	C. McClellan
1990	D. Stone
1991	M. Miller
1992	B. Turpin
1993	L. Marx
1994	D. Stone
1995	T. Orcutt
1996	L. Marx
1997	J. Burke

Figure Skating
U.S. Women's Singles Champions

1914	Theresa Weld
1915	No contest held
1916	No contest held
1917	No contest held
1918	Rosemary Beresford
1919	No contest held
1920	Theresa Weld
1921	Theresa Weld Blanchard
1922	Theresa Weld Blanchard
1923	Theresa Weld Blanchard
1924	Theresa Weld Blanchard
1925	Beatrix Loughran
1926	Beatrix Loughran
1927	Beatrix Loughran
1928	Maribel Vinson
1929	Maribel Vinson
1930	Maribel Vinson
1931	Maribel Vinson
1932	Maribel Vinson
1933	Maribel Vinson
1934	Suzanne David
1935	Maribel Vinson
1936	Maribel Vinson
1937	Maribel Vinson
1938	Joan Tozzer
1939	Joan Tozzer
1940	Joan Tozzer
1941	Jane Vaughn
1942	Jane Sullivan
1943	Gretchen Merrill
1944	Gretchen Merrill
1945	Gretchen Merrill
1946	Gretchen Merrill
1947	Gretchen Merrill
1948	Gretchen Merrill
1949	Yvonne Sherman
1950	Yvonne Sherman
1951	Sonya Klopfer
1952	Tenley Albright
1953	Tenley Albright
1954	Tenley Albright
1955	Tenley Albright
1956	Tenley Albright
1957	Carol Heiss
1958	Carol Heiss
1959	Carol Heiss
1960	Carol Heiss
1961	Laurence Owen
1962	Barbara Pursley
1963	Lorraine Hanlon
1964	Peggy Fleming
1965	Peggy Fleming

1966	Peggy Fleming
1967	Peggy Fleming
1968	Peggy Fleming
1969	Janet Lynn
1970	Janet Lynn
1971	Janet Lynn
1972	Janet Lynn
1973	Janet Lynn
1974	Dorothy Hamill
1975	Dorothy Hamill
1976	Dorothy Hamill
1977	Linda Fratianne
1978	Linda Fratianne
1979	Linda Fratianne
1980	Linda Fratianne
1981	Elaine Zayak
1982	Rosalyn Sumners
1983	Rosalyn Sumners
1984	Rosalyn Sumners
1985	Tiffany Chin
1986	Debi Thomas
1987	Jill Trenary
1988	Debi Thomas
1989	Jill Trenary
1990	Jill Trenary
1991	Tonya Harding
1992	Kristi Yamaguchi
1993	Nancy Kerrigan
1994	Tonya Harding
1995	Nicole Bobek
1996	Michelle Kwan
1997	Tara Lipinski

Golf—Major Champions
U.S. Women's Open

The U.S. Women's Open began under the direction of the Women's Professional Golf Association in 1946; it then passed to the Ladies Professional Golf Association in 1949 and to the United States Golf Association in 1953. The tournament used a match-play format its first year then switched to stroke play.

a—denotes amateur

1946	Patty Berg
1947	Betty Jameson
1948	Babe Didrikson Zaharias
1949	Louise Suggs
1950	Babe Didrikson Zaharias
1951	Betsy Rawls
1952	Louise Suggs
1953	Betsy Rawls
1954	Babe Didrikson Zaharias
1955	Fay Crocker
1956	Kathy Cornelius
1957	Betsy Rawls
1958	Mickey Wright
1959	Mickey Wright

1960	Betsy Rawls
1961	Mickey Wright
1962	Murle Lindstrom
1963	Mary Mills
1964	Mickey Wright
1965	Carol Mann
1966	Sandra Spuzich
1967	a-Catherine Lacoste
1968	Susie M. Berning
1969	Donna Caponi
1970	Donna Caponi
1971	JoAnne Carner
1972	Susie M. Berning
1973	Susie M. Berning
1974	Sandra Haynie
1975	Sandra Palmer
1976	JoAnne Carner
1977	Hollis Stacy
1978	Hollis Stacy
1979	Jerilyn Britz
1980	Amy Alcott
1981	Pat Bradley
1982	Janet Anderson
1983	Jan Stephenson
1984	Hollis Stacy
1985	Kathy Baker
1986	Jane Geddes
1987	Laura Davies
1988	Liselotte Neumann
1989	Betsy King
1990	Betsy King
1991	Meg Mallon
1992	Patty Sheehan
1993	Lauri Merten
1994	Patty Sheehan
1995	Annika Sorenstam
1996	Annika Sorenstam
1997	Alison Nicholas

LPGA Championship

Officially the Mazda LPGA Championship since 1987, the tournament began in 1955.

1955	Beverly Hanson
1956	Marlene Hagge
1957	Louise Suggs
1958	Mickey Wright
1959	Betsy Rawls
1960	Mickey Wright
1961	Mickey Wright
1962	Judy Kimball
1963	Mickey Wright
1964	Mary Mills
1965	Sandra Haynie
1966	Gloria Ehret
1967	Kathy Whitworth
1968	Sandra Post
1969	Betsy Rawls
1970	Shirley Englehorn
1971	Kathy Whitworth

1972	Kathy Ahern
1973	Mary Mills
1974	Sandra Haynie
1975	Kathy Whitworth
1976	Betty Burfeindt
1977	Chako Higuchi
1978	Nancy Lopez
1979	Donna Caponi
1980	Sally Little
1981	Donna Caponi
1982	Jan Stephenson
1983	Patty Sheehan
1984	Patty Sheehan
1985	Nancy Lopez
1986	Pat Bradley
1987	Jane Geddes
1988	Sherri Turner
1989	Nancy Lopez
1990	Beth Daniel
1991	Meg Mallon
1992	Betsy King
1993	Patty Sheehan
1994	Laura Davies
1995	Kelly Robbins
1996	Laura Davies
1997	Chris Johnson

du Maurier Classic

The tournament began as La Canadienne in 1973; it was renamed the Peter Jackson Classic (1974-83) and is now called the du Maurier Classic. This Canadian stop on the LPGA Tour became the third designated major championship in 1979.

1973	Jacelyne Bourassa
1974	Carole Jo Skala
1975	JoAnne Carner
1976	Donna Caponi
1977	Judy Rankin
1978	JoAnne Carner
1979	Amy Alcott
1980	Pat Bradley
1981	Jan Stephenson
1982	Sandra Haynie
1983	Hollis Stacy
1984	Juli Inkster
1985	Pat Bradley
1986	Pat Bradley
1987	Jody Rosenthal
1988	Sally Little
1989	Tammie Green
1990	Cathy Johnston
1991	Nancy Scranton
1992	Sherri Steinhaur
1993	Brandie Burton
1994	Martha Nause
1995	Jenny Lidback
1996	Laura Davies
1997	Colleen Walker

Nabisco Dinah Shore Classic

Formerly known as the Colgate Dinah Shore Classic from 1972 to 1981, the tournament became the LPGA's fourth designated major championship in 1983.

1972	Jane Blalock
1973	Mickey Wright
1974	Jo Ann Prentice
1975	Sandra Palmer
1976	Judy Rankin
1977	Kathy Whitworth
1978	Sandra Post
1979	Sandra Post
1980	Donna Caponi
1981	Nancy Lopez
1982	Sally Little
1983	Amy Alcott
1984	Juli Inkster
1985	Alice Miller
1986	Pat Bradley
1987	Betsy King
1988	Amy Alcott
1989	Juli Inkster
1990	Betsy King
1991	Amy Alcott
1992	Dottie Mochrie
1993	Helen Alfredsson
1994	Donna Andrews
1995	Nanci Bowen
1996	Patty Sheehan
1997	Betsy King

U.S. Women's Amateur

1895	Mrs. C.S. Brown
1896	Beatrix Hoyt
1897	Beatrix Hoyt
1898	Beatrix Hoyt
1899	Ruth Underhill
1900	Frances Griscom
1901	Genevieve Hecker
1902	Genevieve Hecker
1903	Bessie Anthony
1904	Georgianna Bishop
1905	Pauline Mackay
1906	Harriot Curtis
1907	Margaret Curtis
1908	Katherine Harley
1909	Dorothy Campbell
1910	Dorothy Campbell
1911	Margaret Curtis
1912	Margaret Curtis
1913	Gladys Ravenscroft
1914	Katherine Harley
1915	Florence Vanderbeck
1916	Alexa Stirling
1917	No contest held
1918	No contest held

1919	Alexa Stirling
1920	Alexa Stirling
1921	Marion Hollins
1922	Glenna Collett
1923	Edith Cummings
1924	Dorothy C. Hurd
1925	Glenna Collett
1926	Helen Stetson
1927	Miriam Burns Horn
1928	Glenna Collett
1929	Glenna Collett
1930	Glenna Collett
1931	Helen Hicks
1932	Virginia Van Wie
1933	Virginia Van Wie
1934	Virginia Van Wie
1935	Glenna Collett Vare
1936	Pamela Barton
1937	Estelle Lawson
1938	Patty Berg
1939	Betty Jameson
1940	Betty Jameson
1941	Elizabeth Hicks
1942	No contest held
1943	No contest held
1944	No contest held
1945	No contest held
1946	Babe Didrikson Zaharias
1947	Louise Suggs
1948	Grace Lenczyk
1949	Dorothy Porter
1950	Beverly Hanson
1951	Dorothy Kirby
1952	Jacqueline Pung
1953	Mary Lena Faulk
1954	Barbara Romack
1955	Patricia Lesser
1956	Marlene Stewart
1957	JoAnne Gunderson
1958	Anne Quast
1959	Barbara McIntire
1960	JoAnne Gunderson
1961	Anne Quast Decker
1962	JoAnne Gunderson
1963	Anne Quast Welts
1964	Barbara McIntire
1965	Jean Ashley
1966	JoAnne Carner
1967	Mary Lou Dill
1968	JoAnne Carner
1969	Catherine Lacoste
1970	Martha Wilkinson
1971	Laura Baugh
1972	Mary Budke
1973	Carol Semple
1974	Cynthia Hill
1975	Beth Daniel
1976	Donna Horton
1977	Beth Daniel
1978	Cathy Sherk
1979	Carolyn Hill

1980	Juli Inkster
1981	Juli Inkster
1982	Juli Inkster
1983	Joanne Pacillo
1984	Deb Richard
1985	Michiko Hattori
1986	Kay Cockerill
1987	Kay Cockerill
1988	Pearl Sinn
1989	Vicki Goetze
1990	Pat Hurst
1991	Amy Fruhwirth
1992	Vicki Goetze
1993	Jill McGill
1994	Wendy Ward
1995	Kelli Kuehne
1996	Kelli Kuehne
1997	Silvia Cavalle

Gymnastics
U.S. All-Around Champions

1931	Roberta C. Ranck
1932	No contest held
1933	Consetta Caruccio
1934	Consetta Caruccio
1935	Thera Steppich
1936	Jennie Caputo
1937	Pearl Perkins
1938	Helm McKee
1939	Margaret Weissmann
1940	No contest held
1941	Pearl Perkins Nightingale
1942	No contest held
1943	Pearl Perkins Nightingale
1944	Helm McKee
1945	Clara M. Schroth
1946	Clara M. Schroth
1947	Helen Schifano
1948	Helen Schifano
1949	Clara M. Schroth
1950	Clara M. Schroth
1951	Clara M. Schroth
1952	Clara Schroth Lomady
1953	Ruth Grulkowski
1954	Ruth Grulkowski
1955	Ernestine Russell
1956	Sandra Ruddick
1957	Muriel Davis
1958	Ernestine Russell
1959	Ernestine Russell
1960	Gail Sontgerath
1961	Kazuki Kadaowaki
1962	Dale McClemens
1963	Muriel Grossfeld
1964	Marie Walther
1965	Doris Ruchs Brause
1966	Linda Metheny
1967	Carolyn Hacker
1968	Linda Metheny

1969	Joyce Tanac	
1970	Linda Metheny	
1971	Linda Metheny	
1972	Linda Metheny	
1973	Joan Moore Rice	
1974	Joan Moore Rice	
1975	Ann Carr	
1976	Roxanne Pierce	
1977	Stephanie Willim	
1978	Kathy Johnson	
1979	Leslie Pyfer	
1980	Julianne McNamara	
1981	Tracee Talavera	
1982	Tracee Talavera	
1983	Dianne Durham	
1984	Mary Lou Retton	
1985	Sabrina Mar	
1986	Jennifer Sey	
1987	Kristie Phillips	
1988	Phoebe Mills	
1989	Brandy Johnson	
1990	Kim Zmeskal	
1991	Kim Zmeskal	
1992	Kim Zmeskal	
1993	Shannon Miller	
1994	Dominique Dawes	
1995	Dominique Moceanu	
1996	Shannon Miller	
1997	Vanessa Alter, Kristy Powell (tie)	

Marathon Winners

Boston Marathon

Begun in 1897, the Boston Marathon is America's oldest regularly contested footrace. Women were not allowed to enter the race until 1972.

1972	Nina Kuscsik, USA, 3:08:58
1973	Jacqueline Hansen, USA, 3:05:59
1974	Miki Gorman, USA, 2:47:11
1975	Liane Winter, West Germany, 2:42:24
1976	Kim Merritt, USA, 2:47:10
1977	Miki Gorman, USA, 2:48:33
1978	Gayle Barron, USA, 2:44:52
1979	Joan Benoit, USA, 2:35:15
1980	Jacqueline Gareau, Canada, 2:34:28
1981	Allison Roe, New Zealand, 2:26:46
1982	Charlotte Teske, West Germany, 2:29:33
1983	Joan Benoit, USA, 2:22:43
1984	Lorraine Moller, New Zealand, 2:29:28
1985	Lisa Larsen Weidenbach, USA, 2:34:06
1986	Ingrid Kristiansen, Norway, 2:24:55
1987	Rosa Mota, Portugal, 2:25:21
1988	Rosa Mota, Portugal, 2:24:30
1989	Ingrid Kristiansen, Norway, 2:24:33
1990	Rosa Mota, Portugal, 2:25:23
1991	Wanda Panfil, Poland, 2:24:18
1992	Olga Markova, CIS, 2:23:43

1993	Olga Markova, Russia, 2:25:27
1994	Uta Pippig, Germany, 2:21:45
1995	Uta Pippig, Germany, 2:25:11
1996	Uta Pippig, Germany, 2:27:12
1997	Fatuma Roba, Ethiopia, 2:26:23

Women's Wheelchair Winners

1977	Sharon Rahn, USA, 3:48:51
1978	Susan Schapiro, USA, 3:52:53
1979	Sheryl Bair, USA, 3:27:56
1980	Sharon Limpert, USA, 2:49:04
1981	Candace Cable-Brookes, USA, 2:38:41
1982	Candace Cable-Brookes, USA, 2:12:34
1983	Sherry Ramsey, USA, 2:27:07
1984	Sherry Ramsey, USA, 2:26:51
1985	Candace Cable-Brookes, USA, 2:05:26
1986	Candace Cable-Brookes, USA, 2:09:28
1987	Candace Cable-Brookes, USA, 2:19:55
1988	Candace Cable-Brookes, USA, 2:10:44
1989	Connie Hansen, Denmark, 1:50:06
1990	Jean Driscoll, USA, 1:43:17
1991	Jean Driscoll, USA, 1:42:42
1992	Jean Driscoll, USA, 1:36:52
1993	Jean Driscoll, USA, 1:34:50
1994	Jean Driscoll, USA, 1:34:22
1995	Jean Driscoll, USA, 1:40:41
1996	Jean Driscoll, USA, 1:52:54
1997	Louise Sauvage, Australia, 1:54:29

New York City Marathon

Started in 1970, the New York City Marathon is run in the fall, through all of the city's five boroughs, and finishes in Central Park.

1970	No finisher
1971	Beth Bonner, USA, 2:55:22
1972	Nina Kuscsik, USA, 3:08:41
1973	Nina Kuscsik, USA, 2:57:07
1974	Katherine Switzer, USA, 3:07:29
1975	Kim Merritt, USA, 2:46:14
1976	Miki Gorman, USA, 2:39:11
1977	Miki Gorman, USA, 2:43:10
1978	Grete Waitz, Norway, 2:32:30
1979	Grete Waitz, Norway, 2:27:33
1980	Grete Waitz, Norway, 2:25:41
1981	Allison Roe, New Zealand, 2:25:29
1982	Grete Waitz, Norway, 2:27:14
1983	Grete Waitz, Norway, 2:27:00
1984	Grete Waitz, Norway, 2:29:30
1985	Grete Waitz, Norway, 2:28:34
1986	Grete Waitz, Norway, 2:28:06
1987	Priscilla Welch, Great Britain, 2:30:17
1988	Grete Waitz, Norway, 2:28:07
1989	Ingrid Kristiansen, Norway, 2:25:30
1990	Wanda Panfil, Poland, 2:33:21
1991	Liz McColgan, Scotland, 2:27:23
1992	Lisa Ondieki, Australia, 2:24:40
1993	Uta Pippig, Germany, 2:26:24
1994	Tegla Loroupe, Kenya, 2:27:37

1995	Tegla Loroupe, Kenya, 2:28:06
1996	Anuta Catuna, Romania, 2:28:18
1997	Franziska Roehat-Moser, Switzerland, 2:28:43

Swimming

U.S. Open Champions

Originally called the U.S. International Meet, the U.S. Open changed from short course meters to long course meters in 1985 and began allowing colleges and club teams to compete. The U.S. Open is considered a national championship–caliber meet.

50-Meter Freestyle

1985	Jeanne Doolan
1986	Dara Torres
1987	Tamara Kostache
1988	Allison Bock
1989	Nicole Haislett
1990	Nicole Haislett
1991	Angel Martino
1992	Gitta Jensen
1993	Gitta Jensen
1994	Amy Van Dyken
1995	Amy Van Dyken
1996	Lindsey Farella
1997	Martina Moravcova

100-Meter Freestyle

1985	Conny van Bentum
1986	Dara Torres
1987	Dara Torres
1988	Jenny Thompson
1989	Nicole Haislett
1990	Nicole Haislett
1991	Gitta Jensen
1992	Gitta Jensen
1993	Gitta Jensen
1994	Shannon Shakespeare
1995	Catherine Fox
1996	Martina Moravcova
1997	Martina Moravcova

200-Meter Freestyle

1985	Heike Friedrich
1986	Mary Wayte
1987	Mary Wayte
1988	Stacy Cassiday
1989	Nicole Haislett
1990	Whitney Hedgepeth
1991	Gitta Jensen
1992	Claudia Poll
1993	Gitta Jensen
1994	Cristina Teuscher

1995	Sheila Taomina
1996	Lindsey Farella
1997	Martina Moravcova

400-Meter Freestyle

1985	Tiffany Cohen
1986	Janet Evans
1987	Janet Evans
1988	Stacy Cassiday
1989	Janet Evans
1990	Janet Evans
1991	Kim Small
1992	Claudia Poll
1993	Kim Small
1994	Brooke Bennett
1995	Brooke Bennett
1996	Brooke Bennett
1997	Brooke Bennett

800-Meter Freestyle

1985	Tiffany Cohen
1986	Janet Evans
1987	Janet Evans
1988	Andrea Hayes
1989	Janet Evans
1990	Jane Skillman
1991	Kim Small
1992	Sandra Carn
1993	Kim Small
1994	Brooke Bennett
1995	Jessica Foschi
1996	Brooke Bennett
1997	Diana Munz

100-Meter Backstroke

1985	Betsy Mitchell
1986	Betsy Mitchell
1987	Betsy Mitchell
1988	Krisztina Egerszegi
1989	Janie Wagstaff
1990	Janie Wagstaff
1991	Janie Wagstaff
1992	Sylvia Poll
1993	Alecia Humphrey
1994	Julie Howard
1995	Catherine Fox
1996	Catherine Fox
1997	Lea Maurer

200-Meter Backstroke

1985	Betsy Mitchell
1986	Beth Barr
1987	Krisztina Egerszegi
1988	Krisztina Egerszegi
1989	Janie Wagstaff
1990	Janie Wagstaff
1991	Anna Simcic

1992	Kim Higel
1993	Alecia Humphrey
1994	Beth Botsford
1995	Helene Ricardo
1996	Lia Oberstar
1997	Barbara Bedford

100-Meter Breaststroke

1985	Silke Homer
1986	Silke Homer
1987	Tracey McFarlane
1988	Suki Brownsdon
1989	Toni DeSilvia
1990	Tracy McFarlane
1991	Samantha Riley
1992	Alison Fealey
1993	Michele Schroder
1994	Shannon Shakespeare
1995	Amanda Beard
1996	Kristin MacGregor
1997	Kristine Quance

200-Meter Breaststroke

1985	Silke Homer
1986	Susan Johnson
1987	Xiaomin Huang
1988	Annalisa Nisiro
1989	Nathalie Giguere
1990	Anita Nall
1991	Anita Nall
1992	Gabrielle Csepe
1993	Kristine Quance
1994	Rae Abbott
1995	Amanda Beard
1996	Kristine Quance
1997	Kristine Quance

100-Meter Butterfly

1985	Mary T. Meagher
1986	Grace Cornelius
1987	Hong Qian
1988	Pamela Minthorn
1989	Janel Jorgensen
1990	Julie Gorman
1991	Susan O'Neil
1992	Angie Wester-King
1993	Berit Puggaard
1994	Berit Puggaard
1995	Cecile Jeanson
1996	Misty Hyman
1997	Misty Hyman

200-Meter Butterfly

1985	Mary T. Meagher
1986	Julie Gorman
1987	Stela Pura
1988	Rie Shitou

1989	Summer Sanders
1990	Summer Sanders
1991	Helen Morris
1992	Berit Puggaard
1993	Berit Puggaard
1994	Berit Puggaard
1995	Cecile Jeanson
1996	Misty Hyman
1997	Kristine Quance

200-Meter Individual Medley

1985	Michelle Griglione
1986	Mary Wayte
1987	Michelle Griglione
1988	Anna Petricevic
1989	Summer Sanders
1990	Summer Sanders
1991	Jacqui McKenzie
1992	Anne Kampfe
1993	Marianne Limpert
1994	Alison Fealey
1995	Michelle Griglione
1996	Kristine Quance
1997	Martina Moravcova

400-Meter Individual Medley

1985	Michelle Griglione
1986	Janet Evans
1987	Janet Evans
1988	Anna Petricevic
1989	Janet Evans
1990	Summer Sanders
1991	Jacqui McKenzie
1992	Anne Kampfe
1993	Kristine Quance
1994	Whitney Metzler
1995	Whitney Metzler
1996	Kristine Quance
1997	Kristine Quance

Table Tennis

U.S. National Champions

1976	He-Ja Lee
1977	Insook Bhushan
1978	Insook Bhushan
1979	He-Ja Lee
1980	He-Ja Lee
1981	Insook Bhushan
1982	Insook Bhushan
1983	Insook Bhushan
1984	Julie Ou
1985	Insook Bhushan
1986	Insook Bhushan
1987	Insook Bhushan
1988	Insook Bhushan
1989	Insook Bhushan
1990	Wei Wang

1991	Insook Bhushan
1992	Amy Feng
1993	Amy Feng
1994	Amy Feng
1995	Amy Feng
1996	Jun Gao
1997	Jun Gao

Tennis—Grand Slam Champions

Australian Open

The Australian tournament became an Open Championship that opened the tournament to both amateur and professional players and began offering prize money in 1969. Two tournaments were held in 1977, the first in January and the second in December. The tournament was moved back to January in 1987; thus no championship was contested in 1986.

1922	Margaret Molesworth
1923	Margaret Molesworth
1924	Sylvia Lance
1925	Daphne Akhurst
1926	Daphne Akhurst
1927	Esna Boyd
1928	Daphne Akhurst
1929	Daphne Akhurst
1930	Daphne Akhurst
1931	Coral Buttsworth
1932	Coral Buttsworth
1933	Joan Hartigan
1934	Joan Hartigan
1935	Dorothy Round
1936	Joan Hartigan
1937	Nancye Wynne
1938	Dorothy M. Bundy
1939	Emily Westacott
1940	Nancye Wynne
1941-45	No contest held
1946	Nancye Wynne Bolton
1947	Nancye Wynne Bolton
1948	Nancye Wynne Bolton
1949	Doris Hart
1950	Louise Brough
1951	Nancye Wynne Bolton
1952	Thelma Long
1953	Maureen Connolly
1954	Thelma Long
1955	Beryl Pemrose
1956	Mary Carter
1957	Shirley Fry
1958	Angela Mortimer
1959	Mary Reitano
1960	Margaret Smith
1961	Margaret Smith
1962	Margaret Smith
1963	Margaret Smith

1964	Margaret Smith
1965	Margaret Smith
1966	Margaret Smith
1967	Nancy Richey
1968	Billie Jean King
1969	Margaret Smith Court
1970	Margaret Smith Court
1971	Margaret Smith Court
1972	Virginia Wade
1973	Margaret Smith Court
1974	Evonne Goolagong
1975	Evonne Goolagong
1976	Evonne Goolagong Cawley
1977	Kerry Melville Reid, Evonne Goolagong Cawley
1978	Chris O'Neill
1979	Barbara Jordan
1980	Hana Mandlikova
1981	Martina Navratilova
1982	Chris Evert Lloyd
1983	Martina Navratilova
1984	Chris Evert Lloyd
1985	Martina Navratilova
1986	No contest held
1987	Hana Mandlikova
1988	Steffi Graf
1989	Steffi Graf
1990	Steffi Graf
1991	Monica Seles
1992	Monica Seles
1993	Monica Seles
1994	Steffi Graf
1995	Mary Pierce
1996	Monica Seles
1997	Martina Hingis

French Open

Prior to 1925, entry was restricted to members of French clubs. The tournament became an Open Championship in 1968.

1925	Suzanne Lenglen
1926	Suzanne Lenglen
1927	Kea Bouman
1928	Helen Wills
1929	Helen Wills
1930	Helen Wills Moody
1931	Cilly Aussem
1932	Helen Wills Moody
1933	Margaret Scriven
1934	Margaret Scriven
1935	Hilde Sperling
1936	Hilde Sperling
1937	Hilde Sperling
1938	Simone Mathieu
1939	Simone Mathieu
1940-45	No contest held
1946	Margaret Osborne
1947	Patricia Todd

1948	Nelly Landry		1884	Maud Watson
1949	Margaret Osborne duPont		1885	Maud Watson
1950	Doris Hart		1886	Blanche Bingley
1951	Shirley Fry		1887	Charlotte Dod
1952	Doris Hart		1888	Charlotte Dod
1953	Maureen Connolly		1989	Blanche Bingley Hillyard
1954	Maureen Connolly		1890	Lena Rice
1955	Angela Mortimer		1891	Charlotte Dod
1956	Althea Gibson		1892	Charlotte Dod
1957	Shirley Bloomer		1893	Charlotte Dod
1958	Zsuzsi Kormoczy		1894	Blanche Bingley Hillyard
1959	Christine Truman		1895	Charlotte Cooper
1960	Darlene Hard		1896	Charlotte Cooper
1961	Ann Hayden		1897	Blanche Bingley Hillyard
1962	Margaret Smith		1898	Charlotte Cooper
1963	Lesley Turner		1899	Blanche Bingley Hillyard
1964	Margaret Smith		1900	Blanche Bingley Hillyard
1965	Lesley Turner		1901	Charlotte Cooper Sterry
1966	Ann Jones		1902	Muriel Robb
1967	Francoise Durr		1903	Dorothea Douglass
1968	Nancy Richey		1904	Dorothea Douglass
1969	Margaret Smith Court		1905	May Sutton
1970	Margaret Smith Court		1906	Dorothea Douglass
1971	Evonne Goolagong		1907	May Sutton
1972	Billie Jean King		1908	Charlotte Cooper Sterry
1973	Margaret Smith Court		1909	Dora Boothby
1974	Chris Evert		1910	Dorothea Douglass Lambert Chambers
1975	Chris Evert		1911	Dorothea Douglass Lambert Chambers
1976	Sue Barker		1912	Ethel Larcombe
1977	Mima Jausovec		1913	Dorothea Douglass Lambert Chambers
1978	Virginia Ruzici		1914	Dorothea Douglass Lambert Chambers
1979	Chris Evert Lloyd		1915-18	No tournament held
1980	Chris Evert Lloyd		1919	Suzanne Lenglen
1981	Hana Mandlikova		1920	Suzanne Lenglen
1982	Martina Navratilova		1921	Suzanne Lenglen
1983	Chris Evert Lloyd		1922	Suzanne Lenglen
1984	Martina Navratilova		1923	Suzanne Lenglen
1985	Chris Evert Lloyd		1924	Kathleen McKane
1986	Chris Evert Lloyd		1925	Suzanne Lenglen
1987	Steffi Graf		1926	Kathleen Godfree
1988	Steffi Graf		1927	Helen Wills
1989	Arantxa Sanchez Vicario		1928	Helen Wills
1990	Monica Seles		1929	Helen Wills
1991	Monica Seles		1930	Helen Wills Moody
1992	Monica Seles		1931	Cilly Aussem
1993	Steffi Graf		1932	Helen Wills Moody
1994	Arantxa Sanchez Vicario		1933	Helen Wills Moody
1995	Steffi Graf		1934	Dorothy Round
1996	Steffi Graf		1935	Helen Wills Moody
1997	Iva Majdi		1936	Helen Jacobs
			1937	Dorothy Round
			1938	Helen Wills Moody
			1939	Alice Marble
			1940-45	No tournament held
			1946	Pauline Betz
			1947	Margaret Osborne
			1948	Louise Brough
			1949	Louise Brough
			1950	Louise Brough

Wimbledon

This event was officially called "The Lawn Tennis Championships" at the All-English Club, Wimbledon. The challenge round system (defending champion automatically qualifies for following year's final) was used from 1886 to 1921. The tournament became an Open Championship in 1968.

1951	Doris Hart	1891	Mabel Cahill
1952	Maureen Connolly	1892	Mabel Cahill
1953	Maureen Connolly	1893	Aline Terry
1954	Maureen Connolly	1894	Helen Hellwig
1955	Louise Brough	1895	Juliette Atkinson
1956	Shirley Fry	1896	Elisabeth Moore
1957	Althea Gibson	1897	Juliette Atkinson
1958	Althea Gibson	1898	Juliette Atkinson
1959	Maria Bueno	1899	Marion Jones
1960	Maria Bueno	1900	Myrtle McAteer
1961	Anglea Mortimer	1901	Elisabeth Moore
1962	Karen Hantz Susman	1902	Marion Jones
1963	Margaret Smith	1903	Elisabeth Moore
1964	Maria Bueno	1904	May Sutton
1965	Margaret Smith	1905	Elisabeth Moore
1966	Billie Jean King	1906	Helen Homans
1967	Billie Jean King	1907	Evelyn Sears
1968	Billie Jean King	1908	Maud Barger-Wallach
1969	Ann Jones	1909	Hazel Hotchkiss
1970	Margaret Smith Court	1910	Hazel Hotchkiss
1971	Evonne Goolagong	1911	Hazel Hotchkiss
1972	Billie Jean King	1912	Mary K Browne
1973	Billie Jean King	1913	Mary K Browne
1974	Chris Evert	1914	Mary K Browne
1975	Billie Jean King	1915	Molla Bjurstedt
1976	Chris Evert	1916	Molla Bjurstedt
1977	Virginia Wade	1917	Molla Bjurstedt
1978	Martina Navratilova	1918	Molla Bjurstedt
1979	Martina Navratilova	1919	Hazel Hotchkiss Wightman
1980	Evonne Goolagong Cawley	1920	Molla Bjurstedt Mallory
1981	Chris Evert Lloyd	1921	Molla Bjurstedt Mallory
1982	Martina Navratilova	1922	Molla Bjurstedt Mallory
1983	Martina Navratilova	1923	Helen Wills
1984	Martina Navratilova	1924	Helen Wills
1985	Martina Navratilova	1925	Helen Wills
1986	Martina Navratilova	1926	Molla Bjurstedt Mallory
1987	Martina Navratilova	1927	Helen Wills
1988	Steffi Graf	1928	Helen Wills
1989	Steffi Graf	1929	Helen Wills
1990	Martina Navratilova	1930	Betty Nuthall
1991	Steffi Graf	1931	Helen Wills Moody
1992	Steffi Graf	1932	Helen Jacobs
1993	Steffi Graf	1933	Helen Jacobs
1994	Conchita Martinez	1934	Helen Jacobs
1995	Steffi Graf	1935	Helen Jacobs
1996	Steffi Graf	1936	Alice Marble
1997	Martina Hingis	1937	Anita Lizane
		1938	Alice Marble
		1939	Alice Marble
		1940	Alice Marble

U.S. Open

Initially, the U.S. Open was called the U.S. National Championships. Amateur and Open Championships were held in 1968 and 1969. In 1970, the tournament became an exclusively Open Championship.

1887	Ellen Hansell	1941	Sarah Palfrey Cooke
1888	Bertha L. Townsend	1942	Pauline Betz
1889	Bertha L. Townsend	1943	Pauline Betz
1890	Ellen C. Roosevelt	1944	Pauline Betz
		1945	Sarah Palfrey Cooke
		1946	Pauline Betz
		1947	Louise Brough
		1948	Margaret Osborne duPont
		1949	Margaret Osborne duPont
		1950	Margaret Osborne duPont
		1951	Maureen Connolly

1952	Maureen Connolly		1988	Steffi Graf
1953	Maureen Connolly		1989	Steffi Graf
1954	Doris Hart		1990	Gabriela Sabatini
1955	Doris Hart		1991	Monica Seles
1956	Shirley Fry		1992	Monica Seles
1957	Althea Gibson		1993	Steffi Graf
1958	Althea Gibson		1994	Aranxta Sanchez Vicario
1959	Maria Bueno		1995	Steffi Graf
1960	Darlene Hard		1996	Steffi Graf
1961	Darlene Hard		1997	Martina Hingis
1962	Margaret Smith			
1963	Maria Bueno			
1964	Maria Bueno			

Triathlon
Ironman Championships

1965	Margaret Smith			
1966	Maria Bueno		1978	No finishers
1967	Billie Jean King		1979	Lyn Lemaire, 12:55
1968	Virginia Wade		1980	Robin Beck, 11:21:24
1969	Margaret Smith Court		1981	Linda Sweeney, 12:00:32
1970	Margaret Smith Court		1982	Kathleen McCartney, 11:09:40
1971	Billie Jean King		1983	Sylviane Puntous, 10:43:36
1972	Billie Jean King		1984	Sylviane Puntous, 10:25:13
1973	Margaret Smith Court		1985	Joanne Ernst, 10:25:22
1974	Billie Jean King		1986	Paula Newby-Fraser, 9:49:14
1975	Chris Evert		1987	Erin Baker, 9:35:25
1976	Chris Evert		1988	Paula Newby-Fraser, 9:01:01
1977	Chris Evert		1989	Paula Newby-Fraser, 9:00:56
1978	Chris Evert		1990	Erin Baker, 9:13:42
1979	Tracy Austin		1991	Paula Newby-Fraser, 9:07:52
1980	Chris Evert Lloyd		1992	Paula Newby-Fraser, 8:55:28
1981	Tracy Austin		1993	Paula Newby-Fraser, 8:58:23
1982	Chris Evert Lloyd		1994	Paula Newby-Fraser, 9:20:14
1983	Martina Navratilova		1995	Karen Smyers, 9:16:46
1984	Martina Navratilova		1996	Paula Newby-Fraser, 9:06:49
1985	Hana Mandlikova		1997	Heather Fuhr, 9:31:43
1986	Martina Navratilova			
1987	Martina Navratilova			

Appendix C
National Collegiate Athletic
Association (NCAA) Champions—
Division I*

Cross Country

1981	Betty Springs, North Carolina
1982	Lesley Welch, Virginia
1983	Betty Springs, North Carolina
1984	Cathy Branta, Wisconsin
1985	Suzie Tuffey, North Carolina
1986	Angela Chalmers, Northern Arizona
1987	Kimberly Betz, Indiana
1988	Michelle Dekkers, Indiana
1989	Vicki Huber, Villanova
1990	Sonia O'Sullivan, Villanova
1991	Sonia O'Sullivan, Villanova
1992	Carole Zajac, Villanova
1993	Carole Zajac, Villanova
1994	Jen Rhines, Villanova
1995	Kathy Butler, Wisconsin
1996	Amy Skieresz, Arizona
1997	Carrie Tollfeson, Villanova

Fencing

1982	Joy Ellingson, San Jose State
1983	Jana Angelakis, Penn State
1984	Mary Jane O'Neill, Pennsylvania
1985	Caitlin Bilodeaux, Columbia-Barnard
1986	Molly Sullivan, Notre Dame
1987	Caitlin Bilodeaux, Columbia-Barnard
1988	Molly Sullivan, Notre Dame
1989	Yasemin Topcu, Wayne State

Golf

1982	Kathy Baker, Tulsa
1983	Penny Hammel, Miami (Fla.)
1984	Cindy Schreyer, Georgia
1985	Danielle Ammaccapane, Arizona State
1986	Page Dunlap, Florida
1987	Caroline Keggi, New Mexico
1988	Melissa McNamara, Tulsa
1989	Pat Hurst, San Jose State
1990	Susan Slaughter, Arizona
1991	Annika Sorenstam, Arizona
1992	Vicki Goetze, Georgia
1993	Charlotta Sorenstam, Texas
1994	Emilee Klein, Arizona State
1995	Kristel Mourgue d'Algue, Arizona State
1996	Marisa Baena, Arizona
1997	Heather Bowie, Texas

Gymnastics

All-Around

1982	Sue Stednitz, Utah
1983	Megan McCunniff, Utah
1984	Megan Marsden, Utah
1985	Penney Hauschild, Alabama
1986	Penney Hauschild, Alabama
	Jackie Brummer, Arizona State
1987	Kelly Garrison-Steves, Oklahoma
1988	Kelly Garrison-Steves, Oklahoma
1989	Corrinne Wright, Georgia
1990	Dee Dee Foster, Alabama
1991	Hope Spivey, Georgia
1992	Missy Marlowe, Utah
1993	Jenny Hansen, Kentucky
1994	Jenny Hansen, Kentucky
1995	Jenny Hansen, Kentucky
1996	Meredith Willard, Alabama
1997	Kim Arnold, Georgia

*Reprinted from *National Collegiate Championships Records* book with permission from the NCAA.

Balance Beam

1982	Sue Stednitz, Utah
1983	Julie Goewey, California State-Fullerton
1984	Heidi Anderson, Oregon State
1985	Lisa Zeis, Arizona State
1986	Jackie Brummer, Arizona State
1987	Yumi Mordre, Washington
1988	Kelly Garrison-Steves, Oklahoma
1989	Jill Andrews, UCLA
	Joy Selig, Oregon State
1990	Joy Selig, Oregon State
1991	Missy Marlowe, Utah
	Gina Basile, Alabama
1992	Missy Marlowe, Utah
	Dana Dobransky, Alabama
1993	Dana Dobransky, Alabama
1994	Jenny Hansen, Kentucky
1995	Jenny Hansen, Kentucky
1996	Summer Reid, Utah
1997	Summer Reid, Utah
	Elizabeth Reid, Arizona State

Floor Exercise

1982	Mary Ayotte-Law, Oregon State
1983	Kim Neal, Arizona State
1984	Maria Anz, Florida
1985	Lisa Mitzel, Utah
1986	Lisa Zeis, Arizona State
	Penny Hauschild, Alabama
1987	Kim Hamilton, UCLA
1988	Kim Hamilton, UCLA
1989	Corrinne Wright, Georgia
	Kim Hamilton, UCLA
1990	Joy Selig, Oregon State
1991	Hope Spivey, Georgia
1992	Missy Marlowe, Utah
1993	Heather Stepp, Georgia
	Tammy Marshall, Massachusetts
	Amy Durham, Oregon State
1994	Hope Spivey-Shelley, Georgia
1995	Jenny Hansen, Kentucky
	Stella Umeh, UCLA
	Leslie Angeles, Georgia
1996	Kim Kelly, Alabama
	Heidi Hornbeek, Arizona
1997	Leah Brown, Georgia

Uneven Bars

1982	Lisa Shirk, Pittsburgh
1983	Jeri Cameron, Arizona State
1984	Jackie Brummer, Arizona State
1985	Penny Hauschild, Alabama
1986	Lucy Wener, Georgia
1987	Lucy Wener, Georgia
1988	Kelly Garrison-Steves, Oklahoma
1989	Lucy Wener, Georgia
1990	Marie Roethlisberger, Minnesota
1991	Kelly Macy, Georgia
1992	Missy Marlowe, Utah
1993	Agina Simpkins, Georgia
	Beth Wymer, Michigan
1994	Lori Strong, Georgia
	Sandy Woolsey, Utah
	Beth Wymer, Michigan

1995	Beth Wymer, Michigan
1996	Stephanie Woods, Alabama
1997	Jenni Beathard, Georgia

Vault

1982	Elaine Alfano, Utah
1983	Elaine Alfano, Utah
1984	Megan Marsden, Utah
1985	Elaine Alfano, Utah
1986	Kim Neal, Arizona State
	Pam Loree, Penn State
1987	Yumi Mordre, Washington
1988	Jill Andrews, UCLA
1989	Kim Hamilton, UCLA
1990	Michele Bryant, Nebraska
1991	Anna Basaldua, Arizona
	Hope Spivey, Georgia
1992	Tammy Marshall, Massachusetts
	Heather Stepp, Georgia
	Kristen Kenoyer, Utah
1993	Heather Stepp, Georgia
1994	Jenny Hansen, Kentucky
1995	Jenny Hansen, Kentucky
1996	Leah Brown, Georgia
1997	Susan Hines, Florida

Swimming and Diving

50-Yard Freestyle

1982	Diane Johnson, Arizona
1983	Tammy Thomas, Kansas
1984	Krissie Bush, Stanford
1985	Conny Van Bentum, California
1986	Jenna Johnson, Stanford
1987	Jenna Johnson, Stanford
1988	Dara Torres, Florida
	Leigh Ann Fetter, Texas
1989	Leigh Ann Fetter, Texas
1990	Leigh Ann Fetter, Texas
1991	Leigh Ann Fetter, Texas
1992	Jenny Thompson, Stanford
1993	Jenny Thompson, Stanford
1994	Amy Van Dyken, Colorado State
1995	Ashley Tappin, Arizona
1996	Nicole deMan, Tennessee
1997	Catherine Fox, Stanford

100-Yard Freestyle

1982	Amy Caulkins, Florida
1983	Tammy Thomas, Kansas
1984	Agneta Eriksson, Texas
1985	Mary Wayte, Florida
1986	Jenna Johnson, Stanford
1987	Jenna Johnson, Stanford
1988	Dara Torres, Florida
1989	Leigh Ann Fetter, Texas
1990	Leigh Ann Fetter, Texas
1991	Leigh Ann Fetter, Texas
1992	Jenny Thompson, Stanford
1993	Jenny Thompson, Stanford
1994	Jenny Thompson, Stanford
1995	Jenny Thompson, Stanford

1996 Claudia Franco, Stanford
1997 Martina Moravcova, Southern Methodist

200-Yard Freestyle

1982 Marybeth Linzmeier, Stanford
1983 Susan Habernigg, Southern California
1984 Marybeth Linzmeier, Stanford
1985 Susan Habernigg, Southern California
1986 Conny Van Bentum, California
1987 Mitzi Kremer, Clemson
1988 Tami Bruce, Florida
1989 Mitzi Kremer, Clemson
1990 Whitney Hedgepeth, Florida
1991 Nicole Haislett, Florida
1992 Nicole Haislett, Florida
1993 Nicole Haislett, Florida
1994 Nicole Haislett, Florida
1995 Ashley Tappin, Arizona
1996 Martina Moravcova, Southern Methodist
1997 Martina Moravcova, Southern Methodist

500-Yard Freestyle

1982 Marybeth Linzmeier, Stanford
1983 Marybeth Linzmeier, Stanford
1984 Marybeth Linzmeier, Stanford
1985 Tiffany Cohen, Texas
1986 Tami Bruce, Florida
1987 Mitzi Kremer, Clemson
1988 Tami Bruce, Florida
1989 Mitzi Kremer, Clemson
1990 Janet Evans, Stanford
1991 Janet Evans, Stanford
1992 Erika Hansen, Texas
1993 Lisa Jacob, Stanford
1994 Nicole Haislett, Florida
1995 Mimosa McNerney, Florida
1996 Lindsay Benko, Southern California
1997 Lindsay Benko, Southern California

1,650-Yard Freestyle (Mile)

1982 Marybeth Linzmeier, Stanford
1983 Marybeth Linzmeier, Stanford
1984 Marybeth Linzmeier, Stanford
1985 Tiffany Cohen, Texas
1986 Tami Bruce, Florida
1987 Tami Bruce, Florida
1988 Tami Bruce, Florida
1989 Erika Hansen, Georgia
1990 Janet Evans, Stanford
1991 Janet Evans, Stanford
1992 Katy Arris, Texas
1993 Mimosa McNerney, Florida
1994 Tobie Smith, Texas
1995 Mimosa McNerney, Florida
1996 Mimosa McNerney, Florida
1997 Trina Jackson, Arizona

100-Yard Backstroke

1982 Sue Walsh, North Carolina
1983 Sue Walsh, North Carolina
1984 Sue Walsh, North Carolina
1985 Deborah Risen, Texas

1986 Betsy Mitchell, Texas
1987 Betsy Mitchell, Texas
1988 Betsy Mitchell, Texas
1989 Kristen Linehan, Florida
1990 Kristen Linehan, Florida
1991 Jodi Wilson, Texas
1992 Lea Loveless, Stanford
1993 Lea Loveless, Stanford
1994 Lea Loveless, Stanford
1995 Alecia Humphrey, Michigan
1996 Jessica Tong, Stanford
1997 Catherine Fox, Stanford

200-Yard Backstroke

1982 Sue Walsh, North Carolina
1983 Sue Walsh, North Carolina
1984 Sue Walsh, North Carolina
1985 Tori Trees, Texas
1986 Betsy Mitchell, Texas
1987 Betsy Mitchell, Texas
1988 Betsy Mitchell, Texas
1989 Kristen Linehan, Florida
1990 Kristen Linehan, Florida
1991 Beth Barr, Florida
1992 Whitney Hedgepeth, Texas
1993 Lea Loveless, Stanford
1994 Whitney Hedgepeth, Texas
1995 Alecia Humphrey, Michigan
1996 Lindsay Benko, Southern California
1997 Lindsay Benko, Southern California

100-Yard Breaststroke

1982 Kathy Treible, Florida
1983 Jeanne Childs, Hawaii
1984 Tracy Caulkins, Florida
1985 Tracey McFarlane, Texas
1986 Cindy Ounpuu, Florida
1987 Tracey McFarlane, Texas
1988 Tracey McFarlane, Texas
1989 Stephanie Zunich, Florida
1990 Stephanie Zunich, Florida
1991 Lori Heisick, Stanford
1992 Susan Lipscomb, Southern Methodist
1993 Lara Hooiveld, Michigan
1994 Beata Kaszuba, Arizona State
1995 Beata Kaszuba, Arizona State
1996 Penny Heyns, Nebraska
1997 Gretchen Hegener, Minnesota

200-Yard Breaststroke

1982 Kathy Treible, Florida
1983 Jeanne Childs, Hawaii
1984 Susie Rapp, Stanford
1985 Kim Rhodenbaugh, Texas
1986 Cindy Ounpuu, Florida
1987 Susie Rapp, Stanford
1988 Hiroko Nagasaki, California
1989 Ann Colloton, Michigan
1990 Jill Johnson, Stanford
1991 Dorsey Tierney, Texas
1992 Lisa Flood, Villanova
1993 Lara Hooiveld, Michigan
1994 Kristine Quance, Southern California

1995	Beata Kaszuba, Arizona State
1996	Kristine Quance, Southern California
1997	Kristine Quance, Southern California

100-Yard Butterfly

1982	Tracy Caulkins, Florida
1983	Jill Sterkel, Texas
1984	Joan Pennington, Texas
1985	Mary T. Meagher, California
1986	Jenna Johnson, Stanford
1987	Mary T. Meagher, California
1988	Dara Torres, Florida
1989	Jenna Johnson, Stanford
1990	Janel Jorgensen, Stanford
1991	Crissy Ahmann-Leighton, Arizona
1992	Crissy Ahmann-Leighton, Arizona
1993	Janel Jorgensen, Stanford
1994	Jenny Thompson, Stanford
1995	Jenny Thompson, Stanford
1996	Lisa Coole, Georgia
1997	Mimi Bowen, Auburn

200-Yard Butterfly

1982	Tracy Caulkins, Florida
1983	Mary T. Meagher, California
1984	Tracy Caulkins, Florida
1985	Mary T. Meagher, California
1986	Mary T. Meagher, California
1987	Mary T. Meagher, California
1988	Julie Gorman, Florida
1989	Julie Gorman, Florida
1990	Janel Jorgensen, Stanford
1991	Summer Sanders, Stanford
1992	Summer Sanders, Stanford
1993	Janel Jorgensen, Stanford
1994	Berit Puggaard, Southern Methodist
1995	Berit Puggaard, Southern Methodist
1996	Annette Salmeen, UCLA
1997	Lia Oberstar, Southern Methodist

200-Yard Individual Medley

1982	Tracy Caulkins, Florida
1983	Tracy Caulkins, Florida
1984	Tracy Caulkins, Florida
1985	Kim Rhodenbaugh, Texas
1986	Susi Rapp, Stanford
1987	Betsy Mitchell, Texas
1988	Julie Gorman, Florida
1989	Angel Myers, Furman
1990	Janel Jorgensen, Stanford
1991	Summer Sanders, Stanford
1992	Summer Sanders, Stanford
1993	Nicole Haislett, Florida
1994	Kristine Quance, Southern California
1995	Jenny Thompson, Stanford
1996	Kristine Quance, Southern California
1997	Martina Moravcova, Southern Methodist

400-Yard Individual Medley

1982	Tracy Caulkins, Florida
1983	Tracy Caulkins, Florida
1984	Tracy Caulkins, Florida

1985	Mary Wayte, Florida
1986	Patty Sabo, Texas
1987	Janelle Bosse, Ohio State
1988	Julie Gorman, Florida
1989	Michelle Griglione, Florida
1990	Janet Evans, Stanford
1991	Summer Sanders, Stanford
1992	Summer Sanders, Stanford
1993	Mindy Gehrs, Michigan
1994	Kristine Quance, Southern California
1995	Allison Wagner, Florida
1996	Kristine Quance, Southern California
1997	Kristine Quance, Southern California

One-Meter Diving

1982	Megan Neyer, Florida
1983	Megan Neyer, Florida
1984	Megan Neyer, Florida
1985	Wendy Lucero, Southern Illinois
1986	Megan Neyer, Florida
1987	Karen LaFace, Ohio State
1988	Mary Fischbach, Michigan
1989	Alison Maisch, Louisiana State
1990	Julie Farrell, Michigan State
1991	Krista Wilson, Southern Methodist
1992	Cheril Santini, Southern Methodist
1993	Marina Smith, Auburn
1994	Vanessa Thelin, Brigham Young
1995	Cheril Santini, Southern Methodist
1996	Kimiko Hirai, Indiana
1997	Vera Ilyina, Texas

Three-Meter Diving

1982	Megan Neyer, Florida
1983	Megan Neyer, Florida
1984	Megan Neyer, Florida
1985	Robin Ford, Arkansas
1986	Megan Neyer, Florida
1987	Kim Fugett, Ohio State
1988	Mary Fischbach, Michigan
1989	Kelly Jenkins, Texas
1990	Krista Wilson, Southern Methodist
1991	Julie Farrell-Ovenhouse, Michigan State
1992	Eileen Richetelli, Stanford
1993	Eileen Richetelli, Stanford
1994	Robin Carter, Texas
1995	Tracy Bonner, Tennessee
1996	Michelle Rojohn, Kansas

Platform Diving

1990	Courtney Nelson, Brigham Young
1991	Courtney Nelson, Brigham Young
1992	Eileen Richetelli, Stanford
1993	Eileen Richetelli, Stanford
1994	Susie Ryan, Louisiana State
1995	Eileen Richetelli, Stanford
1996	Becky Ruehl, Cincinnati
1997	Laura Wilkinson, Texas

Tennis

| 1982 | Alycia Moulton, Stanford |
| 1983 | Beth Herr, Southern California |

1984	Lisa Spain, Georgia
1985	Linda Gates, Stanford
1986	Patty Fendick, Stanford
1987	Patty Fendick, Stanford
1988	Shaun Stafford, Florida
1989	Sandra Birch, Stanford
1990	Debbie Graham, Stanford
1991	Sandra Birch, Stanford
1992	Lisa Raymond, Florida
1993	Lisa Raymond, Florida
1994	Angela Lettiere, Georgia
1995	Keri Phebus, UCLA
1996	Jill Craybas, Florida
1997	Lilia Osterloh, Stanford

Indoor Track

55-Meter Dash

1983	Janet Burke, Nebraska
1984	Merlene Ottey, Nebraska
1985	Michelle Finn, Florida State
1986	Gwen Torrence, Georgia
1987	Gwen Torrence, Georgia
1988	Carlette Guidry, Texas
1989	Dawn Sowell, Lousiana State
1990	Carlette Guidry, Texas
1991	Carlette Guidry, Texas
1992	Chryste Gaines, Stanford
1993	Holli Hyche, Indiana State
1994	Holli Hyche, Indiana State
1995	Melina Sergent, Texas-El Paso
1996	D'Andre Hill, Louisiana State
1997	Sevatheda Fynes, Eastern Michigan

200-Meter Dash

1988	Pauline Davis, Alabama
1989	Dawn Sowell, LSU
1990	Carlette Guidry, Texas
1991	Carlette Guidry, Texas
1992	Michelle Collins, Houston
1993	Holli Hyche, Indiana State
1994	Holli Hyche, Indiana State
1995	Merlene Frazer, Texas
1996	Debbie Ferguson, Georgia
1997	Nanceen Perry, Texas

400-Meter Dash

1983	Diane Dixon, Ohio State
1984	Ruth Nganga, Arizona
1985	Lillie Leatherwood, Alabama
1988	Terri Dendy, George Mason
1989	Natasha Kaiser, Missouri
1990	Maicel Malone, Arizona State
1991	Maicel Malone, Arizona State
1992	Maicel Malone, Arizona State
1993	Shanelle Porter, Nebraska
1994	Flirtisha Harris, Seton Hall
1995	Youlanda Warren, Louisiana State
1996	Monique Hennagan, North Carolina
1997	LaTorsha Stroman, Louisiana State

800-Meter Run

1983	Joetta Clark, Tennessee
1984	Veronica McIntosh, Villanova
1985	Tina Parrott, Indiana
1988	Karol Davidson, Texas
1989	Edith Nakiyingi, Iowa State
1990	Meredith Rainey, Howard
1991	Edith Nakiyingi, Iowa State
1992	Mireilli Sankatsing, Eastern Michigan
1993	Amy Wickus, Wisconsin
1994	Amy Wickus, Wisconsin
1995	Amy Wickus, Wisconsin
1996	Kristi Kloster, Kansas
1997	Dawn Williams-Sewer, Arkansas-Little Rock

Mile Run

1983	Aisling Molloy, Brigham Young
1984	Linda Detlefsen, Georgia
1985	Tina Krebs, Clemson
1986	Tina Krebs, Clemson
1987	Suzy Favor, Wisconsin
1988	Vicki Huber, Villanova
1989	Suzy Favor, Wisconsin
1990	Suzy Favor, Wisconsin
1991	Jennifer Lanctot, Boston University
1992	Karen Glerum, Iowa
1993	Clair Eichner, Wisconsin
1994	Amy Rudolph, Providence
1995	Trine Pilskog, Arkansas
1996	Joline Staeheli, Georgetown
1997	Becki Wells, Florida

3,000-Meter Run

1983	PattiSue Plumer, Stanford
1984	Cathy Branta, Wisconsin
1985	Christine McMiken, Oklahoma
1986	Stephanie Herbst, Wisconsin
1987	Vicki Huber, Villanova
1988	Vicki Huber, Villanova
1989	Vicki Huber, Villanova
1990	Suzy Favor, Wisconsin
1991	Patty Wiegand, Tennessee
1992	Geraldine Hendricken, Providence
1993	Clare Eichner, Wisconsin
1994	Kay Gooch, Oklahoma
1995	Sarah Schwald, Arkansas
1996	Melody Fairchild, Oregon
1997	Kristine Jost, Villanova

5,000-Meter Run

1989	Jackie Goodman, Oklahoma State
1990	Valerie McGovern, Kentucky
1991	Sonia O'Sullivan, Villanova
1992	Tracy Dahl, Iowa
1993	Tracy Dahl Morris, Iowa
1994	Brenda Sleeuwenhoek, Arizona
1995	Jen Rhine, Villanova
1996	Marie McMahon, Providence
1997	Amy Skieresz, Arizona

55-Meter Hurdles

1983	Candy Young, FDU-Teaneck
1984	Candy Young, FDU-Teaneck
1985	Rhonda Blanford, Nebraska
1986	Rosalind Pendergraft-Council, Auburn
1987	LaVonna Martin, Tennessee
1988	LaVonna Martin, Tennessee
1989	Tananjalyn Stanley, Louisiana State
1990	Lynda Tolbert, Arizona State
1991	Mary Cobb, Louisiana State
1992	Gillian Russell, Miami (Fla.)
1993	Monifa Taylor, Florida
1994	Dionne Rose, Middle Tennessee State
1995	Gillian Russell, Miami (Fla.)
1996	Kim Carson, Louisiana State
1997	Tiffany Lott, Brigham Young

High Jump

1983	Disa Gisladdottir, Alabama
1984	Mary Moore, Washington State
1985	Mary Moore, Washington State
1986	Katrena Johnson, Arizona
1987	Lisa Bernhagen, Stanford
1988	Angie Bradburn, Texas
1989	Paul John, Weber State
1990	Sissy Costner, Auburn
1991	Tanya Hughes, Arizona
1992	Natasha Alleyne, Georgia Tech
1993	J.C. Broughton, Arizona
1994	Amy Acuff, UCLA
1995	Amy Acuff, UCLA
1996	Najuma Fletcher, Pittsburgh
1997	Amy Acuff, UCLA

Long Jump

1983	Carol Lewis, Houston
1984	Angela Thacker, Nebraska
1985	Carol Lewis, Houston
1986	Cynthia Henry, UTEP
1987	Sheila Echols, LSU
1988	Carlette Guidry, Texas
1989	Beatrice Utunda, Texas Southern
1990	Sheila Hudson, California
1991	Diane Guthrie, George Mason
1992	Jackie Edwards, Stanford
1993	Daphnie Saunders, LSU
1994	Daphnie Saunders, LSU
1995	Diane Guthrie-Gresham, George Mason
1996	Angee Henry, Nebraska
1997	Trecia Smith, Pittsburgh

Triple Jump

1985	Esmeralda Garcia, Florida State
1986	Wendy Brown, Southern California
1987	Yvette Bates, Southern California
1988	Yvette Bates, Southern California
1989	Flora Hyacinth, Alabama
1990	Sheila Hudson, California
1991	Leah Kirklin, Florida
1992	Leah Kirklin, Florida
1993	Telisa Young, Texas
1994	Telisa Young, Texas

1995	Najuma Fletcher, Pittsburgh
1996	Nicola Martial, Nebraska
1997	Suzette Lee, Louisiana State

Shot Put

1983	Meg Ritchie, Arizona
1984	Regina Cavanaugh, Rice
1985	Regina Cavanaugh, Rice
1986	Regina Cavanaugh, Rice
1987	Pam Dukes, Stanford
1988	Angela Baker, East Tennessee State
1989	Carla Garrett, Arizona
1990	Tracie Millett, UCLA
1991	Tracie Millett, UCLA
1992	Dawn Dumble, UCLA
1993	Danyel Mitchell, Louisiana State
1994	Eileen Vanisi, Texas
1995	Dawn Dumble, UCLA
1996	Valeyta Althouse, UCLA
1997	Tressa Thompson, Nebraska

Outdoor Track

100-Meter Dash

1982	Merlene Ottey, Nebraska
1983	Merlene Ottey, Nebraska
1984	Randy Givens, Florida State
1985	Michelle Finn, Florida State
1986	Juliet Cuthbert, Texas
1987	Gwen Torrence, Georgia
1988	Gail Devers, UCLA
1989	Dawn Sowell, Louisiana State
1990	Esther Jones, Louisiana State
1991	Carlette Guidry, Texas
1992	Chryste Gaines, Stanford
1993	Holli Hyche, Indiana State
1994	Holli Hyche, Indiana State
1995	D'Andre Hill, Louisiana State
1996	D'Andre Hill, Louisiana State
1997	Sevatheda Fynes, Eastern Michigan

200-Meter Dash

1982	Florence Griffith, UCLA
1983	Merlene Ottey, Nebraska
1984	Randy Givens, Florida State
1985	Juliet Cuthbert, Texas
1986	Juliet Cuthbert, Texas
1987	Gwen Torrence, Georgia
1988	Mary Onyali, Texas Southern
1989	Dawn Sowell, Louisiana State
1990	Esther Jones, Louisiana State
1991	Carlette Guidry, Texas
1992	Dahlia Duhaney, Louisiana State
1993	Holli Hyche, Indiana State
1994	Merlene Frazer, Texas
1995	Sevatheda Fynes, Eastern Michigan
1996	Zundra Feagin, Louisiana State
1997	Sevatheda Fynes, Eastern Michigan

400-Meter Dash

1982	Marita Payne, Florida State
1983	Florence Griffith, UCLA

1984	Marita Payne, Florida State
1985	Sherri Howard, California State-Los Angeles
1986	Lillie Leatherwood, Alabama
1987	Lillie Leatherwood, Alabama
1988	Rochelle Stevens, Morgan State
1989	Pauline Davis, Alabama
1990	Maicel Malone, Arizona State
1991	Ximena Restrepo, Nebraska
1992	Anita Howard, Florida
1993	Juliet Campbell, Auburn
1994	Flirtisha Harris, Seton Hall
1995	Nicole Green, Kansas State
1996	Suziann Reid, Texas
1997	LaTorsha Stroman, Louisiana State

800-Meter Run

1982	Delisa Walton, Tennessee
1983	Joetta Clark, Tennessee
1984	Joetta Clark, Tennessee
1985	Claudette Groenendaal, Oregon
1986	Karen Bakewell, Miami (Ohio)
1987	Julie Jenkins, Brigham Young
1988	Sharon Powell, Nebraska
1989	Meredith Rainey, Harvard
1990	Suzy Favor, Wisconsin
1991	Nekita Beasley, Florida
1992	Nekita Beasley, Florida
1993	Kim Sherman, Wisconsin
1994	Inez Turner, Southwest Texas State
1995	Inez Turner, Southwest Texas State
1996	Monique Hennagan, North Carolina
1997	Dana Riley, Texas

1,500-Meter Run

1982	Leanne Warren, Oregon
1983	Michele Bush, UCLA
1984	Claudette Groenendaal, Oregon
1985	Cathy Branta, Wisconsin
1986	Alisa Harvey, Tennessee
1987	Suzy Favor, Wisconsin
1988	Suzy Favor, Wisconsin
1989	Suzy Favor, Wisconsin
1990	Suzy Favor, Wisconsin
1991	Darcy Arreola, California State-Northridge
1992	Sue Gentes, Wisconsin
1993	Clare Eichner, Wisconsin
1994	Amy Rudolph, Providence
1995	Amy Wickus, Wisconsin
1996	Miesha Marzell, Georgetown
1997	Becki Wells, Florida

3,000-Meter Run

1982	Ceci Hopp, Stanford
1983	Alison Wiley, Stanford
1984	Cathy Branta, Wisconsin
1985	Cathy Branta, Wisconsin
1986	Lisa Breiding, Kentucky
1987	Vicki Huber, Villanova
1988	Vicki Huber, Villanova
1989	Vicki Huber, Villanova
1990	Sonia O'Sullivan, Villanova
1991	Sonia O'Sullivan, Villanova
1992	Nnenna Lynch, Villanova

1993	Clare Eichner, Wisconsin
1994	Karen Hecox, UCLA
1995	Kathy Butler, Wisconsin
1996	Kathy Butler, Wisconsin
1997	Kathy Butler, Wisconsin

5,000-Meter Run

1982	Kathy Bryant, Tennessee
1983	Betty Jo Springs, North Carolina State
1984	PattiSue Plumer, Stanford
1985	Sabrina Dornhoefer, Missouri
1986	Stephanie Herbst, Wisconsin
1987	Annie Schweitzer, Texas
1988	Annette Hand, Oregon
1989	Valerie McGovern, Kentucky
1990	Valerie McGovern, Kentucky
1991	Laurie Gomez, North Carolina State
1992	Monique Ecker, Oklahoma
1993	Kay Gooch, Oklahoma
1994	Jen Rhines, Villanova
1995	Jen Rhines, Villanova
1996	Jen Rhines, Villanova
1997	Amy Skieresz, Arizona

10,000-Meter Run

1982	Kim Schnurpfeil, Stanford
1983	Betty Jo Springs, North Carolina State
1984	Kathy Hayes, Oregon
1985	Nan Doak, Iowa
1986	Stephanie Herbst, Wisconsin
1987	Patricia Murray, Western Illinois
1988	Sylvia Mosqueda, California State-Los Angeles
1989	Jackie Goodman, Oklahoma State
1990	Janet Haskin, Kansas State
1991	Jamie Park, Arkansas
1992	Kim Saddic, George Mason
1993	Carole Zajac, Villanova
1994	Carole Zajac, Villanova
1995	Katie Swords, Southern Methodist
1996	Katie Swords, Southern Methodist
1997	Amy Skieresz, Arizona

100-Meter Hurdles

1982	Benita Fitzgerald, Tennessee
1983	Benita Fitzgerald, Tennessee
1984	Kim Turner, UTEP
1985	Rhonda Blanford, Nebraska
1986	Rosalind Pendergraft-Council, Auburn
1987	LaVonna Martin, Tennessee
1988	Lynda Tolbert, Arizona State
1989	Tananjalyn Stanley, Louisiana State
1990	Lynda Tolbert, Arizona State
1991	Dawn Bowles, Louisiana State
1992	Michelle Freeman, Florida
1993	Gillian Russell, Miami (Fla.)
1994	Gillian Russell, Miami (Fla.)
1995	Gillian Russell, Miami (Fla.)
1996	Kim Carson, Louisiana State
1997	Astia Walker, Louisiana State

400-Meter Hurdles

1982	Tonja Brown, Florida State
1983	Judi Brown, Michigan State

1984	Nawal El Moutawakel, Iowa State
1985	Latanya Sheffield, San Diego State
1986	Maria Usifo, Texas Southern
1987	Linetta Wilson, Nebraska
1988	Schowanda Williams, Louisiana State
1989	Janeene Vickers, UCLA
1990	Janeene Vickers, UCLA
1991	Janeene Vickers, UCLA
1992	Tonja Buford, Illinois
1993	Debbie Parris, Louisiana State
1994	Debbie Parris, Louisiana State
1995	Tonya Williams, Illinois
1996	Tonya Williams, Illinois
1997	Ryan Tolbert, Vanderbilt

High Jump

1982	Disa Gisladdottir, Alabama
1983	Disa Gisladdottir, Alabama
1984	Tonya Alston, UCLA
1985	Katrena Johnson, Arizona
1986	Rita Graves, Kansas State
1987	Mazel Thomas, Abilene Christian
1988	Amber Welty, Arizona State
1989	Melinda Clark, Texas A&M
1990	Angie Bradburn, Texas
1991	Tanya Hughes, Arizona
1992	Tanya Hughes, Arizona
1993	Tanya Hughes, Arizona
1994	Gai Kapernick, LSU
1995	Amy Acuff, UCLA
1996	Amy Acuff, UCLA
1997	Kaysa Bergquist, Southern Methodist

Long Jump

1982	Jennifer Innis, California State-Los Angeles
1983	Carol Lewis, Houston
1984	Gwen Loud, Hawaii
1985	Carol Lewis, Houston
1986	Cynthia Henry, UTEP
1987	Sheila Echols, Louisiana State
1988	Nena Gage, George Mason
1989	Christy Opara, Brigham Young
1990	Sheila Hudson, California
1991	Diane Guthrie, George Mason
1992	Jackie Edwards, Stanford
1993	Daphnie Saunders, Louisiana State
1994	Dedra Davis, Tennessee
1995	Pat Itanyi, West Virginia
1996	Angee Henry, Nebraska
1997	Trecia Smith, Pittsburgh

Triple Jump

1984	Terri Turner, Texas
1985	Esmeralda Garcia, Florida State
1986	Terri Turner, Texas
1987	Sheila Hudson, California
1988	Sheila Hudson, California
1989	Renita Robinson, Nebraska
1990	Sheila Hudson, California
1991	Donna Crumety, St. Joseph's (Pa.)
1992	Leah Kirklin, Florida
1993	Claudia Haywood, Rice
1994	Nicola Martial, Nebraska

1995	Nicola Martial, Nebraska
1996	Suzette Lee, Louisiana State
1997	Suzette Lee, Louisiana State

Discus Throw

1982	Meg Ritchie, Arizona
1983	Leslie Deniz, Arizona State
1984	Carol Cady, Stanford
1985	Laura DeSnoo, San Diego State
1986	Toni Lutjens, UCLA
1987	Laura Lavine, Washington State
1988	Laura Lavine, Washington State
1989	Carla Garrett, Arizona
1990	Tracie Millett, UCLA
1991	Anna Mosdell, Brigham Young
1992	Anna Mosdell, Brigham Young
1993	Danyel Mitchell, Louisiana State
1994	Danyel Mitchell, Louisiana State
1995	Dawn Dumble, UCLA
1996	Anna Soderberg, Northern Arizona
1997	Seilala Sua, UCLA

Javelin Throw

1982	Karin Smith, Cal Poly-San Luis Obispo
1983	Denise Thiemard, Nebraska
1984	Iris Gronfeldt, Alabama
1985	Iris Gronfeldt, Alabama
1986	Helena Uusitalo, Washington
1987	Laverne Eve, Louisiana State
1988	Jill Smith, Oregon
1989	Kim Engel, Georgia
1990	Ashley Selmon, Southern California
1991	Paul Berry, Oregon
1992	Valerie Tulloch, Rice
1993	Ashley Selman, Oregon
1994	Valerie Tolluch, Rice
1995	Valerie Tolluch, Rice
1996	Windy Dean, Southern Methodist
1997	Windy Dean, Southern Methodist

Shot Put

1982	Meg Ritchie, Arizona
1983	Carol Cady, Stanford
1984	Ramona Pagel, San Diego State
1985	Regina Cavanaugh, Rice
1986	Regina Cavanaugh, Rice
1987	Regina Cavanaugh, Rice
1988	Jennifer Ponath, Washington
1989	Carla Garrett, Arizona
1990	Tracie Millett, UCLA
1991	Eileen Vanisi, Texas
1992	Katrin Koch, Indiana
1993	Dawn Dumble, UCLA
1994	Eileen Vanisi, Texas
1995	Valeyta Althouse, UCLA
1996	Teri Steer, Southern Methodist
1997	Tressa Thompson, Nebraska

Heptathlon

1982	Jackie Joyner, UCLA
1983	Jackie Joyner, UCLA
1984	Sheila Tarr, Nevada, Las Vegas

1985	Lauri Young, Northeast Louisiana	1992	Anu Kaljurand, Brigham Young
1986	Jolanda Jones, Houston	1993	Kelly Blair, Oregon
1987	Jolanda Jones, Houston	1994	Diane Guthrie, George Mason
1988	Wendy Brown, Southern California	1995	Diane Guthrie-Gresham, George Mason
1989	Jolanda Jones, Houston	1996	Corissa Yasen, Purdue
1990	Gea Johnson, Arizona State	1997	Tiffany Lott, Brigham Young
1991	Sharon Jaklofsky, Louisiana State		

Appendix D
Athletes Profiled in *Outstanding Women Athletes,* Arranged by Sport

Auto Racing

Janet Guthrie
Shirley Muldowney

Aviation

Amelia Earhart

*Barrel Racing

*Charmayne James

Basketball

Senda Berenson
*Teresa Edwards
Nancy Lieberman-Cline
Ann Meyers
Cheryl Miller
*Vivian Stringer
Patricia Summitt
Lynette Woodard

Bowling

*Lucy Giovinco
Marion Ladewig
Floretta Doty McCutcheon

*Boxing

*Christy Martin

*Bullfighting

*Cristina Sánchez

Cycling

*Juli Furtado
Connie Carpenter-Phinney

Sheila Young (also Speed
   Skating)

Dog Sledding

Susan Butcher

*Fencing

*Helene Mayer

Field Hockey

Constance M.K. Applebee

Figure Skating

Tenley Albright
Peggy Fleming
Dorothy Hamill
Carol Heiss
Sonja Henie
*Kristi Yamaguchi

Golf

Patty Berg
Nancy Lopez
Glenna Collett Vare
Kathy Whitworth
Mickey Wright
Mildred "Babe" Didrikson
   Zaharias (also Track and
   Field)

Gymnastics

Nadia Comaneci
Olga Korbut
*Shannon Miller

Mary Lou Retton
Cathy Rigby

Horse Racing

Julie Krone

*Ice Hockey

*Manon Rheaume

*Mountain Climbing

*Alison Hargreaves

*Racquetball

*Michelle Gould

*Rock Climbing

*Lynn Hill

Skiing

Diana Golden
Andrea Mead Lawrence
Cindy Nelson

*Soccer

*Michelle Akers

Softball

*Lisa Fernandez
Joan Joyce

Speed Skating

*Bonnie Blair
Sheila Young (also Cycling)

---

* Indicates new to this edition (sport & athlete).

Squash

Eleonora Sears

Swimming and Diving

Florence Chadwick
Donna de Varona
Gertrude Ederle
*Janet Evans
Micki King
Patricia McCormick

Tennis

*Tracy Austin
Maureen Connolly
Chris Evert
Althea Gibson
Steffi Graf
Billie Jean King
Alice Marble

Helen Wills Moody
Martina Navratilova
*Monica Seles
Hazel Hotchkiss Wightman

Track and Field

Evelyn Ashford
Fanny Blankers-Koen
*Gail Devers
*Jean Driscoll
*Lynn Jennings
Florence Griffith Joyner
Jackie Joyner-Kersee
Wilma Rudolph
Joan Benoit Samuelson
Mary Decker Slaney
*Francie Larrieu Smith
Wyomia Tyus
Grete Andersen Waitz
Mildred "Babe" Didrikson
   Zaharias (also Golf)

*Triathlon

*Paula Newby-Fraser

Volleyball

Flo Hyman

*Waterskiing

*Camille Duvall

Appendix E
List of Organization Abbreviations

AAGPBL	All-American Girls Professional Baseball League	ECHL	East Coast Hockey League	NAA	National Archery Association
AARA	American Amateur Racquetball Association	FIFA	Federation Internationale de Football Association	NAAF	National Amateur Athletic Federation
AAU	Amateur Athletic Union	FINA	Federation Internationale de Natation Amateur	NAIA	National Association of Intercollegiate Athletics
ABA	American Basketball Association	FIQ	Federation International des Quilleurs	NASCAR	National Association for Stock Car Auto Racing
ABL	American Basketball League	FSFI	Federation Sportive Feminine Internationale	NBA	National Basketball Association
AIAW	Association of Intercollegiate Athletics for Women			NCAA	National Collegiate Athletic Association
AOC	American Olympic Committee	IAAF	International Amateur Athletic Federation	NHL	National Hockey League
APEA	American Physical Education Association	IHL	International Hockey League	NHRA	National Hot Rot Association
ASA	Amateur Softball Association	IIHF	International Ice Hockey Federation	NHSRA	National Handicapped Sports and Recreation Association
ATA	American Tennis Association	IOC	International Olympic Committee	NORBA	National Off-Road Bicycle Association
CIAW	Commission on Intercollegiate Athletics for Women	IRF	International Racquetball Federation	PAL	Police Athletic League
CONCACAF	Confederation of North, Central and Carribean American Football	ISF	International Softball Federation	PGA	Professional Golf Association
		IVA	International Volleyball Association	PITA	Professional International Track Association
CWA	Committee on Women's Athletics	IWPSA	International Women's Professional Softball Association	PWBA	Professional Women's Bowling Association
DGWS	Division for Girls' and Women's Sport	LPGA	Ladies Professional Golf Association	QMJHL	Québec Major Junior Hockey League

RHI	Roller Hockey International	USOC	United States Olympic Committee	WNBA	Woman's National Bowling Association
SCCA	Sports Car Club of America	USRA	United States Racquetball Association	WPA	Works Progress Administration
SEC	South Eastern Conference	USSA	United States Ski Association	WPBA	Women's Professional Billiards Association
SORC	Southern Ocean Racing Circuit	USSS	United States Synchronized Swimming	WPBL	Women's Professional Basketball League
TAC	The Athletics Congress				
UGA	United Golf Association	USTA	United States Tennis Association	WPGA	Women's Professional Golf Association
USAC	United States Auto Club	WBC	World Boxing Council	WPRA	Women's Professional Racquetball Association
USAIGC	United States Association of Independent Gymnastics Clubs	WBCA	Women's Basketball Coaches Association		
		WCTU	Women's Christian Temperance Union	WPRA	Women's Professional Rodeo Association
USBL	United States Basketball League	WIBC	Women's International Bowling Congress	WSA	Women's Swimming Association of New York
USDST	United States Disabled Ski Team	WIRT	Women's International Racquetball Tournament		
USFHA	United States Field Hockey Association			WSF	Women's Sports Foundation
USGA	United States Golf Association	WNBA	Women's National Basketball Association	WTA	Women's Tennis Association
USLTA	United States Lawn Tennis Association			WYRA	Women's Yacht Racing Association

Appendix F
Selected Reference Sources

Many sources were consulted in researching this book, among them a number of newspaper and magazine articles, media guides, sport-specific enyclopedias, biographies and autobiographies, online World Wide Web sites, and assorted reference materials. Following is a selected list of the most frequently used sources.

1995-96 National Collegiate Championships Records. Overland Park, KS: National Collegiate Athletic Association, 1996.

1997 Corel WTA Tour Player Guide. Stamford, CT: Corel WTA Tour, 1997.

1997 LPGA Player Guide. Daytona Beach, FL: Ladies Professional Golf Association, 1997.

1997-98 USOC Fact Book. Colorado Springs, CO: United States Olympic Committee, 1997.

Ashe, Arthur. *A Hard Road to Glory: A History of the African-American Athlete.* New York: Amistad Press, 1988.

Blue, Adrianne. *Faster, Higher, Further: Women's Triumphs and Disasters at the Olympics.* London: Virago Press, 1988.

———. *Grace Under Pressure: The Emergence of Women in Sport.* London: Sidgwick & Jackson, 1987.

Burton, Mariah Nelson. *Are We Winning Yet? How Women Are Changing Sports and Sports Are Changing Women.* New York: Random House, 1991.

———. *The Stronger Women Get, The More Men Love Football: Sexism and the American Culture and Sports.* New York: Avon Books, 1994.

Cahn, Susan K. *Coming on Strong: Gender and Sexuality in Twentieth-Century Sports.* New York: Free Press, 1994.

Condon, Robert J. *Great Women Athletes of the 20th Century.* Jefferson, NC: MacFarland and Company, 1991.

Davis, Michael D. *Black American Women in Olympic Track and Field: A Complete Illustrated Reference.* Jefferson, NC: MacFarland and Company, 1992.

Festle, Nancy Jo. *Playing Nice: Politics and Apologies in Women's Sports.* New York: Columbia University Press, 1996.

Gerber, Ellen W., Jan Felshin, Pearl Berlin, and Waneen Wyrick. *The American Woman in Sport.* Reading, MA: Addison-Wesley Publishing Co., 1974.

Glenn, Rhonda. *The Illustrated History of Women's Golf.* Dallas: Taylor Publishing Co., 1991.

Goodbody, John. *The Illustrated History of Gymnastics.* London: Stanley Paul, 1982.

Gregorich, Barbara. *Women at Play: The Story of Women in Baseball.* San Diego, CA: Harcourt Brace and Company, 1993.

Guttmann, Allen. *Women's Sports: A History.* New York: Columbia University Press, 1991.

Hasson, John, ed. *The 1998 ESPN Information Please Sports Almanac.* Boston: Information Please LLC, 1997.

Heinemann, Sue. *Timelines of American Women's History.* New York: The Berkley Publishing Group, 1996.

Henderschott, Jon. *Track's Greatest Women.* Los Altos, CA: Tafnews Press, 1987.

Hickok, Ralph. *A Who's Who of Sports Champions: Their Stories and Records.* New York: Houghton Mifflin, 1995.

Hollander, Phyllis. *100 Greatest Women in Sports.* New York: Grosset & Dunlap, 1976.

Howell, Reet, ed. *Her Story in Sport: A Historical Anthology of Women in Sports.* West Point, NY: Leisure Press, 1982.

Hult, Joan S., and Marianna Trekell, eds. *A Century of Women's Basketball: From Frailty to Final Four.* Reston, VA: American Alliance for Health, Physical Education, Recreation and Dance, 1991.

Huntington, Anna Seaton. *Making Waves: The Inside Story of Managing and Motivating the First Women's Team to Compete for the America's Cup.* Arlington, TX: The Summitt Publishing Group, 1996.

Johnson, Anne Janette. *Great Women in Sports.* Detroit, MI: Visible Ink Press, 1996.

King, Billie Jean, with Cynthia Starr. *We Have Come a Long Way: The Story of Women's Tennis.* New York: McGraw-Hill Book Co., 1988.

Layden, Joe. *Women in Sports: The Complete Book on the World's Greatest Female Athletes.* Los Angeles: General Publishing Group, 1997.

Leder, Jane. *Grace and Glory: A Century of Women in the Olympics.* Chicago, IL: Triumph Books, 1996.

Lucas John. *The Modern Olympic Games.* South Brunswick, NJ: A.S. Barnes and Company, 1980.

Lumpkin, Angela. *Women's Tennis: A Historical Documentary of the Players and Their Game.* New York: The Whitson Publishing Company, 1981.

Macy, Sue. *Winning Ways: A Photohistory of American Women in Sports.* New York: Henry Holt & Co., 1996.

Mallon, Bill, and Ian Buchanan. *Quest for Gold: The Encyclopedia of American Olympians.* New York: Leisure Press, 1984.

Markel, Robert, and Nancy Brooks Markel. *For the Record: Women in Sports.* New York: World Almanac Publishers, 1985.

Markel, Robert, Susan Waggoner, and Marcella Smith, eds. *The Women's Sports Encyclopedia.* New York: Henry, Holt & Co., 1997.

Miller, Mark, ed. *The Bowlers' Encyclopedia.* Greendale, WI: American Bowling Congress, Women's International Bowling Conrgess, Young American Bowling Alliance, and USA Bowling, 1995.

Nickerson, Elinor. *Golf: A Women's History.* Jefferson, NC: McFarland & Co., Inc., 1987.

Porter, David L., ed. *Biographical Dictionary of American Sports: Outdoor Sports.* Westport, CT: Greenwood Press, 1988.

———, ed. *Biographical Dictionary of American Sports: Basketball and Other Indoor Sports.* Westport, CT: Greenwood Press, 1989.

Rader, Benjamin G. *American Sports: From the Age of Folk Games to the Age of Spectators.* Englewood Cliffs, NJ: Prentice-Hall, Inc., 1982.

Remley, Mary L. *Women in Sport: An Annotated Bibliography and Resource Guide, 1900-1990.* Boston: G.K. Hall & Co., 1991.

Sherrow, Victoria. *Encyclopedia of Women and Sports.* San Diego: ABC-CLIO, Inc., 1996.

Sicherman, Barbara, and Carol Hurd Green, eds. *Notable American Women: The Modern Period.* Cambridge, MA: The Belknap Press, 1980.

Spears, Betty, and Richard Swanson. *History of Sport and Physical Activity in the United States.* Dubuque, IA: Wm. C. Brown Company, 1978.

Stambler, Irwin. *Women in Sports.* New York: Doubleday and Company, 1975.

Tricard, Louise Mead. *American Women's Track and Field: A History, 1895 through 1980.* Jefferson, NC: McFarland and Company, 1996.

Twin, Stephanie L. *Out of the Bleachers*. Old Westbury, NY: Feminist Press, 1979.

United States Lawn Tennis Association. *Official Encyclopedia of Tennis*. New York: Harper and Row, 1972.

Wallechinsky, David. *The Complete Book of the Winter Olympics, 1994 Edition*. Boston, MA: Little, Brown and Company, 1993.

————. *Sports Illustrated Presents the Complete Book of the Summer Olympics*. Boston, MA: Little, Brown and Company, 1996.

Index

by Virgil Diodato

Boldface page numbers indicate presence of main biographical entry.

A League of Their Own, 255
Abbott, Cleveland, 14
Abbott, Margaret, 37, 335
Abbott, Rae, 363
Abbott, Senda Berenson. *See* Berenson, Senda
Abel, Joy, 352
Ackermann, Rosemarie, 341
Acuff, Amy, 373, 375
Adair, Jerrie, 355
Adamek, Donna, 352
Adamovich, T., 357
Adams, Judi, 350
Adams, Rosie, 272
Adler, Kim, 352
Adventurers, 6
African Americans. *See* Blacks
Ahern, Kathy, 359
Ahmann-Leighton, Crissy, 371
Ajunwa, Chioma, 341
Akers, Michelle, **77–79,** 289, 290, 291
Akhurst, Daphne, 364
Akopyan, Arthur, 288
Albertville Olympics (1992), 71–72
Albrecht, Louise, 272
Albright, Tenley, **79–81,** 144
championships won by, 357
in Olympic history, 66, 343
in sports history, 16, 28
Alcott, Amy, 358, 359
Alfano, Elaine, 369
Alfredsson, Helen, 359
All-American Girls Professional Baseball League, 15–16, 252, 253–58

All-American Girls Softball League, 253
All-around athletes
Sears, Eleonora, **216–18**
Zaharias, Mildred "Babe" Didrikson, **245–48**
Allen, Aileen, 355
Alleyne, Natasha, 373
Allison, Stacy, 317
Almeida, Cathy, 352
Alpine skiers
Lawrence, Andrea Mead, **173–75**
Nelson, Cindy, **201–02**
Alpine skiing
champions in, 347–49
in Olympic history, 62–71, 73, 342
in sports history, 16
Alston, Tonya, 375
Alter, Vanessa, 361
Althouse, Valeyta, 373, 375
Altwegg, Jeanette, 343
Alvarez, Delores, 131
Alvarez, Isabel, 255
Amado, Jeanette, 267
Amanar, Simona, 336
Amateur Athlete of the Year. *See* Sullivan Award
Amateur Athletic Foundation, 96
Amateur Athletic Foundation of Los Angeles, 326
Amateur Athletic Union, 26, 252, 326
in Olympic history, 39, 41, 42, 46

in sports history, 9, 12, 13, 14, 16
Amateur Bicycle League of America, 244
Amateur Bowler of the Year, 132
Amateur Fencers League of America, 26
Amateur Skating Union of the United States, 327–28
Amateur Softball Association, 122, 123, 155, 327
Amateur Sports Act of 1978, 21, 105, 166, 252
Amateur Sportswoman of the Year, 109, 160, 161
America³ sailing team, 258–65
American Amateur Baseball Congress, 267
American Amateur Racquetball Association, 135
American Association for Health, Physical Education, and Recreation, 82
American Association for the Advancement of Physical Education, 87
American Athletic Association for the Deaf, 324
American Basketball Association, 188
American Basketball League, 22, 297, 322
American Female Runner of the Year, 154
American Field Hockey Association, 81

American Olympic Committee, 46
American Physical Education Association, 8, 12
American Platform Tennis Association, 328
American Running and Fitness Association, 328
American Softball Association, 268, 269, 304, 305
American Softball Association Hall of Fame, 272–75
American Tennis Association, 9, 11, 128–29
American Water Ski Association, 329
America's Cup, 24, 258–65
Ammaccapane, Danielle, 368
Amos, Diane, 287
Amsterdam Olympics (1928), 40, 43–44
Andersen, Grete. *See* Waitz, Grete Andersen
Andersen, Linda, 341
Anderson, Andrea, 351
Anderson, Beverly, 347, 348, 349
Anderson, Heidi, 369
Anderson, Janet, 358
Anderson, Patrice J., 351
Andersson, Agneta, 333, 334
Andrews, Donna, 359
Andrews, Jill, 369
Andrews, Theresa, 337
Angelakis, Jana, 357, 368
Angeles, Leslie, 369
Anke, Hannelore, 338
Ann, Patty, 352, 353
Anthony, Bessie, 359
Anti-competition movement, 11–12
Anti-Semitism, 45, 183
Antwerp Olympics (1920), 41, 42
Anz, Maria, 369
Aoki, Mayumi, 338
Applebee, Constance M. K., 8, **81–82**
Arba, Rodica, 336
Archery
    champions in, 347–50
    milestone in, 25
    in Olympic history, 37, 57, 58, 333
    organizations for, 322
    in sports history, 6
Arendsen, Kathy, 271, 272
Arizona Athlete of the Year, 305
Armitage-Johnson, Stephanie, 260
Armstrong, Debbie, 70, 342, 349

Armstrong, S., 357
Arnold, Kim, 368
Aronsohn, Liz, 351
Arreola, Darcy, 374
Arris, Katy, 370
Ashford, Evelyn, 57, **82–84,** 339, 347
Ashley, Jean, 360
Associated Press
    Female Athlete of the Decade, 198
    Female Athlete of the Half Decade, 245
    Female Athlete of the Year, 346
Association of Intercollegiate Athletics for Women, 17, 19, 29, 82, 178, 222, 226, 253
Associations, 322–29, 379–80. *See also names of specific associations*
Astakhova, Polina, 335
Athens
    1896 Olympics, 36
    1906 Olympics, 38
Athlete of the Year. *See also* Female Athlete of the Year
    American Amateur Racquetball Association, 135
    Arizona, 305
    Fresno State University, 191
    National Association for Girls and Women in Sports, 188
    Track & Field News, 160–61
    United Press International, 138, 219
    University of California at Los Angeles, 188
    U.S. Olympic Committee, 261
    USA Gymnastics, 288
    Wide World of Sports, 168
Athletic clubs, 4, 8–9
Athletic directors, collegiate, 24, 32, 274
Athletic scholarships, 17, 30
Athletics Congress, 109
Atkinson, Juliette, 366
Atlanta Olympics (1996), 60–61
Ausoni, Olivia, 348
Aussem, Cilly, 364, 365
Austin, Tracy, **85–86,** 219, 346, 367
Auto driving, around the world, 27
Auto racers
    Guthrie, Janet, 21, 30, **138–41**
    Muldowney, Shirley, 30, **195–97**

Auto racing
    bibliography on, 141, 197
    milestones in, 28, 30
Averina, Tatiana, 344
Aviation
    bibliography on, 113
    milestones in, 26, 27, 28
Aviator
    Earhart, Amelia, 10, 27, **110–13**
Award winners, 346–67. *See also names of specific awards*
Ayoatte-Law, Mary, 369
Azzi, Jennifer, 295, 297

Baas-Kaiser, Christina, 344
Babashoff, Shirley, 347
Babb-Sprague, Kristen, 339
Babe Didrikson All-American Basketball team, 14, 247
Babe Zaharias Female Amateur Athlete of the Year, 92
Babilonia, Tai, 70
Backus, Sharron, 272–73
Bacon, Mary, 29
Badders, S., 357
Badea, Laura, 335
Badminton
    champions in, 350–51
    in Olympic history, 52, 59, 60, 333
    organizations for, 322
Baena, Marisa, 368
Bahmann, Angelika, 334
Baier, Ernst, 343
Bair, Sheryl, 361
Baiul, Oksana, 72, 313, 343
Baker, Angela, 373
Baker, Cindy, 351
Baker, Erin, 367
Baker, Kathy, 358, 368
Baker, Mary, 352
Baker-Schultz, Tristan, 355
Bakewell, Karen, 374
Balas, Iolanda, 28, 341
Ballanger, Felicia, 334
Baltzell, Amy, 260
Balukas, Jean, 351
Balzer, Karin, 340
Bancroft, Ann, 31
Bang Soo Hyun, 333
Banks, Nancy, 347, 349
Barash, Julia, 18
Barcelona Olympics (1992), 59–60
Barger-Wallach, Maud, 366
Barinaga, Tyna, 350
Barker, Mrs. J. S., 349

Barker, Sue, 365
Barkhuff, Mrs. Del, 350
Barr, Beth, 362, 370
Barrel racer
    James, Charmayne, **152–53**
Barron, Gayle, 361
Barry, Ceal, 296
Bartlett, Josephine, 355
Barton, Pamela, 360
Basaldua, Anna, 369
Baseball
    bibliography on, 257–58, 271
    milestones in, 25, 27, 30, 31,
        32, 33
    organizations for, 322
    outstanding teams in, 252,
        253–58, 265–71
    in sports history, 6, 14, 15–16,
        24
Baseball players
    Alvarez, Isabel, 255
    Amado, Jeanette, 267
    Braatz, Kim, 267
    Burnham, Elizabeth, 267
    Callaghan, Helen, 255–56
    Clark, K. C., 267
    Coombes, Melissa, 266, 267–
        68
    Cress, Missy, 268
    Croteau, Julie, 266, 268
    Delloso, Michelle, 267, 268
    Faut, Jean, 255, 256
    Foss, Betty, 256
    Gacioch, Rose, 256
    Geatches, Allison, 268
    Gouthro, Laurie, 268
    Heisler, Toni, 268
    Kamenshek, Dorothy, 256
    Ketcham, Lee Anne, 266, 269
    Kropke, Keri, 269
    Kurys, Sophie, 255, 257
    Martinez, Lisa, 269
    McAnany, Michele, 266, 269
    McCann, Rachelle, 269
    Mitchem, Shannan, 266, 270
    Satriano, Gina, 266, 267
    Schaffrath, Pam, 270
    Schroeder, Dorothy, 257
    Sloan, Shae, 270
    Sunny, Stacy, 266, 270
    Venturi, Bridget, 270–71
    Weaver, Joanne, 257
    Wiley, Charlotte, 266, 271
    Williams, Ann, 271
    Wisniewski, Connie, 257
Basile, Gina, 369
Basilio, Enriqueta, 29, 52

Basketball
    bibliography on, 177, 227,
        233, 239, 301, 311
    milestones in, 25, 29, 31, 32,
        33
    in Olympic history, 51, 54, 61,
        333
    organizations for, 322–23
    outstanding teams in, 295–301
    in sports history, 7–8, 13–14,
        21, 22
Basketball coaches
    Stringer, Vivian, **223–25**
    Summitt, Patricia Head, 54,
        188–89, **225–27**
Basketball Hall of Fame, 227
Basketball innovator
    Berenson, Senda, 7, 8, 81, **86–
        87**
Basketball players
    Azzi, Jennifer, 295, 297
    Bolton, Ruthie, 295, 297–98
    Edwards, Teresa, 61, **115–16**,
        226, 295, 296, 298
    Lacey, Venus, 295, 298
    Leslie, Lisa, 295, 297, 298–99
    Lieberman-Cline, Nancy, 54,
        175–77, 188, 199, 347
    Lobo, Rebecca, 295, 297, 299
    McClain, Katrina, 295, 297,
        299
    McCray, Nikki, 295, 299–300
    McGhee, Carla, 295, 300
    Meyers, Ann, 21, 54, **188–89**,
        347
    Miller, Cheryl, **190–91**, 226,
        347
    Staley, Dawn, 295, 297, 300
    Steding, Katy, 295, 300
    Swoopes, Sheryl, 295, 297,
        300–01, 311, 346
    Woodard, Lynette, 31, 226,
        237–39, 347
    Zaharias, Mildred "Babe"
        Didrikson, **245–247**
Bassham, Lanny, 53
Bass'n Gal, 323
Bates, Yvette, 373
Battle of the Sexes
    in horse racing, 31–32
    in tennis, 20, 163
Bauer, Marlene, 346
Bauer, Sybil, 26, 337
Baugh, Laura, 360
Baugniet, Pierre, 343
Bauma, Herma, 341
Bayer, Ernestine, 27

Baylis, A., 26, 356
Bazhanova, Svetlana, 344
Beach volleyball, 52, 60, 333. *See
    also* Volleyball
Beard, Amanda, 363
Bearden, Belinda, 351
Beasley, Nekita, 374
Beathard, Jenni, 369
Beatie, Holly, 351
Beattie, Shelley, 261
Bechdolt, Cherly, 347
Beck Award, 134, 175, 202
Beck, Robin, 367
Becker, Elizabeth, 334
Becker, Ingrid, 341
Becker-Day, Courtenay, 261
Bedard, Myriam, 342
Bedford, Barbara, 363
Beecher, Catherine, 4, 7
Behrendt, Jutta, 336
Beiser, Trude, 65, 342
Bell, Florence, 43
Bell, Robin, 351
Bellutti, Antonella, 334
Belmondo, Stefania, 343
Belote, Melissa, 53, 337, 338
Belousova, Lyudmila, 343
Ben Hogan Award, 90, 248
Benedict, Inga, 353
Benko, Lindsay, 370
Bennett, Brooke, 337, 362
Bennett, Debbie, 352
Benoit, Joan. *See* Samuelson, Joan
    Benoit
Berenson, Senda, 7, 8, 81, **86–87**
Beresford, Rosemary, 357
Berg, Laura, 301, 303
Berg, Patty, 27, **88–90**, 230, 346,
    358, 360
Berger, Alfred, 343
Bergeron, Sarah, 261
Bergquist, Kaysa, 375
Berlin
    1916 Olympics, 39
    1936 Olympics, 45–46
Bernhagen, Lisa, 373
Bernier, Sylvie, 334
Berning, Susie M., 358
Berry, Paul, 375
Berry, Shanda, 296
Bertha Tickey Award, 123, 304
Berthod, Madeleine, 342
Besson, Colette, 339
Bestemianova, Natalia, 343
Betz, Kimberly, 368
Betz, Pauline, 365, 366
Bhushan, Insook, 363, 364

Bianco, Suzannah, 280, 282, 283
Biathlon
    champions in, 351
    in Olympic history, 71, 342
    organization for, 323
Bibliographies, selected, 311–21,
        381–83
Bicyclists. *See* Cyclists
Biebl, Heidi, 342
Billiards, 323, 351
Bilodeaux (Banos), Caitlin, 357,
        368
Bingay, Roberta Gibb, 21, 29
Bingley, Blanche, 365
Bingley, Norman, 38
Biographies, collective, 312
Birch, Sandra, 372
Bischof, Martina, 334
Bishop, Georgianna, 359
Bjedov, Djurdjica, 338
Bjurstedt, Molla, 366
Black, Ann, 347
Black Tennis and Sports
        Foundation, 328
Blackburn, Gail, 348
Blacks. *See also* Color barrier; *and
        names of specific athletes*
    milestones for, 26, 28
    in Rome Olympics, 50
    in sports history, 9, 13, 14
Blackwell, Elizabeth, 4
Blair, Bonnie, **90–92**
    awards won by, 346, 347
    in Olympic history, 71, 72, 344
    in sports history, 22
Blair, Kelly, 376
Blalock, Jane, 315, 359
Blanchard, Theresa Weld, 357
Bland, Harriet, 46
Blanford, Rhonda, 373, 374
Blankers, Jan, 93
Blankers-Koen, Fanny, 47–48,
        92–94, 339, 340, 346
Bleibtrey, Ethelda, 42, 337
Bliss, Karen, 353, 354
Block, Sherry, 350
Bloomer, Shirley, 365
Bloomer teams, 6, 14
Bobby Jones Award, 89–90, 231
Bobek, Nicole, 358
Bocharova, Nina, 335
Bock, Allison, 362
Bodybuilding, 312
Boguinskaia, Svetlana, 336
Boitano, Mary, 30
Boldrick, Evelyn, 350
Bolton, Nancy Wynne, 364
Bolton, Ruthie, 295, 297–98

Bondarenko, Olga, 340
Bone cancer, 132–33
Bonner, Beth, 361
Bonner, Tracy, 371
Boothby, Dora, 365
Borckink, Annie, 344
Borden, Amanda, 285, 286, 287
Borders, Ila, 33
Borner, Jacqueline, 344
Boron, Kathrin, 336
Bosáková, Eva, 335
Bosse, Janelle, 371
Botsford, Beth, 337, 363
Boulmerka, Hassiba, 60, 340
Bouman, Kea, 364
Bourassa, Jacelyne, 359
Bouvia, Gloria, 352
Bowen, Mimi, 371
Bowen, Nanci, 359
Bowie, Heather, 368
Bowlers
    Giovinco, Lucy, **131–32,** 353
    Ladewig, Marion, **171–73,** 352
    McCutcheon, Floretta Doty,
        13, **186–88**
Bowles, Dawn, 374
Bowling
    champions in, 351–53
    milestones in, 26, 27, 32
    organizations for, 323
    in sports history, 9, 13, 16, 17
Bowling Writers Association of
        America, 132, 172
Boxberger, Loa, 352
Boxer
    Martin, Christy, **181–82**
Boxing
    milestones in, 25, 27, 30–31,
        32
    organization for, 323
Boxx, Gillian, 301, 303
Boyarskikh, Claudia, 342, 343
Boycotts, Olympic
    Los Angeles (1984), 56
    Melbourne (1956), 49
    Montreal (1976), 54
    Moscow (1980), 55
Boyd, Esna, 364
Boydstun, Patty, 348
Braatz, Kim, 267
Bradburn, Angie, 373, 375
Bradford, V., 357
Bradley, Debbie, 353
Bradley, Pat, 358, 359
Brady, Lydia, 144
Brady, Pam, 350, 351
Bragina, Lyudmila, 340

Brakettes. *See* Raybestos Brakettes
Brand, Esther, 341
Branta, Cathy, 368, 372, 374
Braun, Ellen, 354
Braun, Maria, 337
Brause, Doris Ruchs, 360
Bray, Janette Burr, 348
Breedlove, Margaret Laneive, 28
Breiding, Lisa, 374
Brennan, Eileen, 353
Briley, Melissa, 356
Brinker, Maureen. *See* Connolly,
        Maureen
Brisco-Hooks, Valerie, 57, 157,
        339
Britz, Jerilyn, 358
Broadcasting. *See* Sportscasting;
        Television
Broderick Cup, 347
Brooks, Mark, 32
Broquedis, Marguerite, 339
Brough, Louise, 127, 129, 130,
        364, 365, 366
Broughton, J. C., 373
Brown, Earlene, 50
Brown, Judi, 374
Brown, Leah, 369
Brown, Mrs. Charles S., 5, 25, 359
Brown, Mrs. Spalding, 6
Brown, Reneé, 296
Brown, Sue, 31
Brown, Tonja, 374
Brown, Wendy, 373, 376
Brown, X., 357
Brown v Board of Education, 17
Browne, Mary K., 194, 366
Brownsdon, Suki, 363
Bruce, Tami, 370
Brummer, Jackie, 368, 369
Brundage, Avery, 46
Brunet, Andrée Joly, 144, 343
Brunet, Pierre, 64, 144, 343
Bryant, Kathy, 374
Bryant, Michele, 369
Bryzguina, Olga, 339
Buckner, Pam, 352
Budd, Zola, 56–57, 153, 221
Budge, Karen, 349
Buding, Edda, 120
Budke, Mary, 360
Bueno, Maria, 163, 346, 366, 367
Buford, Tonja, 375
Bukin, Andrei, 343
Bullfighters
    McCormick, Patricia, 28
    Sánchez, Cristina, **214–15**

Bullfighting, 28
Bundy, Dorothy M., 364
Bundy, May Sutton, 26, 365, 366
Bunn, John, 227
Burcica, Constanta, 336
Burfeindt, Betty, 359
Burger, Heinrich, 343
Burghart, Nancy, 353, 354
Burke, J., 357
Burke, Janet, 372
Burke, Lynn, 337
Burnett, Evelyn, 355
Burnham, Elizabeth, 267
Burns, Mignon, 14
Burr, Janet, 347
Burton, Brandie, 359
Busch, Gundi, 80
Bush, Krissie, 369
Bush, Lesley, 334, 356
Bush, Michele, 374
Butcher, Susan, 77, 94–96
Butler, Kathy, 368, 374
Buttsworth, Coral, 364

Cable-Brookes, Candace, 361
Cabrera, Patricia Guerra, 341
Caddying, 31
Cady, Carol, 375
Cahill, Mabel, 366
Caird, Maureen, 340
Calgary Olympics (1988), 71
California Interscholastic
    Federation, 190
California Soccer Player of the
    Year, 294
Calkins, Tracy, 57
Callaghan, Helen, 15, 255–56
Callen, Gloria, 346
Camber, Irene, 334
Cameron, Jeri, 369
Cameron, Michelle, 339
Campbell, Dorothy, 359
Campbell, Edna, 296
Campbell, Florence, 13
Campbell, Juliet, 374
Camping, 323
Camping Women, 323
Cancer, bone, 132–33
Canoeing
    bibliography on, 312
    in Olympic history, 47, 50,
        56–57, 333–34
    organization for, 324
Cantaline, Anita, 352
Caponi, Donna, 358, 359
Capriati, Jennifer, 339
Caputo, Jennie, 360
Carey, Merritt, 261

Carlson, Jessica, 350
Carn, Sandra, 362
Carner, JoAnne, 358, 359, 360
Carol Eckman Award, 224
Carpenter-Phinney, Connie, 57,
    96–98, 334, 353, 354
Carr, Ann, 361
Carr, Cathy, 338
Carruthers, Kitty, 70
Carruthers, Peter, 70
Carson, Kim, 373, 374
Carter, Belvia, 350
Carter, LaVerne, 352
Carter, Mary, 364
Carter, Paula Sperber, 352
Carter, Robin, 371
Carton, Cheryl, 351
Caruccio, Consetta, 360
Casals, Rosie, 121, 162, 163
Case, Harriet, 349
Cashman, Patti, 353
Cáslavská, Vera, 335
Cassidy, Stacy, 362
Catherwood, Ethel, 341
Catuna, Anuta, 362
Caulkins, Amy, 369
Caulkins, Tracy, 338, 347, 370,
    371
Cavalle, Silvia, 360
Cavanagh, Sarah, 261
Cavanaugh, Regina, 373, 375
Cawley, Evonne Goolagong. See
    Goolagong, Evonne
Cerra, M., 356
Chadwick, Florence, 28, **98–99**
Chalmers, Angela, 368
Chambers, Dorothea Douglass
    Lambert, 339, 365
Chamonix Olympics (1924), 62–
    63
Champions, lists of, 347–76
Chandler, Jennifer, 334, 354, 355
Channels, Isadore, 14
Charameda, Laura, 353
Charles, Lisa, 261
Chastain, Brandi, 289, 291–92
Cheeseborough, Chandra, 277,
    278
Chen Yueling, 340
Cherjazona, Lina, 343
Chi Cheng, 29, 346
Chicago Golf Club, 5
Chicago Sports Club, 8–9
Childs, Jeanne, 370
Chilova, Irina, 337
Chin, Tiffany, 358
Chizhova, Nadezhda, 341

Cho Min-sun, 336
Cho Youn-jeon, 333
Chorkina, Svetlana, 335
Chouchounova, Elena, 335
Chouinard, Yvon, 150
Chow, Amy, 60, 285, 286, 287
Choynowski-Liskiewicz,
    Krystyna, 30
Christophel, Bertha, 26
Chronic fatigue syndrome, 78, 79
Chubina, Maria, 334
Chun Lee-Kyung, 344
Chung So-young, 333
Churchill, Elinor, 26
Civil rights, 17–18. See also
    Women's rights
Civil Rights Act of 1960, 17
Civil War, 4
Clark, Ann, 350
Clark, Joetta, 372, 374
Clark, K. C., 267
Clark, Kristen, 349
Clark, Mary Ellen, 356
Clark, Melinda, 375
Cleland, Tammy, 280, 282, 283
Clubs, 4, 8–9
Coach of the Year
    basketball coaches as, 224, 227
    track and field coach as, 278
Coaches. See also Instructors
    baseball, 265, 266
    basketball, 116, 191, 223–25,
        225–27, 296, 298
    bowling, 131, 171
    diving, 165, 166
    field hockey, 81–82
    figure skating, 80, 124, 125,
        142, 144, 241, 242
    golf, 88, 234
    gymnastics, 100, 101, 167,
        168, 192, 204, 205, 206,
        285, 287–89
    sailing, 258
    skiing, 133, 134
    soccer, 291, 292
    softball, 272
    speed skating, 90, 91
    swimming, 118, 280
    tennis, 102, 103, 137, 161, 162,
        180, 199
    track and field, 82, 93, 106,
        108, 157, 159, 211, 213,
        222, 227–28, 229, 276–
        77, 278
    volleyball, 151
Coaching, milestones in, 32, 33
Coachman, Alice, 48, 341
Coakes, Marion, 53

Coats, Beth, 351
Cobb, Mary, 373
Coburn (-Carroll), Cindy, 352
Cochran, Barbara, 68, 342, 348
Cochran, Lindy, 348
Cochran, Marilyn, 348, 349
Cockerill, Kay, 360
Cohen, Tiffany, 337, 362, 370
Cold War politics, 46–47
Coleman, Georgia, 45, 334, 355
Collective biographies, 312
Colledge, Cecilia, 147
College sports, history of, x, 7–8,
    11–13, 16–19, 24
Collegiate Synchronized Swimmer
    of the Year, 284
Collegiate Woman Athlete of the
    Year, 188
Collett, Glenna. *See* Vare, Glenna
    Collett
Colliard, Renée, 342
Collier, Jeanne, 355
Collins, Deitre, 347
Collins, Jennifer, 349
Collins, Michelle, 372
Colloton, Ann, 370
Color barrier, 9, 17
    in golf, 130
    Nazi Olympics and, 45
    in tennis, 127, 181
    in track and field, 227
    in volleyball, 151
Colorado Silver Bullets, 24, 32,
    33, 253, 265–71, 322
Colorado Sports Hall of Fame,
    187
Colorado Sportswoman of the
    Year, 97
Comaneci, Nadia, 19, 54, 55, **99–
    102**, 335, 346
Commission on Intercollegiate
    Athletics for Women, 17
Committee on Women's
    Athletics, 8, 12, 16, 41
Compagnoni, Deborah, 342
Compartment syndrome, 220
Computerization, 67
Cone, Carin, 49
Confederation of North Central
    and Carribean American
    Football, 290–94
Connolly, Maureen, **102–03**
    awards won by, 346
    Brinker Foundation and, 103,
        328
    championships won by, 364,
        365, 366, 367

in sports history, 16, 28
Connolly, Pat, 82
Conradt, Jody, 33, 227
Cook, Betty, 30
Cook, Mrs. E. C., 349
Cook, Myrtle, 43
Cook, Victoria, 350
Cooke, Sarah Palfrey, 366
Cooksey, P. J., 170
Coole, Lisa, 371
Coombes, Melissa, 266, 267–68
Cooper, Charlotte, 37, 339, 365
Cooper, Christin, 70, 348
Cooper, Linda, 356
Copeland, Lillian, 340
Corcoran, Fred, 89
Cordery, Violet, 27
Cornelius, Grace, 363
Cornelius, Kathy, 358
Cornell, Sheila, 272, 301, 302, 303
Corrock, Susie, 348
Cortina d'Ampezzo
    1944 Olympics, 65
    1956 Olympics, 66
Costello, Pat, 352
Costie, Candy, 339
Costner, Sissy, 373
Coubertin, Pierre de, 35, 38, 40
Country clubs, 4–5
Court, Margaret Smith, 119, 162,
    199, 320
    championships won by, 364,
        365, 366, 367
    in sports history, 22
Cox, Katherine, 347, 349
Cox, Lynne, 30
Cranz, Christl, 64, 342
Crapp, Lorraine, 337
Craus, P., 356
Crawford, Judy, 349
Crawley, Sylvia, 296
Craybas, Jill, 372
Cress, Missy, 268
Crew, 27, 31
Crienkovich, Helen, 355, 356
Crocker, Fay, 358
Cromwell, Doris Duke, 47
Croquet, 6, 324
Cross-country running, 153–54,
    368. *See also* Marathon
    running
Cross-country skiing, 66–70, 72,
    342–43
Croteau, Julie, 24, 31, 266, 268
Crumety, Donna, 375
Crump, Diane, 21, 29
Csák, Ibolya, 341

Csepe, Gabrielle, 363
Cummings, Dorothy, 350
Cummings, Edith, 360
Curling, 28, 73, 324, 343
Curtis, Ann, 27, 48, 185, 337, 346
Curtis, Harriot, 359
Curtis, Margaret, 359
Cusmir-Stanciu, Anisoara, 341
Cuthbert, Betty, 339
Cuthbert, Juliet, 60, 373
Cycling
    bibliography on, 245, 313
    champions in, 353–54
    milestones in, 25, 27, 29
    in Olympic history, 36, 51, 57,
        58, 59, 60, 334
    organizations for, 324
    in sports history, 6–7
Cyclists
    Carpenter-Phinney, Connie,
        57, **96–98,** 334, 353, 354
    Furtado, Juli, **126–27,** 353
    Young, Sheila, 21, 96, **243–45,**
        347, 353
Czechoslovakian Tennis
    Federation, 199

Dafovska, Yekaterina, 342
Dahl, Tracy, 372
d'Algue, Kristel Mourgue, 368
Dalton, M., 356
Dancing, 3–4
Dangalakova, Tania, 338
Daniel, Beth, 346, 359, 360
Daniels, Cheryl, 352
Daniels, Isabelle, 211, 277, 278
Danilova, Olga, 343
Danzig, Sarah Palfrey, 164
Darsch, Nancy, 296
Daughton, Rebecca, 353
Davenport, Lindsay, 339
David, Suzanne, 357
Davidova, Elena, 101
Davidson, Dede, 352
Davidson, Karol, 372
Davidson, Owen, 163
Davies, Laura, 358, 359
Davies, Mrs. T., 349
Davis, Betsy, 353, 354
Davis, Dedra, 375
Davis, Muriel, 360
Davis, Pauline, 372, 374
Davis, Willis, 217
Davydova, Yelena, 55, 335
Dawes, Dominique, 60, 285, 286,
    287–88, 361
de Alvarez, Lili, 27
de Filippis, Maria-Teresa, 28

de Leeuw, Dianne, 142
de Rover, Jolanda, 338
de Seminario, Gladys, 52
De Tuscan, J., 356
de Varona, Donna, 19, 21, 51, **103–05,** 338, 347
Deafness, 114
Dean, Christopher, 70, 343
Dean, Windy, 375
Deaver, Sally, 348
Decker, Anne Quast, 360
Decker, Mary. *See* Slaney, Mary Decker
Decugis, Marie, 339
Decugis, Max, 339
DeFrantz, Anita, 24, 31
Dekkers, Michelle, 368
Delloso, Michelle, 267, 268
deMan, Nicole, 369
DeMattei, Susan, 127
Dementyeva, Yelisaveta, 333
Demet, Dede, 353
Dendy, Terri, 372
Deng Yaping, 339
Deniz, Leslie, 375
Dennis, Clare, 338
Depression, economic, 13
DeShong, Andrea, 182
DeSilvia, Toni, 363
DeSnoo, Laura, 375
Destivelle, Catherine, 149
Detlefsen, Linda, 372
Devers, Gail, 60, 61, **105–07,** 339, 347, 373
Devlin, Judy, 350
Dewar, W. H., 356
Di Centa, Manuela, 72, 343
Dial Award, 193
DiCicco, Tony, 291
Didrikson, Mildred "Babe." *See* Zaharias, Mildred "Babe" Didrikson
Diers, Ines, 337
Dijkstra, Sjoukje, 68, 343
Dill, Mary Lou, 360
Dillinger, Ree, 350
Dinnehey, Helen, 26
Disabled Athlete of the Year, 109
Disabled athletes
  Driscoll, Jean, **107–09**
  Golden, Diana, **132–34**
Disabled in sports, organizations for, 324–25
Discrimination. *See* Anti-Semitism; Color barrier
Discus throw, 340–41, 375
Diseases. *See* Medical conditions

Distinguished Flying Cross, 112–13
Distinguished Service Award, 82
Divers
  King, Micki, 21, **164–66,** 334, 354, 355, 356
  McCormick, Patricia, 49, **184–85,** 334, 346, 354, 355, 356
Diving
  champions in, 354–56, 371
  milestones in, 33
  in Olympic history, 39, 41–43, 45, 48–50, 334
  organization for, 328
  in sports history, 9
Division for Girls' and Women's Sport, 17
Dix, Tammy, 348
Dixon, Charles Percy, 339
Dixon, Diane, 372
Dixon, Richard, 38
Dmitriev, Artur, 343
Doak, Nan, 374
Doan, Catriona LeMay, 344
Dobransky, Dana, 369
Dod, Charlotte, 365
Dog sledding. *See also* Sled dog racers
  bibliography on, 96, 313
  milestone in, 31
Doherty, Reginald, 37, 339
Donkova, Jordanka, 340
Donovan, Anne, 226
Doolan, Jeanne, 362
Doom, Debbie, 123
Dorio, Gabriella, 340
Dornhoefer, Sabrina, 374
Dorsey, Becky, 348
Douglas, Doris K., 26
Douglass, Dorothea, 365
Dow, Helena Mroczkowska, 183, 356
Drag racer
  Muldowney, Shirley, **195–97**
Dragila, Stacy, 33
Draves, Victoria, 48, 334, 356
Drechsler, Heiki, 160, 341
Dreglen, Suzanne, 26
Dress reform, ix, 4, 36
  in baseball, 254
  in cycling, 6–7
  in equestrian events, 26
  in figure skating, 63
  in swimming, 26
  in tennis, 10–11, 26, 27, 194, 235, 236, 237
  in walking, 217

Driscoll, Jean, **107–09,** 361
Driving around the world, 27
Drysdale, Ann. *See* Meyers, Ann
du Pont, Margaret Osborne, 365, 366
Duchková, Milena, 334
Dudley, Eleanor, 27
Duenkel, Virginia, 337
Dufresne, Begona Via, 341
Duggan, Anne Marie, 352
Duhaney, Dahlia, 373
Dukes, Pam, 373
Dumble, Dawn, 373, 375
Dunfield, Sonya Klopfer, 142, 357
Dunlap, Page, 368
Dunne, Karen, 354
Dupont, Helen, 51
Duprel, Renee, 354
Durack, Fanny, 337
Durham, Amy, 369
Durham, Dianne, 361
Durr, Francoise, 119, 365
Duvall, Camille, **109–10**
Duvall, Edith McGuire, 47, 228, 278, 339
Dykman, Janet, 350
Dyroen-Lancer, Becky, 280, 281, 282, 283

Earhart, Amelia, 10, 27, **110–13**
Easterly, Doris Glenn, 355
Eastlake-Smith, Gwendoline, 339
Eaton, Hubert, 128, 129
Echols, Sheila, 373, 375
Ecker, Monique, 374
Eckert, Barbel, 339
Eckert, Claudia, 355
Eckman, Carol, 224
Ecroth, Kathy, 354
Ederle, Gertrude, 10, 27, 43, 98, **113–15**
Education Amendments of 1972, 18. *See also* Title IX
Edwards, Jackie, 373, 375
Edwards, Teresa, 61, **115–16,** 226, 295, 296, 298
Egarova, Lyubov, 342
Egerszegi, Krisztina, 337, 338, 362
Egnot, Leslie, 262
Egorova, Lyubov, 343
Ehret, Gloria, 358
Ehrhardt, Annelie, 340
Eichner, Clair, 372, 374
Eickhoff, Janie, 354
Eighteenth Amendment, 10
Eisel, Mary Ann, 120

Elek, Ilona, 334
Ellingson, Joy, 368
Ellingsworth, Karen, 352
Ellis, Betty, 31
Ely, Janet, 356
Emery, Elizabeth, 353
Emery, Gail, 280
Emoto, Yuko, 336
Encyclopedias, 313
Ender, Kornelia, 337, 338
Enderlein, Ortrun, 344
Engel, Kim, 375
Engel-Krämer, Ingrid, 334
Englehorn, Shirley, 358
Enke, Karin, 70, 344
Enquist, Ludmila, 340
Epple, Irene, 348
Epstein-Barr virus, 78
Equal rights for women. *See*
    Women's rights
Equestrian athlete. *See also* Jockey
    Sears, Eleonora, 216, 217
Equestrian events. *See also* Horse
    racing
    bibliography on, 317
    milestone in, 26
    in Olympic history, 39, 49, 51,
        52, 53, 54, 57, 59
    organizations for, 325
Equipment, advances in, 24
Eriksson, Agneta, 369
Ernst, Joanne, 367
Errath, Christine, 142
Erv Lind Award, 305
Esser, Roswitha, 334
Estep, Mike, 199
Esther Williams Creative
    Achievement Award, 284
Ethridge, Kamie, 347
Ettien, Jo, 173
Evans, Christy, 262
Evans, Janet, **117–18,** 347
    championships won by, 362,
        363, 370, 371
    in Olympic history, 58, 337,
        338
    in sports history, 22
Eve, Laverne, 375
Evert, Chris, 22, 58, **119–21**
    Austin, Tracy and, 85
    awards won by, 346, 347
    championships won by, 364,
        365, 366, 367
    Graf, Steffi and, 136, 137
    Navratilova, Martina and, 199
    Seles, Monica and, 218
Exercise, history of, 4, 7

Fabyan, Sarah Palfrey, 180
Faggs, Mae. *See* Starr, May Faggs
Fairbanks, Jo Ann, 32
Fairchild, Melody, 372
Fairhall, Neroli, 57
Falck, Hildegard, 340
Falk, Paul, 343
Falk, Ria, 343
Faminow, Cathy Priestner, 90
Far Western Amateur Athletic
    Union, 104
Farella, Lindsey, 362
Farrell, Julie, 371
Farrell-Ovenhouse, Julie, 371
Fashion. *See* Dress reform
Fassi, Carlo, 125, 142
Faulk, Mary Lena, 360
Faut, Jean, 16, 255, 256
Favor, Suzy, 347, 372, 374
Fawcett, Joy, 289, 291, 292
Feagin, Zundra, 373
Fealey, Alison, 363
Federation Internationale de
    Football Association, 78, 79,
    290–94
Federation Internationale de
    Natation Amateur, 282–83
Federation Internationale des
    Quilleurs, 131, 132
Fédération Sportive Féminine
    Internationale, 40, 41
Feigel, Ann, 352
Felke, Petra, 341
Female Alpine Skier of the Year,
    134
Female Athlete of the Decade
    Associated Press, 198
    Los Angeles Times, 204
    National Sports Review, 198
    United Press International,
        198
    University of California at
        Santa Barbara, 292
Female Athlete of the World, 96
Female Athlete of the Year. *See
    also* Athlete of the Year
    Associated Press, 346
    Fresno State University, 305
    National Wheelchair Athletic
        Association, 109
    U.S. Cycling Federation, 127
    U.S. Olympic Committee, 123,
        132, 193
    U.S. Rowing Association, 262,
        263
    U.S. Soccer Federation, 78,
        291, 292, 293

USA Basketball, 116, 298, 299,
    300
Female College Athlete of the
    Year, 191
Female College Basketball Player
    of the Year, 299, 300
Female Cyclist of the Year, 127
Female Runner of the Year, 154
Female Skier of the Year, 134
Femininity, 15, 93, 254
Fencer
    Mayer, Helene, 45, **183,** 334
Fencing
    champions in, 356–57, 368
    milestones in, 26, 29, 33
    in Olympic history, 39, 42, 45,
        50, 60, 334–35
    organization for, 325
Fendick, Patty, 372
Feng, Amy, 364
Fergus, Lillian, 355
Ferguson, Cathy, 337
Ferguson, Debbie, 372
Fernandez, Gigi, 339
Fernandez, Lisa, **122–23,** 272, 347
    on national softball team, 301,
        302, 303–04
    in Olympic history, 61
Fernandez, Mary Joe, 339
Fetter, Leigh Ann, 369
Fichtel, Anja, 335
Fiebig, Cora, 352
Field hockey
    in Olympic history, 51, 55, 335
    organization for, 325
    in sports history, 8, 21
Field hockey coach
    Applebee, Constance M. K., 8,
        81–82
Figini, Michela, 342
Figure skaters. *See also index entries
    under each skater's name*
    Albright, Tenley, **79–81**
    Fleming, Peggy, **124–26**
    Hamill, Dorothy, **141–43**
    Heiss, Carol, **144–46**
    Henie, Sonja, **146–48**
    Yamaguchi, Kristi, **241–43**
Figure skating
    bibliography on, 126, 143,
        146, 148, 313–14
    champions in, 357–58
    milestones in, 28, 32, 33
    in Olympic history, 38, 39, 41,
        42, 62–73, 343
    organization for, 325
    in sports history, 16
Fikotová, Olga, 318, 340

Finn, Michelle, 372, 373
Finneran, Sharon, 51
Fischbach, Mary, 371
Fischer, Birgit, 333
Fish, Jennifer, 68
Fisher, Allison, 351
Fisher, Wendy, 349
Fishing, 314, 323
Fitness, in sports history, ix, 11, 15, 21
Fitzgerald (-Brown), Benita, 340, 374
Flanders, Holly, 348
Fleckenstein, Vicki, 348
Fleischer, Tilly, 341
Fleming, Peggy, **124–26,** 146, 346
    championships won by, 357, 358
    in Olympic history, 68, 343
    in sports history, 19
Flessel, Laura, 334
Fletcher, Mrs. P., 349
Fletcher, Najuma, 373
Fletcher, Pam, 348, 349
Fleury, Catherine, 336
Flint, William, 25
Flintoff-King, Debra, 340
Flo Hyman Award, 347
"FloJo." See Joyner, Florence "FloJo" Griffith
Flood, Lisa, 370
Florence Griffith Joyner Youth Foundation, 158
Florida Women's Bowling Hall of Fame, 132
Flying. See Aviation
"Flying Dutch Housewife," 94
Foley, Esther, 355
Foli, Noni, 348
Football, 29, 31, 33
Ford, Michelle, 337
Ford, Robin, 371
Forrest, Stephanie, 347, 349
Fortna, Rosie, 349
Fortner, Nell, 296
Foschi, Jessica, 362
Foss, Betty, 256
Foster, Dee Dee, 368
Fothergill, Dotty, 352
Foudy, Julie, 289, 290, 292
Fox, Catherine, 362, 369, 370
Foyt, A. J., 140
Franco, Claudia, 370
Franke, N. Tomlinson, 357
Fraser, Dawn, 51, 337, 346
Fraser, Gretchen, 65, 342, 348, 349

Fratianne, Linda, 70, 347, 358
Frazer, Merlene, 372, 373
Frederick, Marcia, 30
Freeman, Michelle, 374
Freestyle skiing, 71, 72
French Legion of Honor, 113
Freshman Player of the Year, 237, 292
Friedrich, Doris, 348
Friedrich, Heike, 337, 362
Fruhwirth, Amy, 360
Fry, Shirley, 364, 365, 366, 367
Fryland-Clausen, Stefani, 334
Fu Mingxia, 334
Fuchs, Ruth, 341
Fugett, Kim, 371
Fuhr, Heather, 367
Fuller, Amy, 262
Fung, Lori, 336
Furtado, Juli, **126–27,** 353
Fynes, Sevatheda, 372, 373

Gabarra, Carin, 289, 290, 292
Gacioch, Rose, 256
Gage, Nena, 375
Gaines, Chryste, 372, 373
Galindo, Rudy, 241, 242
Gao Min, 334
Garcia, Esmeralda, 373, 375
Gardiner, Tenley. See Albright, Tenley
Gardner, Julie, 353
Gardner, Maureen, 94
Gardner, Randy, 70
Gareau, Jacqueline, 361
Garmisch-Partenkirchen Olympics (1936), 64
Garms, Shirley, 352
Garrett, Carla, 373, 375
Garrison, Zina, 339
Garrison-Steves, Kelly, 368, 369
Gates, Linda, 372
Ge Fei, 333
Geatches, Allison, 268
Geddes, Jane, 358, 359
Gehring, A., 356
Gehrs, Mindy, 371
Geijssen, Carolina, 344
Geissler, Ines, 338
Genauss, Carsta, 334
Gentes, Sue, 374
Georgia Sports Hall of Fame, 278
Gera, Bernice, 30
Gerety, Megan, 348
Gerg, Hilde, 342
German Tennis Federation, 137
Gernay, Collette, 354
Gestring, Marjorie, 334, 355, 356

Geweniger, Ute, 338
Gianotti, Carol, 352
Gibbes, Mrs. A. H., 349
Gibson, Althea, **127–30,** 181, 346
    championships won by, 365, 366, 367
    in sports history, 17, 28
Giguere, Nathalie, 363
Gil Young-ah, 333
Gillis, Rhona W., 348
Gilman, Michelle. See Gould, Michelle
Giovinco, Lucy, **131–32,** 353
Gisladdottir, Disa, 373, 375
Givens, Randy, 373
Gjanotti-Black, Carol, 352
Glerum, Karen, 372
Gnauck, Maxi, 335
Goalkeeper of the Year, 293
Godden, Norma, 348
Godfree, Kathleen, 365
Goetze, Vicki, 360, 368
Goewey, Julie, 369
Gogarty, Deirdre, 182
Göhr, Marlies, 83–84
Goitschel, Christine, 67, 342
Goitschel, Marielle, 67, 342, 348
Golay, Jeanne, 353
Gold Boot Winner, 78
Gold medalists, Olympic, 333–44
Golden, Diana, **132–34,** 347
Golden Age of Sport in America, 10–11
Golden Ball Award, 292
Golden Cyclone Athletic Club, 14, 246
Golden Rule, 134
Goles, Sabrina, 137
Golf
    bibliography on, 90, 179, 235, 248, 315–16
    champions in, 358–60, 368
    milestones in, 25, 27, 28, 30, 31, 32, 33
    in Olympic history, 37, 39, 335
    organization for, 325
    in sports history, 5, 6, 9, 10, 15, 16, 17–18, 20, 22, 130
Golfer of the Decade, 89, 179
Golfers
    Berg, Patty, 27, **88–90,** 230, 346, 358, 360
    Lopez, Nancy, 20, **177–79,** 346, 347, 359
    Vare, Glenna Collett, 10, 89, **229–31,** 360
    Whitworth, Kathy, 77, **233–35,** 240, 346, 358, 359

Golfers *(continued)*
  Wright, Mickey, 233, 234,
    239–40, 346, 358, 359
  Zaharias, Mildred "Babe"
    Didrikson, **245–48.** *See
    also* Zaharias, Mildred
    "Babe" Didrikson
Gomez, Laurie, 374
Gonzalez, Driulis, 336
Gooch, Kay, 372, 374
Goodman, Jackie, 372, 374
Goolagong, Evonne, 320, 346,
  364, 365, 366
Gopova, Nina, 334
Gordeeva, Ekaterina, 343
Gordon-Dick, Teresa, 33
Gorman, Julie, 363, 371
Gorman, Miki, 361
Gorokhovskaya, Maria, 335
Gorshkov, Aleksandr, 343
Gossick, Sue, 334, 355
Göthenburg International Ladies
  Games (1926), 40
Gould, Michelle, **135–36**
Gould, Shane, 337, 338
Gouthro, Laurie, 268
Governor of Florida's Award, 140
Graber, Phyllis, 18
Graf, Peter, 136, 137
Graf, Steffi, **136–38,** 346
  Austin, Tracy and, 86
  championships won by, 364,
    365, 366, 367
  Navratilova, Martina and, 200
  in Olympic history, 58, 339
  Seles, Monica and, 218, 219
  in sports history, 22
Graham, Debbie, 372
Graham, Linda, 353
Granger, Michele, 61, 123, 272,
  301, 302, 304
Grasegger, Kathe, 64
Graves' disease, 106
Graves, Rita, 375
Gray, Clinton, 211
Gray, Mrs. B. P., 349
Greatest Woman Athlete (of last
  25 years), 119
Green, Nicole, 374
Green, Phyllis, 27
Green, Tammie, 359
Greene, Elizabeth, 349
Greene, Marilyn, 348
Greene, Nancy, 342, 347, 348,
  349
Gregory, Anne, 17
Gregory, Kathy, 21

Grenoble Olympics (1968), 68
Grieco, Jessica, 354
Griffin, Ellen, 27
Griffith Joyner, Florence. *See*
  Joyner, Florence "FloJo"
  Griffith
Griglione, Michelle, 363, 371
Grimes, Betty, 355
Grinham, Judith, 337
Grinkov, Sergie, 343
Griscom, Frances, 359
Gritschuk, Oksana, 343
Groenendaal, Claudette, 374
Gronfeldt, Iris, 375
Grossfeld, Muriel, 360
Grouicheva, Stoyanka, 336
Grubbs, Audrey, 350
Grulkowski, Ruth, 360
Gu Jun, 333
Guarino, Mary, 351
Guecheva, Vania, 333
Guest, Amy Phipps, 111
Guetschow, Joan, 351
Guidry, Carlette, 372, 373
Gummel, Margitta, 341
Gunderson, JoAnne, 360
Gunnarsson, Susanne, 334
Gunnell, Sally, 340
Gusakova, Claudia, 343
Guseva, Klara, 344
Gustafsson, Toini, 342, 343
Guthrie, Diane, 373, 375, 376
Guthrie, Janet, 21, 30, **138–41**
Guthrie-Gresham, Diane, 373,
  376
Gutsu, Tatyana, 192, 335
Gyarmati, Olga, 341
Gyenge, Valéria, 337
Gymnastics
  bibliography on, 102, 168,
    194, 206, 210, 289, 316
  champions in, 360–61, 368–69
  milestones in, 30, 32
  in Olympic history, 39, 44, 46,
    48, 54, 55, 57, 59–60,
    335–36
  organization for, 325
  outstanding team in, 285–89
  in sports history, 20
Gymnasts. *See also index entries
  under each gymnast's name*
  Borden, Amanda, 285, 286,
    287
  Chow, Amy, 285, 286, 287
  Comaneci, Nadia, **99–102**
  Dawes, Dominique, 285, 286,
    287–88

  Korbut, Olga, **166–68**
  Miller, Shannon, **192–94**
  Moceanu, Dominique, 285,
    286, 288
  Phelps, Jaycie, 285, 286, 287,
    288
  Retton Mary Lou, **204–06**
  Rigby, Cathy, **208–10**
  Strug, Kerri, 285, 286, 287,
    288–89

Haas, Christl, 342
Haase, Helga, 344
Habernigg, Susan, 370
Hacker, Carolyn, 360
Haemaelaeinen, Marja-Liisa, 70
Hagge, Marlene, 358
Hain, Michele, 355
Haislett, Nicole, 337, 362, 370,
  371
Hales, Diane, 350
Hall, Kaye, 337
Hall, Mrs. H., 349
Halls of fame
  auto racer in, 141
  aviator in, 113
  barrel racer in, 153
  basketball coach in, 227
  basketball innovator in, 87
  basketball players in, 87, 177,
    188, 189, 191
  bowlers in, 132, 173, 187
  cyclists in, 97, 245
  divers in, 166, 185
  field hockey player in, 82
  figure skaters in, 81, 125, 143,
    145
  golfers in, 89, 179, 231, 234,
    240, 248
  gymnasts in, 168, 206
  in history of sports, 21
  racquetball player in, 136
  skiers in, 175, 202
  softball players in, 156, 272–
    75
  speed skater in, 245
  swimmers in, 99, 104, 114
  tennis players in, 85, 103, 121,
    130, 164, 180, 195, 200,
    237
  track and field athletes in, 94,
    158, 212, 229, 233, 248,
    278, 279, 280
Hämäläinen, Marja-Liisa, 70, 342
Hamill, Dorothy, **141–43,** 146,
  243
  championships won by, 358
  in Olympic history, 69, 343
  in sports history, 19

Hamilton, Kim, 369
Hamm, Mia, 79, 289, 290, 291, 292–93, 347
Hammel, Penny, 368
Hammer, Gladys, 350
Hammond, Harriet D., 26
Hanchette, Ilda, 350
Hand, Annette, 374
Handball, 51, 54, 328, 336
Handicapped athletes. *See* Disabled athletes
Handley, Debi, 348
Hang gliding, 327
Hanlon, Lorraine, 357
Hannam, Edith, 339
Hansell, Ellen, 5, 366
Hansen, Connie, 361
Hansen, Erika, 370
Hansen, Jacqueline, 361
Hansen, Jenny, 368, 369
Hanson, Beverly, 358, 360
Hantze, Karen, 162, 163
Happe, Ursula, 338
Hard, Darlene, 130, 365, 367
Harding, Tonya, 32, 72, 242, 358
Hardwick, Mary, 181
Hardy, Catherine, 48–49
Hargreaves, Alison, 24, **143–44**
Harland, Rose, 25
Harlem Globetrotters, 31, 177, 237, 238–39
Harley, Katherine, 359
Harman, Janet, 352
Harrigan, Lori, 301, 302, 304
Harris, Dionna, 301, 304
Harris, Flirtisha, 372, 374
Harris, Luisa, 347
Harris, Suzanne, 349
Harris, Tom, 276
Harrison, Joan, 337
Harrison, Pat, 273
Hart, Doris, 102, 320, 364, 365, 366, 367
Hartel, Lis, 49
Hartigan, Joan, 364
Harup, Karen-Margrete, 337
Harvey, Alisa, 374
Harvey, Mary, 289, 293
Hase, Dagmar, 337
Hashman, Judy Devlin, 350
Haskin, Janet, 374
Hattestad, Stine Lisa, 343
Hattori, Michiko, 360
Hauschild, Penney, 368, 369
Hawks, Frank, 111
Hayden, Ann, 365
Hayes, Andrea, 362

Hayes, Kathy, 374
Haynie, Sandra, 358, 359
Haywood, Claudia, 375
He-Ja Lee, 363
Head, Patricia Summitt. *See* Summitt, Patricia Head
Health, quality of, 4, 7
Healy, Pam, 262
Heaston, Liz, 33
Heath, Clarity, 349
Hecker, Genevieve, 359
Hecox, Karen, 374
Heddle, Kathleen, 336
Heddy, Kathy, 347
Hedgepeth, Whitney, 362, 370
Hedges, Barbara, 24, 32
Hedrick, Sharon, 58, 341
Hegener, Gretchen, 370
Heggtveit, Anne, 342, 348
Heiden, Beth, 70, 347, 353
Heisick, Lori, 370
Heisler, Toni, 268
Heiss, Carol, 80, **144–46**
    championships won by, 357
    in Olympic history, 66, 67, 343
    in sports history, 16
Heldman, Gladys, 20, 29
Hellmann, Martina, 341
Hellwig, Helen, 366
Helms Athletic Foundation Sports Halls of Fame, 172–73
Helsinki
    1940 Olympics, 46
    1952 Olympics, 48–49
Hemmings, Deon, 340
Hemond-Dent, Susan, 262
Hendricken, Geraldine, 372
Henie, Sonja, 62, 63, 64, **146–48,** 343
Henkel, Heiki, 341
Hennagan, Monique, 372, 374
Henne, Jan, 337
Henning, Anne, 68, 96, 344
Henrotin, Sylvia, 217
Henry, Amanda, 354
Henry, Angee, 373, 375
Henry, Cynthia, 373, 375
Heptathlete
    Joyner-Kersee, Jackie, **158–61**
Heptathlon, 158–61, 341
Herber, Maxi, 343
Herbst, Stephanie, 372, 374
Hermann Award, 78, 293
Herr, Beth, 371
Heyns, Penny, 338, 370
Hicks, Elizabeth, 27, 360

Hicks, Helen, 360
Higel, Kim, 363
High jump, 341, 373, 375
High school sports, 18, 311
Higuchi, Chako, 359
Hilgertova, Stepanka, 334
Hill, Carolyn, 360
Hill, Cynthia, 360
Hill, D'Andre, 372, 373
Hill, Dorothy Poynton, 334
Hill, Kelli, 288
Hill, Lucile E., 81
Hill, Lynn, 24, 148–50
Hillyard, Blanche Bingley, 365
Hines, Phyllis, 353
Hines, Susan, 369
Hingis, Martina, 86, 138, 346, 364, 366, 367
Hintzen, Barbara, 353
Hirai, Kimiko, 371
Hirch, Mary, 27
History
    bibliography on, 316–17
    of civil rights, 17–18
    of college sports, x, 7–8, 11–13, 16–19, 24
    of dress reform, ix, 4, 6–7, 10–11, 26, 27, 36
    of media coverage, 19–20, 22
    milestones in, 25–33
    of the Olympics, x, 35–73, 333–45
    of recreation, 3–4
    nineteenth century, 4–8
    twentieth century, ix–x, 8–25
Hitler, Adolf, 45, 64
Hockey. *See* Field hockey; Ice hockey
Hodgert, Ruth, 350
Hodgson, Beatrice, 350
Hoerger, Mary, 355
Hoff, Karen, 333
Hofstatter, Gerda, 351
Hogan, Ben, 90, 239, 248
Hogshead, Nancy, 57, 337
Hogue, Micki King. *See* King, Micki
Holden, Mari, 353
Holes, Tammy, 33
Holland, Nancy, 348, 349
Hollins, Marion, 360
Holm, Eleanor, 46, 98, 337
Holmes, Phyllis, 31
Holum, Dianne, 68, 96, 344
Homans, Amy Morris, 319
Homans, Helen, 366
Homeghi, Olga, 336

Homer, Silke, 363
Honda Award, 293
Honda Broderick Cup, 347
Hong Qian, 363
Hooiveld, Lara, 370
Hoover, Lou Henry, 11
Hope, Bob, 265
Hopp, Ceci, 374
Hopper, I., 356
Horn, Miriam Burns, 360
Hornbeck, Heidi, 369
Hörner, Silke, 338
Horse racing, 30. *See also*
    Equestrian events; Jockey
    bibliography on, 171, 317
    milestones in, 25, 27, 29, 31,
        32
    organizations for, 325
    in sports history, 21
Horse show riding, 26
Horseshoe pitching, 26
Horton, Donna, 360
Horvat, Elena, 336
Hotchkiss, Hazel. *See* Wightman,
    Hazel Hotchkiss
Howard, Anita, 374
Howard, Julie, 362
Howard, Sherri, 374
Howell, Lida, 37, 333
Howell, Lydia Scott, 6
Howell, Mrs. M. C., 349
Hoyt, Beatrix, 5, 359
Hristova, Ivanka, 341
Huber, Vicki, 347, 368, 372, 374
Hübler, Anna, 343
Hudson, Martha, 277, 278
Hudson, Sheila, 373, 375
Hughes, Tanya, 373, 375
Hulick, Jim, 241, 242
Hull, Helen. *See* Jacobs, Helen
    Hull
Humphrey, Alecia, 362, 363, 370
Hunger, Daniela, 338
Hunter, Peggy, 351
Huntington, Anna Seaton, 258,
    259, 262
Hunyady, Emese, 344
Hurd, Dorothy C., 360
Hurdles, in track and field, 340,
    373, 374–75
Hurst, Pat, 360, 368
Hwang Hye-young, 333
Hyacinth, Flora, 373
Hyang-Soon Seo, 333
Hyche, Holli, 372, 373
Hyman, Flo, **150–52,** 347
Hyman, Misty, 363

Ice dancing, 70, 343
Ice hockey
    milestones in, 32, 33
    in Olympic history, 73, 344
    in sports history, 24
Ice hockey goalie
    Rheaume, Manon, 24, 32,
        207–08
Ice skating. *See* Figure skating;
    Speed skating
Illnesses. *See* Medical conditions
Ilyina, Vera, 371
Inahashi, Kazue, 352
Industrialization, 4
Infantile paralysis, 79
Inkster, Juli, 32, 359, 360
Innis, Jennifer, 375
Innsbruck
    1964 Olympics, 67–68
    1976 Olympics, 69
Instructors. *See also* Coaches
    bowling, 186, 187
    tennis, 235, 236–37
Intercollegiate sports. *See* College
    sports
International Academy of Sports,
    96
International Amateur Athletic
    Federation, 40, 41
International Cyclist of the Year,
    127
International Gymnastics
    Foundation, 100
International Ice Hockey
    Federation, 207
International Lawn Tennis
    Federation, 28
International Olympic Commit-
    tee, 24, 31, 35, 36
    Summer Games and, 38, 40,
        41, 52
    Winter Games and, 62
International Racquetball
    Federation, 135
International Softball Federation,
    122, 271, 275, 303–06
International Swimming
    Federation, 39
International Swimming Hall of
    Fame, 99, 104, 114, 166, 185
International Tennis Hall of
    Fame, 85, 103, 130, 164,
    180, 195, 237
International Volleyball Associa-
    tion, 21
International Winter Sports Week,
    62

International Women in Boating,
    263
International Women's
    Boardsailing Association,
    327
International Women's Fishing
    Association, 323
International Women's Hall of
    Fame, 113
International Women's Profes-
    sional Softball Association,
    20, 156, 163
International Women's Sports
    Hall of Fame, 21
    auto racer in, 141
    aviator in, 113
    basketball coach in, 227
    basketball innovator in, 87
    basketball players in, 189, 191
    bowler in, 173
    cyclists in, 97, 245
    divers in, 166, 185
    figure skaters in, 81, 125, 145
    golfers in, 89, 231, 234, 240,
        248
    gymnasts in, 168, 206
    skiier in, 175
    softball players in, 156, 273,
        274
    speed skater, 245
    swimmers in, 99, 104, 114
    tennis players in, 103, 121,
        130, 164, 200
    track and field athletes in, 94,
        212, 229, 233, 248, 279,
        280
Irish, Carrie, 355
"Iron Woman," 257
Irwin, Juno, 356
Isler, J. J., 259, 262–63
Itanyi, Pat, 375
Ivan, Paula, 340
Ivosev, Aleksandra, 337
Iwasaki, Kyoko, 338

Jackson, Marjorie, 339
Jackson, Trina, 370
Jacob, Lisa, 370
Jacobs, Helen (Hull), 235, 346,
    365, 366
Jacobsen, D. D., 352
Jacobsen D'Asaro, G., 357
Jahl, Evelin Schlaak, 340
Jaklofsky, Shaon, 376
Jakobsson, Ludovika, 343
Jakobsson, Walter, 343
James, Charmayne, **152–53**
Jameson, Betty, 27, 358, 360
Jankowski, Patrice, 351

Janz, Karin, 335
Jäschke, Martina, 334
Jaunzeme, Inese, 341
Jausovec, Mima, 365
Javelin throw, 341, 375
Jeanson, Ceclie, 363
Jenkins, Carol Heiss. *See* Heiss, Carol
Jenkins, Julie, 374
Jenkins, Kelly, 371
Jenkins, Louisa, 353
Jennings, Carin. *See* Gabarra, Carin
Jennings, Lynn, **153–54,** 347
Jensen, Bjorg Eva, 344
Jensen, Gitta, 362
Jesse Owens Award, 158, 160, 161, 221
Jessup, Marian, 194
Jewell, Lynne, 59, 341
Jews, discrimination against, 45, 183
Jimenez, Odalys Reve, 336
Jing Chen, 339
Jo Ettien Trophy, 173
Jochum-Beiser, Trude, 342
Jockey. *See also* Horse racing
Krone, Julie, 31–32, **169–71**
Jockey Club of the United States, 27
Johansson, Greta, 334
John Bunn Award, 227
John, Paul, 373
Johnson, Beverly, 31
Johnson, Brandy, 361
Johnson, Chris, 359
Johnson, Diane, 369
Johnson, Gea, 376
Johnson, Jenna, 369, 371
Johnson, Jill, 370
Johnson, Judy, 27
Johnson, Kathy, 361
Johnson, Katrena, 373, 375
Johnson, Liz, 352, 353
Johnson, Lynette, 350
Johnson, Mrs. Robert, 350
Johnson, Robert, 128, 129
Johnson, Tish, 352
Johnston, Cathy, 359
Johson, Susan, 363
Jolly, Allison, 59, 341
Joly, Andrée, 64, 343
Jones, Ann, 365, 366
Jones, Barbara, 48, 49, 278–79
Jones, Bobby, 89–90, 231
Jones, Esther, 373
Jones, Jolanda, 376

Jones, Loree Jon, 351
Jones, Marion, 366
Jordan, Barbara, 364
Jorgensen, Janel, 363, 371
Josephson, Karen, 339
Josephson, Sarah, 339
Jost, Kristine, 372
Journalism. *See* Sportscasting; Sportswriting
Joyce, Joan, 20, **155–56,** 271, 273–74
Joyner, Al, 159
Joyner, Florence "FloJo" Griffith, 84, **156–58**
awards won by, 346, 347
championships won by, 373
in Olympic history, 58, 339
in sports history, 22
Joyner-Kersee, Jackie, 157, **158–61**
awards won by, 346, 347
championships won by, 375
in Olympic history, 58, 61, 341
in sports history, 22
Judo, 52, 59, 336
Julin, Madga, 343
Jump, Ruth, 355, 356
Jun Gao, 364
Jung-Hwa Hyun, 339

Kaciusyté, Lina, 338
Kadaowaki, Kazuki, 360
Kahn, Paula, 347
Kaiser, Natasha, 372
Kalinchuk, Yekaterina, 335
Kalinina, Irina, 334
Kalitta, Connie, 196, 197
Kaljurand, Anu, 376
Kamenshek, Dorothy, 256
Kampfe, Anne, 363
Kane, Kristen, 355
Kania, Karen, 91
Kapernick, Gai, 375
Karen Krantzcke Sportsmanship Award, 120
Karolyi, Bela, 100, 101, 205, 206, 289
Karolyi, Marta, 100, 289
Karponosov, Gennady, 343
Kaszuba, Beata, 370, 371
Kayaking
bibliography on, 312
in Olympic history, 333–34
organization for, 324
Kazakova, Oksana, 343
Kazankina, Tatyana, 340
Keggi, Caroline, 368
Kelbecheva, Siika, 336

Keleti, Ágnes, 335
Kelleher, Jennie, 27
Keller, Patricia. *See* McCormick, Patricia
Kellerman, Annette, 26
Kellers, Peggy, 274
Kelly, Judianne, 351
Kelly, Kim, 369
Kendall, Barbara, 342
Kennedy, Jennifer, 134
Kenoyer, Kristen, 369
Keplar, Deborah, 356
Kern, Mrs. Albert, 349
Kerrigan, Nancy, 72, 242, 314, 358
Kersee, Bob, 106, 157, 159
Kessler, Jeanne, 356
Ketcham, Lee Anne, 266, 269
Khloptseva, Yelena, 336
Khodotovich, Yekaterina, 336
Khvedosyuk, Lyudmila, 333
Kidd, Willie, Sr., 88
Kiehl, Marina, 342
Kim Dong-mon, 333
Kim Kyung-wook, 333
Kim Mi-jung, 336
Kim, Nelli, 100, 335
Kimball, Dick, 165
Kimball, Judy, 358
Kinard, Utami, 351
King, Betsy, 358, 359
King, Billie Jean, **161–64,** 320
awards won by, 346, 347
championships won by, 364, 365, 366, 367
Evert, Chris and, 119, 120, 121
Joyce, Joan and, 156
in sports history, 20, 21, 22, 29
King, H., 357
King, Kathryn (Sis), 274
King, Micki, 21, **164–66,** 334, 354, 355, 356
Kingsbury, Thelma, 350
Kinmont, Jill, 319, 348
Kipp, Billy, 124
Kirby, Dorothy, 360
Kirk, Hazel, 26
Kirklin, Leah, 373, 375
Kitzmiller, Joy, 351
Kjarsgaard-Ness, Christy, 242
Klein, Emilee, 368
Klein, Krista, 355
Klier, Cornelia, 336
Klimova, Marina, 343
Klochneva, Olga, 336
Klopfer, Sonya. *See* Dunfield, Sonya Klopfer

Kloska, Jeanne, 353
Kloster, Kristi, 372
Klybert, Diana, 263
Knape, Ulrika, 334
Knapp, Barbara, 129
Knaushaar, Silke, 344
Knight, Bobby, 227
Knol, Monique, 334
Knysh, Renald, 167
Koban, Rita, 334
Koch, Bill, 258, 259
Koch, Katrin, 375
Koch, Lorrie, 352
Koch, Marita, 339
Koen, Francina. *See* Blankers-
    Koen, Fanny
Koester, Mrs. A. J., 26
Kok, Ada, 338
Kolb, Claudia, 53, 338
Kolpakova, Tatiana, 341
Komen, Susan G., 223
Komisova, Vera, 340
Kondratyeva, Lyudmila, 339
Konopacka, Halina, 340
Koppen, Kerstin, 336
Kopsky, Doris, 27
Korbut, Olga, **166–68,** 346
    Comaneci, Nadia and, 99, 101
    in Olympic history, 54, 335
    in sports history, 19–20, 22
Köring, Dora, 339
Kormoczy, Zsuzsi, 130, 365
Korondi, Margi, 335
Koshevaia, Marina, 338
Kostache, Tamara, 362
Kostadinova, Stefka, 341
Kosyreva, Lyubov, 342
Koznick, Kristina, 348
Krämer, Ingrid, 50, 334
Krantzcke, Karen, 120
Krause, Barbara, 55, 337
Kraves, Iness, 341
Krebs, Tina, 372
Kreft, Galina, 334
Kreiner, Kathy, 342
Kreiner, Laurie, 348
Kremer, Mitzi, 370
Krepkina, Vyera, 341
Kristiansen, Ingrid, 232, 361
Krivaleva, Svetlana, 341
Kronberger, Petra, 342
Krone, Julie, 31–32, **169–71**
Krone, Kristin, 349
Kropke, Keri, 269
Krzesinska, Elzbieta, 341
Kuchinskaya, Natalya, 335
Kuczynski, Betty, 352

Kuehne, Kelli, 360
Kukleva, Galina, 342
Kulakova, Galina, 342, 343
Kumbernuss, Astrid, 341
Kurys, Sophie, 15–16, 255, 257
Kuryshko, Ekaterina, 334
Kuscsik, Nina, 21, 30, 361
Kusner, Kathy, 29
Kwan, Michelle, 73, 314, 358
Kye Sun, 336

Lacey, Venus, 295, 298
Lackie, Ethel, 337
Lacoste, Catherine, 358, 360
Lacrosse, 325
Lacrosse Foundation and Hall of
    Fame, 325
Ladenburg, Mrs. Adolph, 25–26
Ladewig, Marion, 171–73, 352
Ladies Club for Outdoor Sports,
    4, 25
Ladies' Day, 25
Ladies League Baseball, 322
Ladies Professional Bowlers Tour,
    131, 323
Ladies Professional Golf
    Association, 177, 178, 233,
    325
    awards by, 179, 231, 234
    Berg, Patty and, 88, 89, 90
    Blacks and, 130
    founding of, 245, 247
    Hall of Fame, 89, 179, 234,
        240, 248
    in sports history, 16, 20, 22, 28
LaFace, Karen, 371
Lake Placid
    1932 Olympics, 63–64
    1980 Olympics, 69–70
Lakkarinen, Marjut, 342
Lance, Sylvia, 364
Lancien, Nathalie, 334
Lanctot, Jennifer, 372
Landry, Nelly, 364
Lannoy, Micheline, 343
Larcombe, Ethel, 365
LaRoche, Lucie, 348
Larrieu Smith, Francie. *See* Smith,
    Francie Larrieu
Larsen, Elizabeth, 353
Latimore, Sarah, 13
Latynina, Larissa, 335
Lavine, Laura, 375
Lawn tennis, 5. *See also* Tennis
Lawn Tennis Association, 43
Lawrence, Andrea Mead, **173–75**
    championships won by, 347,
        348, 349

    in Olympic history, 66, 342
    in sports history, 16
Lawson, Estelle, 360
Lazutina, Larissa, 342
Le Jingyi, 337
Leach, Marie, 13
Leadership positions, 24
Leatherwood, Lillie, 372, 374
Lechner, Erica, 68, 344
Lee, Jean, 350
Lee, Jeanette, 351
Lee, Judy, 352
Lee, Mabel, 12, 319
Lee, Suzette, 373, 375
Lee-Gartner, Kerrin, 342
Lee Lai-Shan, 342
Leitch, Cecil, 230
Lemaire, Lyn, 353, 367
Lenczyk, Grace, 360
Lenglen, Suzanne, 26, 339, 364,
    365
Lenzi, Joel, 355
Leslie, Lisa, 295, 297, 298–99
Lesser, Patricia, 360
LeSueur, Emily Porter, 280, 282,
    283–84
Lettiere, Angela, 372
Lewis, Carol, 373, 375
Li Duihong, 337
Lidback, Jenny, 359
Liddick, Peggy, 288
Lieberman-Cline, Nancy, 54, **175–
    77,** 188, 199, 347
Lillehammer Olympics (1994), 72
Lilly, Kristine, 289, 293
Limpert, Marianne, 363
Limpert, Sharon, 361
Lin Li, 338
Lind, Erv, 305
Lindbergh, Charles, 110, 112
Lindh, Hilary, 348, 349
Lindley, G. C., 347, 348
Lindquist, Linda, 259, 263
Lindstrom, Murle, 358
Line Basket Ball for Women, 87
Linehan, Kristen, 370
Linichuk, Natalia, 343
Linsenhoff, Liselott, 49, 54
Linzmeier, Marybeth, 370
Lipa, Elisabeth, 336
Lipinski, Tara, 33, 73, 314, 343,
    347, 358
Lipscomb, Susan, 370
Lisovskaya, Natalia, 341
Little, Sally, 359
Little League baseball, 30
"Little Miss Poker Face," 10

"Little Mo," 102
Livermore, David, 133
Living Legacy Award, 99
Livingston, Karen Bliss, 353
Lizane, Anita, 366
Lloyd, Chris Evert. *See* Evert, Chris
Lloyd, M., 356
Lobatch, Marina, 336
Lobo, Rebecca, 295, 297, 299, 346, 347
Locke, Bernadette, 24, 32
Locke, D., 356
Logvinenko, Marina, 336
Lolk, Nina, 351
Lomady, Clara Schroth, 360
London
    1908 Olympics, 38
    1934 Women's World Games, 41
    1944 Olympics, 46
    1948 Olympics, 47–48
Long Island Sports Car Association, 140
Long jump, 341, 373, 375
Long, Thelma, 364
Longo-Ciprelli, Jeannie, 334
Longvinenko, Marina, 337
Lonsbrough, Anita, 338
Loock, Christine, 355, 356
Lopez, Nancy, 20, **177–79**, 346, 347, 359
Lopiano, Donna, 271, 274
Loree, Pam, 369
Lorenson, Irene, 350
Loroupe, Tegla, 361, 362
Los Angeles
    1932 Olympics, 41, 44–45
    1984 Olympics, 56–57
Losaberidze, Keto, 333
Losch, Natalia, 341
Lott, Tiffany, 373, 376
Loud, Gwen, 375
Loughran, Beatrix, 62, 357
Loveless, Lea, 370
Low, Carrie, 5
Lu Li, 335
Lucas, Theresa Zabell, 341
Lucero, Wendy, 355, 371
Ludington, Nancy, 70
Ludington, Ron, 70
Ludtke, Melissa, 31
Luge
    in Olympic history, 67, 68, 72, 344
    organization for, 326
Lussi, Gustave, 142

Lutjens, Toni, 375
Lynch, Nnenna, 374
Lynn, Janet, 358
Lysenko, Tatyana, 335

Ma Yanhong, 335
Maass, Peggy, 353, 354
MacDonald, Irene, 354, 355
MacGregor, Kristin, 363
Mackay, Pauline, 359
MacMillan, Shannon, 289, 293
Macoviciuc, Camelia, 336
Macpherson, Wendy, 352
Macy, Kelly, 369
Madison, Helene, 27, 337, 346
Madsen, Beth, 349
Maehata, Hideko, 338
Magnificient Seven (gymnasts), 285–89
Magoni, Paoletta, 342
Maher, Kim, 301, 302, 304–05
Maisch, Alison, 371
Majdi, Iva, 365
Mako, Gene, 180
Maleeva, Magdalena, 219
Mallon, Meg, 240, 358, 359
Mallory, Molla Bjurstedt, 194, 217, 366
Malloy, Dalls, 32
Malone, Maicel, 372, 374
Mandilkova, Hana, 364, 365, 367
Manley, Elizabeth, 71
Mann, Carol, 358
Mann, Horace, 7
Mann, Shelly, 338
Manning, Harry, 112
Manning, Madeline. *See* Mims, Madeline Manning
Manoliu, Lia, 340
Mar, Sabrina, 361
Marathon runners
    Jennings, Lynn, **153–54**
    Samuelson, Joan Benoit, **213–14**
    Waitz, Grete Andersen, **231–33**
Marathon running
    champions in, 361–62
    milestones in, 29, 30
    in Olympic history, 57, 340
    in sports history, 21
Marathon walker
    Sears, Eleonora, 217
Marble, Alice, 129, 162, **179–81,** 346, 365, 366
Marfan's syndrome, 151
Margolin, Stacy, 85
Markova, Olga, 361

Marlowe, Missy, 347, 368, 369
Marsden, Megan, 368, 369
Marsh, A., 357
Marshall, Ethel, 350
Marshall, Jane, 353
Marshall, Tammy, 369
Martell, Belle, 27
Marten, Maritza, 341
Martial arts, 326
Martial, Nicola, 373, 375
Martin, Christy, **181–82**
Martin, LaVonna, 373, 374
Martin, Steffi, 344
Martinez, Almudena Muñoz, 336
Martinez, Conchita, 366
Martinez, Lisa, 269
Martino, Angel, 362
Martorella, Millie, 352
Marx, L., 357
Mary Lou Retton Award, 206
Marzell, Miesha, 374
Massey, Phyllis, 352
Mastenbroek, Rie, 337
Masterkova, Svetlana, 340
Mataya, Ewa, 351
Mathews, Margaret, 211, 277, 279
Mathieu, Simone, 364
Matikainen, Marjo, 342
Matthes, Ruthie, 353
Matthews, Merle, 352
Mauer, Renata, 337
Mauermayer, Gisela, 340
Maureen Connolly Brinker Foundation, 103, 328
Maurer, Lea, 362
Maxwell-Pierson, Stephanie, 263
Mayer, Helene, 45, **183,** 334, 356
Mayfield, Mindee, 354
McAlister, Barbara, 355, 356
McAnany, Michele, 266, 269
McAteer, Myrtle, 366
McBean, Marnie, 336
McCann, Rachelle, 269
McCartney, Kathleen, 367
McClain, Katrina, 295, 297, 299
McClellan, C., 357
McClemens, Dale, 360
McClements, Lynette, 338
McColgan, Liz, 361
McCormick, Kelly, 185, 354, 355
McCormick, Patricia (bullfighter), 28
McCormick, Patricia (diver), **184–85,** 346
    championships won by, 354, 355, 356
    in Olympic history, 49, 334

McCoy, Cathy. *See* Rigby, Cathy
McCoy, Penny, 348
McCray, Nikki, 295, 299–300
McCunniff, Megan, 368
McCutcheon, Floretta Doty, 13, **186–88**
McDaniel, Heather, 33
McDaniel, Mildred, 49, 341
McDonald, Shirley, 347
McElmury, Audrey, 29, 353, 354
McFarlane, Tracey, 363, 370
McGhee, Carla, 295, 300
McGill, Jill, 360
McGovern, Valerie, 372, 374
McGrath, Ellen, 356
McGuire, Edith. *See* Duvall, Edith McGuire
McIntire, Barbara, 360
McIntosh, Veronica, 372
McKane, Kathleen, 365
McKane, Kitty, 339
McKean, Marian, 347, 349
McKee, Helm, 360
McKenzie, Jacqui, 363
McKinney, Tamara, 347, 348
McMahon, Marie, 372
McMiken, Christine, 372
McMillan, Kathy, 277, 279
McNair, Winifred, 339
McNamara, Julianne, 361
McNamara, Melissa, 368
McNerney, Mimosa, 370
McTiernan, Kerri, 24
Mead, Andrea. *See* Lawrence, Andrea Mead
Meadowbrook Club, 5, 25
Meagher, Mary T., 57, 338, 347, 363, 371
Meany, Helen, 334, 355
Media coverage, 19–20, 22, 47, 50, 66
Medical conditions
    bone cancer, 132–33
    chronic fatigue syndrome, 78, 79
    compartment syndrome, 220
    deafness, 114
    Graves' disease, 106
    Marfan's syndrome, 151
    pneumonia, 210
    polio, 79, 210
    scarlet fever, 210
    spina bifida, 108
    tuberculosis, 180
Meili, Launi, 337
Meinhart, Carole, 350
Melander, Ann, 348

Melbourne Olympics (1956), 49
Melinte, Doina, 340
Melnik, Faina, 340
Melpomene, 36
Mercatanti, Pat, 352
Merrill, Gretchen, 357
Merritt, Kim, 361
Merten, Lauri, 358
Metheny, Linda, 210, 360, 361
Metschuck, Caren, 338
Metzger, Debra, 350
Metzler, Whitney, 363
Mexico City Olympics (1968), 52–53
Meyer, Debbie, 53, 337, 346
Meyer, Elana, 154
Meyers, Ann, 21, 31, 54, **188–89,** 347
Meyers, Linda, 347, 348, 349
Meyers, Mary, 68
Meyfarth, Ulrike, 341
Meynell, Alicia, 25
Michigan Sports Hall of Fame, 173
Middle class, and industrialization, 4
Mighty Mary, 24
Milbrett, Tiffeny, 289, 291, 293
Milestones, 1803-1997, 25–33
Miller, Alice, 359
Miller, Cheryl, **190–91,** 226, 347
Miller, Dana, 352
Miller, M., 357
Miller, Madi S., 349
Miller, Shannon, **192–94,** 361
    in Olympic history, 59–60, 335
    on U.S. gymnastics team, 285, 286, 287, 288
Miller Lite/Women's Sports Foundation survey, xii
Miller-Mackie, Dana, 352
Millett, Tracie, 373, 375
Milliat, Alice, 40
Mills, Ardelle, 350
Mills, Mary, 358, 359
Mills, Phoebe, 361
Milosovici, Lavinia, 335, 336
Mims, Madeline Manning, 30, 47, 53, 279, 340
Mins, Donna Mae, 28
Minthorn, Pamela, 363
Minuzzo, Guiliana, 66
Misersky, Antje, 342
Mishkutienak, Natalya, 343
Mitchell, Betsy, 362, 370, 371
Mitchell, Danyel, 373, 375

Mitchell, M., 356
Mitchell, Michele, 356
Mitchell, Verne "Jackie," 27
Mitchem, Shannan, 266, 270
Mittermaier, Rosi, 202, 342
Mitzel, Lisa, 369
Moceanu, Dominique, 285, 286, 288, 316, 361
Mochrie, Dottie, 359
Mock, Jerrie, 28
Moe, Karen, 338
Moffitt, Billie Jean. *See* King, Billie Jean
Molesworth, Margaret, 364
Moller, Lorraine, 361
Molloy, Aisling, 372
Monplaisir, S., 357
Monterosso, Irene, 352
Montreal Olympics (1976), 54
Moody, Helen Wills, **194–95,** 198, 235, 346
    championships won by, 364, 365, 366
    in Olympic history, 43, 339
    in sports history, 10, 11
Moore, Elisabeth, 366
Moore, Lavinia, 13
Moore, Mary, 373
Moravcova, Martina, 362, 363, 370, 371
Mordre, Yumi, 369
Moreau, Janet, 48
Morgan, Helen C., 355
Morris, Betty, 352
Morris, Helen, 363
Morris, Tracy Dahl, 372
Morris County Golf Club, 5
Morrissey, William T., Sr., 171
Morse, Marty, 108
Mortimer, Angela, 364, 365, 366
Morton, Lucy, 338
Moscow Olympics (1980), 55
Mosdell, Anna, 375
Moser-Pröll, Annemarie, 69, 342
Moses, Melisa, 355
Mosqueda, Sylvia, 374
Mota, Rosa, 340, 361
Motorboat racing, 30
Motorcycling, 326
Motormaids, Inc., 326
Moulton, Alycia, 371
Mountain bike racer
    Furtado, Juli, **126–27**
Mountain climber. *See also* Rock climber
    Hargreaves, Alison, 24, **143–44**

Mountaineering, 6, 24, 31
  bibliography on, 317–18
  organizations for, 323
El Moutawakel, Nawal, 340, 375
Mroczkowska Dow, Helena. *See*
  Dow, Helena Mroczkowska
Mudd, Mrs. Desales, 350
Mueller, Leah, 70
Mueller, Peter, 91
Mukhina, Elena, 101
Muldowney, Jack, 196
Muldowney, Shirley, 30, **195–97**
Mullen, Michelle, 352
Müller, Anna-Maria, 344
Munich Olympics (1972), 53–54
Munz, Diana, 362
Murdock, Margaret, 53
Murray, Patricia, 374
Mustonen, Kaija, 344
Myers, Angel, 371
Myers, Paula Jean, 354, 355, 356
Myler, Cammy, 72
Myrick, Nancy, 350
Myths
  on loss of femininity, 93
  on physical limitations, 22, 77,
    207

Nadig, Marie-Theres, 342
Nagano Olympics (1998), 73
Nagasaki, Hiroko, 370
Nagel, Judy, 348, 349
Nairn, Susie Leech, 263
Naismith Coach of the Year, 227
Naismith, James, 86, 87
Naismith Memorial Basketball
  Hall of Fame, 87, 177, 188,
    189, 191
Naismith National Player of the
  Year, 297
Naismith Trophy, 191
Nakiyingi, Edith, 372
Nall, Anita, 363
National Amateur Athletic
  Federation, 11–12, 16, 17
National Amateur Bicycling
  Association, 27
National Archery Association, 6,
  322
National Association for Girls
  and Women in Sports, 188,
    191, 326
National Association for Stock
  Car Auto Racing, 140
National Association of Intercol-
  legiate Athletics, 31, 267, 326
National Association of Profes-
  sional Baseball Leagues, 24

National Basketball Association,
  188, 189
National Coach of the Year, 224,
  278
National Collegiate Athletic
  Association, 19, 24, 31, 32,
    326
  awards by, 304, 305
  champions of, 368–76
National Cowgirl Hall of Fame,
  153
National Female College
  Basketball Player of the
  Year, 299, 300
National Field Archery Associa-
  tion, 322
National Foundation of Wheel-
  chair Tennis, 324
National Geographic Society, 113
National Girls and Women in
  Sports Day, 31
National Goalkeeper of the Year,
  293
National Handicapped Sports,
  324
National Handicapped Sports and
  Recreation Association, 133
National High School Athletic
  Coaches Association, 278
National Hockey League, 24, 207
National Hot Rod Association,
  196–97
National Junior College Athletic
  Association, 131
National Off-Road Bicycle
  Association, 127
National Player of the Year, 299
National Rifle Association, 28
National Ski Hall of Fame, 175
National Softball Hall of Fame,
  156, 272–75
National Track and Field Hall of
  Fame, 158, 212, 229, 248
National Wheelchair Athletic
  Association, 109, 324
National Women Bowling
  Writers' Association, 173
National Women in Sports Day,
  24–25
National Women's Baseball
  Association, 322
National Women's Basketball
  Committee, 8
National Women's Martial Arts
  Federation, 326
National Women's Sailing
  Association, 327

Nause, Martha, 359
Navratilova, Martina, 77, **198–200**
  Austin, Tracy and, 86
  awards won by, 346, 347
  championships won by, 364,
    365, 366, 367
  Evert, Chris and, 120
  Graf, Steffi and, 136, 137
  King, Billie Jean and, 163
  Lieberman-Cline, Nancy and,
    176
  Moody, Helen Wills and, 194
  in sports history, 22
Nazi Olympics, 45
Neal, Kim, 369
Neall, Gail, 338
Neidlinger, Sally, 349
Neilson, Sandra, 337
Nelson, Annie, 263–64
Nelson, Cindy, **201–02**, 348
Nelson, Courtney, 371
Nelson, Frankie, 25
Nelson, Heather, 352
Németh, Angéla, 341
Neumann, Liselotte, 358
Neuner, Doris, 344
Newall, Sybil, 333
Newby-Fraser, Paula, 24, **203–04,**
  367
Newell, Betty Hicks, 346
Newman, Julie, 351
Neyer, Megan, 355, 371
Nganga, Ruth, 372
Nicholas, Alison, 358
Nichols, Lorrie, 352
Niekro, Phil, 265, 266
Niemann (-Stirnemann), Gunda,
  344
Nightingale, Pearl Perkins, 360
Nikolayeva, Margaita, 335
Nineteenth Amendment, 10
Ninety-Nines organization, 112
Ninikolayeve, Yelena, 340
Nisiro, Annalisa, 363
Nobis, Shannon, 349
Noonan, Fred, 112
Nord, Kathleen, 338
Nordheim, Pam, 351
Norelius, Martha, 337
Norman, Carol, 352
Norry, Linda, 353
Norwood, Lori, 32
Notaro, Phyllis, 352
Nothnagel, Anke, 334
Novara, Sue, 353
Novikova, Yelena, 335
Nowak, Cecile, 336

Nunn, Glynis, 159, 341
Nunno, Steve, 192, 285, 286, 288
Nuthall, Betty, 366
Nyad, Diana, 30, 321

Oak, Cindy, 348
Oberstar, Lia, 363, 371
O'Brien, Leah, 301, 305
Ochowicz, Sheila Young. *See* Young, Sheila
Ochs, Debra, 350
O'Connell, Joel, 354
Odom, Sandra Jo, 352
O'Donnell Russell, A., 357
Officials, sports, 27, 30–31, 32, 33
Olavarri, Cindy, 353, 354
Oleniuc, Elisabeta, 336
Olga Korbut Foundation, 168
Olizarenko, Nadezhda, 340
Olsen, Zoe Ann, 354, 355
Olsson, Anna, 334
Olympic ceremonies
    flag carriers in, 29, 52, 185
    flame carriers in, 118, 175
    flame lighter in, 52
    oath reciters in, 66, 115
Olympic Development Committee, 17
Olympic Summer Games
    1896-1912 organization period, 36–39
    1920-1936 struggle for inclusion, 39–46
    1948-1964 postwar Games, 46–51
    1968-2000 revolution, 51–61
    gold medalists in, 333–42
Olympic Winter Games
    gold medalists in, 342–44
    history of, 61–73
Olympics
    bibliography on, 318–19
    gold medalists in, 333–44
    history of, 35–73, 333–45
    in sports history, x, 9, 14, 17, 19–22, 24
    team sports and, 252–53, 280–306
    Women's, 14, 40–41
Ondieki, Lisa, 361
O'Neil, Susan, 363
O'Neill, Chris, 364
O'Neill, Dorothy, 350
O'Neill, M. J., 357
O'Neill, Mary Jane, 368
O'Neill, Susan, 338
Onyali, Mary, 373
Opara, Christy, 375

Oppelt, Kurt, 343
Orcutt, T., 357
Organizations, 322–29, 379–80. *See also names of specific organizations*
Ortiz-Del Valle, Sandra, 32
Osborne, Margaret, 364, 365, 366
Osipowich, Albina, 337
Osius, Alison, 150
Oslo Olympics (1952), 66
Ostergren, Mary, 351
Osterloh, Lilia, 372
Ostermeyer, Micheline, 340, 341
Osüer, Ellen, 334
O'Sullivan, Sonia, 368, 372, 374
Otsetova, Svetla, 336
Ott-Crepin, Margi, 59
Ottenbrite, Anne, 338
Ottey, Merlene, 60, 107, 372, 373
Otto, Kristin, 58, 337, 338
Ou, Julie, 363
Ounpuu, Cindy, 370
Outerbridge, Mary Ewing, 5
Outstanding Female Athlete of the World, 96
Overbeck, Carla, 289, 293–94
Owen, Laurence, 357
Owens, Jesse, 158, 160, 161, 221
Ozolina, Elvira, 341

Pace, Kate, 348
Pacillo, Joanne, 360
Packer, Ann, 340
Pagel, Ramona, 375
Pakhomova, Lyudmila, 343
Palfrey, Sarah, 235
Palinkas, Pat, 29
Pall, Olga, 342
Palm, Merritt, 264
Palmer, Gladys, 16–17
Palmer, Sandra, 358, 359
Panfil, Wanda, 361
Paralympics, 109
Paraskevin (-Young), Connie, 353, 354
Paris
    1900 Olympics, 37
    1922 Women's Olympic Games, 40, 41
    1924 Olympics, 42–43
Parisien, Julie, 349
Park, Jamie, 374
Parker, Denise, 350
Parks, Janelle, 353
Parlow, Cindy, 289, 294
Parma, George, 199
Parris, Debbie, 375
Parrott, Tina, 372

Partenkirchen Olympics (1936), 64
Pascoe, Heidi, 33
Patoulidou, Paraskevi, 340
Patterson, Susie, 348
Patty Berg Award, 90
Pauca, Simona, 335
Paul, Robert, 67, 142, 343
Paulsen, Mari, 353
Payne, Marita, 373, 374
Pearl Archery Club, 25
Pease, Heather, 280, 282, 284
Pechstein, Claudia, 344
Pecjak, Sharon, 347
Peck, Anne Smith, 6
Pelletier, Monique, 348, 349
Pemrose, Beryl, 364
Pendergraft-Council, Rosalind, 373, 374
Penes, Mihaela, 341
Penick, Harvey, 234
Penn, Sharon, 354
Pennington, Joan, 371
Pentathlon, 32
Peppler, Mary Jo, 20
Perec, Marie-Jose, 339
Perkins, Pearl, 360
Perreault, Annie, 344
Perry, Nanceen, 372
Pesho, Terri, 350
Peter, Birgit, 336
Peters, Mary, 341
Peters, Roumania, 128
Peterson, Ann, 356
Petricevic, Anna, 363
Petruseva, Natalia, 344
Pettibone, Debbie, 264
Pettibone, Katie, 264
Petzold, Barbara, 343
Pezzo, Paola, 334
Pfeiffer, Nancy, 350
Pflug, Monika, 344
PGA/World Golf Hall of Fame, 179, 248
Phebus, Keri, 372
Phelps, Jaycie, 285, 286, 287, 288
Philadelphia Cricket Club, 5
Phillips, Kristie, 361
Phillips, Mrs. A. M., 349
Phinney, Connie Carpenter. *See* Carpenter-Phinney, Connie
Physical education
    bibliography on, 319
    in Olympic history, 41, 44, 47
    in sports history, 7–8, 11–12, 16–17
    team sports and, 252

Physical limitations, myth on, 22, 77, 207
Pierce, Mary, 364
Pierce, Norma, 350
Pierce, Roxanne, 361
Pieseynski, Janette, 353
Pieterse, Zola. *See* Budd, Zola
Pilskog, Trine, 372
Pinayeva, Lyudmila, 333, 334
Pinkston, Elizabeth Becker, 334
Pippig, Uta, 361
Pires, Sandra, 333
Planck-Szabê, Herma, 62, 343
Platov, Yevgeny, 343
Play days, 12
Player of the Decade, 305
Player of the Year, 191
   AAGPBL, 256, 257
   Basketball Weekly, 237
   California Soccer, 294
   LPGA, 179, 234
   Naismith National, 297
   NCAA, 304
   Sports Illustrated, 300
   Street and Smith's, 237
   Temple University, 304
   U.S. Basketball Writers' Association, 299
   USA Today, 300
   Women's Tennis Association, 86, 138, 200, 219
Player of the Year, Freshman, 237, 292
Player Service Award, 120
Plessy v. Ferguson case, 9
Plumer, PattiSue, 372, 374
Pneumonia, 210
Podkopayeva, Lilia, 335
Poetzsch, Anett, 70
Polio, 79, 210
Poll, Claudia, 337, 362
Poll, Sylvia, 362
Pollack, Andrea, 338
Polo, 216, 217
Ponath, Jennifer, 375
Ponomarenko, Sergie, 343
Ponomaryeva, Nina, 340
Popescu, Marioara, 336
Popova, Larissa, 336
Porter, Dorothy, 360
Porter, Marci, 264
Porter, Shanelle, 372
Porters, Lula, 14
Portwich, Ramona, 334
Post, Sandra, 358, 359
Postma, Sandra, 352
Potter (McIngvale), Cynthia, 354, 355, 356

Pötzsch, Anett, 343
Poulsen, Sandra, 348
Powell Award, 179
Powell, Cindy, 352
Powell, Kristy, 361
Powell, Sharon, 374
Poynton (Hill), Dorothy, 334, 355
Prague Women's World Games (1930), 41
Preis, Ellen, 334
Prentice, Jo Ann, 359
Press, Irina, 51, 340, 341
Press, Tamara, 340, 341
Prevost, Helen, 37
Pringle, Jim, 88
Privalova, Irna, 60
Professional Female Athlete of the Decade, 204
Professional Golf Association, 31
Professional Golf Association Hall of Fame, 89
Professional International Track Association, 20, 229
Professional Rodeo Cowboys Association, 325
Professional Rodeo Hall of Fame, 153
Professional Ski Instructors of America, 134
Professional Sportswoman of the Year, 96, 110, 138, 204, 239
Professional Women's Bowling Association, 16, 173
Prohibition (Eighteenth Amendment), 10
Protopopov, Oleg, 343
Prozumenshikova, Galina, 338
Pueblo (CO) Sports Association Hall of Fame, 187
Puggaard, Berit, 363, 371
Puica, Maricica, 57, 340
Pung, Jacqueline, 360
Puntous, Sylviane, 367
Pura, Stela, 363
Purdy, Melissa, 264
Pursley, Barbara, 357
Pyfer, Leslie, 361
Pyle, J., 356

Qian Hong, 338
Qiao Hong, 339
Quance, Kristine, 363, 370, 371
Quast, Anne, 360
"Queen Mother of Tennis," 235
"Queen of Swimming," 105
Quigley, Jane, 354
Quinn, Terry, 350

Racial discrimination. *See* Color barrier
Racilla, Valeria, 336
Racing. *See* Auto racing; Horse racing
Racquetball, 326
Racquetball player
   Gould, Michelle, **135–36**
Radcliffe, Mary, 236
Radke, Lina, 43, 340
Rafaloski, Gary, 204
Ragno-Lonzi, Antonella, 335
Rahn, Sharon, 361
Rainey, Meredith, 372, 374
Ramsey, Sherry, 361
Ranck, Roberta, 26, 360
Rand, Mary, 341
Randriantefy, Dally, 219
Rankin, Judy, 30, 359
Rantanen, Heli, 341
Rapp, Susie, 370, 371
Ravenscroft, Gladys, 359
Rawls, Betsy, 358
Rawls, Katherine, 346, 355
Raybestos Brakettes, 21, 252, 271–75
Raybestos Girl All-Stars, 271
Raymond, Lisa, 372
Recreation, history of, 3–4
Redington, Joe, 95
Reece, Gabrielle, 321
Referees. *See* Officials, sports
Reggi, Raffaella, 58
Reichert, Ossi, 342
Reid, Elizabeth, 369
Reid, John, 5
Reid, Kerry Melville, 364
Reid, Mrs., 5
Reid, Summer, 369
Reid, Suziann, 374
Reinalda, Barbara, 271
Reinhart, Nicole, 354
Reinholdt, Majorie, 356
Reinisch, Rica, 337, 338
Reitano, Mary, 364
Renk, Silke, 341
Reoch, Mary Jane, 353, 354
Restoux, Marie-Claire, 336
Restrepo, Ximena, 374
Retton, Mary Lou, **204–06,** 214, 285, 361
   awards won by, 346, 347
   in Olympic history, 57, 335
   in sports history, 22
Reynolds, Nancy, 347, 348, 349
Rezková, Miloslava, 341
Reztsova, Anfisa, 342
Rheaume, Manon, 24, 32, **207–08**

Rhine, Jen, 368, 372, 374
Rhodenbaugh, Kim, 370, 371
Ribeiro, Fernanda, 340
Ribot-Canales, Veronica, 355
Ricardo, Helene, 363
Rice, Joan Moore, 361
Rice, Lena, 365
Richard, Deb, 360
Richards, Renee, 199
Richardson, Carmen, 353
Richardson, Dot, 61, 272, 301,
    302, 305, 319
Richetelli, Eileen, 355, 371
Richey, Nancy, 119, 364, 365
Richter, Annegret, 339
Richter, Ulrike, 337, 338
Riddles, Libby, 31, 95, 313
Riding. *See* Equestrian events
Rigby, Cathy, **208–10**
Riggin, Aileen, 42, 43, 334, 355
Riggs, Bobby, 20, 163
Riley, Dana, 374
Riley, Dawn, 258, 264–65
Riley, Samantha, 363
Risen, Deborah, 370
Ritchie, Meg, 373, 375
Ritter, Louise, 341
Rivett-Carnac, Charles, 38
Rivett-Carnac, Frances Cytie, 38
Rizzotti, Jennifer, 347
Road Runners Club of America,
    328–29
Roba, Fatuma, 340, 361
Robb, Muriel, 365
Robbins, Kelly, 359
Roberts, Amelia C., 14
Roberts, Lindsey, 348
Roberts, Tiffany, 289, 294
Robinson, Elizabeth, 43, 46, 339
Robinson, Jane, 353
Robinson, Renita, 375
Robison, Corrine, 14
Rock climber. *See also* Mountain
    climber
    Hill, Lynn, 24, **148–50**
Rodeos, 28, 152–53, 317, 325
Rodgers, Shari, 353
Rodman, Charmayne. *See* James,
    Charmayne
Rodnina, Irina, 70, 343
Rodolph, Katy, 347, 348, 349
Roe, Allison, 361
Roehat-Moser, Franziska, 362
Roethlisberger, Marie, 369
Roffe (-Steinrotter), Diann, 342,
    348, 349
Rogers, Annette, 46

Rojohn, Michelle, 371
Roldan, P., 356
Role models, xii, 10, 35, 161
    baseball players as, 267
    basketball coach as, 227
    basketball players as, 297
    bowler as, 187
    figure skater as, 243
    golfer as, 235
    hockey player as, 208
    mother as, 198
    sailors as, 259
    tennis players as, 237
    triathlete as, 204
Rolinska, Eulalia, 52
Roller skating, 327
Rom, Dagmar, 174
Romack, Barbara, 360
Romanova, Yelena, 340
Romary, Janice Lee York, 29, 52
Romaschkova, Nina, 340
Rome Olympics (1960), 50
Romeo, Robin, 352
Roosevelt, Ellen C., 366
Roques, Shirley. *See* Muldowney,
    Shirley
Rose, Dionne, 373
Rosendahl, Heidemarie, 341
Rosenfield, Fanny, 43
Rosenthal, Jody, 359
Ross, Ann, 355
Ross, Lillian, 14
Rossner, Petra, 334
Rothenburger, Christa, 344
Rothhammer, Keena, 337
Roug, Kristine, 341
Round, Dorothy, 364, 365
Rowe, Ruth, 350
Rowing
    bibliography on, 312
    in Olympic history, 51, 54, 60,
        336
    organization for, 327
    in sports history, 27
Roze, Willie, 274
Rubin, Barbara Jo, 29
Ruby, Karine, 344
Ruddick, Sandra, 360
Rudkovskaya, Yelena, 338
Rudolph, Amy, 372, 374
Rudolph, Wilma, **210–12**
    awards won by, 346
    in Olympic history, 47, 50, 339
    in sports history, 18, 19
    on TSU Tigerbelles, 277, 279
Rüegg, Yvonne, 342
Ruehl, Becky, 356, 371

Rueñes, Maria Colon, 341
Ruiz, Tracie, 339
Running. *See also* Track and field
    champions in, 361–62, 372–75
    milestones in, 29, 30
    in Olympic history, 339–40
    in sports history, 21
Rupert, Frances, 26
Rush, Debbie, 356
Russell, Ernestine, 360
Russell, Gillian, 373, 374
Ruuska, Sylvia, 49
Ruzici, Virginia, 365
Ryabchinskaya, Yulia, 333
Ryan, Elizabeth, 194
Ryan, Susie, 371
Ryon, Luann, 333, 350

Sabatini, Gabriela, 58–59, 137,
    367
Sabo, Patty, 371
Saddic, Kim, 374
Safarik-Tong, Linda, 351
Safety bicycle, 6
Sailing. *See also* Yachting
    bibliography on, 265
    milestones in, 29, 30
    in Olympic history, 37
    organizations for, 327
    outstanding team in, 258–65
    in sports history, 24
    terminology in, 260
Sailors
    Armitage-Johnson, Stephanie,
        260
    Baltzell, Amy, 260
    Beattie, Shelley, 261
    Becker-Day, Courtenay, 261
    Bergeron, Sarah, 261
    Carey, Merritt, 261
    Cavanagh, Sarah, 261
    Charles, Lisa, 261
    Egnot, Leslie, 262
    Evans, Christy, 262
    Fuller, Amy, 262
    Hemond-Dent, Susan, 262
    Huntington, Anna Seaton,
        258, 259, 262
    Isler, J. J., 259, 262–63
    Klybert, Diana, 263
    Lindquist, Linda, 259, 263
    Maxwell-Pierson, Stephanie,
        263
    Nairn, Susie Leech, 263
    Nelson, Annie, 263–64
    Palm, Merritt, 264
    Pettibone, Debbie, 264
    Pettibone, Katie, 264

Porter, Marci, 264
Purdy, Melissa, 264
Riley, Dawn, 258, 264–65
Smith, Suzette Hau'oli, 265
Swett, Hannah, 265
Touchette, Joan Lee, 265
Saimo, Sylvi, 333
Saitoh, Shinobu, 352
Salmeen, Annette, 371
Salmi, Esther, 353
Salness, Kit, 356
Saloukvadze, Nino, 337
Saloumae, Erika, 334
Salt Lake City Olympics (2002),
      73
Salter, Christy. *See* Martin, Christy
Samaranch, Juan Antonio, 59
Samaritan Award, 179
Samolenko, Tatiana, 340
Samuelson, Joan Benoit, **213–14,**
      232
   championships won by, 361
   in Olympic history, 57, 340
   in sports history, 22
San Diego Hall of Champions, 99
Sánchez, Cristina, **214–15**
Sanchez, Emilio, 200
Sanders, Summer, 338, 363, 371
Sanderson, Tessa, 341
Sankatsing, Mireilli, 372
Santini, Cheril, 371
Sapporo
   1940 Olympics, 65
   1972 Olympics, 68–69
Sarah Palfrey Danzig Award, 164
Sarajevo Olympics (1984), 70
Sarazen, Gene, 14, 247
Satoya, Tae, 343
Satriano, Gina, 266, 270
Saubert, Jean, 347, 348, 349
Saunders, Daphnie, 373, 375
Saunders, Nell, 25
Saunders, Tricia, 32
Sauvage, Louise, 361
Savery, Jill, 280, 281, 282, 284
Scamper, 152–53
Scarlet fever, 210
Schacherer-Elek, Ilona, 45, 183,
      334
Schaffrath, Pam, 270
Schaller, Johanna, 340
Schapiro, Susan, 361
Scheiblich, Christine, 336
Schifano, Helen, 360
Schlaak, Evelin, 340
Schlegel, Tonia, 31
Schlunegger, Hedy, 65, 342
Schmid, Heidi, 334

Schmidinger, Krista, 349
Schmidt, Birgit, 334
Schmidt, Jan, 352
Schneider, Petra, 338
Schneider, Vreni, 342
Schneyder, Nathalie, 280, 281,
      282, 284
Schnurpfeil, Kim, 374
Scholarships, 17, 30
Schomburgk, Heinrich, 339
Schone, Andrea Mitscherlich, 344
Schoonmaker, F., 356
Schrader, Hildegard, 338
Schreyer, Cindy, 368
Schroder, Michele, 363
Schroeder, Dorothy, 257
Schroeter, Martina, 336
Schroth, Clara M., 360
Schuba, Beatrix, 343
Schubert, Mark, 118
Schuler, Carolyn, 338
Schumacher, Diane, 274–75
Schumann, Margit, 344
Schut, Johanna, 344
Schwald, Sarah, 372
Schwarczenberger, Ildikê, 335
Schwartz, Elisabeth, 343
Schweitzer, Annie, 374
Scott, Barbara Ann, 65, 343
Scott, Blanche, 26
Scranton, Nancy, 359
Scriven, Margaret, 364
Scurry, Briana, 289, 294
Sears, Eleonora, 27, **216–18**
Sears, Evelyn, 366
Sebasteanski, Kris, 351
Seignious, Hope, 27
Seizinger, Katja, 73, 342
Sekaric, Jasna, 336
Seles, Monica, 86, 138, **218–19**
   awards won by, 346
   championships won by, 364,
      365, 367
Selig, Joy, 369
Selinger, Arie, 151
Selman, Ashley, 375
Selmon, Ashley, 375
Semanska, Agnes, 198
Semple, Carol, 360
Senff, Nida, 337
Seo-Nyung Kim, 333
Seoul Olympics (1988), 58–59
Separate but equal doctrine, 9
Serebryanskaya, Ekaterina, 336
Seredina, Antonina, 333, 334
Serena, Shiroki, 293
Sergent, Melina, 372
Service Bowl award, 237

Sex testing, 52
Sey, Jennifer, 361
Seyfert, Gabriele, 124, 125
Shain, Eva, 30
Shakespeare, Shannon, 362, 363
Shaposhnikova, Natalya, 335
Shaw, Marilyn, 348, 349
Shaw, Winnie, 120
Shea, Julie, 347
Sheehan, Patty, 347, 358, 359
Sheen, Gillian, 334
Sheffield, Latanya, 375
Sheinberg, Carrie, 349
Shellworth, Sandra, 348
Sherk, Cathy, 360
Sherman, Kim, 374
Sherman, Yvonne, 357
Shevtsova, Lyudmila, 340
Shi, Cindy, 351
Shiley, Jean, 44, 45, 341
Shinnecock Hills Golf Club, 5
Shirk, Lisa, 369
Shitou, Rie, 363
Shoemaker, Willie, 32, 170
Shooting events
   milestone in, 28
   in Olympic history, 52–53, 56,
      58, 60, 61, 336–37
   organization for, 327
Shot put, 341, 373, 375
Shouaa, Ghada, 341
Shriver, Pam, 200, 320, 339
Shuttleworth, Pamela, 31
Siegl, Siegrun, 341
Sierens, Gayle, 31
Sigourney, Lydia Huntley, 7
Silivas, Daniela, 335
Sill, Aleta, 352
Silva, Diana, 352
Silva, Jackie, 333
Silver Bullets. *See* Colorado Silver
      Bullets
Simburg, Wyomia. *See* Tyus,
      Wyomia
Simcic, Anna, 362
Simeoni, Sara, 341
Simiriotou, Esmee, 339
Simmons-Carrasco, Heather, 280,
      281, 282, 284
Simpkins, Agina, 369
Simpson, Bill, 271
Simpson, Joey, 353
Sinn, Pearl, 360
Sites, Sharon, 29
Skala, Carole Jo, 359
Skating. *See* Figure skating; Roller
      skating; Speed skating
Skieresz, Amy, 368, 372, 374

Skiers
  Golden, Diana, **132–34**, 347
  Lawrence, Andrea Mead, 66,
    173–75, 342, 347, 348,
    349
  Nelson, Cindy, **201–02**, 348
Skiing. *See also* Alpine skiing;
    Cross-country skiing;
    Waterskiing
  bibliography on, 175, 202, 319
  organization for, 327
Skillman, Jane, 362
Skinner, Ntala, 351
Skoblikova, Lydia, 67, 344
Skydiving, 327
Slaney, Mary Decker, 56–57, **220–
    21**, 223, 346, 347
Slatter, Kate, 336
Slattery, Ann, 352
Slaughter, Susan, 368
Sled Dog Racer of the Decade, 96
Sled dog racers. *See also* Dog
    sledding
  Butcher, Susan, 77, **94–96**
  Riddles, Libby, 31, 95, 313
Sleeuwenhoek, Brenda, 372
Sloan, Shae, 270
Slowe, Lucy Diggs, 9, 26
Slupianek, Ilona, 341
Small, Kim, 362
Smetanina, Raisa, 72, 342
Smith, Caroline, 334
Smith, Dorothy, 350
Smith, Ethel, 43
Smith, Francie Larrieu, **222–23**
Smith, Jill, 375
Smith, Jimmy, 186
Smith, Joan, 351
Smith, Julie, 301, 305
Smith, Karin, 375
Smith, Katie, 296
Smith, Margaret. *See* Court,
    Margaret Smith
Smith, Marina, 371
Smith, Melanie, 347
Smith, Michele, 301, 302, 305–06
Smith, Michelle, 337, 338
Smith, Mrs. L. C., 350
Smith, Robyn, 30
Smith, Suzette Hau'oli, 265
Smith, Tobie, 370
Smith, Trecia, 373, 375
Smyers, Karen, 367
Smythe, Patricia, 49
Snook, Neta, 111
Snowboarding, 73, 327, 344

Soccer
  bibliography on, 319
  milestones in, 31, 32
  in Olympic history, 52, 61, 337
  organization for, 327
  outstanding team in, 289–94
Soccer Player of the Year,
    California, 294
Soccer players
  Akers, Michelle, **77–79**, 289,
    290, 291
  Chastain, Brandi, 289, 291–92
  Fawcett, Joy, 289, 291, 292
  Foudy, Julie, 289, 290, 292
  Gabarra, Carin, 289, 290, 292
  Hamm, Mia, 79, 289, 290, 291,
    292–93, 347
  Harvey, Mary, 289, 293
  Lilly, Kristine, 289, 293
  MacMillan, Shannon, 289, 293
  Milbrett, Tiffeny, 289, 291,
    293
  Overbeck, Carla, 289, 293–94
  Parlow, Cindy, 289, 294
  Roberts, Tiffany, 289, 294
  Scurry, Briana, 289, 294
  Venturini, Tisha, 289, 291, 294
  Wilson, Staci, 289, 294
Soderberg, Anna, 375
Sodoma, Deanna, 109
Softball
  bibliography on, 156, 306, 319
  in Olympic history, 52, 61, 337
  organization for, 327
  outstanding teams in, 252,
    253, 271–75, 301–06
  in sports history, 14, 20, 21
Softball players
  Adams, Rosie, 272
  Albrecht, Louise, 272
  Arendsen, Kathy, 271, 272
  Backus, Sharron, 272–73
  Berg, Laura, 301, 303
  Boxx, Gillian, 301, 303
  Cornell, Sheila, 272, 301, 302,
    303
  Fernandez, Lisa, 61, **122–23**,
    272, 301, 302, 303–04,
    347
  Granger, Michele, 61, 123,
    272, 301, 302, 304
  Harrigan, Lori, 301, 302, 304
  Harris, Dionna, 301, 304
  Harrison, Pat, 273
  Joyce, Joan, 20, **155–56**, 271,
    273–74
  Kellers, Peggy, 274

King, Kathryn (Sis), 274
Lopiano, Donna, 271, 274
Maher, Kim, 301, 302, 304–05
O'Brien, Leah, 301, 305
Richardson, Dot, 61, 272, 301,
    302, 305, 319
Roze, Willie, 274
Schumacher, Diane, 274–75
Smith, Julie, 301, 305
Smith, Michele, 301, 302, 305–
    06
Stokes, Shelley, 301, 306
Stratton, Mickey, 271, 275
Tickey, Bertha, 123, 155, 271,
    275, 304
Topley, Shirley, 275
Tyler, Dani, 301, 306
Vecchione, Gina, 275
Williams, Christa, 301, 302,
    306
Softball Sportswoman of the
    Year, 306
Sonnerup, Anna, 351
Sontgerath, Gail, 360
Sorenstam, Annika, 358, 368
Sorenstam, Charlotta, 368
Sorgi, Erica, 355
Soto, Miriam Blasco, 336
Soutar, Judy, 352
Sowell, Dawn, 372, 373
Spain, Lisa, 372
Spaulding Brown, Mrs., 349
Special Olympics International,
    245, 324
Spectators
  Ladies' Day for, 25
  women as, 4
Speed skaters
  Blair, Bonnie, 22, 71, 72, **90–
    92**, 344, 346, 347
  Young, Sheila, 21, 69, **243–45**,
    344, 347
Speed skating
  bibliography on, 92, 245
  in Olympic history, 64, 67–72,
    344
  organizations for, 327–28
Speed Skating Hall of Fame, 245
Spelterina, Maria, 25
Sperber, Paula, 352
Sperber, Silvia, 337
Sperling, Hilde, 364
Spina bifida, 108
Spivey (-Shelley), Hope, 368, 369
Sports Car Club of America, 140
Sports days, 12, 13
Sports medicine, 22, 24

Sportscasting. *See also*
    Sportswriting; Television
    athletes in, 104, 105, 145, 176,
        189, 191
    milestones in, 31, 33
Sportsman of the Year, 121, 164,
    206
Sportsperson of the Year, 288
Sportswoman, The, 82
Sportswoman of the Year
    Colorado, 97
    European sportswriters, 100
    U.S. Olympic Committee, 347
    Women's Sports and Fitness, 232
    Women's Sports Foundation,
        86, 92, 116, 121, 123,
        200, 214, 221, 299, 304
Sportswoman of the Year,
    Amateur, 109, 160, 161
Sportswoman of the Year,
    Professional, 96, 110, 138,
        204, 239
Sportswriting. *See also*
    Sportscasting
    bibliography on, 319–20
    milestones in, 29, 31
Springs, Betty, 368, 374
Sprinters. *See also* Track and field
    athletes
    Ashford, Evelyn, **82–84**
    Devers, Gail, **105–07**
    Joyner, Florence Griffith, **156–
        58**
    Rudolph, Wilma, **210–12**
    Tyus, Wyomia, **227–29**
Spurgin, Pat, 337
Spuzich, Sandra, 358
Squash, 27, 328
Squash player
    Sears, Eleonora, 27, 216, 217
Squaw Valley Olympics (1960), 67
St. Andrews Golf Club, 5
St. Louis Olympics (1904), 37
St. Moritz
    1928 Olympics, 63
    1940 Olympics, 65
    1948 Olympics, 65
Stacy, Hollis, 358, 359
Staeheli, Joline, 372
Stafford, Shaun, 372
Staley, Dawn, 295, 297, 300, 347
Stalman, Ria, 341
Standards, history of, 8, 17
Stanley, Tananjalyn, 373, 374
Starr, May Faggs, 18, 48, 211,
    276–77, 279–80

Staten Island Cricket and Baseball
    Club, 5
Stearns, Sally, 27
Stecher, Renate, 339
Steding, Katy, 295, 300
Stednitz, Sue, 368, 369
Steer, Teri, 375
Stein, Linda, 353
Steindorf, Ute, 336
Steinhaur, Sherri, 359
Steinseifer, Carrie, 337
Stepanskaya, Galina, 344
Stephens, Helen, 46, 339, 346
Stephenson, Jan, 358, 359
Stepp, Heather, 369
Steppich, Thera, 360
Sterkel, Jill, 347, 371
Stern, S., 356
Sterry, Charlotte Cooper, 365
Stetson, Helen, 360
Steurer, Florence, 348, 349
Steuri, Erna, 349
Stevens, Rochelle, 374
Stevenson, Angie, 351
Stewart, Dana, 352
Stewart, Marlene, 360
Still, Megan, 336
Stimson, M., 356
Stirling, Alexa, 359, 360
Stives, Karen, 57
Stockholm Olympics (1912), 39,
    41
Stockton, Pam, 351
Stokes, Shelley, 301, 306
Stone, D., 357
Stone, Nikki, 343
Stouder, Sharon, 338
Stove, Betty, 85, 163
Stratford Brakettes, 272
Stratton, Mickey, 271, 275
Street, Picabo, 73, 342, 347, 348,
    349
Strickland, Shirley, 340
Stringer, Vivian, 223–25
Stroman, LaTorsha, 372, 374
Strong, Lori, 369
Strug, Kerri, 60, 285, 286, 287,
    288–89, 316
Stuckelberger, Christine, 59
Sua, Seilala, 375
Subert, Jana, 198
Sudduth, Jill, 280, 281, 282, 284
Suefert, Chris, 355
Suffrage, 10
Suggs, Louise, 358, 360
Sugimoto, Katsuko, 352
Sullivan, J. V., 349

Sullivan, James E., 27, 41. *See also*
    Sullivan Award
Sullivan, Jane, 357
Sullivan, M., 357
Sullivan, Molly, 368
Sullivan Award, 27
    to diver, 185
    to speed skater, 91
    to swimmer, 118
    to track and field athletes, 158,
        160, 221
Sullivan Memorial Trophy, 212,
    214, 279
Summer Games, Olympic, 36–61,
    333–42
Summitt, Patricia Head, 54, 188–
    89, 225–27
Sumners, Rosalyn, 358
Sun Fuming, 336
Sunny, Stacy, 266, 270
Susan G. Komen Foundation,
    223
Susanti, Susi, 333
Susman, Karen Hantz, 366
Sutton, May. *See* Bundy, May
    Sutton
Sweeney, Linda, 367
Sweeney, P., 356
Sweet, Judy, 24, 32
Swenson, Kari, 351
Swett, Hannah, 265
Swimmers
    Bianco, Suzannah, 280, 282,
        283
    Chadwick, Florence, 28, 98–99
    Cleland, Tammy, 280, 282,
        283
    de Varona, Donna, 19, 21, 51,
        103–05, 338, 347
    Dyroen-Lancer, Becky, 280,
        281, 282, 283
    Ederle, Gertrude, 10, 27, 43,
        98, 113–15
    Evans, Janet, 117–18. *See also*
        Evans, Janet
    LeSueur, Emily Porter, 280,
        282, 283–84
    Pease, Heather, 280, 282, 284
    Savery, Jill, 280, 281, 282, 284
    Schneyder, Nathalie, 280, 281,
        282, 284
    Simmons-Carrasco, Heather,
        280, 281, 282, 284
    Sudduth, Jill, 280, 281, 282,
        284
    Thien, Margot, 280, 282, 284–
        85

Swimming
    bibliography on, 321
    champions in, 362–63, 369–71
    milestones in, 26, 27, 28, 30
    in Olympic history, 39, 41–43,
        45, 46, 48–53, 55, 57, 58,
        61, 337–39
    organization for, 328
    in sports history, 9, 10
    synchronized team in, 280–85
Switzer, Kathrine, 21, 29, 361
Swoopes, Sheryl, 295, 297, 300–
    01, 311, 346
Swords, Katie, 374
Sydney Olympics (2000), 61
Syers, Madge, 343
Synchronized Swimmer of the
    Year, 284
Synchronized swimming
    in Olympic history, 339
    organization for, 328
    U.S. Olympic team in, 280–85
Szabê, Ecaterina, 335, 336
Székely, Éva, 338
Szewinska, Irena Kirszenstein,
    339
Szöke, Katalin, 337

Tabb, Mary Decker. See Slaney,
    Mary Decker
Table tennis, 51–52, 58
    champions in, 363–64
    in Olympic history, 339
    organization for, 328
Tae kwon do, 61, 326
Takalo, Helena, 342
Takeuchi, E., 357
Talavera, Tracee, 361
Talmage, Barbara, 355, 356
Tanac, Joyce, 361
Tang, Yeping, 351
Taomina, Sheila, 362
Tappin, Ashley, 369, 370
Tarr, Sheila, 375
Tauber, Ulrike, 338
Tayler, Mrs. Witwer, 349
Taylor, Madelaine, 350
Taylor, Monifa, 373
Taylor, Mrs. J. S., 349
Tchepalova, Yulia, 343
Tchistiakova, Galina, 160
Team Sportswoman of the Year,
    116, 123, 299, 304
Teams
    baseball, 252, 253–58, 265–71
    basketball, 295–301
    gymnastics, 285–89
    sailing, 258–65

soccer, 289–94
softball, 252, 253, 271–75,
    301–06
    in sports history, 21, 252–53
    swimming, 280–85
    track and field, 252, 276–80
Teeples, Shirley, 356
Telegraphic meets, 12
Television, viii, 19–20, 255
    athletes as commentators on,
        104, 105, 145, 176
    in Olympic history, 47, 50, 66
    in sports history, 121
Temple, Ed, 47, 211, 227–28,
    276–77
Temple University Player of the
    Year, 304
Tennant, Eleanor "Teach," 102,
    180, 320
Tennessee Sports Hall of Fame,
    278
Tennessee State University
    Tigerbelles, 252, 276–80
Tenney, Jean, 350
Tennis
    "Battle of the Sexes" in, 20
    bibliography on, 86, 121, 130,
        138, 164, 181, 195, 200,
        219, 320–21
    champions in, 364–67, 371–72
    color barrier in, 127
    milestones in, 26, 27, 28, 29,
        30
    in Olympic history, 37, 38, 39,
        42, 43, 52, 58–59, 339
    organizations for, 328
    in sports history, 5, 6, 8, 9, 10–
        11, 13, 16, 17, 20, 22
Tennis Hall of Fame, 121
Tennis players, 161–64. See also
    index entries under each player's
    name
    Austin, Tracy, 85–86
    Connolly, Maureen, 102–03
    Evert, Chris, 119–21
    Gibson, Althea, 127–30
    Graf, Steffi, 136–38
    King, Billie Jean, 161–64
    Marble, Alice, 179–81
    Moody, Helen Wills, 194–95
    Navratilova, Martina, 198–200
    Sears, Eleonora, 216–17
    Seles, Monica, 218–19
    Wightman, Hazel Hotchkiss,
        235–37
Terry, Aline, 366
Terwillegar, Erica, 72

Terzian, Kristi, 348, 349
Teske, Charlotte, 361
Teuscher, Cristina, 362
Texas Cowgirl Hall of Fame, 153
Texas Sports Hall of Fame, 234
Texas Women's Golf Association,
    247
Teyssier, Clara, 354
Thacker, Angela, 373
Thelin, Vanessa, 371
Thiemard, Denise, 375
Thien, Margot, 280, 282, 284–85
Thom, Linda, 337
Thomas, Debi, 71, 358
Thomas, Mazel, 375
Thomas, Tammy, 369
Thompson, Inga, 353
Thompson, Jenny, 362, 369, 371
Thompson, Marie, 9
Thompson, Tressa, 373, 375
Thornton, Helen, 350
Thost, Nicola, 344
Thümer, Petra, 337
Tickey, Bertha, 123, 155, 271,
    275, 304
Tierney, Dorsey, 370
Tigerbelles. See Tennessee State
    University Tigerbelles
Tikhonova, Tamara, 343
Timmer, Marianne, 344
Title IX, ix, x
    history of, 18–19, 21–24, 30
    lobbying for, 105
    team sports and, 252
Titova, Lyudmila, 344
Tkachenko, Nadezhda, 341
Tobias, Donna, 353
Tobin, Katrin, 353
Todd, Jan, 30
Todd, Patricia, 364
Tokyo
    1940 Olympics, 46
    1964 Olympics, 51
Tolbert, Lynda, 373, 374
Tolbert, Ryan, 375
Toma, Sanda, 336
Tomlinson Franke, N., 357
Tong, Jessica, 370
Topcu, Yasemin, 368
Topley, Shirley, 275
Torrence, Gwen, 60, 339, 372,
    373
Torres, Dara, 362, 369, 371
Torvill, Jayne, 70, 343
Touchette, Joan Lee, 265
Tourischeva, Lyudmila, 100, 101,
    335

Townsend, Bertha, 5, 366
Tozzer, Joan, 357
Track and field
    bibliography on, 158, 161,
        212, 214, 221, 248, 321
    champions in, 361–62, 368,
        372–76
    milestones in, 26, 27, 28, 29,
        33
    in Olympic history, 40, 41,
        43–51, 53, 55, 56–58, 60,
        61, 339–41
    organizations for, 328–29
    outstanding team in, 252, 276–
        80
    in sports history, 14, 20, 22
Track and Field Athlete of the
    Year, 84
Track and field athletes. *See also*
    index entries under each athlete's
    name
    Ashford, Evelyn, **82–84**
    Blankers-Koen, Fanny, **92–94**
    Cheeseborough, Chandra, 277,
        278
    Daniels, Isabelle, 277, 278
    Devers, Gail, **105–07**
    Driscoll, Jean, **107–09**
    Duvall, Edith McGuire, 278
    Hudson, Martha, 277, 278
    Jennings, Lynn, **153–54**
    Jones, Barbara, 278–79
    Joyner, Florence Griffith,
        156–58
    Joyner-Kersee, Jackie, **158–61**
    Mathews, Margaret, 277, 279
    McMillan, Kathy, 277, 279
    Mims, Madeline Manning, 279
    Rudolph, Wilma, **210–12**
    Samuelson, Joan Benoit,
        213–14
    Slaney, Mary Decker, **220–21**
    Smith, Francie Larrieu, **222–23**
    Starr, May Faggs, 279–80
    Tyus, Wyomia, **227–29**
    Waitz, Grete Andersen,
        231–33
    White, Willye, 277, 280
    Williams, Lucinda, 277, 280
    Zaharias, Mildred "Babe"
        Didrikson, 44–45,
        245–48
Tracy, Mary Lee, 287, 288
Training, advances in, 24
Trapshooting, 26
Trees, Tori, 370
Treible, Kathy, 370

Trenary, Jill, 358
Triathlete
    Newby-Fraser, Paula, 24,
        203–04, 367
Triathlete of the Year, 204
Triathlon
    champions in, 367
    in Olympic history, 61
    organization for, 329
Trilling, Blanche, 12
Trillini, Giovanna, 335
Trinquet, Pascale, 335
Triple jump, 341, 373, 375
Truman, Christine, 130, 365
Tuberculosis, 180
Tuffey, Suzie, 368
Tulloch, Valerie, 375
Tulu, Derartu, 154, 340
Turgeon, Melanie, 349
Turner, Cathy, 71, 344
Turner, Inez, 374
Turner, Kim, 374
Turner, Lesley, 365
Turner, Sherri, 359
Turner, Terri, 375
Turpin, B., 357
Twardokens, Eva, 348, 349
Twedberg, Eva, 351
Twigg, Rebecca, 57, 96, 97, 353,
    354
Tyler, Dani, 301, 306
Tyler, Dorothy Odam, 48
Tyler, Lucy, 354
Tymochenko, Oleksandra, 336
Tyshkevich, Tamara, 341
Tyus, Wyomia, **227–29,** 280
    in Olympic history, 47, 53, 339
    in sports history, 18, 19, 20, 21

Ujlaki-Rejtö, Ildikê, 334
Ulanov, Aleksei, 343
Umeh, Stella, 369
Underhill, Ruth, 359
United Golf Association, 9
University sports. *See* College
    sports, history of
Upham, Henry, 5
Uphoff, Nicole, 59
U.S. Amateur Confederation of
    Roller Skating, 327
U.S. Association for Blind
    Athletes, 324–25
U.S. Association of Independent
    Gymnastics Clubs, 192
U.S. Auto Club, 140
U.S. Badminton Association, 322
U.S. Basketball Writers' Associa-
    tion, 299

U.S. Biathlon Association, 323
U.S. Canoe and Kayak Team,
    Inc., 324
U.S. Croquet Association, 324
U.S. Curling Association, 324
U.S. Cycling Federation, 127, 245
U.S. Cycling Federation Hall of
    Fame, 245
U.S. Disabled Ski Team, 133–34
U.S. Diving, 166, 328
U.S. Equestrian Team, Inc., 325
U.S. Female Alpine Skier of the
    Year, 134
U.S. Female Athlete of the Year,
    107
U.S. Fencing Association, 325
U.S. Field Hockey Association,
    82, 325
U.S. Figure Skating Association,
    325
U.S. Figure Skating Hall of Fame,
    143
U.S. Golf Association, 5, 17, 230,
    239, 247
U.S. Hang Gliding Association,
    327
U.S. Judo Association, 326
U.S. Lawn Tennis Association, 5,
    20, 120, 127–29, 181, 236,
    237
U.S. Luge Association, 326
U.S. National Ski Hall of Fame,
    202
U.S. National Track and Field
    Hall of Fame, 278, 279, 280
U.S. Olympic Committee
    Advisory Council of, 132
    awards by, 107, 123, 132, 134,
        193, 206, 347
    team sports and, 252–53
U.S. Olympic Hall of Fame, 97,
    104, 125, 143, 166, 185, 206,
    212, 248, 279
U.S. Olympic Synchronized
    Swimming Team, 280–85
U.S. Olympic Women's Basket-
    ball Team, 295–301
U.S. Parachute Association, 327
U.S. Racquetball Association, 136,
    326
U.S. Rowing Association, 262,
    263, 327
U.S. Sailing Association, 264, 327
U.S. Shooting Team, 327
U.S. Ski and Snowboard
    Association, 327
U.S. Ski Association, 134

U.S. Soccer Federation, 78, 289, 291, 292, 293, 327
U.S. Speed Skating Association, 328
U.S. Squash Racquets Association Inc., 328
U.S. Swimming, 328
U.S. Synchronized Swimming, Inc., 281, 283, 284, 285, 328
U.S. Table Tennis Association, 328
U.S. Taekwondo Union, 326
U.S. Team Handball Federation, 328
U.S. Tennis Association, 30, 121, 328
U.S. Volleyball Association, 151, 329
U.S. Women's Curling Association, 324
U.S. Women's Cycling Federation, 324
U.S. Women's Gymnastics Team, 285–89
U.S. Women's Lacrosse Association, 325
U.S. Women's National Soccer Team, 289–94
U.S. Women's Squash Racquets Association, 217
USA Basketball, 116, 322–23
USA Basketball Women's National Team, 295–301
USA Bowling, 323
USA Gymnastics, 286, 288, 325
USA Softball Women's National Team, 301–06
USA Track & Field, 329
USA Triathlon, 329
Usifo, Maria, 375
Utunda, Beatrice, 373
Uusitalo, Helena, 375

Vahlensieck, Christa, 232
Valla, Trebisonda, 340
Valova, Elena, 70, 343
van Bentum, Conny, 362, 369, 370
Van Buskirk, E., 356
Van Dyken, Amy
    awards won by, 346, 347
    championships won by, 362, 369
    in Olympic history, 60, 337, 338
van Gennip, Therese, 71
Van Gennip, Yvonne, 344
van Langen, Ellen, 340

van Staveren, Petra, 338
van Vliet, Petronella, 338
Van Wie, Virginia, 346, 360
Vanderbeck, Florence, 359
VanDerveer, Tara, 116, 296, 311
Vanisi, Eileen, 373, 375
Vare, Glenna Collett, 10, 89, 229–31, 360
Vare Trophy, 89, 179, 231, 234, 240, 247
Varner, Margaret, 350
Vasiliev, Oleg, 70, 343
Vaughan, Robert, 222
Vaughn, Jane, 357
Vaytsekhovskaya, Elena, 334
Vecchione, Gina, 275
Venciene, Vida, 343
Venturi, Bridget, 270–71
Venturini, Tisha, 289, 291, 294
Vicario, Arantxa Sanchez, 138, 365, 367
Vickers, Janeene, 375
Victorian ideal, 4
Villarreal, Vivian, 351
Vinnicombe, Lucy, 354
Vinson, Maribel, 80, 357
Virginia Slims tournament, 20, 29, 163
Viscopoleanu, Viorica, 341
Vitalis Award, 84
Voelker, Heidi, 349
Voigt, Angela, 341
Volleyball
    bibliography on, 321
    in Olympic history, 46, 51, 52, 60, 333
    organizations for, 329
    in sports history, 21
Volleyball player
    Hyman, Flo, 150–52
Vollstedt, Rolla, 140
von Rosen, Clarence, 39
Von Saltza, Christine, 50, 337
von Seck, Anke, 334
Vonderheide, Nancy, 350
Voorhees, A., 356
Voorhies, Marjorie, 26
Voting, right to, 10

Wachter, Anita, 342
Wade Trophy, 176, 191, 238, 297
Wade, Virginia, 120, 364, 366, 367
Wagner, Allison, 371
Wagner, Barbara, 67, 343
Wagner, Lisa, 352
Wagstaff, Janie, 362
Waitz, Grete Andersen, 57, 214, 231–33, 337, 361

Wake Robin Golf Club, 9
Walasiewicz, Stanislawa, 339
Waldman, Suzyn, 33
Waldo, Carolyn, 339
Walker, Astia, 374
Walker, Colleen, 359
Walker, Gladys, 13
Walker, Gloria, 351
Walker, long-distance
    Sears, Eleonora, 217
Walking, Olympic gold in, 340
Walsh, Stella, 46, 212, 339
Walsh, Sue, 370
Walter, Steffi Martin, 344
Walther, Marie, 360
Walton, Delisa, 374
Walton, F., 356
Walton, Starr, 349
Wang Junxia, 340
Waples, D., 357
Ward, Wendy, 360
Warren, Leanne, 374
Warren, Youlanda, 372
Washington, Evelyn. See Ashford, Evelyn
Washington, Marian, 296
Washington, Ora, 11, 13
Water polo, 61
Waterskier
    Duvall, Camille, 109–10
Waterskiing, 329
Watson, Lillian, 338
Watson, Maud, 365
Wayman, Agnes, 12
Wayte, Mary, 337, 362, 363, 369, 371
Weatherspoon, Teresa, 296, 347
Weaver, Joanne, 257
Webb, Karrie, 33
Weber, Ann, 350
Wei Wang, 363
Weidenbach, Lisa Larsen, 361
Weightlifting, 30, 61
Weinbrecht, Donna, 343
Weinstein, Barb, 356
Weiss, Pam, 351
Weissensteiner, Gerda, 344
Weissmann, Margaret, 360
Welch, Lesley, 368
Welch, Priscilla, 361
Weld, Theresa, 357
Wells, Becki, 372, 374
Welts, Anne Quast, 360
Welty, Amber, 375
Wene, Sylvia, 352
Wener, Lucy, 369
Wenzel, Hanni, 69, 342

Werbrouck, Ulla, 336
Wesson, Cynthia, 349, 350
Westacott, Emily, 364
Wester-King, Angie, 363
Wheelchair athlete
  Driscoll, Jean, **107–09**
Wheelchair sports, 341, 361
Wheelchair Sports USA, 325
White, R., 357
White, Willye, 277, 280
White Stag Trophy, 175
Whitemore, Mary E., 350
Whitfield, Beverley, 338
Whitworth, Kathy, 77, **233–35,** 240, 346, 358, 359
Wibert, Pernilla, 342
Wichman, Sharon, 338
Wickham, Tracey, 117
Wickus, Amy, 372, 374
Wideman, Lydia, 342
Wiegand, Patty, 372
Wightman, Hazel Hotchkiss, **235–37**
  championships won by, 366
  Moody, Helen Wills and, 194
  in Olympic history, 43, 339
  Sears, Eleonora and, 216–17
  in sports history, 13, 26
Wilbur, Doreen, 333, 350
Wilcox, Lisa, 348
Wiley, Alison, 374
Wiley, Charlotte, 266, 271
Wilkinson, Dorothy, 352
Wilkinson, Laura, 355, 356, 371
Wilkinson, Martha, 360
Willard, Frances, 6–7
Willard, Meredith, 368
Willard, Patsy, 354, 355, 356
Williams, Ann, 271
Williams, Christa, 301, 302, 306
Williams, Esther, 284
Williams, Lucinda, 277, 280
Williams, R. Norris, 43, 339
Williams, Schowanda, 375
Williams, Terry, 30
Williams, Tonya, 375
Williams, Wendy Lian, 355, 356
Williams, Yvette, 341
Williams-Sewer, Dawn, 372
Willim, Stephanie, 361
Wills, Helen. *See* Moody, Helen Wills
Wills, Virginia, 14
Wilma Rudolph Foundation, 212
Wilson, Jodi, 370
Wilson, Krista, 355, 371
Wilson, Linette, 375

Wilson, Myrtle, 13
Wilson, Rose, 13
Wilson, Staci, 289, 294
Winn, Anne, 348
Winter Games, Olympic, 61–73, 342–44
Winter, Liane, 361
Wisniewski, Connie, 257
Wisser, Maria, 353
Witt, Katarina, 71, 343
Witt, Kathryn, 334
Witty, Chris, 354
Wockel, Barbel Eckert, 339
Wodars, Sigrun, 340
Wolbert, Babe, 26
Wolf, Sigrid, 342
Wolters, Kara, 296
Woman Bowler of the Year, 172
Woman of the Year, 125
Women's Advisory Board, 47
Women's All-Star (Bowling) Association, 323
Women's American Basketball Association, 176
Women's Basketball Coaches Association, 191, 224, 227, 323
Women's Basketball League, 176
Women's Basketball Rules Committee, 8
Women's Board, Olympic Development Committee, 17
Women's Bureau, U.S. Department of Labor, 15
Women's Christian Temperance Union, 6–7
Women's Curling Association, 28
Women's Division, 11–12, 41, 42, 44, 47
Women's International Bowling Congress, 132, 172, 173, 323
  Hall of Fame, 187
  in sports history, 9, 17, 26, 32
Women's International Boxing Federation, 323
Women's International Motorcycle Association, 326
Women's Mountain Bike & Tea Society, 324
Women's movement, x, 36
Women's National Basketball Association, 22, 177, 191, 239, 297, 323
Women's National Bowling Association, 9, 26
Women's Olympic Games, 14, 40–41

Women's Professional Basketball League, 31, 189
Women's Professional Billiards Association, 323
Women's Professional Golf Association, 27, 247
Women's Professional Racquetball Association, 135–36, 326
Women's Professional Rodeo Association, 153, 325
Women's Professional Volleyball Association, 329
Women's rights
  promoters of, 103, 105, 161–62
  in sports history, 4, 17–18
Women's Sports and Fitness, 163
Women's Sports Foundation, 21, 326. *See also* Flo Hyman Award; Sportswoman of the Year
  executive director of, 274
  founding of, 104, 105, 163, 166, 229, 245, 280
  Greatest Woman Athlete award by, 119
Women's Swimming Association, 113
Women's Swimming Association of New York, 9
Women's Tennis Association, 137, 161, 200, 328
  awards by, 86, 120, 138, 200, 219
  founding of, 163
Women's World Games, 41
Women's Yacht Racing Association, 264
Woodard, Lynette, 31, 226, **237–39,** 347
Woodhead, Cynthia, 347
Woodruff, Mrs. C. E., 349
Woods, Stephanie, 369
Woods, Virginia, 13
Woodswomen, 323
Woodworth, Lois, 349
Woolsey, Elizabeth, 347
Woolsey, Sandy, 369
World Boxing Council, 182
World Figure Skating Hall of Fame, 125, 145
World Golf Hall of Fame, 231, 234, 240
World Synchronized Swimmer of the Year, 284

World Trophy (sled dog racing), 96
World War I, 10
World War II, 15–16, 46, 65
Wrestling, 32, 33
Wright, Catherine, 26
Wright, Corrinne, 368, 369
Wright, Mickey, 233, 234, **239–40,** 346, 358, 359
Wrigley, Philip K., 15, 253
Wu Xiaoxuan, 337
Wuilloud, Madeleine, 347
Wurtele, Rhoda, 347, 348, 349
Wyland, Wendy, 356
Wyludda, Ilke, 341
Wymer, Beth, 369
Wynne, Nancye, 364

Xiaomin Huang, 363
Xu Yanmei, 334

Yachting. *See also* Sailing
    Olympic gold for, 341–42
    in Olympic history, 37, 38, 42, 50, 52, 54, 56, 59
Yachtswoman of the Year
    Hawaii Yacht Club, 265
    Rolex, 261, 263
Yamaguchi, Kristi, 22, 71–72, **241–43,** 343, 358

Yang Wenyi, 337
Yarborough, Cale, 140
Yasen, Corissa, 376
Yegorova, Valentina, 340
Yeo Kab-Soon, 337
Yordanova, Zdravka, 336
York, J., 356
York, Teri, 356
York-Romary, J., 356, 357
Young, Candy, 373
Young, Laurette, 350
Young, Lauri, 376
Young, Mark, 287
Young, Sheila, **243–45**
    as cyclist, 96, 347, 353
    as speed skater, 69, 344, 347
    in sports history, 21
Young, Telisa, 373
Young-Ja Yang, 339
Younger, Kathleen, 28
Yu, Jen, 357

Zabell, Theresa, 341
Zabirova, Zulfiya, 334
Zack, Sally, 353
Zaharias, George, 89
Zaharias, Mildred "Babe" Didrikson, 240, **245–48**

awards won by, 346
Berg, Patty and, 88, 89, 90
championships won by, 358, 360
in Olympic history, 44–45, 340, 341
in sports history, 14–15, 16, 28
Zaitsev, Aleksandr, 70, 343
Zajac, Carole, 368, 374
Zarse, Carrie, 355
Zátopková, Dana, 341
Zayak, Elaine, 358
Zehrt, Monika, 339
Zeis, Lisa, 369
Zhou Jihong, 334
Zhuang Xiaoyan, 336
Zhuang Young, 337
Zimmerman, F., 357
Zimmerman, Iris, 33, 357
Zimmermann, Annemarie, 334
Zirzow, Carola, 333
Zmeskal, Kim, 32, 316, 347, 361
Zozulia, Vera, 344
Zunich, Stephanie, 370
Zvereva, Natalia, 137
Zybina, Galina, 341